*Rick.*

# PORTUGAL

# CONTENTS

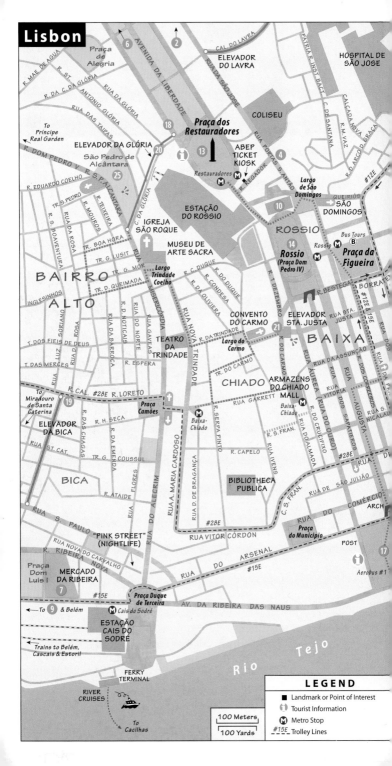

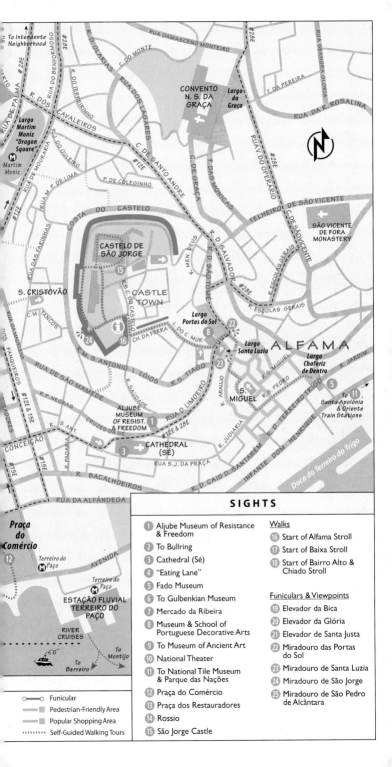

**To Intendente Neighborhood**

RUA DAMASCENO MONTEIRO

CONVENTO N. S. DA GRAÇA

Largo da Graça

RUA DA R. ROSALINA

T. DA PEREIRA

RUA V. DO OPERARIO

T. DAS MONICAS

SÃO VICENTE DE FORA MONASTERY

TELHEIRO DE SÃO VICENTE

C. DE S. VICENTE

R. ESCOLAS GERAIS

Largo Martim Moniz "Dragon Square"

Martim Moniz

#12E

RUA DE PALMA

R. DOS CAVALEIROS

RUA DO BENFORMOSO

R. DA OLARIAS

R. DOS LAGARES

C. DO MONTE

R. DO TERREIRINHO

R. DO QUELRO

RUA DE MOURARIA

RUA M. P. DE LIMA

P. DE COLEGINHO

C. DE SANTO ANDRE

C. DE GRAÇA

#12E

COSTA DO CASTELO

CASTELO DE SÃO JORGE

R. MEN. PEUS

R. D. SÃO TOMÉ

R. D. SALVADOR

R. ESCOLAS GERAIS

S. CRISTOVÃO

RUA DAS FARINHAS

C. M. TANCOS

CASTLE TOWN

Largo Portas do Sol

ALFAMA

RUA DAMAGENA

FANQUEIROS

#12E & 15E

R. B. C. DO CASTELO

CH. DA FERRA

R. DO C. MOR.

Largo Santa Luzia

Largo Chafariz de Dentro

R. JARDIM

R. S. ANTONIO L. LÓIOS

RUA DE SÃO MAMEDE

R. SAUDADE

R. S. TIAGO

R. ARAUJO

S. MIGUEL

R. S. MIGUEL

R. S. PEDRO

R. D. TERREIRO TRIGO

To Santa Apolónia & Oriente Train Stations

R. F. NEGRAS

R. S. ANT.

ALJUBE MUSEUM OF RESIST. & FREEDOM

RUA D. LIMOEIRO

R. JUDIARIA

INFANTE DOM HENRIQUE

CONCEIÇÃO

R. PADARIA

CRUZES DA SÉ

#12E & 28E

CATHEDRAL (SÉ)

RUA S. J. DA PRAÇA

#15E

R. BACALHOEIROS

R. D. CAIS D. SANTAREM

Doca do Terreiro do Trigo

RUA DA ALFÂNDEGA

Praça do Comércio

Terreiro do Paço

AVENIDA

Terreiro do Paço

ESTAÇÃO FLUVIAL TERREIRO DO PAÇO

RIVER CRUISES

To Montijo

To Barreiro

○—○ Funicular

Pedestrian-Friendly Area

Popular Shopping Area

•••••••• Self-Guided Walking Tours

## SIGHTS

1. Aljube Museum of Resistance & Freedom
2. To Bullring
3. Cathedral (Sé)
4. "Eating Lane"
5. Fado Museum
6. To Gulbenkian Museum
7. Mercado da Ribeira
8. Museum & School of Portuguese Decorative Arts
9. To Museum of Ancient Art
10. National Theater
11. To National Tile Museum & Parque das Nações
12. Praça do Comércio
13. Praça dos Restauradores
14. Rossio
15. São Jorge Castle

### Walks

16. Start of Alfama Stroll
17. Start of Baixa Stroll
18. Start of Bairro Alto & Chiado Stroll

### Funiculars & Viewpoints

19. Elevador da Bica
20. Elevador da Glória
21. Elevador de Santa Justa
22. Miradouro das Portas do Sol
23. Miradouro de Santa Luzia
24. Miradouro de São Jorge
25. Miradouro de São Pedro de Alcântara

*Lisbon at night*

*Market vendor*

*Futebol on Nazaré's beach*

*Terraced vineyards in the Douro Valley*

*Fado—songs of sadness and hope*

# Rick Steves®

# PORTUGAL

# Top Destinations in Portugal

PORTO

DOURO VALLEY

COIMBRA

*Atlantic Ocean*

NAZARÉ & CENTRAL PORTUGAL

SINTRA
LISBON

ÉVORA

THE ALGARVE

# INTRODUCTION

Tucked into a far corner of the Continent, Portugal preserves a traditional culture of widows in black and fishermen mending nets. But along with the old, you'll also find the modern—rejuvenated cityscapes, trendy boutiques, and a surging foodie culture—especially in the culturally rich capital of Lisbon and the second city of Porto. If your idea of good travel includes friendly locals (who generally speak English), exotic architecture, windswept castles, thriving towns and cities, appealingly authentic seaside resort towns, and fresh seafood with chilled wine on a beach at sunset...you've chosen the right destination. And it's affordable—Portugal is one of the cheapest places to travel in Western Europe.

This book breaks Portugal into its top big-city, small-town, and rural destinations, giving you all the information and opinions necessary to wring the maximum value out of your limited time and money. Experiencing Portugal's culture, people, and natural wonders economically and hassle-free has been my goal for more than three decades of traveling, guiding tours, and travel writing. With this new edition, I pass on to you the lessons I've learned.

While including the predictable biggies, this book also mixes in a healthy dose of "Back Door" intimacy. You'll eat barnacles washed down with green wine, recharge your solar cells in an Algarve fishing village, and wax nostalgic over bluesy fado music. This book is selective. For example, while there are plenty of Algarve beach towns, I recommend only the top stops: Salema, Lagos, and Tavira.

The best is, of course, only my opinion. But after spending half my adult life exploring and researching Europe, I've developed a sixth sense for what travelers enjoy. Just thinking about the places featured in this book makes me want to while away an evening in a fado bar.

INTRODUCTION

## Map Legend

| | | | | | |
|---|---|---|---|---|---|
| ⅛ | Viewpoint | ✈ | Airport | ⟶ | One-way |
| ↑ | Entrance | ⊤ | Taxi Stand | | Pedestrian Zone |
| ⊕ | Tourist Info | ⊤ | Tram Stop | ------ | Railway |
| WC | Restroom | ⊞ | Bus Stop | ············ | Ferry/Boat Route |
| ♜ | Castle | M | Metro Stop | •▰▰• | Funicular |
| ⌂ | Church | P | Parking | ⅢⅢⅢ | Stairs |
| ▪ | Statue/Point of Interest | 🚲 | Bike Rental | - - - - - | Walk/Tour Route |
| ⊠ | Elevator | | Park | - - - - - | Trail |

*Use this legend to help you navigate the maps in this book.*

## ABOUT THIS BOOK

*Rick Steves Portugal* is a personal tour guide in your pocket. This book is organized by destinations. Each is a minivacation on its own, filled with exciting sights, strollable neighborhoods, affordable places to stay, and memorable places to eat. For destinations covered in this book, you'll find these sections:

**Planning Your Time** suggests a schedule for how to best use your limited time.

**Orientation** has specifics on public transportation, helpful hints, local tour options, easy-to-read maps, and tourist information.

**Sights** describes the top attractions and includes their cost and hours. Major sights have self-guided tours.

**Self-Guided Walks** take you through interesting neighborhoods, pointing out sights and fun stops.

**Sleeping** describes my favorite hotels, from good-value deals to cushy splurges.

**Eating** serves up a buffet of options, from inexpensive eateries to fancy restaurants.

**Connections** outlines your options for traveling to destinations by train, bus, or plane, and suggests route tips for drivers.

**Portugal: Past and Present** gives you a quick overview of Portugal, from its prehistoric beginnings to the issues it faces today.

The **Practicalities** chapter near the end of this book is a traveler's tool kit, with my best advice about money, sightseeing, sleeping, eating, staying connected, and transportation (trains, buses, driving, and flights).

The **appendix** has the nuts-and-bolts: useful phone numbers and websites, a holiday and festival list, recommended books and films, a climate chart, a handy packing checklist, and Portuguese survival phrases.

## Key to This Book

### Updates
This book is updated regularly—but things change. For the latest, visit www.ricksteves.com/update.

### Abbreviations and Times
I use the following symbols and abbreviations in this book:

Sights are rated:

| | |
|---|---|
| ▲▲▲ | **Don't miss** |
| ▲▲ | **Try hard to see** |
| ▲ | **Worthwhile if you can make it** |
| **No rating** | **Worth knowing about** |

Tourist information offices are abbreviated as **TI,** and bathrooms are **WCs.** Accommodations are categorized with a **Sleep Code** (described on page 405); eateries are classified with a **Restaurant Price Code** (page 413). To indicate discounts for my readers, I include **RS%** in the listings.

Like Portugal, this book uses the **24-hour clock.** It's the same through 12:00 noon, then keeps going: 13:00, 14:00, and so on. For anything over 12, subtract 12 and add p.m. (14:00 is 2:00 p.m.).

When giving **opening times,** I include both peak season and off-season hours, if they differ. So, if a museum is listed as "May-Oct daily 9:00-16:00," it should be open from 9 a.m. until 4 p.m. from the first day of May until the last day of October (but expect exceptions).

For **transit** or **tour departures,** I first list the frequency, then the duration. So, a train connection listed as "2/hour, 1.5 hours" departs twice each hour, and the journey lasts an hour and a half.

Throughout this book, you'll find money- and time-saving tips for sightseeing, transportation, and more. Some businesses—especially hotels and walking tour companies—offer special discounts to my readers, indicated in their listings.

Browse through this book, choose your favorite destinations, and link them up. Then have a great trip! Traveling like a temporary local, you'll get the absolute most of every mile, minute, and dollar. As you visit places I know and love, I'm happy that you'll be meeting some of my favorite Portuguese people.

## Planning

This section will help you get started planning your trip—with advice on trip costs, when to go, and what you should know before you take off.

# Portugal's Best Two-Week Trip by Car

| Day | Plan | Sleep in |
|---|---|---|
| 1 | Arrive in Lisbon | Lisbon |
| 2 | Lisbon | Lisbon |
| 3 | Side-trip to Sintra (by train) | Lisbon |
| 4 | More time in Lisbon; afternoon/ evening, pick up car and drive to Salema (3 hours) | Salema |
| 5 | Beach day in Salema | Salema |
| 6 | Side-trip to Cape Sagres and more beach time | Salema |
| 7 | To Lagos (30 minutes), then Évora (3 hours) | Évora |
| 8 | Morning in Évora; afternoon to Nazaré via Óbidos (2.5 hours) | Nazaré |
| 9 | Nazaré | Nazaré |
| 10 | To Coimbra (1.5 hours) with stops in Alcobaça, Batalha, and Fátima | Coimbra |
| 11 | Coimbra | Coimbra |
| 12 | To Douro Valley (2.5 hours) | Douro Valley |
| 13 | To Porto (2 hours), drop off car* | Porto |
| 14 | Porto | Porto |
| 15 | Fly home | |

**Notes:** Driving times are estimates and could be longer in bad traffic. Try to avoid being in Lisbon or Porto on a Monday, when many major sights are closed.

If, after touring Portugal, you're continuing to the Spanish destinations of Salamanca or Madrid, it's better to visit Porto and the Douro Valley before Coimbra.

*Drivers who prefer to fly home from Lisbon can park their car while in Porto, then drive it back to the Lisbon airport (about 3 hours).

**By Train and Bus:** This itinerary designed for a car can also be done by train and bus. To use public transportation, take the bus to and from Salema with a change in Lagos. To get from Évora to Nazaré, you'll have to change in Lisbon. See the sights near Nazaré by bus, using Nazaré as your home base (consider adding an extra night there to fit everything in)—then take the bus straight to Coimbra. From Coimbra, catch the bus or train to Porto; you can skip the Douro Valley or, if you love wineries and scenery, you can side-trip to the valley from Porto (or even spend the night).

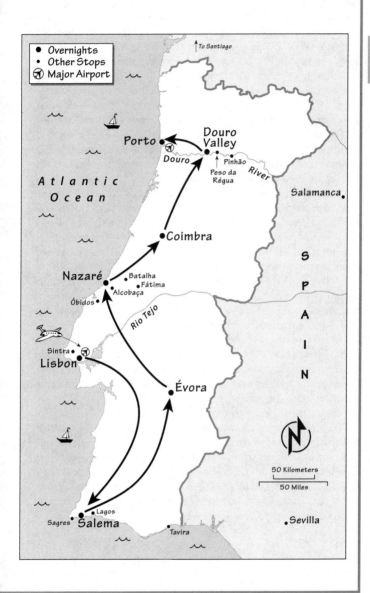

- Overnights
- Other Stops
- Major Airport

To Santiago

Porto

Douro Valley

Douro

Pinhão

Peso da Régua

River

Salamanca

Atlantic Ocean

Coimbra

Nazaré

Batalha
Fátima
Alcobaça

Óbidos

Rio Tejo

S P A I N

Sintra
Lisbon

Évora

Lagos
Sagres Salema

Tavira

Sevilla

N

50 Kilometers

50 Miles

## TRAVEL SMART

Your trip to Portugal is like a complex play—it's easier to follow and really appreciate on a second viewing. While no one does the same trip twice to gain that advantage, reading this book in its entirety before your trip accomplishes much the same thing.

Design an itinerary that enables you to visit sights at the best possible times. Note holidays, festivals, specifics on sights, and days when sights are closed (all covered in this book). For example, many museums and sights close on Mondays. Hotels are most crowded on Fridays and Saturdays, especially in resort towns. To connect the dots smoothly, read the tips in Practicalities on taking trains and buses, or renting a car and driving. Designing a smart trip is a fun, doable, and worthwhile challenge.

Make your itinerary a mix of intense and relaxed stretches. To maximize rootedness, minimize one-night stands. It's worth taking a long drive after dinner (or a train ride with a dinner picnic) to get settled in a town for two nights. Every trip—and every traveler—needs slack time (for laundry, picnics, people-watching, and so on). Pace yourself. Assume you will return.

Reread this book as you travel, and visit local tourist information offices (abbreviated as TI in this book). Upon arrival in a new town, lay the groundwork for a smooth departure; confirm the train, bus, or road you'll take when you leave.

Even with the best-planned itinerary, you'll need to be flexible. Update your plans as you travel. Get online or call ahead to learn the latest on sights (special events, tour schedules, and so on), book tickets and tours, make reservations, reconfirm hotels, and research transportation connections.

Enjoy the friendliness of the Portuguese people. Connect with the culture. Set up your own quest for the best cod dish, cloister, fado bar, or custard tart. Slow down and be open to unexpected experiences. Ask questions—most locals are eager to point you in their idea of the right direction. Keep a notepad in your pocket for confirming prices, noting directions, and organizing your thoughts. Wear your money belt, learn the currency, and figure out how to estimate prices in dollars. Those who expect to travel smart, do.

## TRIP COSTS

Five components make up your trip costs: airfare to Europe, transportation in Europe, room and board, sightseeing and entertainment, and shopping and miscellany.

**Airfare to Europe:** A basic round-trip flight from the US to Lisbon can cost, on average, about $1,000-2,000 total, depending on where you fly from and when (cheaper in winter). Consider saving time and money by flying into one city and out of another; for instance, into Lisbon and out of Porto. Overall, Kayak.com is the

# Portugal at a Glance

▲▲▲**Lisbon** Lively, hilly port and capital, with historic trolleys, grand squares, fado clubs, fine art, and a salty sailors' quarter topped by a castle.

▲▲**Sintra** Aristocratic retreat just outside Lisbon, known for its striking setting, fairy-tale castles, and beautiful gardens.

▲▲▲**The Algarve** Portugal's sunny southern coast, strung with the simple fishing village of Salema, the historic "end of the road" of Cape Sagres, the beach-party town of Lagos, and Moroccan-flavored Tavira.

▲▲**Évora** Whitewashed college town with big Roman, Moorish, and Portuguese history encircled by its medieval wall, in the rustic Alentejo heartland.

▲▲**Nazaré & Central Portugal** Traditional fishing village turned small-town resort, and jumping-off point for day trips to the monastery at Batalha, the pilgrimage site of Fátima, Portugal's largest church in Alcobaça, and the photogenic walled town of Óbidos.

▲▲**Coimbra** Portugal's Oxford, home to a user-friendly old town and bustling with students from its prestigious university.

▲▲**Porto** Gritty but rejuvenated second city with scenic riverfront, steep and picturesque neighborhoods, lively shopping streets, and port-wine tastings.

▲**Douro Valley** Terraced valley and birthplace of port wine, with functional towns of Peso da Régua and Pinhão, and ample countryside *quintas* for tastings and accommodations.

best place to start searching for flights on a combination of mainstream and budget carriers.

**Transportation in Europe:** For a two-week whirlwind trip of my recommended destinations by public transportation, allow $300 per person. If you plan to rent a car, allow $230 per week, not including tolls, gas, and supplemental insurance. If you'll be keeping the car for three weeks or more, look into leasing, which, for trips of this length, can save you money on insurance and taxes. Car rentals and leases are cheapest if arranged from the US. Rail passes normally must be purchased outside Europe but are a waste of money for a Portugal-only trip. It's more economical to buy bus and train tickets as you go. Buses are often more flexible and affordable than trains in Portugal. If combining Portugal with other European destinations, don't hesitate to consider flying—a short flight can be cheaper than the train (check www.skyscanner.com for intra-European flights). For more on public transportation and car rental, see "Transportation" in Practicalities.

**Room and Board:** You can thrive in Portugal on $120 a day per person for room and board (less in villages). This allows $15 for lunch, $30 for dinner, and $75 for lodging (based on two people splitting the cost of a $150 double room that includes breakfast). Students and tightwads can enjoy Portugal for as little as $60 a day ($30 for a bed, $30 for meals).

**Sightseeing and Entertainment:** You'll pay about $6-12 per major sight (museums, churches), $4-5 for minor ones (climbing towers), and $30-60 for splurge experiences (fado concerts, food tours). An overall average of $30 a day works for most people. Don't skimp here. After all, this category is the driving force behind your trip—you came to sightsee, enjoy, and experience Portugal.

**Shopping and Miscellany:** Figure $3 per coffee, beer, ice-cream cone, and postcard. Shopping can vary in cost from nearly nothing to a small fortune. Good budget travelers find that this category has little to do with assembling a trip full of lifelong memories.

## SIGHTSEEING PRIORITIES

So much to see, so little time. How to choose? Depending on the length of your trip, and taking geographic proximity into account, here are my recommended priorities.

| | |
|---|---|
| 3 days: | Lisbon, Sintra |
| 6 days, add: | The Algarve (Salema, Lagos, Cape Sagres) |
| 8 days, add: | Coimbra, slow down |
| 10 days, add: | Nazaré and nearby sights (Óbidos, Alcobaça, Batalha, Fátima) |
| 12 days, add: | Porto |
| 14 days, add: | Évora, Douro Valley |
| More time: | Add Tavira and slow down |

## WHEN TO GO

Spring and fall offer the best combination of good weather, light crowds, long days, and plenty of tourist and cultural activities.

Summer months are the most crowded and expensive in the coastal areas. Beach towns (such as Nazaré or along the Algarve) are packed with vacationers in July and especially in August—when rates go sky-high and it can be tough to find a room. Those same towns are a delight in shoulder season (mid-May-June and Sept-mid-Oct), when the weather is nearly as good and the crowds subside—but they're almost too quiet in the winter. While Portu-

## ∩ **Rick Steves Audio Europe** ∩

My free **Rick Steves Audio Europe app** is a great tool for enjoying Europe. This app makes it easy to download my audio tours of top attractions, plus hours of travel interviews, all organized into destination-specific playlists.

My self-guided **audio tours** of major sights and neighborhoods across Europe are user-friendly, fun, and informative. Among these tours is my Lisbon City Walk, which is marked with this symbol: ∩. These audio tours are hard to beat: Nobody will stand you up, your eyes are free to appreciate the sights, you can take the tour exactly when you like, and the price is right.

The Rick Steves Audio Europe app also offers a far-reaching library of insightful **travel interviews** from my public radio show with experts from around the globe—including many of the places in this book.

This app and all of its content are entirely free. (And new content is added about twice a year.) You can download Rick Steves Audio Europe via Apple's App Store, Google Play, or the Amazon Appstore. For more information, see www. ricksteves.com/audioeurope.

gal is not nearly as hot as Spain (except in the Alentejo region), an air-conditioned room is worth it in summer.

In the off-season (roughly November through March), expect shorter hours, more lunchtime breaks at sights, and fewer activities (confirm your sightseeing plans locally).

For weather specifics, see the climate chart in the appendix.

## KNOW BEFORE YOU GO

Check this list of things to arrange while you're still at home.

You need a **passport**—but no visa or shots—to travel in Portugal. You may be denied entry into certain European countries if your passport is due to expire within six months of your ticketed date of return. Get it renewed if you'll be cutting it close. It can take up to six weeks to get or renew a passport (for more on passports and requirements for Portugal, see www.travel.state.gov). Pack a photocopy of your passport in your luggage in case the original is lost or stolen.

**Book rooms well in advance** if you'll be traveling during peak season (May-Sept) or any major holidays (see page 440).

Call your **debit- and credit-card companies** to let them know the countries you'll be visiting, to ask about fees, and to request your PIN if you don't already know it. See page 399 for details.

Do your homework if you're considering **travel insurance.**

## How Was Your Trip?

Were your travels fun, smooth, and meaningful? You can share tips, concerns, and discoveries at www.ricksteves.com/feedback. To check out readers' hotel and restaurant reviews—or leave one yourself—visit my travel forum at www.ricksteves.com/travel-forum. I value your feedback. Thanks in advance.

Compare the cost of the insurance to the cost of your potential loss. Also check whether your existing insurance (health, homeowners, or renters) covers you and your possessions overseas. For more tips, see www.ricksteves.com/insurance.

If you're planning on **renting a car,** be aware that Portugal has one of the highest rates of automobile accidents in Europe—but also delightfully uncrowded highways outside major cities.

If you plan to hire a **local guide,** reserve ahead by email. Popular guides can get booked up.

If you're bringing a **mobile device,** consider signing up for an international plan for cheaper calls, texts, and data (see page 419). Download any apps you might want to use on the road, such as translators, maps, transit schedules, and **Rick Steves Audio Europe** (see sidebar).

Check for recent **updates to this book** at www.ricksteves.com/update.

## Traveling as a Temporary Local

We travel all the way to Portugal to enjoy differences—to become temporary locals. You'll experience frustrations. Certain truths that we find "God-given" or "self-evident," such as cold beer, ice in drinks, bottomless cups of coffee, "the customer is king," and bigger being better, are suddenly not so true. One of the benefits of travel is the eye-opening realization that there are logical, civil, and even better alternatives. A willingness to go local ensures that you'll enjoy a full dose of Portuguese hospitality. And with an eagerness to go local, you'll have even more fun.

Europeans generally like Americans. But if there is a negative aspect to the Portuguese image of Americans, it's that we are loud, wasteful, ethnocentric, too informal (which can seem disrespectful), and a bit naive.

While the Portuguese look bemusedly at some of our Yankee

excesses—and worriedly at others—they nearly always afford us individual travelers all the warmth we deserve.

Judging from all the happy feedback I receive from travelers who have used this book, it's safe to assume you'll enjoy a great, affordable vacation—with the finesse of an independent, experienced traveler.

Thanks, and *boa viagem!*

*Rick Steves*

# Back Door Travel Philosophy

**From *Rick Steves Europe Through the Back Door***

Travel is intensified living—maximum thrills per minute and one of the last great sources of legal adventure. Travel is freedom. It's recess, and we need it.

Experiencing the real Europe requires catching it by surprise, going casual..."through the Back Door."

Affording travel is a matter of priorities. (Make do with the old car.) You can eat and sleep—simply, safely, and enjoyably—anywhere in Europe for $100 a day plus transportation costs. In many ways, spending more money only builds a thicker wall between you and what you traveled so far to see. Europe is a cultural carnival, and time after time, you'll find that its best acts are free and the best seats are the cheap ones.

A tight budget forces you to travel close to the ground, meeting and communicating with the people. Never sacrifice sleep, nutrition, safety, or cleanliness to save money. Simply enjoy the local-style alternatives to expensive hotels and restaurants.

Connecting with people carbonates your experience. Extroverts have more fun. If your trip is low on magic moments, kick yourself and make things happen. If you don't enjoy a place, maybe you don't know enough about it. Seek the truth. Recognize tourist traps. Give a culture the benefit of your open mind. See things as different, but not better or worse. Any culture has plenty to share. When an opportunity presents itself, make it a habit to say "yes."

Of course, travel, like the world, is a series of hills and valleys. Be fanatically positive and militantly optimistic. If something's not to your liking, change your liking.

Travel can make you a happier American, as well as a citizen of the world. Our Earth is home to seven billion equally precious people. It's humbling to travel and find that other people don't have the "American Dream"—they have their own dreams. Europeans like us, but with all due respect, they wouldn't trade passports.

Thoughtful travel engages us with the world. It reminds us what is truly important. By broadening perspectives, travel teaches new ways to measure quality of life.

Globetrotting destroys ethnocentricity, helping us understand and appreciate other cultures. Rather than fear the diversity on this planet, celebrate it. Among your most prized souvenirs will be the strands of different cultures you choose to knit into your own character. The world is a cultural yarn shop, and Back Door travelers are weaving the ultimate tapestry. Join in!

# PORTUGAL

Portugal is underrated. The country seems somewhere just beyond Europe—prices are a bit cheaper, and the pace of life is noticeably slower. While membership in the European Union has brought sweeping changes to Portugal, the traditional economy is still based on fishing, cork, wine, textiles, and tourism. And yet, Portuguese cities have a worldly buzz: You can munch barnacles bought from a petticoat-clad street vendor on a breezy tiled square, or, a few steps away, sit down with gastronomic pilgrims for a trendy neo-Portuguese feast.

From a traveler's perspective, Portugal is greater than the sum of its parts. The country has few, if any, "blockbuster" sights. Its gritty cities—while increasingly rejuvenated—still come with rough edges. Even its "ritziest" coastal towns are relatively humble, lacking major attractions. And yet, the country offers a heady mix—warmhearted people, vivid culture, laid-back attitude, vertical cityscapes with dramatic viewpoints, gnarled cork trees and terraced vineyards, and (of course) sun-drenched beaches—that conspires to make traveling here a delight.

The easygoing locals, not jaded by tourists, will greet you with warmth—especially if you learn at least a few words of Portuguese, instead of launching into Spanish (see "Portuguese Survival Phrases" in the appendix). But if you do speak some Spanish, it can help—people here are generally gracious, patient, and eager to communicate.

Get your bearings to Portugal's major regions: Lisbon, the capital, is a world unto itself, with an easy sidetrip to the over-the-top royal pleasure palaces at Sintra. To the south is the arid Alentejo region, known for its rugged landscape, cork groves, hearty cuisine, and historic college town of Évora. And at the southern fringe of Portugal is the Algarve—a storied coastline with sandy beaches framed by striped cliffs and jagged sea stacks,

# Portugal Almanac

**Official Name:** It's República Portuguesa, but locals just say "Portugal."

**Population:** Nearly 11 million people. Most Portuguese are Roman Catholic (81 percent), with indigenous Mediterranean roots; there are a few black Africans and Brazilians (from former colonies) and some Eastern Europeans.

**Latitude and Longitude:** 39°N and 8°W (similar latitude to Washington, D.C. or San Francisco).

**Area:** 35,000 square miles, which includes the Azores and Madeira, two island groups in the Atlantic.

**Geography:** Portugal is rectangular, 325 miles long and 125 miles wide. (It's roughly the size and shape of Indiana.) The half of the country north of Lisbon is more mountainous, cool, and rainy. The south consists of rolling plains, where it's hot and dry. Portugal has 350 miles of coastline, much of it sandy beaches.

**Rivers:** The major rivers, most notably the Rio Tejo (or Tagus River, 600 miles long, spilling into the Atlantic at Lisbon) and the Douro (100 miles, flowing through wine country, ending at Porto), run east-west from Spain.

**Mountains:** Serra da Estrela, at 6,500 feet, is the highest point on the mainland (and synonymous with its best cheese), but Portugal's highest peak is Mt. Pico (7,713 feet) in the Azores.

**Biggest Cities:** Lisbon (the capital, 548,000 in the core, with more than 3 million in greater Lisbon), Porto (238,000 in the core, with 1.7 million total), and Coimbra and Braga (each with 144,000 in the core).

**Economy:** The Gross Domestic Product is about $290 billion, and the GDP per capita is around $28,000. Some major money-mak-

beach towns both big (Lagos, Tavira) and small (Salema), and the "end of the earth" point of Europe at Cape Sagres.

Heading north from Lisbon, you pass through the attraction-studded region of central Portugal, with student-packed Coimbra, beachy Nazaré, the grand monasteries at Batalha and Alcobaça, charming little Óbidos, and the famous pilgrimage site at Fátima. And up in the north—with a cooler climate and a famously businesslike attitude—are the hardworking city of Porto and the terraced Douro Valley. While this sounds like a lot—and it is—Portugal is compact and well-connected by good roads; everything mentioned here is within a three-hour drive of the capital.

Wherever you go, you're never far from the sea. The Atlantic Ocean was the source of Portugal's seafaring wealth long ago, and remains the draw for tourists today. From fresh seafood to luxurious beaches, Portugal's maritime spirit is intact.

ers for Portugal are fish (canned sardines), cork, budget clothes and shoes, port wine, and tourism. More than 25 percent of Portugal's foreign trade is with Spain. Still recovering from the Great Recession, Portugal's unemployment hovers around 11 percent. One in 10 Portuguese works in agriculture, 70 percent work in service jobs, and 25 percent in industry. The minimum monthly wage is €580, and the average rent is €400.

**Government:** The prime minister—currently the left-wing António Costa—is the chief executive, having assumed power as the head of the leading vote-getting party in legislative elections. President Marcelo Rebelo de Sousa commands the military and can dissolve the Parliament when he sees fit (it's rarely done, but he has the power). There are 230 legislators, elected to four-year terms, making up the single-house Assembly. Regionally, Portugal is divided into 18 districts (Lisbon, Coimbra, Porto, etc.).

**Flag:** The flag is two-fifths green and three-fifths red, united by the Portuguese coat of arms—a shield atop a navigator's armillary sphere.

**Soccer:** The three most popular teams are Sporting CP Lisbon, Benfica (also from Lisbon), and FC Porto.

**The Average *Senhor* and *Senhora*:** The average Portuguese is 41 years old and will live 79 years. Two in five Portuguese live near either Lisbon or Porto, and slightly less than two in three own a car.

Over the centuries, Portugal and Spain have had a love-hate, on-again-off-again relationship, but they have almost always remained separate, each with their own distinct language and culture. The Portuguese seem humbler and friendlier than the Spanish. Visitors to Spain sometimes feel like they can't do anything right; in Portugal you'll feel like you can't do anything wrong. Portugal is also more ethnically diverse than Spain, as it's inhabited by many people from its former colonies in Brazil, Africa, and Asia. The Portuguese continue to have a special affinity for their Brazilian cousins.

Long before Spain famously expelled its North African Muslim rulers, Portugal bucked the Moors, establishing its present-day borders 800 years ago. A couple of centuries later, the Age of Discovery (1400-1600) made Portugal one of the world's richest nations. Portugal's Prince Henry the Navigator sponsored the explorers who voyaged to Africa seeking a trade route to India: Gil Eanes, Bartolomeu Dias, and Vasco da Gama. Another legendary explorer, Ferdinand Magellan, sailed under the auspices of Spain, but was born in Portugal.

The wealth from Portugal's colonies financed an explosion of the arts back home. The finest architecture from Portugal's Golden Age is in Lisbon, represented by Belém's tower and monastery (in a style now called "Manueline," after then King Manuel I). Other great monasteries—with grand tombs and restful tiled cloisters—are in Batalha and Alcobaça. But no country can corner the market on trade for long, and as with Spain, Portugal underwent a long decline.

*Saudade*—a deep, yearning nostalgia for something you love but that's forever gone—is a distinctive characteristic of the Portuguese people. Portugal peaked in the 15th century, and it's all been downhill from there. These days, Portugal is small..."just us and the Atlantic Ocean," they say. Poets and artists see *saudade* in melancholy people, ornate buildings, lampposts, fado, and even in port wine.

Along with Spain, in the 20th century Portugal suffered through fascism longer than the rest of Europe: From 1932 to 1974, Portugal endured the repressive regime of António de Oliveira Salazar and his successor Marcello Caetano—the longest dictatorship in western European history. This put Portugal in an economic hole that it's still digging out of. When Portugal became part of the European Union (just 12 years after the end of the dictatorship), it was western Europe's poorest country.

The EU spurred great investment in Portugal, helping to bring its economy up to speed. But that money came with strings attached, and—especially following the Great Recession—Portugal finds itself struggling with austerity measures to repay EU loans. It's proved challenging to maintain generous social services, keep taxes reasonable, and reduce unemployment.

Poverty still exists—particularly in rural areas—but overall, the country feels more prosperous than a generation ago. Cities like Lisbon and Porto have sprung to life, with improved infrastructure, rejuvenated cityscapes, and the lively bustle of commerce: foodie restaurants, trendy design shops, and stay-a-while cafés on *azulejo*-slathered squares.

Speaking of *azulejos*, those colorful tiles are one of the many Portuguese icons you'll never tire of seeing. As practical in this hot climate (for their cooling properties) as they are beautiful, *azulejos* decorate seemingly every surface (see page 99).

While you're at it, don't miss these other items on the "Portuguese claims to fame" checklist: cork (that famously versatile material grown in the arid Alentejo region); haunting fado music, sung by nostalgic fishermen's wives in Lisbon and lusty students in Coimbra; colorful cans of preserved fish, called *conserves*; port, the fortified and aged wine produced in the north; and the lovably rickety old trolleys that trundle footsore commuters up and down the hills of Lisbon and Porto. While seemingly clichéd, these are all authentic slices of Portuguese life—each with its own backstory, which proud locals love to tell.

All over Portugal, you'll see the country's mascot: the Rooster of Barcelos, with colorful designs on his black body and a proud red pompadour. Inspired by the legend of a rooster who came back from the dead to prove the innocence of an unjustly accused man, it symbolizes justice and good luck—and is a souvenir-stand staple.

With a rich culture, friendly people, affordable prices, and a salty setting on the edge of Europe, Portugal understandably remains a rewarding destination for travelers.

# LISBON

*Lisboa*

Lisbon is ramshackle, trendy, and charming all at once—an endearing mix of now and then. Vintage trolleys shiver up and down its hills, bird-stained statues mark grand squares, taxis rattle and screech through cobbled lanes, and Art Nouveau cafés are filled equally with well-worn and well-dressed locals—nursing their coffees side-by-side. It's a city of proud ironwork balconies, multicolored tiles, and mosaic sidewalks; of bougainvillea and red-tiled roofs with antique TV antennas; and of foodie haunts and designer boutiques.

Lisbon, Portugal's capital, is the country's banking and manufacturing center. Residents call their city Lisboa (leezh-BOH-ah), which comes from the Phoenician *Alis Ubbo,* meaning "calm port." A port city on the yawning mouth of the Rio Tejo (REE-oo TAY-zhoo—the Tagus River), Lisbon welcomes large ships to its waters and state-of-the-art dry docks. And more recently, it has become a hugely popular stop with cruise ships.

Romans (2nd century B.C.) and Moors (8th century) were the earliest settlers in Lisbon, but the city's glory days were in the 15th and 16th centuries, when explorers such as Vasco da Gama opened new trade routes around Africa to India, making Lisbon one of Europe's richest cities. Portugal's Age of Discovery fueled rapid economic growth, which sparked the flamboyant art boom called the Manueline period—named for King Manuel I (r. 1495-1521).

On the morning of All Saints' Day in 1755, a tremendous earthquake hit Lisbon, followed by a devastating tsunami and days of fires. (For more on this cataclysmic event, see page 54.) Chief Minister Marquês de Pombal rebuilt downtown Lisbon on a grid plan, with broad boulevards and generous squares. It's this

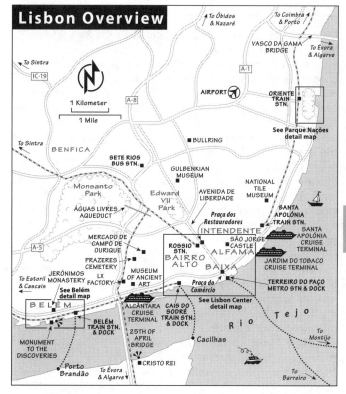

# Lisbon Overview

To Óbidos & Nazaré

To Coimbra & Porto

VASCO DA GAMA BRIDGE

To Évora & Algarve

To Sintra

IC-19

A-1

N

1 Kilometer

1 Mile

AIRPORT

A-8

ORIENTE TRAIN STN.

See Parque Nações detail map

To Sintra

BENFICA

BULLRING

SETE RIOS BUS STN.

GULBENKIAN MUSEUM

NATIONAL TILE MUSEUM

Monsanto Park

Edward VII Park

AVENIDA DE LIBERDADE

SANTA APOLÓNIA TRAIN STN.

ÁGUAS LIVRES AQUEDUCT

A-5

Praça dos Restauradores

INTENDENTE

SANTA APOLÓNIA CRUISE TERMINAL

MERCADO DE CAMPO DE OURIQUE

ROSSIO STN.

SÃO JORGE CASTLE

ALFAMA

PRAZERES CEMETERY

BAIRRO ALTO

BAIXA

JARDIM DO TOBACO CRUISE TERMINAL

To Estoril & Cascais

JERÓNIMOS MONASTERY

LX FACTORY

MUSEUM OF ANCIENT ART

Praça do Comércio

TERREIRO DO PAÇO METRO STN & DOCK

See Belém detail map

BELÉM

ALCÂNTARA CRUISE TERMINAL

CAIS DO SODRÉ TRAIN STN. & DOCK

See Lisbon Center detail map

Rio Tejo

To Montijo

MONUMENT TO THE DISCOVERIES

BELÉM TRAIN STN. & DOCK

25TH OF APRIL BRIDGE

Cacilhas

To Barreiro

Porto Brandão

To Évora & Algarve

CRISTO REI

LISBON

"Pombaline"-era neighborhood where you'll spend much of your time, though remnants of Lisbon's preearthquake charm survive in Belém, the Alfama, and the Bairro Alto district. The bulk of your sightseeing will likely be in these neighborhoods.

As the Paris of the Portuguese-speaking world, Lisbon (pop. 548,000 in the core) is the Old World capital of its former empire—some 100 million people stretching from Europe to Brazil to Africa to China. Portugal remains on largely good terms with its former colonies—and immigrants from places such as Mozambique and Angola add diversity and flavor to the city, making it as likely that you'll hear African music as much as Portuguese fado.

With its characteristic hills, trolleys, famous suspension bridge, and rolling fog, Lisbon has a San Francisco feel. Enjoy all this world-class city has to offer: elegant outdoor cafés, exciting art, fun-to-browse shops, stunning vistas, delicious food, entertaining museums, and a salty sailors' quarter with a hill-capping castle.

## PLANNING YOUR TIME

Lisbon merits at least three days, including a day for a side-trip to Sintra. If you have more time, there's plenty to do.

**Day 1:** Get oriented to Lisbon's three downtown neighborhoods (following my three self-guided walks; see page 40): Alfama, Baixa, and Bairro Alto/Chiado. Start where the city did, at its castle (hop a taxi or Uber to get there at 9:00, before the crowds hit). After surveying the city from the highest viewpoint in town, walk downhill into the characteristic Alfama neighborhood and end at the Fado Museum. From there, zip over to the big main square (Praça do Comércio) to explore the Baixa, then ride up the Elevador da Glória funicular to begin the Bairro Alto and Chiado walk. Art lovers can then hop a taxi to the Gulbenkian Museum (open until 18:00, closed Tue), while shoppers can browse the boutiques of the Chiado and Príncipe Real. Consider dinner at a fado show in the Bairro Alto or the Alfama. For more evening options, see "Entertainment in Lisbon" (page 108).

**Day 2:** Trolley to Belém and tour the monastery, tower, and National Coach Museum. Have lunch in Belém, then tour the Museum of Ancient Art on your way back to Lisbon.

**Day 3:** Side-trip to Sintra to tour the Pena Palace and explore the ruined Moorish castle.

**More Time:** An extra day (or more) lets you slow down and relax—potentially spreading the "Day 1" activities over two days. Use the extra time to explore and window-shop characteristic neighborhoods and nurse drinks bought from kiosks on relaxing squares. You could also head to the Parque das Nações and/or National Tile Museum, or take a food tour.

**Monday Options:** Many top sights are closed on Monday, particularly in Belém. That'd be a good day to choose among the following options: Take my self-guided neighborhood walks; daytrip to Sintra (where all of the major sights are open); go on a guided walking tour with Lisbon Walker or Inside Lisbon (see page 35); or head to Parque das Nações for a dose of modern Lisbon.

# Orientation to Lisbon

## LISBON: A VERBAL MAP

Greater Lisbon has close to three million people and intimidating sprawl. But most visitors spend virtually all their time in the old city center, a delightful series of parks, boulevards, and squares in a crusty, well-preserved architectural shell. But on even a brief visit, you'll also want to venture to Belém, the riverfront suburb with many top sights.

Here's an overview of the city's layout:

**Baixa** (Lower Town): Downtown Lisbon fills a valley flanked by two hills along the banks of the Rio Tejo. In that valley the neighborhood called Baixa (BYE-shah), stretches from the main squares—Rossio (roh-SEE-oo) and Praça da Figueira (PRAH-sah dah fee-GAY-rah)—to the waterfront. The Baixa is a flat, pleasant shopping area of grid-patterned streets. As Lisbon's main cross-roads and transportation hub, touristy Baixa has lots of hotels, venerable cafés and pastry shops, and kitschy souvenir stands.

**Alfama:** The hill to the east of the Baixa is the Alfama (al-FAH-mah), a colorful tangle of medieval streets, topped by São Jorge Castle. The lower slopes of the Alfama are a spilled spaghetti of old sailors' homes.

**Bairro Alto** (High Town): The hill to the west of the Baixa is capped by the Bairro Alto (BYE-roh AHL-too), with a tight grid of steep, narrow, and characteristic lanes. Downhill toward the Baixa, the Bairro Alto fades into the trendy and inviting **Chiado** (shee-AH-doo), with linger-a-while squares, upmarket restaurants, and high-fashion stores.

**Modern Lisbon:** From this historic core, the modern city stretches north (sloping uphill) along wide Avenida da Liberdade and beyond (way beyond), where you find Edward VII Park, the Gulbenkian Museum, breezy botanical gardens, the bullring, and the airport.

**Away from the Center:** Along the riverfront are two worthwhile areas. Three miles west of the center is the suburb of **Belém** (beh-LAYNG), home to much of Lisbon's best sightseeing, with several Age of Discovery sights (particularly the Monastery of Jerónimos)—and you can visit the Museum of Ancient Art along the way. Five miles north of the center is **Parque das Nações,** site of the Expo '98 world's fair and now a modern shopping complex and riverfront promenade (the National Tile Museum is about halfway there).

Few tourists venture **across the Rio Tejo,** but public ferries sail to the little port communities of Cacilhas (from downtown; connected by bus to the towering Cristo Rei statue) or Porto Brandão (from Belém)—both have popular fish restaurants.

## TOURIST INFORMATION

Lisbon has several tourist offices—all branded "ask me Lisboa"—and additional information kiosks sprout around town during the busy summer months (www.visitlisboa.com). The main TIs are strategically located on **Praça dos Restauradores** at Palácio Foz (daily 9:00-20:00, tel. 213-463-314; TI for rest of Portugal in same office; there's also a kiosk across the street); on **Praça do Comércio** (two locations; both daily 10:00-20:00, tel. 210-312-810); and at the **airport** (daily 7:00-24:00, tel. 218-450-660). Smaller TI kiosks are at the bottom (south end) of **Rossio** (daily 10:00-13:00

LISBON

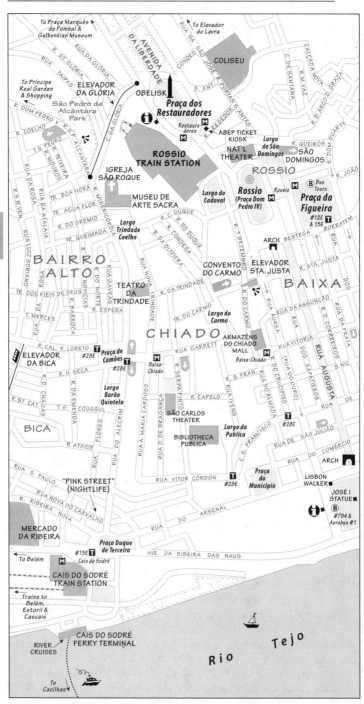

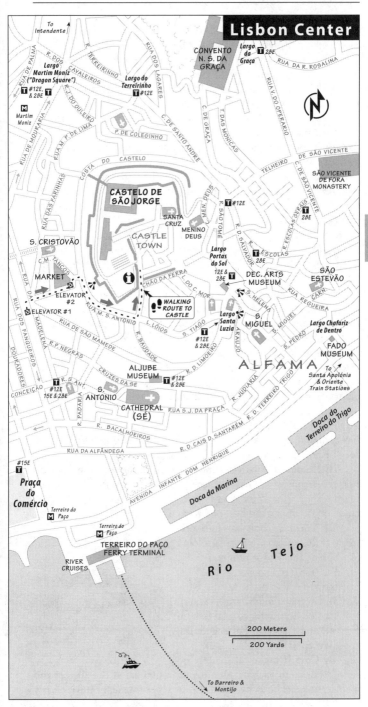

# Lisbon Center

To Intendente

CONVENTO N. S. DA GRAÇA

Largo da Graça · T 28E

RUA DA R. ROSALINA

R. DOS CAVALEIROS

TERREIRINHO

RUA DOS LAGARES

R. DE PALMA

Largo Martim Moniz ("Dragon Square") · T #12E & 28E · T

Largo do Terreirinho · T #12E

R. J. DO OUTEIRO

RUA P.e DE LIMA

M Martim Moniz

RUA DE MOURARIA

RUA DAS FARINHAS

P. DE COLEGINHO

C. DE SANTO ANDRE

C. DE GRAÇA

T. DAS MONICAS

RUA Y. DO OPERARIO

DE SÃO VICENTE

SÃO VICENTE DE FORA MONASTERY

COSTA DO CASTELO

CASTELO DE SÃO JORGE

CASTLE TOWN

SANTA CRUZ

MENINO DEUS

T #12E

C. MEN DEUS

SÃO TOMÉ

TELHEIRO

C. DE SÃO VICENTE

T 28E

R. ESCOLAS GERAIS

S. CRISTOVÃO

C.M. TANCOS

MARKET

R. DA PADARIA

RUA DOS FANQUEIROS

ELEVATOR #2

ELEVATOR #1

RUA DA MADALENA

R.P. NEGRAS

CRUZES DA SÉ

CHÃO DA FEIRA

L. DO C. MOR

RUA M. S. ANTONIO

RUA DE SÃO MAMEDE

R. SAUDADE

RUA LÓIOS

S. TIAGO

WALKING ROUTE TO CASTLE

Largo Portas do Sol · 12E & 28E · T

R. D. SALVADOR

ESCOLAS · T

DEC. ARTS MUSEUM

S. HELENA

R. S. MIGUEL

Largo Santa Luzia · T #12E & 28E

S. MIGUEL

R. ARAUJO

SÃO ESTEVÃO

RUA REGUEIRA

Largo Chafariz de Dentro

S. PEDRO

ALFAMA

FADO MUSEUM

To Santa Apolónia & Oriente Train Stations

ALJUBE MUSEUM · T #12E & 28E

S. ANTONIO · T R.S. ANT. 15E & 28E

CATHEDRAL (SÉ)

RUA S.J. DA PRAÇA

R.D. LIMOEIRO

R. JUDIARIA

R.D. TERREIRO TRIGO

R. BACALHOEIROS

R.D. CAIS D. SANTARÉM

RUA DA ALFÂNDEGA

CONCEIÇÃO

R. DOURADORES

Doca do Terreiro do Trigo

#15E · T

Praça do Comércio

Terreiro do Paço M

Terreiro do Paço M

AVENIDA INFANTE DOM HENRIQUE

Doca da Marina

TERREIRO DO PAÇO FERRY TERMINAL

RIVER CRUISES

Rio Tejo

To Barreiro & Montijo

200 Meters

200 Yards

LISBON

& 14:00-18:00, mobile 910-517-914); across the street from the monastery in **Belém** (Tue-Sat 10:00-13:00 & 14:00-18:00, closed Sun-Mon, tel. 213-658-435); at **Parque das Nações**, in front of the Vasco da Gama mall toward the riverfront (daily 10:00-13:00 & 14:00-19:00, Oct-March until 18:00); and inside **Santa Apolónia train station** (open only Tue-Sat 7:00-9:00, closed Sun-Mon, to-ward the end of track 3). At any TI, you can buy a LisboaCard (see next) and pick up the free city map and information-packed *Follow Me Lisboa* booklet (monthly, cultural and museum listings—also available at www.visitlisboa.com, "Publications" tab).

**LisboaCard:** This card covers all public transportation (as well as trains to Sintra and Cascais) and free entry to many museums (including the Museum of Ancient Art, National Tile Museum, National Coach Museum, Monastery of Jerónimos, and Belém Tower). It also provides discounts on many museums (including sights at Sintra), city tours, and river cruises. You can buy the card at Lisbon's TIs (including the airport TI), but not at participating sights. If you plan to museum-hop, the card is a good value, par-ticularly for a day in Belém (covers your transportation and most sightseeing). The card is unnecessary if you're a student or senior, for whom most sights are free or half-price. When considering the card, remember that many sights are closed on Monday and free on the first Sunday of each month. Carry the LisboaCard booklet with you—some discounts require coupons contained inside (€19/24 hours, €32/48 hours, €39/72 hours, kids 5-11 nearly half-price, in-cludes excellent explanatory guidebook, www.askmelisboa.com).

## ARRIVAL IN LISBON

For complete information on arriving at or departing from Lisbon, see "Lisbon Connections" at the end of this chapter.

**By Plane:** International and domestic flights arrive at Lisbon's Portela Airport. On arrival, check in at the handy TI—it's a smart place to buy your LisboaCard. Options for getting into town in-clude taxis, Uber, Aerobus, or Metro (all described on page 137).

**By Train:** Lisbon has four pri-mary train stations: Santa Apolónia (to Spain and most points north), Oriente (for the Algarve, Évora, Sin-tra, and fast trains to the north), Ros-sio (for Sintra, Óbidos, and Nazaré), and Cais do Sodré (for coastal Belém, Estoril, and Cascais). For schedules, see www.cp.pt.

**By Car:** It makes absolutely no sense to drive in Lisbon. Dump your rental car at the airport and connect to your hotel by a €10 taxi or Uber ride (car return clearly marked; the airport is also a good place to pick up a car on your way out of town).

If you must drive and are entering Lisbon from the north, a series of boulevards takes you into the center. Navigate by following signs to *Centro, Avenida da República, Marquês de Pombal, Avenida da Liberdade, Praça dos Restauradores, Rossio,* and *Praça do Comércio.* If coming from the east over the Vasco da Gama Bridge and heading for the airport, take the first exit after the bridge.

**Parking:** There are many safe underground pay parking lots in Lisbon (follow blue *P* signs), but they discourage anything but short stays by getting more expensive by the hour. Expect to pay €20 per day (the most central Praça dos Restauradores costs €17.50/24 hours if you pay when you arrive).

## HELPFUL HINTS

**Exchange Rate:** €1 = about $1.10

**Country Calling Code:** 351 (see page 422 for dialing instructions)

**Theft Alert:** Lisbon has piles of people doing illegal business on the street. While the city is generally safe, if you're looking for trouble—especially after dark—you may find it.

Pickpockets target tourists on the trolleys, elevators, and funiculars. Enjoy the sightseeing, but be aware. Wear your money belt and keep your pack zipped up. Some thieves pose as tourists by wearing cameras and toting maps. Be on guard whenever you're in a crush of people, or jostled as you enter or leave a tram or bus. And be wary of beggars in the street—some are scammers and pickpockets.

**Pedestrian Warning:** Lisbon's unique black-and-white pattered tile pavement, while picturesque, can be very slippery. And trams can be quiet and sneak up on you if you're not paying attention. Even some of the tuk-tuks are "eco" (electric) and can zip up behind you silently.

**Free Days and Monday Closures:** National museums are free on the first Sunday of each month (all day or until 14:00); the (private) Gulbenkian Museum is free every Sunday after 14:00. Many major sights are closed on Monday, including Lisbon's Museum of Ancient Art, National Tile Museum, and Fado Museum, as well as Belém's Monastery of Jerónimos, Coach Museum, and Belém Tower.

**Market Days:** Tuesdays and Saturdays are flea- and food-market days in the Alfama's Campo de Santa Clara. On Sundays, the LxFactory zone, in the shadow of the 25th of April Bridge, hosts a lively farmers market (9:30-16:00; for location, see "Lisbon Overview" map).

**Useful App:** ∩ For a free audio tour that covers portions of my self-guided walks in this book, get the **Rick Steves' Audio Europe** app (for details, see page 9).

**Post Office:** Modern, user-friendly post offices (*correios* or *CTT*) are at Praça dos Restauradores 58 (closed Sun) and on Rua da Santa Justa 15 (closed Sat-Sun).

**Laundry:** Drop off clothes at centrally located **5àSec Lavandaria** (€7.50/kilo, same-day wash-and-dry service usually possible if you drop off early, Mon-Fri 8:00-20:00, Sat 10:00-20:00, closed Sun, next to the bottom level of the Armazéns do Chiado mall and lower entrance to Baixa-Chiado Metro stop at Rua do Crucifixo 99, tel. 213-479-599).

**Travel Agency: GeoStar** is handy and helpful for train tickets (Portugal only) and flights (Mon-Fri 9:30-18:30, closed Sat-Sun, Praça dos Restauradores 14, tel. 213-245-240).

**Ticket Kiosk:** The green **ABEP kiosk** at the bottom end of Praça dos Restauradores is a handy spot to buy a city transit pass, LisboaCard, and tickets to bullfights, soccer games, concerts, and other events (daily 9:00-20:00, across from TI).

## GETTING AROUND LISBON

If you have a LisboaCard, you can use it to ride Lisbon's public transit (see next page). Otherwise, you'll have to buy tickets.

**Ticket Options:** Transit tickets are issued on a scannable **Viva Viagem** card, which works on the Metro, funiculars, trolleys, buses, Santa Justa elevator, and some short-distance trains. The card itself costs €0.50 and is reloadable, but it's not share-able—each rider needs one. You can buy or reload the card at ticket windows or machines in Metro stations (touch "without a reusable card" for first-time users, or "with a reusable card" to top up). Keep your Viva Viagem card handy—you'll need to place it on the magnetic pad when entering and leaving the system.

You can use the Viva Viagem in three ways:

1. A **single-ride ticket** costs €1.40 (good for one hour of travel within Zone 1). But if you're taking even a few rides, "zapping" is a much better deal (see below).

2. A **24-hour pass** costs €6 (this version does not cover trains). If you're side-tripping to Sintra or Cascais, consider the €10 version, which includes trains to those towns (but does not include the bus at Sintra). Skip the €9 version of the 24-hour pass, which adds the ferry across the Tejo to Cacilhas (it's cheaper to simply buy separately).

3. **"Zapping"** lets you preload the card with anywhere from €3 to €40, and lowers the per-ride cost to €1.25. Figure out how much you'll need, and load it up (estimate conservatively—you can always top up later, but leftover credit is nonrefundable). If you'll be taking fewer than five rides in one day, zapping is your best deal

(and it's fun to say). Unlike the €6 24-hour pass, zapping can be used for trains to Sintra and Cascais.

Although it's possible to **pay the driver** as you board buses (€1.80), trolleys (€2.85), funiculars (€3.60), and the Santa Justa elevator (€5), only suckers do that. It's much cheaper if you get comfortable zapping with Viva Viagem.

For transit information, see www.carris.pt.

## By Metro

Lisbon's simple, fast, and color-coded subway system is a delight to use (runs daily 6:30-1:00 in the morning). Though it's not nec-

essary for getting around the historic downtown, the Metro is handy for trips to or from Rossio (M: Rossio or Restauradores), Praça do Comércio (M: Terreiro do Paço), the Gulbenkian Museum (M: São Sebastião), the Chiado neighborhood (M: Baixa-Chiado), Parque das Nações and the Oriente train station (both at M: Oriente), Sete Rios bus and train

stations (M: Jardim Zoológico), and the airport (M: Aeroporto). Metro stops are marked above ground with a red "M." *Saída* means "exit." You can find a Metro map at any Metro stop, on most city maps, and on the Metro website (www.metrolisboa.pt).

## By Trolley, Funicular, and Bus

Lisbon's buses are fine, but for fun and practical public transportation, use the trolleys and funiculars. These are cheapest zapping with a Viva Viagem card (see above for ticketing options).

Like San Francisco, Lisbon sees its classic **trolleys** as part of its heritage, and has kept a few in use: Trolleys #12E (circling the Alfama) and #28E (a scenic ride across the old town) use vintage cars; #15E (to Belém) uses a modern, air-conditioned version. Buy a ticket, have a pass, validate your Viva Viagem card as you enter... or risk a big fine on the spot. Please be mindful of locals—especially little old Alfama ladies—who need a seat. Trolleys rattle by every 10 minutes or so (or every 15-20 minutes after 19:00) and run until about 23:00. For much more on using and enjoying Lisbon's delightful trolleys, see page 30.

## By Taxi or Uber

Lisbon is a great taxi town except at the airport and cruise terminals, which attract greedy cabbies (for tips on dodging their scams, see "Lisbon Connections"). Otherwise, especially if you're with a companion, Lisbon's cabs are a cheap time-saver. Rides start at €4,

LISBON

# Lisbon Public Transportation

**Legend:**
- —M— Blue Line (Seagull)
- —M— Yellow (Sunflower)
- —M— Green (Sail)
- —M— Red Line (Compass)
- ·········· Rail
- - - - - Bus Routes
- ———•——— Tram Lines & Stops
- ▰▰▰ Elevador (Funicular)

Not all lines, stops or stations are shown

YELLOW LINE
Odevelas M

Campo Grande M

Telheiras M
GREEN LINE

Entre Campos M

BULL RING

Amedora Este M
BLUE LINE

Jardim Zoológico
SETE RIOS BUS STN.
Aerobus #2

GULBENKIAN MUSEUM
Campo Pequeno M

To Sintra

Sete Rios
Aerobus #2

Praça de Espanha

San Sebastião
RED LINE
Campolide

Saldanha M

Picoas M
Aerobus #1

Parque M

Marqués de Pombal M

Rato M
YELLOW LINE

Outurela

#714

Restelo

MERCADO DE CAMPO DE OURIQUE
ESTRELA BASILICA & PARK
Sta. Caterina

PRAZERES CEMETERY
Campo Ourique
#28E
SANTA CATERINA VIEWPOINT

#714 & 728

BELÉM

Centro Cultural Belém

Alcântara Terra
MUSEUM OF ANCIENT ART
BICA

To Cascais & Estoril

JERÓNIMOS MONASTERY
COACH MUSEUM
#15E

Cais Rocha
Santos
Bus #714 & 728

Largo Princesa

#15E

Algés

Largo Jerónimos

BELÉM STATION

Alcântara Mar
CAIS DO SODRÉ TRAIN STN.
GREEN LINE

BELÉM TOWER
MONUMENT TO THE DISCOVERIES
BELÉM RIVER STN.

ALCÂNTARA

ALCÂNTARA CRUISE TERMINAL
CAIS DO SODRÉ RIVER STATION

25TH OF APRIL BRIDGE

*Rio Tejo*

To Porto Brandão

To Évora & Algarve

To Cacilhas

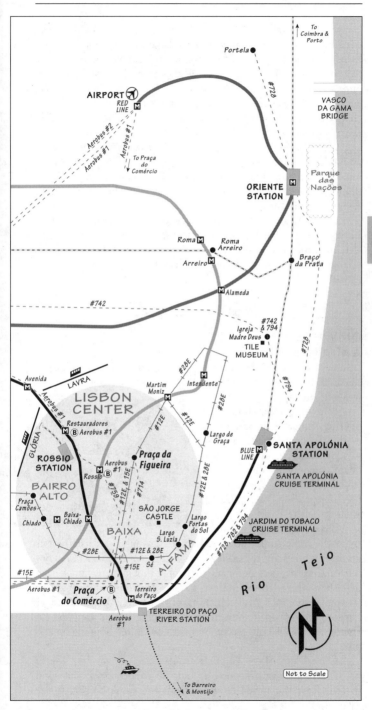

LISBON

and you can go anywhere in the center for around €6. Decals on the window clearly spell out all charges in English. Be sure your driver turns on the meter; it should start at about €4 and be set to *Tarifa 1* (Mon-Fri 6:00-21:00, including the airport) or *Tarifa 2* (same drop rate, a little more per kilometer; for nights, weekends, and holidays). If the meter reads *Tarifa 3, 4,* or *5,* simply ask the cabbie to change it, unless you're going to Belém, which is considered outside the city limits.

Cabs are generally easy to hail on the street (green light means available, lit number on the roof indicates it's taken). If you're having a hard time flagging one down, ask a passerby for the location of the nearest taxi stand: *praça de taxi* (PRAH-sah duh taxi). They're all over the town center.

Lisbon is also an excellent **Uber** town. The ride-sharing app works here just like back home; it's at least as affordable as a taxi (often cheaper, except during "surge" pricing); and the drivers and their cars are generally of great quality. If you've never tried Uber abroad, do it here.

# Tours in Lisbon

## ON WHEELS
### ▲▲Trolleys

Lisbon's trolleys—many of them vintage models from the 1920s—shake and shiver through the old parts of town, somehow safely weaving within inches of parked cars, climbing steep hills, and offering sightseers breezy views of the city (rubberneck out the window and you die). As you board, swipe your Viva Viagem card (see "Getting Around Lisbon") or pay the driver (€2.85), and take a seat.

Buses and trolleys usually share the same stops and routes. Signs for bus stops list the bus number, while signs for trolley stops include an E (for *eléctrico*) before or after the route number. Remember that most pickpocketing in Lisbon takes place on trolleys, so enjoy the ride, but keep an eye on your belongings. You can think of trolleys #28E and #12E as hop-on, hop-off do-it-yourself tours (zapping tickets are good for an hour, and a 24-hour pass comes with unlimited hopping on and off).

**Crowd Warning:** Lisbon's trolleys are an absolute joy...*if* you're sitting down and looking out the window with the wind in your face. But if you have to stand, you won't be able to see

## Lisbon's Best Viewpoints

The first three viewpoints are included in the self-guided walks described in this chapter:

- Miradouro de São Pedro de Alcântara (view terrace in Bairro Alto, at top of Elevador da Glória funicular; see "The Bairro Alto and Chiado Stroll," page 59)
- São Jorge Castle (on top of the Alfama; see photo above and "The Alfama Stroll and the Castle," page 40)
- Miradouro das Portas do Sol (south slope of Alfama; see "The Alfama Stroll and the Castle," page 40)
- Elevador de Santa Justa (in the Baixa, page 64)
- Cristo Rei (statue on hillside across the Rio Tejo, page 100)
- Edward VII Park (at north end of Avenida da Liberdade)
- Bica Miradouro (atop the Elevador da Bica funicular)

out the (low) windows, and you'll spend the jostling ride trying to steady yourself. At peak times, hordes of tourists wait at trolley stops (particularly at starting points, such as on Praça da Figueira for route #12E). My advice is, rather than being determined to take a particular trolley at a particular time, keep an eye on trolleys as they roll by...and if you see an empty one pull up, hop on and take advantage of the open space.

### Trolley #28E

Trolley #28E is a San Francisco-style Lisbon joyride. In the center of town, this trolley is often extremely crowded. To enjoy a seat for the entire scenic ride, consider taking a taxi to Mercado de Campo de Ourique for a meal or to the Prazeres Cemetery (both described next) and catching the #28E from there, where it embarks on its route across town. The following are notable trolley stops from west to east:

**Campo Ourique:** The **Prazeres Cemetery,** at the western terminus of route #28E, is a vast park-like necropolis dense with the mausoleums of leading Lisbon families and historic figures dating back to the 19th century (daily 9:00-17:00).

**Igreja Sto. Condestável:** The first stop after the cemetery is next to an angular modern church. Hiding just behind the church is the **Mercado de Campo de Ourique,** a 19th-century iron-and-glass market that's now a trendy food circus (see page 129).

**Estrela:** Two stops later, the trolley pulls up in front of another large church (on the right). The 18th-century, late Baroque **Estrela Basilica** has stairs winding up to the roof for a view both out and down into the church (€4, daily 10:00-18:00). Across the street is the gate into **Estrela Park,** a cozy neighborhood scene with exotic plants, a pond-side café, and a playground.

**Torre de Tombo:** At the next stop, you'll see a garden poking up on the left behind a high wall (which hides the prime minister's residence). Next up is the huge, stately **Assembly of the Republic** building—home to Portugal's parliament. Soon after, the trolley enters a relatively narrow street at the edge of the Bairro Alto.

**Santa Catarina:** A couple of stops into the Bairro Alto, this area is enjoyable for a stroll through characteristic streets downhill to the **Miradouro de Santa Catarina,** a view terrace with inviting cafés and bars.

**Calhariz-Bica:** Keep an eye on the streets to your right. You'll spot the top of the **Elevador da Bica funicular,** which drops steeply through a rough-and-tumble neighborhood to the riverfront.

**City-Center Stops:** From here, the downtown stops come fast and furious—**Chiado** (at Chiado's main square, Lisbon's café meeting-place); **Baixa** (on Rua da Conceição between Augusta and Prata); **Sé** (the cathedral); **Miradouro das Portas do Sol** (the Alfama viewpoint); **Campo de Santa Clara** (flea market on Tue and Sat); and the pleasant and untouristy **Graça** district (with another excellent viewpoint).

### Trolley #12E

For a colorful, 20-minute loop around the castle and the Alfama, catch trolley #12E on Praça da Figueira (departs every few minutes from the stop at corner of square closest to castle). The driver can tell you when to get out for the Miradouro das Portas do Sol viewpoint near the castle (about three-quarters of the way up the hill), or you can stay on the trolley and be dropped back where you started. Here's what you'll see on this loop ride:

Leaving Praça da Figueira, you enter **Largo de Martim Moniz**—named for a knight who died heroically while using his body as a doorjamb to leave the castle gate open, allowing his Christian Portuguese comrades to get in and capture Lisbon from the Moors in 1147. These days, this gathering point is nicknamed

"Dragon Square" for the modern sculpture erected in the middle by the local Chinese community to celebrate the Year of the Dragon.

At the next stop, on the right, is the picturesque **Centro Comercial da Mouraria,** a marketplace filled with products and aromas from around the world. The big, maroon-colored building capping the hill on the left was a Jesuit monastery until 1769, when the dictatorial Marquês de Pombal booted the pesky order out of Portugal and turned the building into the Hospital São Jose. Today, this is an immigrant neighborhood with lots of cheap import shops. (The trendy **Intendente** neighborhood is just up the street—see page 109.)

Turning right onto Rua de Cavaleiros, you climb through the atmospheric **Mouraria neighborhood** on a street so narrow that a single trolley track is all that fits. Notice how the colorful mix of neighbors who fill the trolley all seem to know each other. If the trolley's path is blocked and can't pass, lots of horn-honking and shouts from passengers ensue until your journey resumes. Look up the skinny side streets. Marvel at the creative parking and classic laundry scenes. This was the area given to the Moors after they were driven out of the castle and Alfama. Natives know it as the home of the legendary fado singer Maria Severa as well as modern-day singer Mariza. The majority of residents these days are immigrants from Asia, making this Lisbon's version of Chinatown and Bollywood wrapped up in one.

At the crest of the hill—at the square called **Largo Rodrigues de Freitas**—you can get out to explore, eat at a cheap restaurant (see "Eating in Lisbon," later), or follow Rua de Santa Marinha to the Campo de Santa Clara flea market (Tue and Sat).

When you see the river, you're at **Largo das Portas do Sol** (Gates of the Sun), where you'll also see the remains of one of the seven old Moorish gates of Lisbon. The driver usually announces *"castelo"* (cahzh-TAY-loo) at this point. Hop out here if you want to visit the Museum and School of Portuguese Decorative Arts (see page 46), enjoy the most scenic cup of coffee in town, explore the **Alfama,** or tour the **castle.**

The trolley continues downhill. First you'll pass (on the right) the stout building called **Aljube**—a prison built on a site dating from Roman times that, more recently, housed political opponents of Portugal's fascist dictator Salazar (now housing a museum about that regime; see page 71). Just downhill is the fortress-like **Lisbon Cathedral** (on left—see page 69). And finally you roll into the **Baixa** (grid-planned Pombaline city—get off here to take my self-guided Baixa walk—see page 49). After a few blocks, you're back where you started—Praça da Figueira.

### Private Trolley Tours

Yellow Bus—the dominant local tour operator (see next)—operates a hop-on, hop-off trolley tour around Lisbon. There are two lines: Hills Tramcar Tour (€19/24 hours, red, year-round) and the shorter Castle Tramcar Tour (€12/24 hours, green, summer only). These use the same tracks and stops as the cheap, easy, and frequent public trolleys described above, but cost much more. But they may be less crowded, and they come with recorded commentary (€18, 1.5-hour tour with five stops, runs every 20 minutes June-Sept 9:15-19:00, fewer off-season).

## Hop-on, Hop-off Bus Tours

Various companies operate hop-on, hop-off bus tours around Lisbon. While uninspiring and not cheap—and Lisbon's sights are compact enough to easily see on your own—these tours can be handy and run daily year-round.

**Yellow Bus** (www.yellowbustours.com) and **Gray Line** (www. cityrama.pt) run multiple loops through town, targeted on different sights; figure around €15 for 24 hours on one loop, or about €25 for 48-hour access to all loops. Each company also offers a dizzying array of combination tickets (trolley tours, tuk-tuks, boat trips, Segway tours, discounts to city sights, and so on). Buses depart from Praça da Figueira (buy tickets from driver). When comparing your options, note that Yellow Bus tickets include some Lisbon city transit as well (public trolleys, buses, Elevador de Santa Justa, and funiculars, but not the Metro).

## Tuk-Tuks

Goofy little tuk-tuks—Indian-style, three-wheel motorcycles—have invaded Lisbon. You'll see them parked in front of tourist landmarks all over town (especially in front of the cathedral and on Praça do Figueira). They have no meter—negotiate with the driver for a tour, or hire one for a point-to-point ride (they can be a little cheaper than a taxi and fit up to three). Tuk-tuks are most practical as a way to tailor your own private tour (€45/hour, €30 if demand is slow and the driver owns his own rig). The key is finding a likeable driver with good language skills and a little charm. The upside: They come with light guiding, can get you into little back lanes, let you hop on and off for quick visits and photo stops, and leave you where you like. The downside: You're contributing to something akin to an invasive weed that is blanketing the city with an annoying presence. Most are noisy and smelly, but you'll also see a few green, silent, electric "eco-tuk-tuks" that are more enticing (and more expensive).

# Ways to Get from the Baixa Up to the Bairro Alto and Chiado

- Ride the Elevador da Glória funicular (a few blocks north of Rossio on Avenida da Liberdade, opposite the Hard Rock Café), or hike alongside the tracks if the funicular isn't running.
- Walk up lots of stairs from Rossio (due west of the central column).
- Taxi or Uber to the Miradouro de São Pedro de Alcântara.
- Take the escalators at the Baixa-Chiado Metro stop. You'll first ride down, then walk past the turnstiles for the Metro entrance, then ride back up, up, up.
- Catch trolley #28E from Rua da Conceição.
- Hike up Rua do Carmo from Rossio to Rua Garrett.
- Take the elevators inside the Armazéns mall (go through the low-profile doors at Rua do Crucifixo 89 or 113); ride to floor 5, and pop out at the bottom of Rua Garrett.
- Take the Elevador de Santa Justa, which goes right by the Convento do Carmo and the Chiado (can have long lines at busy times—but if it's jammed, other options are nearby).

**LISBON**

## BY BOAT

To get out on the Rio Tejo, take a sightseeing cruise or ride a public ferry. Either way, the main destination across the river is the port of Cacilhas (kah-SEE-lahsh). You can also hop a public ferry from Belém to Porto Brandão; see page 95.

**Tourist Cruise:** Yellow Boat—part of the big Yellow Bus tour company—offers a 1.5-hour loop that links Terreiro do Paço (near Praça do Comércio), Cacilhas, and Belém. You can hop on and off, but there are just five boats per day (€19/24 hours, discounts and combo-tickets with their bus tours and other offerings, mid-March-Oct only, details at www.yellowbustours.com).

**Public Ferry Ride to Cacilhas:** For a quick, cheap trip across the river with great city and bridge views in the company of Lisbon commuters rather than tourists, hop the ferry to Cacilhas from the Cais do Sodré station (a 10-minute walk from Praça do Comércio). At the terminal, follow signs to *Cacilhas*, not *Montijo* (€1.20 each way, 4/hour weekdays, fewer on weekends, signs say *partida*—departure—and *destino*). Either hop out for a look at the rough little industrial port, or stay on the boat for a 25-minute round-trip.

## ON FOOT

Two walking-tour companies—Lisbon Walker and Inside Lisbon—offer excellent, affordable tours led by young, top-notch guides with a passion for sharing insights about their hometown.

Both have an easygoing style and small groups (generally 2-12 people); with either, you'll likely feel you've made a friend in your guide. These tours are time and money very well spent (both give my readers a discount).

### Lisbon Walker

Standard tours include "Lisbon Revelation" (best 3-hour overview, with good coverage of Baixa and main squares, quick look at Bairro Alto, and trolley ride across town to Portas do Sol viewpoint); "Old Town" (2.5-hour walk through Alfama that examines the origins of Lisbon); and "Downtown" (2-3 hours, covers 1755 earthquake and rebirth of Lisbon). Each tour includes a shot of *ginjinha* or a tasty *pastel de nata*—two edible icons of Lisbon (€20/person, €15 with this book; tours run daily year-round—check schedule online; meet at northwest corner of Praça do Comércio near Rua do Arsenal, in front of the TI—see map on page 120, tel. 218-861-840, www.lisbonwalker.com).

### Inside Lisbon

Tours include the "Best of Lisbon Walk" (good 3-hour highlights tour of the main squares, Chiado, and Alfama; €18/person, €13 with this book; daily year-round at 10:00) and food and wine tours (see "Food Tours," below). Most tours meet at the statue of Dom Pedro IV in the center of Rossio and last three to four hours (reserve a day ahead via website or phone, mobile 968-412-612, www.insidelisbon.com). They also offer daily private tours and day trips by minivan (€65/person, €60 with this book) to Sintra/Cascais (8 hours) and Obidos/Fátima (9 hours). You can organize a private city tour with them, or use their helpful website as a resource for seeing Lisbon on your own.

### Lisbon Chill-Out Free Walking Tours

If you're looking for a free tour, choose from this young and creative group of local guides (skip Sandeman's, the big expat-led free tour company in town). Your Chill-Out guide is a local who will share cultural insights as you walk through the Bairro Alto, across the Baixa, and into the Alfama. It's refreshing to get a hometown perspective, and they are upfront about "it's not really free—you tip what you like at the end." Three-hour walks start in the Bairro Alto at the statue on Praça de Camões (look for the guide wearing the yellow travel bag) daily at 10:00 and 15:00 (www.lisbonfreetour.blogspot.pt).

## FOOD TOURS

Guided food tours are trendy these days. Several companies offer three- to four-hour multistop tours that introduce you to lots of local food culture while filling your stomach at the same time. This is a quickly evolving scene, so it pays to do a little homework on the latest offerings. But I've enjoyed tours by several good outfits, listed below. In each case, the groups are small, the teaching is good, and—when you figure in the cost of the meal—the tours are a solid value.

**Inside Lisbon** offers three food-related itineraries: Their "Food and Wine Walk" makes five to six short, tasty, and memorable stand-up stops (€40/person, €35 with this book, 3 hours, Mon-Sat at 16:30). The "Sunset, Fado, and Tapas" walk includes an evening stroll and samples of local food and music (€65/person, €60 with this book, 4 hours, departs at 19:00, 5/week in summer, 2/week in winter). And their "Lisbon Experience Walk" is a tour through the Mouraria neighborhood with some food stops mixed in, ending with a ferry to Cacilhas for seafood (€45/person, €40 with this book, 4 hours, Mon-Sat at 10:30; www.insidelisbon.com).

**Culinary Backstreets** is slower-paced but more top-end, taking its time to delve into Lisbon's food scene and its culture. "Culinary Backstreets Essentials" focuses on the Mercado do Ribeira and nearby eateries and shops, ending in the Chiado. Because this company offers food tours throughout the world, it sets its prices in dollars ($95-110/person, 3.5 hours); their longer "Lisbon Awakens" tour passes through more neighborhoods ($130/person, 5.5 hours; www.culinarybackstreets.com).

**Eat Drink Walk** does a €70 tapas walk (5-6 stops in the Baixa), as well as a €85 "gourmet" walk (finer places in the Chiado; www.eatdrinkwalk.pt).

## LOCAL GUIDES

Hiring a private local guide in Lisbon can be a wonderful luxury: Your guide will meet you at your hotel and tailor a tour to your interests. Especially with a small group, this can be a fine value. Guides charge roughly the same rates (€125/half-day, €200/day; car and driver options available). Delightful **Alex Almeida** runs **Your Friend in Lisbon** (group of 4 guides, mobile 919-292-151, www.yourfriendinlisbon.com, alex@yourfriendinlisbon.com). **Cristina Duarte** leads tours for my company and knows Lisbon well (mobile 919-316-242, www.lisbonbeyond.pt, acrismduarte@gmail.com). **Claudia da Costa,** who appears on my Lisbon TV show, is also excellent (mobile 965-560-216, claudiadacosta@hotmail.com). **Cristina Quental** is another fine local guide (mobile 919-922-480, anacristinaquental@hotmail.com).

LISBON

# Lisbon at a Glance

## In Lisbon

▲▲▲**Alfama Stroll and the Castle** Tangled medieval streets topped by São Jorge Castle. See page 40.

▲▲▲**Baixa Stroll** The lower town—Lisbon's historic downtown—gridded with streets and dotted with major squares. See page 49.

▲▲▲**Bairro Alto and Chiado Stroll** The high town's views, churches, and Chiado fashion district. See page 59.

▲▲**Gulbenkian Museum** Lisbon's best museum, featuring an art collection spanning 5,000 years, from ancient Egypt to Impressionism to Art Nouveau. **Hours:** Wed-Mon 10:00-18:00, closed Tue. See page 72.

▲▲**Museum of Ancient Art** Portuguese paintings from the 15th- and 16th-century glory days. **Hours:** Tue-Sun 10:00-18:00, closed Mon. See page 76.

▲▲**Parque das Nações** Inviting waterfront park with a long promenade, modern mall, aquarium, and the Expo '98 fairgrounds. **Hours:** Park always open. See page 96.

▲**Fado Museum** The story of Portuguese folk music. **Hours:** Tue-Sun 10:00-18:00, closed Mon. See page 48.

▲**São Roque Church and Museum** Fine 16th-century Jesuit church with false dome ceiling, chapel made of precious stones, and a less-interesting museum. **Hours:** Mon 14:00-18:00, Tue-Sun 9:00-19:00—until 18:00 in winter, Thu until 20:00. See page 61.

▲**Lisbon Cathedral** From the outside, an impressive Romanesque fortress of God; inside, not much. **Hours:** Tue-Sat 9:00-19:00, Sun-Mon until 17:00. See page 69.

**National Tile Museum** Tons of artistic tiles, including a panorama of preearthquake Lisbon. **Hours:** Tue-Sun 10:00-18:00, closed Mon. See page 98.

**Solar do Vinho do Porto** Plush place selling tastes of the world's greatest selection of ports. **Hours:** Mon-Fri 11:00-24:00, Sat 14:00-24:00, closed Sun. See page 135.

**São Jorge Castle** Originally an eighth-century bastion, first built by the Moors, with kingly views at the highest point in town. **Hours:** Daily March-Oct 9:00-21:00, Nov-Feb until 18:00. See page 43.

**Museum and School of Portuguese Decorative Arts** Aristocratic household richly decorated in 15th- to 18th-century styles. **Hours:** Wed-Mon 10:00-17:00, closed Tue. See page 46.

**Elevador de Santa Justa** 150-foot-tall iron elevator offering a glittering city vista. **Hours:** Daily 7:00-23:00, until 22:00 in winter. See page 64.

LISBON

## In Belém
Note that all of these sights—except the Monument to the Discoveries—are closed on Monday year-round.

▲▲▲**Monastery of Jerónimos** King Manuel's giant 16th-century, white limestone church and monastery, with remarkable cloister and the explorer Vasco da Gama's tomb. **Hours:** Tue-Sun 10:00-18:30, Oct-April until 17:30, closed Mon. See page 84.

▲▲**National Coach Museum** Dozens of carriages, from simple to opulent, displaying the evolution of coaches from 1600 on. **Hours:** Tue-Sun 10:00-18:00, closed Mon. See page 81.

▲**Maritime Museum** Salty selection of exhibits on the ships and navigational tools of the Age of Discovery. **Hours:** Daily 10:00-18:00, Oct-April until 17:00. See page 90.

▲**Monument to the Discoveries** Giant riverside monument honoring the explorers who brought Portugal great power and riches centuries ago. **Hours:** May-Sept daily 10:00-19:00; Oct-April Tue-Sun 10:00-18:00, closed Mon. See page 91.

▲**Belém Tower** Consummate Manueline building with a worthwhile view up 120 steps. **Hours:** May-Sept Tue-Sun 10:00-18:30, off-season until 17:30, closed Mon. See page 94.

# Neighborhood Walks in Lisbon

The essential Lisbon is easily and enjoyably covered in three ▲▲▲ self-guided walking tours through three downtown neighborhoods: Alfama, Baixa, and Bairro Alto/Chiado. You can do them as individual walks, or lace them together into a single tour (allow a minimum of five hours for all three, but could be done as a more leisurely all-day experience—or, for maximum lingering, spread it over two days). You can do the walks in any order, but starting with the Alfama lets you get to the castle before the crowds hit (and avoid ticket lines), kicking things off with a grand city view from Lisbon's fortified birthplace. And you'll finish in the liveliest quarter for evening fun—the Bairro Alto/Chiado.

∩ You can download a free Rick Steves audio tour that covers some of the same territory as these walks, from Praça do Comércio through the Baixa, and up through the highlights of the Bairro Alto.

## ALFAMA STROLL AND THE CASTLE

On this ▲▲▲ walk, you'll explore the Alfama, the colorful sailors' quarter that dates back to the age of Visigoth occupation, from the sixth to eighth centuries A.D. This was a bustling district during the Moorish period, and eventually became the home of Lisbon's fishermen and mariners (and of the poet Luís de Camões, who wrote, "Our lips meet easily, high across the narrow street"). The Alfama's tangled street plan, one of the few features of Lisbon to survive the 1755 earthquake, helps make the neighborhood a cobbled playground of Old World color. The best times to visit are during the busy midmorning market, or in the cooler late afternoon or early evening, when the streets teem with residents. While much of the Alfama's grittiness has been cleaned up in recent years, it remains one of Europe's more photogenic neighborhoods.

**Getting There:** This walk begins at the highest point in town, São Jorge Castle. Get to the castle gate by **taxi** (€6); by **minibus #737** from Praça da Figueira; or by two free **elevator rides** up from the Baixa and then a short uphill walk. To find the elevators, head to Rua dos Fanqueiros and go through the easy-to-miss door at #178 (for location, see map on page 50; you'll see faint, white lettering spelling out *elevador castelo* on the red rooftop—illuminated at night). Ride the elevator to the top floor and exit, angling left across the street and through the little square. Then head up Largo Chão do Loureiro, where you'll see the second elevator (*elevador castelo;* handy supermarket with WC at bottom, view café and fine panoramic terrace at top). When exiting the second elevator, simply follow brown *Castelo de S. Jorge* signs up to the castle (right, then hooking left; about 8 minutes uphill).

Alternatively, **trolleys** #28E and #12E go to Largo Santa Luzia and Largo das Portas do Sol, respectively, a few blocks below the walk's starting point—it's a fun trip, but still a steep hike up to the castle.

## ➊ São Jorge Castle Gate and Fortified Castle Town

The formidable gate to the castle is part of a fortification that, these days, surrounds three things: the view terrace, the small town that stood within the walls, and the castle itself. The ticket office and the turnstile are situated so that those without a ticket are kept away from the view terrace and castle proper (castle entry-€8.50, daily March-Oct 9:00-21:00, Nov-Feb until 18:00).

If money is tight, the castle and view are skippable—the castle is just stark, rebuilt ruins from the Salazar era, and while the hill-capping park has a commanding view, there are other fine views coming up...just jump ahead to stop #4 on this walk.

• *If you decide to go in, follow the cobbles uphill past the first lanes of old Lisbon to the yellow ticket office, and then into the...*

## ➋ Miradouro de São Jorge (Viewpoint)

Enjoy the grand view. The Rio Tejo is one of five main rivers in Portugal, four of which come from Spain. (Only the Mondego  River, which passes through Coimbra, originates inside Portuguese territory, in the Serra de Estrela.) While Portugal and Spain generally have very good relations, a major sore point is the control of all this water. From here, you have a good view of the Golden Gate-like 25th of April Bridge, which leads south to the Cristo Rei statue (described on page 100). Past the bridge, on a clear day, you can barely see the Monument to the Discoveries and the Belém Tower (under and past the bridge on north side).

Look up at the statue marking the center of this terrace. **Afonso Henriques,** a warlord with a strong personal army, was the founder of Portugal. In 1147, he besieged this former Moorish castle until the hungry, thirsty residents gave in. Every Portuguese school-kid knows the story of this man—a Reconquista hero and their country's first king.

Stroll inland along the **ramparts** for a more extensive view of Pombal's Lisbon, described in a circa 1963, tiled panorama-chart (which lacks the big 25th of April Bridge—it was built in 1969). From Praça do Comércio on the water, the grid streets of the Baixa lead up to the tree-lined Avenida da Liberdade and the big Edward

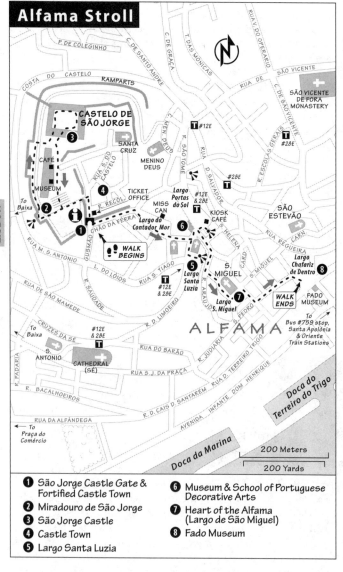

# Alfama Stroll

1 São Jorge Castle Gate & Fortified Castle Town
2 Miradouro de São Jorge
3 São Jorge Castle
4 Castle Town
5 Largo Santa Luzia
6 Museum & School of Portuguese Decorative Arts
7 Heart of the Alfama (Largo de São Miguel)
8 Fado Museum

VII Park, on the far right. Locate city landmarks, such as the Elevador de Santa Justa (the Eiffel-style elevator in front of the ruined Convento do Carmo) and the sloping white roof of Rossio station.
• *Continue walking along the viewpoint, passing several old cannons. Just after going under the second arch (just before the café terrace), take a right into the mostly ruined courtyard of...*

### ❸ São Jorge Castle

While the first settlements here go back to the 7th century B.C., this castle dates to the 11th century when Moors built it to house

their army and provide a safe haven for their elites in times of siege. After Afonso Henriques took the castle in 1147, Portugal's royalty lived here for several centuries. The sloping walls—typical of castles from this period—were designed to withstand 14th-century cannonballs. In the 16th century, the kings moved to their palace on Praça do Comércio, and the castle became a military garrison. Despite suffering major damage in the 1755 earthquake, the castle later served another stint as a military garrison. In the 20th century, it became a national monument.

The strolling **peacocks** remind visitors that exotic birds like these came to Lisbon originally as trophies of the great 16th-century voyages and discoveries. (Today the jaded birds ignore the tourists and cry as if to remember some long-forgotten castle captives.)

Bear left to find the **inner castle**—the largely intact, boxy, crenelated fort in the middle. There's little to see inside the empty shell, but it's fun to climb up the steep stone steps to scramble around the top of the ramparts and towers, with ever-changing views of Lisbon, the Alfama, and the castle itself. (Up top, you'll also find a thrillingly low-tech camera obscura, which is demonstrated twice hourly—times and languages posted.)

As you explore the castle's inner sanctum, imagine it lined with simple wooden huts. The imposing part of the castle is the exterior. The builders' strategy was to focus on making the castle appear so formidable that its very existence was enough to discourage any attack. If you know where to look, you can still see stones laid by ancient Romans, Visigoths, and Moors. The Portuguese made the most substantial contribution, with a wall reaching all the way to the river to withstand anticipated Spanish attacks.

When finished, head back out the inner castle gate, and continue straight ahead toward the castle's entrance. On your right, you'll pass the café, then the humble **museum**. This houses archaeological finds from the 7th century B.C. to the 18th century, with emphasis on the Moorish period in the 11th and 12th centuries. You'll also see 18th-century tiles from an age when Portugal was flush with money from the gold, diamonds, and sugarcane of its colony Brazil. While simple, the museum has nice displays and descriptions.

• *Leave the castle. Across the ramp from the castle entrance is a tidy little castle district, worth a wander for its peaceful lanes and a chance to enjoy the Manueline architecture.*

## ❹ Castle Town

Just outside the castle turnstile is the tiny neighborhood within the castle walls built to give Moorish elites refuge from sieges and, later, for Portuguese nobles to live close to their king. While it's partly taken over by cute shops and cafés, if you wander up Rua de Santa Cruz do Castelo (to the left as you exit the castle) and stroll into its back lanes, you can enjoy a peaceful bit of Portugal's past. (Make a big clockwise loop back to where you entered—you can't get lost, as it's within the walls and there's only one way in or out.) Most of the houses date from the Middle Ages. Poking around, go on a cultural scavenger hunt. Look for: 1) clever, space-efficient, triangular contraptions for drying clothes (hint: see the glass bottle bottoms in the wall used to prop the sticks out when in use); 2) Benfica soccer team flag (that's the team favored by Lisbon's working class—an indication that the upper class no longer chooses to live here); 3) short doors that were tall enough for people back when these houses were built; and 4) noble family crests over doors—dating to when important families wanted to be close to the king.

When you're ready to leave, make your way back to where you started, and head down the ramp to return to the real world. On your way out, just before exiting the lower gate, notice the little statue in the niche on your right. This is the castle's namesake: **St. George** (São Jorge; pronounced "sow ZHOR-zh") hailed from Turkey and was known for fighting valiantly (he's often portrayed slaying a dragon). When the Christian noble Afonso Henriques called for help to eliminate the Moors from his newly founded country of Portugal, the Crusaders who helped him prayed to St. George...and won.

• *Exiting the castle complex grounds, bear left and walk along the wall, then turn right down the second street, Travessa do Chão da Feira. Follow this striped lane downhill through **Largo do Contador Mor**. This small, car-clogged square has a Parisian ambience, some touristy outdoor restaurants serving grilled sardines, and the inviting little **Miss Can** shop and eatery—where traditional Portuguese canned fish gets a modern twist (for ideas on lunching here, see page 131).*

*Exit the square at the bottom, continue downhill 50 yards farther, pass the trolley tracks, and jog right around the little church to reach a superb Alfama viewpoint at...*

## ❺ Largo Santa Luzia

From this square (with a stop for trolleys #12E and #28E), admire the panoramic view from the small terrace, **Miradouro de Santa**

## Pombal's Lisbon

In 1750, lazy King José I (r. 1750-1777) turned the government over to a minor noble, the Marquês de Pombal (1699-1782). Talented, ambitious, and handsome, Pombal was praised as a reformer, but reviled for his ruthless tactics. Having learned modern ways as the ambassador to Britain, he battled Church repression and promoted the democratic ideals of the Enlightenment, but enforced his policies with arrests, torture, and executions. He expelled the Jesuits to keep them from monopolizing the education system, put the bishop of Coimbra in prison, and broke off relations with the pope. When the earthquake of 1755 leveled the city, within a month Pombal had kicked off major rebuilding in much of today's historic downtown—featuring a grid plan for the world's first quake-proof buildings. In 1777, the king died, and the controversial Pombal was dismissed.

**Luzia**, where old-timers play cards and Romeos strum their guitars amid lots of tiles.

In the distance to the left, the **Vasco da Gama Bridge** (opened in 1998, described on page 98) connects Lisbon with new, modern bedroom communities south of the river.

At your feet sprawls the **Alfama** neighborhood. We'll head that way soon, to explore its twisty lanes. Where the Alfama hits the river, notice the recently built embankment. It reclaimed 100 yards of land from the river to make a modern port, used these days to accommodate Lisbon's growing cruise ship industry.

On the wall of the church behind you, notice two 18th-century **tiles.** The one on the left shows the preearthquake Praça do Comércio, with the royal palace (on the left)—it was completely destroyed in the 1755 quake. The other tile (ten steps away, to the right) depicts the reconquest of Lisbon from the Moors by Afonso Henriques. You can see the Portuguese hero, Martim Moniz, who let himself be crushed in the castle door to hold it open for his comrades. Notice the panicky Moors inside realizing that their castle is about to be breeched by invading Crusaders. It was a bad day for the Moors. (A stairway here leads up to a tiny view terrace with a café.)

For an even better city view, hike back around the church and walk out to the seaside end of the **Miradouro das Portas do Sol** catwalk. The huge, frilly building dominating the ridge on the far left is the Monastery of São Vicente, constructed around 1600 by the Spanish king Philip II, who left his mark here with this tribute to St. Vincent. A few steps away, next to a statue of St. Vincent, is a kiosk café where you can enjoy perhaps the most scenic cup of coffee in town.

• *Across the street from the café, you'll find the...*

## ➏ Museum and School of Portuguese Decorative Arts

The Museum and School of Portuguese Decorative Arts (Museu Escola de Artes Decorativas Portuguesas) offers a stroll through

a richly decorated, aristocratic household. The palace, filled with 15th- to 18th-century fine art, offers the best chance for visitors to experience what a noble home looked like during Lisbon's glory days. Inside, a coach on the ground level is "Berlin style," with a state-of-the-art suspension system, on leather straps. The grand stairway leads upstairs past 18th-century glazed tiles (Chinese-style blue-and-white was in vogue) into a world of colonial riches. Portuguese aristocrats had a special taste for "Indo-Portuguese" decorative arts: objects of exotic woods such as teak or rosewood, and inlaid with shell or ivory, made along the sea routes of the age (€4, Wed-Mon 10:00-17:00, closed Tue, Largo das Portas do Sol 2, tel. 218-814-640, www.fress.pt).

From here, it's downhill all the way. From Largo das Portas do Sol (the plaza with the statue of local patron St. Vincent, near the

kiosk café on the terrace), go down the loooong **stairs** (Rua Norberto de Araújo, between the church and the catwalk). A few steps down on the left, under the big arch, notice the public WCs and the fun, vivid **cartoon mural** illustrating Lisbon's history (if you know the key dates, you can enjoy it even without understanding Portuguese).

The massive eighth-century **fortified wall** (on the right of the staircase) once marked the boundary of Moorish Lisbon. Consider that the great stones on your right were stacked here over a thousand years ago. At the bottom of the wall, continue downhill, then turn left at the railing...and go down more stairs.

*• Explore downhill from here. The main thoroughfare, a concrete stepped lane called Escadinhas de São Miguel, funnels you to the Alfama's main square.*

### ❼ The Heart of the Alfama

This square, **Largo de São Miguel,** is the best place to observe a slice of Alfama life. When city leaders rebuilt the rest of Lisbon

after the 1755 quake, this neighborhood was left out and consequently retains its tangled medieval streets.

If you've got the time, **explore the Alfama** from this central square. Its urban-jungle roads are squeezed into confusing alleys—the labyrinthine street plan was designed to frustrate invaders (and guidebook researchers trying to get up to the castle). What was defensive then is atmospheric now. Bent houses comfort each other in their romantic shabbiness, and the air drips with laundry and the smell of clams. Get lost. Poke aimlessly, peek through windows, buy a fish. Locals hang plastic water bags from windows in the summer to try to keep away the flies. Favorite saints decorate doors to protect families. St. Peter, protector of fishermen, is big in the Alfama. Churches are generally closed, since they share a priest. As children have very little usable land for a good soccer game, goalposts are painted onto the stairs.

The tiny balconies were limited to "one-and-a-half hands" in width. A strictly enforced health initiative was designed to keep the town open and well-ventilated. If you see carpets hanging out to dry, it means a laundry is nearby. Because few homes have their own, every neighborhood has a public laundry and bathroom. Until recently, in the early morning hours, the streets were busy with residents in pajamas, heading for these public baths. Today, many are choosing to live elsewhere, lured by modern conveniences unavailable here, and the old flats became congested with immigrant laborers who came during the construction boom a decade ago. Today, with the bad economy, they are moving on in search of employment. In just a couple of generations, the demographics have changed—from fishermen's families to immigrants to young bohemians.

Traditionally the neighborhood here was tightly knit, with

**LISBON**

families routinely sitting down to communal dinners in the streets. Feuds, friendships, and gossip were all intense. Historically, when a woman's husband died, she wore black for the rest of her life—a tradition that's just about gone.

The Alfama hosts Lisbon's most popular outdoor party on St. Anthony's Day (June 13). Imagine tables set up everywhere, bands playing, bright plastic flowers strung across the squares, and all the grilled sardines *(sardinhas grelhadas)* you can eat. The rustic paintings of festive characters (with hints of Moorish style) remind locals of past parties, and strings and wires overhead await future festival dates when the neighborhood will again be festooned with colorful streamers.

While there are plenty of traditional festivals here, the most action on the Alfama calendar is the insane, annual mountain-bike street race from the castle to the sea (which you can see hurtle by in two minutes on YouTube; search "Lisboa downtown race").

Continue exploring downhill from here. Just below the square you'll see the recommended amateur fado restaurant (A Baiuca). Then, a few steps further downhill, you'll hit the cobbled pedestrian lane, **Rua São Pedro.** This darkest of the Alfama's streets, in nearly perpetual shade, was the logical choice for the neighborhood's fish market. Modern hygiene requirements (which forbid outdoor stalls) killed the market, but it's still a characteristic lane to explore.

• *Turn left and follow Rua São Pedro out of the Alfama to the square called Largo do Chafariz de Dentro and, across the street, the...*

## ❽ Fado Museum

This museum, rated ▲, tells the story of fado in English—with a great chance to hear these wailing fisherwomen's blues. Three levels of wall murals show three generations of local fado stars, and the audioguide lets you listen to the Billie Holidays of Portugal (€5, includes audioguide, Tue-Sun 10:00-18:00, closed Mon, Largo do Chafariz de Dentro, tel. 218-823-470, www.museudofado.pt).

• *This walk is over. To get back downtown (or to Praça do Comércio, where the next walk starts), walk a block to the main waterfront drag and cruise-ship harbor (facing the museum, go left around it) where busy Avenida Infante Dom Henrique leads back to Praça do Comércio (to the right). While it's a 15-minute walk or quick taxi ride to Praça do Comércio, just to the left is a bus stop; hop on any bus for two stops, and you're there in moments. (Also, bus #759 goes on to Praça dos Restauradores.)*

## BAIXA STROLL

This ▲▲▲ walk covers the highlights of Lisbon's historic downtown, the Baixa, which fills a flat valley between two hills. The

district slopes gently from the waterfront up to the Rossio, Praça dos Restauradores, Avenida da Liberdade, and the newer town. The walk starts at Praça do Comércio and ends at Praça dos Restauradores.

• *Start your walk at the statue of King José I in the center of Praça do Comércio. Find a spot of shade in José's shadow (or take cover under the arcades) and read a bit about the Baixa's history.*

**Background:** After the disastrous 1755 earthquake, the Baixa district was rebuilt on a grid street plan. The uniform and utilitarian Pombaline architecture (named after the Marquês de Pombal, the chief minister who rebuilt the city—see sidebar, earlier) feels almost military. That's because it is. The Baixa was constructed by military engineers who had experience building garrison towns overseas. The new Lisbon featured the architecture of conquest— simple to assemble, economical, with all the pieces easy to ship. The 18th-century buildings you'd see in Mozambique and Brazil are interchangeable with those in Lisbon.

The buildings are all uniform, with the same number of floors and standard facades. They were designed to survive the next earthquake, with stone firewalls and wooden frameworks that had flexible crisscross beams. The priorities were to rebuild fast, cheap, and shake-proof.

If it had been left up to the people, who believed the earthquake was a punishment from God, they would have rebuilt their churches bigger and more impressive than ever. But Pombal was a practical military man with a budget, a timeline, and an awareness of his society's limits. He didn't want church-building to compromise the needs of the people. In those austere postearthquake days, Pombal got his way.

The Baixa has three squares—two preearthquake (Comércio and Rossio) and one added later (Figueira)—and three main streets: Prata (silver), Aurea (gold), and Augusta (relating the Portuguese king to a Roman emperor). The former maze of the Jewish quarter was eliminated, but the area has many streets named for the crafts and shops once found there.

The Baixa's pedestrian streets, inviting cafés, bustling shops, and elegant old storefronts give the district a certain charm. City-government subsidies make sure the old businesses stay around, but modern ones find a way to creep in. I find myself doing laps up

LISBON

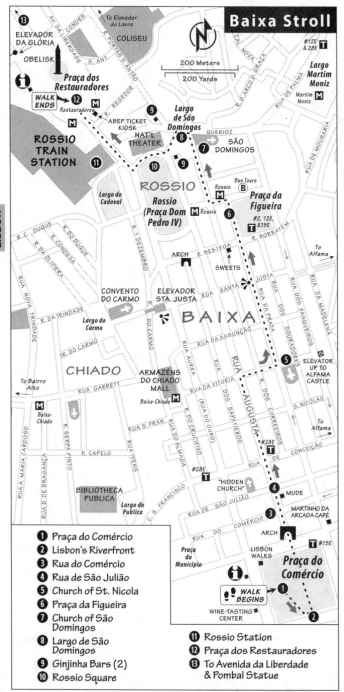

**Baixa Stroll**

200 Meters
200 Yards

1 Praça do Comércio
2 Lisbon's Riverfront
3 Rua do Comércio
4 Rua de São Julião
5 Church of St. Nicola
6 Praça da Figueira
7 Church of São Domingos
8 Largo de São Domingos
9 Ginjinha Bars (2)
10 Rossio Square
11 Rossio Station
12 Praça dos Restauradores
13 To Avenida da Liberdade & Pombal Statue

and down Rua Augusta in a people-watching stupor. Its delightful ambience is perfect for strolling.

• *Now turn your attention to the square itself.*

### ❶ Praça do Comércio (Commerce Square)

At this riverfront square bordering the Baixa—along the gateway to Lisbon—ships used to dock and sell their goods. This was the site of Portugal's royal palace for 200 preearthquake years, but after the 1755 earthquake/tsunami/fire, the jittery king fled to more stable Belém, never to return. These days, government ministries ring Praça do Comércio. It's also the departure point for city bus and tram tours, and boats that cruise along the Rio Tejo. The area opposite the harbor was conceived as a residential neighborhood for the upper class, but they chose the suburbs. Today, the square has two names ("Palace Square" and "Commerce Square") and little real life. Locals consider it just a big place to pass through.

The statue is **José I**, the king who gave control of the government to his chief minister, the Marquês de Pombal. Built 20 years after the quake, it shows the king on his horse, with Pombal (on the medallion), looking at their port. The horse (symbolic of triumph) stomps on snakes (symbolic of evil—perhaps Protestants... or troublemaking noble families), while the elephant represents the Portuguese empire's colonies in India and Africa. In its glory days, this city was where east met west.

The big arch marking the inland side of the square is Lisbon's **Arch of Triumph** (with Vasco da Gama on the left and Pombal on the right). Disregarding his usual austerity, Pombal restored some of the city's Parisian-style grandeur at this central approach into downtown.

Facing the Arch of Triumph, get oriented to a few landmarks on the square (moving from left to right):

At 9 o'clock is the **Wines of Portugal Tasting Room**, a nonprofit wine-appreciation venue. Sixteen local wines are offered with English descriptions above each tap, with a helpful attendant happy to explain things. To taste, you buy a chip card (€3 minimum), take a glass, and serve yourself samples of eight whites, eight reds, a green *(vinho verde),* and a port (each €0.50 and up; Mon-Thu 11:00-19:00, Fri-Sat until 20:00, closed Sun).

At 10 o'clock is the **TI.**

At 2 o'clock, under the arcade just right of the arch, is **Martinho da Arcada,** a fine option for a coffee, pastry, or snack. It was founded in 1782—when the wealthy would come here to savor early ice cream made with mountain snow, lemon, and spices. While it has a fancy restaurant, I'd enjoy just a coffee and pastry in its café bar. This place was one of poet Fernando Pessoa's old haunts (they display a few Pessoa artifacts, lots of old photos, and a shrine-like table that was his favorite). In the early 20th century, painters, writers, and dreamers shared revolutionary ideas here over coffee (Praça do Comércio 8, at the corner of Rua da Prata).

At 3 o'clock is the much-promoted **"Lisbon Story Center,"** a childish exhibit with no artifacts—you pay €8 to stand for an hour looking at animated history on computer screens. Nearby is another branch of the **TI** (in case the first one is too crowded).

And at 5 o'clock is the **Terreiro do Paço Metro stop** (see the red *M* on a post).

• *Before moving on, use the crosswalk at the bottom of the big square for a quick look at...*

## ❷ Lisbon's Riverfront

An inviting balustrade and a pair of Pombaline pillars—symbolizing Lisbon's gateway to the sea—mark a little pier (called the Cais das Colunas) that offers a fine, water-level view of the Tejo riverscape. To your left is the busy Terreiro do Paço ferry terminal—one of many that connect commuters to the far side of the river. To your right are the 25th of April Bridge and Cristo Rei statue. Down here at water level, you can really see that the Tejo is a tidal river—the Atlantic is just around the bend (past the bridge). At low tide, the humble little rocky beach reveals worlds of sea life in rocky pools. Any tide poolers out today?

• *Now, head back up through the square, cross the busy street, pass under the big arch, and walk down Rua Augusta into the Baixa district. (Skip the chance to pay to go to the top of the arch—it affords only a mediocre view from its empty rooftop.)*

*The first cross-street you meet is...*

## ❸ Rua do Comércio

Look right to see the old **cathedral** with its Romanesque fortress-like crenellations (described on page 69). Notice that many of the surrounding buildings are in the austere architectural style adopted immediately after the earthquake. Exterior decoration was adopted here in Lisbon only in the 19th century, after the Portuguese in colonial Brazil found that the tiles protected against humidity.

The characteristic black-and-white cobbled **sidewalk** *(calçada)* is uniquely Portuguese. These mosaic limestone and basalt cobbles were first cut and laid by 19th-century prison laborers. To this day patterns are chosen from a book of acceptable designs. As the stones are slippery and expensive to maintain, the city government is talking about replacing them with modern pavement. And locals are crying out to keep the tradition.

Across the street, on the right, you'll pass the **MUDE,** Lisbon's museum of design (free, Tue-Sun 10:00-18:00, closed Mon). Filling the Art Deco ground floor of a former bank, it offers a quick, well-described-in-English, one-floor stroll through 20th-century fashion. Special exhibits are on other floors, and a huge bank vault in the basement is often part of the show.

• *The next cross-street is...*

LISBON

## ❹ Rua de São Julião

**Churches** are scarce in the postearthquake Baixa. There's one about 30 yards to the left down Rua de São Julião (on right side of street—it's hiding; look for the triangular pediment over the door). Only a few of the quake-destroyed churches were rebuilt, and those were incorporated into the prevailing no-nonsense facades to better match the rest of the street. You'll notice that the Baixa district is struggling to stay vital, with the upper floors of many buildings now mostly empty. Look up for evidence of how downtown Lisbon's population is shrinking, as more people move to the suburbs.

At the next block, **Rua da Conceição,** there's a stop for the handy trolley #28E. Ahead on the right (in the windows of the Millennium Bank) are Roman artifacts—a reminder that Lisbon's history goes way back.

• *Go two more blocks to the intersection with Rua da Vitoria. Turn right and walk two blocks to Rua da Prata, where you'll see the camouflaged...*

## ❺ Church of St. Nicola (Igreja de São Nicolau)

Notice how a typical church facade was allowed to face the square, but on the street-front side, the entire exterior is disguised with green tiles, as just another stretch of post-earthquake Baixa architecture. Several of the fine, tiled buildings on this square have

## The Lisbon Earthquake of 1755

At 9:40 in the morning on Sunday, November 1—All Saints' Day—an underwater earthquake estimated to be close to 9.0 in magnitude occurred off the southern Portuguese coast. Massive tremors rumbled through Lisbon, punctuated by three main jolts. The quake came midway through Mass, when devout locals filled the churches. Ten minutes later, thousands lay dead under the rubble.

Along the waterfront, shaken survivors scrambled aboard boats to sail to safety. They were met by a 20-foot wall of water, the first wave of a tsunami that rushed up the Rio Tejo. The ravaging water capsized ships, swept people off the docks, crested over the seawall, and crashed 800 feet inland.

The violent tremors were felt throughout Europe—as far away as Finland. Imagine a disaster similar to 2004's Indian Ocean earthquake and tsunami, devastating Portugal's capital city.

After the quake, the city turned into an inferno, as overturned cooking fires and fallen church candles ignited raging fires. The flames blazed for five days, ravaging the downtown from the Bairro Alto across Rossio to the castle atop the Alfama.

Of Lisbon's 270,000 citizens, over 10,000 may have perished, and two-thirds of the city was leveled. The city's biggest buildings—its churches, designed to connect earth with heaven—had simply collapsed, crushing the faithful. Understandably, the quake shook conservative Portugal's moral and spiritual underpinnings. Had God punished Lisbon for the Inquisition killings carried out on nearby Praça do Comércio? To the people of the time, it must have felt like the Apocalypse.

King José I was so affected by the earthquake that he moved his entire court to an elaborate complex of tents in the foothills of Belém and resisted living indoors for the rest of his life. He left his energetic (and eventually dictatorial) second-in-command—his chief minister Marquês de Pombal—the task of rebuilding. For more on Pombal, see "Pombal's Lisbon," earlier.

been refurbished. In fact, the one at the very top of the square hides a free elevator that takes you partway up to the castle atop the Alfama.

• *Head left down Rua da Prata toward the statue marking Praça da Figueira. At Rua de Santa Justa, look left for a good view of Elevador de Santa Justa before continuing straight to the square.*

### ❻ Praça da Figueira (Fig Tree Square)

This was the site of a huge hospital destroyed in the earthquake. With no money to replace the hospital, the space was left open

until the late 1880s, when it was filled with a big iron-framed market (similar to Barcelona's La Boqueria). That structure was torn down decades ago, leaving the square you see today.

The big building on the left is run-down—after 50 years of rent control, many landowners are demoralized and do nothing to fix up their property. Buildings like this are often either vacant or occupied by old pensioners living out their lives amid increasingly decrepit conditions. By contrast, the right side (under the castle) is more lived-in and vibrant.

The nearby **Confeitaria Nacional** shop (on the corner of the square, 20 yards to your left) is a venerable palace of sweets little changed since the 19th century. In the window is a display of *"conventuel* sweets"—special nun-made treats often consisting of sugar and egg yolks (historically, the nuns, who used the egg whites to starch their laundry, had an abundance of yolks). Consider a light lunch here in the upstairs dining room (see page 124 for details).

The square is a transportation hub, with stops for minibus #737 to the castle; the old trolley #12E to the Alfama viewpoint (see page 32 for a self-guided trolley tour); the modern trolley #15E and bus #714 heading out to Belém; and the touristic hop-on, hop-off buses.

Walk to the far-left corner of the square, past skateboarders oblivious to its historical statue—Portugal's King João I on a horse. Continue straight out of the square on **Rua Dom Antão de Almada**. This lane has several characteristic shops. Pop into the classic cod shop (on the left at #1C—you'll smell it). Cod *(bacalhau)* is part of Portugal's heritage as a nation of seafaring explorers: Salted cod could keep for a year on a ship. Just soak in water to rinse out the salt and enjoy. The adjacent ham counter serves *pata negra (presunto ibérico)* from acorn-fed pigs—the very best. The *alheira* sausage, made with game instead of pork, was a favorite among Lisbon's Jews back when they needed to fake being Christians (during the forced conversions of the Inquisition era).

• *At the end of the lane stands a big church facing another square.*

### ❼ Church of São Domingos

A center of the Inquisition in the 1600s, this is now one of Lisbon's most active churches (daily 7:30-19:00). The evocative interior—

more or less rebuilt from the ruins left by the 1755 earthquake—reminds visitors of that horrible All Saints' Day Sunday, when most of the city was at Mass and the earth rolled. Across the city, heavy stone church walls like these collapsed on their congregants. Standing at the back of the nave, you can see which parts of the original stone walls remained standing. The black soot on the walls and the charred stonework at the altar recalls the horrible fires that followed the earthquake. Our Lady of Fátima is Portugal's most popular saint, and her chapel (in the left rear of the church) always has the most candles. Her statue is accompanied by two of the three children to whom she miraculously appeared (the third was still alive when this chapel was made and so is not shown in heaven with the saint).

• *Step into the square just beyond the church.*

## ❽ Largo de São Domingos

This area was just outside of the old town walls—long a place where people gathered to keep watering holes busy and enjoy bohemian entertainment. Today the square is home to classic old bars (like the *ginjinha* bar described next) and a busy "eating lane," Rua das Portas de Santo Antão (kitty-corner from where you entered the square, to the right of the National Theater on the far side of the square).

A stone monument on the square remembers the Jewish massacre of 1506. Many Jews expelled from Spain in 1492 took refuge in Portugal. But when a drought ravaged the country, Lisbonites killed several thousand of them on this square.

The city's 16th-century slave market also took place here, but the square is now a meeting point for the city's African community—immigrants from former Portuguese colonies such as Angola, Mozambique, and Portuguese Guinea. They hang out, trade news from home, and watch the tourists go by.

• *At the corner nearest the big adjoining square, find the colorful little hole-in-the-wall tavern serving a traditional berry brandy.*

## ❾ Liquid Sightseeing

*Ginjinha* (zheen-ZHEEN-yah) is a favorite Lisbon drink. While nuns baked sweets, the monks took care of quenching thirsts

with this sweet liquor, made from the *ginja* berry (like a sour cherry), sugar, cinnamon, and brandy. It's now sold for €1.40 a shot in funky old shops throughout downtown. Buy it with or without berries (*com elas* or *sem elas*—that's "with them" or "without them") and *gelada* (if you want it poured from a chilled bottle). In Portugal, when people are impressed by the taste of something, they say, *"Sabe que nem ginjas"*—literally "It tastes like *ginja*," but meaning "finger-lickin' good." The oldest *ginjinha* joint in town is a colorful hole-in-the-wall at Largo de São Domingos 8. If you hang around the bar long enough, you'll see them refill the bottle from an enormous vat. (Another *ginjinha* bar, Ginjinha sem Rival, serves the prized *eduardinho* liqueur, considered the most authentic; it's just across the square, at the start of the restaurant row—Rua das Portas de Santo Antão—at #7.)

• *The big square around the corner (fronting the National Theater) is called...*

## ❿ Rossio

Lisbon's historic center, Rossio, is still the city's bustling cultural heart. Given its elongated shape, historians believe it was a Roman

racetrack 2,000 years ago; these days, cars circle the loop instead of chariots. It's home to the colonnaded National Theater, American fast-food chains, and street vendors who can shine your shoes, laminate your documents, and sell you cheap watches, autumn chestnuts, and lottery tickets. The column in the square's center honors Pedro IV—king of Portugal and emperor of Brazil. (Many maps refer to the square as Praça Dom Pedro IV, but residents always just

call it Rossio, for the train station at one corner.)

The square once held a palace that functioned as the headquarters of the Inquisition. It was demolished, and in an attempt to erase its memory, the National Theater was built in its place.

From here you can see the Elevador de Santa Justa and the ruined convent breaking the city skyline. Notice the fine stone patterns in the pavement—evoking waves encountered by the great explorers. (If you're prone to seasickness, don't look down as you cross the square.)

• *Crossing the square in front of the National Theater, you see Rossio station.*

## ⓫ Rossio Station

The circa-1900 facade of Rossio station is Neo-Manueline. You can read the words *"Estação Central"* (central station) carved on its striking horseshoe arches. Find the statue of King Sebastian in the center of two arches (he may be temporarily gone for restoration). This romantic, dashing, and young soldier-king was lost in 1580 in an ill-fated crusade to Africa. As Sebastian left no direct heir, the crown ended up with Philip II of Spain, who became Philip I of

Portugal. The Spanish king promised to give back the throne if Sebastian ever turned up—and ever since, the Portuguese have dreamed that Sebastian will return, restoring their national greatness. Even today, in a crisis, the Portuguese like to think that their Sebastian will save the day—he's the symbol of being ridiculously hopeful.

• *Just uphill from Rossio station is Praça dos Restauradores, at the bottom of Lisbon's long and grand Avenida da Liberdade. Between Rossio station and the square is Lisbon's oldest hotel, the **Avenida Palace**. Built as a terminus hotel at the same time as Rossio station, it has a fun interior, with an elegant yet inviting oasis of a bar/lounge—popular with WWII spies in the 20th century, and tourists needing a little break in the 21st century (nice after this walk).*

## ⓬ Praça dos Restauradores

This monumental square connects Rossio with Avenida da Liberdade. The obelisk at its centerpiece celebrates the restoration of

Portuguese independence from Spain in 1640 (without any help from the still-missing Sebastian mentioned earlier).

Overlooking the square is the 1920s Art Deco facade of the Eden Theater. About 100 yards farther up the boulevard (past a Metro station and TI, on the left) is the Elevador da Glória funicular that climbs to the Bairro Alto.

• *While this walk ends here, you can stroll up Avenida da Liberdade for a good look at another facet of this fine city. The next walk (Bairro Alto and Chiado Stroll) starts at the funicular just up the street on your left.*

## ⓭ Avenida da Liberdade

This tree-lined grand boulevard, running north from Rossio, connects the old town (where most of the sightseeing action is) with the newer upper town. Before the great earthquake, this was the city's royal promenade. After 1755, it was the grand boulevard of Pombal's new Lisbon—originally limited to the aristocracy. The present street, built in the 1880s and inspired by Paris' Champs-Elysées, is lined with banks, airline offices, nondescript office buildings...and eight noisy lanes of traffic. The grand "rotunda"—as the roundabout formally known as Marquês de Pombal is called—tops off the Avenida da Liberdade with a commanding statue of Pombal. Allegorical symbols of his impressive accomplishments decorate the statue. (A single-minded dictator can do a lot in 27 years.) Beyond that lies the fine Edward VII Park. From the Rotunda (M: Marquês de Pombal), it's an enjoyable 20-minute downhill walk along the mile-long avenue back to the Baixa.

## BAIRRO ALTO AND CHIADO STROLL

The Old Word-feeling Bairro Alto ("High Town") and trendy Chiado perch just above the busy Baixa. This walk (rated ▲▲▲) connects dramatic viewpoints, leafy parks with inviting kiosk cafés, skinny streets lined with fado clubs, a dramatic church, an earthquake-toppled convent, the Chiado's trendy dining and shopping scene, and a classic coffee house.

Rise above the Baixa on the funicular called Elevador da Glória, located near the obelisk at Praça dos Restauradores (opposite the Hard Rock Café, €3.60 if you pay driver, €1.25 if zapping with Viva Viagem card, 6/hour); you can also hike up alongside the tracks.

• *Leaving the funicular on top, turn right (go 100 yards, up into a park) to enjoy the city view from the...*

## ❶ Miradouro de São Pedro de Alcântara (Viewpoint)

A tile map guides you through the view, which stretches from the twin towers of the cathedral (on far right, near the river), to the ramparts of the castle birthplace of Lisbon (capping the hill, on right), to another quaint, tree-topped viewpoint in Graça (directly across, end of trolley #28E), to the skyscraper towers of the new city in the distance (far left). Whenever you see a big old building in Lisbon, it's often a former convent or monastery. With the dissolution of monastic religious orders in 1834, these buildings were

LISBON

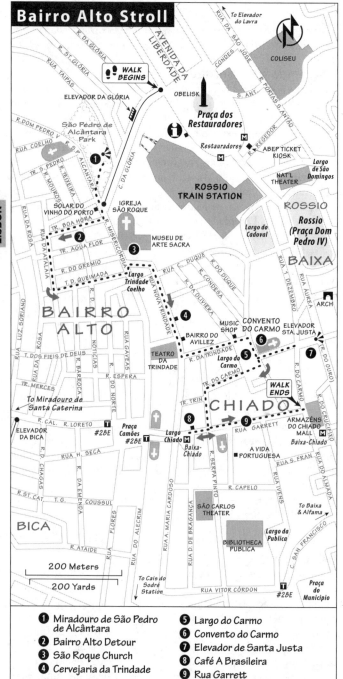

# Bairro Alto Stroll

To Elevador do Lavra

RUA DA SÃO JOSÉ

COLISEU

WALK BEGINS

OBELISK

Praça dos Restauradores

Restauradores

ABEP TICKET KIOSK

Largo de São Domingos

ELEVADOR DA GLÓRIA

São Pedro de Alcântara Park

NAT'L THEATER

ROSSIO TRAIN STATION

ROSSIO

SOLAR DO VINHO DO PORTO

IGREJA SÃO ROQUE

Rossio (Praça Dom Pedro IV)

Largo do Cadoval

MUSEU DE ARTE SACRA

BAIXA

Largo Trindade Coelho

ARCH

BAIRRO ALTO

MUSIC SHOP

CONVENTO DO CARMO

ELEVADOR STA. JUSTA

BAIRRO DO AVILLEZ

TEATRO DA TRINDADE

Largo do Carmo

WALK ENDS

To Miradouro de Santa Caterina

CHIADO

ELEVADOR DA BICA

Praça Camões #28E

ARMAZÉNS DO CHIADO MALL

Larго Chiado

Baixa-Chiado

A VIDA PORTUGUESA

Baixa-Chiado

BICA

SÃO CARLOS THEATER

Largo da Publica

To Baixa & Alfama

BIBLIOTHECA PUBLICA

200 Meters

200 Yards

To Cais do Sodré Station

RUA VITOR CÓRDON

#28E

Praça do Município

1 Miradouro de São Pedro de Alcântara
2 Bairro Alto Detour
3 São Roque Church
4 Cervejaria da Trindade

5 Largo do Carmo
6 Convento do Carmo
7 Elevador de Santa Justa
8 Café A Brasileira
9 Rua Garrett

nationalized and are now occupied by hospitals, schools, or the military.

In the park, a bust honors a 19th-century local journalist (founder of Lisbon's first daily newspaper) and a charming, barefooted delivery boy. This district is famous for its writers, poets, publishers, and bohemians.

• *Directly across the street from where you got off the Elevador da Glória is* **Solar do Vinho do Porto,** *run by the Port Wine Institute—the best place in town to sample the famous fortified wine from northern Portugal. Step inside or consider returning later for an educational tasting (for a description, see page 135).*

*Next, side-trip directly across from the top of the funicular into the old grid-plan streets of the Bairro Alto.*

## ❷ Bairro Alto Detour

The Bairro Alto, or "High Town," is one of the most characteristic and charming districts in Lisbon. Designed in the 16th century with a very modern (at the time) grid-plan layout, the district housed ship workers back when Portugal was a world power and its ships planted the Portuguese flag all around the globe. Today, the Bairro Alto is quiet in the morning, but buzzes with a thriving restaurant scene in the evening.

While it's fun to wander, follow this route for a good sampling: Go two blocks gently uphill on Travessa da Boa-Hora, turn left on Rua da Atalaia, continue three blocks, and then head left down Travessa da Queimada until you cross the big street (leaving the Bairro Alto) and reach the small square, Largo Trindade Coelho.

• *On Largo Trindade Coelho is the...*

## ❸ São Roque Church

Step inside and sit in a pew in the middle to take it all in (free; Mon 14:00-18:00, Tue-Sun 9:00-19:00—until 18:00 in winter, Thu until 20:00). Built in the 16th century, the ▲ church of St. Roque—dedicated to the saint who protects the faithful from disease and plagues—is one of Portugal's first Jesuit churches. The painted-wood, false-domed ceiling is perfectly flat. The acoustics here are top-notch, important in a Jesuit church, where the emphasis is on the sermon (given from twin stone pulpits midnave). The numbered panels on the floor were tombs, nameless because they were for lots of people. They're empty now—the practice was stopped in the 19th century when parishioners didn't want plague victims rotting under their feet.

## Lisbon's Kiosks

The kiosk—that's *quiosque* in Portuguese—is a standard feature of squares and viewpoints all over town. These little pavilions got their start in the 19th century selling snacks and drinks. But they fell out of favor, with some being converted to newsstands or lottery sales points. Now they're back, with outdoor cafés turning parks and squares into neighborhood hangouts and meeting points. Older kiosks have been restored, and new ones are being built all the time and can be quite trendy.

Survey the rich side chapels. The highlight is the **Chapel of St. John the Baptist** (left of altar, gold and blue lapis lazuli columns). It looks like it came right out of the Vatican...because it did. Made in Rome from precious materials, the chapel was the site of one papal Mass before it was disassembled and shipped to Lisbon. Per square inch, it was the most costly chapel ever constructed in Portugal. No-

tice the mosaic floor (with the spherical symbol of Portugal) and, on the walls, three intricate, beautiful mosaics—a Vatican specialty, designed to take the place of real paintings, which were vulnerable to damage from candle smoke and incense. Notice also the delicate "sliced marble" symmetry and imagine the labor involved in so artfully cutting that stone five centuries ago.

To the right of the chapel, a glass case is filled with relics trying to grab your attention. The chapel to the left of St. John the Baptist features a riot of babies. Individual chapels—each for a different noble family—seem to be in competition. Keep in mind that the tiles are considered as extravagant as the gold leaf and silver.

To the right of the Chapel of St. John the Baptist, find the **sacristy** where, along with huge chests of drawers for vestments, you can see a series of 17th-century paintings illustrating scenes from the life of St. Frances Xavier—cofounder of the Jesuit order with St. Ignatius of Loyola.

On your way out, you might pop a coin into a rack of fake candles and power a prayer.

The **São Roque Museum** (to the left as you leave the church) is more interesting than your typical small church museum. It's filled with perhaps the best-presented collection of 16th- and 17th-century church art in town, and is well described in English. The church and this art, rare survivors of the 1755 earthquake, illustrate the religious passion that accompanied Portugal's Age of Discovery, with themes including the mission of the Jesuits and their response to the Reformation; devotion to relics; and devotion to the Virgin (€2.50, same hours as the church).

• *Back outside in the church square (charming WC underground), visit the statue of a friendly lottery-ticket salesman. Two lottery kiosks are nearby. Locals who buy into the* totoloto *(which, like national lotteries everywhere, is a form of taxation on gamblers that helps fund government social programs) rub the statue's well-polished ticket for good luck.*

*Continue (kitty-corner left across the square) downhill along Rua Nova da Trindade, following the tram tracks. At #20 (on the left), pop into...*

## ❹ Cervejaria da Trindade

The famous "oldest beer hall in Lisbon" is worth a visit for a look at its 19th-century tiles. The beautifully tiled main room, once a dining hall for monks, still holds the pulpit from which the Bible was read as the monks ate. After monastic orders were abolished in 1834, the monastery became a brewery—you'll notice that while the oldest tiles have Christian themes, the later ones (from around 1860) are all about the beer. Among the Portuguese beers on tap are Sagres, the standard lager; Sagres Preta, a good dark beer (like a porter); and Bohemia, which is sweet, with more alcohol. At the bar in front you can get a snack and beer, while more expensive dining is in the back (see page 134).

• *Continue down the hill. You'll pass the recommended **Bairro do Avillez**—one of several Lisbon eateries owned by celebrity chef José Avillez, who is helping to bring traditional recipes (like the ones at the* cervejaria *we just left) into the 21st century (see page 133 for more on his restaurants).*

*Continue until the next intersection, where signs point left to the ruined Convento do Carmo. Follow the inside trolley tracks downhill and to the left. Just before you reach the square, notice (on the left) the well-stocked music shop—selling (among other instruments) the unique Portuguese guitars used to perform fado music.*

*You'll wind up in the leafy, inviting square called...*

## ❺ Largo do Carmo

On this square decorated with an old fountain, lots of pigeons, and jacaranda trees from South America (with purple blossoms in June),

police officers guard the headquarters of the National Guard. Famous among residents, this was the last refuge of the dictatorial Salazar regime. The Portuguese people won their freedom in 1974, in a peaceful uprising called the Carnation Revolution. The name came when revolutionaries placed flowers in the guns of the soldiers, making it clear it was time for democracy here. For more history, see the sidebar.

• *On Largo do Carmo, check out the ruins of...*

## ❻ Convento do Carmo

After the convent was destroyed by the 1755 earthquake, the Marquês de Pombal directed that the delicate Gothic arches of its

church be left standing—supporting nothing but open sky—as a permanent reminder of that disastrous event. If you pay to enter, you'll see a fine memorial park in what was the nave, and (filling the former apse at the far end) a simple museum with Bronze Age and Roman artifacts, medieval royal sarcophagi, and a couple of Peruvian mummies—all

explained in English (€3.50—cheapskates can do a deep knee-bend at the ticket desk, sneak a peek, and then crawl away; Mon-Sat 10:00-19:00, Oct-May until 18:00, closed Sun year-round).

• *Facing the convent, take the little lane that cuts around its right side. Head up the stairs next to the Bella Lisa Elevador restaurant to reach the gray, iron...*

## ❼ Elevador de Santa Justa

In 1902, an architect who had studied under Gustav Eiffel completed this 150-foot-tall iron elevator, connecting the lower and upper parts of town. The elevator's Neo-Gothic motifs are an attempt to match the ruined church near its top. It's free to peer through the railings from the entry-level ramp, but I'd spring for a ticket (€1.50) to climb the spiral stairs up to the top-floor lookout—with unobstructed views over the city. (Elevator and rooftop deck-€5;

## The Carnation Revolution

António Salazar, who ruled Portugal from 1926 to 1968, was modern Europe's longest-ruling dictator (he died in 1970). Salazar's authoritarian regime, the Estado Novo, continued in power under Prime Minister Marcelo Caetano until 1974.

By the 1970s, fighting in Portugal's far-flung colonies over the previous decade had demoralized much of Salazar's military, and at home, there was a growing appetite for a modern democracy. On April 25, 1974, several prominent members of the military reluctantly sided with a growing popular movement to oust the government. Their withdrawal of support spelled the end of the Salazar era. Five people died that April day, in a well-planned, relatively bloodless coup. Citizens spilled into the streets to cheer and put flowers in soldiers' rifle barrels, giving the event its name: the Carnation Revolution. Suddenly, people were free to speak aloud what they formerly could only whisper in private.

In the revolution's aftermath, the country struggled to get the hang of democratic practices. Its economy suffered as overseas colonies fell to nationalist uprisings, flooding the country with some 800,000 immigrants. For colonial overlords, life went from "shrimp day and night" to a sudden collapse of the empire; for their own safety, they fled back to Portugal. A good number of these "returnees" didn't fit into their newly democratic old country. Feeling like people without a homeland, many ultimately left Portugal (joining Salazar's henchmen, who took refuge in Brazil). Even those who stayed were generally pro-dictator and angry about the revolution, contributing to a polarization of modern Portuguese society that exists to this day.

In 1976, the Portuguese adopted a constitution that separated church and state. These changes helped to break down an almost medieval class system and established parliamentary law. Mario Soares, a former enemy of the Salazar regime, became the new prime minister, ruling as a stabilizing presence through much of the next two decades. Today, Portugal is enthusiastically democratic.

LISBON

also covered—without the deck—by 24-hour Viva Viagem card, or €1.25 with zapping; daily 7:00-23:00, until 22:00 in winter.)

Stroll around this celebration of the Industrial Age, enjoy the view, then retrace your steps to the square in front of the convent. (The nearby Leitaria Académica, a venerable little working-class eatery with tables spilling onto the delightful square, can be handy for a snack or drink.)

• *Continue straight up through Largo do Carmo, walking a block slightly uphill on Travessa do Carmo. At the next square, take a left on Rua Serpa Pinto, walking downhill to Rua Garrett, where—in the little*

# Portugal's Greatest Poets

The Portuguese are justifiably proud of their two most famous poets, whose names, works, and memorials you may encounter in your travels.

Portugal's most important poet, **Luís de Camões** (1524-1580), was a Renaissance-age equivalent of ancient Greece's Homer. Camões' masterpiece, *The Lusiads (Os Lusíadas)*, tells the story of an explorer far from home. But instead of Odysseus, this epic poem describes the journey of Vasco da Gama, the man who found the route from Europe to India. Camões—who had sailed to Morocco to fight the Moors (where he lost an eye), to Goa (where he was imprisoned for debt), and to China (where he was shipwrecked)—was uniquely qualified to write about Portugal's pursuit of empire on the high seas. For more on Camões, see page 86.

**Fernando Pessoa** (1888-1935) used multiple personas in his poetry. He'd take on the voice of a simple countryman and express his love of nature in free verse. Or he'd write as an erudite scholar, sharing philosophical thoughts in a more formal style. By varying his voice, he was able to more easily explore different viewpoints and truths. While Pessoa loved the classics—reading Milton, Byron, Shelley, and Poe—he was a true 20th-century bohemian at heart. Café A Brasileira, where he'd often meet with friends, has a statue of Pessoa outside. Today, fado musicians still remember Pessoa, paying homage to him by putting his poetry into the Portuguese version of the blues.

*pedestrian zone 50 yards uphill on the right—you'll find a famous old café across from the Baixa-Chiado Metro stop.*

## ❽ Café A Brasileira

Slinky with Art Nouveau decor, this café is a 100-year-old institution for coffeehouse junkies. A Brasileira was originally a shop selling Brazilian products, a reminder that this has long been the city's shopping zone. Drop in for a *bica* (Lisbon slang for an espresso) or a *pingado* (with a dollop of steamed milk; either costs €0.70 at the bar). A *pastel de nata* custard tart costs just €1.30—but the

best place in town for one is just a short walk away (see "Exploring More of the Bairro Alto," later). WCs are down the stairs near the entrance.

The statue out front is of the poet **Fernando Pessoa** (see sidebar), making him a perpetual regular at this café. He was the literary and creative soul of Lisbon in the 1920s and 1930s, when the country's avant-garde poets, writers, and painters would hang out here.

At the neighboring **Baixa-Chiado Metro stop,** a slick series of escalators whisks people effortlessly between Chiado Square and the Baixa. It's a free and fun way to survey a long, long line of Portuguese—but for now, we'll stay in the Chiado neighborhood. (If you'll be coming for fado in the evening—recommended places are nearby—consider getting here by zipping up the escalator.)

LISBON

• *The Chiado district is popular for its shopping and theaters. Browse downhill on...*

## ❾ Rua Garrett

As you stroll, notice the mosaic sidewalks, ironwork balconies, and fine shops. The street lamps you see are decorated with the sym-

bol of Lisbon: a ship, carrying the remains of St. Vincent, guarded by two ravens.

As you walk, peek into classy stores, such as the fabric-lover's paradise **Paris em Lisboa**—imagine how this would have been the ultimate in *oh là là* fashion in the 19th century (at #77, on the right). The next cross street, Rua Serpa Pinto, leads (in one block) to the **São Carlos Theater**—Lisbon's opera house. Celebrity chef José Avillez, whose eatery we passed earlier, and his culinary rivals have revitalized this sleepy quarter with several restaurants. (Avillez's Belcanto has often appeared high on the list of the "50 Best Restaurants in the World.") Between here and the theater is the recommended **Loja da Burel,** selling traditional and modern Portuguese woolens (see "Shopping in Lisbon").

Continuing along Rua Garrett, at the next corner (after the church, at #73) is the venerable **Bertrand** bookstore—with English books and a good guidebook selection. **A Vida Portuguesa**—my favorite shop for Portuguese gifts (quality textiles, soaps, home decor, sardines, wine, and so on) is at the end of the street behind the bookstore (daily 10:00-20:00, Rua Anchieta 11).

Along the main drag, you'll start to see more and more international chains before Rua Garrett ends abruptly at the entrance of the big **Armazéns do Chiado mall.** This grand, six-floor shopping center connects Lisbon's lower and upper towns with a world of ways to spend money (including a handy food court on the sixth floor). For Italian-style gelato, locals like **Santini em Casa,** a few steps downhill to the left as you face the mall (at #9).

• *This walk is over. Whether you leave the Bairro Alto or stay to explore, directions are below.*

    ***Leaving the Bairro Alto:*** *To get from the mall to the Baixa—the lower town—take the elevator (press 1) down to the ground level. To get from the mall to the Metro, exit through the lowest floor of the mall, turn right, and walk 50 yards to the Baixa-Chiado Metro stop.*

    *Or, if you have time and interest, consider...*

## Exploring More of the Bairro Alto

A short walk from the mall gives you a more complete look at this high-altitude neighborhood and a scenic viewpoint. Backtrack (heading west) up Rua Garrett to the square **Praça Luís de Camões,** where the great writer stands on

a pillar, leaning on a sword—more warrior than poet.

Behind Camões, bear west along Rua do Loreto. Just where the square and street meet, on the right at #2, notice the hubbub at the recommended **Manteigaria**—the best spot in town for a *pastel de nata* custard tart. Even if it looks crowded, you'll typically get served quickly (cashiers come along the line to take your order). Pastry in hand, shimmy down the narrow hall inside, where you can stand at the counter and watch the pastry chefs in action—perpetually cutting cross-sections of delicate dough, pressing it into little tins, filling the pastries with gooey custard, and popping big trays into the oven (at 750 degrees Fahr-

enheit, to get just the right amount of caramelizing on top). Be sure to sprinkle your piping-hot pastry with powdered sugar and cinnamon.

Continue three more blocks on Rua do Loreto, passing the picturesque **Elevador da Bica funicular.**

Then, one block farther, turn left on Rua Marechal Saldanha to reach the **Miradouro de Santa Catarina** (a.k.a. the "Bica mirador"), a terrace—flanked by bars—that overlooks the city's harbor and river. This is a popular hangout for the dreadlocked granola crowd on a balmy evening. You'll see a monument to the Cape of Good Hope (a.k.a. the Cape of Torment) that personifies the cape as a monster. This mythic treatment was popularized by poet Camões' *The Lusiads,* which celebrated and nearly deified the great explorers of Portugal's Age of Discovery (such as Vasco da Gama, portrayed as Ulysses), who had to overcome such demons in their conquest of the sea.

# Sights in Lisbon

## CENTRAL LISBON

LISBON

To get a full picture of the best of central Lisbon, take the three neighborhood walks (covering the Bairro Alto, Alfama, and Baixa; see earlier). Several central Lisbon sights are described in detail in those self-guided walks: São Jorge Castle, the Museum and School of Portuguese Decorative Arts, and the Fado Museum (in "Alfama Stroll and the Castle"), and the São Roque Church and Museum (in "Bairro Alto and Chiado Stroll").

### ▲Lisbon Cathedral (Sé de Lisboa)

The cathedral, just a few blocks east of Praça do Comércio, is not much on the inside, but its fortress-like exterior—solid enough to survive the 1755 earthquake—is a textbook example of the stark and powerful Romanesque "fortress of God" so typical of its age. Twin, castle-like, crenellated towers solidly frame an impressive rose window.

**Cost and Hours:** Free, Tue-Sat 9:00-19:00, Sun-Mon until 17:00. You can pay extra to visit the cloister (€2.50, closed Sun) and treasury (€2.50)—but I'd skip them. It's on Largo da Sé, several blocks east of the Baixa—take Rua da Conceição east, which turns into Rua de Santo António da Sé. Trolleys #12E and #28E stop right out front, where the square is clogged with tuk-tuks offering tours around town.

**Visiting the Church:** Started in 1150, this was the first place of worship that Christians built after they retook Lisbon from the Moors. Located on the former site of a mosque, it made a powerful statement: The Reconquista was here to stay. The church is also the site of the 1195 baptism of St. Anthony—a favorite saint of Portugal (locals appeal to him for help in finding a parking spot, true love, and lost objects). Naturally for Portugal, tile panels around the baptismal font (in the back-left corner) portray St. Anthony preaching to the fish. Also, some of St. Vincent is buried here—

# António Salazar

**Q:** What do you get when you cross a lawyer, an economist, and a dictator?

**A:** António Salazar, who was all three—a dictator who ruled Portugal through harsh laws and a strict budget that hurt the poor.

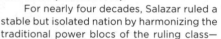

Shortly after a 1926 military coup "saved" Portugal's floundering democracy from itself, General Oscar Carmona appointed António de Olivei-ra Salazar (1889-1970) as finance minister. A former professor of economics and law at the University of Coimbra, Salazar balanced the budget and the interests of the country's often-warring factions. His skill and his repu-tation as a clean-living, fair-minded patriot earned him a promotion. In 1932, he became prime minister, and he set about creating his New State (Estado Novo).

For nearly four decades, Salazar ruled a stable but isolated nation by harmonizing the traditional power blocs of the ruling class— the military, big business, large landowners, and the Catholic Church. He enforced his Christian fascism with the backing of the military—and his secret police.

As a person, Salazar was respected, but not loved. The son of a farm manager, he originally studied to be a priest be-fore going on to become a scholar and writer. He never mar-ried. Quiet, low-key, and unassuming, he attended church reg-ularly and lived a nonmaterialistic existence. But when faced with opposition, he was ruthless, and his secret police became an object of fear and hatred.

Salazar steered Portugal through the turmoil of Spain's Civil War (1936-1939), remaining officially neutral while secret-ly supporting Franco's fascists. He detested Nazi Germany's "pagan" leaders, but respected Mussolini for reconciling with the pope. In World War II, Portugal was officially neutral, but was often friendly with longtime ally Britain and used as a base for espionage. After the war, Salazar's regime benefited great-ly from the United States' Marshall Plan for economic recovery (which Spain missed out on during Franco's rule). The country joined NATO in 1949.

Salazar distracted his poor and isolated masses with a cynical credo: "*Fado, Fátima, and Futebol*" (the three "Fs"). Salazar was undone by two factors: the liberal 1960s and the unpopular, draining wars Portugal fought abroad to try to keep its colonial empire intact. When Salazar died in 1970, the regime that followed became increasingly less credible, lead-ing to the liberating events of the Carnation Revolution in 1974 (see "The Carnation Revolution" sidebar, earlier).

legend has it that in the 12th century, his remains were brought to Lisbon on a ship guarded by two sacred black ravens, the symbol of the city. Take a stroll through the vast, dark interior—with rounded arches and a dim, windowless nave, it's quintessentially Romanesque. Near the altar, the darkness gives way to a slightly lighter Gothic zone. Here you can choose to pay to enter the ambulatory and peaceful **cloister** (an archaeological work-in-progress—they're currently uncovering Roman ruins). The humble **treasury,** back near the entrance, is worth its fee only if you want to support the church and climb some stairs.

### ▲Aljube Museum of Resistance and Freedom (Museu do Aljube)

This new museum is the best place to learn about Portugal's troubled mid-20th century. It fills a stern building called the **Aljube** (from a Moorish word meaning "waterless well"), immediately behind the cathedral. Once a Muslim prison, then a jail during the Inquisition (and on a site that dates back to Roman times), the Aljube later became the main political prison of Portugal's fascist regime under António Salazar. Today, it houses a modern, well-presented, three-floor exhibit detailing Salazar's rise to power, the creation of the Estado Novo, crimes against the Portuguese people, and the eventual end of the regime with the 1974 Carnation Revolution. Exhibits tell the story (in English) with photos and subtitled video clips, as well as some original documents and other artifacts. While often overshadowed by Franco in Spain and the communist regimes of eastern Europe, Salazar was hardly a Boy Scout—and this long-overdue museum documents his abuses. It fills a much-needed gap for those with an appetite for recent history.

**Cost and Hours:** €3, free Sun before 13:00, open Tue-Sun 10:00-18:00, closed Mon, Rua de Augusto Rosa 42, tel. 218-172-400, www.museudoaljube.pt. The entrance is tucked under a tall staircase, on a little square with a stop for trolleys #12E and #28E, between the cathedral and the Alfama.

### Elevador de Santa Justa

This 150-foot-tall iron tower, built in 1902, connects the flat Baixa district with the Bairro Alto/Chiado districts up above. One of the city's main landmarks, it offers a sweat-free connection to the upper town, as well as a fine city view up top. You can climb to the rooftop lookout alone (and skip the elevator ride) if you're already in the Bairro Alto/Chiado.

During busy times, the long line (which wraps up the stairs and around be-

hind the elevator's base) moves slowly. If it's backed up, skip it or come back at a quieter time. Two much faster routes up to Chiado are nearby: the elevators inside Armazéns do Chiado mall, or the escalators inside the Baixa-Chiado Metro station (see "Ways to Get from the Baixa Up to the Bairro Alto and Chiado," page 35).

**Cost and Hours:** Elevator—€5 (round-trip tickets only), rooftop view deck—€1.50; free with 24-hour Viva Viagem card or €1.25 with zapping; departures every 10 minutes, daily 7:00-23:00, until 22:00 in winter, http://carris.transporteslisboa.pt.

## NORTH LISBON

A visit to this North Lisbon sight can be combined with sightseeing in Belém, a quick €8 taxi ride away.

### ▲▲Gulbenkian Museum (Museu Calouste Gulbenkian)

This is the best of Lisbon's 40 museums, and it's worth the trip for art lovers (two miles north of the city center). Calouste Gulbenkian (1869-1955), an Armenian oil tycoon, gave Portugal his art collection (or "harem," as he called it) in gratitude for the hospitable asylum granted him in Lisbon during World War II (where he lived from 1942 until his death). The Portuguese consider Gulbenkian an inspirational model of how to be thoughtfully wealthy: He made a habit of "tithing for art," spending 10 percent of his income on

things of beauty, and his billion-dollar estate is still a vital arts foundation promoting culture in Portugal. The foundation/museum, with its classy modern building set in a delightful garden, often hosts classical music concerts in the museum's auditoriums.

Gulbenkian's wide-ranging collection, spanning 5,000 years of European, Egyptian, Islamic, and Asian art, offers the most purely enjoyable museum-going experience in Iberia—it's both educational and just plain beautiful. Art Nouveau fans should take note of the museum's stunning Lalique jewelry collection. The Gulbenkian is cool, uncrowded, gorgeously lit, and easy to grasp, displaying only a few select and exquisite works from each epoch. Walk through five millennia of human history, appreciating our ancestors by seeing objects they treasured.

**Cost and Hours:** €10, includes main branch and Modern Collection (located across park; see later), free on Sun after 14:00; open Wed-Mon 10:00-18:00, closed Tue; pleasant gardens, good air-conditioned cafeteria; Berna 45, tel. 217-823-000, www.museu.gulbenkian.pt.

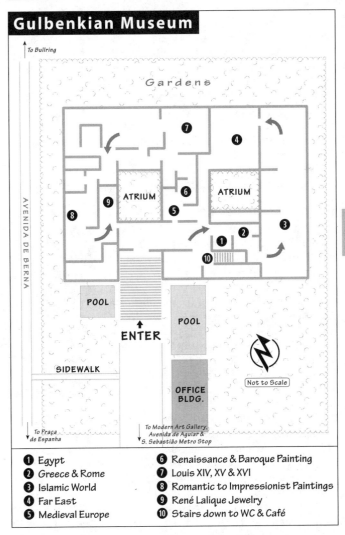

# Gulbenkian Museum

To Bullring

Gardens

ATRIUM

ATRIUM

AVENIDA DE BERNA

POOL

POOL

**ENTER**

SIDEWALK

OFFICE BLDG.

Not to Scale

To Praça de Espanha

To Modern Art Gallery, Avenida de Aguiar & S. Sebastião Metro Stop

LISBON

| | | |
|---|---|---|
| ❶ Egypt | ❻ Renaissance & Baroque Painting |
| ❷ Greece & Rome | ❼ Louis XIV, XV & XVI |
| ❸ Islamic World | ❽ Romantic to Impressionist Paintings |
| ❹ Far East | ❾ René Lalique Jewelry |
| ❺ Medieval Europe | ❿ Stairs down to WC & Café |

**Getting There:** From downtown, hop a cab (€7) or take the Metro from Restauradores to the São Sebastião stop; leave the platform by following *Avenida de Aguiar (norte)* signs. Then, to leave the station, follow signs to *Avenida de Aguiar (nascente)*. Once at street level, it's about a five-minute walk: Go a long block downhill on Avenida de Aguiar with the massive El Corte Inglés department store behind you. Just before the roundabout (across from the funky, pink Spanish embassy on the left), you'll see a small sign pointing right to the *fundação*—the museum entrance is up the stairs and straight ahead through this park, past a long concrete office building, about 100 yards away.

The Gulbenkian's **Modern Collection (Coleção Moderna)** is a five-minute walk from the main branch: Go straight ahead from the main door, and take the path through the park on your left just before the busy road.

**◐ Self-Guided Tour:** From the entrance lobby, there are two wings, covering roughly pre-1500 and post-1500. Following the museum's mostly chronological layout, you'll pass through the following sections:

**❶ Egypt** (2500-500 B.C.): Ancient Egyptians, believing that life really began after death, carved statues to preserve the memory of the deceased, whether it be a prince (*Statue of the Official Bes*, 660-610 B.C., with an inscription calling him "the king's friend") or a family pet. The cat statue nurses her kittens atop a coffin that once held the cat's mummy, preserved for the afterlife. Egyptians honored cats—even giving them gold earrings (notice this statue's ears are pierced). They believed cats helped the goddess Bastet keep watch over the household. Now, thousands of years later, we remember the Egyptians for these sturdy, dignified statues, built for eternity.

**❷ Greece and Rome** (500 B.C.-A.D. 500): The black-and-red Greek vase (calyx-crater), decorated with scenes of half-human satyrs chasing human women, reminds us of the rational Greeks' struggle to overcome their barbarian, animal-like urges as they invented Western civilization. Alexander the Great (r. 336-323 B.C., seen on a coin) used war to spread Greek culture throughout the Mediterranean, creating a cultural empire that would soon be taken over by Roman emperors (seen on medallions).

Journey even further back in time to Mesopotamia (modern Iraq) and the very roots of civilization. The Assyrian relief of Ashurnasirpal II (884-859 B.C.) evokes this distant culture, which invented writing.

**❸ Islamic World** (700-1500): The Muslims who lived in Portugal—as far west of Mecca as you could get back then—might have decorated their homes with furnishings from all over the Islamic world. Imagine a Moorish sultan, dressed in a shirt from Syria, sitting on a carpet from Persia in a courtyard with Moroccan tiles. By a bubbling fountain, he puffs on a hookah.

The culture of Moorish Iberia (711-1492) was among Europe's most sophisticated after the Fall of Rome. The intricate patterns on the glass mosque lamps (behind the partition on the left) are not only beautiful...they're actually Arabic quotes from the Quran, such as "Allah is the light of the world, shining like a flame in a glass lamp, as bright as a star." Explore this large and rich collection, and then head a few thousand miles east.

**❹ Far East** (1368-1644): For almost 300 years, the Ming dynasty ruled China, having reclaimed the country from Genghis Khan and his sons. When Portuguese traders reached the Orient, they brought back blue-and-white ceramics such as these. They became all the rage, inspiring the creation of both Portuguese tiles and Dutch Delftware. Writing utensils fill elaborately decorated boxes from Japan. Another type of box—a Japanese *bento*—was the ultimate picnic basket, perfect for an excursion to the Japanese countryside.

Crossing into the next wing, you enter the section on European art.

**❺ Medieval Europe** (500-1500): While China was thriving and inventing, Europe was stuck in a thousand-year medieval funk (with the exception of Muslim Arab-ruled Iberia). Most Europeans from the "Age of Faith" channeled their spirituality into objects of Christian devotion. A priest on a business trip could pack a portable altarpiece in his backpack, travel to a remote village that had no church, and deliver a sermon carved in ivory. In monasteries, the monks with the best penmanship laboriously copied books (illuminated manuscripts) and decorated them with scenes from the text—and left wacky doodles in the margins. These books are virtual time capsules, preserving the knowledge of Greece and Rome until it could emerge again, a thousand years later, in the Renaissance.

**❻ Renaissance and Baroque Painting** (1500-1700): Around 1500, a cultural revolution was taking place—the birth of humanism. Painters saw God in the faces of ordinary people, whether in Domenico Ghirlandaio's fresh-faced maiden, Frans Hals' wrinkled old woman, or Rembrandt's portrait of an old man, whose crease-lined hands tell the story of his life. Also in this section are lesser works by Van der Weyden, Van Dyck, and Rubens.

**❼ Louis XIV, XV, XVI** (1700-1800): After the Italian-born Renaissance, Europe's focus shifted northward to the luxurious court of France, where a new secular culture was blossoming. In one tapestry, love is in the air (see cupids flying overhead) as Venus rides her barge through a landscaped garden. Powder-wigged nobles in their palaces enjoyed the luxury of viewing art like this pagan scene, while relaxing in chairs like the kind you see here. This furniture, once owned by French kings (and Marie-Antoinette and Madame de Pompadour), is a royal home show. Anything heavy, ornate, and gilded (or that includes curved legs and animal-clawed feet) is from the time of Louis XIV. The Louis XV style is lighter and daintier, with Asian motifs, while furniture from the Louis XVI era is stripped-down, straight-legged, tapered, and more modern. Listen to find out which clocks still work. The one with a globe supported by cherubs, and the time marked by a golden snake tongue, is particularly striking...and the loudest.

❽ **Romantic to Impressionist Paintings** (1700-2000): Europe ruled the world, and art became increasingly refined. Young British aristocrats (Thomas Gainsborough portrait) traveled Europe on the Grand Tour to see great sights like Venice (an entire room of Guardi landscapes). Follow the progression in styles from stormy Romanticism (J. M. W. Turner's tumultuous shipwreck) to Realism's breath-of-fresh-air simplicity (Manet's bubble-blower, Degas' portraits) to the glinting, shimmering Impressionism of Monet and Renoir.

❾ **René Lalique Jewelry:** Finish your visit with the stunning, sumptuous Art Nouveau glasswork and jewelry of French designer René Lalique (1860-1945). Fragile beauty like this, from the elegant turn-of-the-century belle époque, was about to be shattered by the tumultuous 20th century. Art Nouveau borrowed forms from nature, and valued the organic and artisanal over the mass-produced. Ordinary dragonflies, orchids, and beetles become breathtaking when transformed into jewelry. The work of Lalique—just another of Gulbenkian's circle of friends—is a fitting finale to this museum of history and beauty.

## WEST LISBON
The next museum, west of downtown, is halfway to Belém and can be combined with an excursion there.

### ▲▲Museum of Ancient Art
### (Museu Nacional de Arte Antiga)
Not "ancient" as in Roman and Greek—but "antique" as in Age of Discovery—this is Portugal's finest museum for artwork from the time when the Portuguese ruled the seas: the 15th and 16th centuries. (Most of these works were gathered from Lisbon's abbeys and convents after their dissolution in 1834.) You'll also find a rich

collection of furniture, as well as paintings by renowned European masters such as Hieronymus Bosch, Jan van Eyck, and Raphael—all in a grand palace that's sleekly renovated and well-presented.

**Cost and Hours:** €6, free first Sun of month; open Tue-Sun 10:00-18:00, closed Mon; good cafeteria with shaded garden seating that overlooks the river, Rua das Janeles Verdes 9, tel. 213-912-800, www.museudearteantiga.pt.

**Getting There:** It's about a mile west of downtown Lisbon. From Praça da Figueira, take trolley #15E to Cais Rocha, cross the street, and walk up a lot of steps. To stop right in front, take bus #714 from either Praça da Figueira or Praça do Comércio. Note that trolley #15E and bus #714 both continue to the sights in Belém; if you have time when returning at the end of your Belém day and aren't museumed out, this is a handy choice.

**Visiting the Museum:** Here are some of the museum's highlights, starting on the top floor. (But note that a planned renovation in 2017 may cause some changes.) From the ticket desk, turn right to find the elevator and press button 2.

**Top Floor, Portuguese Painting and Sculpture:** From the elevator, veer right through the atrium and find the big, red room at the far end. *The Panels of St. Vincent* are a multipart altarpiece by the late-15th-century master Nuno Gonçalves. A gang of 60 real people—everyone from royalty to sailors and beggars—surrounds Lisbon's patron saint. Of note is the only recognized portrait of Prince Henry the Navigator, responsible for setting Portugal on the path to exploration. Find him in the middle—an elder gentleman dressed in black with a wide-brimmed hat, hands together almost in prayer.

Explore the rest of the floor: Head back into the atrium, turn right, then turn right again into the long room. If you've visited the sights in Belém, you'll recognize the Monastery of Jerónimos before it was fully decorated (1657 painting by Felipe Lobo). Two rooms away, find an exceptional portrait of the baby-faced King Sebastian—who died young when he led an incursion into Africa. The armor is typical of Iberia for the era, as is the royal jaw and pursed lips caused by Habsburg inbreeding.

Before you head down the stairs (in the middle of the atrium) to the next floor, notice the statue of a pregnant Mary (*The Virgin of Expectation*, c. 1340-1350). This unusual theme was common in rural parts of Portugal (such as the Alentejo, the close-to-the-ground region in the southeast), where the Virgin's fertility was her most persuasive quality in recruiting local followers.

**Middle Floor, Art from the Portuguese Discoveries:** This floor collects items that Portuguese explorers brought home from their far-flung travels. Coming down the stairs, bear left, then right, to find the room with large, enchanting Namban screen paintings (*Namban*, meaning "southern barbarians," the catch-all term the Japanese applied to all foreigners). These show the Portuguese from a 16th-century Japanese perspective—with long noses, dark complexions, and great skill at climbing rigging, like acrobats. The Portuguese, the first Europeans to make contact with Japan, gave the Japanese guns, Catholicism (Nagasaki was founded by Portuguese Jesuits), and a new deep-frying technique we now know as tempura.

Now do a counterclockwise circle around this floor, stocked with furniture, large vases, ivory carvings, fine china, and ceram-ics. Imagine how astonishing these treasures must have seemed when the early explorers returned with them. Facing the atrium are some beautiful tiles from Damascus—a gift from Calouste Gulbenkian (founder of the Gulbenkian Museum listed above). Eventually you reach a treasury of gold and silver items. Look for the freestanding glass case with a gorgeous golden monstrance, with its carrying case displayed just behind it—the bejeweled Rococo Communion-host holder was made for Lisbon's Bemposta Palace. Farther along is the even more exquisite  Monstrance of Belém, commissioned by Manuel I and made from East African tribute gold brought back by Vasco da Gama. Squint at the fine enamel creatures filling a tide pool on the base, the 12 apostles gathered around the glass case for the Communion wafer (the fancy top pops off), and the white dove hanging like a mobile under the all-powerful God bidding us peace on earth.

Heading back to the atrium, don't miss the small, dimly lit room (on the left) displaying an impressive jewelry collection, including pieces decorated with the red cross of the affluent Order of Christ, whose members helped plan and fund Portuguese explorations.

Back in the atrium, before continuing downstairs, stop to admire a 17th-century painting of Lisbon before the 1755 earthquake. Notice the royal palace on Praça do Comércio and the ship-clogged Rio Tejo.

**Ground Floor, European Paintings:** Pass through the gift shop, veer left, and follow the one-way route through paintings from all over Europe. A few rooms in, note the larger-than-life paintings of the twelve apostles by the Spanish master Zurburán.

Continue to the end of the hall, then find the room with Bosch's *Temptations of St. Anthony* (a three-paneled altarpiece fantasy, c. 1500) and Albrecht Dürer's *St. Jerome*. St. Jerome—you'll see other portraits of him in this collection, always with a skull—is all-important to Lisbon as the primary figure behind the Monastery of Jerónimos in Belém. Finally, exit through the few remnants of the palace. Note the Pombal coat-of-arms that decorates the elaborate, Baroque doorway (find the star); the palace was originally purchased by the brother of the powerful Marquês de Pombal.

## BELÉM DISTRICT

About five miles west of downtown Lisbon, the Belém district is a stately pincushion of important sights from Portugal's Golden Age, when Vasco da Gama and company turned the country into Europe's wealthiest power. Belém was the sending-off point for voyages in the Age of Discovery. Before embarking, sailors would stay and pray at the Monastery of Jerónimos, and when they returned, the Belém Tower welcomed them home. The grand buildings of Belém survived the great 1755 earthquake, so this is the best place to experience the Manueline architectural style (see sidebar on page 89). After the earthquake, safety-conscious (and rattled) royalty chose to live here—in wooden rather than stone buildings. The modern-day president of Portugal calls Belém home.

To celebrate the 300th anniversary of independence from Spain, a grand exhibition was held here in 1940, resulting in fine parks, fountains, and monuments.

**Getting to Belém:** You have multiple options: By **taxi** or **Uber**, figure no more than about 20 minutes and €10 from downtown. **Buses** #714 and #728 serve Belém, and the coastal train line running from Lisbon's **Cais do Sodré station** gets you there in about 10 minutes.

But if you have the time, I prefer riding the slower **trolley** #15E (30-40 minutes, catch at Praça da Figueira or Praça do Comércio). In Belém, the first trolley stop is at the National Coach Museum (stop is called simply "Belém"—you'll see the brown sign for *Museu dos Coches* just before the stop); the second stop (Belém-Jerónimos) is at the Monastery of Jerónimos; and another (Pedrouços) is two stops farther, at a little square two blocks inland from the Belém Tower. Even if you miss the first stop, you can't miss the second stop at the massive monastery.

**Planning Your Time:** Nearly all of Belém's museums are closed on Monday (though the Monument to the Discoveries is open Mon May-Sept). And be aware that the sights can be mobbed by cruise travelers in the morning.

Consider doing Belém's sights from east to west, in the order

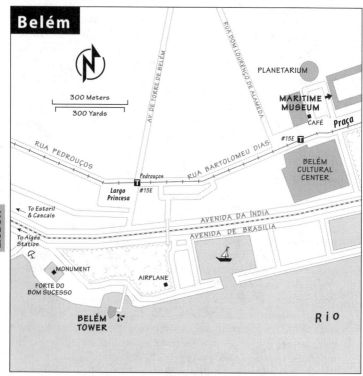

you'll reach them from the tram or train: the National Coach Museum, pastry and coffee break, Monastery of Jerónimos, Maritime Museum (if interested) and/or lunch at its cafeteria (public access, museum entry not required), Monument to the Discoveries, and Belém Tower. If arriving by taxi, you could start at Belém Tower—the farthest point—and do the recommended lineup in reverse, ending at the National Coach Museum (which has easier public transit connections than the tower). Belém also has a cultural center, a children's museum, and a planetarium—not priorities for a quick visit. For recommended eateries in this area, see page 83.

**Returning to Downtown:** When you're through, hop on trolley #15E or bus #714 to return to Praça da Figueira or Praça do Comércio, or ride the coastal train back to Cais do Sodré. If you have time and energy left, you could hop off the trolley or bus to tour the Museum of Ancient Art on the way home (see page 76). Bus #728 takes you to Santa Apolónia station, and continues to Parque das Nações and Oriente station.

**Tourist Information:** A little TI kiosk is directly across the street from the entrance to the monastery (Tue-Sat 10:00-13:00 & 14:00-18:00, closed Sun-Mon, tel. 213-658-437).

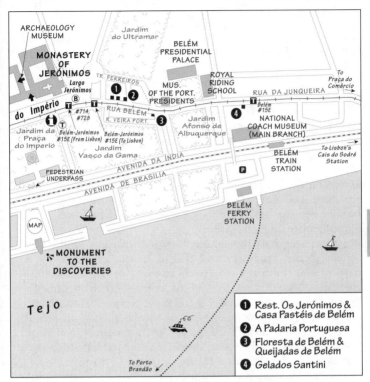

Map legend:

- ARCHAEOLOGY MUSEUM
- Jardim do Ultramar
- BELÉM PRESIDENTIAL PALACE
- MONASTERY OF JERÓNIMOS
- Largo Jerónimos
- TR. FERREIROS
- MUS. OF THE PORT. PRESIDENTS
- ROYAL RIDING SCHOOL
- To Praça do Comércio
- RUA DA JUNQUEIRA
- do Império
- #714, #728
- RUA BELÉM
- R. VEIRA PORT.
- Belém #15E
- Jardim da Praça do Imperio
- Belém-Jerónimos #15E (From Lisbon)
- Belém-Jerónimos #15E (To Lisbon)
- Jardim Afonso de Albuquerque
- NATIONAL COACH MUSEUM (MAIN BRANCH)
- Jardim Vasco da Gama
- AVENIDA DA INDIA
- BELÉM TRAIN STATION
- To Lisbon's Cais do Sodré Station
- PEDESTRIAN UNDERPASS
- AVENIDA DE BRASILIA
- BELÉM FERRY STATION
- MAP
- MONUMENT TO THE DISCOVERIES
- LISBON
- Tejo
- To Porto Brandão

- **1** Rest. Os Jerónimos & Casa Pastéis de Belém
- **2** A Padaria Portuguesa
- **3** Floresta de Belém & Queijadas de Belém
- **4** Gelados Santini

## ▲▲National Coach Museum (Museu Nacional dos Coches)

In 1905, the last queen of Portugal saw that cars would soon obliterate horse-drawn carriages as a form of transportation. She de-

cided to preserve her fine collection of royal coaches, which became today's National Coach Museum. The impressive collection is split between two buildings, each with its own ticket. The main branch—in a huge, blocky, concrete building closer to the river—has the bulk of the collection, with 70 dazzling coaches, all described in English. The Royal Riding School, closer to the tram tracks, is a historical space with a gorgeous interior but only about a half-dozen coaches on display. If you want to really appreciate the coaches themselves, focus on the main branch. But to see regal spaces (which are rare in Lisbon), add on the Royal Riding School.

**Cost and Hours:** Main branch—€6, Royal Riding School—€4, €8 combo-ticket covers both, free first Sun of month, open Tue-Sun 10:00-18:00, closed Mon, tel. 213-610-850, www.museudoscoches.pt.

**Visiting the Main Branch:** The museum is right across the street from the Belém tram stop (on one side) and the Belém train station (on the other). Find the steps down directly to the ticket office under the building, then ride an elevator up to the collection, where you'll loop through two rooms.

The first coach dates from around 1600. This crude and simple vehicle was once used by Philip II, king of Spain and Portugal, to shuttle between Madrid and Lisbon. Notice that the coach has no driver's seat—its drivers would actually ride the horses. You'll have to trust me on this, but if you lift up the cushion from the passengers' seat, you'll find a potty hole—also handy for road sickness. Imagine how slow and rough the ride would be with bad roads and a crude leather-strap suspension.

From here, walk through the historical collection, displayed chronologically. Study the evolution of suspension technology, starting with the first coach, made in the 15th century in the Hungarian town of Kocs (pronounced "coach"—hence the name). By the 17th century—when this collection begins—coaches had caught on in a big way in Portugal, which was an early adopter. Trace the improvements made through the next century, noticing that as the decoration increases, so does the comfort. A Portuguese coat of arms indicates that a carriage was part of the royal fleet. Ornamentation often includes a folk festival of exotic faces from Portugal's distant colonies.

In the middle of the hall shines the lumbering Oceans Coach, as ornate as it is long. At the stern, gold figures symbolize the Atlantic and Indian Oceans holding hands, a reminder of Portugal's mastery of the sea. The Oceans Coach is flanked by two equally stunning coaches with similar symbols of ocean exploration. These were part of a thematic convoy sent by King João V to Pope Clement XI in 1716.

Next you'll see the Exchange of the Princesses carriages, which were used for a ceremonial procession to the Portuguese-Spanish border to swap royal kids for marriage (to shore up the two kingdoms' diplomatic relations after Portugal's 1640 independence). At the far end of the hall, peek inside the Table coach, which must have been a cozy place to hang out and wait for the exchange.

The next room organizes its carriages by theme. First you'll see "Berlins"—a new coach type (pioneered in that city, in the late 17th century) that suspended the main compartment on thick leather straps to improve the ride. You'll see ecclesiastical coaches (suggesting the high status of clergy); single-horse chaise and cabriolet coaches (including some sleek, black leather, 19th-century, Sherlock Holmes-style ones); hunting vehicles; sedan chairs;

# Eating in Belém

You'll find snack bars at Belém Tower, a cafeteria at the Maritime Museum, and fun little restaurants along Rua de Belém, between the National Coach Museum and the monastery. Here are a few other eateries worth checking out:

**$$ Restaurante Os Jerónimos** is a busy little place good for fresh fish, where hardworking Carlos treats his customers well and serves fine, affordable meals and a fish-of-the-day special (Sun-Fri 12:00-21:30, closed Sat, Rua de Belém 74, tel. 213-638-423, next to renowned Casa Pastéis de Belém pastry café, see page 84).

**$ A Padaria Portuguesa,** a respected fast-food chain with fine fresh-baked bread, hearty sandwiches, and salads, is next door at #46 (daily 7:30-20:00).

**Restaurant Row:** Many more fine places with outdoor seating are in the restaurant row beyond the McDonald's facing the park, including **$$ Floresta de Belém,** the local favorite for their home-style Portuguese cooking, such as tasty grilled sardines and *feijoada* bean stew. They have minimal seating inside, but two cozy terraces outside (closed Sun dinner, all day Mon, and Sept; Praça Afonso de Albuquerque 1A, tel. 213-636-307). Next door, **$$ Queijadas de Belém** is a good bet for its salads, sardines, and outside seating (daily, Rua de Belém 1, tel. 213-630-034).

**Dessert:** In addition to the original *pastel de Belém* place (**Casa Pastéis de Belém,** described on page 84), **Gelados Santini**—a local favorite for gelato—is across the street from the National Coach Museum.

scaled-down play carriages for kids who had everything; and mail coaches. You'll also see the "Landau of the Regicide"—the coach in which King Carlos I and his heir were shot and killed on February 1, 1908. You can still see the bullet holes. (This carriage is sometimes on loan to a countryside branch; if it's not here, you'll see a model instead, with a video telling the story.)

**Visiting the Royal Riding School:** You'll find this regal building along the trolley tracks through Belém, kitty-corner from the main museum. The elegant old riding room with its dramatically painted ceiling is as remarkable as the carriages. Under that ceiling, you'll see a handful of fine specimens (but if you've already been to the main branch, this is a rerun). Wander upstairs to get a glimpse of velvet-covered saddles and special riding gear designed for the royal kids. A spectacular view of the entire building interior is picture-perfect (no flash). The portrait gallery covering most of Portugal's royalty is handy for putting a face to all the movers and shakers you've read about so far.

**Nearby:** Just past the Royal Riding School, on the landscaped hill behind the wall, is the stately, pink **Belém Palace**—the residence of Portugal's president. The palace interior is tourable only on Saturdays (€5, most tours in Portuguese), but if you're fascinated by Portuguese history, you can drop in anytime at the modern little **Museum of the Portuguese Presidents** (Museu da Presidència da Repùblica). It offers a little lesson on each of Portugal's democracy-era presidents (since 1910) and lots of state gifts (€2.50, Tue-Sun 10:00-18:00, closed Mon, look for entrance just west of Royal Riding School and palace gate).

### ▲Casa Pastéis de Belém

The Casa Pastéis de Belém café is the birthplace of the wonderful custard tart that's called *pastel de nata* throughout Portugal, but here it's dubbed *pastel de Belém*. You can explore this sprawling temple to Portugal's beloved custard tart like a museum, with a peek at the bakery in the rear. Since 1837, residents have been coming to this café to get their tarts fresh. Its popularity stems mainly from the fact that their recipe is a closely guarded secret—supposedly only three people know the exact proportions of the ingredients. While the recipe is fine, my hunch is that their undeniable goodness is simply because the café cranks out 20,000 or so a day—you get them fresh and crunchy, literally hot out of the oven. (Take one back to your hotel and eat it tonight and it'll taste just like any other in town.) Sit down and enjoy one with a *café com leite*. Sprinkle on as much cinnamon and powdered sugar as you like.

Tarts are €1 whether you eat in or carry out. There's often a line for take-away, but it moves quickly (pay, then take your receipt to the mob at the counter to claim your tart). If the line is extremely long, consider finding a table inside the café, which may have faster service (daily 8:00-24:00, Rua de Belém 84, tel. 213-637-423).

### ▲▲▲Monastery of Jerónimos

This giant, white limestone church and monastery stretches for 300 impressive yards along the Belém waterfront. King Manuel (who ruled from 1495) erected it as a "thank you" for the discoveries made by early Portuguese explorers. It was financed in part with "pepper money," a 5 percent tax on spices brought back from India. Manuel built the church near the site of a humble chapel where sailors spent their last night ashore in prayer before embarking on frightening voyages. What is the style of Manuel's church? Manueline.

**Cost and Hours:** Church—free, cloister—€10, includes audioguide, €12 combo-ticket with Belém Tower (cloister and tower are free on first Sun of month); monastery open Tue-Sun 10:00-18:30, Oct-April until 17:30, closed Mon year-round, www.mosteirojeronimos.pt. There's often a long line to visit the cloister,

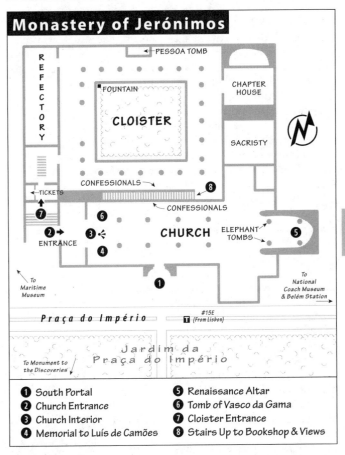

# Monastery of Jerónimos

- REFECTORY
- PESSOA TOMB
- FOUNTAIN
- CLOISTER
- CHAPTER HOUSE
- SACRISTY
- CONFESSIONALS
- TICKETS
- CONFESSIONALS
- **8**
- **7**
- **6**
- **2** ENTRANCE
- **3**
- CHURCH
- ELEPHANT TOMBS
- **5**
- **4**
- **1**
- To Maritime Museum
- To National Coach Museum & Belém Station
- *Praça do Império*
- #15E (From Lisbon)
- *Jardim da Praça do Império*
- To Monument to the Discoveries

**1** South Portal
**2** Church Entrance
**3** Church Interior
**4** Memorial to Luís de Camões
**5** Renaissance Altar
**6** Tomb of Vasco da Gama
**7** Cloister Entrance
**8** Stairs Up to Bookshop & Views

LISBON

but you can cut through it to get immediately to the church entrance.

**Background:** As you circle around the complex, ponder the great history of this serene place. Monks often accompanied the sailor-pirates on their trading/pillaging trips, hoping to convert the heathens to Christianity. Many expeditions were financed by the Order of Christ, a brotherhood of soldier-monks. (The monks who inhabited this cloister were Hieronymites—followers of St. Jerome, hence the monastery name of Jerónimos.)

King Manuel, who did so much to promote exploration, was also the man who forcibly expelled all Jews from the country. (In 1497, the Spanish *Reyes Católicos*—Ferdinand and Isabel—agreed to allow him to marry one of their daughters on the condition that he deport the Jews.) Francis Xavier, a founder of the Spanish Jesuit order, did much of his missionary work traveling in Asia in the service of Portugal.

It was a time of extreme Christian faith. The sheer size of this religious complex is a testament to the religious motivation that—along with money—propelled the Age of Discovery.

◐ **Self-Guided Tour:** Start outside the monastery:

❶ **South Portal:** The fancy portal, facing the street, is textbook Manueline. Henry the Navigator stands between the doors with the king's patron saint, St. Jerome (above on the left, with the lion). Henry (Manuel's uncle) built the original sailors' chapel on this site. This door is only used when Mass lets out or for Saturday weddings. (The electronic snapping sound you hear is designed to keep the pigeons away.)

• *To the left of the portal is the...*

❷ **Church Entrance:** As you approach the main entrance, the church is on your right and the cloister is straight ahead. Flanking the church door are kneeling statues of King Manuel I, the Fortunate (left of door, with St. Jerome), and his Spanish wife, María (right, with John the Baptist).

❸ **Church Interior:** The Manueline style is on the cusp of the Renaissance. The space is more open than earlier medieval churches. Slender, palm-tree-like columns don't break the interior space (as Gothic columns would), and the ceiling is all one height. Motifs from the sea hide in the decor. The sea brought Portugal 16th-century wealth and power, making this art possible. You'll see rope-like arches, ships, and monsters that evoke the mystery of undiscovered lands. Artichokes, eaten for their vitamin C to fend off scurvy, remind us of the hardships sailors faced at sea.

• *On your right as you face the altar is the...*

❹ **Memorial to Luís de Camões:** Camões (kah-MOISH, 1524-1580) is Portugal's Shakespeare and Casanova rolled into one, an adventurer and writer whose heroic poems, glorifying the nation's sailing exploits, live on today. It was Camões who described Portugal as the place "where land ends and the sea begins."

After college at Coimbra, Camões was banished from the court (1546) for flirting with the noble lady Dona Caterina. He lost an eye soldiering in Morocco (he's always portrayed squinting), served jail time for brawling with a bureaucrat, and then caught a ship to India and China, surviving a shipwreck on the way. While

serving as a colonial administrator in India, he plugged away at the epic poem that would become his masterpiece. Returning to Portugal, he published *The Lusiads* (*Os Lusíadas*, 1572), winning minor recognition and a small pension.

The long poem describes Vasco da Gama's first voyage to India in heroic terms, on the scale of Homer's *Odyssey*. *The Lusiads* begins:

> *Arms and the heroes, from Lisbon's shore,*
> *sailed through seas never dared before,*
> *with awesome courage, forging their way*
> *to the glorious kingdoms of the rising day.*

LISBON

The poem goes on to recite many events in Portuguese history, from the time of the Lusiads (the original pre-Roman natives) onward. Even today, Camões' words are quoted by modern Portuguese politicians in search of a heroic sound bite. And Portugal's national holiday, June 10, is known as Camões Day, remembering the day in 1580 when the great poet died. The stone monument here—with literary rather than maritime motifs—is an empty tomb (his actual burial spot is unknown).

• *Now head up to the front of the church, and the...*

❺ **Renaissance Altar:** Nearly everything here survived the 1755 earthquake, except for the stained glass (the replacement glass is from 1940). In the niches surrounding the main altar, elephants—a Far Eastern symbol of power, more powerful and kingly than the lion—support two kings and two queens (King Manuel I is front-left). Many Portuguese churches (such as the cathedrals in downtown Lisbon and Évora) were renovated in Renaissance and Baroque times, resulting in an odd mix of dark, older naves and pretty pastel altars.

Skip the **sacristy** (entrance in the corner), a single-columned room wrapped in paintings on wood featuring scenes from the life of St. Jerome (not worth the admission fee). Instead, do an about-face and head up the aisle on the right, back toward the entrance (noticing more elephants in the transept). You'll pass **seven wooden confessional doors** (on your right). Notice the ornamental carving around the second one: a festival of faces from newly discovered corners of the world. Head back toward the entry.

• *Under a ceiling that's a veritable* Boy Scout's Handbook *of rope and knots is the...*

❻ **Tomb of Vasco da Gama:** On the night of July 7, 1497, in the small chapel that once stood here, da Gama (1460-1524) prayed for a safe voyage. The next day, he set sail from Belém with four ships (see the caravel carved in the middle of the tomb's side) and 150 men. He was armed with state-of-the-art maps and sailing technology, such as the carved armillary sphere (to the right of the caravel)—a globe surrounded by movable rings designed to deter-

mine the positions of the sun or other stars to help sailors track their location on earth. (Some say its diagonal slash is symbolic of the unwritten pact and ambition of Spain and Portugal to split the world evenly, but it actually represents the path of the planets as they move across the heavens.)

Da Gama's mission? To confirm what earlier navigators had hypothesized—that the ocean recently discovered when Bartolomeu Dias rounded Africa's Cape of Good Hope was the same one seen by overland travelers to India. Hopefully, da Gama would find a direct sea route to the vast, untapped wealth of Asia. The symbols on the tomb show the icons of the period—the cross (symbolizing the religious military order of the soldier-monks who funded these voyages), the caravel (representing the method of travel), and Portugal's trading power around the globe (the result).

By Christmas, da Gama rounded the Cape of Good Hope. After battling hostile Arabs in Mozambique, he hired an Arab guide to pilot the ships to India, arriving on the southwest coast in Calicut (from which we get the word "calico") in May 1498. He traded for spices, networked with the locals for future outposts, battled belligerent chiefs, and then headed back home. Da Gama and his crew arrived home to Lisbon in September 1499 (after two years and two months on the seas) and were greeted with all-out Vasco-mania. The few spices he'd returned with (many were lost in transit) were worth a staggering fortune. Portugal's Golden Age was launched.

King Manuel dubbed da Gama "Admiral of the Sea of India" and sent him out again, this time to subdue the Indian people, establish more trade outposts, and again return home to wealth and honor. Da Gama died on Christmas Eve 1524, in India. His memory lives on due to the tribute of two men: Manuel, who built this large church, and Luís de Camões (honored opposite Vasco), who turned da Gama's history-making voyage into an epic poem.

• *Leave the church, turn right, purchase your ticket, pick up the included audioguide, and enter the...*

❼ **Cloister:** This restored cloister is the architectural highlight of Belém. The lacy arcade is Manueline; the simpler diamond and decorative rose frieze above the top floor is Renaissance. Study

# Manueline Architecture, c. 1480-1580

Portugal's unique decorative style (from its peak of power under King Manuel I, the Fortunate, r. 1495-1521) reflects the wealth of the times and the many cultural influences of the Age of Discovery. It is more an ornamental than structural style, blending late Gothic features with Mudejar (Moorish) elements. Craftsmen applied it equally to buildings with pointed Gothic or rounded Renaissance arches; you'll see elaborate Manueline carved stonework particularly around windows and doors.

The Manueline aesthetic is ornate, elaborate, and intertwined, often featuring symbols from a family's coat of arms (shields with castles, crosses, lions, banners, and crowns) or motifs from the sea (rope-like columns or borders, knots, shells, coral, anchors, and nets). Manuel's personal symbol was the armillary sphere—a celestial globe—which was an indispensable navigational aid for sailors. You'll also see imports of the age, from opium poppies to exotic animals.

Architecture students will recognize elements from Gothic's elaborate tracery, the abstract designs of Moorish culture, similarities to Spain's intricate Plateresque style (which dates from the same time), and the elongated excesses of Italian Mannerism.

LISBON

the carvings, especially the gargoyles above the lower set of arches. Among these functioning rainspouts, find a monkey, a kitten, and a cricket.

Heads of state are often received in the cloister with a warm welcome. This is also the site of many important treaty signings, such as Portugal's admittance to the European Union in 1986. Turn left and do a clockwise spin around this fine space.

In the first corner, a small lion-topped basin (where the monks washed up before meals) marks the entrance to the **refectory**, or dining hall—today an occasional concert venue—lined with fine 18th-century tiles. The tiles are considered textbook Rococo, which ignores the parameters set by the architecture (unlike Baroque, which works within the structure).

Halfway down the next stretch of cloister, on the left, is the burial spot of Portugal's most revered modern poet, **Fernando Pessoa** (see sidebar on page 66).

Continuing around, the former **chapter house** contains an exhibit of the lengthy restoration process, as well as the tomb of Alexandre Herculano, a Romantic 19th-century historian and poet. Quotes from Herculano adorn his tomb: "Sleep? Only the cold cadaver that doesn't feel sleeps. The soul flies and wraps itself around the feet of the All-Powerful."

· *Continuing around the cloister, find the stairs up.*

❽ **Upstairs:** At the top of the stairs, on the left, step into the Upper Choir (above the main door)—peering down into the vast sanctuary, at the feet of a powerful crucifix.

Back out in the upper cloister, circle around to find a bookshop (and the exit). All the way around are great cloister views. At the far end of the cloister is an exhibition that juxtaposes the historical timeline of this monastery and Portugal with contemporaneous world events (but no real artifacts).

## ▲Maritime Museum (Museu de Marinha)

If you're interested in Portugal's historic ships and navigational tools, this museum, which fills the west wing of the Monastery of Jerónimos (listed above), is worth a look. It's refreshingly uncrowded, and sailors love it.

**Cost and Hours:** €6.50, free first Sun of month, open daily 10:00-18:00, Oct-April until 17:00. It's at the far end of the long monastery building; facing the planetarium, the museum entrance is to your right, and its good **$$** cafeteria (open to the public) is to your left.

**Visiting the Museum:** You'll enter past huge statues of great explorers, then follow the one-way route (with English explanations) through the sprawling collection, offering a well-presented recap of an age when Portugal ruled the waves. And it's loaded with actual artifacts: nautical paintings, model ships, cannons, uniforms, and maps illustrating Portuguese explorations. The exhibit takes you right up to the present day, covering not just explorers and military vessels but also the fishing industry. You'll see the reconstructed king's and queen's staterooms from aboard King Carlos I's royal yacht *Amélia*. Then you'll walk outside (under a gallery) to reach a vast warehouse of actual boats—from rustic *rabelos* (see page 375) to yawls to ceremonial royal barges. The centerpiece is the massive barge of King João VI, with 38 oars pulled by some 80 oarsmen, and plush royal quarters at the stern.

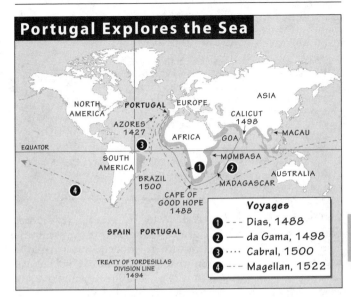

## Portugal Explores the Sea

**Voyages**
- ❶ - - - Dias, 1488
- ❷ ——— da Gama, 1498
- ❸ ···· Cabral, 1500
- ❹ - - - Magellan, 1522

### ▲Monument to the Discoveries
### (Padrão dos Descobrimentos)

In 1960, the city honored the 500th anniversary of the death of Prince Henry the Navigator by rebuilding this giant riverside

monument, which had originally been constructed for a 1940 world's fair. It takes the shape of a huge caravel ship, in full sail, with Henry at the helm and the great navigators, sailors, and explorers on board behind him. The elevator inside takes you up to the tip-top for a tingly vista—including a fine aerial view down over the mural in front.

**Cost and Hours:** €4; May-Sept daily 10:00-19:00; Oct-April Tue-Sun 10:00-18:00, closed Mon, tel. 213-031-950, www.padraodosdescobrimentos.pt.

**Visiting the Monument:** To get here, find the pedestrian tunnel under the busy boulevard, then walk around the huge monument. The 170-foot concrete structure shows that exploring the world was a team effort. The men who braved the unknown stand on the pointed, raised prow of a caravel, about to be launched into the Rio Tejo.

Leading the charge is Prince Henry the Navigator (for more about him, see page 183), holding a model of a caravel and a map, followed by kneeling kings and soldiers who Christianized foreign

## Caravels

These easily maneuverable trading ships were fast, small (80 feet), and light (100 tons), with few guns and three triangular-shaped sails (called lateen-rigged sails) that could pivot quickly to catch the wind. They were ideal for sailing along coastlines. Many oceangoing caravels were also rigged with a square foresail for stability. (This photo shows the model held by Prince Henry on Belém's Monument to the Discoveries.) Columbus' *Niña* and *Pinta* were rerigged caravels.

LISBON

lands with the sword. Behind Henry (on the west side, away from bridge), find the men who financed the voyages (King Manuel I, holding an armillary sphere, his personal symbol), those who glorified it in poems and paintings (like Luís de Camões, holding his famous poem *The Lusiads* on a scroll), and at the very end, the only woman, Philippa of Lancaster, Henry's British mother.

On the east side (closest to bridge—as you walk, notice the optical illusion of waves on the flat cobbled surface), Vasco da Gama stands with his eyes on the horizon and his hand on his sword. Magellan holds a circle, representing the round earth his ship circumnavigated, while in front of him, Pedro Cabral puts his hand to his heart, thankful to have (perhaps accidentally) discovered Brazil. Various monks, navigators with maps, and crusaders with flags complete the crew. Check out the pillory, decorated with the Portuguese coat of arms and a cross, erected in each place discovered by the Portuguese—leaving no doubt as to who was in charge.

In the **marble map in the pavement** (a gift from South Africa) in front of the Monument to the Discoveries, follow Portugal's explorers as they inched out into monster-infested waters at the edge of the world. From their tiny, isolated nation in Europe, the Portuguese first headed south to the coast of Morocco, conquering the Muslims of Ceuta in God's name (1415), and gaining strategic control of the mouth of the Mediterranean. They braved the open Atlantic to the west and southwest, stumbling on the Madeiras (1420), which Prince Henry planted with vineyards, and the remote Azore Islands (Açores, 1427).

Meanwhile, the Portuguese slowly moved southward, hugging the African coast, each voyage building on the knowledge from previous expeditions. They cleared the biggest psychological hump when Gil Eanes sailed around Cape Bojador (western Sahara, 1434)—the border of the known world—and into the equatorial seas where it was thought that sea monsters lurked, no winds blew, and ships would be incinerated in the hot sun. Eanes survived, re-

## The Age of Discovery, 1400-1600

In 1560, you could sail from Lisbon to China without ever losing sight of land explored by Portugal. The riches of the world poured into the tiny nation—spices from India and Java (black pepper, cinnamon); ivory, diamonds, and slaves (sold to New World plantations) from Africa; sugarcane, gold, and diamonds from Brazil; and, from everywhere, knowledge of new plants, animals, and customs. How did tiny Portugal pull this off?

First, its people were motivated by greed, hoping to break the Arab and Venetian monopoly on Eastern luxury goods (the price of pepper was jacked up 1,000 percent by the time it reached European dinner tables). They were also driven by a crusading Christian spirit, a love of science, and a spirit of adventure. An entire 15th-century generation was obsessed with finding the legendary kingdom of the fabulously wealthy Christian named "Prester John," supposedly located in either India or Africa. (The legend may be based on a historical figure from around 1120 who visited the pope in Rome as "patriarch of India.")

Portugal also had certain natural advantages. Its Atlantic location led to a strong maritime tradition. A unified nation-state (one of Europe's first) financed and coordinated expeditions. And a core of technology-savvy men used and developed their expansive knowledge of navigational devices, astronomy, maps, shipbuilding, and languages.

turning home with 200 Africans in chains, the first of what would become a lucrative, abhorrent commodity. Two generations later, Bartolomeu Dias rounded the southern tip of Africa (Cabo da Boa Esperança, 1488), discovering the sea route to Asia that Vasco da Gama (1498) and others would exploit to colonize India, Indonesia, Japan, and China (Macao in 1557, on the south coast).

In 1500, Pedro Cabral (along with Dias and 1,200 men) took a wi-i-i-ide right turn on the way down the African coast, hoping to avoid windless seas, and landed on the tip of Brazil. The country proved to be an agricultural goldmine for Portugal, which profited from sugar plantations worked by African slaves. Two hundred years later, gold and gemstones were discovered in Brazil, jump-starting the Portuguese economy again.

In 1520, Portuguese Ferdinand Magellan, employed by Spain, sailed west with five ships and 270 men, broke for R&R in Rio, continued through the Straits of Magellan (tip of South America), and suffered through mutinies, scurvy, and dinners of sawdust and ship rats before touching land in Guam. Magellan was killed in battle in the Philippines, but one remaining ship continued west and arrived back in Europe, having circumnavigated the globe after 30 months at sea.

By 1560, Portugal's global empire had peaked. Tiny-but-filthy-rich Portugal claimed (though they didn't actually occupy) the entire coastline of Africa, Arabia, India, the Philippines, and south China—a continuous stretch from Lisbon to Macao—plus Brazil. The Treaty of Tordesillas (1494) with Spain divvied up the colonial world between the two nations, split at 45 degrees west longitude (bisecting South America—and explaining why Brazil speaks Portuguese and the rest of the continent speaks Spanish) and 135 degrees east longitude (bisecting the Philippines and Australia).

But all that wealth was wasted on Portugal's ruling class, who neglected to reinvest it in the future. Easy money ruined the traditional economy and stunted industry, hurting the poor. Over the next four centuries, one by one, Portugal's colonies were lost to other European nations or to local revolutions. Today, only the (largely autonomous) islands of the Azores and Madeiras remain from the once-global empire.

### ▲Belém Tower (Torre de Belém)

Perhaps the purest Manueline building in Portugal (built 1515-1520), this white tower protected Lisbon's harbor. Today it symbolizes the voyages that made Lisbon powerful, with carved stone representing ropes, Manuel's coat of arms, armillary spheres, and shields with the cross of the Order of Christ, charged with spreading the faith in new territories.

**Cost and Hours:** €6, €12 combo-ticket with Monastery of Jerónimos, free first Sun of month, Tue-Sun 10:00-18:30, Oct-April until 17:30, closed Mon; from the monument it's a pretty, 10-minute waterfront walk, but be ready to detour around the big yacht marina; tel. 213-620-034, www.torrebelem.pt.

**Visiting the Tower:** This was the last sight sailors saw as they left their homeland, and the first as they returned, loaded with gold, spices, and social diseases. When the tower was built, the river went nearly to the walls of the monastery, and the tower was midriver. Its interior is pretty bare, but the views of the bridge, river, and Cristo Rei statue are worth the 120 steps.

The floatplane on the grassy lawn is a monument to the first flight across the South Atlantic (Portugal to Brazil) in 1922. The original plane (which beat Charles Lindbergh's *Spirit of Saint Louis* across the North Atlantic by five years) is in Belém's Maritime Museum.

If you're choosing between towers, the Monument to the Discoveries is probably the better choice, because it offers a better view of the monastery. Both towers are interesting to see from the outside, whether or not you go up.

### Ferry from Belém to Porto Brandão

For a delightfully untouristy little adventure, consider having lunch across the river in **Porto Brandão.** The ferry terminal is immediately in front of the National Coach Museum, across a busy road and train tracks (€1.65 each way—or €1.15 zapping with Viva Viagem card, 8-minute cruise, ferries depart on the hour and half hour except hourly from 13:30-15:30, last ferry departs 23:00 weekdays and 22:00 weekends; for a memorable Tejo experience, tall men can use the urinal while sticking their head out the porthole). Boats continue to Trafaria before returning to Belém via Porto Brandão. Upon arrival, carefully confirm return times.

Porto Brandão is a tiny (and dead) three-street town whose harborfront square has several good fish restaurants. I like cozy, blue-and-white-tiled **$$$ Restaurante Porto Brandão.** Their *bacalhau à lagareiro* is for garlic lovers. The *cataplana* (a traditional fish-and-veggie stew) and seafood fondue meals are made for two but stuff three (daily 12:00-15:00 & 18:00-23:00, Rua Bento Jesus Caraça 25, tel. 212-959-145).

## MODERN LISBON

Lisbon celebrated the 500th anniversary of Vasco da Gama's voyage to India by hosting Expo '98 here at Parque das Nações. The theme was "The Ocean and the Seas," emphasizing the global importance of healthy, clean waters. And today, the city has thoughtfully repurposed the fairgrounds into a park and shopping mall. To get out of the quaint, Pombal-esque old town and enjoy a peek at some modern architecture, ride the Metro to Oriente station. From here, you can stroll through an airy shopping mall, explore the sprawling site of the 1998 world's fair, and promenade with locals along the Rio Tejo riverfront park. It's worth a visit any day, but makes sense on Monday (when most museums in town are closed). It's also particularly vibrant when people are out early on summer evenings and weekends.

• *Your visit begins when you step off the train, inside...*

### Oriente Train Station (Gare do Oriente)

*Oriente* means "facing east." This impressive hub ties together trains (to the Algarve and Évora), the Metro, and buses under a swooping concrete roof designed by the Spanish architect Santiago Calatrava.

• *Facing Oriente station across the street is...*

### Vasco da Gama Mall

The inviting, soaring glass facade of Lisbon's top shopping mall—originally the grand entrance to Expo '98—was also designed by Calatrava (daily 9:00-24:00). Stepping into the mall, you'll see that its design seems to have been inspired by the main hall of a luxury cruise ship. Notice the water cascading down the glass roof—a clever and eye-pleasing way to keep things cool and avoid any greenhouse effect. From the mall's entrance, climb the stairs to a small outdoor terrace for a good view back at the train station. Look up at the two skyscraping luxury condo buildings. With fine transportation connections and modern office space, this area holds lots of promise, both for residences and businesses. Microsoft set up its Portuguese headquarters here, and the Portuguese national court occupies contemporary new buildings nearby.

Now stroll through the upper level of the mall to the opposite end, where you can step out to another outdoor terrace. From here you can look toward the river and survey Parque das Nações—the grounds for Expo '98. Straight ahead are the flags lining the Grand Esplanade (described next). The striped oval dome to the left, once the Atlantic Pavilion (Pavilhão Atlântico), is now an 18,000-seat concert hall. The oil refinery tower far to the right marks the west end of the park and is a remnant of the industrial wasteland that was here before the fair.

• *Exiting the mall at the far end from the train station, you'll be smack-dab in the middle of...*

### ▲▲Parque das Nações

From the Vasco de Gama Mall, you're at the top of the Grand Esplanade (Rossio Olivais), lined by 155 flags—one for each country represented at Expo '98. The flags are arranged in alphabetical order, so the first ones are South Africa (Africa dul Sul), Albania, and Germany (Alemanha). In the middle you'll find the US (Estados Unidos), Spain (Espanha), and Estonia side by side.

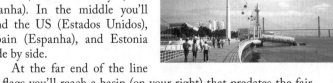

At the far end of the line of flags you'll reach a basin (on your right) that predates the fair.

Back before World War II, this was a watery "parking lot" (just 1.5 yards deep) for seaplanes. Across the basin to your right, the blocky building that resembles an aircraft carrier with a spiky rooftop is the Lisbon Oceanarium (described next)—the big hit of the fair and still the park's major attraction. From behind that the cable car (€4 one-way, €6 round-trip, nothing special, daily 11:00-19:00) drifts east to the Vasco da Gama Tower, which marks that end of the park. Two miles away, built as part of the 1998 celebrations, is the Vasco da Gama Bridge. A delightful promenade (Caminho dos Pinheiros; "The Way of the Pine Trees") runs along the riverfront from the marina all the way to a park at the base of the Vasco de Gama Bridge.

### Lisbon Oceanarium (Oceanário de Lisboa)

Europe's largest aquarium—housed in what looks like a drilling platform or a big, modern ship at sea—simulates four different oceanic underwater and shoreline environments, from the Atlantic to the Pacific to the Indian to the Arctic. You'll circle around the upper level, seeing surface dwellers from each climate (such as, otters, puffins, penguins, and other sea birds). Then you'll head downstairs and do another loop, this time seeing underwater creatures. The centerpiece—which you'll keep circling back to—is an enormous and mesmerizing central tank crammed full of fascinating fish big and small, including several sharks. Weekday-morning school groups are also happily on display.

**Cost and Hours:** €14, €9 for kids 4-12, daily 10:00-20:00, Nov-March until 19:00, last entry one hour before closing, tel. 218-917-000, www.oceanario.pt.

### Vasco da Gama Bridge (Ponte Vasco da Gama)

Europe's longest bridge (10.7 miles) was opened in 1998 to connect the Expo '98 grounds with the south side of the Rio Tejo, and to alleviate the traffic jams on Lisbon's only other bridge over the river, the 25th of April Bridge. The Vasco de Gama Bridge helped connect north and south Portugal, back when a freeway was a big deal in this late-to-develop European nation. Built low to the water, the bridge's towers and cables are meant to suggest the sails of a caravel ship.

## EAST LISBON

### National Tile Museum (Museu Nacional do Azulejo)

Filling the Convento da Madre de Deus, the museum features piles of tiles, which, as you've probably noticed, are an art form in Portugal. They've tried to show-  case the tiles as they would have originally appeared (note the diamond-shaped staircase tiles), but the presentation is low-tech, and the posted English explanations are dry. You can see more exciting tiles in situ throughout Portugal. But for aficionados this is a handy one-stop survey. And the circa-1700 tile panorama of Lisbon (upstairs) is fascinating, letting you pick out landmarks that were toppled in the 1755 quake.

**Cost and Hours:** €5, free first Sun of month; open Tue-Sun 10:00-18:00, closed Mon; located about a mile east of Praça do Comércio—15 minutes on bus #794 from Praça do Comércio or bus #742 from near the Gulbenkian Museum (bus leaves around the corner from São Sebastião Metro station—along Rua Marquês de Fronteira), both buses stop right at museum entrance on Rua da Madre de Deus 4, tel. 218-100-340, mnazulejo.im-ip.pt.

LISBON

# Azulejos

During visits to neighboring Spain, King Manuel I not only ac-

quired wives, but he also obtained several thousand tiles to decorate palaces throughout Portugal. Vibrant colors must have attracted the king's attention, and some examples from his visits can still be seen in the National Palace in Sintra. It wasn't long before Portuguese artists began producing them for local clients, and the tiles—called *azulejos* (ah-zoo-LAY-zhoos, from an Arab word meaning "small polished stone")—became synonymous with the seafaring empire.

The biggest challenge for early artisans was keeping colors from running together during firing. A number of techniques developed to solve this problem: *Alicatados* are mosaic pieces, cut after firing, to form intricate geometric patterns; *corda seca* fills thick outlines of manganese oxide with different colors, like a children's coloring book; and *aresta* sculpts color wells directly into the tile. The biggest breakthrough came with the development of *majólica*, or *faiança*—the undecorated clay tile is baked first, then covered with an opaque glaze that makes a canvas for the painted design, which is set by a second firing.

Brazilians loved tilework, too, and after the return of the Portuguese king to European shores, factories began producing tilework for the masses. But tilework began to fall out of fashion by the early 20th century. Then Lisbon's 1959 Metro system gave tile artists a new playground. While not originally in the budget, artist Maria Keil could not bear to see the walls vacant. Her original designs are still on display, and future artists continue to make the Metro an underground art museum.

Unfortunately, others have noticed the beauty (and profitability) of historic tilework panels. Theft is common—often for resale on the black market—and many of Lisbon's older panels are at risk. In the past decade, local watch groups have documented several hundred cases of missing panels and helped recover several of them. Think twice before purchasing tilework at the Feira da Ladra flea market.

To go on your own *azulejo* scavenger hunt, check out Endless Mile's tile guide to Lisbon that lists nearly 100 of the city's best tile panels (www.endlessmile.com).

## SOUTH OF LISBON, ACROSS THE RIVER

### ▲25th of April Bridge (Ponte 25 de Abril)

Imagine that before 1966, there was no way across the Rio Tejo except by ferry. This suspension bridge—1.5 miles long (3,280 feet between the towers—bears an uncanny re-  semblance to San Francisco's Golden Gate Bridge (it was built in 1966 by the same company that made its famous cousin—but notice the lower deck for train tracks). The foundations are sunk 260 feet below the sur- face into the riverbed, making it the world's deepest bridge. Originally named for the dictator Salazar, the bridge was renamed for the date of Portugal's 1974 revolution and liberation. For a generation, natives would show their political colors by choosing which name to use. While conservative Portuguese called it the "Salazar Bridge," liberals referred to it as the "25th of April Bridge" (just as Washington, D.C.'s airport is still called "National" by some and "Reagan" by others).

### Cristo Rei Statue (Christ the King)

A huge, 330-foot concrete statue of Christ (à la Rio de Janeiro, in the former Portuguese colony of Brazil) overlooks Lisbon from across the Rio Tejo, stretching its arms wide to  symbolically bless the city (or, as less reverent Por- tuguese say, "to dive into the river"). Lisbon's car- dinal, inspired by a visit to Rio de Janeiro in 1936, wanted a replica built back home. Increased sup- port came after an appeal was made to Our Lady of Fátima in 1940 to keep Portugal out of World War II. Portugal survived the war relatively unscathed, and funds were collected to build this statue in ap- preciation. After 10 years of construction, it opened to the public in 1959. It's now a sanctuary and pil- grimage site, and the chapel inside holds regular Sunday Mass. The statue was designed to be seen from a distance, and there's little reason to go to the trouble of actually visiting it. If you do visit, an elevator will take you to the top for a panoramic view: From left to right, see Belém, the 25th of April Bridge, downtown Lisbon (Praça do Comércio and the green Alfama hilltop with the castle), and the long Vasco da Gama Bridge.

**Cost and Hours:** €5, daily 9:30-18:15, slightly later in sum- mer, tel. 212-751-000, www.cristorei.pt.

**Getting There:** To get to Cristo Rei, catch the 10-min- ute ferry from downtown Lisbon to Cacilhas (4/hour, see

"Public Ferry Ride to Cacilhas" on page 35), then hop on the bus marked *101 Cristo Rei* (3/hour, exit ferry dock left into the maze of bus stops to find the #20 stop with the "101 Cristo Rei" schedule under the awning, 15-minute ride). Because of bridge tolls to enter Lisbon, taxis from the site are expensive. Consider taking a late-morning ferry-and-bus connection to Cristo Rei; catch a taxi from the statue to Porto Brandão and have lunch there (see page 95); and ferry direct to Belém and see the sights. For drivers, the most efficient visit is a quick stop on your way to or from Évora or the Algarve.

## WEST OF LISBON, ON THE COAST
### Cascais

The seafront resort town of Cascais (kahsh-KAYSH), about 17 miles due west of Lisbon, provides a fun and quick escape from

the big city of Lisbon. Before the rise of the Algarve, Cascais was the haunt of Portugal's rich and beautiful. Today it's an elegant and inviting escape from the city with pleasant beaches and a relaxing ambience (see map on page 143).

Before the 20th century, aristocrats wanted to avoid the sun and exaggerate their lily-white skin—and a day at the beach made just no sense. But about 1900, the Portuguese queen Maria Pia (daughter of King Victor Emmanuel II of Italy) made Cascais her summer vacation getaway—and Portugal's high society followed. A train line made Cascais easily accessible from the city, and between the world wars, the area was developed as a kind of Portuguese answer to the French Riviera.

**Getting There:** Just hop the train at Lisbon's Cais do Sodré station (M: Cais do Sodré) and you're in Cascais in 40 minutes or less (3/hour, www.cp.pt).

**Visiting Cascais:** The Cascais station (the last stop on the Cais do Sodré line) faces the town center. From there, the main cobbled street, Rua Frederico Arouca, parallels the waterfront past shops and eateries to Largo Cidade Vitória, where you'll find a helpful TI kiosk (daily 9:00-18:00).

Cascais still has a fishing industry. Adjacent to the TI, you'll find the Serviços de Pescado, a wholesale fish market where most days at 17:00 visitors can witness the quick fish auction as local retailers snap up the day's catch. Just beyond is the main beach and a palm-lined promenade leading to an old fort. Deeper into town are several little museums; the Museu do Maris is best for the story of the town and its relationship with the sea (free, Tue-Sun 10:00-17:00, closed Mon, about 10 minutes from the center at Rua Júlio Pereira de Mello, www.cm-cascais.pt/museumar).

**Returning to Lisbon via Estoril:** A paved seaside promenade leads from Cascais past several beaches to **Estoril,** its sister beach resort town (a half-hour stroll away). Of the several small sandy beaches, Praia da Conceição and Praia das Moitas conveniently have showers. If you have time and like seaside strolls, I'd recommend walking this strip and catching the train back to Lisbon from Estoril (all trains stop at both Estoril and Cascais).

Estoril is famous for its casino and many grand hotels. From the Lisbon-Cascais train you can look past the Estoril station and across the park at the modern casino. Ian Fleming hatched his first 007 story here in the early days of World War II, when Portugal was neutral and this area was a hotbed of spies. The Estoril casino where Fleming gambled must have been part of the inspiration for his first James Bond novel, *Casino Royale.* But Cascais rather than Estoril is clearly the most rewarding stop for today's traveler.

# Shopping in Lisbon

Lisbon is a marvelous shopping city: creative, with a trendy vibe but also respectful of tradition—and it's cheap. My suggestions below focus on one-off shops that specialize in unique slices of Lisbon life. I've also included a few big malls for handy one-stop shopping.

## SOUVENIR IDEAS

The shops mentioned here are scattered around central Lisbon, but most are concentrated in the hip and artsy Chiado district.

### Cork

Portugal is famous for its cork, a versatile material that can be put to hundreds of uses (see sidebar on page 235). Shops all over town show off practical and eye-pleasing items made of cork, from handbags to wallets to umbrellas. For fashionable, top-end products, head up to the flagship store of the internationally respected **Pelcor,** in the Príncipe Real shopping zone (closed Sun, Pátio do Tijolo 4, just off Rua Dom Pedro V, www.pelcor.pt). In the Bairro Alto, **Cork & Co** is a more affordable little boutique with a wider array of products—including jewelry (closed Sun, Rua das Salgadeiras 6-10, www.corkandcompany.pt).

### Wine

If you're in the market to buy some fine bottles of wine to enjoy in Portugal or to ship home, two handy options sit near each other just below the cathedral. While touristy—and with somewhat inflated prices—both have helpful staff who can talk you through your options and arrange shipping. (They may suggest that you make your selection in the shop, then place your order on their website.) **Napoleão Wine Shop** has free samples of three unique Portuguese options: port, *vinho verde,* and *ginjinha* (daily, main branch at Rua Conceição 16 specializes in Portuguese wines, second branch across the street also has international booze; www.napoleao.eu). **Garrafeira Nacional** has a similar set-up in the Baixa (closed Sun, Rua da Conceição 20/26) and a user-friendly location inside Mercado da Ribeira (www.garrafeiranacional.com).

### Azulejos (Colored Tiles)

Portugal's iconic colored tiles make vivid souvenirs—for use as trivets, wall hangings, or even (for the ambitious) a backsplash renovation project. It's easy to find affordable, basic, painted replicas of classic *azulejo* designs—many souvenir shops stock a small selection. For better-quality replica *azulejos,* try **Viúva Lamego** (closed Sat-Sun, in the trendy Intendente neighborhood at Largo do Intendente 25; for more on Intendente, see page 109), **Fábrica Sant'Anna** (closed Sun, in the Chiado at Rua do Alecrim 95), or the more tourist-oriented **Loja dos Descobrimentos** (daily, below the cathedral at Rua dos Bacalhoeiros 12). If you're shopping for authentic antique tiles, try **d'Orey Azulejos** (closed Sun, in the Chiado at Rua do Alecrim 68) or the cramped **Antiquário Solar** (a.k.a. Albuquerque e Sousa; closed Sat afternoon and all day Sun, in the Bairro Alto at Rua Dom Pedro V 68-70).

### Conservas (Canned Fish)

Canned fish (collectively called *conservas*) is a Portuguese staple, are not the harsh, cured-in-salt sardines you might think of back home. This is quality fish in olive oil (sardines, cod, mackerel, and tuna are most common), often mixed with herbs, spices, or infused oils to impart extra flavor. Best of all, colorful packaging turns the cans into great souvenirs or gifts, and makes window-shopping a delight. The best *conservas* place in town—near Mercado da Ribeira—is **Loja Das Conservas,** with shelves upon shelves of attractively decorated cans from all over Portugal. This shop is operated by a local consortium, and prides itself on educating its customers (daily, Rua do Arsenal 130). In the upper part of the Alfama, just below the castle, **Miss Can** sells a small selection of their own production, with clever packaging and a little café where you can enjoy a light meal (see "Eating in Lisbon," daily, Largo do Contador Mor 19). And in the Chiado, you'll find the upscale **Conserveira da Trinidade,** with a carefully curated selection and the option to nibble right there (daily, Rua Nova da Trinidade 11).

LISBON

**1** To Pelcor
**2** Cork & Co.
**3** Napoleão Wine Shop
**4** Garrafeira Nacional (2)
**5** To Viúva Lamego
**6** Fábrica Sant'Anna
**7** Loja dos Descobrimentos
**8** d'Orey Azulejos

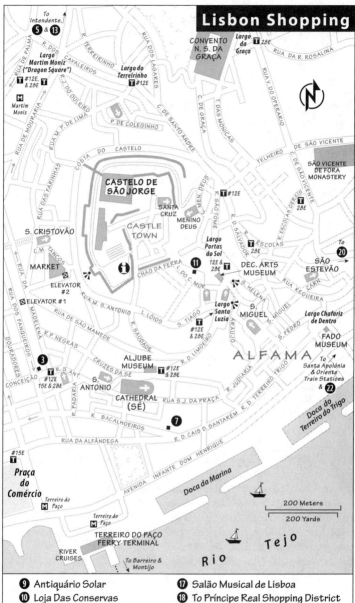

**Lisbon Shopping**

9 Antiquário Solar
10 Loja Das Conservas
11 Miss Can
12 Conserveira da Trinidade
13 A Vida Portuguesa (3)
14 Lisbon Shop (2)
15 Loja da Burel
16 Luvaria Ulisses
17 Salão Musical de Lisboa
18 To Príncipe Real Shopping District
19 Mercado da Ribeira
20 To Feira da Ladra Flea Market
21 Armazéns do Chiado Mall
22 To Vasco da Gama Mall
23 To El Corte Inglés

### Other Quality Portuguese Souvenirs

**A Vida Portuguesa** is the best shop in town for a well-chosen selection of high-quality, artisanal Portuguese products—everything from stationery and toiletries to housewares and decorative objects to toys and jewelry (daily, Rua Anchieta 11, www.avidaportuguesa.com). They have two other locations: a bigger flagship store in the Intendente neighborhood (daily, Largo do Intendente 23), and a smaller location inside the Mercado do Ribeira.

If you're in a pinch for souvenirs, local TIs have a small but nicely stocked **"Lisbon Shop"** with some basic items emblazoned with Lisbon's trademarks—sardines, fado, or trolleys—as well as fado CDs, at prices typically better than elsewhere in the Baixa (daily, main branch in Praça do Comércio TI, smaller selection at the TI on Praça das Restauradores).

**Woolens:** The delightful **Loja da Burel** boutique showcases fashionable items made from the heavy Portuguese wool called *burel*. This company took over an abandoned wool factory high in the mountains and brought back skilled but out-of-work old-timers to revive a dormant industry. Today the factory churns out high-quality blankets, handbags, coats, shoes, and other products with a mix of traditional and contemporary style (daily, Rua Serpa Pinto 15B, www.burelfactory.com).

**Leather Gloves:** The Lisbon institution **Luvaria Ulisses** sells top-quality leather gloves *(luvas)* one pair at a time, with individual attention to help you find just the right style and fit. The shop is nestled into a tiny storefront just a few steps off Rossio. You squeeze into the shop, then the clerks squeeze your hands into the gloves: they'll nest your elbow on a dainty little pillow, squirt a puff of talcum powder into the glove, then massage your fingers in, one at a time (after a visit here, you'll suddenly appreciate the expression "fits like a glove"). While popular with tourists from faraway lands (expect to wait at busy times), they're still cranking out quality gloves at decent prices (many pairs around €50-60, closed Sun, Rua do Carmo 87, www.luvariaulisses.com).

**Musical Instruments:** If you're captivated by fado and want to check out a Portuguese guitar, **Salão Musical de Lisboa** has a fine selection and a handy location, right on the charming Campo de Carmo square (closed Sun, Rua da Oliveira ao Carmo 2, www.salaomusical.com).

## SHOPPING ZONES

For a focused shopping spree, consider one of these areas. Intendente, described in "Entertainment in Lisbon," also has a few fun shops.

### Príncipe Real Shopping District

For cutting-edge fashion and design, and one of Lisbon's most appealing little green parks, head to the Príncipe Real Garden at the top of the Chiado (about a five-minute walk or speedy bus trip from the top of the Elevador da Glória funicular).

The anchor of this area is the **Embaixada** complex, across the street from the park. Young entrepreneurs have taken over a grand 19th-century Arabian-style townhouse, given it a modern makeover, and filled its two floors with an array of high-end local designers and vendors that attract hipsters, well-dressed urbanites, and in-the-know tourists. You'll see fashion, home decor, kidswear, high-end tailors,

art galleries, pop-up shops, and much more. Climb the grand old staircase, on scuffed tiles and under peeling plaster ceilings, to feel the artful "ramshackle chic" vibe. In the atrium, the Less café has affordable light meals and a gin bar; there's also a little garden café out back (daily 12:00-20:00, Praça do Príncipe Real 26).

Just a few doors down (walking with the park on your left), at the smaller but similarly chic **REAL "Slow Retail" Concept Store,** creative local vendors display their wares in a clean, cool, industrial-mod space. You'll see stacks of coffee-table books, creative housewares, summer dresses, burlap backpacks, colorful shoes and sandals, hipster toddler garb, and horn-rimmed sunglasses (Mon-Wed 10:30-20:00, Thu-Sat until 23:00, closed Sun, Praça do Príncipe Real 20).

A bit farther down are more fun shops, including **Corallo,** where Bettina and Niccolò make their own chocolates and roast their own coffee (closed Sun, Rua da Escola Politécnica 4), and the old-school **Príncipe Real Enxovais,** specializing in top-quality linens for the home (daily, Rua da Escola Politécnica 12). And in the opposite direction, a block up Rua Dom Pedro V back toward the heart of the Chiado, is the **Pelcor** cork products flagship store (see earlier, under "Cork").

This is also a great part of town to get a bite; for details, see the Chiado listings in "Eating in Lisbon," later.

### Mercado da Ribeira (a.k.a. Time Out Market)

This recently renovated market hall offers Lisbon's best one-stop shopping for culinary souvenirs (it's described in detail on page 128). In addition to bottles of wine, chocolates, canned fish, and other edible goodies, it has an outpost of Lisbon's best souvenir shop, A Vida Portuguesa. And, of course, it's also great for a meal. Most stalls are open daily from 12:00 to 24:00. Note that the Loja Das Conservas canned-fish shop is just down the street (see earlier, under *"Conservas"*).

### Flea Markets

On Tuesdays and Saturdays, the **Feira da Ladra flea market** attracts bargain hunters to Campo de Santa Clara in the Alfama (8:00-15:00, best in morning). A Sunday-morning **coin market** jingles at Mercado da Ribeira, listed above (9:00-13:00).

### Shopping Malls and Department Stores

Lisbon has several malls and huge department stores (all open long hours daily). Most central is **Armazéns do Chiado,** with six modern floors—and handy elevators connecting the Baixa and the Chiado (food court on the sixth floor, www.armazensdochiado.com). North of downtown, **Vasco da Gama Mall** fills the grand entryway to the Expo '98 site at the Oriente train/Metro station (described on page 96). And the Spanish megadepartment store, **El Corte Inglés,** has a huge branch at the top of Edward VII Park (near Gulbenkian Museum at Avenida António Augusto de Aguiar 31, M: São Sebastião).

# Entertainment in Lisbon

## NIGHTLIFE

The Baixa is quiet at night, with a few touristy al fresco restaurants and not much else. Head instead up to the Bairro Alto for fado halls, bars, and the Miradouro de São Pedro de Alcântara (view terrace), a pleasant place to hang out. Nearby Rua Diario de Noticias is lined with busy bars and fun crowds spilling onto the street.

### Rua Nova do Carvalho
### (a.k.a. Pink Street)

This happening, crazy street is a short walk downhill from the Chiado in the Cais do Sodré neighborhood (just behind Mercado da Ribeira). Rua Nova do Carvalho, otherwise known as "Pink Street," was once notorious as the sailors' red-light zone. Now the prostitutes are just painted onto the walls, and the made-over street is painted a bright pink. After the bars in other neighborhoods

close, late-night revelers hike 10 minutes from the Chiado down Rua do Alecrim to reach Pink Street. Surrounded by largely uninhabited Pombaline buildings, Pink Street's four bars are allowed to make noise—and they do—until very late into the night. Many of the nightspots here are rowdy, youthful dance halls with names like Tokyo, Musicbox, Viking, and Sabotage Rock Club, with a few striptease clubs mixed in. But the following places—lively earlier and accessible to a wider clientele—are my Pink Street picks.

**Pensão Amor** ("House of Love") is a velvety place for a cocktail. Wallpapered with sexy memories of the days when it was a brothel, it's a grungy tangle of corners to hang out in and enjoy a drink (or just stare at the graffiti), often against a backdrop of live jazz. It even has a sexy library if you feel like reading (no food, Rua Nova do Carvalho 38, also possible to enter from along the bridge at Rua do Alecrim 19, tel. 213-143-399).

**Sol e Pesca Bar,** a nostalgic reminder of the sailor-and-fisherman heritage of this street, sells drinks and preserved food in tins. Just browse the shelves of classic tinned seafood—from pâté and sardines to caviar—and wash down your salty seafood tapas with a glass of wine amid the lures and nets (Rua Nova do Carvalho 44, tel. 213-467-203).

**Povo Lisboa** is a trendy little bar serving delightful Portuguese tapas (from 18:00) and enlivening things with fado (from 20:00 weekdays or from 21:00 weekends, closed Mon, no cover— just buy a drink, light food, Rua Nova do Carvalho 32, tel. 213-473-403).

### LxFactory

LxFactory is a typical riverside industrial zone gone shabby-chic. Passing through the factory gate (under the 25th of April Bridge), you'll find a youthful crowd sorting through a collection of restaurants, clubs, shops, and galleries. LxFactory is lively each night and all day on weekends (www.lxfactory.com).

### Intendente

Intendente—just north of the Baixa—is emerging as a hip and happening zone, with a mellower energy (and fewer partying tourists) than the raucous Pink Street described earlier. This is where Lisbon's artsy hipsters gather to sip a drink, smoke a cigarette, and just hang out. Until recently a place locals avoided at night, today Intendente has impromptu cultural happenings and intriguing little bars and cafés. The epicenter is the main square, Largo do Intendente, which is tucked just off the main drag.

**Getting There:** Ride the Metro (M: Intendente) or walk 15 minutes up Rua de Palma from the top of Praça da Figueira. You'll pass through the entertaining Praça Martim Moniz, nicknamed "Dragon Square" (at M: Martim Moniz). This parklike neighborhood square comes with some basic world food stalls (including Brazilian) and a family-friendly vibe during the day.

**Visiting Intendente:** On the once-seedy Largo do Intendente—ringed with classic old buildings in various stages of deterioration and renovation—you'll find several cafés and shops. **Casa Independente,** a cultural venue with a chill and alternative vibe, has a nondescript entrance—but climb up the stairs to discover a ramshackle-chic bar and patio with light bites and cocktails (Tue-Sat 14:00-24:00, closed Sun-Mon, no sign, upstairs at Largo do Intendente 45, tel. 218-872-842, www.casaindependente.com). Other characteristic, pretentiously casual cafés have seating on the square, including the artsy **O das Jonas** (with light meals, closed Tue, at #28, tel. 218-879-401) and the divey **Largo Café Estudio** (closed Mon, live music every Thu night, at #16).

Shopping is enjoyable here, especially at the flagship branch of **A Vida Portuguesa**—a stylish boutique celebrating made-in-Portugal gifts that feels a bit mainstream amid all this edginess (daily, on the square at #23). Next door—in the lavishly *azulejo*-slathered building at #25—is **Viúva Lamego,** selling quality Portuguese tiles (closed Sat-Sun—for more on both stores, see "Shopping in Lisbon").

If you want a bite beyond the basic light fare at the cafés on the square, along the main street is **$$$ Cervejaria Ramiro**—an old-school but newly in-vogue restaurant serving well-respected seafood and steak. It's hugely popular and becoming quite touristy—you can't miss the long line out front—but it's still a good choice (Tue-Sun 12:00-24:00, closed Mon, Avenida Almirante Reis 1H, tel. 218-851-024).

### Evening Stroll

While not as big a deal as in Spain, the people of Lisbon enjoy a paseo-like early evening stroll after work and before dinner when the weather is balmy. When it comes to weather, Lisboners are pretty spoiled. If it's even a little blustery, they'll likely stay in. But when it's nice, in the summer, you'll find lots of people out strolling. Here are four good places to join them: Rua Augusta through the heart of the Baixa district; along the seaside promenade near Belém Tower; along the fine riverfront promenade at Parque das Nações; and the river walk at Ribeira das Naus (from the water at Praça do Comércio to Cais do Sodré).

## FADO MUSIC

Fado is the ▲▲ folk music of Lisbon's back streets. Since the mid-1800s, it's been the Lisbon blues—mournfully beautiful and haunting ballads about lost sailors, broken hearts, and bittersweet romance. While generally sad, fado can also be jaunty—in a nostalgic way—and captivating. A stout 60-year-old widow singing fado can be invitingly sexy.

While authentically traditional, most Lisbon fado bars cater to tourists these days. Don't expect to find a truly "local" scene. Even the seemingly homemade "fado tonight" *(fado esta noite)* signs are mostly for tourist shows. Still, if you choose well—and can find a convivial restaurant with relatively reasonable prices and fewer tour groups—it's a very memorable evening. (And be wary of your hotel's recommendations, which are often skewed by hefty kickbacks.)

The two main areas for fado in Lisbon are on either side of the Baixa: the Bairro Alto and the Alfama. Below, I've listed options in each neighborhood. For locations, see the maps on page 126 and page 132. To avoid disappointment, it's smart to reserve ahead.

**Ways to See Fado:** Your basic choices are a polished restaurant with a professional-quality staged show; or—my preference—a more rustic place with *fado vadio,* a kind of open-mic fado evening when suspiciously talented "amateurs" line up at the door of neighborhood dives for their chance to warble. Waiters—hired more for their vocal skills than hospitality—sometimes take a turn entertaining the crowd.

Most people combine fado with a late dinner. The music typically begins between 20:00 and 21:00; arrive a bit earlier to be seated and order. Night owls can have a cheaper dinner elsewhere, then show up for fado when the first round of diners are paying their bills (around 22:30 or 23:00). Both elegant, high-end places and holes-in-the-wall generally let nondiners in late for the cost of an overpriced drink and/or a €10-15 cover charge.

**Prices for Fado:** Prices for a fado performance vary greatly, but assume you won't leave any fado experience without spending at least €30 per person—and more like €50-60 per person for the fancier restaurants. Many places have a cover charge, others just expect you to buy a steeply priced meal, and some enforce a €25-30 per person minimum. Remember, as throughout Portugal, appetizers, bread, or cheese that appear on your table aren't free—if you don't want these (exorbitantly priced) appetizers, it's safest to send them back.

### Fado in the Bairro Alto

In the Bairro Alto, wander around Rua Diario de Noticias and neighboring streets.

**Canto do Camões,** while touristy, is romantic, candlelit, and classic. Run by friendly, English-speaking Gabriel, it's easy to reserve and has good music and tasty food. Call ahead to assure a seat. When it's busy, the room feels like a stage show, with 25 or 30 tables all enjoying classic fado. Relax, spend some time, and

# Fado

Fado songs reflect Portugal's bittersweet relationship with the sea. Fado means "fate"—how fate deals with Portugal's adventurers...and the women they leave behind. These are songs of both sadness and hope, a bittersweet emotion called *saudade* (meaning yearning or nostalgia). The lyrics reflect the pining for a loved one across the water, hopes for a future reunion, remembrances of a rosy past or dreams of a better future, and the yearning for what might have been if fate had not intervened. (Fado can also be bright and happy when the song is about the virtues of cities such as Lisbon or Coimbra, or of the warmth of a typical *casa portuguesa*.)

The songs are often in a minor key. The singer *(fadista)* is accompanied by a 12-string Portuguese *guitarra* (with a round body like a mandolin) or other stringed instruments unique to Portugal. Many singers crescendo into the first word of the verse, like a moan emerging from deep inside. Though the songs are often sad, the singers rarely overact—they plant themselves firmly and sing stoically in the face of fate.

A verse from a typical fado song goes:

*O waves of the salty sea,*
*where do you get your salt?*
*From the tears shed by the women in black*
*on the beaches of Portugal.*

close your eyes, or make eye contact with the singer. Let the music and wine collaborate (open at 20:00, music from 20:30 until after midnight; no cover but €27 meal required—includes appetizer, 3 courses, water, and wine; after 22:00 €12 minimum for two drinks; from Rua da Misericordia, go 2 blocks uphill on Travessa da Espera to #38; tel. 213-465-464, www.cantodocamoes.pt).

**Restaurante Adega do Ribatejo** is a homey place crowded with locals and tourists nightly (except Sun) from around 20:00 to 24:00. It's just around the corner from Canto do Camões, and less touristy. This is a good budget alternative: just pay for your meal (main courses around €15) and drinks with no cover or required minimum (Mon-Sat from 19:00, closed Sun, Rua Diario de Noticias 23, tel. 213-468-343). After 22:30, you're welcome to just buy a drink and enjoy the music.

**O Faia** is a top-end fado experience, in a classy dining room under heavy, graceful arches. It's pricey (plan on €60/person for dinner and drinks), but the food and the fado are both professional and top-quality. If you come after dinner (23:00) for just drinks and music, there's a €25 minimum. Filled with an older, well-dressed, international clientele, it's a memorable evening (open Mon-Sat for dinner at 20:00, fado begins at 21:30, closed Sun, Rua da Barroca 54-56, tel. 213-426-742, www.ofaia.com).

**Concert Alternative: Fado in Chiado,** a sterile 50-minute performance in a small modern theater, is for tourists who don't want to stay out late or mess with a restaurant. Sitting with other tourists and without food or drink, you'll enjoy four musicians: a man and a woman singing, a guitarist, and a man on the Portuguese guitar, which gives fado its balalaika charm (€17, daily at 19:00 except Sun, conveniently located in Chiado at Rua da Misericordia 14, on second floor of in Cine Theatro Gymnasio, tel. 961-717-778, www.fadoinchiado.com).

**Trendier Alternative:** In the hip Pink Street nightlife zone, just downhill from the Bairro Alto and Chiado toward the river, **Povo Lisboa** has fado most nights (closed Mon, see listing on page 109).

### Fado in the Alfama

While often pretty lonely and dead after dark, the Alfama has several bars offering fado with their meals—just head uphill from the Fado Museum. Some bars are geared for tourists and tour groups, but others feel organic, spontaneous, and part of the neighborhood culture. While schedules at any particular place can be inconsistent, if you hike up Rua São Pedro de Alcântara to the Church of São Miguel, you'll hear the music wafting out from hole-in-the-wall eateries and be greeted by men hustling business for their fado restaurants. Generally, you simply pay for the meal and enjoy the music as included entertainment. If it's late and there's room, you can just buy a drink. For locations, see map on page 132.

**A Baiuca,** a tiny fun-loving restaurant, offers my favorite Alfama fado experience. A Baiuca—the name means a very rough tavern—packs people in and serves up spirited *fado vadio* (open mic for amateurs) with overpriced, basic food and lots of wine. As the English-speaking manager, Isabel, likes to say, "Fado needs wine." This intimate place is a neighborhood affair and has surround sound—as everyone seems to get into the music (€25 minimum—and be careful with the very pricey appetizers and bottles of wine that can push the bill much higher). If you come very late you can just buy a drink (music Thu-Mon 20:00-24:00, closed Tue-Wed, reservations smart, in the heart of the Alfama, just off Rua São Pedro up the hill from Fado Museum at Rua de São Miguel 20, tel. 218-867-284). When the door is closed, they're full, but you can peek at the action through the window around to the left.

**Clube de Fado** is much classier—one of the best places in town to hear quality fado. While expensive, there's not a bad seat in the house. Music plays nightly in this formal yet intimate setting. When busy, the musicians switch between two adjacent halls, giving waiters time to serve between sets, and diners get music about half the time (plan on €50/person for dinner with wine, plus €7.50 cover charge, meals from 20:00, dinner reservations required, music 21:30 until after midnight; after 23:00, pay just €10 cover plus cost of a drink; around corner from cathedral at Rua São João da Praça 94, tel. 218-852-704, www.clube-de-fado.com).

**Casa de Linhares,** a block downhill from Clube de Fado, offers similar quality fado and an even nicer space, with dinner served under the stone vaults of a 16th-century palace (€15 cover for music, plan about €40/person for dinner, music nightly from 20:00, after 22:00 just cover plus drink purchase, Beco dos Armazéns Do Linho 2, tel. 218-865-088, www.casadelinhares.com).

**Concerts at the Fado Museum:** At the base of the Alfama, the Fado Museum hosts occasional live, free concerts that let you focus on the music (check schedule at www.museudofado.pt). Taking in a show here, then having a budget dinner elsewhere, lets you enjoy Alfama fado on the cheap.

LISBON

## BULLFIGHTS, SOCCER, CONCERTS, AND MOVIES

Tickets to bullfights, concerts, and other events are sold at the green **ABEP kiosk** at the southern end of Praça dos Restauradores (daily 9:00-20:00).

### ▲Portuguese Bullfight

If you always felt sorry for the bull, this is Toro's Revenge: In a Portuguese bullfight, the matador is brutalized along with the bull. Lisbon hosts only about a dozen fights a year, but if you're in town for one, it's an unforgettable experience.

In Act I, the horseman *(cavaleiro)* skillfully plants four beribboned barbs in the bull's back while trying to avoid the leather-padded horns. The horses are the short, stocky Lusitano breed, with excellent balance. In Act II, a colorfully clad eight-man suicide squad (called *forçados*) enters the ring and lines up single file facing the bull. With testosterone sloshing everywhere, the leader taunts the bull—slapping his knees and yelling, *"touro!"*—then braces himself for a collision that can be heard all the way up in the cheap  seats. As he hangs onto the bull's head, his buddies pile on, trying to wrestle the bull to a standstill. Finally, one guy hangs on to *o touro*'s tail and "water-skis" behind him. (In Act III, the *ambulân-cia* arrives.)

Unlike the Spanish *corrida de toros,* the bull is not killed in front of the crowd at the Portuguese *tourada*...but it is killed later. (Some brave bulls with only superficial wounds are spared to fight another day.) Spanish aficionados insist that Portuguese fights are actually crueler, since they humiliate the bull, rather than fight him as a fellow warrior. Animal-rights groups enliven the scene before each fight.

Fights are held at the **Campo Pequeno,** a spectacular, Moorish-domed brick structure that bears a resemblance to Madrid's bullring. The ring is small, so there are no bad seats. To sit nearly at ringside, try the cheapest *bancada* seats, on the generally half-empty and unmonitored main floor. Underneath the ring there's a shopping mall, and overhead there's a retractable roof for concerts. It hosts a variety of restaurants inside, including an Argentine steak restaurant. Maybe the beef served was in the ring earlier?

**Cost and Hours:** Tickets are always available at the door (€20-50); they're also sold at the ABEP kiosk on Praça dos Restauradores (10 percent surcharge). Fights are generally held from Easter through September, typically on Thursday evenings at 22:00; bullring is north of the Baixa in the Campo Pequeno district (M: Campo Pequeno); tel. 217-932-143, www.campopequeno.com.

**Important note:** Half the fights are simply Spanish-type *corridas* without the killing. For the real slam-bam Portuguese-style fight, confirm that there will be *grupo de forçados* ("bull grabbers").

### Soccer

Lisbon is home to two *futebol* teams, Benfica and Sporting CP, which means there are lots of games (1-2/week Aug-May, tickets €20 and up) and lots of team spirit. Benfica, with the red jerseys, plays at the 65,400-seat Stadium of Light, north of the city center (Estádio da Luz; M: Colegio Militar/Luz, www.slbenfica.pt). Sporting CP, with the green-and-white jerseys, plays at the 50,000-seat Estádio José Alvalade, which is also north of Lisbon's center (M: Campo Grande, www.sporting.pt). Tickets are generally available at the stadiums or at the ABEP kiosk on Praça dos Restauradores.

### Concerts

The Gulbenkian Museum runs a classical concert season with about 180 events a year (www.gulbenkian.pt/musica; see page 72). You can hear classical music by national and city orchestras at the cultural center in Belém (www.ccb.pt). Traditional Portuguese theater plays in the National Theater on Rossio and in theaters along Rua das Portas de Santo Antão (the "eating lane"—see page 128) stretching north from Rossio. For popular music, these days you're more likely to find rock, jazz, Brazilian, and African music than traditional fado (which is more for tourists). The monthly *Agenda Cultural* provides the most up-to-date listing of world music, arts, and entertainment (free at TI, €0.50 at newsstands, online at www. agendalx.pt, in Portuguese only).

### Movies

In Lisbon, unlike in Spain, most films are shown in the original language with subtitles. (That's one reason the Portuguese speak better English than the Spanish.) Many of Lisbon's theaters are classy, complete with assigned seats, ushers, and intermissions. The top places don't allow eating or drinking in the theater. Check the newspaper or online to see what's playing. Modern options are in malls like El Corte Inglés (M: São Sebastião) or at the Monumental complex in the ritzy Saldanha neighborhood (M: Saldanha).

# Sleeping in Lisbon

Lisbon has a wide variety of accommodations. I've focused on a few categories: chic, international-style hotels offering a comfortable refuge at a high price; cheap, dingy, but affordable and safe old guesthouses (often up creaky old staircases in grimy buildings); newer boutique hotels offering a compromise between cost and comfort; and some famously classy hostels, which welcome travelers of all ages. For locations of accommodations, see the map on page 120.

Lisbon has become increasingly popular, and rates have increased accordingly—especially on weekends (Thu-Sun), when many Brits and other Europeans fly in for brief urban vacations. Conventions can clog Lisbon at any time, and the busiest time is during the Festas de Lisboa (the last three weeks of June)—when parades, street parties, concerts, and fireworks draw crowds to the city.

## IN THE BAIXA

Central as can be, the grid-planned, easy-to-navigate Baixa district bustles with shops, traffic, tourists, commuters, street musicians, pedestrian areas, and urban intensity. It's close to Rossio station, and the Aerobus to and from the airport cuts right through its middle. And it's handy to all of your sightseeing—wedged between the Alfama and the Bairro Alto/Chiado, with vintage trolleys zipping through every few minutes.

### Upscale Hotels

**$$$$ My Story Hotel Rossio** rents 46 well-equipped, stylish, efficient rooms in a couldn't-be-better location, tucked behind a strip of cafés facing bustling Rossio (air-con, elevator, Praça Dom Pedro IV 59, tel. 213-400-380, www.mystoryhotels.com, fom.rossio@mystoryhotels.com).

**$$$$ Internacional Design Hotel** has 55 small, chic rooms centrally located at the southeast corner of Rossio. Each of its four floors has a different theme—pop, Zen, tribal, and urban. Having breakfast in their expansive restaurant overlooking Rossio is a fine way to start the day (air-con, elevator, underground pay parking nearby, Rua da Betesga 3, tel. 213-240-990, www.idesignhotel.com, book@idesignhotel.com.

**$$$$ Hotel Avenida Palace,** the most characteristic five-star splurge in town, was built with Rossio station in 1892 to greet big-shot travelers. Back then, trains were new, and Rossio was the only station in town. The lounges are sumptuous, dripping with chandeliers, and the 82 rooms—while a bit faded—still mix elegance with modern comforts (air-con, elevator, free parking, hotel's sign is on Praça dos Restauradores but entrance is at Rua 1 de Dezembro 123—down a small alleyway next to Starbucks, tel. 213-218-121, www.hotelavenidapalace.pt, reservas@hotelavenidapalace.pt).

**$$$ My Story Hotel Ouro** has 51 rooms decorated in gold tones—*ouro* in Portuguese. Outside-facing rooms have great views over the busy Baixa streets below, but for maximum quiet, ask for an inside room (air-con, elevator, Rua Áurea 100, tel. 213-400-340, www.mystoryhotels.com, ouro@mystoryhotels.com).

## Dumpy but Affordable Dives

Basically a notch up from a hostel, these are worth considering if you're on a tight budget and want a handy Baixa location. Keep in mind that you get what you pay for—these are the best I've found in this price bracket.

**$ Pensão Praça da Figueira** is a backpacker place on a quiet back street with youth-hostel prices, a kitchen on every floor, a slick modern lobby overlooking Praça da Figueira, and 32 basic but colorfully updated rooms—some with views on the square (cheaper rooms have shared bath but no air-con, 2 flights up with no elevator, entrance is at Travessa Nova de São Domingos 9, tel. 213-426-757, www.pensaopracadafigueira.com, pensaofigueira@clix.pt).

**$ Residencial Florescente** rents 67 straightforward rooms on the thriving, traffic-free "eating lane," a block off Praça dos Restauradores (air-con, elevator, Rua das Portas de Santo Antão 99, tel. 213-426-609, www.residencialflorescente.com, geral@residencialflorescente.com).

**$ Pensão Residencial Gerês** is a throwback, renting 20 well-worn, no-frills rooms with double-paned windows. The sweet Nogueira family speaks some English (RS%, cheaper rooms with private bathroom down the hall, no breakfast, uphill a block off

## Sleep Code

Hotels are classified based on the average price of a standard double room with breakfast in high season.

| | |
|---|---|
| **$$$$** | **Splurge:** Most rooms over €150 |
| **$$$** | **Pricier:** €100-150 |
| **$$** | **Moderate:** €70-100 |
| **$** | **Budget:** €40-70 |
| **¢** | **Backpacker:** Under €40 |
| **RS%** | **Rick Steves discount** |

Unless otherwise noted, credit cards are accepted, hotel staff speak basic English, and free Wi-Fi is available. Comparison-shop by checking prices at several hotels (on each hotel's own website, on a booking site, or by email). For the best deal, *book directly with the hotel*. Ask for a discount if paying in cash; if the listing includes **RS%**, request a Rick Steves discount.

northeast corner of Rossio, Calçada do Garcia 6, tel. 215-958-368, no website but book at www.booking.com, infogereslx@gmail. com).

## Boutique Hostels in the Baixa

Among hostel aficionados, Lisbon is famous for having the best hostels anywhere. They welcome travelers of any age, come with an artistic flair, and, besides the usual dorm beds, have plenty of double rooms (except Home Lisbon Hostel). These come with extras like bike rental, movie nights, and cheap or "free" (tip-based) city tours and excursions out of town.

**¢ Lisbon Destination Hostel** feels designed for backpackers—young and old—who appreciate style, peace, and quiet. Located upstairs in the Rossio train station (literally next to the platforms), it provides a wonderful value and experience. The astroturfed lounge—with beanbag chairs and hammocks—sprawls beneath an Industrial Age glass canopy (many private rooms available, movie night in lounge, Largo do Duque de Cadaval 17, tel. 213-466-457, www.destinationhostels.com, lisbon@destinationhostels.com).

**¢ Home Lisbon Hostel** is a little more rough and homey, with a loose camaraderie and friendly management. The hostel is dominated by its classic old wooden bar—an inviting place to socialize (all dorms—no private rooms, on the second floor at Rua de São Nicolau 13, near corner of Rua dos Fanqueiros, M: Baixa-Chiado, tel. 218-885-312, www.homelisbonhostel.com, info@ homelisbonhostel.com).

**¢ Living Lounge Hostel** is clean, modern, and centrally located near the Baixa-Chiado Metro stop. Each room is uniquely decorated (private rooms including singles, some rooms with air-con, Rua Crucifixo 116, second floor, tel. 213-461-078, www.livingloungehostel.com, info@livingloungehostel.com).

¢ **Lisbon Lounge Hostel,** run by the same folks as the Living Lounge Hostel above, is roughly midway between Praça da Figueira and Praça do Comércio (private rooms but no singles, Rua de São Nicolau 41, tel. 213-462-061, www.lisbonloungehostel.com, info@lisbonloungehostel.com).

## IN THE CHIADO

The Chiado district feels like Lisbon's "uptown." For many, it's the best of all worlds: It's handy to the Baixa and Rossio area (just a few steps downhill), and to the artfully seedy Bairro Alto fado zone (just a few steps uphill), but it feels less touristy and congested than either. It's also a prime location for Lisbon's up-and-coming foodie restaurants and hipster shopping scene, making this a fun place simply to wander, graze, and window-shop. If I were buying an apartment in Lisbon...I'd look in the Chiado. This area specializes in fresher, small, conscientiously run boutique hotels—often upstairs in big buildings without elevators (expect lots of stairs).

**$$$$ Casa Balthazar** is an enticing splurge—an oasis-like private compound of stately old townhouses tucked amid characteristic, restaurant-lined stepped lanes just above Rossio, on the way up into the heart of the Chiado. Classy and modern but still homey, each of its 17 rooms is different—some with views, terraces, and/or private whirlpool baths. There's an inviting little swimming pool, and breakfast is served in your room (air-con, Rua do Duque 26, mobile 917-085-568, www.casabalthazarlisbon.com, reservas@casabalthazarlisbon.com).

**$$$$ Lisboa Carmo Hotel** is bigger and has less personality than the others listed here, but it's in an appealing location: a few steps from the Chiado's charming Largo do Carmo. It has 45 sleek, straightforward, business-class rooms, not much in the way of public spaces, and the only elevator among my Chiado listings (air-con, elevator, Rua da Oliveira ao Carmo 1A, tel. 213-264-710, carmo.luxhotels.pt, carmo.reservas@luxhotels.pt). Their newer sister property, **$$$$ Lisboa Pessoa Hotel,** has similar rooms and a swimming pool just up the street in a neatly tiled building.

**$$$ Casa do Barão** is a delightful little refuge on a tame sidestreet just a block below the bustling Praça Luís de Camões in the heart of the Chiado. Its 12 tidy, well-appointed, modern rooms share several fine common spaces, including a cozy library, winter-garden breakfast room, gravel patio, and tiny swimming pool. Complimentary coffee, tea, and snacks are available all day. At the lower end of this price range, it's a terrific value and a comfortable home base in Lisbon. As it's not staffed 24 hours a day, confirm

# Lisbon Center Hotels

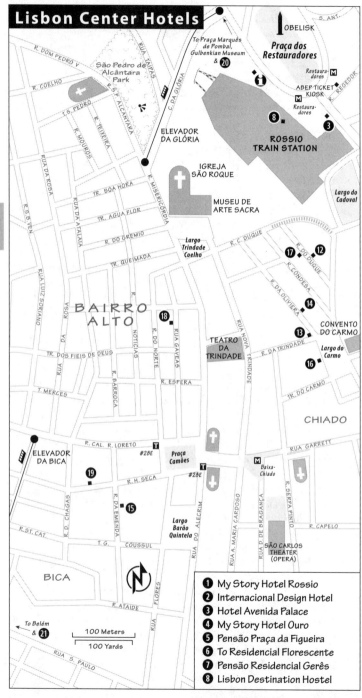

OBELISK

*Praça dos Restauradores*

R. DOM PEDRO V

RUA TAIPAS

To Praça Marquês de Pombal, Gulbenkian Museum & **20**

São Pedro de Alcântara Park

R. COELHO

R. SP. ALCÄNTARA

C. DA GLORIA

S. ANT.

Restaura-dores

ABEP TICKET KIOSK

R. REGEDOR

Restaura-dores

T.S. PEDRO

R. TEIXEIRA

R. MOUROS

ELEVADOR DA GLÓRIA

**8**

ROSSIO TRAIN STATION

**3**

RUA DA ROSA

RUA DA ATALAIA

R.S. BTEN.

IGREJA SÃO ROQUE

MUSEU DE ARTE SACRA

Largo do Cadoval

TR. BOA HORA

TR. AGUA FLOR

R. DO GREMIO

Largo Trindade Coelho

R. C. DUQUE

R. DO DUQUE

**17**  **12**

R. CONDESA

TR. QUEIMADA

R. DA OLIVERA

**14**

R. MISERICORDIA

**BAIRRO ALTO**

RUA DA ROSA

R. DO NORTE

R. NOTICIAS

**18**

RUA GAVEAS

TEATRO DA TRINDADE

RUA NOVA TRINDADE

CONVENTO DO CARMO

**13**

R. DA TRINDADE

Largo do Carmo

**16**

TR. DOS FIEIS DE DEUS

R. BARROCA

R. ESPERA

TR. DO CARMO

T. MERCES

**CHIADO**

RUA LUIZ SORIANO

R. DA.

ELEVADOR DA BICA

R. CAL. R. LORETO

#28E

Praça Camões

RUA GARRETT

Baixa-Chiado

#28E

**19**

R.H. SECA

R. D. CHAGAS

R. DA EMENDA

**15**

RUA A. MARIA CARDOSO

RUA D. DE BRAGANÇA

R. SERPA PINTO

R. CAPELO

R. ST. CAT.

T.G. COUSSUL

Largo Barão Quintela

RUA DO ALECRIM

SÃO CARLOS THEATER (OPERA)

**BICA**

R. ATAIDE

RUA FLORES

To Belém & **21**

100 Meters

100 Yards

RUA S. PAULO

**1** My Story Hotel Rossio
**2** Internacional Design Hotel
**3** Hotel Avenida Palace
**4** My Story Hotel Ouro
**5** Pensão Praça da Figueira
**6** To Residencial Florescente
**7** Pensão Residencial Gerês
**8** Lisbon Destination Hostel

LISBON

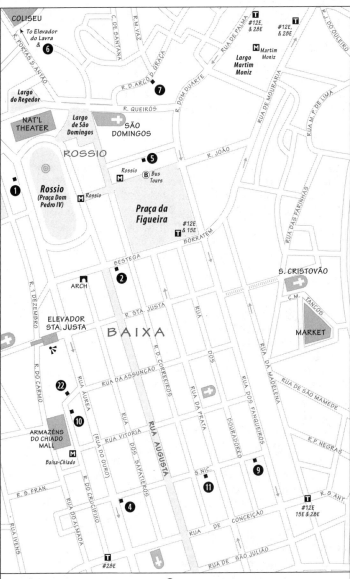

**9** Home Lisbon Hostel

**10** Living Lounge Hostel

**11** Lisbon Lounge Hostel

**12** Casa Balthazar

**13** Lisboa Carmo Hotel

**14** Lisboa Pessoa Hotel

**15** Casa do Barão

**16** Feeling Chiado 15

**17** Zuza Guest House & Zuzabed & Breakfast

**18** Zuzabed Lisbon Suites

**19** Chiado 44

**20** To Avenida da Liberdade Area Hotels

**21** To Hotel As Janelas Verdes

**22** Laundry

your arrival details (air-con, Rua da Emenda 84, mobile 967-944-143, www.casadobarao.com, casasdobarao@gmail.com).

**$$$ Feeling Chiado 15** is a fourth-floor walk-up with eight rooms high above the Chiado's most appealing little leafy square, Largo do Carmo. Four of the rooms—at the cheaper end of this price range—look down over a residential patio; the pricier, "deluxe" rooms have views over Lisbon's rooftops and castle (most rooms have air-con, Largo do Carmo 15, tel. 213-470-845, www.feelingchiado.com, feelingchiado@gmail.com).

**Zuza,** run by entrepreneurial Luis Zuzarte, has rooms in three different buildings around the Chiado. The main branch, **$ Zuza Guest House,** has eight basic but neatly outfitted rooms with shared bathrooms in a creaky old building (no air-con, Rua do Duque 41). A few doors down, **$$ Zuzabed & Breakfast** has four rooms with bathrooms and castle views (air-con, Calçada do Duque 29). And a short walk away, up in the Bairro Alto, **$$$ Zuzabed Lisbon Suites** has seven classy rooms with vintage furnishings (Rua das Gáveas 81). Let them know when you'll arrive: If coming in the morning, you'll likely check in at the Rua do Duque location, but in the afternoon you'll head to the location you're sleeping at (contact for all: mobile 934-445-500, www.zuzabed.com, zuzabed@zuzabed.com).

**$$ Chiado 44** is a simple place in a great location, just below Praça Luís de Camões. Its 11 small, basic, but comfortable rooms fill a historic building—expect plenty of stairs (air-con, Rua Horta Seca 44, mobile 918-352-901, www.chiado44.pt, info@chiado44.pt, Fabian).

## ALONG AVENIDA DA LIBERDADE

Avenida da Liberdade is an upscale neighborhood facing a broad, tree-lined, very European-feeling boulevard. Most of my listings are a block or so off the main street. While it's a residential area, there are also lots of hotels—it's where many of Lisbon's tourists go to sleep. For this reason, it's a bit less characteristically "Lisbon" than some other neighborhoods...but for the sake of a quiet night's sleep, some consider that a good thing. These listings are a 10-minute walk or short Metro ride from the center. Most are near the Avenida Metro stop; Lisbon Dreams is closer to the Rato station.

### High-End Chain Hotels

The **Hoteis Heritage Lisboa** chain has several branches, most near Avenida da Liberdade. These hotels distinguish themselves with classy public spaces and rooms, professional staff, and top-notch amenities (air-con, elevator, pay parking); guests are entitled to sightseeing deals—ask for details. Each hotel has its own style and personality (website for all: www.heritage.pt).

**$$$$ Hotel Britania** maintains its 1940s Art Deco charm throughout its 33 spacious rooms, offering a clean and professional haven on a workaday street one block off Avenida da Liberdade. Three top-floor rooms are decorated in a luxurious Mod Deco style (Rua Rodrigues Sampaio 17, tel. 213-155-016, britania.hotel@ heritage.pt).

**$$$$ Heritage Avenida Liberdade** is the most contemporary, the only one actually on the leafy boulevard, and the closest to the center (a 5-minute walk from Rossio). Its stylish lobby/breakfast room is inviting, and the 42 rooms feel upscale-urban (Avenida da Liberdade 28, tel. 213-404-040, avliberdade@heritage.pt).

**$$$$ Hotel As Janelas Verdes** is farther out—west of the center, next door to the Museum of Ancient Art, filling an 18th-century mansion with 29 cushy rooms and comfortably elegant public spaces. The third-floor library overlooks the river (Rua das Janeles Verdes 7, bus #714 stops nearby, tel. 213-968-143, janelas. verdes@heritage.pt).

**$$$ Hotel Lisboa Plaza**—a large, plush gem—mixes traditional style with bright-pastel classiness. Its 112 rooms are on a quiet street off busy Avenida da Liberdade, a block from the Avenida Metro station (free port wine after 18:00, Travessa do Salitre 7, tel. 213-218-218, plaza@heritage.pt).

## Other Avenida Liberdade Hotels

**$$$ Hotel Alegria** faces a quiet, inviting park in a peaceful neighborhood 200 yards from the Avenida Metro station. Its bright, inviting public spaces and 30 comfortable, well-appointed rooms have hardwood floors varnished like a ship's deck (breakfast extra, air-con, elevator, Praça da Alegria 12, tel. 213-220-670, www. hotelalegria.pt, info@hotelalegria.pt).

**$ Lisbon Dreams Guest House** has 18 fresh, relaxing, Ikea-style rooms, occupying three apartments and sharing seven bathrooms (shared kitchen and terraces; M: Marquês de Pombal, then take Rua Alexandre Herculano uphill and turn left on Rua Rodrigo da Fonesca, or M: Rato, take Rua Alexandre Herculano downhill, then right to reach Rua Rodrigo da Fonesca 29, tel. 213-872-393, www.lisbondreams.com, info@lisbondreams.com).

# Eating in Lisbon

Each district of the city comes with fun and characteristic restaurants. (Good eateries in Belém are described on page 83.) Ideally, have one dinner with a fado performance—several good options for music with your meal are listed in this section, with more fado options described earlier, under "Entertainment in Lisbon." Note that some smaller, family-run places take a few weeks off in the late summer or early fall—don't be surprised to find a handwritten *fechado para férias* (closed for vacation) sign taped to the window.

**Snack Bars:** Lisbon seems enthusiastic about serving quick, light meals at characteristic bars. On just about any street, you can belly up to a bar, observe, and order what looks good for a tasty, memorable, and extremely cheap meal. You'll see lots of *pastel de bacalhau,* Lisbon's ubiquitous and delicious cod cake. Other good standbys are *prego* (steak sandwich) and *bifana* (pork sandwich), each made with a secret sauce to give them character.

**Food Tours in Lisbon:** To simultaneously eat good food, learn about Portuguese cuisine, and meet a knowledgeable local guide, consider taking one of the food tours (described on page 36). These tours are informative, tasty, and a good value—filling you in while filling you up.

## IN THE BAIXA
### Near Rossio

My first few listings here are nice, sit-down eateries, while the rest are good for a quick bite. The area around Rossio station, with plenty of practical, inexpensive eateries, caters to busy locals commuting in and out by train.

**$$$ Bastardo Restaurante**—upstairs in the recommended Internacional Design Hotel—is a simple, solid, no-stress option for Portuguese cuisine with a modern twist overlooking the square. The space is fresh, bright, and accessible, like the menu. It can be smart to reserve (vegan options, daily 12:30-15:00 & 19:30-23:00, Rua da Betesga 3, facing Rossio, tel. 213-240-993, http://restaurantebastardo.com).

**$$$$ Pinóquio Restaurante,** a venerable seafood beer hall famous for its clams (€22 splittable portion), has a good local energy. You'll dine with a smart crowd at white-tableclothed tables yet with no pretense—the focus is on simple quality (daily 12:00-24:00, big portions, dine inside or outside facing the busy square, Praça dos Restauradores 79, tel. 213-465-106).

**$$ Confeitaria Nacional** has been proudly satisfying sweet tooths for 180 years, and was once the favorite of Portuguese royalty. Stop in for a tasty pastry downstairs. Or, for a peaceful and inexpensive lunch, go upstairs, where you'll choose between a cheaper meal in the cafeteria or pay a little extra for service and Old World sophistication in the elegant dining room (Mon-Sat 8:00-20:00, pastry counter open Sun but upstairs may be closed, Praça da Figueira 18, tel. 213-424-470).

**$ Restaurante Beira-Gare** is my choice for a quick, cheap meal immediately across the street from Rossio station. A classic greasy-spoon diner, it dishes out cod and vegetables prepared faster than a Big Mac and served with more energy than a soccer team.

---

## Restaurant Price Code

I've assigned each eatery a price category, based on the average cost of a typical main course. Drinks, desserts, and splurge items (steak and seafood) can raise the price considerably.

| | |
|---|---|
| **$$$$** | **Splurge:** Most main courses over €17 |
| **$$$** | **Pricier:** €12-17 |
| **$$** | **Moderate:** €7-12 |
| **$** | **Budget:** Under €7 |

In Portugal, takeout food is **$**; a basic sit-down eatery is **$$**; a casual but more upscale restaurant is **$$$**; and a swanky splurge is **$$$$**.

---

The house specialty is a pork sandwich *(bifana no pão)*. Consider their soup-and-sandwich special (Mon-Sat 6:00-24:00, closed Sun, stand at the bar or grab a table, Rua 1 de Dezembro, tel. 213-420-405).

**$ Casa Brasileira** offers a characteristic budget snack or meal in a classic local scene. Fast, cheap lunch deals are served only at the bar, or choose the sidewalk tables with a higher-priced menu. And their *pastel de nata* (custard tart), made downstairs, is as tasty as those that people line up for in Belém (daily 7:00-24:00, 100 yards from Rossio at Rua Augusta 265, tel. 213-459-713).

**$ A Tendinha do Rossio,** established in 1840 and run by Calheiros and Carmo, is a classic *ginjinha* bar that also sells soups, sandwiches, and fishy snacks. While it's pretty dumpy, it's notable because it offers the only cheap tables on Rossio. Prices are dirt-cheap and the same whether you sit with the drunks at the bar, grab a tiny table inside, or serve yourself and sit outside overlooking Rossio (Mon-Sat 7:00-21:00, closed Sun, Praça Dom Pedro IV 6, tel. 213-468-156).

**Rua 1 de Dezembro:** This street, which is active during the workday and dead after hours, is lined with cheap restaurants that make self-service speed a priority for busy office workers who eat here. Walk the street from Rossio station to the Elevador de Santa Justa to determine the prevailing menu of the day. **$$ Leão d'Ouro** has a fancy and expensive sit-down restaurant, but their handy self-service cafeteria next door (at #97) offers an affordable lunch or dinner buffet (daily 12:00-23:00). There are also two grocery stores on this street (open long hours daily): the straightforward **Pingo Doce supermarket** (at #73, with very cheap 9-stool cafeteria), and—across the street—the organic/health-food alternative, **Celeiro,** which also has a self-service vegetarian lunch joint (called Tasquinha do Celeiro, at #53, Mon-Fri 8:00-18:00, closed Sat-Sun).

**$ Armazéns do Chiado Mall:** The sixth-floor food court at

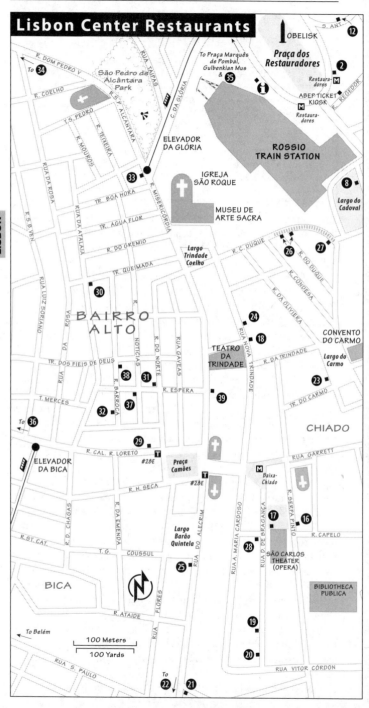

# Lisbon Center Restaurants

OBELISK

To Praça Marquês de Pombal, Gulbenkian Mus & ... 35

Praça dos Restauradores

S. ANT 12

2

Restaura-dores

ABEP TICKET KIOSK

Restauradores

ROSSIO TRAIN STATION

R. DOM PEDRO V

To 34

São Pedro de Alcântara Park

R. COELHO

T. S. PEDRO

R. TEIXEIRA

R. F. ALCÂNTARA

RUA TIPAS

C. DA GLÓRIA

ELEVADOR DA GLÓRIA

33

IGREJA SÃO ROQUE

MUSEU DE ARTE SACRA

8

Largo do Cadoval

R. MOUROS

RUA DA ROSA

R. S. B. VEN.

TR. BOA HORA

TR. AGUA FLOR

R. DO GREMIO

Largo Trindade Coelho

R. C. DUQUE

26

27

E. DO DUQUE

R. CONDESA

R. DA OLIVEIRA

TR. QUEIMADA

30

BAIRRO ALTO

R. DA ROSA

R. LUIZ SORIANO

NOTICIAS

R. DO NORTE

RUA GAVEAS

24

18

TEATRO DA TRINDADE

RUA NOVA TRINDADE

R. DA TRINDADE

CONVENTO DO CARMO

Largo do Carmo

23

R. DO CARMO

TR. DOS FIEIS DE DEUS

38

31

R. ESPERA

T. MERCES

R. BARROCA

32

37

39

CHIADO

29

R. CAL. R. LORETO

T #28E

Praça Camões

T #28E

RUA GARRETT

M Baixa-Chiado

ELEVADOR DA BICA

To 36

R. D. CHAGAS

R. DA EMENDA

R. H. SECA

Largo Barão Quintela

RUA DO ALECRIM

RUA A. MARIA CARDOSO

RUA D. DE BRAGANÇA

R. SERPA PINTO

17

16

R. CAPELO

R. ST. CAT.

T. G. COUSSUL

25

28

SÃO CARLOS THEATER (OPERA)

BIBLIOTHECA PUBLICA

BICA

FLORES

RUA

R. ATAIDE

To Belém

100 Meters

100 Yards

19

20

RUA S. PAULO

To 22

21

RUA VITOR CORDON

1. Bastardo Restaurante
2. Pinóquio Restaurante
3. Confeitaria Nacional
4. Restaurante Beira-Gare
5. Casa Brasileira
6. A Tendinha do Rossio
7. Rua 1 de Dezembro Eateries
8. Leão d'Ouro Rest./Café
9. Pingo Doce Supermarket
10. Celeiro
11. Armazéns do Chiado Mall Eateries
12. Bonjardim Restaurante
13. Casa do Alentejo Restaurante/Bar
14. To Rest. Solar dos Presuntos & Cantinho São José
15. To Nova Pombalina
16. Belcanto
17. Café Lisboa
18. Bairro do Avillez
19. Cantinho do Avillez
20. Pizzaria Lisboa
21. Restaurante Vicente
22. To "Pink Street" Nightlife
23. Carmo Restaurante & Bar
24. Cervejaria da Trindade
25. By the Wine
26. Café Buenos Aires & Solar do Duque
27. El Rei D'Frango
28. Café no Chiado
29. Manteigaria
30. Restaurante Bota Alta
31. A Primavera do Jerónimo & Canto do Camões Rest. & Fado
32. Lisbon Winery
33. Solar do Vinho do Porto
34. To Príncipe Real Garden Eateries
35. To Cervejaria Ribadouro & Restaurante A Gina
36. To Mercado de Campo de Ourique
37. Restaurante Adega do Ribatejo Fado
38. O Faia Fado
39. Fado in Chiado
40. Wines of Portugal Tasting Room
41. To Martinho da Arcada Café Bar

LISBON

## Lisbon's Gourmet Food-Circus Markets

The big news on Lisbon's eating scene is the transformation of traditional farmers markets into gourmet food circuses. These combine the stalls of traditional food-market vendors (selling produce, meat, fish, spices, etc.) with a food court filled with eateries run by locally respected chefs. If you love food—or even if you don't—these are fun to explore.

### Mercado da Ribeira (a.k.a. Time Out Market)

Located at Cais do Sodré (between the Chiado and the river), this is two markets in one: The boisterous and venerable market survives in one half of the Industrial Age, iron-and-glass market hall, while the other half has become a trendy food court curated by *Time Out* magazine, which has invited a few dozen quality restaurants to open outposts here. Eating here on disposable plates and long, noisy picnic tables is far from romantic, but the quality and prices are great. The produce and fish market is open from 7:00 to 13:00 (closed Sun and no fish Mon), while the restaurants are open daily from 12:00 to 24:00. This place is no secret—to avoid a mob scene at dinnertime, arrive before 19:00.

**Getting There:** The Mercado da Ribeira (like many locals, I resist calling this venerable market by its new "Time Out" name) is across the street from the Cais do Sodré train station. It's conveniently served by the Metro (Cais do Sodré stop) and tram #15E (on the way to/from Belém), and it's about a 10-minute walk from Praça do Comércio. If you're here for dinner, note that the crazy Pink Street—lined with clubs and bars—is just two blocks inland and lively late (described in "Entertainment in Lisbon," earlier).

**Eating at Mercado da Ribeira:** Entering the market from the main entrance (facing Cais do Sodré), the workaday market

this shopping center, between the Bairro Alto and the Baixa, offers a selection of fun eateries—mostly fast food and chain restaurants you'd find in any modern mall, but a few are actual restaurants with castle views (daily 12:00-23:00, between Rua Garrett and Rua da Assunção; from the lower town, find the inconspicuous elevator at Rua do Crucifixo 89 or 113, next to the Baixa-Chiado Metro entrance). **$ Loja das Sopas** has hearty soups with cheap fixed-price meals. **$ Companhia das Sandes** offers up hearty sandwiches and healthy, big-bowl pasta salads topped with tropical fruits. **$$ Restaurant Chimarrão** serves Brazilian cuisine and offers an impressive *rodizio:* an all-you-can-eat buffet of salad, veggies, and endless beef, ham, pork, sausage, and chicken (€11 for weekday lunch, €13 for dinner and on weekends).

## Lisbon's "Eating Lane"

Just north of Rossio, Rua das Portas de Santo Antão is Lisbon's stalls are on your right, while the foodie festival is on your left. In the food court, join the young, trendy, hungry, and thirsty crowd grazing among a wide variety of options. Assemble a sampling of local treats, and grab a seat at the big, shared tables in the middle. The north wall is a row of stalls run by big-name Lisbon chefs offering quality dishes at reasonable prices (enticing dinner plates for €10). And there are also branches of Honorato (a local "gourmet burger" chain), O Prego da Peixaria (fish and steak sandwiches), Sea Me (a Chiado institution for seafood), Aloma (in the west outer aisle, for the best pastries), and Santini (the venerable Portuguese gelateria). Get wine and beer from separate stalls in the center. You may find affordable *percebes* (barnacles) at several seafood stalls.

### Mercado de Campo de Ourique

A trendy marketplace fills this 19th-century iron-and-glass market. Compared to Mercado da Ribera, it's less crowded and more purely local. Produce stalls, fishmongers, and bakeries sell everything from pigs' ears to fragrant bunches of cilantro (most close in the evening). At lunch and dinner, local diners pick up meals from whichever counter appeals: pork, seafood, Japanese, wine, beer, coffee, meat, produce, artisanal gelato, and so on (most eateries open daily 10:00-23:00).

**Getting There:** It's a couple of miles west of Rossio. Take a taxi or Uber, or hop on trolley #28E and ride to the second-to-last stop (Igreja Sto. Condestável; market is behind the big church). Lisbon's most interesting cemetery is one stop farther, at the end of the trolley line.

"eating lane"—a galaxy of eateries, many specializing in seafood (off the northeast corner of Rossio). While the waiters are pushy and it's all very touristy, the lane—lively with happy eaters—is enjoyable to browse. This is a fine spot to down a beer, snack on some snails, and watch people go by. The last two options are just beyond the end of the eating lane, and therefore less touristy (they're also handier to hotels on Avenida da Liberdade).

**$$ Bonjardim,** a family-friendly diner on a small side street, is known for its tasty rotisserie chicken—paint on some spicy African *piri-piri* sauce (Tue 19:00-23:00, Wed-Sun 12:00-23:00, closed Mon, Travessa do Santo Antão 7 or 10, both branches run by same owner, tel. 213-427-424).

**$$$ Casa do Alentejo Restaurante** specializes in Alentejo cuisine and fills an old, second-floor dining hall. The Moorish-looking building is a cultural and social center for transplants from the Alentejo, the traditional southern province of Portugal (and historically the poorest region in the country). While the food is mainly hearty and simple, come for the ambience. It's a good place to try regional specialties such as pork with clams, or the super-sweet, eggy almond dessert called *charcada*. The full-bodied Alentejo red wine is cheap and solid (lunch specials, Tue-Sun 12:00-15:00 & 19:00-22:00, Mon 19:00-22:00, slip into the closed-looking building at Rua das Portas de Santo Antão 58 and climb stairs to the right, tel. 213-469-231). They host folk singing in the grand ballroom (often on Sat from 15:00) and ballroom dancing (on many Sun from 15:00 to 19:00), except in summer when it's too hot (mid-June–mid-Sept).

**$ Casa do Alentejo Bar,** in the same building, serves cheap bar food and wine, either in the sleek-and-trendy interior or out on the little patio (spicy meat dishes, hearty cheeses, other tapas; daily 12:00-23:00, to the right of the stairs, look for *taberna* sign on main floor).

**$$$$ Restaurante Solar dos Presuntos** keeps the theater crowd happily fed with meat and seafood specialties. Its upstairs is more elegant, while the downstairs—with a colorful, open kitchen—is higher energy. Photos of Lisbon's celebrities and politicians who eat here enliven the walls. This place can take advantage of its popularity and bulldoze tourists into spending a lot—order cautiously and know what you're paying for. Reservations are smart (big splittable portions, good wine list, see daily suggestions, Mon-Sat 12:00-15:30 & 19:00-23:00, closed Sun, at the top end of Rua das Portas de Santo Antão at #150, tel. 213-424-253, www. solardospresuntos.com).

**$ Cantinho São José** is a wonderfully untouristy, cheap-and-cheery hole-in-the-wall a block beyond the main restaurant zone. Its extremely tight, tiled interior is jammed with tiny tables filled by big locals ordering hearty, splittable portions of Portuguese classics—for pennies on the dollar compared to the tourist traps nearby (Sun-Fri 9:00-24:00, closed Sat, Rusa São José 94, tel. 213-427-866).

### Below the Cathedral

These places are at the southeast corner of the Baixa, on the way to the Alfama.

**$ Nova Pombalina** is a busy little joint that serves quick sandwiches, soups, and exotic fresh-squeezed juices. It's famous among office workers for its suckling pig sandwich *(sandes de leitão)*. They have good *piri-piri* sauce on request. From Praça do Comércio, it's five blocks toward the castle, on the corner of Rua do Comércio and Rua da Madalena (Mon-Sat 8:00-19:00, closed Sun, Rua do Comércio 2, for location see map on page 126, tel. 218-874-360).

**$$ Mesa Kreol** offers a lively taste of Portugal's former over-

## Appetizers Aren't Free

Remember: In Portugal, there's no such thing as a free munch. Appetizers brought to your table before you order (such as olives, bread, and fancy pâtés) are not free. So if you don't want to pay for them, just push them aside or wave them away when the waiter brings them. Don't eat any of it—not even one olive—or you'll be charged (only €1-2 for the simpler appetizers, but it's disturbing if you don't expect it).

seas colonies—with cuisine from Cape Verde, Mozambique, Angola, and Brazil. Its interior is small, cozy, and nondescript, but the cuisine is a bold and flavorful change of pace. Manager Ju enjoys helping his guests navigate the menu, and there's often live music (Tue-Sun 19:00-24:00, closed Mon, Arco das Portas do Mar 29, for location see map on page 132, mobile 910-629-690).

### IN THE ALFAMA

These are listed geographically, from just below the castle at the top to the Fado Museum at the bottom.

**Lunch on Largo do Contador Mor:** This leafy and picturesque square, just under the castle, has a few interchangeable **$$** restaurants serving up decent plates of grilled sardines *(sardinhas grelhadas)*. But the real star of the square is **$ Miss Can,** an engaging, colorful, and stylish little shop that's injecting some contemporary class into the beloved Portuguese tradition of canned fish. Three young, hip Lisboners have returned to their roots (their families have been in the sardine biz for generations) to create fresh new packaging for a variety of canned sardines, mackerel, and cod. Peruse their shop, and pick a can or two to eat with bread, salad, and a drink at one of their inviting little café tables (daily 11:00-19:00, at #17, mobile 910-007-004, www.miss-can.com).

**Near the Santa Luzia Viewpoint: $$$ Farol de Santa Luzia,** which offers a nice seafood feast with a delicate and delightful dining area, is a favorite of mine for dinner at the top of the Alfama. A family-run place with a local clientele, it offers the Algarve *cataplana* style of cooking—simmered in a copper pot (€27 big *cataplana* of meat, fish, or shellfish for two; indoor seating only, Mon-Sat 17:30-23:00, closed Sun, Largo Santa Luzia 5, across from Santa Luzia viewpoint terrace, tiny sign, tel. 218-863-884; Andre, Luis, and family).

**Near Largo Rodrigues de Freitas:** For more of an adventure with your meal, walk past Largo das Portas do Sol and follow the trolley tracks along Rua de São Tomé to a square called Largo Rodrigues de Freitas—if riding trolley #12E, it's the first stop over the big hill. On this square, **$$ Restaurante Frei Papinhas** is a

LISBON

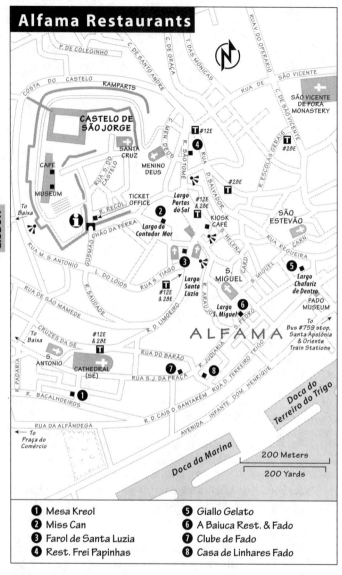

**Alfama Restaurants**

- ❶ Mesa Kreol
- ❷ Miss Can
- ❸ Farol de Santa Luzia
- ❹ Rest. Frei Papinhas
- ❺ Giallo Gelato
- ❻ A Baiuca Rest. & Fado
- ❼ Clube de Fado
- ❽ Casa de Linhares Fado

classic, family-run, hole-in-the-wall where you can feast on fresh seafood with the neighborhood crowd. Dine inside, or at rickety tables across the street in a charming square—where you can watch the trolleys rattle by (daily 12:00-16:00 & 19:00-24:00, Rua de São Tome 13, tel. 218-866-471).

**Fado Deep in the Alfama:** While the Bairro Alto is far livelier at night and has a better energy, the Alfama still has a unique charm. My favorite places for dinner with fado are described earlier, under "Entertainment in Lisbon."

**Ice Cream: Giallo,** across Campo de Ourique from the Fado Museum, has an enticing array of high-quality artisanal gelato.

## IN THE CHIADO

The Chiado has some of Lisbon's trendiest restaurants. If you don't mind paying a bit more to experience the city's burgeoning food scene (rather than the old-school, fill-the-tank, and tourist-focused places in other neighborhoods), venture up into these inviting streets. When considering these listings, remember that the more traditional Bairro Alto neighborhood—covered in the next section—is just a few minutes' walk away.

**José Avillez Restaurants:** One of Portugal's top celebrity chefs, José Avillez, has elevated and modernized Portuguese classics with international influences and techniques. He runs a growing empire of pricey but excellent destination restaurants in Lisbon (reservations recommended for all; www.joseavillez.pt). His flagship location is the Michelin-starred **$$$$ Belcanto,** a top-end splurge (with €125-145 tasting *menus*, closed Sun-Mon, Largo de São Carlos 10, tel. 213-420-607). But other nearby locations offer far more affordable tastes. **$$$ Café Lisboa,** directly across the square from Belcanto (in front of the opera house), has indoor and outdoor seating, uneven service, and delicious modern Portuguese dishes (daily 12:00-24:00, Largo de São Carlos 23, tel. 211-914-498). A couple of blocks away, **Bairro do Avillez** is bright and boisterous. There's a lively **$$$** *taberna* up front with small plates, main courses, casual seating, and lots of well-dressed urbanites mingling at the bar; in back, the **$$$$** *páteo* under a glass skylight offers a full menu of pricier fish and seafood dishes (both open daily 12:00-24:00 but no meals served in *páteo* 15:30-19:00, Rua Nova da Trinidade 18, tel. 211-992-369). Two more, less expensive Avillez eateries are just downhill (toward the river) on Rua dos Duques de Bragança: **$$$ Cantinho do Avillez,** with a casual vibe and a more international menu (daily, at #7), and **$$$ Pizzaria Lisboa** (daily, at #5).

**$$$ Restaurante Vicente,** at the southern edge of the Chiado (downhill from the main zone, halfway to Mercado da Ribeira), fills a former brick-arched coal warehouse with rustic-trendy decor and excellent Alentejo cuisine from Portugal's arid southern heartland. The hearty, delicious meals come with real history: Traditionally, coal cellars like this one came with a crow named "Vicente" to act as an early-warning system for polluted air—like the proverbial canary in a coal mine (Mon-Fri 12:30-15:30 & 19:30-24:00, Sat-Sun 19:30-24:00, Rua das Flores 6, tel. 218-066-142).

**$$ Carmo Restaurante and Bar** offers delicious updated

Portuguese cooking. You can share a few *petiscos* (Portuguese-style tapas), or get well-presented main courses. In good weather, sit out on the inviting square, under a leafy canopy. Otherwise, take advantage of the chic-but-homey setting, with a series of smaller rooms that help you get away from the crowds (weekday lunch deals, tempting desserts, daily 12:00-23:00, Largo do Carmo 11, tel. 213-460-088).

**$$$ Cervejaria da Trindade**—a bright, boisterous, beer hall—is full of historic tiles, seafood, and tourists. While over-priced and in all the guidebooks, it's a historic landmark (see description on page 63). The seafood is charged by weight—clarify prices when you order (daily 12:00-24:00, liveliest 20:00-22:00, air-con, courtyard, a block down from São Roque Church at Rua Nova da Trindade 20C, tel. 213-423-506).

**$$$ By the Wine** is a trendy yet accessible wine bar, filling a cellar under a green-bottled vaulted ceiling. They serve a few dozen Portuguese wines by the glass, thoughtfully paired with local cold cuts and cheeses, small plates, and main dishes. It's less intimate and informative than Lisbon Winery (described later), but busier, more atmospheric, and more food-focused (Mon 18:00-24:00, Tue-Sun 12:00-24:00, Rua das Flores 41-43, tel. 213-420-319).

**$$$ Café Buenos Aires** is a friendly place serving Argentinian cuisine (lots of red meat), hearty dinner salads, vegetarian homemade pasta, and famous chocolate cake. Dine in the charming and intimate woody interior, or at fun tables outside on a characteristic, stepped pedestrian lane with views across to the Alfama (daily 18:00-24:00, Rua do Duque 31, tel. 213-420-739). Above this place and on the same lane is **$$ Solar do Duque,** a typical Portuguese eatery with romantic tables on the stepped lane (daily, Rua do Duque 67, tel. 213-426-901).

**$ El Rei D'Frango** ("King of Chicken") is a local favorite for huge portions of affordable, stick-to-your-ribs grilled meat and fish specialties (but, strangely, little to no chicken), served in an unpretentious little hole-in-the-wall. It's on the steep stepped lanes at the very bottom of the Chiado, just above the back end of the Baixa, behind Rossio station (Mon-Sat 10:00-22:00, closed Sun, Calçada do Duque 5, tel. 213-424-066).

**$$$ Café no Chiado** is perched on an upper street overlooking the square in front of the **São Carlos** opera house (find the stairs up next to the recommended Café Lisboa). It's a local favorite for its brief, accessible menu. The interior is casual-classy, and the outdoor tables—on a tiny square under red-and-black awnings—feels very European (daily 12:00-24:00, Largo do Picadeiro, tel. 213-460-502).

**Dessert: $ Manteigaria** is simply the best place in town for *pastel de nata*—everyone's favorite local pastry. They serve only this one treat, constantly churning the lovable little €1 custard pies out of the oven so you eat them not "reheated warm"...but literally hot from the oven. While here, enjoy a look at the busy little kitchen (daily until 24:00, Rua Loreto 2 just off Praça Camões).

## IN THE BAIRRO ALTO

For a characteristic meal in Old World surroundings, the Bairro Alto is hard to beat.

**Fado with Dinner in Bairro Alto:** For a most memorable dining experience with live fado music in the Bairro Alto, consider **Canto do Camões** (more formal and subdued, Travessa da Espera 38), **Restaurante Adega do Ribatejo** (more rough and casual, Rua Diario de Noticias 23), or **O Faia** (top-end splurge with quality food and fado, Rua da Barroca 54-56). All are described under "Entertainment in Lisbon" on page 111; for locations, see map on page 126.

**$$ Restaurante Bota Alta** ("The Old Boot") is a classic—if a bit touristy—little eatery with a timeless Portuguese ambience, tight seating, and reliably good food. Portions are big, and Paulo offers a fun dessert sampler plate. Reservations are smart. (Mon-Sat 12:00-14:30, 19:00-23:00, closed Sun, at corner of Travessa da Queimada and Rua da Atalaia, tel. 213-427-959).

**$$ A Primavera do Jerónimo** is a quintessential Bairro Alto joint serving traditional home-style plates in a jam-packed, joyfully characteristic scene. Rafael and Helena love serving stuffed squid and Brás-style cod—whipped into a frittata with potatoes and onions (Mon-Sat opens at 19:30, closed Sun; reserve, come early, or wait; at Travessa da Espera 38, a few steps below recommended fado place Canto do Camões, tel. 213-420-477).

**$$$ Lisbon Winery,** a modern, casual little wine bar and tapas place, has a passion for the best wines, cheeses, and meats. With quality local ingredients, cork walls, and fado music playing, it's a perfect storm of Portuguese culture. Sommelier Alex is evangelical about Portuguese wines and ports, and how to complement them with tasty foods. Just tell him your budget, and he'll work within it. For a memorable and educational light meal, two people can pay €20 each for a complete array of cheeses, meats, and wines. Cap your experience by tossing a cork into the 500 year-old cistern (Tue-Sun 15:00-24:00, closed Mon, Rua da Barroca 13, tel. 218-260-132, www.lisbonwinery.com. They also do wine tastings (€50-60/person, typically at 15:30, but confirm).

## Serious Port Wine Tastings

**Solar do Vinho do Porto,** run by the Port Wine Institute, has perhaps the world's greatest selection of port—the famous fortified wine that takes its name from the city of Porto. If you're not headed to Porto, this is your best chance for a serious lesson. The plush, air-conditioned, Old World living room is furnished with leather chairs (this is not a shorts-and-T-shirt kind of place). You can order from a selection of more than 150 different ports (€2-22/glass), generally poured by an English-speaking bartender. Read the instructive menu for an education in port. Fans of port describe it as "a liquid symphony playing on the palate." Browse through the easy menu. Start white and sweet (cheapest), taste your way through spicy and ruby, and finish mellow and tawny. A *colheita* (single harvest) is particularly good. Appetizers *(aperitivos)* are listed in the menu with small photographs. As these are government employees and their jobs are secure, smiles or help navigating the menu are unnecessary. Table service can be slow and disinterested when it's busy; to be served without a long wait, go to the bar (Mon-Fri 11:00-24:00, Sat 14:00-24:00, closed Sun, directly across from the top of the Elevador da Glória funicular at Rua São Pedro de Alcântara 45). For much more on port, see page 348.

## Príncipe Real Garden Eateries (Jardim do Príncipe Real)

This delightful parklike square is just a five-minute hike up Rua Dom Pedro V above the top of the Elevador da Glória funicular and the Bairro Alto. While this area is becoming known as a shopping mecca (see under "Shopping in Lisbon," earlier), it also has a delightful array of eateries.

The park itself has an unforgettable cedar tree shaped into a canopy over shady benches and a *quiosque* that doubles as a trendy, youthful wine and beer hangout. Also below the tree's canopy is **$$$ Esplanada do Príncipe Real,** with delightful seating—either at outdoor tables under shady branches or in the glassed-in interior. Skip the pricey, forgettable food—I'd just order a drink and savor the ambience (tel. 210-965-699).

A block away (along Rua Dom Pedro V back toward the Bairro Alto) is the neighborhood's big foodie draw: **$$$ A Cevicheria,** where (under a giant stuffed octopus) Chef Kiko serves elegant Peruvian/Portuguese dishes—specializing in flavorfully marinated raw fish and seafood ceviche. This deservedly popular place takes no reservations; arrive early or expect to wait (daily 12:00-24:00, Rua Dom Pedro V 129, tel. 218-038-815, www.acevicheria.pt).

For a huge contrast, a few doors down is **$$ Pavilhão Chines** ("Chinese Pavilion")—an eccentric, smoky, private museum-like bar with room after room slathered with an enormous collection of esoteric treasures. Come here to settle into a club chair and sip a drink rather than to eat (daily from 18:00, Rua Dom Pedro V 89, billiards in back).

## ON AVENIDA DA LIBERDADE

**$$$$ Cervejaria Ribadouro** is a favorite splurge for locals because of its quality meat and shellfish (daily 12:00–24:00, Avenida da Liberdade 155, at intersection with Rua do Salitre, M: Avenida, tel. 213-549-411). Seafood prices are listed by weight—the waiter can help you determine the cost of a portion. For a fun, quick, €14 per-person meal, order a small draught beer *(uma imperial),* 100 grams (about a quarter-pound) of *percebes* (barnacles), and *pão torrado com manteiga* (toasted bread with butter).

**$$$ Restaurante A Gina,** glowing like a mirage in a vacant lot that used to be a theater zone, is one of my favorite places for a good dinner in Lisbon. It's a lunchtime hit with local office workers, who tuck in cloth bibs embroidered with Gina's name to appreciate the tasty traditional Portuguese grilled meat and fish. Gina and her staff scramble to give this wonderful place a genuine friendliness. Two minutes off of Avenida da Liberdade (directly behind recommended Hotel Lisboa Plaza—go between the white pillars and look left), it feels worlds away from the tourist crowds (daily 12:00–15:00 & 18:00–24:00, reservations recommended, tel. 213-420-296). The son, Rui, speaks English. Diners with this book get a free dessert port.

# Lisbon Connections

## BY PLANE

Lisbon's easy-to-manage Portela Airport is five miles northeast of downtown (airport code: LIS; for airport info, see www.aeroportolisboa.pt or call 218-413-700 or 800-201-201).

### Getting Between the Airport and Downtown

Getting to and from the airport is a snap. Figure on 20 to 30 minutes by taxi, Uber, or bus (depending on traffic) or 30 to 40 minutes by Metro.

**By Taxi or Uber:** Taxis line up on the curb at the airport, but are notoriously aggressive in gouging arriving travelers. You're more likely to get a fair price—and skip any line—by going upstairs to the departures curb and hopping into a cab as it drops off its riders. Better yet, request a ride using Uber. Either way, a ride to or from town should cost no more than €10 to the center. If taking a taxi, insist on using the meter—it should start at around €4 and be set to *Tarifa 1* (or *Tarifa 2* for nights, weekends, and holidays). There is no "airport fee" supplement, but there is a legitimate €1.60 fee for your luggage (not per bag).

To return to the airport from downtown, simply use Uber or hail a cab on the street. Skip the outrageously overpriced "taxi vouchers" sold by the airport TI—these are for rides outside the center and more than double your cost.

**By Bus:** While dirt-cheap public buses leave from the airport curb, they are not intended for people with luggage. The Aerobus shuttle is faster and nearly as cheap (€3.50, 3/hour, runs 7:00-23:20, departs outside arrival level at bus stop marked "Aerobus #1," www.aerobus.pt). Be sure to use Aerobus #1, which heads to the city center, with stops at Marquês de Pombal, Avenida da Liberdade, Restauradores, Rossio, Praça do Comércio, and Cais do Sodré. Route #2 avoids the downtown and ends in the financial district, but makes a handy stop at the bus station at Sete Rios if you plan to go elsewhere immediately (see "By Bus," page 140). Aerobus tickets are sold at the airport TI or on the bus for the same price. (But for three passengers, a taxi or Uber is likely cheaper than this bus.)

**By Metro:** The Metro gets you into town affordably (for the price of a single transit ticket) and avoids traffic. But to reach central Lisbon, you'll have to change from the airport's suburb-focused red line to the green line (at Alameda)—it's time-consuming (figure 30-40 minutes total) and inconvenient if you're packing heavy. To find the Metro, exit the airport arrivals hall and turn right to find the Aeroporto stop. Before boarding, buy a reloadable Viva Viagem card and your choice of ticket (zapping, single-ride, or all-day) at the ticket machine (see details under "Getting Around Lisbon" on page 26).

## BY TRAIN

All of Lisbon's train stations are connected to the Metro system, making departures and arrivals a breeze. For train info, call 808-208-208, visit www.cp.pt, or check Germany's excellent all-Europe website, www.bahn.com.

**Santa Apolónia** station covers international trains and nearly all of Portugal. Located just east of the Alfama, it has ATMs, a morning-only TI, baggage storage, a Pingo Doce supermarket, and good Metro and bus connections to the town center. A taxi or Uber from Santa Apolónia to any of my recommended hotels costs roughly €8. Bus #728, #759, #782, and #794 go to or near Praça do Comércio, and bus #759 continues to Rossio and Praça dos Restauradores. To get to the bus stop from the station, look for the Metro sign, walk past the escalators to exit the station, and go right along busy Avenida Infante Dom Henrique to the bus stop.

Most trains using Santa Apolónia also stop at **Oriente** station, farther from the center, near Parque das Nações (M: Oriente; for more on this architecturally interesting station, see page 96).

**Rossio** station, which is in the town center and an easy walk from most recommended hotels, handles the most convenient trains to Sintra (direct, 2/hour, 40 minutes, buy tickets from machines at track level on second floor). It also has trains to Óbidos and Nazaré (but since both destinations require a transfer, the bus is a better option). The all-Portugal ticket office on the ground floor (next to Starbucks) sells long-distance and international train tickets (Mon-Fri 8:00-14:30 & 15:30-19:00, closed Sat-Sun, cash only).

**Cais do Sodré** station, near the waterfront just west of Praça do Comércio (M: Cais do Sodré), is the terminus for a short regional line that runs along the coast from Lisbon, making stops at Belém (10 minutes), Estoril (30 minutes), and Cascais (40 minutes).

## Train Connections

Note: Any train leaving from Santa Apolónia passes through Oriente station a few minutes later.

**From Lisbon by Train to: Madrid** (1/day, "Lusitânia" night train, 11 hours, departs from Santa Apolónia station, arrives at Madrid's Chamartín station), **Évora** (4/day, 1.5 hours, departs Oriente), **Lagos** (5/day, 4 hours, departs Oriente, transfer in Tunes or Faro), **Tavira** (5/day, 4-5 hours, departs Oriente, change at Faro), **Coimbra** (almost hourly, 2 hours, departs Santa

Apolónia), **Nazaré/Valado** (3-5/day, 4 hours, involves 2-3 transfers; bus is better—see below), **Óbidos** (3/day, 2.5 hours, transfer in Sete Rios, departs Oriente; also 5/day, 2.5 hours, transfer in Mira Sintra-Melecas or Cacém, departs Rossio), **Porto** (almost hourly, 3 hours, departs Oriente), **Sintra** (2/hour, 40 minutes, departs Rossio; 4/hour, 50 minutes, departs Oriente).

**To Salema:** To reach Salema, you'll first need to get to **Lagos,** which is about 4 hours from Lisbon by train (see above) or bus (see next). Trains from Lisbon to the Algarve leave from Oriente station on the Lisboa-Faro line. At Tunes, a transfer to a local train takes you as far as Lagos. From there, it's a cheap bus ride or a pricier taxi ride to Salema (see page 199 for details).

## BY BUS

Lisbon's efficient Sete Rios bus station is in the modern part of the city, three miles inland. It has ATMs, schedules, self-service info kiosks, and two information offices—one for buses within Portugal, the other for international routes (InterCentro Lines, which sells tickets for routes—including to Spain—even if operated by other companies). While it's possible to buy bus tickets up to a week in advance, you can almost always buy a ticket just a few minutes before departure. The EVA company covers the south of Portugal (www.eva-bus.com), while Rede Nacional de Expressos does the rest of the country (www.rede-expressos.pt; bus info for both companies—toll tel. 707-223-344).

The bus station is across the street from the large Sete Rios train station, which sits above the Jardim Zoológico Metro stop. To get from the bus station to downtown Lisbon, it's a €6 taxi or Uber ride or a short Metro trip on the blue line (from bus station, walk down and across to enter the Sete Rios train station, then follow signs for *Metro: Jardim Zoológico*).

**From Lisbon by Bus to: Coimbra** (hourly, 2.5 hours), **Nazaré** (6/day, 2 hours), **Fátima** (hourly, 1.5-2.5 hours), **Batalha** (5/day, 2 hours), **Alcobaça** (6/day, 2 hours, some transfer in Caldas da Rainha), **Óbidos** (hourly, 1 hour, departs from near Campo Grande Metro stop), **Porto** (at least hourly, 3 hours), **Évora** (almost hourly, 1.5 hours), **Lagos** (12 buses/day direct, 4 hours, easier than train, must book ahead, get details at TI), **Tavira** (5/day direct, 4.25 hours), **Madrid** (2-3/day, 8-9 hours, overnight option, www.avanzabus.com), **Sevilla** (2/day, 7 hours, overnight option, may be fewer off-season, run by Alsa, www.alsa.es).

## BY CRUISE SHIP

Lisbon's port is the busiest on Europe's Atlantic coast, with most cruise ships docking at one of three terminals: Jardim do Tabaco (immediately below the Alfama), Santa Apolónia (near the train station of the same name, just beyond the Alfama), or Alcântara (about two miles west of downtown, between the center and Belém).

The taxis that wait at cruise terminals are notoriously dishonest. You may be better off using Uber, walking a block or two away from the terminal and hailing a passing cab on the street (not at a taxi stand), or riding a cruise-line shuttle service to Praça da Figueira. Hop-on, hop-off bus tours, which conveniently link up major sights—stop at the cruise terminals (see "Tours in Lisbon" earlier in this chapter).

From **Alcântara,** you can hop on trolley #15E (use pedestrian underpass to reach trolley stop) or bus #728—either way, it's about a 15-minute ride. (Both of these also go—in the opposite direction—to the sights in Belém.)

**Jardim do Tobaco** and **Santa Apolónia** are close enough to walk to the Baixa (15-20 minutes)—just go along busy Avenida Infante Dom Henrique with the river on your left, until you reach Praça do Comércio. Or you can take bus #728 from near either terminal to Praça do Comércio (at Santa Apolónia, the bus stop is in front of the train station, across the street).

# SINTRA

For centuries, Portugal's aristocracy considered Sintra (SEEN-trah)—just 15 miles northwest of Lisbon—the perfect place to escape from city life. Now tourists do, too. Sintra is a mix of natural and manmade beauty: fantasy castles set amid exotic tropical plants, lush green valleys, and craggy hilltops with hazy views of the Atlantic and Lisbon. This was the summer getaway of Portugal's kings. Those with money and a desire to be close to royalty built their palaces amid luxuriant gardens in the same neighborhood. Lord Byron called this bundle of royal fancies and aristocratic dreams a "glorious Eden," and even though it's mobbed with tourists today, it's still magnificent.

With extra time, explore the rugged and picturesque westernmost tip of Portugal at Cabo da Roca.

## PLANNING YOUR TIME

Sintra makes a great day trip from Lisbon. Here you can romp along the ruined ramparts of a deserted Moorish castle, and climb through the Versailles of Portugal—the Pena Palace—on a neighboring hilltop.

It's such an ideal side-trip, in fact, that Sintra can be miserably mobbed (especially July through Sept). Saturdays and Sundays are popular with Portuguese, while foreign tourists clog the town on Mondays (when many Lisbon museums are closed, but all major Sintra sights are open). Crowds are a bit lighter on Tuesdays through Fridays. Sintra's complicated landscape—with lots of hills and one-way roads between the big sights—adds to the challenge. A trip here requires patience and a flexible schedule. For the most stress-free visit possible, consider this good one-day plan:

**Near Lisbon**

To Coimbra & Porto

Cabo da Roca

**Sintra**

N-247

N-9

A-8

A-1

A-9

PARQUE DAS NAÇÕES

IC-19

**Lisboa**

Rio Tejo

VASCO DA GAMA BRIDGE

Guincho Beach

N-9

N-247

A-5

**Belém**

Cacilhas

A-12

**Cascais**

Estoril

25TH OF APRIL BRIDGE

CRISTO REI MON.

Barreiro

Pinhal Novo

To Évora

Costa da Caparica

A-2

A-6

To Algarve (by expressway)

*Atlantic Ocean*

Setúbal

IC-1

N-379

To Algarve (by scenic coastal route)

Portinho da Arrábida

Cabo Espichel

5 Km
5 Miles

**Major Train Stations**
❶ Santa Apolónia
❷ Oriente
❸ Rossio
❹ Cais do Sodré

**Other**
❺ Belem to Porto Brandão Ferry

**SINTRA**

Leave Lisbon around 8:30 to arrive in Sintra by 9:15 (most major sights open between 9:30 and 9:45—if you arrive much later, you'll be hopelessly mired in crowds all day). Pick up a map at the TI in Sintra's train station, and catch bus #434 in front of the station to Pena Palace. Visit the palace, walk down to the Moorish Castle ruins, scramble over its ramparts, then hike about 45 minutes back down to town via Vila Sassetti (or take bus #434). Have lunch (unless you already had a picnic, or lunched at the Pena Palace's café), explore the town, and—if you're not exhausted yet—visit the National Palace (right in town) or the Quinta da Regaleira (a 10-minute walk). Finally, catch the train back to Lisbon in time for dinner. This general plan also works well for drivers, who ideally should leave their car in Lisbon (or at least park in Sintra) and take advantage of public transportation.

Spending the night in Sintra is an intriguing option. This lets you get an earlier start, or visit the sights later in the day as crowds subside (the Moorish Castle is even better at closing time, with the sun low in the sky)—and also lets you savor the small town after dark, when it's quieter. Drivers in particular could consider overnighting in Sintra on the way to or from Lisbon.

## GETTING TO SINTRA

Catch the **train** to Sintra from Lisbon's central Rossio station (direct, 2/hour, 40 minutes; also 4/hour from the less central Oriente station, 50 minutes). The trip is covered by the LisboaCard or the €10 version of Lisbon's all-day transit pass; if "zapping" with a Viva Viagem card, it's €2.15 each way (see page 26). Note that none of these passes work on local buses once you're in Sintra.

To avoid early-morning lines at the station in Lisbon, buy or charge up your card the night before (otherwise, buy it when you get to Rossio station—using the ticket machines or windows upstairs, at track level). During your ride, take in the views of the 18th-century aqueduct (on the left) and the workaday Lisbon suburbs. Relax...Sintra is at the end of the line.

Sintra is far easier by train than by **car** from Lisbon. Consider waiting until after you visit Sintra to pick up your rental car. If you do drive to Sintra, see "Route Tips for Drivers" on page 161.

# Orientation to Sintra

Sintra is small. The town itself sprawls at the foot of a hill, an easy 10-minute walk (or quick bus ride) from the train station. The National Palace, with its unmistakable pair of cone-shaped chimneys, is in the center of the town, a block from the TI, and the Quinta da Regaleira is a 10-minute walk away. But the other two main sights—Pena Palace and the Moorish Castle—hover on the hilltop above (you can see the castle's serrated wall on the hilltop). Most people take the bus up, but avid hikers enjoy the walk (figure

an hour steeply uphill; see "Hiking Between Sintra and the Castles," later.)

## TOURIST INFORMATION

Sintra has two TIs: a small one in the train station (daily 10:00-13:00 & 14:00-18:00, tel. 211-932-545) and a larger one a block off the main square in the Museu Regional building (daily 10:00-18:00, Aug until 19:00, tel. 219-231-157, www.askmelisboa.com). Pick up a free map with information on sights and a local Scotturb bus schedule. Hikers can download walking routes from the city website (www.cm-sintra.pt).

## ARRIVAL IN SINTRA

**By Train:** Upon arrival, stop at the TI in the station. To **bus** to the town center, hop on Scotturb #434 (exit the station to the right to

reach the nearest stop, buy €5 all-day ticket from driver, schedules posted at stop; there's also a Scotturb office across the street from the station but it's extremely crowded in the morning; for more bus info, see "Getting Around Sintra," later). The bus stops in town first (at the National Palace, then near the main TI) before heading up to the Moorish Castle and Pena Palace, then loops back down to the station and town.

You can also reach the town center easily on **foot** (exit the station and go left, then turn left when you hit the turreted town hall)—it's about a 10-minute walk along a mostly level road along the lip of a ravine. Along the way you'll see modern "art" and hippies selling handmade trinkets.

**By Car:** See "Route Tips for Drivers" on page 161.

## HELPFUL HINTS

**Exchange Rate:** €1 = about $1.10

**Country Calling Code:** 351 (see page 422 for dialing instructions)

**LisboaCard:** This sightseeing pass gets you discounts on the Pena Palace, Moorish Castle, National Palace, and the Monserrate gardens. It also covers the train ride from Lisbon to Sintra, but not the bus within Sintra (buy the LisboaCard at a Lisbon TI before you visit Sintra—see page 24). Be sure to bring the LisboaCard booklet, which contains coupons required for some of the discounts.

**Festivals:** The lively Festival de Sintra music and dance festival runs from late May to early July (www.festivaldesintra.pt).

**Money:** You'll find a few ATMs near the train station, another inside the main TI, and one on Rua das Padarias, just up the hill from the recommended Casa Piriquita.

**WCs:** The only free WC in town—other than at restaurants—is located near the small, central parking lot where horse carriages wait (Calçada do Pelourinho).

**Bring a Picnic:** If saving a few euros is important, consider bringing a picnic from Lisbon—restaurants here can be pricey, though there is a very basic grocery store (see "Eating in Sintra," later).

**Local Guide: Cristina Quental** works mainly in Lisbon, but lives near Sintra and can meet you at the station (Mon-Fri €150/half-day, €210/day; mobile 919-922-480, anacristinaquental@hotmail.com).

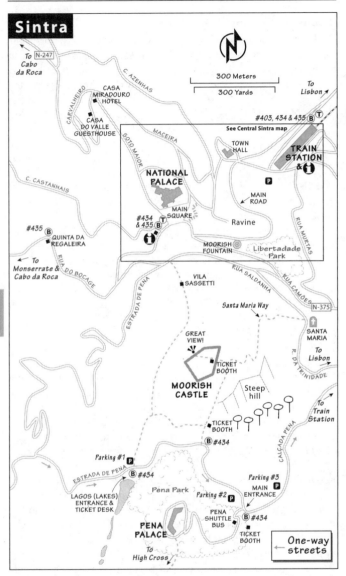

## GETTING AROUND SINTRA

Whether you're driving, taking the bus, riding a taxi, or hopping in a tuk-tuk, you'll take the same very congested, single-lane, one-way road that loops up the hill and passes the main monuments. That means that no way is faster than any other—maybe just a bit more comfortable.

The best choice for most is **Scotturb Bus #434,** which loops together all the important stops—the train station, the town center (stops at the National Palace, then at the TI), the Moorish Castle ruins, and the Pena Palace—before heading back to town and the train station (4/hour—subject to traffic; €5 ticket good all day for one loop with stops, buy from driver or Scotturb staffer at stop near TI in town; first bus departs train station at 9:15; last bus leaves station at 19:50; entire circuit takes 30 minutes without traffic). A different bus, **#435,** goes from the train station to Quinta da Regaleira and the Monserrate gardens (1-3/hour, €2.50 one-way, also stops at TI, not covered by loop ticket).

Busy days bring very long lines at popular bus stops. Here are some **crowd-beating tips:** If there's a long line at the train station bus stop, consider walking into town and catching the bus at the National Palace instead. When returning to town from the Pena Palace, consider walking about 10 minutes (mostly downhill) back along the road to the Moorish Castle bus stop, where there's usually no line.

If the bus is a mob scene, you have alternatives. Noisy, bouncy, but fun **tuk-tuks** are all over Sintra, charging €5 per person for a breezy ride from town or the station to the Moorish Castle, Pena Palace, or Quinta da Regaleira (you can also book tuk-tuks for a "guided tour" loop). Or figure €10 for a **taxi** from the center up to any one of the sights.

Clip-clop **horse carriages** cost about €30 for 25 minutes. They can take you anywhere; you'll likely see them waiting on the little square near the bus stop just in front of the National Palace.

## Sights in Sintra

Combo-tickets are available for the Pena Palace, Moorish Castle, and National Palace, but savings are minimal (about 5 percent)—ask when you buy your first ticket. Unless you're 100 percent certain you'll make it to all three sights, the combo deal is probably not worthwhile.

### ON THE HILL ABOVE SINTRA

These sights cap the hill high above Sintra—connected by bus #434. If walking between them, figure 10 minutes between the Pena Palace main entrance and the Moorish Castle, and another 10 minutes to the Pena Palace's lower "Lakes/Lagos" entrance. Be careful walking along the congested road, with its narrow shoulder and ankle-twisting cobbles.

## ▲▲Pena Palace (Palácio de Pena)

This magical hilltop palace sits high above Sintra, above the Moorish Castle ruins. In the 19th century, Portugal had a very romantic prince, the German-born Prince Ferdinand. A contemporary and cousin of Bavaria's "Mad" King Ludwig (of Disneyesque Neuschwanstein Castle fame), Ferdinand was also a cousin of England's Prince Albert (Queen Victoria's husband). Flamboyant Ferdinand hired a German architect to build a fantasy castle, mixing elements of German and Portuguese style.

He ended up with a crazy Neo-fortified casserole of Gothic towers, Renaissance domes, Moorish minarets, Manueline carvings, Disneyland playfulness, and an *azulejo* (tile) toilet for his wife.

**Cost and Hours:** Palace and gardens—€14, shuttle bus—€3 round-trip (buy with your palace ticket); daily May-mid-Sept 9:30-19:00, last entry 45 minutes before closing, gardens stay open an hour after palace closing time, shorter hours off-season; tel. 219-105-340, www.parquesdesintra.pt.

**Getting In:** There are two entrances to the castle grounds: the lower "Lakes/Lagos" entrance (at the bottom of the park, across from the first parking lot you come to), and the main entrance (just below the castle itself). It's a 20-minute walk between these two (you'll pass the Moorish Castle ticket booth between them). While the lower entrance is less crowded, it's best to use the main entrance if possible, since it's closer to the castle.

At the main entrance, purchase your ticket at the small hut next to the gate (if there's a long line, look for ticket machines just downhill—toward the Moorish Castle). To avoid the 15-minute uphill climb from the entrance to the palace (and enjoy a lift back down later), catch the green shuttle bus, which departs from straight ahead as you enter (€3 round-trip, buy with your palace ticket—or inside gift shop—but *not* from driver, departs about every 10 minutes).

**Eating:** The palace has an inexpensive **$** view café and a pricier **$$** restaurant. If you brought your lunch with you, enjoy it in the picnic-perfect gardens either before or after your visit—with views fit for a king.

**❍ Self-Guided Tour:** English descriptions throughout the palace give meaning to the rooms. Be sure to pick up the *Parques e Palácios* map, with a helpful illustration of the castle on one side and a circular, 1.5-hour walking route of the park on the other. For even more info, rent the €3 audioguide.

The palace, built in the mid- to late-1800s, is so well-preserved that it feels as if it's the day after the royal family fled Portugal in 1910 (during a popular revolt that eventually made way for today's modern republic). This gives the place a charming intimacy rarely seen in palaces. Here are the highlights.

• *After you hop off the green shuttle bus, hike up the ramp and show your ticket at the Moorish archway with alligator decor. Cross the drawbridge that doesn't draw, and join a slack-jawed world of tourists frozen in deep knee-bends with their cameras cocked.*

**Palace Interior:** Show your ticket again to enter the palace itself. Inside, at the base of the stairs, you'll see King Ferdinand, who built this castle from 1840 until his death in 1885. Though German, he was a romantic proponent of his adopted culture and did much to preserve Portugal's architectural and artistic heritage.

• *Next you'll pop out into the...*

**Courtyard:** The palace was built on the site of a 16th-century monastery; the courtyard was the former location of the cloister. In spite of its plushness, the palace retains the monkish coziness of several small rooms gathered in two levels around the cloister.

Like its big brother in Belém, the monastery housed followers of St. Jerome, the hermit monk. Like their namesake, the monks wanted to be isolated, and this was about as isolated as you could be around here 500 years ago. The spot was also a popular pilgrimage destination for its statue of "Our Lady of the Feathers" (*pena* means feather—hence the palace's name). In 1498 King Manuel was up here enjoying the view when he spied Vasco da Gama sailing up the river, returning safely from his great voyage. To celebrate and give thanks, the king turned what was a humble wooden monastery into a fine stone palace.

• *From here, follow the one-way route counterclockwise around the courtyard, dipping into a variety of rooms. These are especially worthy of attention.*

**Dining Room and Pantry:** Stuck into a cozy corner, the monastery's original refectory was decked out with the royal family's finest tableware and ceiling tiles.

**Atelier (Workshop) of King Carlos I:** With a shaky empire crumbling around him, King Carlos found refuge in art—specifically the latest style, Art Nouveau. Unfinished paintings and sketches eerily predict the king's unfinished rule.

SINTRA

**King's Bedroom and Bathroom:** The king enjoyed cutting-edge comforts, including a shower/tub imported from England, and even a telephone to listen to the opera when he couldn't face the Lisbon commute. The bedroom is decorated in classic Romantic style—dark, heavy, and crowded with knickknacks.

• *Now head upstairs (gripping the funky dragon-like handrail). Circling around the courtyard, you'll enter the wing called the Piano Nobile ("noble floor"). Go through a few daintily decorated rooms that belonged to ladies-in-waiting, and then enter the...*

**Queen's Bedroom and Dressing Room:** Study the melancholy photos of Queen Amelia (Amélie of Orléans), King Carlos, and their family in this room. The early 1900s were a rocky time for Portugal's royal family. The king and his eldest son were assassinated in 1908. His youngest son, Manuel II, became king until he, his mother the queen, and other members of the royal family fled Portugal during the 1910 revolution.

As you shuffle through the palace, you'll see state-of-the-art conveniences—such as the first flush toilets and hot shower in Portugal, and even a telephone room. The whole place is lovingly cluttered, typical of the Victorian horror of empty spaces.

• *At the end of this floor, step out onto the...*

**Queen's Terrace:** Enjoy a sweeping view from Lisbon to the mouth of the Rio Tejo. Find the Cristo Rei statue and the 25th of April Bridge. The statue on the distant ridge honors the palace's architect.

• *Heading back inside, you'll pass through some smaller rooms, then enter...*

**The New Wing:** This spacious addition to the original series of rooms around the cloister includes the apartments of the last king, the smoking room (with a tiled ceiling), and the fantastically furnished Great Hall.

On your way down the spiral staircase, take a detour to see the **Stag Room**—with well-antlered walls and a dramatic dome supported by a stout, palm-tree-like column. From here, you'll head down to see the abundant kitchen.

Just after, a view café conveniently welcomes us peasants. While many people take this as a sign to leave, we haven't yet seen some of the most scenic parts of the castle.

• *From the café, turn left and walk alongside the palace, then duck through one of the two huge, ornamental gateways on your left (the second one has a scowling Triton overhead). You'll emerge into the...*

**Inner Patio:** Take the stairs up to the pointed dome covered in green and white tiles (in front of the tallest red tower). This was the royal family's sumptuous private **chapel,** decorated in a variety of styles. The structure is Manueline, reminiscent of the Monastery of Jerónimos in Belém.

• *Heading back down into the patio, don't miss the little door under the chapel marked...*

**The Wall Walk:** Follow this for a rampart ramble with great views—of the onion-domed balustrade, of the palace itself, and of the surrounding countryside—including the Moorish Castle on an adjacent hilltop. You'll circle all the way around the outside of the palace, and wind up back at the entrance.

• *From here, you can return directly to the main entrance (walk 10 minutes or catch the green shuttle bus—your ticket covers the round-trip), or detour for a self-guided tour of the park.*

**Pena Palace Park:** The lush, captivating, and sprawling palace grounds—rated ▲—are dotted with romantic surprises. Several landmarks within the park are signposted near the shuttle bus stop. Highlights include the High Cross (highest point around, with commanding views), chapels, a temple, lakes, giant sequoia trees, and exotic plants. To walk through the park after you tour the palace, take a 40-minute stroll downhill (following the map that came with your palace entry) to the lower park gate, at the Lakes/Lagos entry, where you'll find a bus stop and the Estrada de Pena loop road. From here, it's a ten-minute hike uphill to the Moorish Castle, or a 20-minute hike back to the Pena Palace's main entrance.

### ▲Moorish Castle (Castelo dos Mouros)

Sintra's thousand-year-old ruins of a Moorish castle are lost in an enchanted forest and alive with winds of the past. They're a castle

lover's dream come true, and a great place for a picnic with a panoramic Atlantic view. Though built by the Moors, the castle was taken by Christian forces in 1147. It's one of the most classically perfect castles you'll find anywhere, with two hills capped by hardy forts, connected by a crenellated wall walkway. (It's so idealized because it was significantly restored in the 19th century.)

**Cost and Hours:** €8, daily 9:30-20:00, last entry one hour before closing, tel. 219-237-300, www.parquesdesintra.pt.

**Getting In:** From the main ticket booth (near the bus stop) to the castle entrance, it's an atmospheric 10-minute stroll—mostly downhill—through a forested canyon, passing a few small exhibits and information plaques. If the main ticket booth is crowded, bypass it and simply continue to the castle itself, where there's another ticket booth that rarely has a wait. Either way, be sure to pick up the well-illustrated map, which has lots of insightful information.

**Visiting the Castle:** You'll enter the castle in a terraced area with a cafeteria, shop, and WCs, all sitting on top of a cistern. The castle walls and towers climb hills on either side of you. Do a hardy counterclockwise hike, conquering the lower one first, then heading up to the higher one.

From where you entered, go right and take the stony stairs up to the keep. From the top tower, you can see how the wall twists and turns—following the contours of the land—as it connects over to the taller hilltop tower. Follow the crenellated path, with delirious views over Sintra down below and as far as the Atlantic. You'll go down, then back up the other side, ascending higher and higher to the top of the Royal Tower. From the summit, you enjoy great views across to Pena Palace, perched on its adjacent hilltop. From this pinnacle, you can gingerly descend to the cafeteria and entrance—having conquered the castle.

### Hiking Between Sintra and the Castles

It's a steep one-hour hike from town up to the Moorish Castle and Pena Palace—challenging even for hardy hikers. But hiking back down to town after your hilltop visits (rather than cramming into an overstuffed bus) is an appealing 45-minute possibility for those with strong knees. Be sure to equip yourself with the TI's invaluable *Pedestrian Route* map—and get their advice—before you set out (maps may also be available at Moorish Castle or Pena Palace ticket offices).

The best route is to take a terraced path directly below the Moorish Castle, which leads past the **Vila Sassetti.** You'll find the trailhead at the end of the parking lot directly across from the Lakes/Lagos lower entrance of the Pena Palace grounds, and you'll also find a trail connecting to it near the Moorish Castle main ticket booth (near the bus stop). From here, the trail curls around the bottom of the Moorish Castle's rocky perch, then enters the grounds of the Vila Sassetti (open daily 10:00-18:00, or until 17:00 off-season). Designed by theater set decorator Luigi Manini (who also did the Quinta da Regaleira, described later), the Vila Sassetti looks like an old Roman house with a terra cotta roof. You'll hike down to the villa itself, then traipse through its lower gardens into Sintra. (If the Villa is closed, you can also drop down—on steep steps—to footpaths that run through the woods above the main road.)

Yet another option is to walk down on the **"Santa Maria Way,"** which forks off in the opposite direction from the Moorish Castle entrance. However, this trail is mostly through thick woods and less scenic.

## IN TOWN
These sights are all within easy walking distance of the town center.

### ▲National Palace (Palácio Nacional)
While the palace dates back to Moorish times, most of what you'll see is from the 15th-century reign of King João I, with later Manueline architectural ornamentation from the 16th century. This oldest surviving royal palace in Portugal is still used for official receptions. Having housed royalty for 500 years (until 1910), it's fragrant with history.

**Cost and Hours:** €10, daily 9:30-19:00; look for white, double-coned building in town center, 10-minute walk from train station, photos OK, tel. 219-237-300, www.parquesdesintra.pt.

**❍ Self-Guided Tour:** The palace is a one-way romp with little information provided. The €3 audioguide is informative, but as dry as an Alentejo summer; free English tours depart the entrance at 14:30. If touring on your own, read the brief descriptions in each room, and tune into the following notable parts of the palace.

• *Show your ticket, then head upstairs into...*

**Swan Room:** This first room is the palace's banquet room. A king's daughter—who loved swans—married into a royal house in Belgium. The king missed the princess so much that he decorated the ceiling with her favorite animal. These aren't the only creatures in the room, though. Check out the ceramic soup tureens designed in the shape of your favorite barnyard animal.

**Central Patio:** This was a fortified medieval palace, so rather than having fancy gardens outside, it has a stay-awhile courtyard within its protective walls. Notice the unique chimneys. They provide powerful suction that removes the smoke from the kitchen and also create a marvelous open-domed feeling (as you'll see at the end of your tour).

**Magpie Room:** The queen caught King João I being a little too friendly with a lady-in-waiting. Frustrated by his court—abuzz with gossip—João had this ceiling painted with magpies. But to defend his honor, he illustrated each magpie quoting the king's slogan—*Por bem*, "For good." The 15th-century Moorish tiles are from Spain, brought in before the development of the famous, ubiquitous Portuguese tiles, and are considered some of the finest Moorish-Spanish tiles in all of Iberia.

SINTRA

**Bedchamber of King Sebastian** (Dom Sebastião): The king portrayed on the wall (to the right of where you enter) is King Sebastian, a gung-ho, medieval-type monarch who went to battle in Africa, following the Moors even after they were chased out of Europe. He disappeared in 1578 at age 24 (although he was almost certainly killed in Morocco, "Sebastianists" awaited his mythical return into the 19th century). With the king missing, Portugal was left in unstable times with only Sebastian's great uncle (King Henrique) as heir. The new king died within two years, and the throne passed to his great uncle, King Philip II of Spain, leading to 60 years of Spanish rule (1580-1640).

Note the ebony, silver, and painted copper headboard of the Italian Renaissance bed. The tiles in this room are considered the first Portuguese tiles—from the time of Manuel I. The corn-on-the-cob motif topping the tilework is a reminder of American discoveries.

**More Main-Floor Rooms:** From here, you'll walk through the **Julius Caesar Room,** with a Flemish tapestry of the Roman general-turned-ruler; the **Goddess Diana Courtyard;** and up the stairs to the **Galleon Room,** whose ceiling is painted with ships flying the flags of the great nautical powers of the day. Step out onto the balcony for views of a forested hillside scattered with the villas of aristocrats—and capped by the serrated wall of the Moorish Castle. Then, head up the stairs to walk through some smaller, simpler apartments with a few original furnishings.

• *Finally, you step into the glorious...*

**Blazons Hall** (a.k.a. Coat of Arms Room): The most striking room in the palace—under a golden dome and slathered in blue tiles—honors Portugal's loyal nobility. Study the richly decorated ceiling. The king's coat of arms at the top is surrounded by the coats of arms of his children; below that is a ring of stags; and finally, at the bottom, are the coats of arms of all but one of Portugal's noble families (the omitted family had schemed a revolt, so received only a blank niche). The Latin phrase circling the room reads, "Honoring all the noble families who've been loyal to the king." The 18th-century tiles hang from the walls like tapestries. Enjoy the view: a garden-like countryside dotted with mansions of nobility who clamored to  be near their king, the hill-capping castle, and the wide-open Atlantic. You're in the westernmost room of the westernmost palace on the European continent.

• *Continue through the upper halls, peeking into the...*

**Bedchamber and Prison of Alfonso VI:** This king suffered from a fever as a child that left him mentally unstable. After he became king, he was removed by his wife and his brother—who became King Pedro II, locked him in this room for the rest of his life, and married his queen.

**Yet More Rooms:** As you continue, you'll pass through the **Chinese Room** (with an exquisite ivory-and-bone model of a Chinese pagoda). Downstairs, you can step out onto a private balcony and peer down into the **Palatine Chapel,** with a Mudejar wood-carved ceiling. Then you'll pass through a room of coffers (literal treasure chests) and head downstairs to the **Arab Room**—decorated with Moorish tiles, and with a little fountain in the middle; this was the preferred bedroom of João I. From here, you'll walk through a fancy **guest room** and into the **kitchen.** With all the latest in cooking technology, the palace chef could roast an entire cow on the spit, keep the king's plates warm in the iron dish warmer (with drawers below for the charcoal), and get really dizzy by looking up and spinning around three times.

On your way out, as you step back into the big entry hall, be sure to detour left into the **Manueline Room,** with carved-stone ropes over the doors and a grand chandelier, and a handy WC in the corner. You'll walk back through the Central Patio (peek into the blue-tiled **Grotto of the Baths** in the corner) and head for the exit. On your way out, watch for the easy-to-miss door on the right that lets you explore the manicured, terraced **gardens** surrounding the palace.

## SOUTHWEST OF THE CENTER

These two sights line up on a road southwest of central Sintra. You can walk to Quinta da Regaleira, but Monserrate is quite a bit farther. Bus #435 stops at each one (see details earlier, under "Getting Around Sintra"), or you can take a tuk-tuk or taxi.

### ▲▲Quinta da Regaleira

This Neo-Everything (Manueline/ Gothic/Renaissance) 1912 mansion and garden has mystical and Masonic twists. It was designed by Italian opera-set designer Luigi Manini for a wealthy but disgruntled monarchist two years after the royal family was deposed. While the mansion—prickly with spires—is striking from the outside, its interior is nothing compared to the Pena Palace or National Palace. But the grounds are an utter delight to

SINTRA

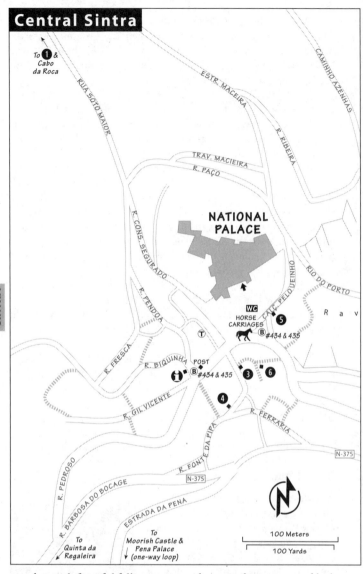

# Central Sintra

wander, with fanciful follies, secret underground passages, and lush landscaping. Many travelers (especially younger ones) find romping around these grounds more enjoyable than shuffling around the crowded interiors of the more famous palaces. Ask a local to pronounce "Regaleira" for you, and just try to repeat it.

**Cost and Hours:** €6, daily 10:00-20:00, closes earlier off-season, last entry one hour before closing, 10-minute walk from downtown Sintra, café, tel. 219-106-650, www.regaleira.pt.

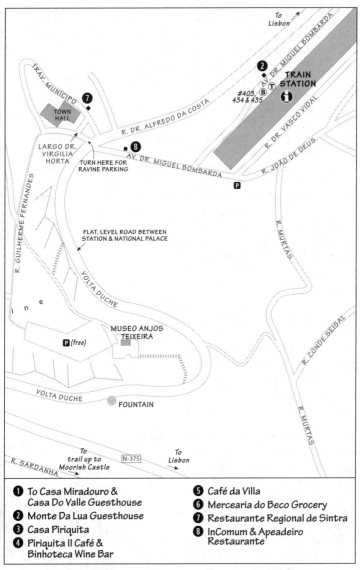

**SINTRA**

❶ To Casa Miradouro & Casa Do Valle Guesthouse
❷ Monte Da Lua Guesthouse
❸ Casa Piriquita
❹ Piriquita II Café & Binhoteca Wine Bar
❺ Café da Villa
❻ Mercearia do Beco Grocery
❼ Restaurante Regional de Sintra
❽ InComum & Apeadeiro Restaurante

**Tours:** Excellent two-hour English tours fill up, so book ahead online or by phone (€10, includes entry, about hourly April-Sept, fewer off-season). The tour focuses on the garden, but can be longish unless you're into quirky Masonic esoterica.

**Visiting the Quinta:** As you enter, be sure to pick up the superb illustrated map of both the house and the gardens.

The **mansion** itself is striking—as it was designed to be. (In fact, that was its sole purpose.) You'll enter through the finest space, the Hunting Room, with an outrageously carved fireplace. From here you can explore three floors, filled mostly with well-presented exhibits on the design and construction of the place, and biographical sketches of the aristocrat and the architect who brought it to life. At the top floor, find the tight spiral stone staircase up to the view terrace.

The real highlight is the playful **gardens,** which stretch uphill from the mansion. Work your way up, past the elaborate private chapel, then to higher and higher crenellated viewpoints. Follow *Waterfall* signs to reach a refreshing artificial canyon with ponds and a cascade. Stepping stones lead across the main pond to the grottos that hide beneath, giving you a unique perspective. From the top of the waterfall, continue up to the "Portal of the Guardians"; inside, secret tunnels lead to the dramatic, spiral-staircase-wrapped well—burrowed 90 feet down into the hillside, and, like the rest of Quinta da Regaleira, more about showing off than about being functional. From here, more tunnels lead to other parts of the property; use your map to explore to your heart's content.

### Monserrate

About 2.5 miles outside of Sintra—on the road past the Quinta da Regaleira—are the wonderful gardens of Monserrate. If you like tropical plants and exotic landscaping, a visit is time well-spent, though many find that the gardens at Pena Palace or the Quinta da Regaleira are just as good as these more famous grounds.

**Cost and Hours:** €8, park open daily 9:30-20:00, palace open until 19:00, last ticket sold for each one hour before closing, tel. 219-237-300, www.parquesdesintra.pt.

## WEST OF SINTRA, ON THE COAST
### Cabo da Roca

Wind-beaten, tourist-infested Cabo da Roca (KAH-boo dah ROH-kah) is the westernmost point in Europe, perhaps the inspiration for the Portuguese poet Luís de Camões' line, *"Onde a terra se acaba e o mar começa"* ("Where land ends and the sea begins"). It has a little shop, a café, and a tiny TI that sells an expensive "proof of being here" certificate. Take a photo instead (tel. 219-280-801). Nearby, on the road south to Cascais, you'll pass a good beach for wind, waves, sand, and the chance to  be the last person in Europe to see the sun set. For a remote beach, drive to Praia Adraga (north of Cabo da Roca).

## Sleep Code

Hotels are classified based on the average price of a standard double room with breakfast in high season.

| | |
|---|---|
| **$$$$** | **Splurge:** Most rooms over €150 |
| **$$$** | **Pricier:** €100-150 |
| **$$** | **Moderate:** €70-100 |
| **$** | **Budget:** €40-70 |
| **¢** | **Backpacker:** Under €40 |
| **RS%** | **Rick Steves discount** |

Unless otherwise noted, credit cards are accepted, hotel staff speaks basic English, and free Wi-Fi is available. Comparison-shop by checking prices at several hotels (on each hotel's own website, on a booking site, or by email). For the best deal, *book directly with the hotel*. Ask for a discount if paying in cash; if the listing includes **RS%**, request a Rick Steves discount.

# Sleeping in Sintra

Sintra works well as an overnight—allowing you to beat the crowds by tackling the sights early or late, and having the charming town to yourself after hours. To reach the first two places, you'll head into town, turn right to pass in front of the National Palace, then continue steeply downhill on the road past Hotel Tivoli; they face each other at the very bottom of the street (free street parking, steep 10-minute hike back up to the town center). The final listing—cheaper and handier for train travelers—is directly across the street from the train station.

**$$$ Casa Miradouro** is a beautifully restored mansion from 1893, now run by Belgian expat Charlotte Lambregts. The creaky old house feels like a homey, upscale British B&B, with eight spacious, stylish rooms, an elegant lounge, castle and sea views, and a wonderful garden (good breakfast extra, Rua Sotto Major 55, mobile 914-292-203, www.casa-miradouro.com, mail@casa-miradouro.com).

**$$ Casa Do Valle Guesthouse** offers 11 comfortable, modern rooms on several levels in a peaceful hillside location. They have a lovely garden and large deck with valley and castle views, a swimming pool, and a shared kitchen (extra for continental breakfast in your room, reception open until 18:30, behind Casa Miradouro at Rua da Paderna 5, tel. 219-244-699, www.casadovalle.com, info@casadovalle.com).

**$ Monte Da Lua Guesthouse** has seven clean, simple rooms with shiny hardwood floors; some rooms face the train station, while others face a quieter ravine in the back (cheaper rooms with shared bath, no breakfast, Avenida Dr. Miguel Bombarda 51, tel. 210-129-659, www.montedalua.net, montedalua51@gmail.com).

# Eating in Sintra

All of these listings are in the town of Sintra. To eat at the hilltop sights, there are cafés at both Pena Palace and the Moorish Palace, or you can pack a picnic.

## LIGHT MEALS

Most of these (except Café da Villa) are on or near Rua das Padarias, the touristy little cobbled lane across the street from the National Palace. The sit-down restaurants in this zone are very pricey and touristy, but these are handy for a light, quick meal.

**$ Casa Piriquita** bills itself as "the" *antiga fabrica de queijadas*—historic maker of tiny, tasty tarts with a cheesy filling. It's good for a sweet and a coffee or a simple lunch, such as toasted sandwiches. Take a seat in the café (up a few steps) to avoid groups who rush in to get pastries to go, or do battle and grab a half-dozen for about €5 (Tue-Thu 8:30-22:00, closed Wed, Rua das Padarias 1, tel. 219-230-626).

**$ Piriquita II,** sister to Casa Piriquita, is a block farther up the lane and may have less commotion. It has a more extensive menu and a view terrace (Wed-Mon 8:30-20:00, closed Tue, Rua das Padarias 18).

**$$ Binhoteca,** a welcoming little *enoteca*, provides wine lovers with an astonishing array of Portuguese wines and ports available by the glass (starting at €5), along with tasty meat-and-cheese plates, sandwiches, and salads. The knowledgeable staff is happy to explain what you're enjoying. It's a fun experience, but prices can add up (daily 10:00-19:00—and often later, Rua das Padarias 16, tel. 219-230-444).

**$$ Café da Villa,** a favorite of bus drivers and tour guides, offers generous portions of homemade-style soups and salads in a homey pub-like setting. It's good for a quiet, inexpensive lunch, with a variety of fixed-price meal options (daily 12:00-24:00, facing the little bus-stop square in front of the National Palace at Calçada do Pelourinho 2, tel. 219-241-174).

**Groceries: Mercearia do Beco,** just a few steps off Rua das Padarias, is a basic grocery store where you can assemble a picnic (daily 9:00-22:00, Rua Arco do Teixeira 17).

## DINING

While there are plenty of tourist eateries in Sintra's old center, for a serious meal I'd head a couple of blocks away to the station area.

**$$ Restaurante Regional de Sintra,** which feeds locals and

> ## Restaurant Price Code
>
> I've assigned each eatery a price category, based on the aver-
> age cost of a typical main course. Drinks, desserts, and splurge
> items (steak and seafood) can raise the price considerably.
>
> **$$$$**    **Splurge:** Most main courses over €17
> **$$$**    **Pricier:** €12-17
> **$$**    **Moderate:** €7-12
> **$**    **Budget:** Under €7
>
> In Portugal, takeout food is **$**; a basic sit-down eatery is **$$**;
> a casual but more upscale restaurant is **$$$**; and a swanky
> splurge is **$$$$**.

tourists very well, is my favorite place for dinner in Sintra. Gentle
Paulo speaks English and serves huge, splittable portions (Tue-
Thu 12:00-16:00 & 19:00-22:30, closed Wed, tucked to the right
of the turreted town hall at Travessa do Municipio 2, tel. 219-
234-444).

**$$$ InComum** is working hard to bring a modern sensi-
bility to traditional Portuguese cooking. The owners, who lived
in Switzerland, pride themselves on serving Portuguese-inspired
dishes with updated, international flair. The minimalist dining
room is especially popular at lunchtime, when the weekday lunch
special offers an affordable taste of their cooking (daily 12:00-
24:00, Rua Dr. Alfredo Coasta 22, tel. 219-243-719, www.
incomumbyluissantos.pt).

**$$ Apeadeiro Restaurante,** named for the platform along
the track at the train station just a block away, is a quality eatery
serving good food at good prices. Their daily specials can be split,
allowing two to eat affordably (Fri-Wed 9:00-24:00, closed Thu,
Avenida Dr. Miguel Bombarda 3, tel. 219-231-804).

# Sintra Connections

**From Sintra by Train and Bus to: Lisbon** (2 trains/hour to Rossio station, 40 minutes; 4 trains/hour to Oriente station, 50 minutes), **Cascais** (bus #403 via Cabo da Roca, 45-60 minutes, 1-2/
hour; express bus #417, 30 minutes, hourly; both buses fewer on
weekends, catch either one at the Sintra train station).

## ROUTE TIPS
### Sintra Day Trip from Lisbon by Car
Cars are the curse of Sintra—all traffic, from cars to buses to
tuk-tuks, has to nudge through town on a two-lane road, and
parking is difficult (especially up at the hilltop castles).

If you insist on taking a car to Sintra, take the IC-19 freeway out of Lisbon (allow 30 minutes, not counting traffic delays). When you arrive in Sintra, follow *Centro Histórico* signs. It's probably smartest to simply park your car and use bus #434 to get around. The road into town (Volta do Duche) has some pay-and-display parking—see what you can find (4-hour maximum). And there's free parking on the road just behind the train station.

If you anticipate crowds and don't want to hunt for a space, park in the (relatively) large lot down in the ravine between the train station and the TI. As you come into town, watch for the colorful, turreted town hall building on your right; take the tiny lane immediately after that building (the *no entry* signs are just for campers) and head down to the lot next to the Museu Anjos Teixeira. Climb up the stairs next to the museum, and you're on the main road into town.

It's tempting to drive up the **Moorish Castle** and **Pena Palace,** but be warned that parking up top is very limited and fills up fast (often jammed already by about 10:00 on busy days). The road makes a very long, one-way loop with no backtracking, so if you don't find a space you'll have to complete the loop and return back to the center. But if you're feeling lucky, here's the plan: Head up the road with every other car and bus in town. You'll twist up, up, up on a dozen switchbacks. Approaching the sights, there are three marked parking lots (one by the lower Lakes/Lagos entrance to Pena Palace; another just before the main entrance to Pena Palace—this is probably your most convenient choice, if it has space; and a third one, just past the main entrance to Pena Palace). Monitors along the road suggest which lots might have space, and which are *completo*. All along the congested, cobbled road are a few well-marked roadside spaces. It's best to park as soon as you find something—anything—and then walk the rest of the way to connect the sights.

It's possible to make a **70-mile circular trip** and drive to all the destinations near Lisbon within a day (Lisbon–Belém–Sintra–Cabo da Roca–Cascais–Lisbon), but traffic congestion around Sintra, especially on weekends and during rush hour, can slow you down.

## Loop Trip by Public Transportation

If you're bent on seeing sights west of Lisbon—Sintra, Cabo da Roca, and Cascais)—in a single long day, it can be done using public transportation. Start at the Sintra train station and buy a day pass for the Scotturb **bus** (€12). Use the pass to take bus #434 to Sintra's sights, then go to Cabo da Roca on bus #403. When you're ready, catch the next bus #403 for the jaunt to Cascais and a seafood dinner on the waterfront (for more on Cascais, see

page 101). If you want to head from Sintra straight to Cascais—
without the Cabo da Roca detour—take the faster bus #417.

From Cascais, returning to Lisbon is a snap—just buy a one-
way **train** ticket to Lisbon at the train station. You'll get off at
the last stop on the line (Cais de Sodré Station), a five-minute
walk from Praça do Comércio in downtown Lisbon. Or, to return to Sintra, hop on bus #417.

# THE ALGARVE

*Salema • Cape Sagres • Lagos • Tavira*

The Algarve—Portugal's warm and dry south coast, stretching for some 100 miles—was once known as Europe's last uncharted tourist frontier. Today's Algarve is far from undiscovered—and in some places can be miserably crowded and overdeveloped—but it does still hold some gems ideal for a relaxing beach break.

You won't be the first one seeking the sun here. When the Moors ruled Portugal, they chose not to live in the rainy north, but here—where warm, sandy beaches framed by jagged rocks give way to rolling green hills dotted with orchards. They called this land Al-Gharb Al-Andalus ("to the west of Andalucía"), and made it the westernmost fringe of the huge Islamic world at the time. Today, perceptive visitors notice echoes of Muslim culture all along the Algarve: groves of almond and orange trees, and white-domed buildings with blue trim, traditional *azulejos* (tiles), and pointy chimneys—reflecting the region's minaret heritage.

Choose your home base carefully. If you go to the places featured in tour brochures (the middle stretch, roughly between Faro and Lagos), you'll find it much like Spain's Costa del Sol: paved, packed, and pretty stressful. Two worthwhile, midsize resort towns offer a better experience: In the west is Lagos, an urban resort with a vibrant old town, a youthful surfing buzz, and dramatically scenic beaches. And in the east—amid lagoon estuaries, just this side of Spain—is pleasant Tavira, a whitewashed town with a real soul, a fun-to-explore cobbled townscape, and boats to an island-beach getaway.

But even Lagos and Tavira are secondary to this region's best destination: the laid-back beach village of Salema. For some rig-

orous rest and intensive re-
laxation, make Salema your
Algarve hideaway. Here the
tourists and the fishermen sport
the same stubble. It's just you, a
beach with weathered fishing
boats, no must-see attractions,
and a few other globetrotting
experts in lethargy. Salema is where surfing beach bums meet a
famously lenient Portuguese drug policy (you'll smell marijuana
everywhere). Nearby is Cape Sagres, Europe's "Land's End" and
home of the scant remains of Henry the Navigator's famous navigation school. But unless you're out for the extra credit, you could
just stick around sleepy Salema...work on a tan and see how slow
your pulse can get. If not now, when? If not you, who?

## PLANNING YOUR TIME

The Algarve is your vacation from your vacation. How much time
does it deserve? It depends upon how much time you have, and how
much time you need to recharge your solar batteries. On a two-
week trip of Portugal, I'd give it three nights and two days. After a
full day of sightseeing in Lisbon (or Sevilla, if you're arriving from
Spain), I'd push it by driving to Salema around dinnertime to gain
an entirely free beach day. With two full days, I'd spend one enjoying side trips to Cape Sagres and Lagos, and another just lingering in Salema. The only other Algarve stop to consider is Tavira,
farther to the east and most logical on the way to or from Spain.
(If you're visiting in winter, Tavira—which is lively year-round—
makes a better stop than tiny Salema, which slows way down.)

## GETTING AROUND THE ALGARVE

Trains and buses connect the main towns along the south coast
(skimpy service on weekends and off-season). Buses take you west
from Lagos, where trains don't go. The freeway crossing the Algarve from Lagos to the Spanish border (and on to Sevilla, Spain)
makes driving quick and easy. (See "Route Tips for Drivers," at the
end of this chapter.)

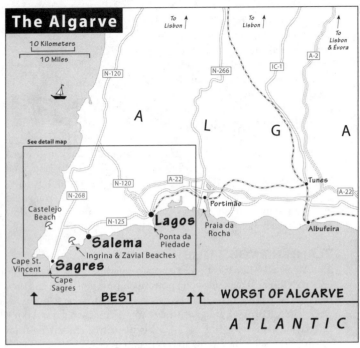

## The Algarve

10 Kilometers
10 Miles

To Lisbon
To Lisbon
To Lisbon & Évora

N-120
N-266
IC-1
A-2

A   L   G   A

See detail map

N-120
A-22
Tunes
A-22
N-268
Portimão
N-125
Castelejo Beach
**Lagos**
Praia da Rocha
Ponta da Piedade
Albufeira
**Salema**
Ingrina & Zavial Beaches
Cape St. Vincent
**Sagres**
Cape Sagres

↑ BEST ↑↑ WORST OF ALGARVE

A T L A N T I C

**ALGARVE**

# Salema

One bit of old Algarve magic still glitters quietly in the sun: Salema. Fronting a fine sandy beach, it's at the end of a small road just off the main drag between the big city of Lagos and the rugged southwest tip of Europe, Cape Sagres.

Salema (sah-LAY-mah) is changing but is still charming. The fishermen are fading into the past, the younger generation is moving to the big city, and the economy is evolving. Salema now draws visitors from nearby gated resorts and golfing clubs seeking local character and atmospheric restaurants. Yet Salema is still a place that will reward you with a great beach-town experience.

This simple fishing village has three beachside streets, a dozen or so restaurants, a few hotels, time-share condos up the road, a couple of bars, a paved promenade, and endless summer sun. Most important, it has a long, broad, gorgeous beach—luxurious with powder-fine sand, framed off by steep vivid-yellow cliffs, and rela-

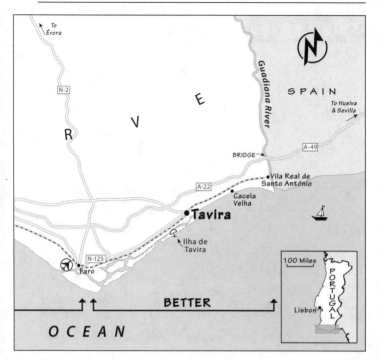

tively untrampled by rowdy tourists. For my money, it may be the most purely enjoyable beach in all of Europe.

# Orientation to Salema

Tiny Salema meets the water at the parking-lot square called Largo da Liberdade. Most of my recommended accommodations and restaurants are within a few minutes' walk of here; a few are a steep but scenic walk above town.

## TOURIST INFORMATION

Salema lacks a real TI, but people in the bars, restaurants, and pensions (and Romeu at the Salema Market—see "Eating in Salema," later) have heard all the questions and are happy to provide answers. There's a little information online at www.salema4u.com, and the TIs in nearby Sagres or Lagos offer some help for Salema as well.

## ARRIVAL IN SALEMA

**By Train and Bus:** To get to Salema, you'll arrive first at Lagos, the western Algarve's transportation hub (with the closest train and bus stations; see "Lagos Connections" on page 199). From there, buses go every hour or two between Lagos and Sagres—Salema is about halfway between the two (30-minute ride, last bus de-

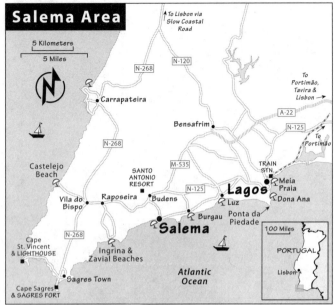

parts Lagos at 20:30, fewer buses on weekends, schedules at www.algarvebus.info and www.eva-bus.com).

About half the buses conveniently go right into the village of Salema (these are usually marked *Salema Village*). You should confirm with the driver by asking: *"Você vai à praia de Salema?"* (voh-say vie ah pry-ah deh Salema).

The rest of the buses—marked with a cross ("X") in the schedule—stop at the top of the road, a 20-minute downhill walk into town. (If you're on one of these buses, it's better to stay on and get off at the next stop, Figueira. From there you can backtrack 20 yards, then follow the sign for *Salema*. It's the same distance as the first downhill walk, but there's a sidewalk, so it's safer and easier.)

**By Car:** From the A-22 freeway that parallels the coast, take the Lagos exit (marked *Lagos/Vila do Bispo/Sagres*), then follow *Sagres/Vila do Bispo* signs. The Salema turnoff (marked with just one small white sign) is at the roundabout after Budens and before Figueira. In Salema, parking is free just about everywhere—there are several handy spots on the main square, steps above the beach, and a larger overflow gravel lot over the little bridge at the top of the square.

To stop in **Lagos** before continuing to Salema, take the exit marked *Lagos/Vila do Bispo/Sagres,* but follow signs to *Lagos centro*. When ready to continue to Salema, leave Lagos on Avenida dos Descobrimentos, and follow signs to *Sagres/Vila do Bispo*.

**By Taxi:** A cab from Lagos to Salema takes 20 minutes and costs about €30 (metered, but ask for an estimate first; see below).

## HELPFUL HINTS

**Exchange Rate:** €1 = about $1.10

**Country Calling Code:** 351 (see page 422 for dialing instructions)

**Money:** It's helpful to stock up on cash before coming to Salema. Many places don't accept credit cards, and there's just one real ATM in town (tucked around the corner from the main square, by the public WC). The well-lit "ATM" across the square is run by a money-changing outfit—not a bank—and offers terrible rates.

**WCs:** You'll find free public WCs in the little, white municipal building at the top of the main square/parking lot (just around the corner to the right of Bistro Central). The fountain in front of the building is a reminder of the old days. When water to the village was cut off, this was always running.

**Taxi:** Your hotel can arrange a taxi, but I'd rather work directly with a local couple, **José and Isabel,** who (along with their sons) have four- to eight-seat taxis. Rates can vary with the number of people—try to split the cost: about €30 to Lagos; €70 for a two-hour guided tour of Cape Sagres (add €10 for wait time to explore more); and about €400 to Sevilla, Évora, or Lisbon. They all speak English and are happy to answer your questions about the area; Isabel is a former tour guide. They can also take you to desolate beaches. Call or email in advance to reserve (mobile 919-385-139 or 919-422-061, www.vibeltaxisairporttransfers.com info@vibeltaxisairporttransfers.com).

# Sights in Salema

Salema has a split personality: The whitewashed Old Town is for locals, and the other half was built for tourists. Both groups pursue a policy of peaceful coexistence. Tourists laze in the sun, while locals grab the shade.

It's a small town where everyone seems connected in one way or another. (As the saying goes, "When you kick one person, everyone limps.") A good percentage of the population has the surname Duarte, and people have nicknames like Cucumber Ze and Bread Roll Paulo. Several of the local men married visiting German women back in

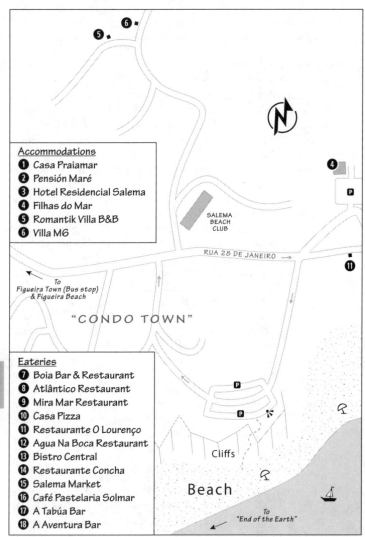

**Accommodations**

1. Casa Praiamar
2. Pensión Maré
3. Hotel Residencial Salema
4. Filhas do Mar
5. Romantik Villa B&B
6. Villa M6

**Eateries**

7. Boia Bar & Restaurant
8. Atlântico Restaurant
9. Mira Mar Restaurant
10. Casa Pizza
11. Restaurante O Lourenço
12. Agua Na Boca Restaurant
13. Bistro Central
14. Restaurante Concha
15. Salema Market
16. Café Pastelaria Solmar
17. A Tabúa Bar
18. A Aventura Bar

the 1980s, demonstrating the town knack for making tourists feel welcome.

**Fishing Scene**

Salema is still a fishing village—but just barely. There are six or eight working boats, but it's a far cry from the days—just a generation ago—when the town's main drag, Rua dos Pescadores, was, as its name suggests, literally the street of the fishermen. While the fishermen's hut no longer hosts a fish auction, you'll still see old-timers enjoying its shade on rickety old plastic chairs, in front of the

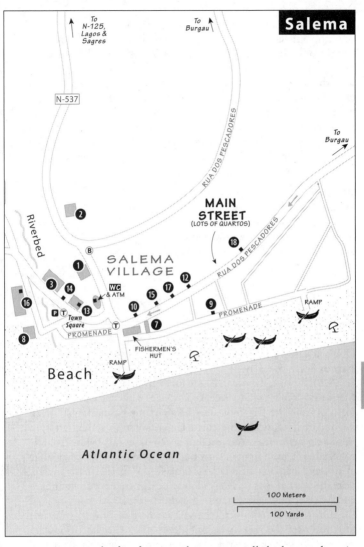

community-subsidized tractor they use to pull the boats ashore in the winter. (In the days before tractors, boat-hauling was a 10-person chore.) In the calm of the summer, boats are left out on buoys. Oblivious to tourists, the old salts mend their nets and reminisce about the good ol' days when life was "only fish and hunger." To get permission before taking their photo, ask *"Posso tirar uma foto, por favor?"* (paw-soo teer-ar oo-mah foh-too poor fah-vor).

At night you'll see evenly spaced lights bobbing on the horizon: these are fishing boats out in search of squid, sardines, and the main catch—octopi. The pottery jars stacked everywhere are traps; owners take care to keep them clean because octopi prefer smooth, barnacle-free pots. Unwritten tradition allocates different chunks of undersea territory to each Salema family. The traps are tied about 15 feet apart in long lines and dropped offshore. Octopi, thinking these jars would make a cozy place to set an ambush, climb in and get ambushed themselves. (They also take refuge in pots during a storm.) When the fishermen hoist them in, the octopi hang on—unaware they've made their final mistake. The fishermen mace them out of their pots with a squirt of bleach. The octopi flop angrily into the boat, bound for the market and—who knows—maybe onto your dinner plate.

## Beach Scene

Sunbathers enjoy the beach May through early October. Knowing their tourist-based economy sits on a foundation of sand, locals hope and pray that the sand returns after being washed away each winter (some winters leave the beach just a pile of rocks).

A walk the length of the beach, tracing the edge of the wet sand from the rocks in the west to the rocks in the east, is a peaceful experience. Doing it early or late is a fine way to start or finish your day.

Locals claim the ocean is safe for swimming, and in summer a lifeguard is often on duty (marked by signs), but the water is rarely really warm. The flag indicates the swimming conditions: Green is good, yellow means the current merits extra caution, and red means no swimming. You can rent beach items just below Atlântico restaurant, or in front of Boia Bar (lounge chair-€5/day, 2 lounge chairs and bamboo sunshade-€10/day). Up on the main square, near the start of Rua dos Pescadores, local entrepreneurs rent one- and two-person kayaks, stand-up paddleboards, and more.

On the west end of the beach, at low tide, you may be able to climb over the rocks past tiny tide pools to secluded Figueira Beach. (But be aware of when the tide comes in, or your route back will have to be over land.) While the old days of black-clad widows chasing topless Nordic women off the beach are gone, topless bathing is still considered somewhat risqué: Northern European sun worshippers do so with discretion, sometimes tucking in at the end of the beach among the rocks.

## Hiking

From Salema, several beautiful hikes go along the beach and through the countryside out to neighboring villages such as Figueira. For routes, ask at your hotel, or see the walks and hikes described at www. salema4u.com/tours.

**Near Salema**

The whole peninsula (west of Lagos) has been declared a natural park, and further development close to the beach is forbidden. But the village of Salema is becoming less and less ramshackle as it's gradually bought up by northern Euro-

peans for vacation or retirement homes. Salema will live with past mistakes, such as the huge hotel in the town center that pulled some mysterious strings to go two stories over code. Up the street is a sprawling community of condos and Club Med-type vacationers who rarely leave their air-conditioned bars and swimming pools.

Across the highway and two miles inland is a big golf resort, **Santo Antonio at Parque da Floresta,** where several well-known European soccer players have snapped up holiday homes. Visitors can pay a daily rate to use the spa, gym, outdoor pool, golf course, and tennis courts (spa tel. 282-690-086, golf tel. 282-690-054, www.saresorts.com; for golf see parquedaflorestagolfclub.com).

## Sleeping in Salema

Salema has a limited number of hotels; you'll feel the pinch in the busy summer months of July through mid-September (August is horribly packed). Prices jump in July and especially in August, when rates can spike well above the ranges suggested here. Many Salema accommodations lack air-conditioning—locals insist they don't need it, thanks to stiff, cooling Atlantic winds that blow through most evenings. Salema is partially closed down in winter, when just a couple of restaurants stay open.

### IN OR NEAR THE TOWN CENTER

**$$$ Casa Praiamar**—in a newer building just above the main square, with a pool and Astroturf—feels fresh and slick by Salema standards. It rents 10 modern rooms, most with kitchens and half with sea views and balconies (RS%, family rooms, no breakfast, air-con, mobile 962-619-037, www.casapraiamarsalema.com, casapraiamar@gmail.com).

**$$ Pensión Maré,** a blue-and-white building overlooking the village along the main road into town, is the best hotel value in Salema. It's run by friendly Bettina, who offers six comfortable rooms, three fully equipped apartments, and an inviting breakfast terrace in a tidy paradise (RS%, air-con in some rooms, laundry

## Sleep Code

Hotels are classified based on the average price of a standard double room with breakfast in high season.

| | |
|---|---|
| **$$$$** | **Splurge:** Most rooms over €150 |
| **$$$** | **Pricier:** €100-150 |
| **$$** | **Moderate:** €70-100 |
| **$** | **Budget:** €40-70 |
| **¢** | **Backpacker:** Under €40 |
| **RS%** | **Rick Steves discount** |

Unless otherwise noted, credit cards are accepted, hotel staff speaks basic English, and free Wi-Fi is available. Comparison-shop by checking prices at several hotels (on each hotel's own website, on a booking site, or by email). For the best deal, *book directly with the hotel*. Ask for a discount if paying in cash; if the listing includes **RS%,** request a Rick Steves discount.

service, tel. 282-695-165, bettina@the-mare.com, www.the-mare. com).

**$$ Hotel Residencial Salema** rents basic, comfortable rooms handy to the beach. Their 32 rooms all have air-conditioning, balconies, and partial views (RS%, usually closed Nov-Easter, elevator, Wi-Fi only in lobby, tel. 282-695-328, www.hotelsalema.com, info@hotelsalema.com, Andrea).

**$$ Filhas do Mar,** run by Dutch transplant Peter, has four big, multiroom apartments and two studios in a modern building tucked at the back end of town. While the location is more practical than romantic, this is a decent option if the others are full (some rooms have modest views, no breakfast, air-con, tel. 282-695-943, www.filhasdomar.com).

**$ Quartos:** For economy, the experience, and an opportunity to practice your Portuguese, you can stay in a *quarto* (private room for rent). These typically can't be reserved in advance—if you're brave, show up without a reservation and ask around for a room (Romeu at Salema Market is a good person to ask; otherwise try restaurants or any local along the waterfront). Most options line the main residential street, Rua dos Pescadores. For general info on staying at a *quarto,* see page 409.

### ABOVE TOWN

These two places perch on the bluff overlooking town. Plan on a steep 10- to 15-minute walk up. To get here by foot, head up from the beach past Restaurante O Lourenço, take a right just after the *Salema Beach Club* sign, and carry on steeply uphill (with the white condos on your left). When you reach a fork at the big, rounded, white wall (and *Villa Oceanis* sign), bear left to find Romantik Villa or right to find Villa M6.

Because of one-way streets, drivers take a slightly different route: Take the first left past Restaurante O Lourenço, and loop around past the parking lot over the beach; then, when you get back to the main road at the stop sign, turn right (back downhill) for a few yards, then take the first left. From there, follow the directions above.

**$$ Romantik Villa B&B** is a chic, artsy house on top of the hill with one room, two apartments, a beautiful garden, and a swimming pool. Conscientiously run (with an eco-focus) by warm French couple Olivier and Geraldine, it's a tastefully decorated, serene, seaview retreat. This is a great option for those who don't mind the steep walk up from town (room includes breakfast and daily cleaning; apartments have a three-night minimum, come with kitchens, and offer breakfast and cleaning for extra charge; self-service laundry, tel. 282-695-670, mobile 967-059-806, www.romantikvilla.com, romantikvilla@sapo.pt).

**$$ Villa M6** is a simpler, no-frills alternative just around the corner. Heiwi (from Germany) rents four rooms, and there's a fine swimming-pool terrace with sea views (cheaper rooms with shared bath, some rooms with view, kitchen, tel. 282-698-684, www.algarve-salema.de).

## Eating in Salema

Eat fresh seafood here. The local specialty is *cataplana*—fish, tomatoes, potatoes, onions, and whatever else is available—cooked a long time in a traditional copper pot (somewhere between a pressure cooker and a steamer). Costing around €25, a single *cataplana* is enough food for two (or three). Also look for grilled golden bream *(dourada grelhada)* and giant prawns *(camarões)*. For wine, try *vinho verde* (a refreshing young white wine).

For such a small town, Salema seems to specialize in good restaurants. Dinner with a view is tempting here; Boia Bar, Atlântico, and Casa Pizza all have modern glass fronts so you can be both comfortable and seaside in cold weather. The Mira Mar is right on the beach and can be chilly at dinnertime.

For a memorable last course at any of these places, consider taking your port, *moscatel* (dessert wine), *caipirinha* (Brazilian sugarcane liquor mixed with lime), or coffee to the beach for some stardust on the side.

**$$ Boia Bar and Restaurant,** at the base of the Rua dos Pescadores residential street, has a classy beachfront setting, noteworthy service by a friendly gang, and a knack for doing whitefish just right (always with free seconds on vegetables). Their vegetarian la-

## Restaurant Price Code

I've assigned each eatery a price category, based on the average cost of a typical main course. Drinks, desserts, and splurge items (steak and seafood) can raise the price considerably.

|        |                                         |
|--------|-----------------------------------------|
| **$$$$** | **Splurge:** Most main courses over €17 |
| **$$$**  | **Pricier:** €12-17                     |
| **$$**   | **Moderate:** €7-12                     |
| **$**    | **Budget:** Under €7                    |

In Portugal, takeout food is **$**; a basic sit-down eatery is **$$**; a casual but more upscale restaurant is **$$$**; and a swanky splurge is **$$$$**.

sagna and salads are popular (daily 10:00-24:00, tel. 282-695-382, Anibal, Rui, and Carla).

The **$$$ Atlântico**—big, busy, and right on the beach—has long dominated the Salema scene and comes with a fun energy. It's known for tasty fish (see the daily board), friendly service, and a wonderful beachside terrace (daily 12:00-22:00, also rents lounge chairs and bamboo sunshades, tel. 282-695-142, Cristiano and his sister Sandra run the place).

**$$$ Mira Mar,** easily accessed from the promenade, is actually on the beach. Dieter (a German who adopted Salema as his hometown decades ago) offers a creative rotating menu for those venturing away from seafood. He serves hearty salads for lunch and always has a vegetarian option. As tables are outside on a covered patio facing the beach, it can be cool, but they have blankets (Sun-Fri 12:30-15:30 & 18:30-22:00, closed Sat, cash only, no reservations—try to arrive by 19:00 to nab a table).

**$$ Casa Pizza,** across the street from the Boia Bar, isn't on the beach, but its upper deck has a great view. Run by Stelios and family, it serves a variety of tasty pizzas, salads, and fresh fish, as well as meat and pasta dishes (Wed-Mon 12:00-15:00 & 18:00-24:00, closed Tue, Rua dos Pescadores 100, tel. 282-697-968). You can get a pizza to go, and eat it on the beach for the best view in town.

**$$$ Restaurante O Lourenço,** a block up the hill, has no ambience or view (choose between the dining room or the covered terrace across the street), but offers good-value meals and is popular with both locals and tourists. Paulo fishes and serves what he catches, while his mother Aldina cooks. A fish dinner for two here will cost around €35; Paulo can knowledgeably explain the story and cost of each fish (Mon-Sat lunch from noon and dinner from 18:00, closed Sun, cash only; from Hotel Residencial Salema cross the bridge, restaurant is a half-block uphill; tel. 282-698-622).

**$$$ Agua Na Boca** ("Mouth Watering"), a sophisticated, atmospheric, and noisy eatery run by Paulo and his wife-and-chef Irene, serves up-market local cuisine complemented by an extensive wine list. It's always busy, especially with the fancy golf-club crowd, so reserve ahead. Dishes are innovative—more than the standard grilled fish—and their special plates are huge and splittable. For about €60 you can enjoy a three-course meal for two people with wine (April-Sept daily from 18:00, Oct-May closed Sun, on Rua dos Pescadores 82, tel. 282-695-651).

**Cafés on the Main Square:** While these options lack a view, they are handy for a quick bite for those who want to take a break from the beach. **$$$ Bistro Central** has a mix of Portuguese and international dishes (good wine list, homemade desserts, Tue-Sun 10:30-24:00, closed Mon, mobile 934-194-215, Luisa and Natalia). The simpler **$$ Restaurante Concha** is run by smiley Sérgio (an avid surf photographer) and his Polish wife Marlena, who serve a long menu of basic fare—including some tasty traditional Polish meals (try Marlena's *mięso babuni*—"granny's meat," pork slow-roasted in savory spices; Tue-Sun 9:00-23:00, closed Mon, mobile 916-280-783).

**Picnics:** Romeu's **Salema Market** has all the fixings for a great picnic to take with you to a secluded beach or Cape Sagres. Look for fresh fruits, veggies, bread, sheep's cheese, sausage, and *vinho verde*. Helpful Romeu also gives travel and *quarto* advice (daily 9:00-20:00—later in summer, Nov-April closes 13:00-15:00, on Rua dos Pescadores).

**For drivers:** Drivers who want a memorable meal outside of town should consider the elegant **Vila Velha Restaurante** in Sagres or the more rustic, beachfront **Castelejo Restaurante** at the surreal Praia do Castelejo (both described later).

### Breakfast in Salema

*Quartos* and some hotels don't serve breakfast. Three options are on the main square: **$ Café Pastelaria Solmar** (in the strip facing Hotel Residencial Salema) serves coffee and pastries from 7:00. Others start serving after the bread guy arrives. The recommended **Restaurante Concha** (from 9:00) and **Bistro Central** (from 10:30) both offer full English breakfasts for around €9. Meanwhile, for beach scenery, **$$ Boia Bar** serves a big €8 breakfast all day (from 10:00).

# Nightlife in Salema

Salema's two late-night bars are each worth a visit to sample local drinks. *Armarguinha* (ar-mar-GWEEN-yah) is a sweet, likeable almond liqueur. *Licor beirão* (LIK-kor bay-ROW, rhymes with "cow") is Portuguese amaretto, a "double distillation of diverse plants and aromatic seeds in accordance with a secret old formula." *Caipirinha* (kay-peer-EEN-yah), tasty and powerful, is made of fermented Brazilian sugarcane with lime, sugar, and crushed ice. And *moscatel* is the local sweet dessert wine.

The two bars stand within a few steps of each other on the main street. **A Tabúa Bar** serves a popular sangria and feels a bit younger and more local (from 17:00). Just up the street, **A Aventura Bar** offers an intimate atmosphere for sipping drinks whipped up by Karl and Zoe, an English couple who prefer the Eagles to hip-hop (from 18:00).

I enjoy capping my dinner by taking a drink from any beachside restaurant and grabbing a bench on the promenade or a place on the beach to peacefully ponder the moon and the waves.

# Cape Sagres

In the days before Columbus, when the world was presumed to be flat, this rugged southwestern tip of Portugal was the spot closest to the edge of the Earth. Prince Henry the Navigator, determined to broaden Europe's horizons and spread Catholicism, founded his navigators' school here and sent sailors ever farther into the unknown. Shipwrecked and frustrated explorers were carefully debriefed as they washed ashore.

Today, Cape Sagres (KAH-peh SAH-gresh) is popular among two sets of travelers: Those who want photographic evidence that they've been to the "end of Europe" (before retreating to the comfort of their concrete resorts); and a young, international crowd drawn by the strong surf, who settle into humble guest houses in the town of Sagres and keep its many bars hopping. While the Henry the Navigator sights are worth a quick visit, and some of the surrounding sea cliffs are dramatic, the town itself is scrappy, humble, and visually underwhelming. It smells like sea spray, surfer B.O., and sweet wafts of marijuana...making it nirvana for some, and a hold-your-breath pass-through for others.

## Orientation to Cape Sagres

Portugal's end of the road is two distinct capes. **Cape Sagres,** with its old fort and Henry the Navigator lore, is the more historic cape of the two. Windy **Cape St. Vincent** is actually the most southwestern tip. At either cape, look for daredevil windsurfers and fishermen casting from the cliffs.

Lashed tightly to the windswept landscape is the salty **town of Sagres,** above a harbor of fishing boats. Sagres (pop. 1,900)—which really does feel like the last town in Europe—is basically a scruffy main street (Avenida Comandante Matoso) with plenty of places to eat and sleep. The main square is a broad expanse called Jardim de Sagres, with the TI, a statue of Henry the Navigator wearing a rakish hat, and bus stops. The square—and the town—sits on a bluff above the shoreline, with cliffs on the horizon in all directions. At one end of town is Cape Sagres, and at the other is a hardworking fishing port with an auction (Docapesca, described below) and a few leisure boats. Running underneath the town is a fine crescent beach, with a good beachside restaurant.

**Arrival in Sagres:** If arriving by **bus,** hop off at the main square, near the TI. **Drivers** pass through tacky low-rise concrete sprawl before reaching the roundabout at the start of town. Here you have three choices: right for Cape St. Vincent; straight to Cape Sagres and the fortress *(fortaleza);* or left onto the main drag, which passes the main square (with free street parking), then goes through the middle of town before ending at the twisty road down to the port.

**Tourist Information:** The TI is on the main street (hours flex with demand, generally Mon-Fri 9:30-13:00 & 14:00-17:30, closed Sat-Sun, tel. 282-624-873).

## Sights in Cape Sagres

Tourism here is all about surfing. When the surf's up, things are busy and there's a hip and youthful vibe. In low season, it feels pretty dead.

### Docapesca

Sagres harbor hosts the biggest fish auction west of Lagos (Mon-Fri at 7:30 and 15:00). Snack Bar A Sereia is perched above the action, and from its big windows you can watch the fishy action as restaurateurs fill the two-dozen chairs above the conveyor belt and bid against each other for the best fish.

### ▲Cape Sagres Fort (Fortaleza de Sagres) and Navigators' School

The former "end of the world" is a craggy, windswept, wedge-shaped point that juts into the Atlantic (a short drive or 15-minute walk from Sagres; follow brown signs for *fortaleza).* In 1420, Prince Henry the Navigator used his order's funds to establish a school here for navigators. It was devastated by the 1755 earthquake (which also destroyed Lisbon), the center of which was 50 miles

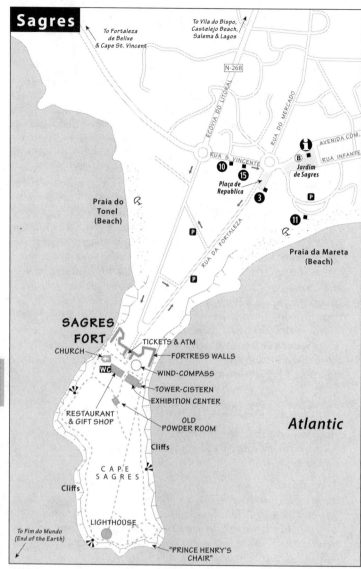

**Sagres**

To Fortaleza de Belixe & Cape St. Vincent

To Vila do Bispo, Castelejo Beach, Salema & Lagos

N-268

ECOVIA DO LITORAL

RUA S. VICENTE

RUA DO MERCADO

AVENIDA COM.

RUA INFANTE

Jardim de Sagres

10

15

Plaça de Republica

3

11

Praia do Tonel (Beach)

RUA DA FORTALEZA

Praia da Mareta (Beach)

**SAGRES FORT**

TICKETS & ATM

CHURCH

FORTRESS WALLS

WC

WIND-COMPASS

TOWER-CISTERN

EXHIBITION CENTER

RESTAURANT & GIFT SHOP

OLD POWDER ROOM

*Atlantic*

Cliffs

CAPE SAGRES

Cliffs

To Fim do Mundo (End of the Earth)

LIGHTHOUSE

"PRINCE HENRY'S CHAIR"

ALGARVE

offshore from here. Today, little remains of Henry's school, except the site of buildings replaced by a few more modern structures. An 18th-century fortress, built on the school's original battlements and whitewashed in the 20th century, dominates the entrance to the point.

**Cost and Hours:** €3, daily 9:30-20:00, Oct-April until 17:30, tel. 282-620-140.

**Visiting the Fort:** After entering through the 18th-century

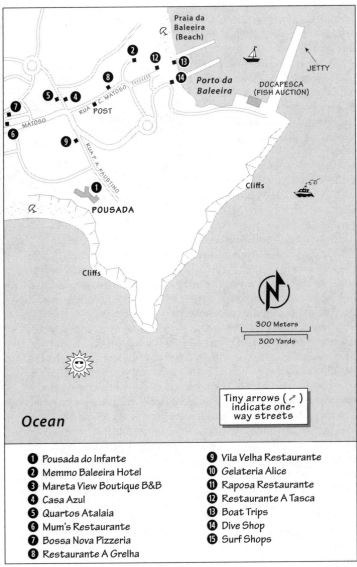

Praia da
Baleeira
(Beach)

JETTY

*Porto da
Baleeira*

DOCAPESCA
(FISH AUCTION)

POST

RUA C. MATOSO

MATOSO

RUA P. A. FAUSTINO

POUSADA

Cliffs

Cliffs

**N**

300 Meters

300 Yards

Tiny arrows ( ↗ )
indicate one-
way streets

*Ocean*

ALGARVE

① Pousada do Infante
② Memmo Baleeira Hotel
③ Mareta View Boutique B&B
④ Casa Azul
⑤ Quartos Atalaia
⑥ Mum's Restaurante
⑦ Bossa Nova Pizzeria
⑧ Restaurante A Grelha

⑨ Vila Velha Restaurante
⑩ Gelateria Alice
⑪ Raposa Restaurante
⑫ Restaurante A Tasca
⑬ Boat Trips
⑭ Dive Shop
⑮ Surf Shops

battlements, turn back and look above the entry arch. Find the carved **stone plaque** that honors Henry. The ship in the plaque is a caravel, one of the small, light craft that was constantly being reinvented by Sagres' shipbuilding grad students. The astrolabe, a compact instrument that uses the stars for navigation, emphasizes Henry's role in the exploration process.

Head a few more steps into the complex and look right. The stone column capped with a **cross** honors Henry, who died here in

1460 (erected on the 500th anniversary of his death). The top is a replica of the stone used by Portugal's great mariners to claim new territory.

Poke around...though there's little to actually see here. Sagres' most impressive sight—a circle on the ground, 100 feet across and outlined by round pebbles—is a mystery. Some think it was a large **wind-compass** *(rosa-dos-ventos)*. A flag flying from the center could immediately announce the wind's direction. Others speculate it's a large sundial. A pole in the center pointing toward the North Star (at a 37-degree angle, Sagres' latitude) would cast a shadow on the dial showing the time of day.

The row of buildings beyond the wind-compass is where Henry's **school** once was. Today these modern buildings house the shop, cafeteria, and a planned exhibition (though a long-delayed renovation means any or all of these may be closed for your visit). At the far-left end, the **tower-cistern** is part of the original dorms. You can climb it for the view. At the far-right end, the small, whitewashed **Church of Our Lady of Grace** (with St. Vincent and St. Francis flanking its humble altar) replaced Henry's church. The **windbreak wall** dates from Henry's time, but is largely rebuilt.

For a better view of the complex, climb up the ramps to the **rooftop of the fortress.** Look out to sea and consider the epic history of this strategic location: The Sagres school taught mapmaking, shipbuilding, sailing, astronomy, and mathematics (for navigating), plus botany, zoology, anthropology, languages, and salesmanship for mingling with the locals. The school welcomed Italians, Scandinavians, and Germans, and included Christians, Muslims, and Jews. Captured Africans gave guest lectures. (The next 15 generations of Africans were not so lucky, being sold into slavery by the tens of thousands.)

Besides being a school, Sagres was Mission Control for the explorers. Returning sailors brought spices, gold, diamonds, silk, and ivory, plus new animals, plants, peoples, customs, communicable diseases, and knowledge of the routes that were added to the maps. Henry ordered every sailor to keep a travel journal that could be studied. Ship designs were analyzed and tweaked, resulting in the square-sailed, oceangoing caravels that replaced the earlier coast-hugging versions.

It's said that Ferdinand Magellan (circumnavigator), Vasco da Gama (found sea route to India), Pedro Cabral (discovered Brazil), and Bartolomeu Dias (Africa-rounder) all studied at Sagres (after

# Prince Henry the Navigator (1394-1460)

No swashbuckling sailor, Infante Dom Henrique (as the Portuguese call him) was a quiet scholar, an organizer, a religious man, and the brains behind Portugal's daring sea voyages. The middle child of King João I of Portugal and Queen Philippa of England, he was one of what was dubbed "The Marvelous Generation" (*Ínclita Geração*) that drove the Age of Discovery. While his brothers and nephews became Portugal's kings, he worked behind the scenes.

At age 21, he planned the logistics for the large-scale ship invasion of the Muslim city of Ceuta (1415) on the north coast of Morocco, taking the city and winning knightly honors. Awed by the wealth of the city—a terminus of the caravan route—and intrigued by the high-quality maps he found there, Henry decided to organize expeditions to explore the Muslim world. He hoped to spread Christianity, contain Islam, tap Muslim wealth, and find Prester John's legendary Christian kingdom, said to exist somewhere in Africa or Asia.

As head of the Order of Christ—a powerful brotherhood of soldier-monks—Henry used their money to found a maritime school at Sagres. While Henry stayed home to update maps, debrief returning sailors, order supplies, and sign paychecks, brave seamen traveled off under Henry's strict orders not to return until they'd explored what was known as the "Sea of Darkness."

They discovered the Madeira Islands (1420), which Henry planted with vineyards, and the Azores (1427), which Henry colonized with criminals. But the next expeditions returned empty-handed, having run into a barrier—both a psychological and physical one. Cape Bojador (at the southwest corner of modern Morocco), with its reefs and currents, was seen as the end of the world. Beyond that, sea serpents roamed, while the hot equatorial sun melted ships, made the sea boil, and turned white men black.

Henry ordered scared, superstitious sailors to press on. After 14 unsuccessful voyages, Gil Eanes' crew returned (1437), unharmed, with new knowledge that was added to corporate Portugal's map library.

Henry gained a reputation as an intelligent, devout, celibate monk. In later years, he spent less time at court in Lisbon and more in desolate Sagres, where he died in 1460. (He's buried in Batalha; see page 252.) Henry died before finding a sea route to Asia and just before his voyages really started paying off commercially. A generation later, Vasco da Gama would sail to India, kicking off Portugal's Golden Age.

Henry's time, though). In May of 1476, the young Italian Christopher Columbus washed ashore here after being shipwrecked by pirates. He went on to study and sail with the Portuguese (and marry a Portuguese woman) before beginning his American voyage. When Portugal denied Columbus' request to sail west, Spain accepted. The rest is history.

Beyond the buildings, the granite **point** itself is windswept, eroded, and largely barren, except for hardy, coarse vegetation admired by botanists. Walk on level paths around the edge of the bluff (a 40-minute round-trip walk), where locals cast lines and tourists squint into the wind. You'll get great seascape views of Cape St. Vincent, with its modern lighthouse on the site of an old convent (described next). At the far end of the Sagres bluff are a naval radio station, a natural cave, and a promontory called "Prince Henry's Chair."

Sit on the point and gaze across the "Sea of Darkness," where monsters roam. Long before Henry's time, Romans dubbed it Promontorium Sacrum—Sacred ("Sagres") Promontory. Pilgrims who came to visit this awe-inducing place were prohibited from spending the night here—it was for the gods alone.

In Portugal's seafaring lore, capes, promontories, and land's ends are metaphors for the edge of the old, and the start of the unknown voyage. Sagres is the greatest of these.

## Cape St. Vincent (Cabo São Vincente)

About a 10-minute drive past Cape Sagres, this spit of land is the actual southwestern tip of Europe. It has a desolate lighthouse that marks what was thought of even in prehistoric times as "the end of the world." Today it's an impossibly tacky tourist trap, with a parking lot jammed with salt-of-the-earth merchants selling seaworthy sweaters and a stand boasting the *"Letzte Bratwurst vor Amerika"* (last hot dog before America).

The cape's tip is marked by the **St. Vincent Lighthouse.** Stepping through the gate of the complex (Tue-Sun 10:00-18:00, until 17:00 Oct-March, closed Mon), on your right you'll see the entrance to a humble little museum, which is worth a few minutes and the modest admission. Its exhibits focus on ship technology, ancient legends, celestial navigation, the evolution of Portuguese lighthouses, and the history this lighthouse in particular. In 1846, you could see the light of the oil lamp from six miles away. Now the beam is one of the strongest in Europe, said to reach 60 miles.

If you'd like to go up to visit the **lantern,** wait at the door marked *Privado No Entry* (directly across from the museum's gift shop), and the lighthouse keeper will eventually show up to take you on a free little tour. (If it's quiet and you want to make sure he's coming, ask at the little gift shop downstairs, near the WCs). Also in the courtyard are a salty café, WCs, and wild views of the often stormy coastline and the adjacent, jagged cliffs. You may see a few intrepid adventure-seekers rock-climbing here—a recent and very dangerous trend that local authorities strongly discourage.

Just off the road—about a half-mile before the lighthouse—you'll see **Fortaleza de Belixe,** the eroded remains of a 16th-century castle hanging precariously on a bluff over the sea. It was used as a kind of headquarters by the English pirate "sir" Francis Drake. Drake, who pillaged with the queen's blessing, waited here for his Mediterranean-bound victims.

### Beaches

In the town of Sagres itself, **Mareta Beach** (Praia da Mareta), just below the town center, has rental gear and showers in the summer

and the fun little recommended Raposo Restaurante.

Drivers can visit many beaches tucked away on the drive **between Salema and Cape Sagres.** Most of them require a short walk after you stop along N-125. In some cases, you leave your car on access roads or cross private property to reach the beach—be considerate. Furnas beach is fully accessible by car. You can access Ingrina and Zavial beaches by turning south in the village of Raposeira. Many beaches have bars (the one at Ingrina beach is famous for its spicy garlic prawns—*camarão piri-piri*).

The best secluded beach in the region is **Praia do Castelejo,** north of Cape Sagres (from the town of Vila do Bispo, drive inland and follow the signs for 15 minutes). If you have a car and didn't grow up in Fiji, this really is worth the drive. Overlooking the deserted beach is **$$$ Castelejo Restaurante,** which specializes in octopus dishes, *percebes* (barnacles), and *cataplana,* the hearty seafood stew (daily 12:00-22:00, 7.5 miles from Salema at Praia do Castelejo, tel. 282-639-777). While beaches between Salema and Sagres offer more of a seaside landscape, beaches north of São Vicente are more rugged and wild because they're exposed to ocean wind and weather. If there's no sand in Castelejo when you visit, blame it on nature and enjoy the rock formations instead.

For a resort beach, consider **Luz** (the first town west of Lagos), which feels like a Portuguese Riviera playground with a fine promenade and all the trappings of a beach-vacation destination.

### Activities

There's no shortage of options for beach fun in Sagres. Several outfitters (renting surfboards, organizing excursions, and so on) line

**ALGARVE**

the streets of town, particularly at the end near the TI. Down at the port, you'll find boat excursions and the diving school.

**Boat Trips:** Two competitive outfits with storefronts at the port sell tourist boat excursions into the waters near Sagres. Popular options include a dolphin-watching cruise (€35/1.5 hours), a seabird-watching tour (€45/2.5 hours—they toss in chum so you can observe the spectacle), a straightforward sightseeing cruise to Cape St. Vincent and back (€20/1.5 hours), fishing trips, and more. Comparison-shop at **Cape Cruiser** (mobile 919-751-175, www.capecruiser.org) and **Mar Ilimitado** (mobile 916-832-625, www.marilimitado.com).

**Diving:** At the port, **Divers Cape Sagres** is a diving school offering dive classes and excursions (mobile 965-559-073, www.diverscape.com).

**Surfing:** Near the entrance to town (between the two main roundabouts, on Rua São Vincente), two companies offer surfing gear and lessons: **Sagres Natura Sport** (tel. 282-624-072, www.sagresnatura.com) and **Pure Surf Camps** (www.puresurfcamps.com).

## Sleeping in Sagres

**$$$$ Pousada do Infante,** with 51 rooms on a bluff overlooking the sea, provides a touch of elegance in Sagres. Like other *pousadas* (historic inns), this is staid, stuffy, and a bit dated—but it enjoys a magnificent setting. At breakfast, you can sip coffee and enjoy the buffet while gazing out to sea (air-con, elevator, tel. 282-620-240, www.pousadas.pt, recepcao.infante@pousadas.pt).

**$$$ Memmo Baleeira Hotel,** with views over the port of Sagres, is your big hotel option—a 144-room resort that caters to groups. While a bit faded, it remains chic and minimalist, with pure white bedrooms—most with sea views (air-con, elevator, beautiful swimming pool terrace, tel. 282-624-212, www.memmohotels.com, baleeira@memmohotels.com).

**$$ Mareta View Boutique B&B,** a delightful and stylish refuge on a quieter back street, is perched on a bluff at the edge of town. Its 17 modern rooms have access to a fine garden and a seaview hot tub (air-con, Beco D. Henrique, tel. 282-620-000, www.maretaview.com, info@sagresholidays.com). Its sister hotel, Mareta Beach (a block closer to town), is bigger, less tranquil, and less appealing.

**$$ Casa Azul**—youthful and cheery—feels like an upgraded old guest house on an urban street, with 11 vivid rooms (each a different color, nearly all with a small private balcony) and four apartments (air-con, just up the street next to the Spar supermarket, tel. 282-624-856, www.casaazulsagres.com).

$ **Quartos Atalaia,** run by English-speaking Jorge, is your budget option—with seven basic rooms and four huge apartments on a workaday corner in the center of town (family rooms, no breakfast, across the street from Caza Azul—see earlier, tel. 282-624-681, mobile 911-046-068, apart.atalaia@gmail.com).

# Eating in Sagres

## ON OR NEAR THE MAIN DRAG

Sagres feels designed to feed visitors, with lots of inviting little eateries along its main drag, Avenida Comandante Matoso. Good choices include **$$$ Mum's,** with a hip retro vibe and a mix of traditional Portuguese and international comfort food (Wed-Mon 18:00-24:00, closed Tue, tel. 968-210-411); **$$ Bossa Nova Pizzeria,** serving tasty pizzas, pastas, salads, and vegetarian dishes in a converted stable (daily 18:00-24:00, closed Sun off-season, tucked down a little pedestrian lane behind the row of bars that includes Paü de Pita and Dromadário, tel. 282-624-219); and the old-school, traditional **$$ Restaurante A Grelha** (Mon-Sat 12:00-15:00 & 19:00-22:00, closed Sun, tel. 282-624-193).

**$$$$ Vila Velha Restaurante,** the pricey top-end option in town, offers wonderful meals—especially their rabbit stew (Tue-Sun 18:30-22:00, closed Mon, reservations smart, a block above the main drag on Rua Patrão Antonio Faustino—on the way up to the *pousada,* tel. 282-624-788, www.vilavelha-sagres.com).

**Ice Cream: Gelateria Alice** has a small selection of freshly made, top-quality gelato—some with interesting flavors—on the little street between the two roundabouts at the start of town (Rua São Vincente).

## WITH A VIEW

**$$$ Raposo Restaurante** ("Fox") is right on the pristine, sandy, and picturesque Mareta Beach. It's a fun spot for snacks (try *percebes*—barnacles), drinks, or a serious meal, inside or outside on a terrace. Have a dip in the sea right after your meal (meals served daily 12:00-21:00, tel. 282-624-168).

**$$$ Restaurante A Tasca,** known for good seafood, has fine indoor seating and a huge, sunny terrace overlooking the harbor. To find it, head to the far (port) end of town, then go down the big staircase (Thu-Tue 8:00-24:00, closed Wed, Porto da Baleeira, tel. 282-624-177).

## Cape Sagres Connections

From Salema, Sagres is a 20-minute drive or a 30-minute bus trip (runs every 1-2 hours, stop is at the edge of town—near the big park and TI, just after the roundabout with the giant anchor). You can check bus times online at www.eva-bus.com or www.algarvebus. info. A handful of buses continue to the Cape St. Vincent (Cabo São Vincente); check schedules beforehand.

A taxi ride from Salema to Sagres costs about €30 (for a Salema-based driver, see page 169).

# Lagos

With a beach-party old town and a jet-ski marina, Lagos (LAH-goosh) is as enjoyable as a big-city resort can be. This major town on the west end of the Algarve was the region's capital in the 13th and 14th centuries. The first great Portuguese maritime expeditions embarked from here, and the first African slave market in Europe was held here. And today, with nothing of earth-shaking importance to see or do, it's just a purely enjoyable little bit of the Algarve.

In some ways, big-city Lagos is the yin to sleepy Salema's yang. While Salema is far more relaxing, even sedate, Lagos attracts a younger and rowdier crowd. The big draw here are Lagos' stunning beaches, which are framed by jagged sandstone-colored sea stacks that poke up, like serrated teeth, from the aquamarine deep. While little Salema's streets are lined with take-your-time fish restaurants and napping cats, Lagos is jammed with funky cafés, hard-partying bars and nightclubs, and sales kiosks hawking all manner of boat, kayak, scuba diving, and other excursions.

Lagos is a whitewashed jumble of pedestrian streets, bars, hippie craft shops, outdoor restaurants, mod fountains and sculptures, and sunburned tourists. Except for a stroll among the rocks on the beach, there are no major sights—though to get your bearings, the town walk (described later) makes for a delightful morning or afternoon. Search out the sea-creature designs laid in the pavement—some of them will probably be on your plate at dinner.

ALGARVE

# Orientation to Lagos

Most visitors to Lagos (pop. 27,000) focus on the **old town.** Defined by its medieval walls, old Lagos stretches between the main

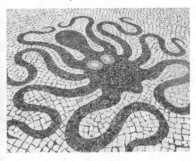

square (Praça Gil Eanes) and the fort. Across the Benasfrim River and just upstream are a colorful marina, excursion boats, and the train station.

The **beaches** with the exotic rock formations begin just past the fort, with easy access on foot via boardwalks and higher trails, or by local buses, taxis, and a tourist train. While the Praia da Batata, next to the old fort, is walkable from the center and perfectly good for a short visit, serious beachgoers may want to head farther out along the point to the south of the old town. This road is lined with scenic beaches (Dona Ana is best), culminating at the Ponta da Piedade viewpoint.

## TOURIST INFORMATION

The TI, which covers the entire Algarve, is in the former City Hall on the south side of Praça Gil Eanes (daily 9:30-17:30, likely closed Sun off-season, tel. 282-763-031, www.visitalgarve.pt).

## ARRIVAL IN LAGOS

**By Train or Bus:** The train and bus stations are a five-minute walk apart, separated by the marina and a ramped pedestrian bridge over a river. Neither station has baggage storage.

**By Car:** From the A-22 freeway, exit at Lagos and follow signs to *centro*. On your way into town, the road forks: turn left (white *centro* signs) to the town center, or carry on straight (brown *praia* signs) for the farther-flung scenic beaches (each is individually signposted).

In town, the most convenient free parking lot is just outside the old city wall off Rua Infante de Sagres. More central (and still affordable) is the large underground parking garage on Avenida dos Descobrimentos, near Praça do Infante. Another pay lot is near the marina. For a short visit, you can pay-and-display anywhere along the harborfront promenade.

## HELPFUL HINTS

**Car Rental:** English-speaking Nuno at **Lagorent Rent-a-Car** can set you up with four wheels for around €45 a day (daily,

ALGARVE

Avenida dos Descobrimentos 43, tel. 282-762-467, www. lagorent.com, info@lagorent.com).

**Local Guide: Carla Andrez de Sousa** is a good licensed guide who lives and works in Lagos (€100/family or group for a two-hour private town tour, longer tours available, mobile 964-670-661, carlasousa64@gmail.com).

# Lagos Town Walk

While the actual sights of Lagos are humble, the town itself has an endearing charm that is best experienced by strolling. This simple self-guided walk, worth ▲▲, takes about an hour (allow more time if you enter the sights along the way) and covers the essence of the city. It starts on the main square, cuts straight up the main street to the town museum, and then down to the site of the slave market and harborfront, where you can walk the promenade and/or hike the exotic beaches.

## Praça Gil Eanes

This city's inviting cobbled pedestrian streets seem to converge in this square around the playful statue of King Sebastian (Sebastião).

The big, yellow building housing the TI is the former City Hall. The local, free-spirited hippie community provides street music, and the cafés are tempting. While Lagos was a regional power from 1578 to 1756—in fact, the capital of the Algarve—today it feels like the capital of not much.

The statue commemorates the romantic **King Sebastian,** the young Portuguese ruler who ventured into Africa to Christianize "the Dark Continent"...and was killed. With his death, Spanish royalty came to power here and Portugal entered into a kind of Spanish-dominated Dark Age (1580-1640). And the Portuguese have never given up hope that somehow, their lost king will return. Sebastian is symbolic of ridiculous hopefulness. When he returns, so will the good times. This statue is particularly poignant because it was inaugurated in 1973, the year before the Carnation Revolution—when the people of Portugal were hungry to toss out their dictator and win their freedom.

• *From the square, head down Lagos' main drag. It's behind Sebastian, leading to the left.*

ALGARVE

## April 25 Street (Rua 25 de Abril)

Forca Portugal, a patriotic soccer gear shop, marks the start of April 25 Street—named for the date of the 1974 military coup. Follow the street through Lagos' restaurant row. Enjoy the colorful tiles on building fronts. This was the town's finest street, and home to its noble families in the 19th century. The crest of the hill marks the start of the most popular night spots, with boisterous bars and popular discos (after hours, the streets just uphill from here are packed).

• *Stroll the street for several blocks. Eventually you'll run into the...*

## ▲Church of St. Anthony (Santo António) and Municipal Museum

Tourists enter the Church of St. Anthony through the Municipal Museum (around the right side). Lagos' humble little museum,

while old-school, has some fascinating exhibits with good English descriptions (€3, ask about a combo-ticket that includes the Slave Market Museum and the fort; open Tue-Sun 10:00-12:30 & 14:00-17:30, closed Mon).

In the **museum,** you'll see ancient Roman mosaics, amphorae, and busts, models of traditional boats, octopus jugs, and other fishing gear. The chimneys, so characteristic of those you see all over the Algarve, are nicknamed "chimneys of the new Christians." According to tour guides, while Muslim Moors forced to convert in the 13th century became nominal Christians, they worshipped privately under chimneys like these, which were inspired by and reminiscent of the minarets of their destroyed mosques.

The **Church of St. Anthony** was first constructed in the 16th century, then rebuilt in the decades following the 1755 earthquake that devastated much of Portugal (and led to Lagos' decline). Considered one of the finest Baroque/Rococo churches in Portugal, it's dedicated to the patron saint of the military. The altar (from 1719, the oldest surviving artifact from the original church) is shiny with Brazilian gold leaf. Paintings show the miracles of St. Anthony (each described in English); the ceiling is a festival of 3-D; and the exuberant cupids are all very expressive.

• *Exit the museum, take two rights, and walk a block downhill to the next church,* **Santa Maria.** *After being rebuilt many times, it's more modern and vibrant.*

*Across the square, with the low-profile, double-arched arcade, is the...*

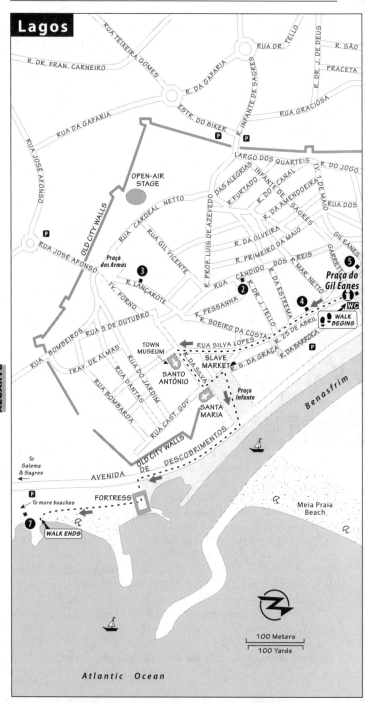

# Lagos

RUA TEIXEIRA GOMES
RUA DR. TELLO
R. SÃO
R. DR. FRAN. CARNEIRO
RUA DR. TELLO
R. DR. R. J. DE DEUS
PRACETA
R. DA GAFARIA
RUA INFANTE DE SAGRES
ESTR. DO BIKER
RUA GRACIOSA
RUA DA GAFARIA
LARGO DOS QUARTEIS
R. DO JOGO
RUA JOSÉ AFONSO
OPEN-AIR STAGE
RUA CARDEAL NETTO
R. FURTADO
R. DO CANAL
TV. 1° DE MAIO
RUA DOS
DAS ALEGRIAS
INFANTE DE SAGRES
R. DA AMENDOEIRA
GIL EANES
GARRETT
OLD CITY WALLS
RUA GIL VICENTE
R. PROF. LUIS DE AZEVEDO
R. DA OLIVEIRA
R. PRIMEIRO DE MAIO
R. MAR. NETTO
5 Praça do Gil Eanes
RUA JOSÉ AFONSO
Praça das Armas
3
TV. FORNO
R. LANÇAROTE
RUA CANDIDO DOS REIS
R. DR. J. TELLO
R. DA ESTREMA
2
4
1
WC
WALK BEGINS
R. PESSANHA
RUA BOMBEIROS
RUA 5 DE OUTUBRO
K. R. SOEIRO DA COSTA
RUA SILVA LOPES
R. 25 DE ABRIL
R. DA BARROCA
TRAV. DE ALMAS
TOWN MUSEUM
DA SILVA
SLAVE MARKET
S. DA GRAÇA
RUA DO JARDIM
SANTO ANTÓNIO
Praça Infante
RUA D'ANTAS
RUA BOMBARDA
RUA CAST. GOV.
SANTA MARIA
Benasfrim
OLD CITY WALLS
DE DESCOBRIMENTOS
To Salema & Sagres
AVENIDA
Meia Praia Beach
FORTRESS
To more beaches
7
WALK ENDS

100 Meters
100 Yards

Atlantic Ocean

ALGARVE

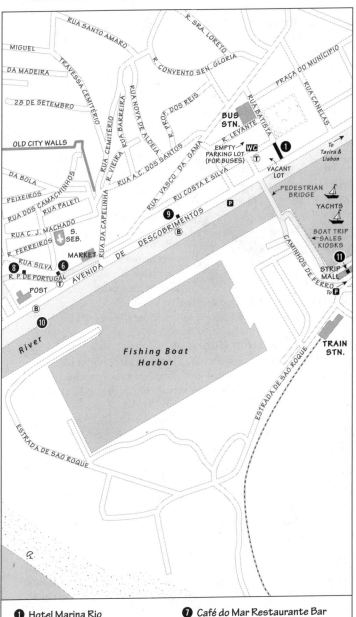

1 Hotel Marina Rio
2 Hotel Riomar
3 Youth Hostel
4 Restaurante Dom Sebastião
5 Restaurante Pescador
6 Casa do Pasto do Zé
7 Café do Mar Restaurante Bar
8 Taquelim Gonçalves House of Regional Sweets
9 Supermarket
10 Promenade & Coastal Boat Tours
11 Bom Dia Boat Trips

## ▲Slave Market Museum (Mercado de Escravos)

This modern **museum,** located on the site of the original Lagos slave market, documents the tragic history of slavery in the region, which began at this very spot in 1444. Displays include 15th-century coins, African ceramics and beads, and a skeleton—one of several sadly found in a nearby rubbish dump (€1.50, Tue-Sun 10:00-12:30 & 14:00-17:30, closed Mon, www.cm-lagos.pt).

In the small **portico** outside, chained slaves were paraded around to be bid on. From 1444 until the mid-1700s, over 100,000

individual people were sold into slavery under these arches. In the early days of Portuguese exploration, the king made a rule that ships needed to bring back dirt, plants, and people from "discovered" lands. Slaves were quarantined for 40 days. Survivors were cleaned up and sold. Under the ceiling are navigational charts showing the slave-trade routes.

• *The square between the slave market and Santa Maria Church is...*

## Praça Infante Dom Henrique

This square honors its namesake, **Henry the Navigator,** with a statue (erected along with the city's fine harborfront promenade in 1960 to celebrate the 500th anniversary of his death; he died just down the coast in Sagres in 1460).

Portugal's age of discovery started in 1415 in Lagos under Prince Henry (before he earned his nickname "the Navigator"). Up to 400 ships would depart on huge royal-sponsored expeditions from this port. The glory days of Lagos lasted through the 1400s, but by 1500 the action shifted to Lisbon. The slave trade enriched the city in the 15th and 16th centuries. Later, Lagos was a tuna-fishing center and the military capital of the Algarve. But the 1755 earthquake/tsunami devastated the city, spelling the end of its importance.

• *From the square, turn right and walk along the old city walls toward the striking fort on the harbor. The* **walls** *of Lagos, measuring nearly two miles, are the longest in the Algarve. Pause at the fortified* **Moorish gate,** *with its stout twin crenelated towers. The first wall here dates from the ninth century. Across the street is the...*

## Fort Ponta da Bandeira

Fort Ponta da Bandeira was a state-of-the-art defense back in the 17th century, built to protect the city against pirates and Spaniards. Today it offers the visitor only stony ramparts and harbor views (€2, Tue-Sun 10:00-12:30 & 14:00-17:30, closed Mon).

• *Continue walking beyond the fort, passing the Lagos Nautical Club (which rents canoes and kayaks), a public WC, and a boardwalk across the sand leading to...*

## Praia da Batata

"Potato Beach" is the most accessible of Lagos' many fine beaches, and a popular student hangout. At low tide, you can enjoy a fascinating beach walk through exotic rocks and tunnels for nearly a mile. (But be careful, as the tide can come in quickly.) At high tide, a stepped and paved path takes you along the beach but higher up, with fine views of remote, photogenic little beaches with striking rock formations.

• *From Praia da Batata, stairs lead up to the recommended **Café do Mar**, which crowns a bluff with wonderful outdoor tables overlooking the harbor and sea.*

# Activities in Lagos

### Lagos Market Hall

The slick and modern market hall faces the harbor as if waiting for the fishermen to unload their catch (as they do almost daily at 8:00 and 11:00; hall open Mon-Sat 9:00-13:00, closed Sun). The Algarve's third-biggest fish market welcomes visitors to peruse an impressive array of fish, all netted within a few miles of town. Upstairs are fresh fruits and vegetables, dried figs, and nuts. You'll also see fun, gifty local products like spicy homemade *piri-piri* sauce and "flower of salt" from Tavira's salt beds, respected all over Europe. Snails *(caracois)*, which come out after rain, are sold by merchants, but their prices are generally undercut by street-sellers.

### ▲Lagos' Promenade

This pedestrian avenue stretches about a mile from the fort to the marina. It's a joy to stroll along the black-and-white patterned cobbles (Portugal's unique *calçada* stonework), with views of palm trees and busy little boats, the occasional sailboat heading out to sea, a soundtrack of gulls and hustlers of various sea activities, and the smell of "the perfume of the Atlantic."

ALGARVE

## Coastal Boat Tours

All over town, you'll be hustled to take a sightseeing cruise. There's plenty of creativity and competition, giving you lots of options. Old fishermen ("who know the nickname of each rock along the coast") sit at anchor on board, while their salespeople on the promenade hawk 45-minute exotic rock-and-cave tours for around €10 (2-person minimum). There are companies specializing in dolphin watching, kayak tours, RIB (high-speed rigid inflatable boat) tours, snorkeling, fishing, and more.

To comparison-shop most easily, you'll find the highest concentration of vendors (and sales pitches) in two places: along the promenade, and lining the marina between the pedestrian bridge and the pink-and-white strip mall. It's actually pleasant to stroll over the bridge and around the marina to consider your options. Some pleasant cafés are in the mall—sip a *sumo de laranja* (fresh orange juice) while observing the comings-and-goings of the yachts.

If you fancy a sailboat trip, **Bom Dia** offers several different tours: a two-hour grotto tour (with a chance to swim) for €25; a half-day BBQ cruise that's basically a grotto tour with a meal for €49; and a three-hour family-friendly fishing trip for €40 (buy tickets at kiosk on the promenade in marina at Lagos 10, WC on board, smart to reserve at least a day ahead in Aug, tel. 282-087-587, www.bomdia-boattrips.com).

## ▲▲Scenic Beaches and Viewpoints

The beaches near Lagos are famed for their dramatic scenery. The soft, sandy-colored land was carved out and artfully shaped by centuries of pounding surf, creating steep strati-fied cliffs and stunning formations just offshore. The easiest choice—giving you a taste of this scenery close to the center—is **Praia da Batata,** just beyond the fort in the heart of town (described at the end of the "Lagos Town Walk," earlier). While smaller and often more crowded, Batata is certainly the handiest for nondrivers.

Other beaches line up along the point just south of town. Along here, **Praia Dona Ana** is perhaps the best combination of scenery (jagged sea stacks) and services (rentable chairs and umbrellas, and a basic restaurant). While it feels (relatively) secluded once you're there, it's tucked below a sprawling resort area with several high-rise hotels. From the big parking lot (pay WC), a wooden staircase takes you down to the beach. Also along this road, **Praia do Camilo** is less busy and less developed—BYO blankets, chairs, and umbrellas.

**Viewpoint:** If you take the beach road to its far end, you'll reach a dusty parking lot at a lighthouse with a tacky café. This popular spot—**Ponta da Piedade**— offers great views down on the dramatic rock formations offshore. Wander (carefully) around the top of the bluff to discover various perspectives on those postcard vistas, which are far more dramatic than the overrated "end of Europe" views from Cape St. Vincent near Sagres. Stairs lead down closer to water level, and "grotto cruise" boat trips offer an even more intimate look at the formations.

**Getting There:** To get there, drivers can follow brown *praias* signs, then track individual beaches (turn-offs individually labeled). Non-drivers can take a long hike to reach the beaches, or hop on the **bus.** Local line #2 departs hourly from along the old town's riverfront embankment (stops are in front of the fish market, at the post office just toward the river from the TI, and just below Henry the Navigator Square) and stops near several beaches (€1.20, buy ticket on board, runs hourly). There's also a **tourist train** that departs from near the old town and loops to the beaches.

## Sleeping in Lagos

Lagos is enjoyable for a resort its size, but it feels very touristy and can be rowdy with young partiers after hours. If that's not your scene—or if you prefer a mellow village experience with even easier beach access (but fewer big-city amenities)—remember that Salema is a short drive, taxi, or bus ride away. My heart lies in Salema, but for some travelers Lagos can be a good choice.

**$$$ Hotel Marina Rio** is big, slick, and comfortable, and faces the marina and the busy main street immediately in front of the bus station. Its 36 modern rooms have all the amenities. Pricier marina views come with noise; somewhat quieter rooms face the bus station in the back. All rooms have twin beds (air-con, elevator, small heated rooftop pool and sun terrace, Avenida dos Descobrimentos, tel. 282-780-830, www.marinario.com, marinario@net. vodafone.pt).

**$ Hotel Riomar,** popular with tour groups, is a dreary, aging, and cheap budget option offering 42 dimly lit rooms in a blocky, 1980s-feeling building. Front-facing rooms come with little balconies but bar noise, while the courtyard-facing rooms are quieter (family rooms, air-con, elevator, Rua Candido dos Reis 83, tel. 282-770-130, www.hotelriomarlagos.com, hotelriomar@sapo.pt).

The **¢ youth hostel** is well-run and nicely located, a couple of blocks above the main drag and near a busy nightlife zone. It offers some budget-priced private rooms and a sunny interior courtyard (Rua Lançarote de Freitas 50, tel. 282-761-970, www.pousadasjuventude.pt, lagos@movijovem.pt).

## Eating in Lagos

You'll find a variety of lively choices for dinner branching out in all directions from Praça Gil Eanes—especially along Rua 25 de Abril. Most offer a similar sampling of grilled fish with plenty of vegetables, but other options range from Italian to Indian. Home-style cooking is likely better closer to the market.

**$$$ Restaurante Dom Sebastião,** with quality cuisine and a huge wine cellar, is busy with expats and tourists ready to indulge. Antonio runs his restaurant in a hands-on way, with thoughtful touches. While the people-watching is great from the outside tables, I like the energy in the air-conditioned interior. Portions are big and you're welcome to split. When shared, the €18 *cataplana* becomes a great value (daily 12:00-22:00, reservations smart, Rua 25 de Abril 20, tel. 282-780-480, www.restaurantedonsebastiao.com).

**$$ Restaurante Pescador,** popular with locals and tourists alike, serves good, inexpensive grilled fish and meat in a simple, bright atmosphere. Portions are large and easily splittable. Hard-working João speaks little English but is eager to please (Tue-Sun 12:00-22:00, until 23:00 in summer, closed Mon, Rua Gil Eanes 6, tel. 282-767-028).

**$$ Casa do Pasto do Zé** is a very traditional, family-run diner facing the harbor next to the market. It's just right if you want to feel like a temporary local and write a poem (daily 12:00-22:00, Rua Portas de Portugal 65, tel. 282-762-038).

**$ Café do Mar Restaurante Bar** is perched on a bluff overlooking the sea and the city, just above the first of the exotic beaches. It's at the end of my town walk and is good for a drink or a bite. There are affordable sandwiches, salads, and omelets; try to sit at the great outdoor tables, not at the nondescript interior seating (daily 10:00-24:00, just above and beyond the fortress overlooking Praia da Batata, tel. 282-788-006).

**Dessert: Taquelim Gonçalves House of Regional Sweets** is the local favorite for fresh-baked pastries, ice cream, and coffee. It offers a fine vantage point on the square for enjoying the scene. Their almond and custard tarts and marzipan are hits (long hours daily, Rua da Porta de Portugal 27, tel. 282-762-882).

Picnics: **Intermarché** supermarket has a wide selection (daily 8:00-21:00, until 22:00 in summer, on the waterfront opposite the marina).

## Lagos Connections

**From Lagos by Train and Bus to: Lisbon** (5 trains/day, 4 hours, transfer in Tunes; 12 buses/day direct, 4 hours), **Évora** (2 trains/day, 5 hours, transfer in Pinhal Novo and Tunes; 2 buses/day direct in July-mid-Sept, otherwise transfer in Albufeira, 5 hours), **Tavira** (8 trains/day, 3 hours, some change in Faro but others simply have long wait there—ask conductor; 6 buses/day, 4 hours, transfer in Faro). Confirm times locally. Train info: tel. 808-208-208, www.cp.pt. Bus info: tel. 289-899-760 or 282-762-944, www.eva-bus.com or www.algarvebus.info.

**From Lagos to Salema:** Take a bus (every 1-2 hours, fewer on weekends, 30 minutes) or a taxi (€30, 20 minutes). In Lagos, to get from the train station to the bus station, exit the station toward the pink-and-white shopping mall. Turn left just before the mall and follow the pleasant pedestrian promenade along the marina, then cross the pedestrian drawbridge. Once across the bridge, jog right to find the bus station. Before heading to Salema, pick up return bus schedules and train schedules for your next destination.

**Connecting Lagos and Sevilla, Spain, by Bus:** There are four buses per day in each direction during summer, and two per day off-season (about 5.5 hours from Lagos bus station to Sevilla's Plaza de Armas bus station). Ask the TI or a local travel agency for the latest bus schedule, or check www.algarvebus.info or www.eva-bus.com. In summer (May-Oct), it's important to book your ticket a day or two in advance. Note that Spanish time is one hour ahead of Portuguese time, so the time you arrive in Lagos is about four and a half hours after you depart Sevilla, and the time you arrive in Sevilla is about six and a half hours after departing Lagos. This bus also stops in Tavira en route—a pleasant town and a nice midway point.

# Tavira

Straddling a river, with a lively park, chatty locals, and boats that share its waterfront center, Tavira (tah-VEE-rah) is a low-rise, easygoing alternative—and a refreshing break—from the more aggressive Algarve resorts. That's because Tavira is a real, living town. Whitewashed, red-roofed, and cobbled, it feels close to Morocco... because it is. More than a glitzy

beach town, Tavira is a mini-Évora, with real culture that runs deeper than its beaches.

Because Tavira has good connections by bus and train (it's on the trans-Algarve train line, with frequent departures both east and west), the town is more accessible than Salema. If you're driving from Sevilla to Salema, it's the perfect midway stop on the four-hour trip (just two miles off the freeway). You can also get to Tavira by bus from Sevilla.

You'll see many churches and fine bits of Renaissance architecture sprinkled throughout the town. These clues are evidence that 500 years ago, Tavira was the largest town on the Algarve (with 1,500 dwellings according to a 1530 census) and an important base for Portuguese adventurers in Africa.

The silting up of its harbor, a plague in 1645, the offshore 1755 earthquake, and the shifting away of its once-lucrative tuna industry left Tavira in a long decline. Today, the town has a wistful charm and lives off its tourists.

## Orientation to Tavira

Tavira (pop. 26,000) straddles the Rio Gilão two miles from the Atlantic. Everything of sightseeing and transportation importance is on the south bank. A clump of historic sights—the ruined castle and main church—fills its tiny fortified hill and tangled Moorish lanes. But today, the action is outside the old fortifications along the riverside Praça da República square and the adjacent, shaded, bench-filled park (with the old market hall at the park's far end). Just beyond that is the boat to Tavira's beach island.

Tavira's south bank is congested with tourists; the old pedestrian-only Roman Bridge leads from Praça da República to the more local-feeling north bank (with most of the evening and restaurant action). With the exception of Clive's fun, fascinating camera obscura show, the town's sights are pretty dull.

## TOURIST INFORMATION

The TI is on the main square, Praça da República, right across from City Hall. They charge €0.50 for a helpful town leaflet (daily 9:00-17:30, may close for lunch off-season, Praça da República 5, tel. 281-322-511).

## ARRIVAL IN TAVIRA

**By Train:** The train station is a 15-minute walk from the town center. To get there, leave the station via the roundabout and follow the signpost to *centro* (center). Follow this road downhill to the river and Praça da República (or take a cab from the station for around €4). The riverside bus station is three blocks from the town center; simply follow the river into town.

**By Car:** Drivers can park on the street in much of the old town. It's pay-and-display for up to two hours (€0.40/hour, Mon-Fri 9:00-19:00, Sat 9:00-14:00, Sun free, look for *zona pago* signs, pay at blue boxes marked *caixa*, change required). Free parking is available farther from the center, including some large lots at the western end of town (near the bus station and fish market).

## HELPFUL HINTS

**Bike Rental: Abilio Bikes** has a great selection, including electric and road bikes, and also run bike tours (basic bike-€7/day, hotel delivery possible for an extra charge; open Mon-Sat 9:00-19:00—except may be closed Sat 13:00-15:00 in summer, closed Sun; Rua João Vaz Corte Real 23A, tel. 281-323-467, www.abiliobikes.com).

**Taxi:** A taxi stand is across the Roman Bridge on Praça Dr. António Padinha; another is in the town center, near the old cinema.

**Shopping Tips:** You can buy your own copper *cataplana* **pot** for about €37 at the yellow hardware store at the far end of Rua Alexandre Herculano (behind City Hall). And for a wonderful selection of port wine and other Portuguese drinks, visit the helpful **Soares Wine Shop** (Mon-Sat 10:00-24:00 in summer, otherwise 10:00-19:00, closed Sun, facing market hall at Rua José Pires Padinha 66).

# Sights in Tavira

I've linked the sights in a logical walking order starting near the TI on Praça da República (the town square).

### Old Town Gate

This unimpressive gate (to the left of the TI) is one of the few sections left from Tavira's 16th-century wall. Check out the gate's

ALGARVE

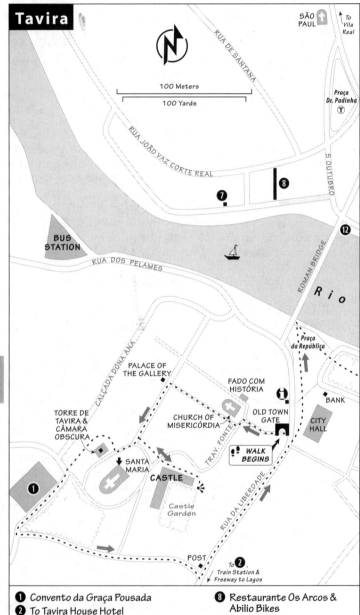

# Tavira

SÃO PAUL

To Vila Real

Praça Dr. Padinha

RUA DE SANTANA

100 Meters
100 Yards

RUA JOÃO VAZ CORTE REAL

5 OUTUBRO

8

7

BUS STATION

RUA DOS PELAMES

ROMAN BRIDGE

Rio

12

CALÇADA DONA ANA

PALACE OF THE GALLERY

Praça da República

FADO COM HISTÓRIA

BANK

TORRE DE TAVIRA & CÂMARA OBSCURA

CHURCH OF MISERICÓRDIA

OLD TOWN GATE

CITY HALL

TRAV. FONTE

SANTA MARIA

1

CASTLE

WALK BEGINS

Castle Garden

RUA DA LIBERDADE

POST

To 2
Train Station & Freeway to Lagos

1 Convento da Graça Pousada
2 To Tavira House Hotel
3 Residencial Marés
4 Residencial Lagôas
5 Hotel Princesa do Gilão
6 Aquasul Restaurante
7 Beira Rio Restaurante

8 Restaurante Os Arcos & Abilio Bikes
9 Supermarket
10 Pasteleria Ramos
11 Soares Wine Shop
12 Tourist Train

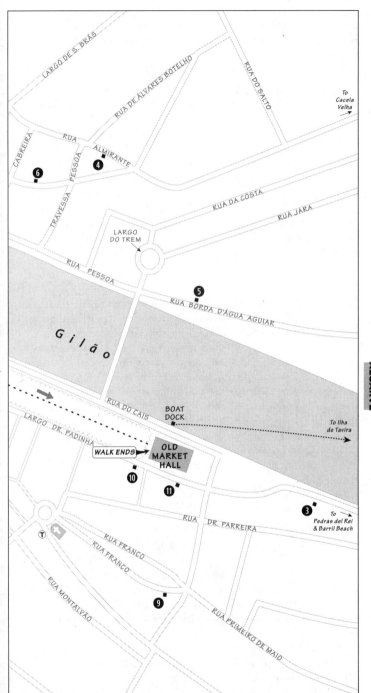

crown and spheres—meant to remind visitors that they are in the kingdom of Portugal—and the holes for bars that once locked the door.

• *At the top of the lane, above the gate, stands a church.*

### Church of Misericórdia

While Tavira has 21 churches, there's only one active priest. Most of the churches—including this one—are open primarily as tourist attractions. Dating from 1541, this church's Renaissance facade is considered the finest in the Algarve. Inside, you'll see a multitude of blue-and-white tile panels that illustrate how to lead a good Christian life and an over-the-top, gold-plated altar. A zealous attendant will make sure you don't take any photos. Throughout the year, the church transforms into a beautiful concert venue. Ask the attendant if any performances are scheduled during your visit.

**Cost and Hours:** Church entry free, generally Mon-Sat 9:30-13:00 & 14:00-17:30, closed Sun.

• *Around the right side of the gate is...*

### Fado com História

This humble but endearing fado show, in a tasteful little theater, is the brainchild of local *fadistas* who grew tired of performing for unappreciative crowds in local restaurants. Their goal is to share the history and beauty of fado with tourists, with a little explanation (in English) before each song. Five times a day, they show an insightful 10-minute film about the history of the form, then perform for about 20 minutes (two guitarists and a singer). While the fado shows in Lisbon and Coimbra are better quality, this is worth considering if it's your only chance to sample Portugal's most beloved musical form.

**Cost and Hours:** €5, 5 performances/day (schedule posted at door), closed Sun and Aug, Rua Damião de Brito Vasconcelos 4, mobile 968-774-613.

• *Back in front of the church, head up the stepped lane on its left side. At the top of the stairs is the...*

### Palace of the Gallery

This 17th-century Baroque palace, nearly the town's highest point, is nicknamed "Tavira's Acropolis." It's the biggest private mansion in town and houses an exhibition center, open to the public, with rotating themes: contemporary art or Tavira's maritime history. Even if you don't go into the museum itself, pop inside the door to see some Phoenician ritual pits, visible through glass covers on the foyer floor (€2, Tue-Sat 9:00-16:30, closed Sun-Mon).

• *Facing the palace, turn left and continue climbing uphill to the big Church of Santa Maria. Before visiting there, look to your left, where you can go through a door in what's left of the castle, and into the...*

### Castle Garden

The base of the castle wall is supposedly Neolithic, while later in-habitants—the Phoenicians in the eighth century B.C., the Moors in the eighth century A.D., and the Portuguese in the thirteenth century—added their own layers. The castle grounds are now a fragrant garden, offering a fine city view. Overlooking the city, notice Tavira's unique "treasury" rooftops—a little roof for each room of a building. Tour guides have two explanations for this: The small roofs were inspired by visions brought home from Asia by local explorers. Or they are the result of this region having a shortage of big trees and therefore using small timbers for beams. (Portugal has long been short on timbers, naming its major colony "Brazil," the Portuguese word for a very valuable type of wood—apparently the colonists were particularly excited about that raw material.) Gaze to the right and see tower-wall remnants sprouting up between houses.

**Cost and Hours:** Free, Mon-Fri 8:00-17:00, Sat-Sun from 10:00, daily until 19:00 in July-Sept.

• *Now visit the church that dominates the square out front. You'll find the small tourist entrance on the right side, as you face it.*

### Church of Santa Maria

Once a mosque, this church was transformed in the 13th century. Buy a ticket and head inside. On the right side (from where you enter) are two inset chapels. The second one—with blue and yellow tiles—is the only part of the church that survived the 1755 earthquake. The other chapel has fine pink columns. The "marble" is actually painted wood, since there was no marble in the Algarve and no money to import it. Facing the church's main altar, notice the little row of seven red crosses on the right side of the apse (inaccessible to the public). These mark the remains of seven near-legendary Reconquista heroes who were ambushed and killed by Moorish forces during a truce—inspiring the Portuguese forces to take up arms and conquer Tavira. Your church ticket also includes a small museum of two rooms with crude but beautiful art.

**Cost and Hours:** €1.50 includes both church and museum, Mon-Fri 10:00-13:00 & 14:00-17:00, Sat 10:00-13:00, closed Sun.

• *Next to the church, you can't miss the tall, white water tower, which has been converted into my favorite sight in town...*

### ▲Camera Obscura in the Tavira Tower
### (Torre de Tavira and Câmara Obscura)

This 1931 water tower has been converted into an elevator-accessible viewpoint, with a darkroom designed to accommodate an early optical device called a camera obscura. This centuries-old technology uses nothing more than a pinhole of light, mirrors, and a well-calibrated lens (from 1899) to project a huge, live image of the town onto a circular canvas. Clive, the British owner, narrates an entertaining and informative 15-minute, 360-degree view of Tavira—a delightful orientation to the entire town, from the comfort of a cool dark room. With his levers and pulleys, Clive masterfully zooms in and out on live images of people walking across the Roman Bridge or boats plying the river. It's not "rain or shine"—without the sun, there's no image. He's planning to open a planetarium at the base of the tower in 2017.

**Cost and Hours:** €3.50; July-Sept Mon-Fri 10:00-17:00, Sat until 13:00, closed Sun; off-season Mon-Fri 10:00-17:00 or 16:00 depending on weather, closed Sat-Sun; www.torredetavira.com.

• *Just beyond the camera obscura is the recommended convent-turned-pousada (Convento da Graça). Go down the little lane directly in front of the pousada, then turn left on Rua da Liberdade, which takes you back to the main square and TI, where we started this walk. Very nearby are a couple more sights. First, just past the TI is the...*

## Roman Bridge

The "Roman Bridge" may not actually be Roman, but at least it was here when the Moors came. The current structure is from 1657, with parts rebuilt after it was knocked over in a 1989 flood. Since it was replaced, it's been a pedestrians-only option for crossing between the two parts of town.

• *Back on the south side of the river, stretching along the riverbank from the TI is the inviting...*

## Riverside Park and Old Market Hall

This is where old folks gossip and children play. Walk past the bandstand to the old market hall. In the 1990s, this was a noisy, colorful fish and produce market. Today, the hall has gift shops, cafés, and eateries with riverside seating.

Beyond the market hall are a few fishing boats. Fishermen are weathering tough times as the "natural park" classification of the coastal areas makes aggressive netting illegal, and Spanish fishermen are selling their catch for far less.

**Nearby: Pasteleria Ramos,** near the market end of the park opposite a green kiosk, produces sweet and sticky almond cakes—

perfect with a *galão* (milky coffee) at their outside tables (daily 8:00-24:00).

# Sights near Tavira

### ▲Tavira's Beach Island (Ilha de Tavira)

Tavira's beach island is a hit with visitors. Ilha de Tavira is an almost treeless, six-mile-long sandbar with a campground, several restaurants, and a sprawling beach. It's an enjoyable boat trip even if you just go round-trip without getting off.

**Getting There:** In summer, it's easiest to hop on a **shuttle boat** (€2 round-trip, June-Sept about hourly 8:00-20:00, timetable at TI, departs from dock just past the old market hall). Off-season, continue a bit farther along the riverbank to find the much pricier but year-round **water taxi** (rates vary but always much more than the shuttle boat, mobile 966-615-071).

The third option—also year-round—is to walk to the **Quatro Aguas ferry.** It's a longer but pleasant riverside stroll: Keep going past the market hall and first boat dock, then take the series of causeways past the salt pans and fish farms (about a mile all together, no shade) out to Quatro Aguas. From here, a five-minute ferry shuttles sunbathers to the beach island (€1.50 one-way, runs constantly year-round with demand, last trip at 19:00 or near midnight in high season to accommodate diners). If you're not up for the walk, you can get to Quatro Aguas by bus, taxi, bike, or cheesy tourist train (tourist train also includes an hour-long tour of Tavira's highlights, one loop—€4, all-day—€6, departs from across the Roman Bridge).

### ▲Barril Beach

This fine beach resort is about three miles from Tavira. Walk, rent a bike, or take a city bus to Pedras del Rei, and then catch the little train (usually runs year-round), or walk 10 minutes through Ria Formosa Natural Park to the beach. Get details at the TI.

### Cacela Velha

This tiny village lies through the orange groves about eight miles east of Tavira (half-mile off the main road and the bus route). It sits happily ignored on a hill with its fort, church, one restaurant, a few *quartos* and apartments, and a beach with the open sea just over the sandbar a short row across its lagoon. The restaurant—**$$ Casa De Igreja**—serves sausages *(chouricos)* and cheese *(queijo)* specialties fried at your table, along with local oysters and *vinho verde* (daily July-Sept, March-June weekends only, closed Oct-Feb, tel. 281-952-126, Patricio speaks English). If you're driving, swing by, if only to enjoy the coastal view and to imagine how nice the Algarve would be if people like you and me had never discovered it.

**ALGARVE**

# Sleeping in Tavira

In Tavira, prices usually shoot up in August.

**$$$$ Convento da Graça** is a *pousada* (government-sponsored historic inn) with 36 elegantly appointed rooms inside a renovated Augustine convent. The cloister is perfect for relaxing, and there's even a pool if you can't tear yourself away to go to the beach. It's at the top of the Old Town, near the castle ruins and camera obscura, a five-minute walk above the main square (air-con, elevator, Rua D. Paio Peres Correia, tel. 210-407-680, www.pousadas. pt, recepcao.conventograca@pestana.com).

**$$$ Tavira House Hotel** is a charming and classy nine-room boutique B&B filling a lovingly renovated army officer's house from 1860. Manager Christophe has given the place a Moroccan flair, with splashes of bright color—especially on the inviting roof terrace. It's out of the busy central area, but just a five-minute walk away (air-con, Rua Miguel Bombardo 47, tel. 281-370-307, www. tavirahousehotel.com).

**$$ Residencial Marés,** on the busy side of the river amid all the strolling and café ambience, is an endearing throwback. Dated but well-maintained, with a dark-wood-and-earth-tone-tile ambience, it has 24 good rooms, a friendly reception, an upscale restaurant, and an inviting rooftop terrace with lounge chairs. Some rooms have balconies overlooking the river, but also come with a little noise from cafés immediately below (air-con, laundry service, sauna extra, Rua José Pires Padinha 134/140—just beyond old market hall, tel. 281-325-815, www.residencialmares.com, maresresidencial@mail.telepac.pt).

**$ Residencial Lagôas** is homey, colorful, and a block off the river. Friendly Claudia and Miquel offer 17 rooms, a communal refrigerator, laundry washboard privileges, and a rooftop patio with a view made for wine and candles (RS%, cheaper rooms with shared bath, no breakfast, cash only, most rooms with air-con, lots of stairs, Rua Almirante Candido dos Reis 24, tel. 281-328-243, al.lagoas@hotmail.com).

**$ Hotel Princesa do Gilão** is a low-energy, budget-priced last resort, offering 22 small, basic rooms in a big concrete building right along the river's north bank. Choose between riverfront or quiet rooms on the back with a terrace (family rooms, air-con, elevator, Rua Borda de Agua de Aguiar 10, cross Roman Bridge and turn right along river, tel. 281-325-171, www.princesa-do-gilao. tavira.hotels-pt.net, geral@hotelprincesadogilao.com).

# Eating in Tavira

Tavira is filled with reasonable restaurants. Most places on the south bank are more touristy; lively, top-end places face the riverbank just beyond the old market hall. Your best bets lie just across the river and inland a couple of blocks (where hole-in-the-wall options offer more fish per dollar). It's fun to walk around and scout out your options; while the ones I recommend are a good start, the choices are ample and locals love to give tips. Trust their advice.

**$$$ Aquasul**—mod, bright, cheery, on a back lane, and open only for dinner—serves a modern fusion of Italian, Mediterranean, and international dishes, including nightly vegetarian specials, good pizzas out of the wood oven, and tasty homemade desserts. Reserve ahead here, particularly if you want to sit out on the pedestrian lane rather than in the less appealing, cave-like interior (Tue-Sat 18:30-22:30, closed Sun-Mon, tucked down an easy-to-miss paved lane at Rua Dr. A. S. Carvalho 13, tel. 281-325-166). If it's full or doesn't do it for you, check out several other appealing places spilling out onto the same street; **$$$ O Tonel** is popular (at #6-8).

**On the River:** For dining along the river, these popular places offer good value (if not top cuisine). To reach both, cross the Roman Bridge, turn left, go through the tunnel, and look for tables on the waterfront. **$$ Beira Rio** is Irish-owned, with a lively Irish pub next door. The menu is an odd mix of international pub-grub standards and lots of local fish (daily 12:00-23:00, Rua Borda d'Agua da Asseca 46, tel. 281-323-165). A bit closer to the Roman Bridge, **$$ Restaurante Os Arcos** is the lowbrow option, with cheap and tasty grilled fish served at rustic little riverside tables—but I'd skip the nondescript old dining hall (Mon-Sat 12:00-15:00 & 19:00-22:00, closed Sun, Rua João Vaz Corte Real 15, tel. 963-583-527).

**Supermarket: Minipreço** has all the groceries you'll need for a good picnic. It's centrally located, a couple of blocks inland from the market hall (daily 9:00-21:00, Rua D. Marcelino Franco 40).

# Tavira Connections

**From Tavira by Train and Bus to: Lisbon** (5 trains/day, 4-5 hours, transfer in Faro, arrive at Oriente; 5 direct buses/day, 4 hours), **Lagos** (8 trains/day, 3 hours, some change in Faro while others simply have a long wait there—ask conductor; 6 buses/day, 4 hours, change in Faro), **Sevilla** (4 buses/day in summer, 2/day in winter, 3-4 hours, check TI or bus station to verify schedules, buy ticket a day or two in advance May-Oct, note that Spain is an hour ahead when calculating arrival times). Luggage storage is not available. Train info: tel. 808-208-208, www.cp.pt. Bus info: tel. 281-322-546, www.eva-bus.com or www.algarvebus.info.

## ROUTE TIPS FOR DRIVERS

**Lisbon to the Algarve** (185 miles, 3.5 hours): A modern freeway, light traffic, and the glory of waking up on the Algarve make doing this drive in the evening after a full day in Lisbon a good option.

Following the blue *Sul Ponte* signs from central Lisbon, drive south over Lisbon's 25th of April Bridge. A short detour just over the bridge takes you to the giant concrete statue of Cristo Rei (Christ in Majesty). Then stay on the A-2 expressway as it heads east toward Alentejo, then bends south toward the Algarve. You'll pass through cork groves, and finally—about 1.5 hours after leaving Lisbon—you'll run into the A-22 expressway (which runs east-west, parallel to the coast). At the A-22 junction, you can choose to head west to Lagos (and beyond it, Salema and Sagres) or east to Tavira and, eventually, Spain (signed for *Espanha*).

If heading to Salema, stay on A-22 to the Lagos/Vila do Bispo exit, and follow signs to *Vila do Bispo* and *Sagres*. Pay close attention to spot the turnoff for Salema before Vila do Bispo.

**Algarve to Sevilla, Spain** (175 miles, 3 hours): Drive east along the Algarve. It's a 1.5-hour drive from Salema to Tavira, with some hills crowned by rotting windmills and others by mobile-phone towers. From Lagos, hit the freeway (A-22, direction: Lisboa/Faro, then Espanha) to Tavira. Leaving Tavira, follow the signs to *Espanha*. You'll cross the bridge into Spain (where it's one hour later) and glide effortlessly (1.5 hours by freeway) into Sevilla. Be aware that there is an electronic tolling system on the A-22 highway from the Spanish border to Lagos.

# ÉVORA

Deep in the heart of Portugal, in the sizzling, arid plains of the southern province of Alentejo, historic Évora (EH-voh-rah) has been a cultural oasis for 2,000 years. With an untouched provincial atmosphere, a fascinating whitewashed old town, museums, a cathedral, a chapel of bones, and even a Roman temple, Évora (pop. 57,000) stands proudly amid groves of cork and olive trees.

From Romans to Moors to Portuguese kings, this little town has a big history. Évora was once a Roman town (second century B.C. to fourth century A.D.), important because of its wealth of wheat and silver, as well as its location on a trade route to Rome. You'll still see Roman sights, including several fragments of an aqueduct and the towering columns of a temple. But most of Évora's Roman past is buried under the houses and hotels of today (often uncovered by accident when plumbing work needs to be done in basements).

The Moors ruled Évora from the 8th to the 12th century. Around the year 1000, Muslim nobles divided the caliphate into small city-states (like Lisbon), with Évora as this region's capital. And during its glory years (15th-16th century), Évora was favored by Portuguese kings, often serving as the home of King João III (1502-1557, Manuel I's son who presided over Portugal's peak of power...and its first decline).

Évora—a traditional, conservative city with a small-town feel—reopened its historic university about 40 years ago. You'll see plenty of black-caped students here, along with lots of retirees, but comparatively few 30- to 40-year olds. There's not much to keep graduates around, and this generation gap gives the town an intriguing mix of old and new—strong traditions underlie its youthful bustle.

## PLANNING YOUR TIME

With easy bus and train connections to Lisbon (buses almost hourly, four trains a day; both take 1.5 hours), Évora makes a decent day trip from Portugal's capital city. Better yet, spend the night—ideally en route to or from the Algarve. Along the way, drivers can explore dusty droves of olive groves, scruffy seas of peeled cork trees, and some dramatic prehistoric monuments.

A day in Évora is enough to fully experience the town. Follow my self-guided walk outlined on page 216, have a quick lunch, see the remaining sights (cathedral, Chapel of Bones, university), and enjoy a leisurely, top-notch dinner. Late in the evening, stroll the back streets and ponder life, like the old-timers of Évora seem to do so expertly.

# Orientation to Évora

Évora's Old Town, contained within a medieval wall, is surrounded by the sprawling newer part of town. The walled center (where you'll spend virtually all your time) is large and quite hilly—it takes about 20 minutes to cross from one end of town to the other, on cobbled streets that are anything but straight. The major sights—the Roman Temple and the cathedral—crowd together at the Old Town's highest point. A subtle yet still-powerful charm is contained within the medieval walls. Find it by losing yourself in the quiet lanes of Évora's far corners.

## TOURIST INFORMATION

Pick up a free map at the TI on the main square at Praça do Giraldo 73 (April-Oct daily 9:00-19:00, Nov-March Mon-Fri 9:00-18:00, Sat-Sun 10:00-14:00 & 15:00-18:00, tel. 266-777-071, www.cm-evora.pt/en).

## ARRIVAL IN ÉVORA

**By Bus:** The bus station is west of the center, on Avenida São Sebastião. To reach the town center, take a short taxi ride (€5) or a 10-minute walk (exit station right, continue straight all the way into town, past the cemetery wall and through the city gates at the halfway point).

**By Train:** The train station is south of the center, on Avenida Dr. Barahona. To get to the center, take a taxi (€7), or walk a long 25 minutes up Avenida Dr. Barahona, continuing straight on Rua da República after you enter the city walls.

**By Car:** Drivers will find Évora's Old Town frustrating because of its tiny one-way streets. Park in one of the big, free parking lots that circle the town just outside the walls (see map on page 215 for locations). The green-and-white Trevo shuttle bus (see below) serves the parking lots and gets you near most hotels, or—if you're packing light—you can walk (though some streets can be steeper than maps suggest).

## HELPFUL HINTS
**Exchange Rate:** €1 = about $1.10
**Country Calling Code:** 351 (see page 422 for dialing instructions)
**Taxis:** Cabs wait on the main square (€3.90 minimum for 2.5 miles—4 kilometers—likely the farthest you'd go in compact Évora).
**Shuttle Bus:** The blue line on the streets marks the route of the green-and-white Trevo shuttle bus that circles through the town, offering tourists easy transport to and from the parking lots outside the walls. Hop on for a city joyride (€1); they stop for anyone who waves.

# Tours in Évora

### Walking Tour
A group of local guides offers excellent two-hour city walks every morning, departing from the TI at 10:00 (€15, 2-person minimum, call ahead to confirm tour will run, mobile 963-702-392, info@alentejoguides.com). The tour hits the sights described in this chapter, but it's a great opportunity to connect with a local and enliven your visit. They are also happy to schedule tours at other times (€95, 2-person minimum).

### Bus Tours
A bus tour is a good option if you want to see the prehistoric sights near Évora, since getting there by public transport is nearly impossible. **Ebora Megalithica Guided Tours** runs an interesting three-hour minivan tour led by archaeologist Mário to Cromeleque dos Almendres, the standing stone of Menhir dos Almendres, and the Zambujeiro burial mound (€25, Mon-Sat at 10:00 and 14:30, no tours Sun, 6-person maximum, reserve a day ahead, mobile 964-808-337, www.eboramegalithica.com, eboramegalithica@gmail.com).

**RSI** offers several half-day bus and minivan tours into the surrounding countryside. Their "Megalithic Circuit Tour" visits the main prehistoric sights, including Cromeleque dos Almendres (€30/half-day, 2-person minimum, discounts for larger groups, smart to reserve a day ahead, tel. 266-747-871, www.rsi-viagens. com, info.evora@rsi-viagens.com).

**ÉVORA**

AQUEDUCT

CIRCULAR A MURALHA

RUA DO MURO

RUA DO MURO

R-114-4

RUA DE CHARTRES

CITY WALLS

AVENIDA DE LISBOA

RUA DOS PENEDOS

AV. SÃO JOÃO BOSCO

To Bus Station

AV. SÃO SEBASTIÃO

ÉVORA

Cemetery

AVENIDA PEREIRA

CITY WALLS

To Megalithic Sites & Lisbon

N-114    AV. ESPANCA

N-380    R. DE VIANA

E-802

BULLRING

Public Garden

AV. GEN.

FORMER ROYAL PALACE

Praça 1 de Maio

ST. FRANCIS & BONE CHAPEL

RUA ROMÃO RAMALHO

RUA DE BERNARDO DE MATOS

RUA DO RAMUNDO

TV. DE PALMEIRA

RUA DOS MERCADORES

RUA DA MOEDA

RUA DE SERPA PINTO

RUA DOS TOUROS

WALK BEGINS & ENDS

Praça do Giraldo

ST. ANTÃO

MILHEIRA

R. DA CAL BRANCA

R. SÃO CRISTÓVÃO

RUA DO TEATRO

R. SÃO DOMINGOS

PEREIRA

MENDES

R. SANTA CATARINA

R. DE DEUS

R. DE CIMA

NOVA

TOWN HALL

POST

Praça do Sertório

SALVADOR

OLIVENÇA

R. JESUS

CORREDOURA

R. MOURARIA

INVERNO

RUA DE JANEIRO

R. FONTES

RESENDE

MORENAS

R. DE AVIZ

SERPE

PASSARINHO

CANO

CARDEAL

NOBRES

SIMÕES

R. OLIVAL

R. MONIZ

R. MOSTARDEIRA

R. DA RODA

RUA SANTA MARIA

Praça Aguiar

R. RAMALHO

R. TRINADADE

R. CALVÁRIO

R. REIS DONZELAS

TORRES

ARMEIRO

CONDESSA

LAGARES

2   3   15   11   14   19   10   13   12   7   8   16   6   17   4   21   23   9

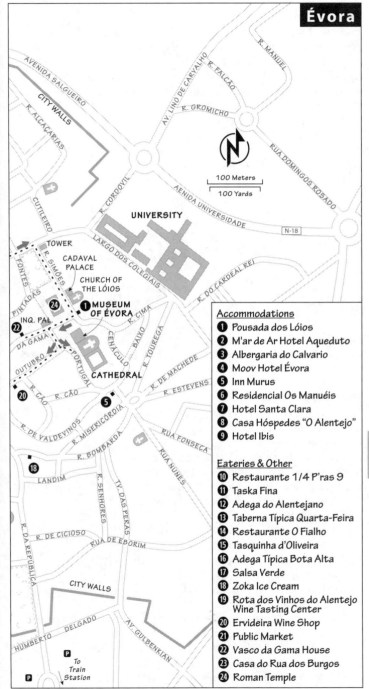

# Évora

100 Meters
100 Yards

CITY WALLS

UNIVERSITY

TOWER
CADAVAL PALACE
CHURCH OF THE LÓIOS
MUSEUM OF ÉVORA
INQ. PAL
CATHEDRAL

CITY WALLS

To Train Station

## Accommodations
1. Pousada dos Lóios
2. M'ar de Ar Hotel Aqueduto
3. Albergaria do Calvario
4. Moov Hotel Évora
5. Inn Murus
6. Residencial Os Manuéis
7. Hotel Santa Clara
8. Casa Hóspedes "O Alentejo"
9. Hotel Ibis

## Eateries & Other
10. Restaurante 1/4 P'ras 9
11. Taska Fina
12. Adega do Alentejano
13. Taberna Típica Quarta-Feira
14. Restaurante O Fialho
15. Tasquinha d'Oliveira
16. Adega Típica Bota Alta
17. Salsa Verde
18. Zoka Ice Cream
19. Rota dos Vinhos do Alentejo Wine Tasting Center
20. Ervideira Wine Shop
21. Public Market
22. Vasco da Gama House
23. Casa do Rua dos Burgos
24. Roman Temple

ÉVORA

## Local Guides

Professor **Libânio Murteira Reis**—who has a passion for his native Alentejo region and loves to share it with others—organizes town and regional tours; he'll even take you around in his car (€120/half-day, €220/day for a family up to 4, transport—when required—and admission fees not included, confirm price on reserving, mobile 917-236-025, but best to contact via email at m.murteira@mail.telepac.pt, www.evora-mm.pt).

**Maria José Pires** does walking tours of Évora as well as car tours of the surrounding area (€95/half-day, €180/day, price of car tours varies with distance, mobile 917-232-147, m-jose-pires@hotmail.com).

# Évora Walk

Évora's walled city is compact, and its key sights are all within a five-minute walk of the main square, Praça do Giraldo (PRA-suh doo zhee-RAHL-doo). This self-guided walk takes about an hour (longer if you visit sights). If it's going to be a hot day, go early in the morning.

• Start at Évora's main square.

## Praça do Giraldo

This square was the market during the Moorish period, and to this day, it remains a center of commerce and conviviality for country folk who come to Évora for their weekly shopping. Until recently, the square hosted a traditional cattle-and-produce market. While ranchers and farmers no longer gather in the square to make deals, old-timers still gravitate here out of habit.

Notice the *C.M. Évora* board (opposite the TI, near the start of Rua Cinco de Outubro), where people gather to see community death notices. You'll see the initials "C.M.E."—Câmara Municipal (municipality) de Évora—all over town, from lampposts to manhole covers.

The square is named for Giraldo the Fearless, the Christian knight who led a surprise attack and retook Évora from the Moors in 1165. As thanks, Giraldo was made governor of the town, and he's become the symbol of the city. (Évora's coat of arms is a knight on a horse, usually walking over two beheaded Moors; see it crowning the lampposts.) On this square, all that's left of several centuries of Moorish rule is their artistry, evidenced by the wrought-iron balconies of the buildings that ring the square. You'll also spot the occasional, distinctive Mudejar "keyhole" window throughout the town.

King João III lived in Évora off and on for 30 years. The TI is inside the **palace** where the king's guests used to stay, but others weren't treated as royally. A fervent proponent of the Inquisition, João was king when its first victims were burned as heretics on this square in 1543.

Speaking of the Inquisition, until the 16th century, the area behind the TI was the **Jewish quarter.** At the time, it was believed that the Bible prohibited Christians from charging interest for loans. Jews did the moneylending instead, and the streets in the Jewish quarter still bear names related to finance, such as Rua da Moeda (Money Street) and Rua dos Mercadores (Merchants' Street).

The characteristic **arcades** you see all around the square suit the weather, providing shelter in the winter and shade in the summer.

The Roman triumphal arch that once stood on this square was demolished in the 16th century to make way for the looming **Church of Santo Antão.** In front of the church is a 16th-century marble fountain— once an important water source for the town (fed by the end of the aqueduct we'll see in a minute) and now a popular hangout for young and old.

Radiating out from this town hub, in every direction, are traditionally decorated cobbled streets. Évora has strictly preserved the old center, and works hard to be people-friendly and inviting. The charming colors you see are traditional in Alentejo: Yellow trim is believed to repel evil spirits, and blue actually does keep away flies. Monster garbage cans hide under elegant smaller ones; at night, trucks lift entire hunks of sidewalk to empty them. Jacaranda trees—imported from Brazil 200 years ago—provide shade through the summer and purple flowers in the spring.

• *Leave the square on Rua Cinco de Outubro (across from the TI). On the first corner, Courelas da Torre is a good little shop for gifty gourmet goodies from the region (daily 10:30-19:30). Outside, note how the back of the shop incorporates the old Roman-Arab wall. From here, head left (past Mr. Pickwick's Restaurante) on Alcárcova de Cima. A few steps*

## Alentejo Region

Southeastern Portugal is very sunny and very dry. The rolling plains of the Alentejo (ah-len-TAY-zhoo) are dotted with large orchards and estates, Stone Age monoliths, Roman aqueducts, Moorish-looking whitewashed villages, and thick-walled, medieval Christian castles.

During the Christian reconquest of the country, Alentejo was the war zone. When Christian conquerors defeated the Muslims, they turned over huge tracts of recaptured land to the care of soldier-monks. These recipients came from various religious-military orders, including the Knights Templar and the Order of Christ (which Prince Henry the Navigator once headed). Évora was governed by the House of Avis, which produced the kings of Portugal's Age of Discovery.

Despite its royal past, the Alentejo (the land "beyond the River Tejo") is the unpretentious terrain of farmers. Having been irrigated since Roman and Moorish times, the region is a major producer of wheat, cattle, wine...and trees. You'll see cork oak trees (green leaves, knotted trunks, red underbark of recently harvested trunks), other types of oak (native to the country, once used to build explorers' caravels), olive (dusty green-silver leaves, major export crop), and eucalyptus (tall, cough drop-smelling trees imported from Australia, grown for pulp).

Today, the Alentejo region is known for being extraordinarily traditional, and it is even considered backward by snooty Lisboans. The people of Alentejo don't mind being the butt of jokes. My friend from Évora said it was the mark of a people's character to be able to laugh at themselves. He asked me, "How can you tell a worker is done for the day in Alentejo?" I didn't know. He said, "When he takes his hands out of his pockets." He continued more philosophically: "In your land, time is money. Here in Alentejo, time is time. We take things slow and enjoy ourselves." I'm impressed when a region that others are inclined to insult has a strong local pride.

*farther on, you'll see another portion of a Roman wall built into the buildings on your right.*

## Roman Remnants

A series of modern windows shows more of the Roman wall, which used to surround what is now the inner core of the town. Through the last window, you can see the red paint of a Roman villa built over by the wall. If you look at your town map, you'll notice how the Roman wall, which surrounded the ancient city, left its footprint in the circle of streets defining the city core. The bulk of the wall that currently encircles Évora is from the 14th century, with a more modern stretch from Portugal's 17th-century fight for independence from Spain.

• *Walk straight, sniffing the wonderful scent of pastries coming from the kitchen of Café Arcada (we'll visit the café at the end of this walk), and cross the intersection to find the...*

## Aqueduct

This blunt granite-columned end of the town's aqueduct is a relic from the 16th century. The Portuguese have such a fondness for their aqueduct reservoirs that they give them a special name—*Mãe d'Agua* (Mother of Water). Notice the abnormally high sidewalk just beyond the columns—it's the aqueduct channel. (On the outskirts of town, the channel sets higher, supported by stone pillars that kept the water flowing downhill.)

• *Return to the intersection at Mãe d'Agua and walk uphill until you reach the large, irregular plaza called Largo de Alexandre Herculano. Turn right and walk to the end of the square; at #5, just as the cobbled lane starts, go through the large green doors on the right.*

## Casa do Rua dos Burgos

This 17th-century house with a Roman foundation contains a small museum, with temporary exhibits on the main floor and a section of Roman wall below (free, Mon-Fri 9:00-12:30 & 14:00-17:30, closed Sat-Sun). The house is also home to a regional cultural organization, and staff at the entrance will point the way inside. Walk through the courtyard to view a small collection of Roman artifacts and a large section of the original town wall (including the other side of the section you saw earlier in this walk).

• *Exit the building left, head back through the little square, and continue straight one block down Rua de S. Tiago (with the church on your right). You'll reach a square that was once congested with parked cars and is now a good example of how the town has become very pedestrian-friendly.*

## Praça de Sertório and the Town Hall

The tallest white building on the square is the town hall. Any up-and-coming project for Évora is displayed inside here, including aerial views and scale models that visualize what the future city will look like (Mon-Fri 8:00-17:30, closed Sat-Sun, free Wi-Fi inside and on the square). Inside the town hall, in the corner on the right, is a view of a Roman bath that was uncovered during a building repair. Step through the glass door to the right of this overlook for a peek at the ongoing excavation.

Exit the town hall to the right. Look up to see a church and convent built into a Roman tower (once part of the Roman wall you saw earlier). The grilled windows at the top of the tower enabled the cloistered sisters to enjoy looking at the busy town without being seen.

• *Take a right turn and walk under the arcades past the post office (signed* CTT) *and take the first left, on Rua de Dona Isabel. You'll immediately see a...*

## Roman Arch

This arch, the Porta de Dona Isabel, was once a main gate in the Roman wall. Below are some of the original Roman pavement stones, large and irregular in size and placement.

When you pass under the Roman wall, you're entering a neighborhood called **Mouraria** (after the Moors). After Giraldo the Fearless retook Évora, the Moors were still allowed to live in the area, but on the other side of this gate, beyond the city walls. They were safe here for centuries...until the Inquisition expelled them in about 1500.

• *Passing under the old arch, turn right, and walk along the road past sod-capped water reservoirs. Turn right immediately before the tower, called the Cinco Esquinas (Five Corners) for its five sides, and walk a block up Rua A. F. Simões to...*

## Évora's Sight-Packed Square

Here, at the town's high point (1,000 feet above sea level), you'll see many of Évora's main landmarks. There's the Roman Temple facing a public garden, the palace, the garden courtyard restaurant, and the private chapel of the powerful local Cadaval clan (on the left side of the square—you can pay a hefty €7 to enter the church, described on page 224). Just beyond the Cadaval chapel is the recommended Pousada dos Lóios, once a 15th-century monastery but now a luxurious hotel with small rooms (blame the monks). At the far end of the square (not visible from here, but we'll go there soon) are even more landmarks and museums.

• *Dominating the scene are the stirring ruins of the...*

## Roman Temple

With 14 Corinthian columns, this temple was part of the Roman forum and the main square in the first century A.D. Today, the town's open-air concerts and events are staged here against an evocative temple backdrop. It's beautifully floodlit at night. While previously known as the Temple of Diana, it was more likely dedicated to the emperor.

• *Continue past the Roman Temple, into the far half of the square. Straight ahead, you'll see the...*

## Museum of Évora

This museum stands where the Roman forum once sprawled. An excavated section of the forum is in the museum's courtyard, surrounded by a delightful mix of Roman finds, medieval statuary, and 16th-century Portuguese, Flemish, Italian, and Spanish paintings. The museum also contains megalithic artifacts, including some found near Évora at the tomb known as the Anta Grande do Zambujeiro (described on page 230; €3, includes audioguide, free first Sun of each month, open May-Sept Tue-Sun 10:00-18:00, Oct-April Tue-Sun 9:30-17:30, closed Mon year-round, Largo Conde de Vila Flor, tel. 266-702-604, www.museudevora.pt).

• *Across the square from the museum (on your right) is a white building with the top windows trimmed in yellow. This is the...*

## Tribunal of the Inquisition

This building stands as a reminder of Évora's notorious past as a tribunal site during Portugal's Inquisition. Here, thousands of innocent people, many of them Jews, were tried and found guilty of crimes against faith. Punishment could be anything from whipping, imprisonment, banishment, slave labor, or, for the most unlucky, death by burning on the main square.

More recently, the structure has been converted into the Fórum Fundação Eugenio de Almeida—a contemporary art museum, with exhibits that change every four months. Art lovers can see what's on and decide whether it's worth the cost of entry (usually €4). You can also pay €1 to get a peek at the 16th-century frescoes inside (Tue-Sun 10:00-19:00, until 18:00 in Oct-April, closed Mon, www.fundacaoeugeniodealmeida.pt).

• *Go a few steps down the lane to the left of the Inquisition headquarters—a little street called...*

## Rua de Vasco da Gama

According to legend, globetrotting da Gama is said to have lived on this street after he discovered the water route to India in 1498. Most historians refute the claim that his house is 30 yards down the street (find the smudged #15 on your right)—but locals still love to tout the connection. Note the fine circa-1500 horseshoe-arch window, above and to the right.

• *Évora's historic **university** building is just a few blocks away. To reach it (either now, or later, when you finish the walk), you'd exit the square to the left of the Museum of Évora and work your way downhill. For a description, see page 227.*

**ÉVORA**

*For now, let's finish our walk. Directly across the square from the former Inquisition building, set on its own little leafy square, is the...*

## Cathedral

Located behind the museum, this cathedral was built after Giraldo's conquest—on the site of the mosque. (For a description of the cathedral, its cloister, and its museum, see "Sights in Évora," next page.)

• *Head downhill on the little street opposite the cathedral's entrance. You're walking on...*

## Rua Cinco de Outubro

This shopping street, which has served this same purpose since Roman times, connects Évora's main sights with its main square. Its name celebrates October 5, 1910, when Portugal shook off royal rule and became a republic. The street is lined with products of the Alentejo region: cork (even used to make postcards), tile, leather, ironwork, and Arraiolos rugs (handmade with a distinctive weave, in the nearby town of the same name).

For a great opportunity to taste Alentejo wines, stop in at the **Ervideira Wine Shop** at #56 (on the left). It sits in the old family home of the Count of Ervideira—look for the shrine remnants holding some of the oldest bottles from the winery (located 20 miles outside Évora). They make crisp whites (even from the red tempranillo grape), earthy reds from a secret family recipe, rosés, and the occasional sparkling wine (€2.50 tasting fee for 4 wines, daily 11:00-19:00, Rua Cinco de Outubro 56, tel. 266-700-402, www.ervideira.pt). If you like what you taste and want to try more local wines—by a wider variety of producers—be sure to visit the Rota dos Vinhos wine-tasting center, described on page 228.

As you stumble down the shopping street, after passing the intersection with Rua de Burgos, look left to see a blue **shrine** protruding from the wall of a building. The town built it as thanks to God for sparing it from the 1755 earthquake that devastated much of Lisbon.

Ahead of you is the main square. The Chapel of Bones and town market are just a few blocks away on your left. But first, stop by the venerable **Café Arcada,** under the arcade near the church. Considered the best pastry shop in town (with the brusquest staff), it serves good coffee and the local specialty: fresh, sweet cheese tarts (*queijada,* kay-ZHAH-duh, pay at the bar).

ÉVORA

# Sights in Évora

## NEAR THE ROMAN TEMPLE

### ▲ Évora Cathedral (Sé de Évora)

Portugal has three archbishops, and one resides here in Évora. This important cathedral of Santa Maria de Évora, built in the late 12th

century, is a transitional mix of Romanesque and Gothic styles. As happened throughout Iberia, this church was built upon a mosque after the Reconquista succeeded here. That mosque was built upon a Christian Visigothic chapel, proving that religious and military tit-for-tat is nothing new.

**Cost and Hours:** There's a dizzying variety of tickets, combining the cathedral interior, the cloisters, the Museum of Sacred Art (called "treasury"/*tesouro*), and the viewpoint (called both terrace/*terraço* and tower/*torre*). Choose what you like; a ticket for the whole shebang is €4.50. Daily 9:00-17:00, closed for lunch Oct-June 12:30-14:00, last entry to the Museum of Sacred Art one hour before closing. There's a WC in the cloister.

**Visiting the Cathedral:** Inside the **cathedral,** in a sumptuous Baroque chapel midway down the nave on the left, is a 15th-

century painted marble statue of a pregnant Mary. It's thought that the first priests, hoping to make converts out of Celtic pagans who worshipped mother goddesses, felt they'd have more success if they kept the focus on fertility. Throughout Alentejo, there's a deeply felt affinity for this ready-to-produce-a-savior Mary. Loved ones of mothers giving birth pray here for blessings during difficult deliveries. Across the aisle, a more realistic Renaissance Gabriel, added a century later, comes to tell Mary her baby won't be just any child.

The 16th-century pipe organ still works, and the 18th-century high altar is Neoclassical. Step up close to the high altar to view the ornately decorated chapel filling the apse. The royal box (high on the right, covered in gold leaf) looks down on the space, which is decorated almost entirely with colored marble. Only the muscular, crucified Jesus is not marble—he's carved in wood, yet matches the marble all around.

ÉVORA

The **Museum of Sacred Art** (Museu de Arte Sacra) is to the right of the main altar. Signage is sparse, but make your way through the chapel reproduction at the entrance, go past the elevator, then turn right. You'll enter a long series of rooms displaying ornaments and artifacts used in the cathedral over the centuries. The highlight (at the end) is a sparkling reliquary heavily laden with more than a thousand gems—diamonds, rubies, emeralds, and sapphires—and supposedly containing pieces of the True Cross (in a cross shape). Backtrack and go up a flight of steps to floor 2 to find an intricate 14th-century, French-made, puzzle-like ivory statue of Mary *(Virgem do Paraiso).* Her "insides" open up to reveal scenes of her life. A photo below shows Mary folded up and ready to travel. Not much else of interest is on this floor except perhaps Our Lady of Good Death—*Nossa Senhora da Boa Morte*—displayed toward the chapel.

Return to the church (scan your ticket again to leave the museum). The entrance to the Gothic **cloister** is past the ticket booth to the left. The cloister's openness and orange trees make it a cool haven, even on the hottest of Alentejo afternoons. Carvings of the four evangelists decorate the corners. Near where you enter, a tight spiral stairway leads to the "roof," with close-up views of the cathedral's fortress-like crenellations and grand views of the Alentejo plains. This "fortress of God" design was typical of the Portuguese Romanesque style. Notice the small relief (carved in the wall to the right as you face the church) showing the local Christian hero Giraldo the Fearless with two severed Muslim heads. Back on ground level, a simple chapel niche (opposite the cloister entry) has a child-sized statue of another pregnant Virgin Mary (midway up wall on left).

For the best views of the plains, return to the ticket booth and climb even more stairs to reach the church's rooftop terrace. Get up close to the church bells and the cathedral's fine lantern tower. Baroque flaming vases provide an interesting foreground to the rolling hills.

### Church of the Lóios and Cadaval Palace (Palacio Cadaval)

This is the palace and lavish mausoleum chapel of the noble Cadavals, who are still a big-time family—which is why they charge a stiff entry price. If you're on a budget, it's skippable, but if you appreciate beautiful and serene churches, the impressive gold altarpiece is worth seeing.

**Cost and Hours:** €7, covers the church and the palace; Tue-Sun 10:00-18:00, closed Mon; on

the square facing the Roman Temple, mobile 967-979-763, www.palaciocadaval.com.

**Visiting the Church and Palace:** Directly in front of the *pousada* (next to the Roman Temple), stairs lead down into the **church.** You'll walk upon Cadaval tombstones throughout your visit; taped chants and liturgical music add to the ambience. Look for the two small trapdoors in the floor that flank the aisle, midway up the church. The one on the right opens up to a deep, dark well (the palace and its church sit upon the remains of a Moorish castle—this was its cistern); the one on the left reveals an ossuary stacked with bones, supposedly belonging to former monks. The noble box (middle of the church, high above the pews) is a reminder that the aristocratic family didn't worship with commoners below. The tilework around the altar is from the 17th century—mere decoration with traditional yellow patterns. Along the nave, the tiles are 18th-century, with scenes illuminating Bible stories. The popularity of these tiles (inspired by the blue-and-white Delft tiles of the Netherlands) coincided with the flourishing of tapestries in France and Belgium that had the same teaching purpose.

The grilled windows allowed the Cadaval family to worship without being seen. The room to the right of the altar contains religious art, including a cleverly painted Crucifixion and rare Muslim tilework.

Your ticket includes—whether you want it or not—a walk through the **Cadaval Palace.** Next to the church entrance, you'll pop into the inviting family courtyard (now filled by a restaurant they operate), and follow signs upstairs and around the courtyard to the palace interior. The rooms are filled with old furniture, portraits, handwritten documents, and other historic icons. All told, it ranks pretty low on a European scale and is skippable unless you have time to kill.

## AT THE SOUTHERN END OF THE OLD TOWN

These sights are within a few steps of each other, about a five-minute walk south of the main square, on Praça 1 de Maio.

### ▲▲Church of St. Francis and the Chapel of Bones (Igreja de São Francisco/Capela dos Ossos)

This church and its Chapel of Bones are worth the stroll to the southern edge of the old town. The main attraction is the macabre chapel, with the skulls and bones of 5,000 monks tightly cemented to the walls, with barely a gap in sight.

**Cost and Hours:** Church-free, Chapel of Bones-€3, daily June-Sept 9:00-18:30, Oct-May 9:00-12:50 & 14:30-17:00.

**Visiting the Church and Chapel:** Imagine the **church** in its original, pure style—simple, as St. Francis would have wanted it.

It's wide, with just a single nave lined by chapels. In the 18th century, it became popular for wealthy families to buy fancy chapels, resulting in today's gold-leaf hodgepodge. The huge Baroque chapel to the left of the altar is dedicated to St. Francis and Claire, his partner in Christ-like simplicity. But they're surrounded by anything but poverty—the chapel is slathered in gold leaf from Brazil. The fine 18th-century tiles tell stories of St. Francis' life.

The entrance to the **bone chapel** (Capela dos Ossos) is outside, to the right of the church entrance. After buying your ticket, head

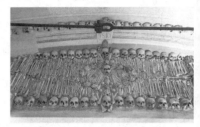

to the right to find the macabre chapel. The message above the door translates: "We bones in here wait for yours to join us." Inside, bones line the walls, and a chorus of skulls stares blankly from walls and arches. They were unearthed from various Évora churchyards. This was the work of three monks who were concerned about society's values at the time. They thought this would provide Évora, a town noted for its wealth in the early 1600s, with a helpful place to meditate on the transience of material things in the undeniable presence of death. The bones of the three Franciscan monks who founded the church in the 13th century are in the small white coffin by the altar.

Your ticket also includes a few sights **upstairs** (entrance back near the ticket desk): a low-impact museum of ecclesiastical art, a nice terrace, and a worthwhile collection of nativity scenes. This exhibit displays just a fraction of the 2,600 pieces donated by a local collector who really, really liked nativity scenes. More than half are from Portugal, but those are joined by examples from around the world. The collection is easy to miss—you have to cross over the terrace (outside) to reach it.

### ▲Public Market (Mercado Público)

Across the square in front of the Church of St. Francis, pop into the modernized yet still charming farmers market. It's busiest in the morning and on Saturday (Tue-Sun 7:00-18:00, generally

closed Mon though a few rogue stands might be open). Wander around. It's a great slice-of-life look at this community. People are proud of their produce. *"Posso provar?"* (POH-soo proo-VAHR) means "Can I try a little?" *Provar* some cheese and stock up for a picnic (perhaps in the adjacent gardens).

### ▲Public Gardens (Jardim Público)

Take a refreshing break in the town's public gardens (main entrance across from market, at the bottom of Praça 1 de Maio). Just inside the gate, Vasco da Gama looks on with excitement as he discovers a little kiosk café nearby selling sandwiches, freshly baked goodies, and drinks. For a quick little lunch, try an *empada de galinha* (tiny chicken pastry) and perhaps a *queijada* (sweet cheese tart— a local favorite). The gardens, bigger than they look, contain an overly restored hunk of the 16th-century Royal Palace (right of the entry gate). Behind the palace, look over the stone balustrade to see a kids' playground and playfields. Life goes on—make no bones about it.

## NORTHEAST OF THE ROMAN TEMPLE

From Évora's Roman Temple and cathedral, the university is about a five-minute walk away.

### ▲University of Évora (Universidade de Évora)

While far less monumental or interesting than Coimbra's (see page 292), Évora's historic university building is worth exploring—especially during the school year, when it offers a chance to rub elbows with students filling its blue-tiled galleries.

**Cost and Hours:** €3, Mon-Sat 9:30-18:00, closed Sun; Largo dos Colegiais 2, tel. 266-740-800, www. uevora.pt.

**Background:** First known as the College of the Holy Spirit, this institution was established as a Jesuit university in 1559 by Henrique, brother of King João III and the cathedral's first archbishop (1512-1580). Henrique later became king himself after his great-nephew Sebastian (Sebastião, who had succeeded João III) died in a disastrous attempt to chase the Moors out of North Africa. Because Henrique was a cardinal—and therefore chaste—he left no direct descendants when he died only two years later. Portugal's throne passed to Sebastian's uncle, King Philip II of Spain, beginning 60 years of Spanish rule—and the start of Évora's decline.

Two hundred years after the founding of the Jesuit university, Marquês de Pombal (see sidebar, page 45), the powerful minister of King José I, decided that the Jesuits had become too rich, too political, and—as the sole teachers of society—too closed to modern thinking. He abolished the Jesuit society in 1759, confiscated their wealth, and closed the university. Another 200 years later, in 1973, it reopened, but this time as a secular university. Inject-

**ÉVORA**

ing 8,000 students into this town of 57,000 people (with 11,000 inside the walls) brought Évora a new vitality—and discos. Unlike an American-style centralized campus, the colleges are scattered throughout the town. But this building is its historic core, and the closest thing to a student union building.

**Visiting the University:** The university's main entrance is the old courtyard on the ground level (downhill from the original Jesuit chapel—facing the grassy quad-like square). Enter the inner courtyard. Attractive blue-and-white tiles (one of the biggest and best-preserved collections south of Lisbon) ring the walls of the courtyard as well as the classrooms lining the courtyard arcades. Explore. If class is not in session, they usually leave the door open for curious tourists to peek in. The tiles within classrooms portray the subject originally taught in each room. Notice the now-ignored pulpits. (Originally, Jesuit priests were the teachers, and information coming from a pulpit was not to be questioned.)

Enter the **ceremonial room** directly across the courtyard from the entrance. Major university events are held here under the watchful eyes of Cardinal Henrique (the painting to the left) and young King Sebastian (to the right).

**Sala 114,** to the right of this room, gives you a great look at more tiles. In the 16th century, this was a classroom for students of astronomy—note the spheres and navigational instruments mingled with cupids and pastoral scenes. Imagine the class back then. Having few books, if any, the students (males only) took notes as the professor taught in Latin from the lectern in the back.

To find the university's **cafeteria,** follow the passage to the right of Sala 114, which connects to a smaller courtyard. The cafeteria (marked *bar)* is in the far-right corner. In the alcove just outside, notice the big marble washbasin. The cafeteria thrives with students and offers anyone super-cheap meals (Mon-Fri 8:30-18:00, closed Sat-Sun, WC).

## NORTHWEST OF THE MAIN SQUARE

This sight sits on Praça Joaquim António de Aguiar, a five-minute walk northwest of the main square.

### ▲Rota dos Vinhos do Alentejo Wine Tasting Center

This inviting place offers free tastings of four to six local wines, bottles of which are available for purchase (most are €5-20). Familiarize yourself with little-known Portuguese grape varietals *(castas)*. Wines change weekly and are posted on the front door. Large info-panels in English hold perfume sprays that capture the essence of each varietal. Try to identify the various scents—it's more difficult than you think. The staff can give you details about the Alentejo wine route and schedule visits to nearby cellars.

**Cost and Hours:** Free, Mon 14:00-19:00, Tue-Fri 11:00-19:00, Sat 10:00-13:00, closed Sun, Praça Joaquim António de Aguiar 20-21, tel. 266-746-498, www.winesofalentejo.com.

## MEGALITHIC SITES NEAR ÉVORA

This region has been a historic crossroads for millennia—the three river basins that intersect here provided a rich, fertile area for pre-

historic people to thrive. Human civilization's long presence here on the plains of Alentejo is marked by megalithic sites—some of the most important such stony configurations in the Iberian Peninsula—dating from 5500-3000 B.C.

Near Évora, you'll find menhirs (solitary standing stones, near Nossa Senhora de Guadalupe and elsewhere), cromlechs (monolith circles, at Cromeleque dos Almendres), and dolmens (stone slabs such as the rock tombs of Anta Grande do Zambujeiro, near Valverde; and Anta Capela de São Brissos—which was later Christianized, capped with a terra cotta roof, and painted white and blue). The most interesting to visit are Cromeleque dos Almendres and the Anta Grande do Zambujeiro, described next. Both of these sights are immersed in classic Alentejo scenery: cork-tree groves and a dusty, parched terrain.

Depending on how much you want to see, you can do a 15- to 45-mile loop from Évora by **bus tour** or hire a **guide** with a car (see "Tours in Évora," earlier), or **rent a car** to do the loop on your own (Évora's TI has a list of rental-car agencies and a map of the sites).

### ▲Cromeleque dos Almendres

This Portuguese Stonehenge, dating from about 5500 B.C., stands in the midst of cork trees down a dirt road.

**Getting There:** It's five miles (20 minutes) west of Évora, down a dirt road that begins in the village of Nossa Senhora de Guadalupe (just south of where N-114 highway meets A-6 expressway). In the village, look for the brown *Almendres* signposts that lead you down a well-tended dirt road through cork trees. It's a bit over a mile to the menhir, then another mile-plus to the cromlech.

**Visiting the Stones:** Heading down the road, first you'll pass the pullout for the less-interesting sight, a lone 10-foot **menhir**—it's about a five-minute walk along a rutted dirt path from the parking pullout. This menhir lines up with the cromlech at sunrise on the summer solstice.

For a more dramatic site, continue to where the road ends, park, and walk a couple of dusty minutes to the **cromlech** (*cromeleque,*

ÉVORA

# Megalithic Sights near Évora

1. Cromeleque dos Almendres
2. Menhir dos Almendres
3. Anta Grande do Zambujeiro
4. Anta Capela de São Brissos

meaning "enclosure")—95 rounded granite stones erected in the shape of an oval. It's the largest megalithic monument in Iberia and one of the oldest in Europe, some 2,000 years older than Stonehenge. Discovered in the 1960s, it was carefully reerected in its current position. Look closely at the stones; some have raised carvings, barely visible, of circles and shapes resembling a shepherd's hook.

Some believe that Stone Age sun-worshippers gathered at this pagan sanctuary in search of harmony between the "micro" environment on earth and the "macro" environment of the entire cosmos. The stones functioned as a celestial calendar, with the far ends of the ellipse lining up with the rising and setting sun on each solstice. A posted description (in English) at the site tells more. Stop and comfort a peeled cork tree, or pet the sheep that are often grazing nearby.

## ▲Anta Grande do Zambujeiro

This large megalithic dolmen, a burial tomb, is one of the tallest of its kind and dates to 4000-3000 B.C.

**Getting There:** The dolmen is located just outside the town of Valverde, a 20-minute drive southwest of Évora on N-380, and just a few minutes' drive from Nossa Senhora de Guadalupe. In Valverde, carefully track the brown *Zambujeiro* signs, which lead through a little industrial zone, then along a poorly maintained dirt road. Drive until the road ends, park, walk over the footbridge, and stroll a few more minutes to the dolmen (easy to see thanks to its modern roof).

**Visiting the Dolmen:** When it was discovered in 1964, the tomb was completely covered by a large mound of dirt. Excavation left the structure exposed to the elements, and although now protected by a roofed enclosure, it's believed the tomb will eventually collapse. Walk up behind the dolmen and look into the bare interior, which once contained one of the largest artifact caches ever found in Iberia. Weapons, ceramics, gold and ivory jewelry, as well as 30 male skeletons had all been buried here over several generations (some of these items are now on display at the Museum of Évora). Off to the side you can see the original capstone, which was blasted off with dynamite during excavation.

## Entertainment in Évora

### Bullfighting
Évora's bullring (Arena d' Évora, just outside the southern city wall) was recently turned into a multipurpose pavilion, and routinely draws crowds as a concert venue. While bullfights are still held here, they're rare (about 4/year), in contrast to nearby towns that advertise fights on Saturday and Sunday throughout the summer (details from TI). Women are on the program now, perhaps to give a tired sport a little kick.

### Fado Music
Although fado is not as popular here as it is in Lisbon or Coimbra, the recommended **Adega Típica Bota Alta** has live fado music on Friday and Saturday evenings (see page 235). The TI can suggest other places to hear fado.

## Sleeping in Évora

$$$$ **Pousada dos Lóios,** formerly a 15th-century monastery, is now a luxury hotel renting 36 well-appointed cells. While the rooms are tiny, this hotel sprawls with fine (if somewhat faded) public spaces, courtyards, and a swimming pool in a peaceful garden (air-con, free parking, Convento dos Lóios, across from Roman Temple, tel. 266-730-070, www.pousadas.pt, recepcao. loios@pousadas.pt.

$$$$ **M'ar de Ar Hotel Aqueduto** is the place if you want a modern, spa-like splurge inside the city walls, with the old Roman aqueduct literally running through its back garden. The hotel has 64 rooms, a spa, an outdoor swimming pool, generous grounds, sleek modern style, and a whiff of snobbery in this otherwise un-

---

## Sleep Code

Hotels are classified based on the average price of a standard double room with breakfast in high season.

| | | |
|---|---|---|
| **$$$$** | **Splurge:** | Most rooms over €150 |
| **$$$** | **Pricier:** | €100-150 |
| **$$** | **Moderate:** | €70-100 |
| **$** | **Budget:** | €40-70 |
| **¢** | **Backpacker:** | Under €40 |
| **RS%** | Rick Steves discount | |

Unless otherwise noted, credit cards are accepted, hotel staff speak basic English, and free Wi-Fi is available. Comparison-shop by checking prices at several hotels (on each hotel's own website, on a booking site, or by email). For the best deal, *book directly with the hotel.* Ask for a discount if paying in cash; if the listing includes **RS%**, request a Rick Steves discount.

---

pretentious town (air-con, elevator, free parking, Rua Cândido dos Reis 72, tel. 266-740-700, www.mardearhotels.com).

**$$$ Albergaria do Calvario** is a stylish 22-room hotel on the site of a 16th-century olive mill. Friendly Peter and Nina will take very good care of you. When you reserve a three-night stay directly and mention this book, they'll throw in one load of free laundry service—and may offer an upgrade (confirmed on arrival) to their best available room (air-con, elevator, free private parking, excellent organic breakfast, just inside the old town walls at the Porta Nova entrance, Travessa dos Lagares 3, tel. 266-745-930, www. adcevora.com, hotel@adcevora.com).

**$ Moov Hotel Évora** is a great value: a minimalist oasis offering 80 small, professional, crisp rooms in a residential part of the walled city. The building incorporates part of the facade of Évora's first bullring, and the decor is equestrian-inspired. An interior patio with a reflecting pool is relaxing even on the hottest of afternoons (breakfast extra, elevator, secure pay garage, Rua do Raimundo 99, tel. 266-240-340, www.hotelmoov.com, evora@hotelmoov.com).

**$ Inn Murus** is a family-friendly guest house with a classic tiled staircase, 11 fresh rooms with modern flair, and a shared terrace and kitchen (cheaper rooms with shared bath, family rooms, breakfast extra, air-con, Rua de São Manços 10, tel. 2660-041-721, www.facebook.com/innmurus, innmurus@gmail.com).

**$ Residencial Os Manuéis** rents 14 cozy, simple rooms surrounding an airy central patio. Breakfast can be served on the terrace with views of the sweeping Alentejo plains, while the Church of St. Francis looms in the distance. Vasco makes you feel at home and loves to share his knowledge of Portugal (RS%, air-con, no elevator, free parking, Rua do Raimundo 35, tel. 266-769-160,

no website but can reserve through booking.com, res.osmanueis@
sapo.pt).

**$ Hotel Santa Clara,** renting 46 comfortable rooms on a
quiet side street, is solid, professional, and tour-friendly. It has
a sterile business-class vibe, but comes with a good location and
price (breakfast extra, air-con, elevator, free parking, Travessa do
Milheira 19, tel. 266-704-141, www.hotelsantaclara.pt, evora@
stayhotels.pt).

**$ Casa Hóspedes "O Alentejo"** feels like a time warp: an old
noble house renting 22 well-worn but thoroughly cared-for rooms,
a homey TV salon, and endearing attention to quaint detail (family
rooms, no breakfast, air-con, Rua Serpa Pinto 74, tel. 266-702-
903, residencial.oalentejo@gmail.com, charming Rosa speaks very
little English).

**$ Hotel Ibis,** a cheap chain hotel, has 87 identical Motel
6-type rooms that are a 15-minute walk from the center, just outside the city walls. Simple to find and offering easy parking, it's a
cinch for drivers—but staying here is like eating at McDonald's
in Paris (family deals, breakfast extra, air-con, elevator, parking, Rua de Viana 18, tel. 266-760-700, www.ibishotel.com,
h1708@accor.com).

# Eating in Évora

You'll notice I list an unusual number of splurges in this otherwise
budget-priced town. That's because the Alentejo region has its own
proud cuisine—rustic and hearty, with lots of game and robust red
wines. (Think of it as the Tuscany of Portugal.) You can sleep and
sightsee cheap here, but consider dining royally. Don't order *vinho
verde* or port here—Alentejo produces some of Portugal's best
wines, which are both full-bodied and fruity. A good local *vinho
licoroso* (sweet dessert wine) is Mouchão.

**$$$ Restaurante 1/4 P'ras 9** ("Quarter to Nine") has a big,
rustic dining room with an open kitchen that steams up with local
families and tourists chowing down on favorites such as *arroz de
tamboril,* a rice and seafood stew, and *açorda de marisco,* a soup with
clams, shrimp, and bread spiced with Alentejo herbs like cilantro.
This is simply good, solid, traditional Alentejo cooking (Thu-Mon
12:30-15:00 & 19:30-22:00, Tue 12:30-15:00, closed Wed, some
outdoor seating, Rua Pedro Simões 9A, near exposed kink in aque-
duct off Rua do Menino Jesus, tel. 266-706-774).

**$$ Taska Fina** is a classic little mom-and-pop eatery with a
tight dining room, red-and-white tablecloths, bullfighting decor,
and a little punch of modern style. The owners are friendly, the
Alentejo classics are delicious, and the price is reasonable—attract-

## Restaurant Price Code

I've assigned each eatery a price category, based on the average cost of a typical main course. Drinks, desserts, and splurge items (steak and seafood) can raise the price considerably.

**$$$$**  **Splurge:** Most main courses over €17
**$$$**  **Pricier:** €12-17
**$$**  **Moderate:** €7-12
**$**  **Budget:** Under €7

In Portugal, takeout food is **$**; a basic sit-down eatery is **$$**; a casual but more upscale restaurant is **$$$**; and a swanky splurge is **$$$$**.

ing a local crowd along with the tourists (Mon-Sat 11:30-23:00, closed Sun, Rua do Apóstolo 10, tel. 266-707-070).

**$$ Adega do Alentejano** is like an aboveground wine cellar. Locals choose from affordable traditional dishes, including tasty pork options. The menu is scrawled on paper tablecloths and chalkboards. Ask to watch them pour your *jarro* of house wine from the large earthenware vats at the back. If you didn't try *ginjinha* in Lisbon or Óbidos, finish your meal with a glass of this housemade cherry liqueur. Come at lunch to avoid crowds, or elbow in at dinnertime for a festive night out (Mon-Sat 12:00-15:00 & 19:00-22:00, closed Sun, Rua Gabriel Victor do Monte Pereira 21A, tel. 266-744-447).

**$$$ Taberna Típica Quarta-Feira** is a rustic 14-table tavern, festooned with patriotic Portuguese decor, where Zé Dias and his family proudly and expertly serve country cooking, including rabbit and partridge in season. Don't expect to order from a menu—they usually serve just the food they felt like cooking that day. Sit down and enjoy the "Trust Zé Special"—he'll bring out the works, offering fun samples of whatever's in season, including his house wine (there's no wine list...just one decent house wine), fine desserts, dessert wine, and coffee. This is no place for vegetarians (Mon 12:30-15:00, Tue-Sat 12:30-15:00 & 19:30-22:00, closed Sun, hidden on a narrow street just north off Rua da Mouraria at Rua do Inverno 16, tel. 266-707-530).

**$$$$ Restaurante O Fialho** is expensive and enjoyably pretentious, with bowtied waiters serving Alentejo cuisine to Bogart-like locals. Enjoy the photos of VIP diners on the wall, or ask for a look at the photo album showing O Fialho's great moments since it opened in 1948. For decades, this was virtually the only fine restaurant in town, and it arguably still offers Évora's best food. Go all-local with your waiter's recommendations. For a delightful mix of nun-inspired sweets, ask for the *misto de convento* (Tue-Sun 12:30-24:00, closed Mon, arrive before 20:00 or make a res-

ÉVORA

## Versatile Cork

The cork extracted from the bottle of wine you're having with dinner is very local. The Alentejo region is known for its cork. (The wine you're drinking is likely local, too—the Alentejo produces lots of wine as well.) Besides bottle-stoppers, cork is used for many things, from bulletin boards to floor tiles, and from car-engine gaskets to the center of a baseball. Cork is a remarkable substance, spongy and pliable but resistant to water.

Cork comes from the bark of the cork oak *(Quercus suber)*, a 30-foot tree with a sprawling canopy and knotty trunk that grows well in dry heat and sandy soil. After 25 years, a tree is mature enough for harvest. The outer bark is stripped from the trunk, leaving a "wound" of red-colored "blushing" inner bark. It takes nine years for the bark to grow back, and then it's harvested again. A cork tree keeps producing for more than 100 years. After harvesting, the bark is boiled to soften it up, then flattened. Machines cut the cork into desired shapes or punch out bottle stoppers.

Portugal produces more than half the world's supply of cork (with Spain making much of the rest). These days, many wine stoppers are made from plastic, which could become a threat to cork production. So far the business remains strong, thanks to cork's insulating and acoustical applications, but some fear that if cork eventually loses its economic value, the survival of the forests—and the special ecosystem they support—will be at risk.

ervation, Travessa das Mascarenhas 16, tel. 266-703-079, www. restaurantefialho.com).

At **$$$$ Tasquinha d'Oliveira,** Manuel (who was a cook for years at O Fialho) and his wife, Carolina, offer an intimate dining experience with all the quality of his mentor's restaurant, but less pretense. In a tiny, 14-seat abode of cooking love, they work with a respect for Alentejo cuisine and heritage. Note that you will be brought several plates of appetizers—if you nibble, you will pay, and some of them are upwards of €15. Just leave them on the table or refuse the dish (main dishes are easily splittable, Mon-Sat 12:30-15:00 & 19:30-22:00, closed Sun, reservations smart, Rua Cândido dos Reis 45, tel. 266-744-841).

**$$$ Adega Típica Bota Alta** is a charming eight-table eatery, worth checking out on weekends for their live fado music. Esperança runs "her house" with a loving passion for the art of fado. (See page 112 for more on fado.) You'll find yourself singing along with the locals. Arrive no later than 20:30 to finish your meal before the music starts at 22:00. You're welcome to come just for fado; you'll pay €10 for a seat (fado music Fri-Sat 22:00-late, open for meals Tue-Sun 13:00-15:00 and 19:00-late, closed Mon and Aug, Rua Serpa Pinto 93, mobile 968-655-166).

**$$ Salsa Verde** is an excellent choice for a light, inexpensive lunch or dinner. This vegetarian cafeteria serves up flavorful salads and meatless versions of Alentejo classics in a crisp, clean, modern setting (Mon-Fri 11:00-15:30 & 19:00-21:30, Sat 11:00-15:30, closed Sun, Rua do Raimundo 93, tel. 266-743-210).

**Ice Cream: Zoka,** a local favorite for ice cream, has tables on a quiet, inviting square just 100 yards off the main square (daily 9:00-22:00, off Largo de S. Vicente, Rua Miguel Bombarda 14, tel. 266-703-133).

## Évora Connections

**From Évora by Bus to: Lisbon** (almost hourly, 1.5 hours), **Lagos** (2/day direct in July-mid-Sept, otherwise transfer in Albufeira, 5 hours), **Coimbra** (2/day direct, 4 hours; otherwise almost hourly with transfer in Lisbon), **Madrid** (in summer daily at 11:15 and 23:15, 7 hours, off-season only the night bus is available, book a day ahead at the bus station—Eurolines/Intersul office, second floor). Portugal bus info (no English spoken): tel. 266-769-410.

**From Évora by Train to: Lisbon** (4/day, 1.5 hours, arrives at Lisbon's Oriente station), **Coimbra** (3/day direct, 4.5 hours, more options with change in Lisbon), **Lagos** (2/day, 5 hours, change in Pinhal Novo and Tunes). Check with TI or online at www.cp.pt for schedules.

# NAZARÉ & CENTRAL PORTUGAL

*Nazaré • Batalha • Fátima • Alcobaça • Óbidos*

Nazaré (nah-zah-RAY), an Atlantic-coast fishing town turned resort, is both black-shawl traditional and beach-friendly. The beach town is just the start of the region called "Centro Portugal." Several worthy sights are within easy day-trip distance: Drop by Batalha to see its monastery, the patriotic pride and architectural joy of Portugal. If the spirit moves you, the pilgrimage site at Fátima is nearby. Alcobaça has Portugal's largest church (and saddest romance). And Portugal's incredibly (almost artificially) cute walled town of Óbidos is just down the road. (The most interesting city in central Portugal, Coimbra, is covered in its own chapter.)

## PLANNING YOUR TIME

While the far north of Portugal has considerable charm, those with limited time can enjoy maximum travel thrills here—in its "Midwest." This area is an ideal stop if you're interested in a small, resort-town side-trip north from Lisbon, or if you're coming in from Salamanca or Madrid, Spain. Expect crowds in July and August,

particularly on weekends. In 2017, Fátima celebrates the 100th anniversary of the visions of the Virgin Mary—be prepared for a multitude of pilgrims.

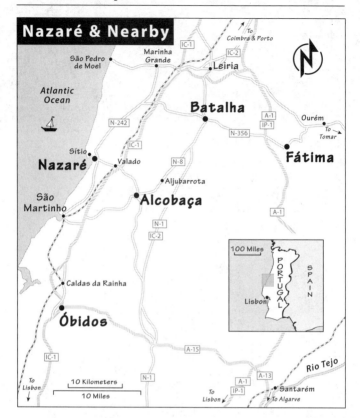

Nazaré & Nearby

On a two-week trip through Portugal, Nazaré merits a day. Another day's worth of sightseeing is in Alcobaça, Batalha, and Fátima (which I'd prioritize in that order). Óbidos is a light palate-cleanser, if you can squeeze it in on the way between Nazaré and Lisbon.

**Day-Tripping from Nazaré by Bus:** If you're traveling by bus, you can see both Alcobaça and Batalha in one day (but not on Sunday, when bus service is sparse). Alcobaça is easy to visit on the way to or from Batalha (and both are connected by bus with Óbidos). Ask at the bus station or TI for schedule information, and be flexible. Fátima has the fewest connections and is farthest away. Without a car, Fátima is not worth the trouble for most, but if you're heading by bus to Coimbra, you can go via Fátima. A taxi from Nazaré to Alcobaça costs a little more than €15; agree on the price before leaving town.

# Nazaré

Nazaré is an ideal place for a Portuguese beach break (especially if you're not making the long drive south to the Algarve). It falls somewhere between a real-life, narrow-laned fishing village and a busy resort with a beach littered with frolicking families. You'll be greeted by the energetic applause of the surf, widows with rooms to rent, and big plates of *percebes* (barnacles). Relax in the Portuguese sun in a land of cork groves, eucalyptus trees, ladies in petticoats, and men who stow cigarettes and fishhooks in their stocking caps.

It seems that most of the town's 15,000 inhabitants are in the tourist trade, but it's not at all hard to find pockets of vivid and  authentic culture. Somehow Nazaré traditions survive, and the townspeople go about their old-school ways. Stroll through the market for some ideal people-watching. Wander the back streets for a fine look at Portuguese family-in-the-street life. Laundry flaps in the wind, kids play soccer, and fish sizzle over tiny curbside hibachis. Squadrons of sun-dried and salted fish are crucified on nets pulled tightly around wooden frames and left under the midday sun. (Locals claim they are delightful...but I wouldn't know.) Off-season Nazaré is almost empty of tourists—inexpensive, colorful, and relaxed, with enough salty fishing-village atmosphere to make you pucker.

Nazaré doesn't have any real "sights." The beach, tasty seafood, and the funicular ride up to the Sítio headland (for a great coastal view) are the bright lights of my lazy Nazaré memories.

Plan some beach time here. Sharing a bottle of chilled *vinho verde* on the beach at sundown is a good way to wrap up the day.

## Orientation to Nazaré

Nazaré is simple: super-skinny streets with three- to five-story apartment blocks stretching away from an extra-long and extra-wide beach. The beach sweeps between the new harbor in the south and the cliffs on the north, which are capped by the old town of Sítio (SEE-tee-oo).

To get your bearings, survey the town from anywhere along the main beachfront drag, Avenida da República. Scan the cliffs. The funicular climbs to Sítio, which boasts breathtaking views over the entire town and its beach. Just below those cliffs, notice the road kinking inland, marked by the yellow balconies of Ribamar

## Nazaré Fashions: Seven Petticoats and Black-Clad Widows

Nazaré is famous for its women who wear skirts with seven petticoats (one for each day, or for the seven colors of the rainbow, or...make up your own legend). While this is partially just a creation for the tourists, there is some element of truth to the tradition. In the old days, women would sit on the beach waiting for their fishermen to sail home. To keep warm in the face of a cold sea wind while staying modestly covered, they'd wear several petticoats so they could fold layers over their heads, backs, and legs. Even today, older and more traditional women wear short skirts made bulky by several—but not seven—petticoats. The ensemble is completed with house slippers, an apron (hand-embroidered by the wearer), a small woolen cape, head scarf, and flamboyant jewelry, including chunky gold earrings (often passed down from generation to generation).

You'll see some women wearing black, a sign of mourning. Traditionally, if your spouse died, you wore black for the rest of your life. While this tradition is still observed, mourning just ain't what it used to be—in the last generation, widows began remarrying.

Hotel. This street marks the main square, Praça Sousa Oliveira (with ATMs). Most of my recommended hotels and restaurants are near this square.

## TOURIST INFORMATION

The TI is next to the entrance to the market hall, a long block off the beach (daily Aug 9:00-21:00, April-July and Sept 9:30-12:30 & 14:30-18:30, Oct-March 9:30-13:00 & 14:30-18:00, Avenida Vieira Guimarães, tel. 262-561-194, www.centerofportugal.com).

## ARRIVAL IN NAZARÉ

The town lacks an official **bus** station, but buses usually arrive along Avenida do Município, a few blocks up from the beach. **Drivers** can pay to park along the beachfront, or in the big lot just south of the market. For free parking, use the lot at the top of town (behind the town hall, near Avenida Vieira Guimarães—except on Friday, when it hosts a flea market); you can also park for free on town streets that aren't along the beachfront, but check signs to confirm

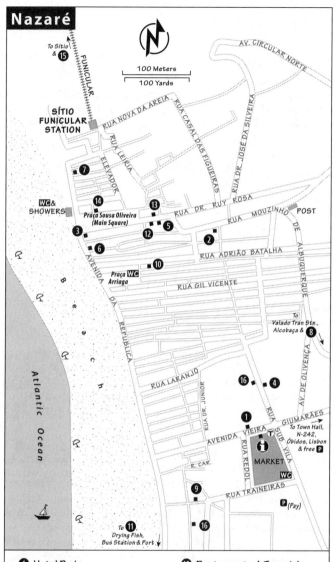

**Nazaré**

1. Hotel Praia
2. Hotel Magic
3. Hotel/Rest. Mar Bravo
4. Hotel Âncora Mar
5. Hotel Maré
6. Ribamar Hotel-Restaurant
7. Hotel A Cubata
8. To Quinta das Rosas
9. Taberna d'Adélia
10. Restaurante A Tasquinha
11. To Taverna "do 8 ó 80"
12. Tosca Gastrobar
13. Mr. Pizza
14. Restaurante O Casalinho
15. To Restaurante O Luis & Sitiado
16. Laundries (2)

that your spot is legal. Most hotels have their own parking or a deal with a nearby garage.

## HELPFUL HINTS

**Exchange Rate:** €1 = about $1.10

**Country Calling Code:** 351 (see page 422 for dialing instructions)

**Laundry:** At **Lavanderia Nazaré,** Fátima will wash, dry, and fold your laundry for pickup the next day (€3.50/load, Mon-Fri 9:00-13:00 & 15:00-19:00—open all day July-Aug, Sat 9:00-13:00, closed Sun, Rua Branco Martins 17, tel. 262-552-761). There's also **self-service launderette** a half-block from the market and TI, just up from the beach (daily 9:00-13:00 & 14:00-19:00, Rua Sub Vila 50, mobile 914-755-365).

**Regional Guide: Manuela Rainho,** who works out of Alcobaça, is a helpful guide for anyone interested in seeing this part of Portugal (€170/day, mobile 968-076-302, manuelarainho@gmail.com).

# Sights in Nazaré

### ▲▲Nazaré's Beach

Nazaré's broad and generous beach is the domain of the summertime tents—a tradition in Portugal. The tents are run as a cooperative by the old women you'll see sitting in the shade ready to collect €6 or more a day. The beach is groomed and guarded, and in the evening, piped music is played. Flags indicate danger level: red (no one allowed in the water), yellow (wading is safe), and green (no problem). The area closest to the cliffs has rougher

surf, and is marked off for surfers. There's also a world of fun water activities—surfing, jet skiing, stand-up paddleboarding, dolphin-seeking boat rides, and more. You'll see sales and rental shacks around the beach, or drop by the TI for details on your options.

If you see a mass of children parading through town to the beach, they're likely from a huge dorm, where poorer kids from inland areas are put up for a summer break.

Boats used to line the beach in summer and fill the squares in winter, but they moved to a big, purpose-built harbor just south of town in 1986. Re-creations line the main square to show the hands-on fishing process of the past (most Sundays in May; confirm days with the TI).

If you stroll south along the promenade toward the new harbor, you'll come to a few **traditional boats** in the sand, with high

prows to cut through the surf. Try to imagine the beach before 1986, littered with boats like these, with old men mending their nets. Oxen (and later, tractors) hauled the boats out each day. (Across the street is the town's Cultural Center—with interesting exhibits.)

Near the boats is a **mackerel crucifixion zone**—where ladies still sun-dry their mackerel and sardines. (They may try to sell them to you, but the fish need to be cooked again before eating.) Preparing and selling fish is the lot of Nazaré women married to fishermen. Stroll to people-watch. Traditions survive even among younger women.

The buildings beyond this point are new. While it may seem that most locals are older than most of the buildings, the town is a Portuguese Coney Island—thriving with young people who flock here for fun-in-the-sun on the beach.

Head back into town. Just under the bluff (near the funicular to Sítio) is the oldest square in Nazaré, **Praça Sousa Oliveira**. This square is lined with the oldest buildings in the lower town.

### ▲Market (Mercado Municipal)

Filling a rusting old industrial hall with slices upon slices of Nazaré life, the town market sits just one long block up from the busy beach (daily 8:00-13:00 except closed Mon Oct-May, Avenida Vieira Guimarães, in the green building just behind the taxi stand). While you'll see traditionally clad locals scattered around town, the market is one-stop shopping for people-watching (and, if you like, assembling a picnic). Most of the main floor has produce, with dried fruits and nuts, butchers, and bakers off to the left. Up a few stairs in the back is the fragrant fish market.

For another slice of local life, on the main street in front of the market (and near the bus station), look for petticoat-clad locals holding *quartos* signs—advertising rooms in private homes. They line the street coming into town, hit up tourists on the beachfront promenade, and meet each bus as it pulls into the station. You may enjoy dropping by for the commotion as the grannies fight over the tourists.

**Flea Market:** A flea market pops up near Nazaré's town hall every Friday, except in August (9:00-13:00, also on Avenida Vieira Guimarães).

### IN SÍTIO

Sitting quietly atop its cliff, the Sítio neighborhood feels like a totally separate village. Its people don't fish; they farm. Take the funicular up to the top for a spectacular view and the exquisitely decorated village church.

**Getting There:** The handy Sítio **funicular** was originally built in 1889—the same year as the Eiffel Tower—by the same disciple of Eiffel who built the much-loved Elevador de Santa Justa in Lisbon. The equipment and stations, however, have been modernized. To get to the lift, follow signs to *ascensor;* it goes every 15 minutes (€1.20 each way, June-Sept 7:30-24:00, Oct-May 7:30-20:30, WCs at each station). Off-season, buses replace funicular service after 20:30, but run only about twice hourly. If dining in Sítio off-season, check bus times at the funicular station before you eat (funicular round-trip ticket valid for bus ride down).

Upon arrival at the top, exit straight ahead, walk downhill, and turn left to reach the main square and the promontory.

### Sítio's Main Square

Historic Sítio seems to gather around its dominant square. The bandstand marking the center of the square is a reminder that this is the main venue for the town's busy festival schedule. In the summer, smoke rises from the many outdoor grills, and the savory fragrance entices you to sit down for a plate of sardines.

• *At the top of the square, check out the…*

### ▲Church of Our Lady of Nazaré

The town's main church, built in the late 16th century and proudly restored by small local donations, is on the pilgrimage trail. The faithful circulate around the ambulatory and then go up to the high altar to venerate the Black Madonna, brought here by two fishermen in the seventh century from Jesus' hometown of Nazareth (hence the name of this town: Nazaré). The Madonna, hidden in nearby rocks throughout the Muslim Moorish rule, was rediscovered during the Christian Reconquista in the 12th century, when interest in the relic led to the establishment of the town. Today the church, with its gilded Baroque-Neoclassical interior and 17th-century Delft tiles (from the Netherlands), is popular for weddings and other family religious occasions (which is why it has lots of flowers). If you'd like to pay your respects at the Black Madonna, you'll first have to pay €1 (to the left of the altar).

On the left side of the nave at the entrance, a large painting shows the story you'll find all over town: Dom Fuas, a noble from the area, was hunting deer and became so absorbed in the chase that he didn't realize he was about to go over the cliff. The Virgin Mary appeared suddenly and stopped him, saving his life. (The unfortunate deer didn't see Mary in time.)

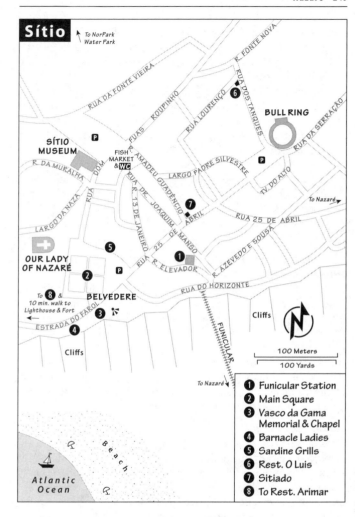

• *In front of the church, admire the view from...*

### ▲▲▲The Belvedere

From the edge of the bluff you can survey Nazaré and its golden beach stretching all the way to the new harbor. In the distance are the mostly uninhabited Berlenga Islands. The pillar on the belvedere ("beautiful view") is a stone **memorial** for Vasco da Gama, erected in 1497 after he stopped

here before leaving Europe for India. The tiny chapel next to the monument sits on the spot where the Black Madonna hid in the rocks for 400 years, as if waiting for the Moors to leave and for the Christians to return.

Several women (mostly from the same family, but competitive nevertheless) camp out here in their over-the-top traditional fashions, selling munchies and Nazaré knickknacks. This can be a fine opportunity to buy *percebes*—boiled, addictively tasty, and ready-to-eat **barnacles.** Two euros will get you 100 grams (that's the size of their tiny wooden box).

From here, it's a 10-minute walk to where the road ends at the **Farol lighthouse,** where you can enjoy panoramic views of the north beach *(praia norte).*

• *If you cross back over the square, then head up the street past the church, soon you'll reach the...*

### Sítio Museum (Museu Dr. Joaquim Manso— Museu da Nazaré)

Dedicated to Dr. Joaquim Manso, this museum is the only place in Nazaré where you can see artifacts of the colorful traditional fishing culture—boats, rustic tools, costumes, historic photos, miniature models of Nazaré's distinctive boats, and so on (but without a word of English).

**Cost and Hours:** Free, Tue-Sun 10:00-12:30 & 14:00-18:00, slightly shorter hours Oct-June, closed Mon year-round, one block inland from Sítio's main square, Rua Dom Fuas Roupinho, tel. 262-562-801, http://mdjm-nazare.blogspot.com.

### Activities in Sítio

Sítio stages Portuguese-style **bullfights** on Saturday nights in summer (typically mid-July-Aug, get schedule at TI, tickets at kiosk in Praça Sousa Oliveira). Sítio's NorPark is a family-friendly **water park** with a pool, slides, and hot tub (open only mid-June-mid-Sept, get details at TI, free shuttle bus if you call ahead, tel. 262-562-282, www.facebook.com/nazaretodoano).

Restaurante Arimar, on the left along the way to the lighthouse, is a good place to **take in the sunset** with drinks or dinner (avoid windy days). For more dining suggestions, see "Eating in Nazaré," later.

## Sleeping in Nazaré

You should have no problem finding a room, except in August, when the crowds, temperatures, and prices are all at their highest (particularly during the Nazaré Beach Party in mid-Aug). Anywhere you stay in Nazaré, lower your expectations—this is a ragtag beach town, not a glitzy resort. And count on noise—from passing

---

# Sleep Code

Hotels are classified based on the average price of a standard double room with breakfast in medium-high season.

| | |
|---|---|
| **$$$$** | **Splurge:** Most rooms over €150 |
| **$$$** | **Pricier:** €100-150 |
| **$$** | **Moderate:** €70-100 |
| **$** | **Budget:** €40-70 |
| **¢** | **Backpacker:** Under €40 |
| **RS%** | Rick Steves discount |

Unless otherwise noted, credit cards are accepted, hotel staff speak basic English, and free Wi-Fi is available. Comparison-shop by checking prices at several hotels (on each hotel's own website, on a booking site, or by email). For the best deal, *book directly with the hotel*. Ask for a discount if paying in cash; if the listing includes **RS%**, request a Rick Steves discount.

---

cars, from karaoke-belting revelers, and from your neighbors (since most buildings in town are cheaply constructed, with thin walls and doors). Bring earplugs and be on vacation.

Prices vary wildly with the season. The price ranges in my listings are based on the cost of a standard double room with no view in medium-high season (approximately June-mid-July and Sept). Expect to pay about 50 percent more from mid-July through mid-August, and much less off-season.

**$$$ Hotel Praia** feels big and muscular, filling two buildings across from the market hall. It's along the main road into town and an easy walk from the beachfront. Its 80 rooms are spacious, if a bit well-worn, with a bright and beachy color scheme. It comes with a rooftop terrace with a pool and its own attached parking garage—free for those who book direct (air-con, elevator, Avenida Vieira Guimarães 39, tel. 262-569-200, www.hotelpraia.com, geral@hotelpraia.com).

**$$ Hotel Magic,** the most stylish choice near Nazaré's beach, is a short walk up from the main square. It has 19 sleek, white, minimalist, well-equipped rooms with splashes of color, as well as an inviting ground-floor lounge with old movie posters. For those more swayed by contemporary chic than Old World kitsch, this "art hotel" is the place to stay (air-con, elevator, Rua Mouzinho de Albuquerque 58, tel. 262-569-040, www.hotelmagic.pt, info@hotelmagic.pt).

**$$ Hotel Mar Bravo** is on the main square and the waterfront. Its 16 comfy rooms are modern, bright, fresh—and they come with balconies, nearly all of them with views (RS%, double-paned windows, view breakfast room, air-con, elevator, recommended restaurant serves good seafood with a sea view, Praça Sousa Oliveira

71-A, tel. 262-569-160, www.marbravo.com, info@marbravo.com, owner Fátima). Parking for the Mar Bravo is several blocks away, at Hotel Praia on Avenida Vieira Guimarães.

**$$ Hotel Âncora Mar** is a big, modern, almost institutional place, with 27 spacious, bright, and functional rooms and a generous roof terrace with a pool. It's on a quiet street a block from the market hall, and still a relatively short walk from the beach (air-con, elevator, limited free parking, Rua Sub-Vila 49, tel. 262-569-010, www.ancoramar.com, info@ancoramar.com).

**$$ Hotel Maré,** just off the main square, is a big, modern, American-style hotel with 46 straightforward rooms (all with balconies), some tour groups, and a rooftop terrace (family deals, double-paned windows, air-con, elevator, pay parking 500 yards away, Rua Mouzinho de Albuquerque 10, tel. 262-550-180, www.hotelmare.pt, geral@hotelmare.pt).

**$$ Ribamar Hotel-Restaurant,** at the lower end of this price range, has a rare Old World atmosphere and 25 small rooms with dark wood. While it feels like a throwback (no air-conditioning, no elevator), you're paying for the prime waterfront location—to spot the hotel from along the beach, just look for its yellow balconies (four rooms have balconies, good attached restaurant downstairs, pay parking; Rua Gomes Freire 9, tel. 262-551-158, www.ribamarnazare.com, reservas@ribmarnazare.com).

**$$ Hotel A Cubata,** a last resort on the waterfront on the north end, has 20 small, nondescript rooms above a noisy bar. To save money and sleep better, forgo a private balcony and take a back room (Avenida da República 6, tel. 262-569-150, www.hotelcubata.com, geral@hotelcubata.com).

**$ *Quartos:*** Private rooms for rent—called *quartos*—are a Nazaré specialty, but most can't be booked in advance. If you're willing to travel without reservations, you can just show up and ask around to find a cheap but modern, comfortable room. Sometimes *quartos* hosts find you first—if you stand around near the bus station with your luggage, you'll likely be approached by a petticoat-clad local with a *quartos* sign. For more on this option, see page 409.

## A TRANQUIL *QUINTA* OVERLOOKING NAZARÉ

**$$ Quinta das Rosas,** perched high above the congestion and chaos of Nazaré (but still just a few minutes' drive away), is a restful retreat thoughtfully run by a Portuguese-Canadian mother-and-daughter team—Anna Maria and Anna. It's a working farm with resident chickens and fine views over Nazaré and its beach. The five rooms are comfortable and country-classy (most with balconies, some with views), the breakfast includes farm-fresh eggs and Algarve-fresh OJ, and your hosts are generous with travel advice (Caminho Real, Pederneira, tel. 262-562-706, www.quintadasrosas.com, reservations@quintadarosas.com. Driving up out of Nazaré, head toward the marina, then drive through the village of Pederneira, following signs for *Miramar Hotel* (the *quinta* is just before the hotel—watch for the gate on the right). They also have three family-friendly apartments with kitchens—called **$$ Seashell Apartments**—in a well-soundproofed building right along the beach in Nazaré.

## Eating in Nazaré

Nazaré is a fishing town, so don't order *hamburguesas*. Fresh seafood is tasty all over town, more expensive (but plenty affordable) along the waterfront, and cheaper farther inland.

In this fishing village, even the snacks come from the sea. *Percebes* are boiled barnacles; in season they're sold as munchies in bars and on the street. Sardines are fresh only in July, August, and the first half of September, but yummy any time of year.

Try Portugal's light, young wine, *vinho verde,* which pairs well with shellfish. *Amêndoa amarga* is the local amaretto. For a tasty pastry, try a *pastel de feijão* (fay-ZHOW) from any café. This small tart with a puff-pastry shell has a filling similar to pecan pie, but made of white beans.

**$$$ Taberna d'Adélia** is a family-run *restaurante típico* popular with Portuguese visitors for its honest service, fresh fish, and unpretentious jovial ambience. Marco and his family pride themselves on respecting the customer (daily 12:00-15:30 & 19:00-22:30, reservations smart in summer, one block off the beach at Rua das Traineiras 12, tel. 262-552-134).

**$$ Restaurante A Tasquinha** dishes up authentic Portuguese cuisine with a cozy blue-and-white-tile, picnic-bench ambience. Friendly, hardworking Carlos and his family serve their fish with the best bread in town and a special sauce that's good on just about everything (Tue-Sun 12:15-15:15 & 19:15-22:15, closed Mon, Rua Adrião Batalha 54, tel. 262-551-945).

**$$$ Taverna "do 8 ó 80"**—with a stylish, modern, wine-and-tapas-bar setting—defies Nazaré's fishing heritage with a menu heavy on beef and pork dishes. But they also have some creative, if hit-or-miss, dishes from the sea. The main attraction is the wine list: With more than 600 different bottles of wine on-site and more than 200 available by the glass, it's a short course in Portuguese enology. Sidewalk tables let you watch the tide roll in (Wed-Mon 12:00-23:00, closed Tue, a five-minute walk along the beachfront south of the colorful boats at Edifício Atlântico, Loja 8, tel. 262-560-490).

**$$$ Tosca Gastrobar** is a foodie option just above the main square. The mod, appealing menu (with both seafood and land

---

## Restaurant Price Code

I've assigned each eatery a price category, based on the average cost of a typical main course. Drinks, desserts, and splurge items (steak and seafood) can raise the price considerably.

  **$$$$** **Splurge:** Most main courses over €17
  **$$$** **Pricier:** €12-17
  **$$** **Moderate:** €7-12
  **$** **Budget:** Under €7

In Portugal, takeout food is **$**; a basic sit-down eatery is **$$**; a casual but more upscale restaurant is **$$$**; and a swanky splurge is **$$$$**.

---

food) combines Portuguese and international flavors with artful presentation (Fri-Tue 12:00-24:00, Thu 19:00-24:00, closed Wed, Rua Mouzinho de Albuquerque 4, tel. 262-562-261).

**$ Mr. Pizza,** just off the main square, has decent pizzas that you can order to go and eat down on the beach (daily 12:00-23:00, across the street from Hotel Maré at Rua Mouzinho de Albuquerque 15, tel. 262-560-999).

**Main Square with a Beach View:** Competitive, pricey restaurants ring the main square. These two offer decent value: **$$$ Mar Bravo**'s friendly staff serves fresh seafood at charming on-square tables overlooking the beach—and offers a 10 percent discount for readers of this guidebook (daily 12:00-23:00, inside hotel of same name, Praça Sousa Oliveira 71-A, tel. 262-569-160). **$$$ Restaurante O Casalinho** has good outdoor seating, plain decor, and a solid reputation (daily 12:00-23:00, Praça Sousa Oliveira 7, tel. 262-551-328).

**Public Market for a Picnic:** To experience the colorful market—described earlier—buy a picnic there and enjoy it on the beach (daily 8:00-13:00, closed Mon Oct-May, a long block up from the beach on Avenida Vieira Guimarães). Other to-go and picnic options can be found in any number of mini-markets along Rua Sub-Vila.

### In Sítio

Remember that off-season, the funicular stops running at 20:30—before settling in for dinner, check the schedule for the bus back down to Nazaré.

**$$ Restaurante O Luis** serves excellent seafood and regional cuisine to an enthusiastic crowd in a cheery atmosphere. While few tourists go here, the friendly white-coated waiters make you feel welcome. This place is worth the funicular ride if you want to eat well (Fri-Wed 12:00-24:00, closed Thu, reserve on weekends, aircon, Rua Dos Tanques 7, tel. 262-551-826, David speaks English).

**$$ Sitiado,** just off the main square, is a bit trendier but retains a respect for tradition, with delicious *petiscos* (Portuguese tapas) served on earthenware plates in a casual bar setting (Wed-Mon 12:30-15:30 & 18:00-24:00, closed Tue, Rua Amadeu Guadêncio 2, tel. 262-087-512).

# Nazaré Connections

## BY BUS

Nazaré's bus station was demolished in 2012 to make way for an apartment building. Since then, a "temporary" ticket office is in a small portable building behind the library on Avenida do Municipio, a few blocks inland from the Cultural Center and beach. Buses merely stop along the avenue. A new, permanent station may be built eventually, but it's anyone's guess when or where. Service diminishes on weekends (especially Sundays), so verify schedules beforehand online or at the TI. Two bus companies serve Nazaré: Rede Expressos, which covers most of Portugal (tel. 707-223-344, www.rede-expressos.pt) and RodoTejo, which focuses on central Portugal (mobile 967-449-868, www.rodotejo.pt). To know all your options, check both sites.

If you're heading to Lisbon, buses are faster and more direct than trains. You will arrive at Lisbon's Sete Rios bus station, a Metro (or taxi) ride away from the center.

**Nazaré by Bus to: Alcobaça** (stopping at Valado, about every half-hour, 20 minutes), **Batalha** (6/day, 1 hour), **Óbidos** (4/day, 1 hour, some direct, most transfer in Caldas da Rainha), **Fátima** (4/day, 1.5 hours), **Coimbra** (5/day, 2 hours), **Lisbon** (6/day, 2 hours). Buses are scarce on Sunday.

## BY TRAIN

The nearest train station is at Valado dos Frades (three miles toward Alcobaça, connected by semiregular buses and reasonable, easy-to-share €8-10 taxis). The train to Lisbon requires a bus or taxi ride from Nazaré to the station in Valado, then several transfers—not worth the hassle. To avoid this train-station headache, consider using intercity buses instead of trains.

**From Nazaré/Valado by Train to: Coimbra** (3/day direct, 2 hours, bus is easier), **Lisbon** (3-5/day, 4 hours, involves 2-3 transfers in Caldas da Rainha, Cacém, and possibly Melecas; bus is better). Train info: Tel. 808-208-208.

# Batalha

The town of Batalha (bah-TAHL-yah) is worth a stop only to see its great Monastery of Santa Maria, considered Portugal's finest architectural achievement. It celebrates a dramatic medieval battle-field victory (hence the town's name, "Battle").

On August 14, 1385, two armies faced off on the rolling plains here to decide Portugal's future—independence or rule by Span-ish kings? King João I of Portugal ordered his 7,000 men to block the road to Lisbon. The Spanish Castilian king, with 32,000 sol-diers and 16 modern cannons, ordered his men to hold their fire. But when the Portuguese knights dismounted from their horses to form a defensive line, some hotheaded Spaniards—enraged by such a display of unsportsmanlike conduct by supposedly chival-rous knights—attacked.

Shoop! From the side came 400 arrows from English archers fighting for Portugal. The confused Castilians sounded the retreat, and the Portuguese chased them, literally, all the way back to Cas-tile. A mere half-hour (and several hundred deaths) after it began, the Battle of Aljubarrota was won. King João I claimed the Por-tuguese crown, and thanked the Virgin Mary with a new church and monastery.

**Tourist Information:** The TI is behind the monastery, along the main road into town (daily 10:00-13:00 & 14:00-18:00, Praça Mouzinho de Albuquerque, tel. 244-765-180, www.visitcentrodeportugal.com.pt). Batalha's market is Monday morn-ing (market is 200 yards behind monastery).

**Arrival in Batalha:** If you take the **bus** to Batalha, you'll be dropped off a block behind the monastery and TI, near an Inter-marché supermarket. To get to the monastery, walk toward the Gothic spires. There's no official luggage storage, but you can leave luggage at the TI if you ask nicely. If you're **driving,** follow the signs to *Batalha*. Once in town, you'll loop around the back end of the huge monastery complex (the Unfinished Chapels), then park in the big, free lot alongside the church (follow *P* and *parque* signs through the first roundabout—by the TI—then take the exit by the tiny chapel at the next roundabout).

## Sights in Batalha

### ▲▲▲MONASTERY OF SANTA MARIA

This monastery, the symbol of Portugal's national pride, was built by King João I after winning the Battle of Aljubarrota. Unfortu-nately, the highway runs directly in front of the monastery, but at least you can't miss it from the road.

**Cost and Hours:** Church—free; worthwhile additional sights (Founders' Chapel, Unfinished Chapels, cloisters)—€6 except free first Sun of every month; open daily April-Sept 9:00-18:00, Oct-March until 17:00, tel. 244-765-497.

○ **Self-Guided Tour:** Here's a walk through Batalha's most important sight.

• *Start by surveying the...*

❶ **Exterior** (1388-1533): The Church of Our Lady of Victory (c. 1388-1550) is a fancy late Gothic (pointed-arch) struc-

ture decorated with lacy Gothic tracery—stained-glass windows, gargoyles, railings, and Flamboyant pinnacles representing the flickering flames of the Holy Spirit. (Inside, we'll see even more elaborate Manueline-style ornamentation, added to-

ward the end of its construction.) The church's limestone has mellowed over time into a warm, rosy, golden color.

The equestrian statue outside the church is of **Nuno Alvares Pereira,** who commanded the Portuguese in the battle and masterminded the victory over Spain.

Before entering the church, study the **carvings** on the main entrance (much-restored after serious damage in the 1755 earthquake). Notice the six lanes of heavenly traffic in the archway over the entrance: inside track—angels with their modesty wings; second track—the angel band with different instruments, including a hillbilly washboard; third—evangelists (those holding scrolls are from the Old Testament, those holding books are from the New Testament); fourth—Biblical kings and secular kings (those with globes in their hands); fifth—doctors of the Church with symbols of their martyrdom; and the express lane—female saints. Overseeing all this traffic is Jesus with the four evangelists in the tympanum. And the 12 apostles provide a foundation for it all. The statues are 19th-century copies of 14th-century originals. At the top of the pointed arch are two small coats of arms: Portugal's on the right and the House of Lancaster's on the left (a reminder of the marriage of João I and Philippa that cemented centuries of friendship between Portugal and England).

• *Enter the church.*

❷ **Church Interior:** The tall pillars leading your eye up to the "praying hands" of pointed arches, the warm light from stained-glass windows, the air of sober simplicity—this is classic Gothic, from Europe's Age of Faith. The church's lack of ornamentation re-

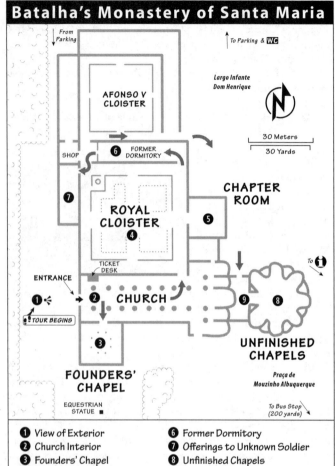

# Batalha's Monastery of Santa Maria

- **1** View of Exterior
- **2** Church Interior
- **3** Founders' Chapel
- **4** Royal Cloister
- **5** Chapter Room & Tomb of the Unknown Soldier
- **6** Former Dormitory
- **7** Offerings to Unknown Soldier
- **8** Unfinished Chapels
- **9** Elaborately Decorated Doorway

flects the vision of the project's first architect, Afonso Domingues (worked 1388-1402). Compared with Alcobaça's monastery (described later), this interior is dimmer and feels more somber, though the stained glass more dramatically colors the floors and columns (only the glass around the altar is original).

• *Buy a ticket for the cloisters and chapels (at the ticket counter on your immediate left as you enter). You'll need it to enter the rest of the sights described here. The first chapel on the right—directly across from the ticket desk—is the...*

**3 Founders' Chapel** (Capela do Fundador): Center-stage is the double sarcophagus (that's English-style) of King João I and his English queen, Philippa. The tomb statues lie together on their backs, holding hands for eternity. This husband-and-wife team ushered in Portugal's two centuries of greatness.

João I (born 1357, ruled 1385-1433), the bastard son of Dom Pedro I (King Peter I, see sidebar on page 269), repelled the Spanish invaders, claimed the throne, consolidated his power by confiscating enemies' land to reward his friends, gave Lisbon's craftsmen a voice in government, and launched Portugal's expansion overseas. His five-decade reign greatly benefited Portugal. João's motto, *"Por bem"* ("For good"), is carved on his tomb. He established the House of Avis (see the coat of arms carved in the tomb) that would rule Portugal through the Golden Age (and eventually challenge the House of Hertz in the car-

rental business). João's descendants—through both the Avis and Bragança lines—would rule Portugal until the last king, in 1910.

João, indebted to English soldiers for their help in the battle, signed the friendship Treaty of Windsor with England (1386). To seal the deal, he was requested to marry Philippa of Lancaster, the granddaughter of England's king. You can see their respective coats of arms carved at the head of the tomb.

Philippa (c. 1360-1415)—intelligent, educated, and moral—had already been rejected in marriage by two kings. João was also reluctant, reminding the English of his vow of celibacy as Grand Master of the Order of the Cross. He retreated to a monastery (with his mistress) before finally agreeing to marry Philippa (1387). Exceeding expectations, Philippa won João's admiration by overseeing domestic policy, boosting trade with England, reconciling Christians and Jews, and spearheading the invasion of Ceuta (1415) that launched the Age of Discovery.

At home, she used her wide knowledge (she was trained personally by Geoffrey Chaucer and John Wycliffe) to inspire her children to greatness. She banished João's mistress to a distant convent, but raised his bastard children almost as her own, thus sparking the rise of the Bragança line that would compete for the throne.

João and Philippa produced a slew of talented sons, some of whom rest in tombs along the nearby wall. These are the golden youth of the Age of Discovery that the Portuguese poet Luís de Camões dubbed "The Marvelous Generation" *(Ínclita Geração)*.

"Henrique" (third from the left, wearing a church for a hat) is Prince Henry the Navigator (1394-1460, see sidebar on page 183). When Philippa was on her deathbed with the plague, she summoned her son Henry to her side and made him swear he would dedicate his life to finding the legendary kingdom of Prester John—sending Henry on his own journey to explore the unknown.

Fernando (tomb on far left), Henry's kid brother, attacked the Muslims at Tangier (1437) and was captured. When his family refused to pay the ransom (which would have meant returning the city of Ceuta), he died in captivity. Son Pedro (tomb on far right), a voracious traveler and student of history, ruled Portugal as regent while his six-year-old nephew Afonso grew to manhood (Afonso's

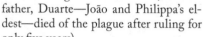

father, Duarte—João and Philippa's eldest—died of the plague after ruling for only five years).

The Founders' Chapel is a square room with an octagonal dome. Gaze up (like João and Philippa) at the ceiling, an eight-pointed star of crisscrossing pointed arches—a masterpiece of the Flamboyant Gothic style—that glow with light from stained glass. The central keystone (with João's coat of arms) holds all the arches-within-arches in place.

Remember this finished chapel—a lantern roof atop tombs in an octagonal space—when you visit the Unfinished Chapels later. Notice that some of the tracery in the arches still have their original red-and-green paint job.

• *Go back into the main part of the church, cross the nave, and bear right to find the entrance to the adjoining...*

❹ **Royal Cloister** (Claustro Real): Architecturally, this open courtyard exemplifies Batalha's essence: Gothic construction from circa 1400 (the pointed arches surrounding the courtyard) filled in with Manueline decoration from circa 1500. The tracery in the arches features the cross of the Order of Christ (headed at one time by Prince Henry the Navigator) and armillary spheres—skeletal "globes" that showed what was then considered the center of the universe: planet Earth.

The tracery is supported by delicate columns with shells, pearls, and coils of rope, plus artichokes and lotus flowers from the recently explored Orient.

Stop here and picture Dominican monks in white robes, blue capes, and tonsured haircuts (shaved crown) meditating as they slowly circled this garden courtyard. They'd stop to wash their

# Portugal's House of Avis and Its Coat of Arms

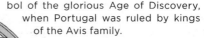

Seen on monuments at Belém, Batalha, Sagres, and even on the modern Portuguese flag, the Avis coat of arms is a symbol of the glorious Age of Discovery, when Portugal was ruled by kings of the Avis family.

In the center of the shield are five smaller shields arranged in the form of a cross. (One theory says that, after several generations of battle, the family shield—passed down from father to son—got beaten up, and the cross ripped apart into five pieces, held there by nails—the dots on the coat of arms.) Around the border are castles, representing Muslim cities conquered by Portugal's Christian kings. (Some versions have fleurs-de-lis and personal emblems of successive kings.)

## Some Important House of Avis Kings

**Pedro I** (Peter I, r. 1357-1367): Buried with his beloved Inês de Castro at Alcobaça (see sidebar on page 269).

**João I** (r. 1385-1433): Pedro's bastard son, who protected Portugal from a Spanish takeover and launched overseas expansion.

**Manuel I** (r. 1495-1521): Ruler when all the overseas expansion began to pay off financially. He built the Monastery of Jerónimos at Belém, decorated in the ornamental style that bears his name (see architecture sidebar on page 89).

**João III** (r. 1521-1557): Ruler during Portugal's peak of power... and at the beginning of its decline.

**Sebastian** (r. 1557-1578): Because he was lost in battle, the nation lost its way, leading to takeover by Spain.

hands at the washbasin (*lavabo*, in the northwest corner, with a great view back at the church) before stepping into the adjoining refectory (dining hall) for a meal.

• *Circle the courtyard counterclockwise, dipping into the...*

❺ **Chapter Room:** The self-supporting star-vaulted ceiling spans 60 feet, an engineering tour-de-force by Master Huguet, a foreigner who became chief architect in 1402. Huguet brought Flamboyant Gothic decoration to the church's sober style. The ceiling was considered so dangerous to build (it collapsed twice) that only prisoners condemned to death were allowed to work on it. (Today, unknowing tourists are allowed to wander under it.) The architect who helped Huguet come up with the strong-enough, interlocking, spider-web design for this vast vault supposedly silenced skeptics by personally spending the night in this room. (It even survived the 1755 earthquake.) He's remembered with a little portrait figurine supporting the column in the far-right corner of the room. Besides this ceiling, Huguet designed the Founders' Chapel and the Unfinished Chapels.

Portugal's **Tomb of the Unknown Soldier** sits under a mutilated crucifix called *Christ of the Trenches*, which accompanied Portuguese soldiers into battle on the western front of World War I. The three small soldiers under the flame—which burns Portuguese olive oil—are dressed to represent the three most valiant chapters in Portuguese military history: fighting Moors in the 12th century, Spaniards in the 14th century, and Germans in the 20th century. Every so often, soldiers goose-step into the room to clear a path for a modest changing of the guard ceremony.

• *Leaving the Chapter Room, turn right and enter the* ❻ *former dormitory through the archway (notice the tiny ornamental knots). Pass through the dormitory while immersing yourself in the walk-through audiovisual history of the church and monastery. Exit left to the refectory, through the door near the fountain in the corner.*

The **refectory** contains a collection of all the ❼ offerings from various countries to the Portuguese unknown soldier. Of particular interest is a photograph taken in the trenches of the WWI crucifix (on the wall of the gift shop; the crucifix itself is the one displayed in the Chapter Room you just visited).

• *Go back past the exit of the former dormitory and continue through the* **Afonso V Cloister**—*not nearly as interesting as the Royal Cloister (although you may see art students learning about sculpture on the far side). Follow the exit signs to a square outside the church. Head right, to the...*

❽ **Unfinished Chapels** (Capelas Imperfeitas): The Unfinished Chapels are called by that name because, well, that's not a Gothic sunroof overhead. This chapel behind the main altar was intended as an octagonal room with seven niches for tombs, topped with a rotunda ceiling (similar to the Founders' Chapel). But only the walls, support pillars for the ceiling, and a double tomb were completed.

King Duarte and his wife, Leonor, lie hand-in-hand on their backs, watching the clouds pass by, blissfully unaware of the work left undone. Duarte (1391-1438), the oldest of João and Philippa's sons, was the golden boy of the charmed family. He wrote a how-to book on courtly manners. When, at age 42, he became king (1433), he called a *cortes* (parliament) to enact much-needed legal reforms. He financed and encouraged his brother Prince Henry's initial overseas explorations. And he began work on these chapels, hoping to make a glorious family burial place. But Duarte died young of the plague, leaving behind an unfinished chapel, a stunned nation, and his six-year-old son, Afonso, as the new king.

Leonor became the regent while Afonso grew up, but she proved unpopular as a ruler, being both Spanish and female. Duarte's brother Pedro then ruled as regent before being banished by rivals.

In 1509, Duarte's grandson, King Manuel I, added the elaborately decorated ❾ **doorway** (by Mateus Fernandes), a masterpiece of the Manueline style. The series of ever larger arches that frame the door are carved in stone so detailed that they look like stucco. See carved coils of rope with knots, some snails along the bottom, artichokes (used to fend off scurvy), corn (from American discoveries), and Indian-inspired motifs (from the land of pepper). Contrast the doorway's Manueline ornamentation with the Renaissance simplicity of the upper-floor balcony that crowns the grand doorway, done in 1533.

Manuel abandoned the chapel after Vasco da Gama's triumphant return from India, channeling Portugal's money and energy instead to building a monument to the Age of Discovery launched by the Avis family—the Jerónimos Monastery in Belém (where both Manuel and, some believe, da Gama are buried).

## Sleeping in Batalha

If you spend the night, don't count on nightlife—this town shuts down early.

**$$ Hotel Villa Batalha** is a big, American-style hotel offering 93 modern rooms with high-class comfort, complete with an in-house spa and swimming pool (air-con, elevator, Rua D. Duarte I 248, tel. 244-240-400, www.hotelvillabatalha.pt, geral@hotelvillabatalha.pt). It's unromantically situated amid distant parking lots: With the monastery behind you, walk left on Rua Dona Filippa de Lencastre, continue straight through the roundabout, and you'll see the hotel.

## Batalha Connections

**From Batalha by Bus to:** Nazaré (6/day, 1 hour), **Alcobaça** (8/day, 30 minutes), **Fátima** (2/day—or 4/day in summer, 1 hour), **Coimbra** (3/day, 2.5 hours, transfer in Leiria), **Porto** (6/day, 3 hours), and **Lisbon** (5/day, 2 hours). Expect fewer buses on weekends. Buy bus tickets at Café Frazão, across the street from the Batalha bus stop (not sold by drivers).

**By Car:** Batalha is an easy 10-mile drive from Fátima. You'll see signs from each site to the other.

# Fátima

On May 13, 1917, three children were tending sheep when the sky lit up and a woman—Mary, the mother of Christ, "a lady brighter than the sun"—appeared standing in an oak tree. (It's the tree to the left of the large basilica.) In the midst of bloody World War I, and with the rise of an atheistic regime in Russia, she brought a message that peace was coming. The war raged on, so on the 13th day of each of the next five months, Mary dropped in again to call for peace and to repeat three messages. Word spread, bringing many curious pilgrims. The three kids—Lucia, Francisco, and Jacinta—were grilled mercilessly by authorities trying to debunk their preposterous visions and were even briefly imprisoned. But the children remained convinced of what they'd seen.

Finally, on October 13, 70,000 people assembled near the oak tree. They were drenched in a rainstorm when suddenly, the sun came out, grew blindingly bright, danced around the sky (writing "God's fiery signature"), then plunged to the earth—spreading fragrant flower petals everywhere. When the crowd came to its senses, the sun was shining and the rain had dried.

In 1930, the Vatican recognized the Virgin of Fátima as legit. And today, tens of thousands of believers come to rejoice in this modern miracle. Many walk from as far away as Lisbon. Depending on the time of year you visit, you may see scores of pilgrims with reflective vests walking along the smaller highways. Fátima, Lourdes (in France), and Međugorje (in Bosnia-Herzegovina) are the three big Mary sights in Europe.

## Orientation to Fátima

The pilgrim-friendly, modern Fátima (FAH-tee-mah) is a huge complex, with two big churches bookending a vast esplanade, adjacent to a practical commercial center. Wandering through the

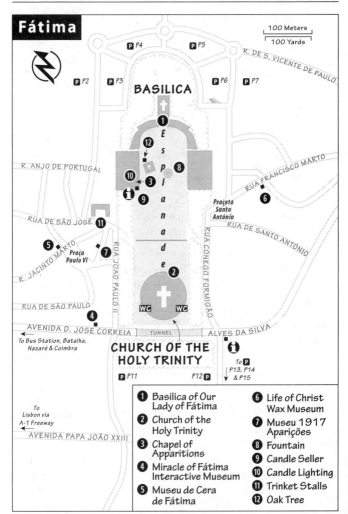

# Fátima

**BASILICA**

*Esplanade*

**CHURCH OF THE HOLY TRINITY**

R. DE S. VICENTE DE PAULO

R. ANJO DE PORTUGAL

RUA FRANCISCO MARTO

Praceta Santo António

RUA DE SANTO ANTÓNIO

RUA DE SÃO JOSÉ

RUA CONEGO FORMIGÃO

RUA DE SÃO PAULO

RUA JOÃO PAULO II

Praça Paulo VI

R. JACINTO MARTO

Praça Paulo VI

AVENIDA D. JOSÉ CORREIA

TUNNEL

ALVES DA SILVA

To Bus Station, Batalha, Nazaré & Coimbra

To P13, P14 & P15

P11

P12

To Lisbon via A-1 Freeway

AVENIDA PAPA JOÃO XXIII

100 Meters
100 Yards

❶ Basilica of Our Lady of Fátima
❷ Church of the Holy Trinity
❸ Chapel of Apparitions
❹ Miracle of Fátima Interactive Museum
❺ Museu de Cera de Fátima
❻ Life of Christ Wax Museum
❼ Museu 1917 Aparições
❽ Fountain
❾ Candle Seller
❿ Candle Lighting
⓫ Trinket Stalls
⓬ Oak Tree

religious and commercial zones, you see the 21st-century equivalent of a medieval pilgrimage center: lots of beds, cheap eateries, fields of picnic tables and parking lots, and countless religious souvenir stands—all ready for the mobs of people who inundate the place each 12th and 13th day of the month from May through October. Any other day, it's just big and empty. In 2017, the Shrine of Fátima celebrates the centennial of the apparitions—expect crowds.

At the start of the commercial zone, browse through the horseshoe-shaped mall of stalls selling religious trinkets—wax body parts, serene statuettes of Mary, rosaries (which pilgrims get blessed after attending Mass here), and so on.

## Mary's Three Messages

1. Peace is coming. World War I is ending. (Later, during World War II, Salazar justified keeping Portugal neutral by saying it was in accordance with Mary's wishes for peace.)

2. Russia will reject God and communism will rise, bringing a second great war.

3. Someone will try to kill a bishop dressed in white.

    The third message was kept a secret for decades, supposedly lying in a sealed envelope in the Vatican. In 1981, on May 13—the year's first pilgrimage day of Fátima—Pope John Paul II was shot. Upon recovering, he became convinced that he was the "bishop" of the prophecy. In the Jubilee Year of 2000, the pope visited Fátima, met with the surviving visionary, beatified the two who had died, and publicly revealed this long-hidden third secret.

**Arrival in Fátima:** From the **bus** station, follow the main road to the right, and in about five minutes you'll hit the back of the big, circular Church of the Holy Trinity (at the bottom of the esplanade). **Drivers** come to a big roundabout, where exits are marked for individual, numbered parking lots. All parking is free; a green *GRATIS* on the directional signs means they have spaces available. The handiest lots are P3, P4, P5, and P6, which cluster just behind the basilica; others are farther out (see map on page 261).

**Tourist Information:** The **town TI** is in a glassy modern kiosk behind the big, round Church of the Holy Trinity (Mon-Fri 9:00-13:00 & 14:00-17:00, Sat-Sun 9:30-13:00 & 14:00-17:30, Avenida José Alves Correia da Silva 213, tel. 249-531-139, www.visitcentrodeportugal.com.pt. For information on the religious sites and the schedule of today's services, check in at the **shrine TI** at the western side of the esplanade, near the candles (Mon-Sat 9:00-18:30, Sun until 18:00, slightly shorter hours off-season, tel. 249-539-600, www.fatima.pt).

# Sights in Fátima

## Esplanade

The huge assembly ground facing the basilica is impressive even without the fanfare of a festival day. The fountain in the middle provides holy water for pilgrims to take home. You'll see the information center; the oak tree and Chapel of the Apparitions marking the spot where Mary appeared; a place

for lighting and leaving candles (with an inferno below where the wax melts into a trench and flows into a vat to be resurrected as new candles—the shrine TI is right near here); and a long, smooth route on the pavement for pilgrims to approach the chapel on their knees.

## Basilica of Our Lady of Fátima

The towering Neoclassical basilica (1928-1953) has a 200-foot spire with a golden crown and crystal cross-shaped beacon on top. Its facade features Mary of the Rosary, flanked by mosaics in the porticoes of the 14 Stations of the Cross (under the statues of the four Portuguese saints). Built into the grand staircase is a covered stage with an open-air altar, cathedra (bishop's chair), and pulpit—all awaiting the next 13th of the month, when the masses will enjoy an outdoor Mass.

Inside, giant letters arc across the ceiling above the altar, offering up a request for Mary in Latin, "Queen of the Holy Rosary of Fátima, pray for us."
A huge painting depicting the vision is flanked by chapels dedicated to the Stations of the Cross and the tombs of the children who saw the vision. Two of the three died in the flu epidemic that swept the world shortly after the visions. Francisco's tomb (died  1919) is to the right of the altar. Jacinta (died 1920) and Lucia rest in a chapel to the left of the altar. Lucia (the only one with whom Mary actually conversed) passed away at the age of 97 in 2005. She lived as a Carmelite nun near Coimbra for most of her life. The basilica is busy with many Masses throughout each day.

**Cost and Hours:** Free, daily 7:00-21:00.

## Church of the Holy Trinity (Igreja da Santíssima Trindade)

Construction of this grand church began in 2004 with its foundation stone, a fragment from St. Peter's actual tomb in the Vatican, given by Pope John Paul II. Completed in late 2007, the church can hold 9,000 devotees, 10 times the capacity of the older basilica. The striking architecture and decoration is intentionally multinational—the architect was Greek; the large orange iron crucifix in front is German; the dazzling, golden mosaic mural inside (the left side depicts Mary with the three children she visited and all the people who witnessed her in the last apparition in October 1917) is Slovenian; and the crucifix at the altar (with the strikingly different Jesus) is Irish. The church is circular, symbolizing the world. Each of its 12 doors is named for an apostle. Outside, statues of two popes kneel facing the esplanade (Paul VI, who was here on the

50th anniversary in 1967, and John Paul II, who had a special place in his heart for Fátima and visited three times). The long, smooth approach for pilgrims making their way to the Chapel of Apparitions on their knees starts here, with a pilgrims' prayer posted.

**Cost and Hours:** Free, daily 9:00-19:00.

## Chapel of Apparitions

This marks the spot where Mary appeared to the three children (located outside the church, next to the big old oak tree, beneath a canopy). Services take place all day long in a variety of languages; check the posted schedule for English.

## Pilgrimage

On the 13th of each month from May through October, and on August 19, up to 100,000 pilgrims come to Fátima. Some shuffle on their knees, traversing the mega-huge, park-lined esplanade (which is more than 160,000 square feet) leading to the church. Torch-lit processions occur on two nights (usually the 12th and 13th). In 1967, on the 50th anniversary of the miracle, 1.5 million pilgrims—including the pope—gathered here; the centennial in 2017 is likely to bring even bigger crowds.

## Museums

Unfortunately, the Catholic Church hasn't yet put together an official exhibition befitting this beautiful sight. Instead, a variety of tacky and overpriced for-profit "museums"  compete for your euros—each within a couple of blocks of the esplanade in the modern town. Each of these is focused on re-creating the narrative of the three young villagers and the visions. The steep admission fees (not one dime of which go to a good cause) make these perhaps the worst sightseeing values in Portugal. And all of these are earnest, evangelical, and pretty cheesy for those not inclined to take Fátima too seriously.

The **Miracle of Fátima Interactive Museum** is the newest and most engaging of the bunch. A guide takes visitors on a 40-minute journey through a series of rooms, where video clips; a 3-D movie; and sound, light, and smell effects enhance the story. Touchscreens encourage you to learn more (€7.50, daily 9:30-19:00, until 18:30 in Nov-March, Avenida José Alves Correia da Silva 123, www.omilagredefatima.com).

The **Museu de Cera de Fátima** is two floors of vignettes in which wax figures illustrate the story of Fátima's visitation one scene at a time. While impressively extensive, it's also expensive and a bit long in the tooth (€7.50, daily April-Oct 9:30-18:30, Nov-

March 10:00-17:00, English leaflet describes each vignette, Rua Jacinta Marto, tel. 249-539-300). The same people also operate a **Life of Christ wax museum,** with 210 wax figures enacting 33 scenes from Jesus' life in a big, sleek, purpose-built facility on the far side of the esplanade (€8.50, daily 9:00-19:00, Rua Francisco Marto, tel. 249-530-680, www.vidadecristo.pt).

The **Museu 1917 Aparições**—the most basic (and cheapest) choice—tells the same story with a 15-minute-long low-tech sound-and-light show (€3.50, daily April-Oct 9:00-19:00, Nov-March 9:00-18:00, deep inside a shopping complex behind enormous Hotel de Fátima, worthless without English soundtrack—request at the ticket window).

## Fátima Connections

**From Fátima by Bus to: Batalha** (2/day—or 4/day in summer, 1 hour), **Alcobaça** (2/day, 1 hour, more frequent with transfer in Batalha), **Coimbra** (hourly, 1 hour), **Nazaré** (4/day, 1.5 hours), and **Lisbon** (hourly, 1.5-2.5 hours, depending on route); service drops on Sunday. Note that the stop closest to the basilica is listed on bus schedules as Cova de Iria, *not* Fátima. Baggage storage is available at the bus station (€2.50/day).

# Alcobaça

This pleasant little town is famous for its church, one of the most interesting in Portugal. I find Alcobaça (ahl-koh-BAH-sah) a better stop than Batalha.

**Tourist Information:** The English-speaking TI is in the shopping district, between the monastery and the market (daily 9:00-12:30 & 14:00-17:30, Rua 16 de Outubro 9, tel. 262-582-377, www.visitcentrodeportugal.com.pt).

**Arrival in Alcobaça:** If you arrive by **bus,** it's a five-minute walk to the town center and monastery. Exit right from the station (on Avenida Manuel da Silva Carolino), walk a half-block uphill (car parking lot visible in distance), take the first right, and continue straight (on Rua Dom Pedro V). Hang a left just after passing a small plaza, and you are in the main square.

If you're arriving by **car,** follow the *Mosteiro* signs. For free parking, use the lot just uphill from the bus station (*estação rodoviárioi* signs). But it's easiest to simply park on the streets in front of the monastery, where the parking is cheap.

**Sweets: Pastelaria Alcôa,** across from the entrance to the monastery, wins awards for their traditional convent pastries, including the best *pastel de nata* in all of Portugal. Do your own taste test (daily 8:00-19:30, Praça 25 de Abril 44, tel. 262-597-474).

# Sights in Alcobaça

### ▲▲Monastery of Santa Maria (Mosteiro de Santa Maria)

This Cistercian abbey church, despite its mainly Baroque facade, represents the best Gothic building in Portugal. It's also the country's largest church, and a clean and bright break from the heavier Iberian norm. Afonso Henriques began construction in 1178 after taking the nearby town of Santarém from the Moors.

The first Cistercian monks arrived in 1228 and proceeded to make this one of the most powerful abbeys of the Cistercian Order and a cultural center of 13th-century Portugal. This simple abbey was designed to be filled with hard work, prayer, and total silence. With finely preserved old dormitories and dining halls, it's the easiest place in Portugal to really envision the life monastic.

**Cost and Hours:** Church and tombs—free; cloisters—€6, free first Sun of every month, daily April-Sept 9:00-19:00, Oct-March until 17:00, tel. 262-505-128, www. mosteiroalcobaca.pt.

● **Self-Guided Tour:** As you view the ❶ **church exterior** from the expansive square facing it, you can sense its former importance. The wings stretching to the right and left from the facade housed monks and pilgrims. As was generally the case, the monastery was an industrial engine (making ceramics and other products), and by the 16th century a town had grown around the abbey. When the abbey was dissolved in 1834, the town declined, too.

Stepping inside, you find a suitably grand yet austere house of prayer—just straight Gothic lines. The only decor is organic (such as leafy capitals).

• *The long and narrow central nave leads to a pair of finely carved tombs that flank the main altar.*

❷ **Tombs of Dom Pedro and** ❸ **Inês:** These 1360 Gothic tombs belong to Portugal's most tragic romantic couple, Dom Pedro (King Peter I, 1320-1367, on the right) and Dona Inês de Castro (c. 1323-1355, on the left). They rest feet-to-feet in each transept, so that on Judgment Day they'll rise and immediately see

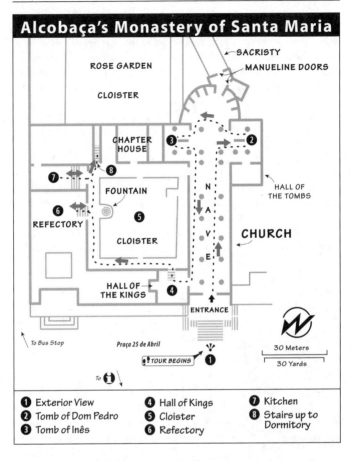

# Alcobaça's Monastery of Santa Maria

- SACRISTY
- MANUELINE DOORS
- ROSE GARDEN
- CLOISTER
- CHAPTER HOUSE
- **❸**
- **❷**
- **❼**
- **❽**
- FOUNTAIN
- **❻**
- **❺**
- REFECTORY
- CLOISTER
- N A V E
- HALL OF THE TOMBS
- CHURCH
- HALL OF THE KINGS
- **❹**
- ENTRANCE
- To Bus Stop
- *Praça 25 de Abril*
- **TOUR BEGINS ❶**
- To **🛈**
- 30 Meters
- 30 Yards

❶ Exterior View
❷ Tomb of Dom Pedro
❸ Tomb of Inês
❹ Hall of Kings
❺ Cloister
❻ Refectory
❼ Kitchen
❽ Stairs up to Dormitory

one another again. Pedro, heir to the Portuguese throne, was hopelessly in love with the Spanish aristocrat Inês (see sidebar on page 269).

Start with **Pedro's** (on the right), and examine the exquisite carvings. Like religious alarm clocks, the attending angels are poised to wake the couple on Judgment Day. Pedro will lie here (as inscribed on the tomb) *"Até ao fim do mundo"*—until the end of the world, when he and Inês are reunited. The "Wheel of Life" below Pedro's finely combed head features the king on the throne at the top and the king in his tomb at the bottom, with the good things in life on the left and the bad things (including Inês' beheading) on the right.

Scenes from the life of St. Bartholomew—famous for being skinned alive (Pedro's patron saint, reflecting his life of sacrifice)—circle the tomb. The martyrdom of St. Bartholomew is depicted on a relief directly below the king's head on his left side—along with the creepy aftermath. Pedro's tomb is supported by lions, a symbol of royalty.

Now check out the tomb of **Inês,** which is supported by the lowly scum who murdered her...one holding a monkey, a symbol of evil. Inês' tomb features vivid scenes from the life of Christ, and the relief at her feet features Heaven up above, the dragon mouth of Hell (pictured at bottom of previous page), and jack-in-the-box coffins on Judgment Day. Although Napoleon's troops vandalized the tombs (that's why so many heads are missing), the story of Pedro and Inês endures *até ao fim do mundo.*

Stroll through the ambulatory (behind the altar) to the sacristy entrance. The two **Manueline doors,** courtesy of King Manuel I, add a touch of grandeur (think of Lisbon's Monastery of Jerónimos) to the rather plain but elegant church.

• *Return toward the entrance and find the doorway on the right to the...*

❹ **Hall of Kings:** This hall features terra-cotta ceramic statues of most of Portugal's kings. The last king portrayed is Joseph, who

ruled when the earthquake hit in 1755. Since then there has been no money for fancy statues. The next empty pedestal (to the left of Joseph) is wider than the rest—in anticipation of the reign of Portugal's first queen, Mary I, and her big fancy dress.

The walls feature 18th-century tiles telling the story of the 12th-century conquest of the Moors and the building of the monastery (each with Latin supertitles and Portuguese subtitles). In the last scene, the first king lays the monastery's first stone.

The biggest sculpture—in its own niche, facing the entrance—features a fantastical image of Afonso Henriques, first king of Portugal and founder of this monastery, being crowned by Pope Innocent III and St. Bernard.

• *From here, steps lead to the...*

❺ **Cloister:** Cistercian monks built the abbey in 40 years, starting in 1178. They inhabited it until 1834 (when the Portuguese king disbanded all monasteries). The monks spent most of their lives in silence, and were allowed to speak only when

# Pedro and Inês

Twenty-year-old Prince Pedro met 17-year-old Inês, a Galician noblewoman, at his wedding to Inês' cousin Constance. The politically motivated marriage was arranged by Pedro's father, the king. Pedro dutifully fathered his son, the future king Fernando, with Constance in Lisbon, while seeing Inês on the side in Coimbra. When Constance died, Pedro settled in with Inês. Concerned about Spanish influence, Pedro's father, Afonso IV, forbade their marriage. You guessed it—they were married secretly, and the couple had four children. When King Afonso, fearing rivals to his ("legitimate") grandson's kingship, had Inês murdered, Prince Pedro went ballistic. He staged an armed uprising (1355) against his father, only settled after much bloodshed.

Once he was crowned King Pedro I the Just (1357), the much-embellished legend begins. Pedro summoned his enemies, exhumed Inês' body, dressed it in a bridal gown, and put it on the throne, making the murderers kneel and kiss its putrid rotting hand. (The legend continues...) Pedro then executed Inês' two murderers—personally—by ripping out their hearts, eating them, and washing them down, it is said, with a fine *vinho verde*. Now that's *amor*.

given permission by the abbot. To enjoy this cloister like the monks did: Meditate, pray, exercise, and connect with nature. As you multitask, circle clockwise until you reach the fountain—where the monks washed up before eating.

• *Traditionally, in any cloister, the fountain marks the entry to the...*

**❻ Refectory** (Dining Hall): Imagine the hall filled with monks eating in silence as one reads from the Bible atop the "Readers' Pulpit." Food was prepared next door.

• *Continue around the cloister and into the...*

**❼ Kitchen:** The 18th-century kitchen's giant three-part oven could roast seven oxen simultaneously. The industrious monks rerouted part of the River Alcoa to bring in running water. This kitchen fed huge numbers: The population of monks here maxed out at 999 (triple the Trinity), and peasants who worked the church-owned land were rewarded with meals here.

• *Head back out into the cloister, turn left, and take the stairs up to the bare...*

**❽ Dormitory:** In the hall where the monks slept, you can peer down on the transept of the church where Inês and Pedro lie buried. On this floor, there is also a terrace onto the adjacent cloister, with a rose garden.

### ▲Mercado Municipal

An Old World version of Safeway is housed happily here under huge steel-and-fiberglass arches. Inside the covered market, black-

clad dried-apple-faced women choose fish, uncaged and feisty chickens, ducks, and rabbits from their respective death rows. Wander among figs, melons, bushels of grain, and nuts (Mon-Sat 9:00-13:00, closed Sun, best on Mon and Sat). Imagine having a lifelong relationship with the person who grows your produce. Women from Nazaré—with their distinctive dress—sell fish in a separate room. The market is a five-minute walk from the TI (just down the block from the bus station); ask a local, *"Mercado municipal?"* Also, a flea market happens Mondays by the Alcoa River.

## Alcobaça Connections

**From Alcobaça by Bus to: Lisbon** (6/day, 2 hours, some transfer in Caldas da Rainha), **Nazaré** (2/hour, 20 minutes, stops at Valado), **Batalha** (8/day, 30 minutes), **Fátima** (2/day, 1 hour, more frequent with transfer in Batalha), **Óbidos** (6/day, 2 hours), **Coimbra** (2/day, 1.5 hours). Bus frequency drops on weekends, especially Sunday. A taxi to the Nazaré/Valado train station costs about €10; to Nazaré, a little over €15. Bus info: Tel. 808-200-370.

# Óbidos

Postcard-perfect Óbidos (OH-bee-doosh) sits atop a hill, its 14th-century wall (45 feet tall) corralling a bouquet of narrow lanes and flower-bedecked whitewashed houses. Its name, dating from ancient Roman times, means—appropriately enough—"walled town." The 16th-century aqueduct connecting it like an umbilical cord to a nearby spring is a reminder of the town's importance during Portugal's boom century. Óbidos—now protected by the government from modern development—is ideal for photographers who want to make Portugal look as pretty as possible.

Founded by Celts (c. 300 B.C.), then ruled by Romans, Visigoths, and Moors, Óbidos was known as Portugal's "wedding city." In 1282, when King Dinis brought his bride Isabel here, she liked the town so much he gave it to her. (Whatta guy.) Later kings carried on the tradition—the perfect gift for a king to give to a queen who has everything. (Beats a toaster.) Today, this medieval walled town

is popular for lowly commoners' weddings. Preserved in its entirety as a national monument since 1951, it survives on tourism. And in 2015, it was named a "City of Literature"—you'll notice a book theme around town, and Óbidos is very proud of its new, annual literary festival.

Óbidos may well be Portugal's prettiest little town—but it's also one of its most touristy...and least authentic. For this reason, a quick visit outside of peak times is ideal. Every summer morning at 9:30, the tour groups flush into town (in August, it's absolutely packed). Ideally, arrive late one day and leave early the next, enjoying the town as you would a beautiful painted tile.

**Tourist Information:** The TI is at Óbidos' main pay parking lot, just outside the main gate (daily May-Sept 9:30-19:30, shorter hours off-season, tel. 262-959-231, www.visitcentrodeportugal. com.pt).

**Arrival in Óbidos:** There's no official place to store luggage in town, so it's smart to travel light.

If you arrive at the **train** station, you're faced with a 20-minute uphill hike into town. The **bus** drops you off much closer, right outside the main gate (upon arrival, go up the steps and through the archway on the right). If leaving by train, you can catch a taxi to the station in the lot outside the main gate (about €10).

If you arrive by car, don't drive into tiny, cobbled Óbidos. Ample tourist parking is provided just outside the main gate. The closest lot—right outside the main gate, near all the tour buses, the TI, and a public WC—is pay-and-display. The huge lot across the street (lined by the 16th-century aqueduct) is usually free, but they may charge during busy times or special events. If you're staying inside the town walls and want to park near your hotel, be sure to get details beforehand. Some hotels inside the walls have one or two spots, but it's generally easier to park outside the walls.

# Óbidos Walk

There's not much to see in Óbidos—the main attraction is the town itself—but this walk covers it. In about 30 minutes, it goes from one end of town (the main gate) to the other (castle-turned-*pousada*).

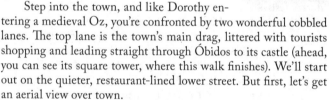

• *From the parking lot or bus stop, enter Óbidos' 14th-century wall through the...*

**Main Gate:** Inside the gate, pause to gaze up at the scenes related to the town's history—depicting centuries of battles and religion in blue-and-white tiles. Tiles like these covered the entire face of the walls here until the 1755 quake shook them down.

Step into the town, and like Dorothy entering a medieval Oz, you're confronted by two wonderful cobbled lanes. The top lane is the town's main drag, littered with tourists shopping and leading straight through Óbidos to its castle (ahead, you can see its square tower, where this walk finishes). We'll start out on the quieter, restaurant-lined lower street. But first, let's get an aerial view over town.

• *From where you walked through the gate, you'll see steep stairs on your left. Hike up for a view from atop the...*

**Town Wall:** Enjoy the panoramas of the city and surrounding countryside from the 45-foot-high walls. This is one of several access points for the scenic sentry path along the wall (other options are near the castle/*pousada*, and uphill from the main church). The west (uphill) wall is best, letting you look over the town's white buildings with red roofs and blue or yellow trim. You can almost gaze all the way to the Atlantic, six miles away. Until the 1100s, when the bay silted up, the ocean was half as far away, making this a hilltop citadel guarding a natural port. The aqueduct is from the 16th century.

• *At the end of our walk, you can stroll along the top of the walls all the way back to this point. But for now, descend the staircase and head into town. At the fork, follow the right/downhill of the two streets...*

**Rua Josefa d'Óbidos:** Along this restaurant row, notice the whitewash that keeps things cool; the bright blue-and-yellow trims, traditionally designed to define property lines; and the potted geraniums, which bloom most of the year, survive the summer sun well, and keep mosquitoes away.

The **Church of St. Peter** has a fine, restored Baroque altar covered with Brazilian gold leaf. The Maltese-type crosses carved into the rock throughout the church are a constant reminder that this

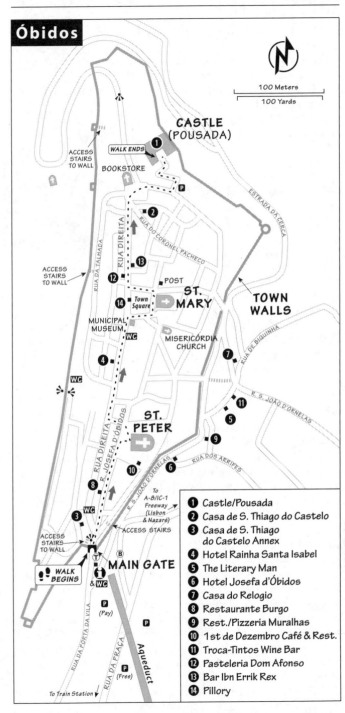

# Óbidos

100 Meters
100 Yards

N

ACCESS STAIRS TO WALL

CASTLE (POUSADA)

**WALK ENDS** ❶

BOOKSTORE

ESTRADA DA CERCA

❷

RUA DO CORONEL PACHECO

RUA DIREITA

RUA DA TALHADA

ACCESS STAIRS TO WALL

❸

❷

POST

ST. MARY

TOWN WALLS

Town Square

❹

MUNICIPAL MUSEUM

WC

MISERICÓRDIA CHURCH

❼

RUA DE BIQUINHA

WC

❹

R. S. JOÃO D'ORNELAS

❶

❺

ST. PETER

❾

RUA DIREITA

R. JOSEFA D'ÓBIDOS

❿

❻

RUA DOS ARRIPES

❽

WC

R. S. JOÃO D'ORNELAS

To A-8/IC-1 Freeway (Lisbon & Nazaré)

ACCESS STAIRS

❸

ACCESS STAIRS TO WALL

**WALK BEGINS**

❶

MAIN GATE

Ⓑ

& WC

P (Pay)

P

RUA DA PORTA DA VILA

RUA DA PRAÇA

P (Free)

Aqueduct

To Train Station

❶ Castle/Pousada
❷ Casa de S. Thiago do Castelo
❸ Casa de S. Thiago do Castelo Annex
❹ Hotel Rainha Santa Isabel
❺ The Literary Man
❻ Hotel Josefa d'Óbidos
❼ Casa do Relogio
❽ Restaurante Burgo
❾ Rest./Pizzeria Muralhas
❿ 1st de Dezembro Café & Rest.
⓫ Troca-Tintos Wine Bar
⓬ Pasteleria Dom Afonso
⓭ Bar Ibn Errik Rex
⓮ Pillory

**NAZARÉ & CENTRAL PORTUGAL**

fine building was "brought to you by your friends in the Order of Christ."

• *After peeking in, exit the church and climb uphill to the main tourist drag, where you'll turn right on...*

**Rua Direita:** Walking toward the castle on this main shopping drag, you'll pass typical shops, a public WC, and the small **Municipal Museum,** not worth the admission fee unless you enjoy stairs, religious art, and Portuguese descriptions.

As you stroll, you'll see stands selling €1 shots of *ginjinha*—Óbidos' famous cherry liqueur. The tiny shots are served in edible chocolate cups (you'll pay a bit more for a shot in a glass, which can fit more booze). This custom, while gimmicky, is practically obligatory. (If you'd rather try one at a particularly atmospheric indoor spot, I've listed a favorite bar later in this walk.)

This is the town's most touristy street. But as you stroll, peek up to your left to notice a lonesome pastel-colored world, draped with flowers, and without a tourist in sight. Consider returning to the main gate (after this walk) on this picturesque upper lane, which is a photographer's delight.

• *Continue on and enter the...*

**Town Square:** The lone column at the side of the road (opposite the church) is the 16th-century **pillory.** Bad boys were tied to this to endure whatever punishment was deemed appropriate. Studying it closely, you'll notice it's capped by Queen Leonor's crown. On the side facing the castle, the carved hanging shrimp net represents how fishermen found the body of 16-year-old Afonso, son of Manuel I and Leonor, in the Rio Tejo after a tragic and mysterious death. The net eventually became part of the queen's coat of arms. The huge pots you see beneath the tile-roofed porch overlooking the square on the left were once in the central market and held olive oil instead of flowers.

• *At the bottom of the square, enter the...*

**Church of St. Mary of Óbidos:** Grab a seat on a front pew, surrounded by classic 17th-century tiles. Notice the fine painted-wood ceiling over each of the three naves. To the left of the altar is a niche with a delicate Portuguese Renaissance tomb, featuring a pietà carved out of local limestone. To the right of the altar are three paintings, including *The Mystical Marriage of St. Catherine,* all by Óbidos' most famous artist, the nun Josefa d'Óbidos (1634-1684).

To peek into another church, exit left and head a few steps

down (behind the terrace bar). Look for Our Lady of Mercy sculpted in blue and white ceramic above the entrance. The **Misericórdia church** was built as part of the queen's charity institution, hence the royal coat-of-arms painted on the ceiling. It's lined with 16th-century "carpet tiles." To the right of the altar you can see one of the "religious floats" and a cross that's carried through town during Holy Week festivities.

• *Return to the main shopping drag and turn right for the...*

**Final Stretch to the Castle:** On the left, pop into the **Pasteleria Dom Afonso** (#113). This welcoming little coffee bar, dominated by a big old grape press, serves good pastries and sandwiches. Try the local version of *pastel de nata,* with chocolate or with the sour-cherry-like berries that go into *ginjinha* (open daily 8:00-19:00).

A few steps farther down the street, **Bar Ibn Errik Rex** (#100, on the right) is the most characteristic indoor spot to sip *ginjinha.* Bruno will take good care of you, with a backdrop of his dad's extensive, 30-year-old collection of liquor bottles. Rather than serve the liqueur in a chocolate cup, he'll give you a more generous (and pricey) pour in a shot glass for €2.50 (Wed-Mon 11:00-24:00, closed Tue—except likely open Tue in July-Aug).

The main drag ends at a big, white church—but it's not a church anymore. Step inside to find a huge and inviting **bookstore,** with giant shelves filling the nave and apse, and a good selection of books in English. This deconsecrated church was repurposed after Óbidos was named a "City of Literature" (daily 10:00-19:00).

• *Facing the big, white church/bookstore, you have a couple of choices: Stairs on the left lead up to the top of the town wall. But for now, instead turn right and follow* pousada *signs. You'll pass the* pousada's *sweet little garden (an inviting spot for a coffee or drink), then continue up the curving stairs to a view terrace (with a telescope) just in front of the former castle.*

**Castle/Pousada:** Óbidos' onetime castle is now a fancy **$$$$** hotel with nine rooms (tel. 262-955-080, www.pousadas.pt). Looking out over these grand views, consider this history: On January 11, 1148, Afonso Henriques (Portugal's first king) led a two-pronged attack to liberate Óbidos from the Moors. Afonso attacked the main gate at the other end of town (where tourists enter), while the Moorish ruler huddled here in his castle. Meanwhile, a band of Afonso's men, disguised as cherry trees, snuck up the steep hillside behind the castle. The doomed Moor ignored his daughter when she turned from the window and asked him, "Daddy, do trees walk?"

After savoring the view, go back down toward the top of Rua Direita and enter the archway to your right. Walk uphill for a minute until you see the town wall. Turn around for a spectacular view of the castle—it's yours for the taking...even if you don't have a cherry-tree costume.

• *You can return to your starting point three ways: hiking along the upper town wall, exploring photogenic side lanes, or shopping and drinking your way back down the main drag.*

# Sleeping in Óbidos

To enjoy Óbidos without tourists, spend the night. There are reasonable values in this overpriced toy of a town. In the first three weeks in August, prices spike up well above those indicted by these price ranges.

## INSIDE THE OLD WALLS

**$$ Casa de S. Thiago do Castelo,** a fancy and characteristic little guesthouse at the base of the *pousada*/castle, rents eight elegantly appointed rooms around a chirpy *Better Homes and Tiles* patio. Lower levels offer three different, welcoming salons to relax in, including one with a classy billiards table (free parking, Largo de S. Thiago, tel. 262-959-587, www.casas-sthiago.com, reservas@casas-sthiago.com, Alice speaks English). They also have an annex near the main gate, where they book overflow guests in six rooms (without breakfast or parking) at busy times.

**$$ Hotel Rainha Santa Isabel** is an old-school hotel marked by flags on the main drag in the center of the old town. It has 20 traditional, musty rooms and a big lounge with comfy leather chairs (air-con, elevator, Wi-Fi in public areas only, minimal breakfast, some street noise, Rua Direita 63, tel. 262-959-323, www.obidoshotel.com, arsio@mail.telepac.pt). If you're driving, call first to let them know you're approaching, stop long enough to drop your bags and get a parking permit, and drive on to the town square to park. If no one's at the front desk, the staff at the Doce Rainha café next door can help.

## JUST BELOW THE OLD WALLS

While still in a cute cobbled zone, these accommodations sit just below the actual walls—so they have easier car access and fewer tourist throngs. All have free, public street parking nearby.

**$$ The Literary Man** was built as a convent, but it was recently remodeled to celebrate Óbidos' proud new literary status. Its 30 rooms come in two types: classic, old-fashioned tiled rooms, and sleek new postmodern rooms with concrete and warm wood. The public spaces—including a funky and delightful breakfast room/bar with books stacked under stout vaults—have books, books, everywhere (air-con, Rua Dom João d'Ornelas, tel.

262-959-217, www.theliteraryman.pt, bookme@theliteraryman.pt).

**$ Hotel Josefa d'Óbidos,** located just outside the town walls, is a great value, with 30 well-appointed, modern rooms and a sense of style rare in this price range (air-con, Rua Dom João d'Ornelas, tel. 262-955-010, www.josefadobidoshotel.com, josefadobidos@iol.pt). The attached **$$$** restaurant serves nice fish and meat dishes, and offers vegetarian options.

**$ Casa do Relogio** is a rustic eight-room place at the down-hill end of town, just outside the wall. It's friendly and easygoing, providing no-stress parking and great comfort for the price. English-speaking Sara offers a big sun terrace and happily does her guests' laundry for no extra charge (RS%, cash only, Rua da Graça 12, tel. 262-959-282, www.casadorelogio.com, reservas@casadorelogio.com).

## Eating in Óbidos

Óbidos is tough on the average tourist's food budget. Consider a picnic or one of the many cafés that offer cheap, basic meals.

**$$$ Restaurante Burgo,** just inside the main gate on the lower road, is a lively place with good seating in the small, stony dining room, or out on the cobbled street (daily 12:00-15:30 & 18:00-22:30, good ice cream, Rua Josefa d'Óbidos 11).

**$$ Restaurante/Pizzaria Muralhas** serves traditional Portuguese and Italian cuisine outside the city wall. Dine indoors, or on the back patio (Thu-Tue 12:00-15:00 & 19:00-22:00, closed Wed—but may be open Wed in July-Aug, closed Tue for dinner in winter, Rua Dom João d'Ornelas 6, tel. 262-958-550).

**$$ 1st de Dezembro Café & Restaurante,** tucked on a little square next to the Church of St. Peter, serves inexpensive pizza, salads, and omelets (Mon-Sat 8:00-24:00, closed Sun, Largo de San Pedro, tel. 262-959-298).

**$$ Troca-Tintos** is a good spot for a glass of wine and light meal of *petiscos* (Portuguese tapas) in an intimate atmosphere. Try to sit at one of the outdoor tables (Mon-Sat 18:00 until late, closed Sun, Rua Dom João d'Ornelas, next to recommended Literary Man, mobile 966-928-689). They have fado weekly (Mon 20:30-23:30, €4 cover, €3 if you buy food).

## Óbidos Connections

**By Bus from Óbidos to: Nazaré** (4 buses/day, 1 hour, some direct, most transfer in Caldas da Rainha), **Alcobaça** (6 buses/day, 2 hours). Far fewer buses run on weekends; be sure to check schedules at the TI.

**By Bus or Train to Lisbon:** The bus (hourly, 1 hour, www.rodotejo.pt) is a much better option than the train (5/day to Lisbon Rossio, 2.5 hours, transfer in Cacém or Mira Sintra-Melecas; also 3/day to Lisbon Oriente, 2.5 hours, transfer in Sete Rios).

**By Car to Lisbon:** From Óbidos, the tollway zips you directly into Lisbon in about an hour.

# COIMBRA

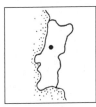

The college town of Coimbra—just two to three hours north of Lisbon by train, bus, or car—is Portugal's Oxford, and the country's easiest-to-enjoy city.

Don't be fooled by the drab suburbs. Culturally and historically, Coimbra (koo-EEM-brah) is second only to Lisbon. It was Portugal's leading city while the Moors controlled Lisbon (8th to 12th century) and the country's capital for more than 100 years (12th to mid-13th century). Only when Portugal's maritime fortunes rose did the ports of Lisbon and Porto manage to surpass landlocked Coimbra.

The earthquake that devastated Lisbon in 1755 spared Coimbra. Coimbra's "earthquake" came much later, in the form of the 20th-century dictator Salazar—who demolished much of the old center for his bombastic building projects.

Today, Coimbra (pop. 144,000) is home to the country's oldest and most prestigious university (founded 1290). When school is in session, this town bustles with the spirited exuberance of youth—although many students go home on Friday, so weekend nights aren't as crazy as you might expect. (Over the summer holidays, it's almost sleepy.) During the school year, you'll see bands of black-caped students hanging out, rushing to class, or gathered in little clusters on the street singing traditional songs—to each other as much as for tourists. Coimbra's fado music also has its own special character: Here, it's performed by college-age men rather than older women (as in Lisbon). Music lovers will want to sample both types.

Any time of year, Coimbra's inviting Arab-flavored old town—a maze of people, narrow streets, and tiny *tascas* (restaurants with just a few tables)—awaits exploration. And its main drag—with glassy marbled stone underfoot, old-timey shops and bakeries winking their neon signs, and more locals than tourists—is a delight to simply wander. But for serious sightseeing, look no further than that historic university, capping the hill above town and offering a busy slate of cultural attractions. By the time you leave town, you'll know why graduating students sing, *"Coimbra tem mais encanto na hora da despedida"* (Coimbra is the most enchanting at the moment you leave her).

## PLANNING YOUR TIME

On a two-week swing through Portugal, give Coimbra two nights and a full day. You could spend the whole day simply following my self-guided walk and dipping into the various sights as you reach them, then wind down the afternoon and evening by strolling and exploring the town, enjoying a good meal, and taking in some fado (the Fado ao Centro show at 18:00 is an ideal introduction).

# Orientation to Coimbra

Coimbra is a mini-Lisbon, with everything good about urban Portugal without the intensity of a big metropolis. I couldn't design a more delightful city for a visit. Skip Coimbra's modern center and stick to the charming old town.

From Largo da Portagem, the main square by the river, everything is within a short (if occasionally steep) walk. Plenty of budget rooms are within several blocks of the train station. The best views are from its low and high points: looking up from the far end of Santa Clara Bridge (Ponte Santa Clara) and looking down from the observation deck of the old university.

Coimbra's old town—a maze of timeworn shops, houses, and stairways—has two parts: the lower (Baixa) and the upper (Alta). The dividing line between these two sections is the main pedestrian street, which is named Visconde da Luz at one end and Rua de Ferreira Borges at the other. It runs from the Praça 8 de Maio to the Mondego River.

To get from this main pedestrian thoroughfare to the university, follow the streets that wind their way up the side of the hill. These little lanes meander like the alleyways of a Moroccan medina up to the city's highest point, the old university. To save yourself some uphill climbing, use Coimbra's elevator, take a taxi, or ride the little electric minibus (see "Getting Around Coimbra," later).

## TOURIST INFORMATION

The TI is a few steps off Largo da Portagem (June-Sept Mon-Fri 9:00-20:00, Sat-Sun 9:00-18:00; Oct-May Mon-Fri 9:00-18:00, Sat-Sun 9:30-13:30 & 14:00-17:30; entrance on Avenida Emídio Navarro—facing the bridge, tel. 239-488-120, www.turismodocentro.pt).

## ARRIVAL IN COIMBRA

### By Train

There are two Coimbra train stations, Station B (Estaçã Velha) and Station A (Estaçã Nova). Think B for "big": Nearly all major trains—such as those to and from Lisbon or Porto—stop only at Station B (some local trains do stop at both). But any ticket to or from Coimbra includes a shuttle train that connects Station B with the more centrally located Station A (5 minutes, 4/hour). To find which train will get you from B to A, check the electronic schedule boards or ask any station employee, *"Para Coimbra A* (ah)*?"* Taxis wait across the tracks from Station B (figure about €5 to Station A or your hotel). Neither has baggage storage.

Upon arrival at Station A, you're within a 10-minute walk of most lower town (Baixa) landmarks. Many recommended hotels are right outside the station, and others aren't much farther.

### By Bus

The bus station, on Avenida Fernão de Magalhães (tel. 239-855-270), has ATMs and baggage storage (closed Sat-Sun). The station is a 15-minute walk from the center; exit the bus station to the right, and follow the busy street into town. There's no need to make a special trip to the station just to get bus schedules or buy tickets (both can be done online, or the TI can print timetables upon request). If you're walking *to* the station to catch a bus to leave Coimbra, take Avenida Fernão de Magalhães almost to its intersection with Cabral, and look to the left—the Neptuno café is by the station's subtle entrance.

### By Car

From Lisbon, it's an easy two-hour straight shot on the slick *auto-estrada* A-1 (toll road). You'll pass convenient exits for Fátima and the Roman ruins of Conímbriga along the way. Leave the freeway on the easy-to-miss first Coimbra exit (Coimbra Sul), then follow the *Centro* signs. Two and a half miles after leaving the freeway, you'll cross the Mondego River. Take Avenida Fernão de Magal-hães directly into town. Most recommended hotels are near Station

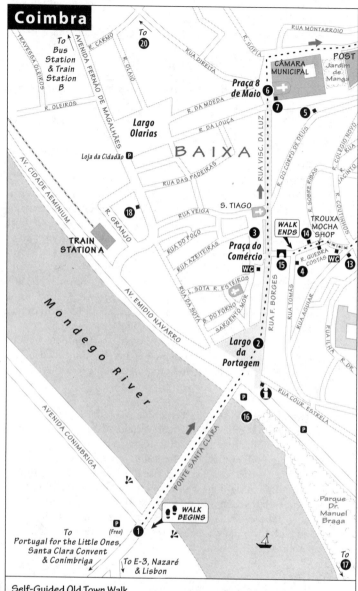

# Coimbra

RUA MONTARROIO

To Bus Station & Train Station B

AVENIDA FERNÃO DE MAGALHÃES

TRAVESSA OLEIROS

R. CARMO

R. OLAIO

R. OLEIROS

To **20**

RUA DIREITA

R. DA MOEDA

R. DA LOUÇA

**Largo Olarias**

Loja da Cidadão **P**

RUA VISC. DA LUZ

RUA DO CORPO DE DEUS

**CÂMARA MUNICIPAL**

**Praça 8 de Maio** **6**
**7**

**POST**

Jardim de Manga

**5**

B A I X A

RUA DAS PADEIRAS

RUA VEIGA

R. GRANJO

**18**

AV. CIDADE AEMINIUM

**TRAIN STATION A**

RUA DO POÇO

RUA AZEITEIRAS

S. TIAGO

**3**

**Praça do Comércio**

**WC**

R. SOBRE RIBAS

R. DO CORPO DE DEUS

R. COLÉGIO NOVO

R. JACINTO

R. COUTINHOS

**WALK ENDS**

**TROUXA MOCHA SHOP**

**14**

**15** R. QUEBRA COSTAS **4** **WC** **13**

RUA F. BORGES

RUA TOMÁS

RUA AGUIAR

RUA ILHA R. DR.

*M o n d e g o   R i v e r*

AV. EMÍDIO NAVARRO

L. SOTA  R. ESTEIROS

R. DA SOTA

B. DO FORNO

SARGENTO MOR

**Largo da Portagem** **2**

**16**

**P**

**i**

RUA COUR. ESTRELA

**P**

AVENIDA CONÍMBRIGA

PONTE SANTA CLARA

**P** (Free)

**WALK BEGINS**

**1**

*Parque Dr. Manuel Braga*

To **17**

To Portugal for the Little Ones, Santa Clara Convent & Conímbriga

To E-3, Nazaré & Lisbon

## Self-Guided Old Town Walk
1. Santa Clara Bridge
2. Largo da Portagem
3. Praça do Comércio
4. Chiado Building/ Municipal Museum
5. À Capella Fado
6. Church of Santa Cruz
7. Café Santa Cruz
8. Mercado Municipal
9. Elevador do Mercado
10. Machado de Castro Museum/ Cryptoporticus

COIMBRA

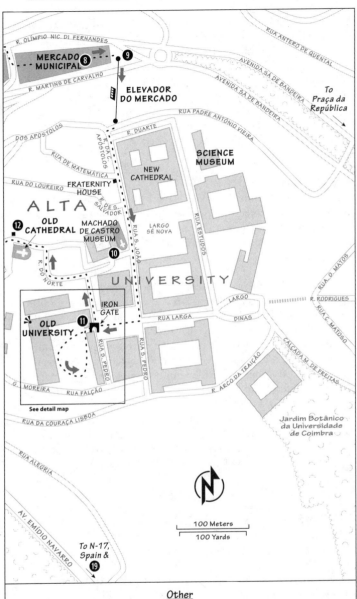

R. OLÍMPIO NIC. DI FERNANDES

RUA ANTERO DE QUENTAL

**MERCADO MUNICIPAL** 8 --- 9

AVENIDA SÁ DE BANDEIRA

R. MARTINS DE CARVALHO

AVENIDA SÁ DE BANDEIRA

*To Praça da República*

**ELEVADOR DO MERCADO**

RUA PADRE ANTÓNIO VIEIRA

DOS APOSTOLOS

R. DUARTE

RUA DAS APOSTOLOS

RUA DE MATEMÁTICA

**NEW CATHEDRAL**

**SCIENCE MUSEUM**

RUA DO LOUREIRO

**FRATERNITY HOUSE**

R. DE S. SALVADOR

**A L T A**

12 **OLD CATHEDRAL**

**MACHADO DE CASTRO MUSEUM** 10

LARGO SÉ NOVA

RUA S. JOÃO

RUA ESTUDOS

R. DO NORTE

**U N I V E R S I T Y**

RUA O. MATOS

R. RODRIGUES

RUA C. MATOS

**IRON GATE**

LARGO DINAS

**OLD UNIVERSITY** 11

RUA LARGA

CALÇADA M. DE FREITAS

RUA S. PEDRO

RUA S. PEDRO

R. ARCO DA TRAIÇÃO

G. MOREIRA

RUA FALCÃO

See detail map

RUA DA COURAÇA LISBOA

*Jardim Botânico da Universidade de Coimbra*

RUA ALEGRIA

AV. EMÍDIO NAVARRO

N

100 Meters
100 Yards

*To N-17, Spain &* 19

11 Iron Gate to Old University

12 Restaurante O Trovador

13 Café Sé Velha

14 Fado ao Centro

15 Arco de Almedina

*Other*

16 River Cruises

17 To Kayak Tours

18 InterVisa Travel Agency (Bus Tickets)

19 To Pedro & Inês Bridge

20 To Launderette

A and the Santa Clara Bridge. If you arrive from northern Portugal or central Spain, follow signs for *Centro/Largo da Portagem*.

The large lot on the south bank of the river offers free parking (but it's not guarded overnight—park at your own risk). In town, you'll find several big, convenient, clearly marked pay garages. The largest is centrally located in the lower old town under the government office called Loja da Cidadão (on Avenida Fernão de Magalhães). Most hotels can provide advice on the best parking options, and many offer parking in city lots (as little as €5/day).

## HELPFUL HINTS

**Exchange Rate:** €1 = about $1.10

**Country Calling Code:** 351 (see page 422 for dialing instructions)

**Laundry:** A modern, self-service **Lavamais** launderette is less than a 10-minute walk north of the main shopping street (daily 8:00-22:00, free Wi-Fi, Rua Mário Pais 22, mobile 914-376-001).

**Long-Distance Bus Tickets:** The **InterVisa travel agency** sells international tickets to Salamanca, Spain, and beyond. They charge a small commission, but it's worth it (Mon-Fri 9:00-13:00 & 14:30-18:30, closed Sat-Sun, Avenida Fernão da Magalhães 11, tel. 239-823-873).

**Local Guides:** I've enjoyed working with three good private guides in Coimbra. Each can give you and your travel partners a private half-day tour in town (€100) or around the region on an outing tailored to your interests: **Cristina Carvalho** (mobile 917-200-180, ccfb64@hotmail.com), **Maria Jose Fernandes** (mobile 934-093-542, mariajf76@gmail.com), and **Rosa Lopez** (mobile 966-103-277, mrosatoscano@gmail.com). **Sara Cruz** and her colleagues at **Go! Leisure & Heritage** lead a variety of cultural town walks, as well as excursions to out-of-town sights (mobile 910-163-118, www.gowalksportugal.com, booking@gowalksportugal.com).

## GETTING AROUND COIMBRA

While most visitors do the entire city on foot, **taxis** are cheap (€4-5 for a short ride) and a good option if you've been up and down too many hills.

Most **buses** skip the old town, but a few run through the university. You can either buy a ticket for €1.60 per ride; or pay €0.50 for a rechargeable Viagem ConVIDA card for cheaper fares (€1/ride; better-value 3-ride, 10-ride, and one-day passes available and shareable; all are sold at kiosks or the Loja SMTUC offices—one is at Santa Clara Bridge directly across from the TI and another is at the Elevador do Mercado, www.smtuc.pt). Bus passes are also valid for Coimbra's Elevador do Mercado that runs between Mercado Municipal and the top of town (described on page 290), and for the electric minibus that shuttles between the lower and upper town (described next).

This cute little electric **minibus** (nicknamed *pantufinhas,* or "grandma's slipper") is silent and easy, designed to get grandmas— and anyone else—up and down the steep hills of the old town. It makes a continuous 20-minute loop through the lower old town (Baixa) and around the upper old town (Alta), passing through Largo da Portagem, down the pedestrian shopping lane to Praça 8 de Maio, past the market and elevator, then circling up to the cathedral (the bus' high point) before returning down to Largo da Portagem. There are just three regular stops—but you can wave down the bus anywhere you like, and the driver will let you off wherever you ask (€1.60, pay driver or use Viagem ConVIDA card).

## Coimbra Old Town Walk

Coimbra is fun on foot, especially along its straight (formerly Roman) pedestrian-only main drag. This self-guided tour takes two to three hours—but if you visit all of the sights en route (including the university), it could fill the better part of a day.

• *Start your walk at the...*

❶ **Santa Clara Bridge** (Ponte Santa Clara): This bridge has been an important link across the Mondego River since Roman times. For centuries, it had a tollgate *(portagem).* The far end of the bridge offers a fine Coimbra view.

Coimbra is redeveloping its long-neglected riverside. A park stretches past several recommended restaurants to the romantic pedestrian bridge, linking the town with the far riverbank, where an improved, people-friendly zone is envisioned. The bridge is named for Dom Pedro and Dona Inês (Portugal's Romeo and Juliet—see page 269).

• *At the end of the bridge on the Coimbra side is the parklike square called...*

❷ **Largo da Portagem:** In the center of the main square is a statue of the prime minister who, in 1834, shut down the city's convents and monasteries, and earned the nickname "friar killer."

Much of the old center is ornamented with fin-de-siècle architecture (circa 1900) from a boom period; on the left side of the square, notice the fancy pink bank building and the exterior of Hotel Astória behind it.

This square is a great place for coffee or a pastry. The best

COIMBRA

## Coimbra in History

**1064**  Coimbra is taken from the Moors.

**1139**  Portugal's first king, Afonso Henriques, makes Coimbra his capital.

**1211**  Portugal's first parliament of nobles (cortes) convenes at Coimbra.

**1256**  Lisbon replaces Coimbra as Portugal's capital.

**1308**  The university (founded in Lisbon in 1290 under King Dinis, r. 1279-1325) moves to Coimbra.

**1537**  The university, after another short stint in Lisbon, resettles permanently in Coimbra under Jesuit administration.

**1810**  Napoleon's French troops sack Coimbra, then England's duke of Wellington drives them out.

**1928**  António Salazar, professor of political economy at Coimbra, becomes minister of finance and eventually dictator of Portugal.

goodies are at Pastelaria Briosa, at the start of the main drag; enjoy their creative window displays. The shop's name, meaning "pure, proud, respectable," is the nickname for the people of Coimbra (and their football team): Go Briosa! Another popular place is Café Montanha, with a big brass palm tree inside and delightful seating on the square. The town's two special treats are *pastel de Santa Clara* (pastry made with almonds and marmalade) and *pastel de Tentúgal* (rolls of puff pastry stuffed with eggs and cream, and dusted with powdered sugar).

• *Stroll down the delightfully pedestrianized Rua de Ferreira Borges. After a 200-yard-long gauntlet of clothing stores, take the stairs (on your left, under the gigantic graffiti portrait of what looks like Sigmund Freud) leading to a terrace overlooking the square below (pay public WC—*sanitários—*are in the stairwell).*

❸ **Praça do Comércio:** This pleasant square is, literally, the place of commerce. It was originally just outside the city walls— a kind of medieval duty-free zone where merchants could trade tax-free. The streets branching off the square were named for the type of product traditionally made or traded there (such as Rua das Azeiteiras, named for olive-oil producers). Two churches book-ending the square are a reminder that religious orders also set up just outside the city walls. Beyond Praça do Comércio stretches the rough end of town.

Look at your map. The circular street pattern outlines the wall used by Romans, Visigoths, Moors, and Christians to protect Coimbra. Historically, only the rich could afford to live within the protective city walls of the Alta, or high town. Even today, the Baixa, or lower town, remains a poorer section, with haggard women rolling wheeled shopping carts, children running barefoot, and men lounging on the square as if wasting time is their life's calling. But it's a fine area for wandering around during the day to explore small shops and eateries, and to get thoroughly disoriented.

• *Return to the pedestrian street.*

Across the way, notice the balconied building trimmed with lacy ironwork. This innovative iron structure, which opened as the ❹ **Chiado** department store in 1909, was big news in town when it was built. (Today it's a museum with textiles and artwork; see page 301.)

Next door is **Casa da Sorte,** a lottery shop—these are much loved in Portugal. Step inside and feel the energy of gamblers unwittingly letting the state take their money to fund social programs. What's the total for the Euromilhões (European-wide "euro millions" lottery)? You may see circles of friends huddling here who've invested collectively in a gambling partnership. (If you like to send postcards, this shop is a convenient place to buy stamps.)

At the corner (on your right), steps lead up through an ancient arched gateway—**Arco de Almedina**—into the old city and to the old cathedral and university. Later, after visiting the university, we'll finish this walk by going downhill through this arch.

A block farther along the pedestrian drag, stop at the picturesque corner (where the building comes to a triangular corner). The steep road climbs into Coimbra's historic former Jewish quarter and the wonderful and recommended ❺ **À Capella** fado nightclub (see "Entertainment in Coimbra," later).

Check out the newsstands, where the daily papers have mostly sport news fixated on football (meaning soccer). The **Bragas men's store** (near the end of the street, on the right at #35), with hats and ties, is one of a shrinking number of old-time shops left on this street. Malls are sucking this kind of business out to the suburbs as a rising tide of tourism changes the character of this venerable street.

As you stroll along, you'll know it's graduation time if students' photos are displayed in photographers' windows. Check out the graduates decked out in their traditional university capes (displaying the time-honored rips on the hem—cuts on the left side are made by family, on the right side by friends, and on the back by girl- or boyfriends) and color-coded sashes indicating their field of study.

• *The pedestrian street ends at Praça 8 de Maio, with the...*

❻ **Church of Santa Cruz** (Mosteiro de Santa Cruz): Enjoy this church's grand facade. While almost invisible, wires on the statuary are electrified to keep pigeons from dumping their corrosive loads on the tender limestone. Go inside; it's the most active religious spot in town (church—free, sacristy—donation requested; Mon-Fri 9:00-17:00, Sat 9:00-12:00 & 14:00-17:00, Sun 16:00-17:30; limited access during Mass).

The musty church is lavishly decorated with 18th-century tiles that tell the stories of the discovery of the Holy Cross (by Roman Emperor Constantine's mother, Saint Helena, on the left) and the life of St. Augustine (on the right; the church is of the Augustinian order).

Head up the nave, pausing at the side altar on the left (under the organ with horizontal trumpets). Here you see St. Anthony of Padua—known locally as St. Anthony of Lisbon—dressed as an Augustinian monk. He studied in Coimbra as a young monk in the 13th century. Just beyond the chapel, the exquisitely carved pulpit is considered one of the finest pieces of Renaissance work in Portugal.

Step behind the altar for a close-up look at two fine 16th-century tombs. On the left lies the first Portuguese king, Afonso Henriques (1095-1185). Afonso "The Conqueror" reclaimed most of Portugal from the Moors, declared himself king, got the pope to approve the title, and settled down in his chosen capital—Coimbra. There, his wife gave birth to young Sancho, who later became king. Sancho I (1154-1211, tomb on right) was known as "The Populator." He saw the destruction that war had brought to the country, and set about rebuilding and repopulating, inviting northern European Crusaders (such as the Knights Templar) to occupy southern Portugal and giving trade privileges to border towns to strengthen his country's economy.

Notice that these tombs are carved in the richly ornamented Manueline style. In the 16th century, while headed on a pilgrimage to Santiago de Compostela, the great King Manuel I dropped by this church and was underwhelmed by the two kings' original tombs. He commissioned these beautifully carved replacements—much more fitting for royalty. Study the intimate faces. Notice how the kings seem only to be resting. (To make themselves more comfortable, they've "hung" their helmets and arm guards just behind them.)

**Church of Santa Cruz Sacristy and Cloister:** For a small donation, you can explore the sacristy (entrance to right of main altar), see the treasures of the church, and pass through the impressive chapter room into the Manueline Cloister of Silence. The first room is the actual sacristy (with "carpet tiles" blanketing the walls and huge banks of drawers for priests' vestments). The room to the right has relics, including the skull of St. Teotonio, the first Portuguese saint. Opposite is the chapter room with St. Teotonio's tomb and a few paintings.

In the chapter room, note the painting of the Augustinian monks. Imagining you are a fellow monk, step outside into the Cloister of Silence, with its fine Manueline arches and late-18th-century tiled scenes of Christ teaching the beatitudes. Walk pensively clockwise, hands folded, pondering worshipfully each parable from Matthew and Luke as a meditative monk would have in this space 200 years ago. Feel the tranquility. Notice that you are walking upon the tombs of the very monks who took this same stroll so long ago—and who chose to be buried so humbly, to be trod upon by those who came after them. You're in the city center, but here, in the Cloister of Silence, about the only sound is the gurgle of the fountain.

• *Exit the church into the main square. Once called the Square of Samson, it was renamed for the date when French Revolutionary ideas arrived in Portugal (a little behind the European trends, as usual) and the state asserted its secular power over the Church—on May 8, 1833. People (and pigeons) survey the Praça 8 de Maio scene from the terrace of the recommended...*

❼ **Café Santa Cruz:** Located to the right of the church, this coffeehouse was originally built as a church. It was abandoned with the dissolution of the monasteries in the 1830s, when the government took possession of many grand religious buildings and their surrounding land. As a café, this was the 19th-century haunt of the town's intellectuals. The altar is now used for lectures, poetry readings, small concerts, and art exhibits (the women's restroom is in a confessional). They offer free fado performances many nights at 22:00.

• *Continue past the church and the City Hall (Câmara Municipal). At the noisy street, turn right, and go a block to find a park with a fountain (once a monastery cloister and Renaissance garden) and the cheap, handy, and recommended self-service restaurant* **Jardim da Manga**. *Keep going uphill along the busy Rua Olímpio Nicolau di Fernandes past the big post office to the...*

❽ **Mercado Municipal:** This modern covered market is fun to explore and great for gathering picnic supplies (Mon-Sat 8:00-14:00, closed Sun, busiest on Tue and Fri). It's clean and hygienic, but maintains the colorful appeal of an old farmers market. See the "salt of the earth" in the faces of the women selling produce (their men are off in the fields...or in the bars—a.k.a. their beloved "little chapels"). These ladies aren't shy about trying to sell their goods, even to tourists. For about the cheapest meal in town, pop into the Bar do Mercado Requinte at the end of the ground floor (menu posted on wall, €7 meals for two, public WC around the corner).

In the bar's sit-down area, check out the photos of the old market on the wall. Then go upstairs for bread, more meat, and veggies. Follow your nose through the glass doors at the far end, with all the fresh fish and dried cod. The Portuguese are the world's biggest cod eaters, but because cod is no longer found in nearby waters, the local favorite is imported from Norway. To the Portuguese, cod *(bacalhau)* tastes

much better dried and salted than fresh. This section housed the original market—you can recognize the wrought-iron work from the photos you've just seen on the ground floor at the bar.

• *Swim through the fish hall and head outside at the far end, where you'll find the sleek city elevator.*

**❾ Elevador do Mercado:** A combination elevator/funicular ride whisks you up the long, steep hill (stop midway to transfer to funicular), offering commanding views of Coimbra en route (€1.60/trip, or €1 with Viagem ConVIDA card, ticket office adjacent or just pay the elevator attendant; Mon-Sat 7:30-21:00, Sun 10:00-21:00).

At the top, jog right, then head straight uphill (on Rua da Couraça Apóstolos) toward the university buildings at the top of the hill. Fifty yards up this lane, at the first intersection, you'll find a fraternity house called Real República Corsários das Ilhas ("Royal Commune of the Island Pirates"). Notice the faded skull-and-crossbones graffiti on the wall, linking McDonald's and the G8 (group of the eight most powerful countries). Look around for other graffiti. These small university frat houses, called *repúblicas*, are communes that traditionally house about a dozen students from the same region or provincial town. While some are highly cultured, the rowdier ones are often decorated with plunder from their pranks—stolen traffic signs and so on—giving rise to the local saying, "At night, many things happen in Coimbra."

• *Walk three blocks. On the right, you'll pass the ❿ Machado de Castro Museum (visit on your way back downhill at the end of this walk; they also have a handy lunch buffet; described on page 299). Across the street and uphill, you'll see the New Cathedral and some stark university buildings.*

*Soon you pop out into the big, fascist-style university square (Praça da Porta Férrea). The ⓫ Iron Gate entry to the old university is on your right.*

**University:** Explore the university (described later, under "Sights in Coimbra"), and then continue this town walk. (If you tour the Science Museum, afterward make your way back to the Machado de Castro Museum to continue the walk.)

• *When you're finished, leave the university: Pass back out through the Iron Gate, turn left—retracing your steps a bit—and, if you like, tour the Machado de Castro Museum. Then you'll take the steps down around the back of the museum, following the steep lanes toward the old cathedral and into the old town. If you've visited the Roman substructure inside the museum, seeing these stout walls and steep slope helps you understand the need for a sturdy foundation to support a sprawling and level market square, or forum. Farther down, look through the metal grates on your right to see the old Roman street and remains of ancient houses.*

**Downhill Streets Through the Upper Town:** As you wander, notice the white-paper squares and diamonds in the windows—they indicate that there's a student room available for rent.

Continuing on, you'll come to the **old cathedral** (Sé Velha, described later, under "Sights in Coimbra"). Facing the cathedral is the ⓬ **Restaurante O Trovador,** offering fado performances nearly every night in summer (reservations essential, see "Entertainment in Coimbra"). The colorful little ⓭ **Café Sé Velha,** on the corner immediately below the cathedral and tiled with traditional Coimbran scenes, is a good place to sit and watch people climb up and down. From here, a very faded blue line on the cobbles marks the route of the electric minibus (described earlier).

Take the steep stairway leading down (past the public WCs) to **Rua Quebra Costas,** the "Street of Broken Ribs." At one time, this lane had no steps, and literally *was* the street of broken ribs. During a strong rain, this becomes a river. The lane's many tourist and gift shops show off the fine local blue-and-white ceramic work called *faiança*.

Descending farther, you emerge into a little square ringed by enticing al fresco cafés and funky shops catering to a mix of tourists and students. On your left, the **Trouxa Mocha** shop has appealing clothes (leather shoes, wool sweaters) and accessories with modern style, but rooted in Portuguese tradition. Just below that shop, notice the charming statue of **Tricana** (the term given for a local woman in traditional folk dress) resting after a trip to the well. She represents the usual target of fado love songs—and student Romeos. Local men from the lower town had a tough time competing for the Tricana of Coimbra with all the rich and witty students... not to mention the talented singers. Across the street from Tricana is the recommended ⓮ **Fado ao Centro,** my favorite place in town for getting a concise and appealing taste of Coimbra's unique take on this Portuguese musical form—consider making a reservation now for a performance (see page 304 for details).

• *Rua Quebra Costas ends at...*

⓯ **Arco de Almedina:** This is the double set of arches (named "Gate to the Medina" in Arabic by the Moors) we saw earlier from the pedestrian street Rua de Ferreira Borges. Part of the old town wall, the arches act as a double gate with a 90-degree kink in the middle for easier defense. Pause at the gift shop between the gates to enjoy the lilting, nostalgic sound of fado and the 12-string Portuguese guitar. That's sweet. But don't linger too long because— look up: In times of attack, soldiers used those two square holes in the ceiling to pour down boiling oil, turning attacking Moors into fritters. The holes are rudely nicknamed *mata-cães* (dog killers).

A few steps farther down, before the second gate, admire from all sides the monument to fado. Featuring the Coimbra-style Portuguese guitar, draped both with the cape of the male student and the shawl of the woman, this bronze statue celebrates how fado connected the all-male-at-the-time university world with the women of the town. Locals say a good musician plays his guitar with art and passion, as if loving a woman.

• *Passing under the second arch, you're back on the pedestrian street near where this walk began.*

## Sights in Coimbra

### ▲▲UNIVERSITY OF COIMBRA (UNIVERSIDADE DE COIMBRA)

This venerable centuries-old university, founded in 1290, was modeled after Bologna's university (Europe's first, founded in 1139).

It occupies a stately three-winged former royal palace (from when Coimbra was the capital), beautifully situated overlooking the city. At first, law, medicine, grammar, and logic were taught. Then, with the rise of seafaring in Portugal, astronomy and geometry were added. While Lisbon's university is much larger, Coimbra's university (with 25,000 students) is still the country's most respected. For visitors, the university marks the top of the old town. While most of it is mid-20th-century sprawl, the old core of the university (*velha universidade*—the palace section, with its iron gate, courtyard, fancy ceremonial halls, chapel, and library) makes for an interesting visit.

**Cost:** Programa 3 costs €10 and covers the Grand Hall, St. Michael's Chapel, and King João's Library at the old university. **Programa 1** is €12 and adds the Science Museum, a 5-minute walk away. You can add €1 to any ticket to climb the tower, but I wouldn't. Buy your ticket at the counter located inside the Biblioteca Geral (the large building to the left as you approach the Iron Gate).

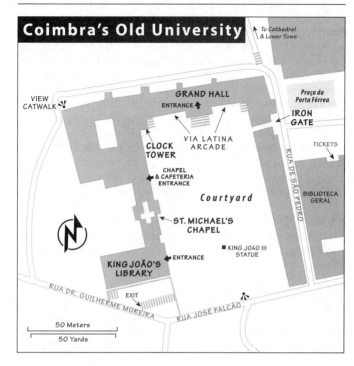

**Coimbra's Old University**

To Cathedral & Lower Town

VIEW CATWALK

GRAND HALL
ENTRANCE

CLOCK TOWER

VIA LATINA ARCADE

CHAPEL & CAFETERIA ENTRANCE

Courtyard

ST. MICHAEL'S CHAPEL

KING JOÃO'S LIBRARY

ENTRANCE

KING JOÃO III STATUE

Praça da Porta Férrea

IRON GATE

TICKETS

RUA DE SÃO PEDRO

BIBLIOTECA GERAL

RUA DR. GUILHERME MOREIRA

EXIT

RUA JOSÉ FALCÃO

50 Meters

50 Yards

**Hours:** April-Oct daily 9:00-19:30, Nov-March Mon-Fri 9:30-13:00 & 14:00-17:30, Sat-Sun 10:00-16:00.

**When to Go:** King João's Library, the complex's highlight, is accessible only via a timed-entry receipt that comes with your ticket. Reservations are not possible; on very busy days, you may have to wait hours. If you anticipate crowds, arrive by 10:00.

**Getting There:** To get to the university, you could take my "Coimbra Old Town Walk" (described earlier), using the elevator from the Mercado Municipal to get to the top of the hill. Or take a taxi to the Iron Gate (on Praça da Porta Férrea), see the university, and then sightsee Coimbra downhill.

**Information:** Tel. 239-242-745, www.uc.pt/en.

**Tours:** The €3 audioguide gives 1.5 hours of info.

### ❍ Self-Guided Tour

• *Begin your visit just outside the entrance to the old campus, at the...*

### Iron Gate (Porta Férrea)

Before entering the old campus, stand with your back to the iron gate and look across the stark, modern square at the fascist architecture of the new university. In the 1940s, in what's considered one of the worst cultural crimes in Portuguese history, the dictator António Salazar tore down half of Coimbra's old town to build these university halls. The grandiose ceremonial approach to the university, bombastic and utilitarian to fit fascist taste, is flanked by the faculties of letters, medicine, science, and the library (with the ticket office). The law school is behind you, inside the old campus.

Salazar, proud that Portugal was the last European power to hang onto its colonial empire, wanted a fittingly monumental university here. After all, Salazar—along with virtually everyone of political influence in Portugal—had been educated at Coimbra, where he studied law and then became an economics professor. If these bold buildings are reminiscent of Mussolini's E.U.R. in Rome, perhaps it's because they were built in part by Italian architects hired by Portugal's "little Mussolini."

OK, now turn and walk through the Iron Gate. Traditionally, freshmen—proudly wearing their black capes for the first time—pass through the Iron Gate to enroll. Also traditionally, they had to pass through an Iron Gate gauntlet of butt kicks from upperclassmen to get out.

### Old University Courtyard

The university's most important sights all face this square: the Grand Hall (up the grand stairway on the right), St. Michael's Chapel (straight ahead, through the door, then to the left), and King João's Library (across the square, farthest door on left, flanked by columns).

The statue in the square is of **King João III** (1502-1557). While the university was established in 1290, it went back and forth between Lisbon and Coimbra (back then, university students were adults, privileged, and a pain to have in your town). In 1537, João III finally established the school permanently in Coimbra. Standing like a good humanist (posing hand on hip, much like we're used to seeing his contemporary, England's King Henry VIII), João modernized Portugal's education system in the Renaissance style. But, unlike Henry, who broke the local power of the Church, João (grandson of the ultra-Catholic Queen Isabel of Spain) empowered the Church. He let the Jesuits—the guardians of orthodoxy—run this university, which became the center of Portugal's Inquisition.

The black capes famously worn by local students originated with the capes worn by Jesuits and clergy during this period. Like the uniforms of students at American Catholic schools, standardized clothing removes the focus on power-dressing and equalizes people of all classes. To this day, standards of modesty prevail, keeping class divisions at a minimum among the students, and between students and professors. (Students, when wearing their gowns, are not allowed to show off by wearing gold.)

Survey the square with your back to the gate. The dreaded sound of the clock tower's bell—named the "baby goat" for its nagging—calls students to class. On several occasions, the clapper has been stolen. (No bell...no class. No class...big party.) A larger bell (the "big goat") rings only on important, formal occasions.

The arcaded passageway (on the right, up the stairs) between the Iron Gate and the clock tower is called Via Latina, from the days when only Latin was spoken in this part of the university.

• *Now visit each of the university's sights, beginning with the...*

## Grand Hall (Sala dos Capelos)

From the middle of the Via Latina, climb the tiled stairway. Follow the route through an ornate room, then trudge around a narrow

hallway, where you can peek out from little balconies into the Grand Hall—the site of the university's major academic ceremonies, such as oral exams and graduations. This regally red room was originally the throne room of the royal palace. Today, the rector's green chair sits like a throne in front. During ceremonies, students in their formal attire fill the benches, and teachers sit along the perimeter as gloomy portraits of Portuguese kings watch from above.

The fine, old, painted ceiling features "Indo-Portuguese" themes, reminding Portugal's next generation of leaders of the global reach of their nation. There is no clapping during these formal rituals, but a brass band (on the wooden platform in the back) punctuates the ceremonies with solemn music.

**View Catwalk** *(Varanda):* Continue past the end of the Grand Hall, to an ornately decorated former royal stateroom (until recently a place where students took their oral exams as portraits of past university rectors looked on). Just past this room a door leads to a narrow observation gallery offering the best views of Coimbra (closed in bad weather). If the door is closed, open it.

From the viewpoint, scan the old town from right to left. Remember, before Salazar's extension of the university, this old town surrounded the university. The Baroque facade breaking the horizon is the "new" cathedral—from the 16th century. Below that, with the fine arcade and modern café terrace, is the Machado de Castro Museum, housed in the former bishop's palace and located

# The Burning of Ribbons

Europe's third-oldest university has long-standing traditions to match. If you're lucky enough to be in Coimbra at the end of the academic year (early to mid-May), you'll witness a big party.

The "Burning of Ribbons" *(Queima das Fitas)* began in the 1850s, when a group of students who passed their final fourth-year exams gathered outside the Iron Gate and marched together to the lower town. They burned their ribbons (which were used to bind and carry their books) in a small fire, representing their passage from student life to professional life. Eventually, that simple event evolved into the biggest academic festival of the year, complete with floats and parades.

Students entering their last year of studies as well as recent graduates *(finalistas)* participate in the party these days, but of course the graduates get the most attention. Women wear simple white shirts with black skirts and black stockings. Men dress more formally in a long black suit, university cape, wide sash with various badges, top hat, and cane.

Different accent colors, proudly displayed on the top hats and canes, represent the different academic departments, indicating which degree the student earned (yellow for medicine, red for law, blue for science, and so on). For good luck after graduation, men take their canes and tap other students' top hats three times. (The taps can get out of control, and lots of students end up losing the tops of their hats.)

Much drinking accompanies this rite of passage. Ribbon-burning parties are also celebrated in Porto, and to a lesser extent in Lisbon. Join the fun, and offer an appropriately colored flower to a new graduate. You may be invited to the party.

atop a Roman site (all described later). And below that, like an armadillo, sits the old cathedral with its tiled cupola.

Gaily painted yellow-and-blue windows mark *república* frat houses. If you visit during late October, November, or May, you might see a student festival: Parades of rowdy students in funny costumes, draped in signs, dragging tin cans—these are all part of the traditional initiation rites marking the beginning and end of the school year. May provides the biggest spectacle, when new students receive—and graduating students burn—the small colored ribbons of their chosen major (see sidebar). Look beyond the houses to the Mondego River, the longest river that flows entirely in Portugal. Over the bridge, beyond the university's sports facilities, stretches the 17th-century Santa Clara Convent—at 590 feet, the longest building in Coimbra.

• *Exiting the building, you'll spot the entrance to the **tower**. Skip it—it's not worth the entry fee or the 184 claustrophobic steps to see views similar to the ones you just saw from the catwalk.*

*Instead, continue straight ahead. Just on the right is the entrance to...*

## St. Michael's Chapel (Capela de São Miguel)

This chapel is behind a 16th-century facade (enter through door to the right of facade—once inside, knock on the door on the left marked *capela*). The architecture of the church interior is Manueline—notice the golden "rope" trimming the arch before the altar. The chapel was begun in 1517, but much of the decor is from a later time. The altar is 17th-century Mannerist, with steps unique to Portugal (and her South American colonies); based on Jacob's Ladder, they symbolize the steps the faithful take on their journey to heaven. The "carpet tiles" covering the walls date from the 17th century and kept the chapel cool in the summer. The 2,100-pipe, 18th-century German-built organ is notable for its horizontal "trumpet" pipes. Found only in Iberia, these help the organist perform the allegorical fight between good and evil—with the horizontal pipes trumpeting the arrival of the good guys. The box seats for the royal family are high above the musicians' loft in the rear. Students and alums enjoy the privilege of having their weddings here.

**Student Cafeteria:** In the corridor just outside the chapel, you'll find WCs and a cheap student-filled café with a lovely view of the river from the terrace (follow signs to *bar*). Visitors are perfectly welcome to eat here. During busy lunch times, every seat gets taken, people share tables, and you may find yourself sitting with law students and their professors.

• *As you face the statue of King João, you'll see his descendant's library poking out into the courtyard, at the end, on the right.*

## ▲King João's Library (Biblioteca Joanina)

In this elegant building, one of Europe's best surviving Baroque libraries displays 55,000 books in 18th-century splendor. The zealous doorkeeper locks the door at every opportunity to keep out humidity. At your appointed time, you'll be allowed into this 300-year-old

temple of thought. (After you enter, watch the doorkeeper use the giant key as a hefty doorknob.)

Inside, at the "high altar," stands the library's founder, the absolute monarch King João V (1698-1750), who considered France's King Louis XIV an inspiration (and they have similar hairstyles).

The reading tables, inlaid with exotic South American woods (and ornamented with silver ink wells), and the precious wood shelves (with clever hideaway staircases) are reminders that Portugal's wealth was great—and imported (mostly from Brazil). Built Baroque, the interior is all wood. Even the "marble" on the arches of triumph that divide the library into rooms is painted wood. (Real marble would add to the humidity.) The small doors with glass windows lead to professors' tiny studies with big windows to read by. The resident bats—who live in the building, but not the library itself—are well cared for and appreciated. They eat insects, providing a chemical-free way of protecting the books, and alert the guard to changing weather with their "eee-eee" cry. Look for

the trompe l'oeil Baroque tricks on the painted ceiling. Gold leaf (from Brazil) is everywhere, and the Chinese themes are pleasantly reminiscent of Portugal's once vast empire. The books, each dating from before 1755, are in Latin, Greek, and Hebrew. Imagine being a student in Coimbra centuries ago, when this temple of learning stored the world's knowledge like a vast filing cabinet (and consider how readily accessible the world of information is to our age).

When it's time to leave, head out the door on the side of the hall and take the stairs down to the "**Academic Prison**"—overflow book stacks under stout arches. Exit this area, turn left, and take the stairs into the main courtyard.

• *The final university sight—skippable for some—is about a five-minute walk away. Exit the courtyard through the Iron Gate, walk to the end of the fascist-style square, then turn left and walk a couple of blocks along Rua Estudos. The last academic building on your right—marked* Laboratorio Chimico—*houses the...*

## Science Museum (Museu da Ciência)

This old-school museum provides a peek into a grand, Old World lecture hall with elegant wood details (across from entry hall). But is most worthwhile for the opportunity to take a 45-minute tour (minimal English) of the Cabinet of Physics, with dusty cases displaying 18th- and 19th-century models, and the Gallery of Zoology, with six rooms of stuffed animals and skeletons—including a

65-foot-long whale skeleton and a herd of African ungulates, arranged by size. Many of these specimens date back 300 years or more, emphasizing the university's rich academic heritage. When you arrive, ask when the next tour of the galleries departs; pass any wait time in the museum.

**Cost and Hours:** €4, covered by €12 Programa 1 ticket, Tue-Sun 10:00-18:00, closed Mon, Largo Marquês de Pombal, tel. 239-854-350, www.museudaciencia.org.

## MORE SIGHTS IN COIMBRA
### ▲▲Machado de Castro Museum and Cryptoporticus of Aeminium

Housed in an elegant old bishop's palace, the huge Machado de Castro Museum (Museu Nacional Machado de Castro) has two

parts: the vast, barren understructure (Criptoportico de Aeminium) of the ancient Roman forum upon which the palace was built; and a fine collection of art through the ages, particularly strong on sculpture (including 14th- to 16th-century statues taken from dissolved monasteries). To save needless climbing, visit this sight before or after the old university (since both are at roughly the same altitude).

**Cost and Hours:** €6 for museum and Roman site, €3 for just the Roman site, free first Sun of every month, Tue 14:00-18:00, Wed-Sun 10:00-18:00, closed Mon, audioguide-€1.50, Largo Dr. José Rodrigues, tel. 239-853-070, www.museumachadocastro.pt.

**Visiting the Museum:** Follow the one-way route through several levels of the sprawling museum. Attendants will keep you on track. Everything is described in English.

Begin by descending to the **Roman ruins.** Aeminium was the Roman city that became Coimbra. Two thousand years ago, its two main streets crossed here, marking the forum. Because the city was built on a slope, a vast understructure was required to provide a level place for the town square (like a modern "daylight basement")—and that "cryptoporticus" is what survives today. Walking through the vast two-level maze of the stout, vaulted galleries, evocative and beautifully lit, will leave you marveling at what you can do with slave labor.

Back up on the main level, you're routed through the extensive, chronologically displayed **art collection,** starting with Roman and Romanesque fragments—a 2,000-year-old rubble layer-cake of Coimbra's past—and on to the museum's strongest collection: statues from the 14th, 15th, and 16th centuries. Many of these are refugees from the dissolution of the monasteries (in the 1830s, following Portugal's Civil War). The highlight is a powerfully realistic 14th-century *Cristo Negro*—an evocative, spindly armed, crucified Jesus—carved in wood. Until a decade ago, when this statue was cleaned (and the candle soot was removed), it was considered to be a portrait of a black Christ. If this dramatic statue has an impact on you today, imagine its power in the 14th century. Gothic lasted here long after the Renaissance hit Italy and France. Just beyond that is the stately Renaissance Treasurer's Chapel, moved here from a now-gone 16th-century monastery. Viewing this, consider how Coimbra with its university was Portugal's center of humanism and the Renaissance.

There's much more to see, but (unless you have a special interest) it's mostly skippable. As you explore, note how aspects of Moorish culture and design were absorbed into the Christian culture that threw them out. Downstairs on floor -1, you'll find terra cotta sculpture, and on floor -2, 17th-century Portuguese sculpture. From there, an elevator zips you up to floor 1: northern European statues and paintings (a reminder of this country's wealth in its Golden Age heyday), Portuguese paintings, precious metals (including some fine gold and silver sculptures), ceramics and tiles, and religious vestments. The finale is the treasury of Queen/St. Isabel, who donated some of her finest possessions to Coimbra's Santa Clara Monastery.

**Eating:** At the entry level, you'll find Loggia, a great restaurant on a terrace with a fine old-town view (described in "Eating in Coimbra," later).

### ▲Old Cathedral (Sé Velha)

Same old story: Christians build a church on a pre-Christian holy spot (Visigoths in sixth century), Moors destroy the church and build a mosque (eighth century), then Christians push out the Moors (1064), tear down their mosque, and build another church (consecrated in 1184).

If this structure reminds you of Lisbon's cathedral, it should. As in Lisbon, this was essentially a church-fortress, built in the middle of the Reconquista and designed by the same French architect. Notice the crenellations along the roof of this Romanesque church; the Moors, though booted out, were still considered a risk.

**Cost and Hours:** Church and cloisters-€2.50, open Mon-Sat 10:00-18:00 and generally Sun 11:00-17:00.

**Visiting the Cathedral:** Before entering, stand back and study the **west portal** (the main entrance, facing downhill). Notice how Moorish-style columns are decorated by neo-Byzantine capitals, but there are no Christian motifs. It is an unbreakable facade—fortified and practical, complete with arrow slits.

The **north portal** (around the left side) was added later, in Renaissance times. Made of soft limestone, it was cheap and easy to carve but hasn't weathered very well.

Study the stone blocks of the main structure, set up in the 12th century. You can see mason's marks and even some Arabic writing (on a block six rows up by the north portal), indicating that the conquered Moors worked within Christian society.

Now enter the **interior.** At the start of the nave, the giant holy-water font shells are a 19th-century gift from Sri Lanka. The walls are lined with some of the oldest tiles in the country—imported in the 16th century from Sevilla, Spain.

Head up the right aisle. At the altar just before the transept is a murky **painting of Queen Isabel** (St. Elizabeth) with a skirt full of roses. This 13th-century Hungarian princess—with family ties to Portugal—is a local favorite with a sweet legend. Against the wishes of the king, she always gave bread to the poor. One day, when he came home early from a trip, she was busy doling out bread from her skirt. She pulled the material up to hide the bread. When the king asked her what was inside (suspecting bread for the poor), the queen—unable to lie—lowered the material and, miraculously, the bread had turned to roses. For this astonishing act, she was canonized as a saint in 1625.

At the front of the church, the **three altars** are each worth a look. The main altar, a fine example of the late Flamboyant Gothic style, was made by Flemish artists (circa 1500). The 16th-century chapel to the right contains one of the best Renaissance altars in the country. The apostles all look to Jesus as he talks, while musical angels flank the holy host. Notice how the Renaissance passion for balance and proportion trumped fact—the composition had room for only 10 apostles. To the left of the main altar, the Chapel of St. Peter shows Peter being crucified upside down.

The peaceful **cloister** (entrance near back of church, near the ticket desk) is the oldest Gothic cloister in Portugal. Well-maintained with an inviting lawn, the courtyard offers a fine, framed view of the cathedral's dome. A tomb from 1064 in the cloister belongs to Coimbra's first Christian post-Reconquista governor.

### Chiado Building/Municipal Museum (Edifício Chiado/Museu Municipal)

Originally the site of Coimbra's first Chiado department store (a chain common throughout Portugal in the early 20th century), this refurbished building is notable for its construction—it was one of the first structures in Portugal to be built around an iron framework, like the then-revolutionary American skyscrapers. It now houses an eclectic assortment of artworks and textiles donated by local collector José Telo de Morais.

**Cost and Hours:** €1.80, Tue-Fri 10:00-18:00, Sat-Sun 10:00-13:00 & 14:00-18:00, closed Mon, Rue Ferreira Borges 85, tel. 239-857-525, www.cm-coimbra.pt ("Cultura" tab).

**Visiting the Museum:** Take the elevator up to the top floor and walk your way down, noticing the exposed iron beams. The third floor has ceramics, drawings, and a collection of silverware. The second floor has 17th- and 18th-century furniture as well as religious paintings and objects. The first floor holds oil and pastel paintings from the 19th and early 20th centuries. The ground floor houses a free temporary exhibit, and the small (and also free) Galeria Almedina, which highlights emerging student artists.

### Parque Dr. Manuel Braga

Coimbra's pleasant riverside park sprawls upstream from the Santa Clara Bridge to the Pedro and Inês Bridge. You'll find boat tours, some recommended restaurants, a strip of trendy evening spots, and the Portuguese Pavilion from the Hannover Expo (2000 World's Fair in Hannover, Germany).

### River Cruise

To take advantage of Coimbra's Mondego River, try a cruise: Basófias boats float up and down the river on a 50-minute joyride (€6.50, April-Sept Tue-Sun, a few departures each afternoon—ask at dock across from TI, no cruises Mon, no narration, mobile 969-830-664, www.odabarca.com).

### Portugal for the Little Ones (Portugal dos Pequenitos)

Across the Santa Clara Bridge is a children's (or tourists') look at the great buildings and monuments of Portugal and its former empire in miniature, scattered through a park a couple of blocks south of town. Wanting to boost national pride, Salazar commissioned architect Cassiano Branco to build these minireplicas in 1940. If you've been through some of Portugal already, it's fun to try to identify the buildings you've already seen. Doll fans may enjoy the recent addition of an enormous Barbie collection, including one of the very first ever produced.

**Cost and Hours:** €9.50, kids 3-13—€6, kids under 3—free, daily March-May 10:00-19:00, June-mid-Sept 9:00-20:00, mid-Sept-Feb 10:00-17:00, Rossio de Santa Clara, tel. 239-801-170, www.portugaldospequenitos.pt.

## NEAR COIMBRA
### ▲Conímbriga Roman Ruins (Conímbriga Ruínas)

Portugal's best Roman sight is impressive...unless you've been to Rome. What remains of the Roman city of Conímbriga is divided

in two, in part because its in-habitants tore down buildings to erect a quick defensive wall against an expected barbarian attack. You'll see what's left of homes, shops, and baths from the second and third centuries A.D. (some remnants are even older), amazingly detailed mo-saic floors, and peaceful gar-

dens. Informative exhibits tell the city's history with excavated artifacts at the on-site museum.

**Cost and Hours:** €4.50 admission covers ruins and museum, daily 10:00-19:00—but in winter the ruins close at 17:30, last entry 45 minutes before closing, www.conimbriga.pt.

**Getting There:** The ruins are nine miles southwest of Co-imbra, just outside the town of Condeixa-a-Nova on the road to Lisbon. **Buses** leave for the ruins across from Coimbra's Station A (€2.45; Mon-Fri at 9:00, 9:30, 12:30, and 15:30; Sat at 9:30, 12:30, and 15:30; Sun at 9:30, 12:30, and 15:00; on the river side, look for the *Joalto* sign, 30-minute trip). Return buses leave from Coním-briga's parking lot (Mon-Fri at 12:55, 16:25, and 17:55; Sat at 13:25 and 18:25; Sun at 13:55 and 18:25). Confirm the destination by asking, *"Vai para Conímbriga?"* Otherwise, you could end up on one of the frequent buses to Condeixa (run twice hourly) that stop a mile short of the ruins. Figure about €20 one-way for a taxi from Coimbra.

**Drivers** find that Conímbriga fits well on a trip between Co-imbra and points south; the Conímbriga freeway exit is clearly marked from the A-1. To get there from the town center, cross the Santa Clara Bridge and go uphill, following signs to *Conde-ixa*. Continue straight through town, and you will see brown signs guiding you to the ruins.

**Eating:** The museum's café is a fine spot to have lunch before catching the return bus to Coimbra. Or bring a picnic lunch—there's a good picnic area between the museum and the ruins.

**Visiting Conímbriga:** Allow at least an hour to tour the site and museum—and be warned that in summer, the ruins can be blazing hot in the afternoon. I prefer to visit the ruins first and then see the museum.

Purchase tickets inside the main building, then walk five minutes to the ruins, tour the site, and return to the main building to visit the museum. Helpful arrows guide you through the site. Explore the remnants of the old town first, and save the mansion—under the protective modern roofing—for the grand finale.

You'll first see remains of different houses and shopping arcades, most with wonderful mosaics intact. Note how the columns are made of preformed wedges.

Dominating the site is a stout wall, which locals hastily built for their own protection...and it shows. Once the Roman Empire retreated from this area, invaders from the north went on the offensive (beginning around A.D. 465). A Christian Germanic tribe conquered the city and built a basilica at the end of this wall.

Just outside the wall, you'll see the surviving arch of an aqueduct. You can also venture farther into the field to find the scant remains of the forum, and beyond that, ruins of a bath (the blocky structure at the edge of the site).

Finish your visit at the most important find (under a protective roof): The **House of the Fountains** is an entire dwelling, with most of its rooms and mosaics intact. Don't spend €0.50 on the lazy fountain show (wait for one of the school groups to do it for you), but enjoy the stories told in the mosaics. Simple portraits, horses, and numerous hunting scenes illustrate the daily routine in this town during Roman times.

Now return to the delightful **museum** that shows the discoveries from decades of excavation. A model at the entrance helps you get your bearings. The room to the left of the ticket counter describes daily life in Conímbriga. You'll see coins, dinnerware, and even grooming utensils (find the spoon-shaped ear cleaners)—all with good English descriptions. The opposite room contains a miniature replica of the forum, along with fine mosaics and a few tombstones. The best mosaic is of the mythological, bull-headed Minotaur—follow the maze from the center until you are safely out.

# Entertainment in Coimbra

### ▲▲Fado Music

Portugal's unique, mournful traditional music—fado—is generally performed by women. But in Coimbra, young men sing fado. The best performers are probably at Fado ao Centro or À Capella. But you may get to enjoy an impromptu concert on the streets: Roving bands of male students—similar to the *tuna* bands in Spain's Salamanca—serenade around town for tips and the hearts of women.

**Fado ao Centro** is an all-male ensemble of current and former Coimbra university students who sing fado in the unique local style. The 50-minute shows, held in a cute little hall, end with a glass of port and a little Q&A time with the musicians (€10, daily at 18:00 and occasionally, with demand, at 19:00). This is a nice alternative to late-night shows, but can be popular with tour groups; reservations are smart in summer (just past the Arco de Almedina on Rua Quebra Costas 7, tel. 239-837-060, www.fadoaocentro. com). Money raised here supports musicians and promotes local culture.

**À Capella,** on the hill above the Church of Santa Cruz, offers an intimate fado nightclub experience. The chapel has been turned into a temple for Coimbra-style traditional music, and it's fado almost every night all year long (three musicians perform from 22:00 to about 24:00). Come for the music, the cool scene, the slick background videos adding context to each song, and the snacks and drinks (€13 cover, reservations wise in summer; at the triangular corner midway down the main drag, climb the steep Rua do Corpo de Deus 100 yards until you see the old chapel on your left; tel. 239-833-985, www. acapella.com.pt). If you're coming to eat, note that the chapel opens nightly at 20:00 and serves snacks and wine by the glass.

**Diligência** is a fado bar famous for its informal music schedule—locals love to come here and just jam (guitar and voice). In fact, all their regular performers started out as customers who came to sing along. The cave-like setting has some basic tapas and drinks. Along with the occasional sing-along, up-and-coming groups often play here. If the music moves you, jump right in (no cover, kitchen opens at 20:00, shows daily 22:30 until late; from Praça 8 de Maio, take Rua Sofia to your second left, Diligência is 2 blocks up on your right at Rua Nova 30; tel. 239-827-667).

**$$$ Restaurante O Trovador** is your best place for dinner with fado. Reservations are essential to eat with the music—ask for a seat with a music view. When busy, the musicians alternate between two dining rooms. During performances, guests must order food—not just drinks (music nearly nightly in June-Aug from 21:00, off-season Fri-Sat only, no cover; meals Mon-Sat 19:30-22:30, closed Sun, facing the old cathedral on Largo de Sé Velha 15, tel. 239-825-475, www.restaurantetrovador.com).

**More Fado:** During the tourist season, you'll find sit-down fado most nights at Café Santa Cruz. The mayor organizes Thursday street concerts that feature fado music through the summer.

**Kayaks and Adventure Sports**

**Kayaking: O Pioneiro do Mondego** buses you from Coimbra to Penacova (15 miles away), where you can kayak down the Mondego River for about four hours back into Coimbra (€24.50, tel. 239-478-385, www.opioneirodomondego.com, Kristien and Jonas speak English). Most people stop to swim or picnic on the way back, so it often turns into an all-day journey. For the first 12.5 miles, you'll go easily with the flow, but you'll get your exercise paddling the remaining stretch. To avoid the workout (and the more boring part of the Mondego River), ask to be picked up 2.5 miles before Coimbra, at Portela do Mondego, where the river's current slows down.

**Adventure Sports:** Located in the nearby town of Foz da Figueira, **Capitão Dureza** specializes in at-your-own-risk activities: rappelling, rafting, mountain biking, hiking, and canyoning (pickup and drop-off in Coimbra, tel. 239-476-701, mobile 918-315-337, www.capitaodureza.com).

# Sleeping in Coimbra

Coimbra's hotels are cheap...in every sense. Don't expect luxury here. These are basic, thin-walled, well-worn hotels where nighttime noise is par for the course. Most of these listings are just outside the central Station A, within a few minutes' walk of the main drag, Santa Clara Bridge, and most recommended restaurants and sights in the lower town.

**$$$ Hotel Tivoli Coimbra,** a classy, Houston-esque skyscraper, is Coimbra's closest thing to contemporary luxury—such as flat-screen TVs and a swimming pool—while still at a reasonable price. It rents 100 spacious (if faded) rooms with all the modern amenities, a 10-minute walk from Station A and the charming core (air-con, elevator, pay parking, Rua João Machado 4, tel. 239-858-300, www.tivolicoimbra.com, htcoimbra@tivolihotels.com).

**$$ Hotel Astória** gives you the experience of staying in the city's finest (but desperately faded) old hotel with Coimbra's first Art Deco lounges. This venerable time warp, with 62 rooms, is overdue for a thorough renovation. In the meantime, it offers historical charm at reasonable prices. Rooms with river views don't cost extra, but come with some street noise. I prefer the quieter city-view rooms at the back (RS%, air-con, elevator, public parking opposite hotel, central as can be at Avenida Emídio

COIMBRA

## Sleep Code

Hotels are classified based on the average price of a standard double room with breakfast in high season.

| | |
|---|---|
| **$$$$** | **Splurge:** Most rooms over €150 |
| **$$$** | **Pricier:** €100-150 |
| **$$** | **Moderate:** €70-100 |
| **$** | **Budget:** €40-70 |
| **¢** | **Backpacker:** Under €40 |
| **RS%** | **Rick Steves discount** |

Unless otherwise noted, credit cards are accepted, hotel staff speak basic English, and free Wi-Fi is available. Comparison-shop by checking prices at several hotels (on each hotel's own website, on a booking site, or by email). For the best deal, *book directly with the hotel.* Ask for a discount if paying in cash; if the listing includes **RS%,** request a Rick Steves discount.

Navarro 21, tel. 239-853-020, www.astoria-coimbra.com, astoria@almedahotels.com).

**$ Hotel Vitória** is a well-located hotel renting 21 modern rooms over a good restaurant, between Station A and the main drag. Some rooms have uphill views to the university. In terms of value, quality, and location, this is the most appealing option in town (air-con, elevator, a block from Station A at Rua da Sota 9, tel. 239-824-049, www.hotelvitoria.pt, reservas@hotelvitoria.pt).

**$ Hotel Bragança**'s brown-on-brown lobby leads to 83 clean if outmoded rooms with modern bathrooms. The wood paneling and furniture transport you to the 1950s (RS%, family rooms, air-con, elevator, free parking in tiny lot at entrance if space available, Largo das Ameias 10 next to Station A, tel. 239-822-171, www.hotel-braganca.com, geral@hotel-braganca.com).

**$ Ibis Hotel,** a modern high-rise, has 110 orderly little rooms that come with all the comforts. Well-located near the riverside Parque Dr. Manuel Braga, this impersonal but reliable chain hotel is three blocks past the Santa Clara Bridge and the old town (breakfast extra, air-con, elevator, easy pay parking, Avenida Emídio Navarro 70, tel. 239-852-130, www.ibishotel.com, h1672@accor.com).

**$ RiverSuites** offers 25 rooms just across the Santa Clara Bridge, overlooking a noisy roundabout. The 10-minute walk from the hotel across the bridge comes with fine views of Coimbra (family rooms, air-con, at the foot of the Santa Clara Bridge at Avenida João das Regras 82, tel. 239-440-582, www.riversuites.pt, geral@riversuites.pt).

**$ Hotel Domus,** tucked away in a corner of a side street near Station A, has 15 cozy rooms with antique furniture, updated

COIMBRA

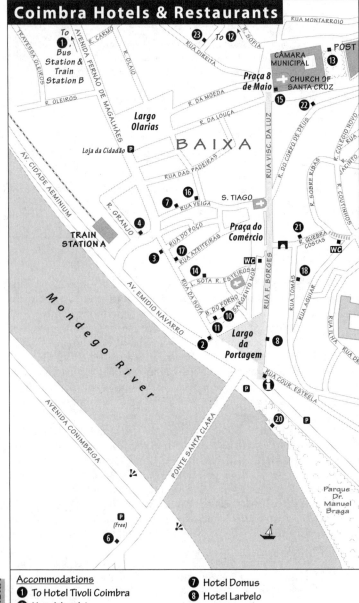

# Coimbra Hotels & Restaurants

Accommodations
1 To Hotel Tivoli Coimbra
2 Hotel Astória
3 Hotel Vitória
4 Hotel Bragança
5 Ibis Hotel
6 RiverSuites
7 Hotel Domus
8 Hotel Larbelo
9 Serenata Hostel

Eateries & Entertainment
10 Restaurante Zé Manel dos Ossos
11 O Bizarro

COIMBRA

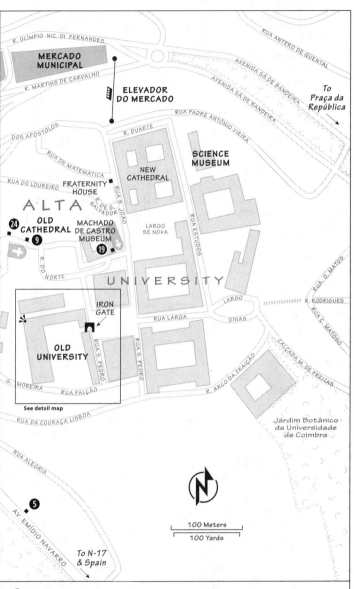

| | |
|---|---|
| ⑫ To Língua | ⑲ Loggia Restaurante |
| ⑬ Restaurante Jardim da Manga | ⑳ Restaurante Itália |
| ⑭ Restaurante O Serenata | ㉑ Fado ao Centro |
| ⑮ Café Santa Cruz | ㉒ À Capella Fado |
| ⑯ Adega Paço do Conde | ㉓ Diligência Fado |
| ⑰ Restaurante Solar do Bacalhau | ㉔ Restaurante O Trovador |
| ⑱ Fangas Mercearia Bar | |

bathrooms, and thin windows (RS%, air-con, pay parking, Rua Adelino Veiga 62, tel. 239-828-584, www.hoteldomus.com.pt, hoteldomus@sapo.pt, Sra. and Sr. Santos).

¢ **Hotel Larbelo,** with Old World character, mixes frumpiness and former elegance in its 17 rooms. Its location couldn't be handier—right on Largo da Portagem, where the main street hits the river. The old-fashioned staircase, classic reception rooms, and gentle non-English-speaking management take you to another age (no breakfast, air-con, Largo da Portagem 33, tel. 239-829-092, www.larbelo.net, residencial.larbelo@sapo.pt.

¢ **Serenata Hostel,** appealingly modern, offers private rooms and dorms with views. It fills a gorgeously restored historic maternity hospital and music conservatory on the often-noisy-with-students square behind the cathedral. The young-at-heart who don't mind wearing earplugs (or request a quieter windowless interior room) may find this preferable to the similarly priced, dreary hotels near the station (cheaper rooms with shared bath, air-con, Largo Sé Velha 21, tel. 239-853-130, www.serenatahostel.com).

# Eating in Coimbra

Specialties of this hilly Beira region include *leitão* (suckling pig), *cabrito* (baby male goat), *chanfana* (goat cooked in wine), *Serra* cheese, and rich, red *Bairrada* and *Dão* wines. For a sweet and herby *digestivo,* try Licor Beirão. The local pastries are *pastel de Santa Clara* (made with almonds and marmalade) and *pastel de Tentúgal* (flaky puff pastry with a sweet egg filling and a dusting of powdered sugar). Be aware that many of these restaurants shut down—along with most of Coimbra—on Sunday.

## IN THE LOWER TOWN (BAIXA)

Several enticing places—including many of my recommendations—are buried in the tight lanes between Hotel Astória and the main walking street.

**$$ Restaurante Zé Manel dos Ossos** is tiny, rustic, and authentic. Judging from the walls—caked with notes from happy eaters—and the line of people waiting hungrily in the alley, this place is a favorite. They serve a dozen good, typical Coimbran dishes. To order, I'd trust Mario, who speaks a lee-tle English. The *ossos*—meaty bones cooked with veggies—are the popular dish here (Mon-Sat 12:30-15:00 & 19:30-22:00, closed Sun and off-season, no reservations—arrive early or wait; Beco do Forno 12, tel. 239-823-790).

**$$ O Bizarro** is a small, family-run, white-tablecloth hole-in-the-wall that serves up tasty Portuguese food at a good price. *Chanfana* (goat simmered in wine) is the house specialty (great

COIMBRA

---

## Restaurant Price Code

I've assigned each eatery a price category, based on the average cost of a typical main course. Drinks, desserts, and splurge items (steak and seafood) can raise the price considerably.

**$$$$**    **Splurge:** Most main courses over €17
**$$$**    **Pricier:** €12-17
**$$**    **Moderate:** €7-12
**$**    **Budget:** Under €7

In Portugal, takeout food is **$**; a basic sit-down eatery is **$$**; a casual but more upscale restaurant is **$$$**; and a swanky splurge is **$$$$**.

---

lunch special, daily 12:00-15:00 & 19:00-22:00, Rua Sargento Mor 44, Rafael speaks English).

**$$$ Língua** ("Tongue") bills itself as a *restaurante lusófono*—a restaurant of the Portuguese-speaking world. The menu—an eclectic mix of exotic, flavorful dishes from former colonies Brazil, Angola, Mozambique, Cape Verde, Goa, and more—provides a break from traditional dishes while staying in the Portuguese cultural orbit. The contemporary dining room—a five-minute walk north of the Church of Santa Cruz—is classy but unfussy, the service is helpful, and the food is high-quality (Tue-Sun 12:00-15:00 & 19:30-23:30, closed Mon, Beco do Fanado 5, tel. 239-158-005).

**$$ Restaurante Jardim da Manga** is handy for a quick, cheap, self-service meal with locals. Sit indoors or outdoors next to a cool and peaceful fountain. It's family-friendly and cheap enough to be a popular choice for children's birthday parties. Just slide a tray down the counter and pick what you like (daily 12:00-15:00 & 19:00-22:00, in the Jardim da Manga garden behind Church of Santa Cruz, tel. 239-829-156).

**$$ Restaurante O Serenata** is country-kitchen cozy, with two-dozen tables and a fresh, bright atmosphere. Hardworking and helpful Pedro serves hearty and splittable meals. Goat, cod, and mixed grill are his fortes (Mon-Sat 12:00-15:00 & 19:00-23:00, closed Sun, Largo da Sota 6, mobile 963-992-545).

**$ Café Santa Cruz,** next to the Church of Santa Cruz and filling one of its former buildings, is Old World elegant, but totally unpretentious. It has great, cheap coffee, simple toasted sandwiches, Wi-Fi, and outdoor tables offering great people-watching over Praça 8 de Maio. Their signature pastry *cruzios* (named for the church's friars) is a new confection inspired by nun-baked sweets (Mon-Sat 7:00-24:00, plus Sun 8:00-20:00 in summer, closed Sun off-season). The café hosts free live fado most nights in season at 22:00 (and sometimes also Thu-Sun at 18:00).

**$ Adega Paço do Conde**—humble but popular—knows how

to grill, and Coimbra's students know it. Choose your seafood or meat selection from the display case as you enter. They'll pop it right on the grill and then bring it to your table. Students, travelers, families, and pigeons like this homey place that just seems right, even without English menus (big, splittable plates, Mon-Sat 11:30-15:00 & 19:00-22:00, closed Sun, Rua Paço do Conde 1—on the small square called Largo Paço do Conde, tel. 239-825-605, Alfredo).

**$$ Restaurante Solar do Bacalhau** serves good Portuguese and Italian meals in a huge, contemporary, stony-chic dining room that feels fancier than the prices (daily 12:00-14:30 & 19:00-24:00, Rua da Sota 12, tel. 239-098-990).

## IN THE UPPER TOWN (ALTA)

These restaurants sit on the slopes above the main drag—the first one lower, the second one higher.

**$$$ Fangas Mercearia Bar,** my Coimbra favorite, is an intimate five-table wine bar where English-speaking Luisa serves delightful *petiscos* (Portuguese tapas) matched by a nice selection of quality Portuguese wines by the glass (3 or 4 tapas will fill 2 people, or try a sampler plate; daily 12:30-16:00 & 19:00-24:00, Rua Fernandes Tomás 45, reserve ahead, tel. 934-093-636, http://fangas. pt). They have a larger second location—**$$$ Fangas Maior**—with the same menu and philosophy, but a bit less coziness, a few steps closer to the main drag (same hours and phone number, Rua Fernandes Tomás 29).

**$$$ Loggia Restaurante** is a dressy place at the Machado de Castro Museum with seating inside or outside on the view terrace overlooking the old town. It's a convenient stop while sightseeing, as it's next to the university, and there's a good-value €9.50 weekday lunch buffet available 12:30-14:30, €11.50 on weekends. And, if you don't mind the long hike above the old town, it's a romantic and classy option for dinner—at higher prices than you'll pay in town, but still reasonable (Tue and Sun open 10:00-18:00 for lunch only, Wed-Sat 10:00-22:30 with dinner from 19:30, closed Mon, tel. 239-853-076).

## ON THE RIVER

**$$$ Restaurante Itália**—at Parque Dr. Manuel Braga, opposite the TI—literally hangs over the river. It serves Italian food—pasta, pizza (also available for carryout), meat, and fish—indoors and out. Dinner reservations are smart (daily 12:00-24:00, riverside tables limited to parties of four when busy, tel. 239-838-863).

**Picnics:** Shop at the colorful covered market (Mercado Municipal), behind the Church of Santa Cruz (Mon-Sat 8:00-14:00, closed Sun) or at tiny *mini-mercados* in the side streets. The well-maintained gardens along the river across from the TI are picnic-pleasant.

# Coimbra Connections

If you're traveling by train, remember that Coimbra has two stations—A and B—but any ticket covers you for the five-minute shuttle train that runs between the stations (see page 281 for details).

**From Coimbra by Bus to: Alcobaça** (2/day, 1.5 hours), **Batalha** (3/day, 2.5 hours, transfer in Leiria), **Fátima** (hourly, 1 hour), **Nazaré** (5/day, 2 hours), **Lisbon** (hourly, 2.5 hours), **Évora** (2/day direct, 4 hours; otherwise almost hourly with transfer in Lisbon), **Porto** (almost hourly, 1.5 hours). Bus info: Tel. 239-855-270, www.rede-expressos.pt. Frequency drops on weekends, especially Sunday.

**By Train to: Nazaré/Valado** (3/day direct, 2 hours; the bus is a better option—see above—because Nazaré/Valado train station is 3 miles outside Nazaré), **Porto** (nearly hourly, 1 hour on Alfa Pendular line or Intercidades service, 2 hours on regional line; most long-distance trains end at Porto's noncentral Campanhã station but include a transfer to the more central São Bento station), **Lisbon** (almost hourly on Alfa Pendular or Intercidades service, 2 hours; regional service equally frequent but takes 4 hours; for Lisbon center, get off at Santa Apolónia Station; for Lisbon airport, hop off at Oriente station and take the Metro to airport; all Coimbra/Porto trains stop at both Lisbon stations, 7 minutes apart). Train info: tel. 808-208-208, www.cp.pt.

**To Salamanca, Spain:** The best option is the direct InterNorte **bus** (usually departs daily at 10:15, arrives at 17:30 in Salamanca on Spain time—add one hour from Portugal). To guarantee a place, book a couple of days in advance. You can confirm schedules and buy your bus ticket by phone or in person at the friendly InterVisa travel agency in Coimbra, near Station A (see "Helpful Hints," page 284) more easily than at Coimbra's bus station (InterCentro office, tel. 239-827-588, no English spoken).

I'd avoid taking the **train** to Salamanca because of its inconvenient early-morning arrival time: One train per day on the Sud-Expresso line departs Coimbra at 23:37 and drops you in Salamanca at 4:56 (4.5 hours).

COIMBRA

# PORTO

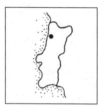

Porto (POR-too)—the capital of the north and Portugal's second city—is fiercely proud of what distinguishes it from its rival, Lisbon. Yes, Porto's a bit less polished. But block for block, it may be even more full of gritty, Old World charm. In many ways, a visit to Portugal isn't complete without experiencing Porto.

Spared by the 1755 earthquake that toppled Lisbon, Porto is charmingly well-preserved. Houses with red-tiled roofs tumble down the hills to the riverbank, prickly church towers dot the skyline, mosaic-patterned stones line streets, and flat-bottomed boats called *rabelos* ply the lazy river.

Internationally, the city is synonymous with the port wine that ages on its riverbanks. But the Portuguese think of Porto as a hardworking engine of industry, with an endearing warts-and-all character. It's a solid city—it seems made entirely of granite—with solid people. The town's two most famous foods—tripe soup and a quadruple-decker sandwich drenched in sauce—say it all: This place is unpretentious. Locals claim they're working too hard to worry about being pretty. As an oft-repeated saying goes, "Coimbra studies, Braga prays, Lisbon parties...and Porto works."

Not long ago, Porto was a somewhat depressed industrial city, but it has enjoyed a cultural renaissance over the past decade. European Union money has poured in, funding a revamping of the public transportation system, infrastructure, and more. Meanwhile, tourism has taken off in a big way (thanks largely to cheap flights attracting weekend vacationers from Britain and the Continent). Locals are rising to the occasion, filling the characteristic streets with trendy eateries and boutiques. Porto is ever-changing, often chaotic, and even more worth a visit.

Porto offers two high-impact sightseeing thrills: the postcard-perfect ambience of the riverfront Ribeira district, and the opportunity to learn more about (and taste) the port wine that ages across the river in Vila Nova de Gaia. (Aficionados of port—or of dramatic scenery—can use Porto as a springboard for visiting the Douro Valley, where grapes grow on dramatic stone terraces; see next chapter.) But you'll discover that Porto also features many unexpected treats: sumptuous Baroque churches and civic buildings, a bustling real-world market hall, atmospheric lanes of glorious *azulejo*-tiled houses, a variety of good restaurants and appealing boutiques, and quirky but worthwhile museums.

The weather is always changing, blown in and out by the steady sea breeze. You're likely to get sun and rain at the same time—causing the locals to exclaim, "A widow's going to remarry."

## PLANNING YOUR TIME

Porto offers one very busy day's worth of sightseeing—or better yet, two relaxed days. Start your day in the market area (when it's most thriving). Then head to the main boulevard, Avenida dos Aliados, and follow my self-guided Porto Walk through the rest of town. If time allows, the activities most worth considering along the way are climbing Clérigos Tower for a visual orientation, touring the Stock Exchange Palace, and visiting the glorious São Francisco Church and its spooky crypt. My walk ends on the Ribeira, a scenic 15-minute walk across the bridge to the opposite riverbank, to do some port wine tastings in Vila Nova de Gaia. Have dinner in the Ribeira (for touristy bustle) or up in the city center (for more interesting local eateries).

With a second day, slow down, taste more port, visit the cathedral, cruise the river, and add a visit to the Serralves Museum, its Art Deco mansion, and its plush park...or just head to the Atlantic beaches at Foz to mellow out.

# Orientation to Porto

Porto (pop. 238,000, with a metro area sprawling to 1.7 million)

blankets the hilly north bank of the Douro River, near where the river meets the Atlantic Ocean. The tourist's Porto is fairly compact but very steep—and therefore tricky to navigate. Even though maps can be deceptive (given the variable terrain), get a good one and use it. Comfortable walking shoes are a must.

PORTO

And don't hesitate to grab a taxi or request an Uber whenever you need a quick connection—they're cheap, fast, and save you lots of climbing.

It helps to think of the tourist's Porto in three parts.

**Ribeira** (ree-BAY-rah): Down along the river, the Ribeira neighborhood has narrow streets and oodles of atmosphere. Praça Infante Dom Henrique (Henry the Navigator Square), two blocks above the Ribeira, hosts two intriguing sights: the Stock Exchange Palace and São Francisco Church.

**City Center:** Ramshackle old townhouses scramble steeply uphill toward the second part of town, the modern city center, which hovers above the Ribeira and surrounds the broad boulevard called Avenida dos Aliados (Avenue of the Allies). This area is the urban business center of Porto, packed with office buildings and shoppers, and peppered with hotels and enticing restaurants. You'll also find a smattering of squares, monuments, and sights (including the market hall and cathedral). Clérigos Tower stands as the city's most recognizable landmark.

**Vila Nova de Gaia:** Across the river shine the neon signs of Porto's main tourist attraction, the port wine cellars *(caves do vinho do porto)* in Vila Nova de Gaia—technically a separate town.

The Douro is spanned by six bridges (two steel, four concrete). The only one you're likely to cross is the monstrous steel **Ponte**

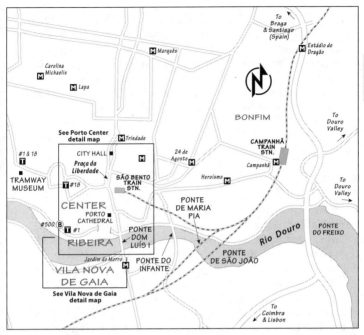

**Dom Luís I** (cars use lower level, Metro trains run along upper level; pedestrians can use either level).

Visitors venturing farther out find Porto to be a city of contrasts. Its outskirts boast bright, spacious, and prim residential neighborhoods, such as the areas surrounding the Boavista Rotunda and the Serralves Museum and park. The upscale Atlantic beach neighborhood, Foz, is a nice escape from the congested center.

## TOURIST INFORMATION

Porto has two main TIs: in the **city center** across from City Hall (at the top of Avenida dos Aliados, Rua Clube dos Fenianos 25), and in the crenellated tower just below **cathedral square** (both open daily 9:00-20:00, until 19:00 off-season, tel. 223-393-472). You'll also find TI kiosks in highly trafficked areas: on the **Ribeira** waterfront (April-Oct daily 10:00-19:00) and near the Imperial McDonald's on **Avenida dos Aliados** (daily 9:30-18:30). Additional TIs are at the **Campanhã train station** (Jun-Aug daily 10:30-18:00) and the **airport** (daily 8:00-23:30, at the arrivals level). **Vila Nova de Gaia** has its own TI, as well (see page 345). Porto's TIs share a website: www.visitporto.travel. Note the many *tourist service* and *tourist info* offices you'll see around town are for-profit agencies in disguise; for an official TI, go to one of the locations mentioned here.

At any TI, pick up the free city map, the list of prices and hours for sights, and the monthly *Programme* of cultural events. All

TIs also sell the Porto Card (described next); the TI near City Hall sells the Andante card (for transit—described later).

**Porto Card:** This card—sold at TIs and travel agencies—offers free entry to some sights and discounts for others, plus discounts on bus tours and some restaurants. You can choose between the Walker version (€6/1 day, €10/2 days) or the Transport version, which includes public transit—but not trolleys (€13/1 day, €20/2 days). Admission prices are reasonable in Porto, and on a short visit you may not take much public transit—so do the math before springing for this card.

## ARRIVAL IN PORTO

**By Train:** Porto has two train stations. Regional trains, including those serving the Douro Valley, use the very central **São Bento** station (a sight in itself for its magnificent tiles; see page 333). Facing the exit in the left corner is the helpful Loja da Mobilidade **transport office,** where you can purchase train tickets as well as the Andante transit card (tel. 808-208-208, www.stcp.pt).

Trains coming from farther away, including Lisbon and Coimbra, arrive at **Campanhã** station, on the east edge of town. If your train stops at both stations, get off at São Bento (closer to central hotels). If you have to get off at Campanhã, you have three options for getting into the center: Take a taxi or Uber directly to your hotel (€7 with luggage to most city-center accommodations); catch another train to São Bento station (6/hour, free with any ticket to Porto); or use the Metro across the street (take it to the Trindade stop, then transfer to the yellow line for either Aliados or São Bento stations).

Note that the Metro does not have a stop directly at the Ribeira, but the neighborhood is a downhill walk from the São Bento Metro stop and train station.

**By Bus:** As each of Porto's many bus companies operates its own garage, there's no central bus station. All the bus garages are more or less in the city center. The main ones are **Rede Expressos** (to Lisbon and Coimbra; Rua Alexandre Herculano 366, tel. 707-223-344, www.rede-expressos.pt); **RENEX** (to Lisbon; Campo Mártires da Pátria 37, tel. 222-003-395, www.renex.pt); **Rodonorte** (to points north; Rua Ateneu Comercial do Porto 19, tel. 222-005-637, www.rodonorte.pt); and **Internorte** (to Spain, including Madrid; Praça da Galiza 96, tel. 226-052-421 or 707-200-512, www.internorte.pt). The Spanish bus company **Autna** runs buses to Vigo, Spain (with connections to Santiago), that leave from in front of the Imperial McDonald's on Avenida dos Aliados (www.autna.com).

**By Car:** Central Porto is a headache by car—the streets are confusing and congested, and parking is very expensive (over €30/

day). Try to pick up your rental on your way out of town (or drop it off on the way in); otherwise, just stow it at your hotel. Approaching from Lisbon and Coimbra on the A-1 expressway, pay a toll and then follow signs for *Ponte da Arrábida*. After crossing the bridge, take the first right and follow *centro* signs (or the little bull's-eyes) into downtown.

**By Plane:** Porto's Francisco Sá Carneiro Airport (airport code: OPO) is 11 miles north of the city center. Since it's an international airport (with connections beyond Iberia), it's used by people throughout northern Portugal and Spain. The Metro connects the airport to the center (3/hour, 30 minutes to the Trindade stop), or catch a taxi or Uber (figure €25). Airport info: Tel. 229-432-400.

## HELPFUL HINTS

**Exchange Rate:** €1 = about $1.10

**Country Calling Code:** 351 (see page 422 for dialing instructions)

**Oporto or Porto?** The British—who've traded with the city for centuries—refer to the city as "Oporto." While various guidebooks and postcards call it this, locals never do.

**Closed Day:** Most Porto museums are closed on Monday. Many traditional shops close early on Saturday and all day Sunday (but trendy or tourist-oriented stores stay open on weekends).

**Festivals:** Porto's big holiday is São João Day (for St. John the Baptist, the city's patron saint) on June 24. Festivities start the night of June 23 with partying and fireworks at Ponte Dom Luís I bridge, and continue on the 24th with a *rabelo* regatta.

**Laundry:** A small **full-service laundry** hides almost underground at the west end of the Ribeira district (between São Francisco Church and the river at the top of Rua da Reboleira, unpredictable hours, tel. 222-084-621). The self-service **Lavanderia do Infante** is just a couple of blocks uphill (daily 8:30-22:00, Rua do Comércio do Porto 43, mobile 968-902-713).

**Best Views:** There are fine views all along the Ribeira riverfront embankment, but they're even better from across the river in Vila Nova de Gaia (looking back toward Porto)—especially from the cable car or Porto Cruz's rooftop bar. You can also enjoy the views from the top of Clérigos Tower, from the terrace next to the cathedral, from the old town wall, or from Mosteiro da Serra do Pilar (the monastery across the river, just above the big steel Ponte Dom Luís I bridge). But the best vantage point of all may be from a boat on the river (see "Cruising the Douro," page 327).

## GETTING AROUND PORTO

While steep, Porto is walkable. On a short visit, it's possible you won't take any public transit (other than getting into town from

PORTO

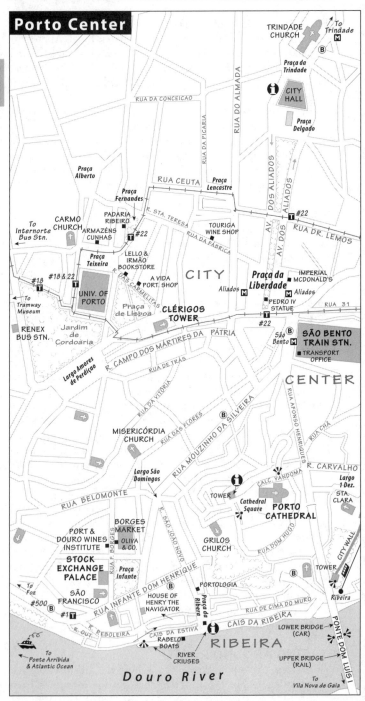

# Porto Center

TRINDADE CHURCH — To Trindade — Ⓜ

Praça da Trindade — Ⓑ

RUA DA CONCEIÇAO

RUA DO ALMADA

RUA DA PICARIA

AV. DOS ALIADOS

ℹ CITY HALL

Praça Delgado

Praça Alberto

RUA CEUTA — Praça Lencastre

Praça Fernandes

R. STA. TERESA

To Internorte Bus Stn. — CARMO CHURCH — ARMAZÉNS CUNHAS — PADARIA RIBEIRO — Ⓣ #22

TOURIGA WINE SHOP

RUA DA FÁBRICA

Ⓣ #22 — RUA DR. LEMOS

LELLO & IRMÃO BOOKSTORE

Praça Teixeira

A VIDA PORT. SHOP

CITY

IMPERIAL MCDONALD'S

#18 & 22 — Ⓣ

R. DAS CARMELITAS

Praça da Liberdade

Aliados — Ⓜ — Aliados

UNIV. OF PORTO

#18 & 22 — Ⓣ

Praça de Lisboa

CLÉRIGOS TOWER

PEDRO IV STATUE

RUA 31

RENEX BUS STN.

Jardim de Cordoaria

Ⓣ #22

São Bento — Ⓑ — Ⓜ — SÃO BENTO TRAIN STN.

To Tramway Museum

R. CAMPO DOS MÁRTIRES DA PÁTRIA

■ TRANSPORT OFFICE

Largo Amores de Perdição

RUA DE TRÁS

CENTER

RUA DA VITÓRIA

RUA CHÃ

RUA AFONSO HENRIQUES

MISERICÓRDIA CHURCH

RUA DAS FLORES

Ⓑ

R. CARVALHO

Largo São Domingos

RUA MOUZINHO DA SILVEIRA

CALÇ. VANDOMA

Largo 1-Dez.

RUA BELOMONTE

TOWER — ℹ

Cathedral Square

PORTO CATHEDRAL

STA. CLARA

BORGES MARKET

R. SÃO JOÃO NOVO

RUA DOM HUGO

PORT & DOURO WINES INSTITUTE

OLIVA & CO.

GRILOS CHURCH

CITY WALL

STOCK EXCHANGE PALACE

RUA F. BORGES

Praça Infante

Ⓑ — TOWER

SÃO FRANCISCO

RUA INFANTE DOM HENRIQUE

PORTOLOGIA

Ribeira

To Foz #500 — Ⓑ — #1 — Ⓣ

R. REBOLEIRA

HOUSE OF HENRY THE NAVIGATOR

Ⓑ

Praça da Ribeira

RUA DE CIMA DO MURO

PONTE DOM LUÍS I

R. OUT.

CAIS DA ESTIVA — RABELO BOATS

ℹ — CAIS DA RIBEIRA

LOWER BRIDGE (CAR)

To Ponte Arrábida & Atlantic Ocean

RIVER CRUISES

RIBEIRA

UPPER BRIDGE (RAIL)

To Vila Nova de Gaia

Douro River

PORTO

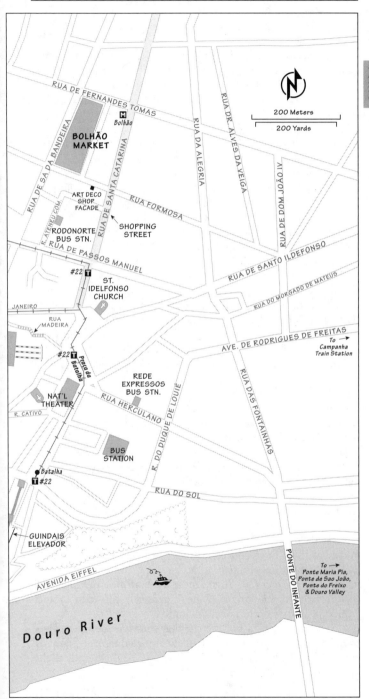

Campanhã station or the airport)—unless you choose to go for a vintage trolley joyride.

The city's public-transit network includes buses and the Metro. A few more interesting options—historical trolleys, a funicular, and the cable car in Vila Nova de Gaia—are privately run and covered by separate tickets. For public-transit info, see www.stcp.pt.

**Andante Card:** To ride the Metro or buses in Porto, you'll pay €0.50 for a non-shareable, reloadable card called Andante (similar to the Via Viagem system in Lisbon—see page 26). It also works for the train linking Campanhã and São Bento stations, but not for the vintage trolleys. You can load the card with as many trips, or *títulos,* you need (you have just over an hour to complete your journey; buy 10 rides and get one free). Virtually everything described in this chapter is covered by a Zone 2 trip (€1.20)—except the airport, for which you'll need to buy a Zone 4 trip (€1.85). It's unlikely you'd need the 24-hour pass, called Andante 24 (€4.15 for Zone 2, €6.40 for Zone 4)—especially because once you use your card for a 24-hour pass, you can't load it with individual trips. I'd also skip the €7 one-day AndanteTour card, which is a rip-off for tourists.

The cards are sold at ticket machines, the TI near City Hall (but not at other TIs), the Loja da Mobilidade transport office in the São Bento station, Andante stores (at the airport and at Trindade station), and at some bus, Metro, and train ticket offices. To use the card, pass it over the scanner on the Metro, bus, or train. If you transfer Metro lines, you must swipe your card again.

## By Bus

Buses #900, #901, and #906 go from São Bento station to the port wine lodges in Vila Nova de Gaia, across the river; bus #500 runs from the Ribeira to Foz; and bus #203 goes from the beach in Foz to the Serralves Museum. Service is generally speedy, but avoid buses during rush hour, when traffic slows to a crawl. If you don't have an Andante card (see earlier), you can pay the driver €1.85 for a ticket.

## By Trolley

Porto has three interconnecting trolley lines for tourists: #1, #18, and #22 (sometimes called "trams"; cars for all three lines are marked *Porto Tram City Tour*). These are both fun and practical, though frequency is limited (2/hour; generally run daily around 9:30-20:00, www.portotramcitytour.pt).

**Trolley #1** uses a historic car that shudders along the river from the Ribeira, past several museums (including the Tramway Museum) to the Jardim do Passeio Alegre, a 10-minute walk to the Foz district and the Atlantic Ocean.

**PORTO**

**Trolley #18** begins at Carmo Church and wobbles to the Tramway Museum.

**Trolley #22** makes a loop through the city center, from the shopping street Rua de Santa Catarina, down Rua de Passos Manuel, cutting through Avenida dos Aliados, and turning near Carmo Church to return along Rua 31 de Janeiro, with a jog across Praça da Batalha to the funicular (see map on page 320).

Trolleys are not covered by the Andante card. Individual tickets cost €2.50 per ride (purchase from driver). You can also buy an €8 pass that covers unlimited rides on all three lines for a 24-hour period.

## By Metro

Metro lines include blue, red, green, purple, and orange; these five connect Campanhã station to the center (www.metrodoporto.pt). All Metro lines converge at the Trindade stop, two blocks behind City Hall and Avenida dos Aliados. The purple line connects the airport to the center and Campanhã station; the yellow line includes São Bento station and Vila Nova de Gaia, across the river. To ride the Metro, you must have an Andante card, described earlier.

## By Funicular

A handy funicular (Elevador dos Guindais) connects the Ribeira district (at the base of the Ponte Dom Luís I bridge) to the top of the steep hill above (at the remains of the city wall, down the Rua de Augusto Rosa from Praça da Batalha, near the terminus for trolley #22). This is the only public-transit option for saving yourself the steep hike between the Ribeira and the city center (€2.50, every 10 minutes; daily 8:00-22:00, in summer sometimes until 24:00; Nov-April until 20:00).

## By Cable Car

The overpriced Teleférico de Gaia cable car soars above Vila Nova de Gaia, connecting the riverfront with the Jardim do Morro, just under the Mosteiro da Serra do Pilar monastery and the upper part of the Ponte Dom Luís I bridge. The five-minute ride gives a unique view over the port wine lodges and across the river to the city, and can be handy for connecting the upper and lower parts of Vila Nova de Gaia (€5 one-way, €8 round-trip, daily 10:00-20:00 in summer, 10:00-18:00 off-season, www.gaiacablecar.com).

## By Taxi or Uber

**Taxis** are a good option in this hilly city. Most rides are fairly short and cost only around €5. For rides within the city limits, the meter should be on "T1" during the day (€2 drop charge) and "T2" at

PORTO

## Porto at a Glance

**▲▲▲Port Wine Lodges in Vila Nova de Gaia** Touring the cellars and sampling Porto's most famous product is this city's top tourist activity, especially for connoisseurs. **Hours:** Vary, but generally daily, last tours at 18:00. See page 345.

**▲▲Porto Walk** A two-part self-guided walk linking the city's top landmarks. **Hours:** Walk—any time; sights and shops—check listings. See page 327.

**▲▲Strolling the Cais da Ribeira** Porto's picturesque riverfront, with arcades and colorful traditional homes. **Hours:** Always open. See page 337.

**▲▲Stock Exchange Palace** Astonishing monument to civic pride, with room after sumptuous room. **Hours:** By tour only, daily April-Oct 9:00-18:30, Nov-March 9:00-12:30 & 14:00-17:30. See page 343.

**▲Cruising the Douro** Lazy one-hour cruises up and down the river, offering the city's top views. **Hours:** Generally daily 10:00-18:30 in summer (until 17:00 off-season). See page 327.

**▲São Francisco Church** Gothic church dripping with Baroque gold. **Hours:** Daily March-Sept 9:00-19:00, Oct-Feb 9:00-17:30. See page 344.

**▲Avenida dos Aliados** Porto's top urban street, where the city goes to work in elaborate buildings. **Hours:** Always open; quiet at night. See page 327.

**▲Clérigos Church and Tower** Porto's towering landmark, with a 225-step climb to sweeping views over the urban sprawl. **Hours:** Daily 9:00-19:00. See page 332.

night (21:00-6:00, €2.50 drop charge). Each kilometer costs about €0.40. A luggage surcharge of €1.60 is legit (per ride, not per piece of luggage). It's easy to find taxi stands, and you'll pay €0.80 more to call one (try Invicta, tel. 225-076-400). Better yet, Porto is an excellent town for using Uber. If you're comfortable with Uber back home, it works just the same here—and typically comes with cleaner cars, friendlier drivers, and cheaper fares than a taxi.

▲**São Bento Train Station** Entry hall decorated with impressive *azulejo* (tile) murals. **Hours:** Always open. See page 333.

▲**Porto Cathedral** Huge church overlooking the town, with fine *azulejo*-decorated cloister and otherwise dull interior. **Hours:** Church—daily in summer 9:00-12:30 & 14:30-19:00, until 18:00 in winter; cloister and sacristy—daily in summer 9:00-12:30 & 14:30-19:00, until 17:30 in winter, closed Sun morning. See page 340.

▲**Rua de Santa Catarina** The main shopping drag, with Art Nouveau and Art Deco landmarks. **Hours:** Traffic-free during the day; quiet at night. See page 339.

▲**Market** Lively old-fashioned produce and meat market...with old-fashioned sanitary conditions. **Hours:** Mon-Fri 7:00-17:00, Sat 7:00-13:00, closed Sun. See page 339.

▲**Serralves Foundation Contemporary Art Museum and Park** Sprawling park with impressive museum, Art Deco mansion, and relaxing grounds. **Hours:** April-Sept Tue-Fri 10:00-19:00, Sat-Sun 10:00-20:00; Oct-March Tue-Fri 10:00-18:00; Sat-Sun 10:00-19:00; closed Mon year-round, except park open July-Sept Mon 10:00-19:00. See page 350.

**Tramway Museum** Collection tracing the history of electrical transport. **Hours:** Mon 14:00-18:00, Tue-Sun 10:00-18:00. See page 350.

**House of Henry the Navigator** Birthplace of the explorer, with history exhibits. **Hours:** Tue-Sun 9:30-13:00 & 14:00-17:30, closed Mon. See page 344.

**House of Music** New Modernist concert hall with performances of jazz, fado, and more. **Hours:** English tours daily at 11:00 and 16:00, concerts nearly nightly. See page 352.

# Tours in Porto

## ON WHEELS

Steep Porto is a good candidate for a bus tour. Three different **hop-on, hop-off bus tour** companies—red, blue, and yellow—do loops through town, connecting the city center, the Ribeira, Vila Nova de Gaia, and the Foz suburb. All of them have open-top buses, headphone commentary, and run twice per hour. If you're also interested in a river cruise—described on page 327—ask about

---

## Lisbon versus Porto: Teams and Terms

Lisbon and Porto are proud rivals. Lisboners, known as "cabbage eaters," drink an *imperial* (as a small glass is called) of Sagres beer while rooting for Benfica (the working-class soccer team) or Sporting (the upper-class rival). Meanwhile, the people of Porto, known as "tripe eaters," drink a *fino* (small glass) of Super Bock beer while rooting for FC Porto. Differences extend to coffee breaks, too. When it's time for a shot of espresso, Lisboners ask for a *bica* while in Porto they request a *cimbalino*.

---

bus-plus-cruise combo-tickets (all three companies offer them). The companies are essentially interchangeable, but the blue bus is slightly cheaper (€10/1 day rather than €13/1 day).

For a cheaper (and more humiliating) option, the "Magic Tour" **tourist train** does a loop around the town center and also includes a stop at a port wine lodge across the river (€8.50, 2/hour, 1.25 hours, leaves from in front of cathedral).

The **tuk-tuk** invasion of Portugal, which began in Lisbon, has reached Porto. You'll see these little three-wheeled taxis (which seat up to three) parked at touristy sights around town, especially in front of Clérigos Tower. Little guided tours around town cost €12-60, depending on length, and rates can be soft. Find a driver you like and go for a spin. While a tuk-tuk ride can be noisy, smelly, and jostling, it can work well for a sweat-free tour around this very vertical city.

### ON FOOT
A good local guide or tour can be well worth the expense.

**Maria Jose Aleixo** is a private guide whom I've found very helpful (€110/half-day per group, mobile 969-468-347, aleixo19@ sapo.pt).

**The City Tailors Tours** are led by your friend in Porto, Ricardo Brochado, who truly loves his work. He tailors half-day Porto experiences for groups of one to six for €75 per person (cheaper for larger groups). This rate includes snacks, drinks, and a light meal along the way (mobile 917-574-983, www.thecitytailors.com, ricardo@thecitytailors.com).

**Taste Porto Food and Wine Tours** is run with gusto by tour guide André, who has a contagious enthusiasm for good food and embracing life Portuguese-style. André takes small groups (up to 10) on a two-mile walk with six tasty stops. It's fun socially, really educational, relaxed, and delicious. André enjoys his work so much he'll happily do the tour if just one person signs up (€59, Tue-Sat at

10:30 and 16:00, 3.5 hours, mobile 920-503-302, www.tasteporto. com, info@tasteporto.com).

## BY BOAT

The city's well-promoted **"Six Bridges" river cruises,** worth ▲, leave from the waterfront in the Ribeira district (see page 336). If you want a longer cruise, consider **day trips along the Douro,** which include boat passage one-way to Peso da Régua or Pinhão and the other way by train, as well as breakfast and/or lunch on board (figure €60-85 to Peso da Régua, €75-100 to Pinhão, price depends on what's included, www.rotadodouro.pt; for details, see the next chapter).

# Porto Walk

This two-part self-guided walk, worth ▲▲, links Porto's top landmarks (see map on page 328). Part 1 is a brief, uphill-downhill loop through the city center, connecting the main square with some relatively untouristed back streets and the city's main landmark (Clérigos Tower). Part 2 begins at the São Bento train station and angles downhill to Porto's finest interiors (Stock Exchange Palace and São Francisco Church) before ending in its characteristic waterfront zone, the Ribeira. Doing the entire two-part walk gives you a great overview of the city's charms. The complete walk takes about two hours (one hour per part), and that's assuming you don't go into any of the sights. If you're very tight on time, just do Part 2.

Porto is decentralized, with important sights scattered on many levels. Along the way I'll point out additional landmarks that you could detour to, if you have the time and interest.

## PART 1: UPPER PORTO—THE CITY CENTER

• *Begin at the equestrian statue that marks the bottom end of Porto's main square-slash-boulevard...*

### ▲Avenida dos Aliados (Avenue of the Allies)

This is the main urban drag of Porto, where Portugal's hardworking second city goes to work. Porto—often invaded, never con-

quered—is known as *cidade invicta,* the "Invincible City." It's also called "The Granite City"—both for its stone-built cityscape and its sturdy, stubborn people (who like to say they have granite in their DNA). Rounding out the defiant symbolism is the dragon—the mascot of the locally beloved soccer team, FC Porto.

PORTO

# Porto Walk

### PART 1
1. Avenida dos Aliados
2. Rua da Fábrica
3. Praça Guilherme Gomes Fernandes
4. Praça de Gomes Teixeira
5. Lello & Irmão Bookstore
6. Praça de Lisboa Park
7. Clérigos Church & Tower

### PART 2
8. São Bento Train Station
9. Rua das Flores
10. Henry the Navigator Square
11. Cais da Ribeira
12. Praça da Ribeira

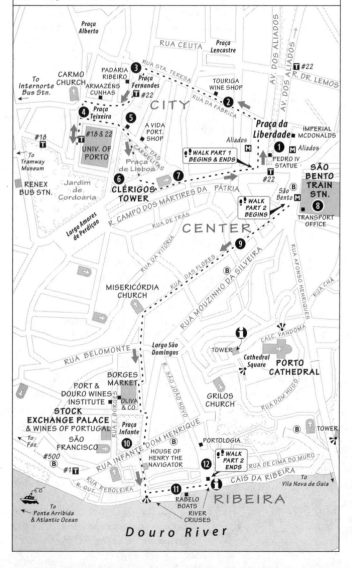

Avenida dos Aliados is named for the alliance created when Portugal joined the winning side before the outbreak of World War I. The wide boulevard, lined with elaborate examples of various architectural eras (mostly Art Nouveau and Art Deco), reminds me of Prague's Wenceslas Square. The twin bank towers flanking the street midway up were designed by Portuguese architect Marques da Silva (circa 1920). And crowning the square is the huge City Hall (Câmara Municipal).

The bottom of the avenue—where you're standing—is **Praça da Liberdade** (Liberty Square). The statue honors King Pedro IV (1798-1834), a hero in the 1832 Civil War, who advocated for a limited constitutional monarchy in Portugal (while maintaining his title as Emperor of Brazil). King Pedro prevailed...and he's holding the constitution to prove it. A true "peoples' king," he left his heart to the people of Porto—literally. (It's buried in a local church.) The square is a strong statement for a secular and modern Portugal: It's topped not by a church, but by the City Hall (which blocks the view of Trindade Church—the namesake of the nearby station where all of Porto's Metro lines converge). Throughout Porto, after the king confiscated church property in the 1830s, large tracts of land that had been the domain of the church became the domain of the people. Then, in the 1920s and 1930s (especially with the coming of the dictator António Salazar), Portugal demonstrated its national pride by razing many characteristic medieval quarters to build bigger squares and bigger buildings (as here).

Directly to the right of King Pedro, hiding behind the trees, is the **"Imperial McDonald's"**—one of the fanciest in Europe (formerly the Imperial Café). Check it out, and ponder the battle of cultural elegance against global economic efficiency.

Now stand at the very bottom of the square, along the busy street. Notice that nothing is level in Porto. Looking uphill, you'll see the blue-tiled church of St. Ildefonso, and just downhill is São Bento station. This walk connects key landmarks, with a little uphill walking (at the start), then lots of downhill walking.

• *When you're ready, head one short block up Avenida dos Aliados, to the over-the-top bank tower on the left side of the square (labeled* Unic— *indeed it is). Angle up the little street just in front of that building (Rua do Dr. Artur de Magalhães Basto). After one short block, continue up the same street, now called...*

## Rua da Fábrica

This street—named for the tobacco factories that once helped power local industry in this town—is one of many appealing shopping lanes in downtown Porto. The city has been transformed in recent years. Not long ago, streets like this were seedy and deserted.

They may still be (artfully) seedy, but they are deserted no more—with clever boutiques and tempting eateries opening all the time.

On the first corner, on the right, notice the big **craft market** with high-quality, locally handcrafted items: leather shoes, jewelry, cork products, sardines, and more. Farther up Rua da Fábrica, on the right at #30, is the handy **Touriga wine shop,** offering tastings and shelves stocked with local wines (see page 360). Across the street at #29 is the **Grande Hotel de Paris Residencial,** a once-classic, now-divey spot that brags it was the first hotel in Porto with running water in its rooms. At the top of the block on the left, at #71, is one of many fine *azulejo*-tiled storefronts in town.

• *Keep going up Rua da Fábrica, huffing your way up three more short but steep blocks. You'll pop out at a cute little triangular square called...*

## Praça Guilherme Gomes Fernandes

Firefighters take note: The square's namesake—honored by a statue in the middle—led the fire brigade that contained an 1888 blaze, which otherwise might have devastated the city.

Guilherme is eyeing the main reason to linger on this cozy square: the recommended **Padaria Ribeiro** pastry shop, a local favorite (closed Sun). Step inside and take your pick from the extensive offerings. You can either order something to go, or make your choice and have them bring it out to you on the square. You've finished the uphill portion of this walk—now's the time for a little pastry break.

• *With the pastry shop at your back, turn right and follow the trolley tracks around the corner to the right. You'll quickly emerge into a grand square called...*

## Praça de Gomes Teixeira

The centerpiece of this square is the Fountain of Lions, and behind that is the main building of the **University of Porto.** The U. Porto is a fairly young school (founded 1911), but the second-biggest in Portugal, with about 30,000 students who give this city—and this neighborhood (one of three main campuses)—a special energy. The square is named for its first rector and a beloved math prof.

At the top of the square (facing the university), the **Armazéns Cunhas** department store demonstrates the sleek Art Deco style that took hold in Porto in the early 20th century—sprucing up a city of granite and *azulejos*. This neon facade, though now faded, might look more at home in Hollywood or Miami Beach. The peacock at the top trumpets the new fashions of the age, and neon announces *novidades—vendemos mais barato* ("new fashions—we sell cheaper!").

Just past the end of the square, you can't miss the brilliant blue *azulejos* on the side of **Carmo Church,** depicting the founding of the Carmelite Order. Circling around to the front, you'll see this is two fine Rococo churches in one: On the right, Carmo Church, once inhabited by friars; on the left, the Carmelite church, once housing an order of Carmelite nuns. These two were connected (by what they like to call the "world's narrowest house"—with the green gate and door) to allow the monks and nuns inside to hunker down in their spiritual sanctuary without venturing into the outside world.

Downhill from the church, in the delightful cobbled square, notice the **trolley stop** for two of Porto's historic lines. As in Lis-

bon, rickety trolleys have long been a part of Porto's history, and the city is committed to bringing them back as an integral part of the public-transit system. In 1872 (40 years after being invented in the US), the first trolleys in Iberia began operating in Porto, pulled by horses and oxen. Dubbed *americanos* based on their origin, the trolley network was electrified in 1904. Essential for connecting suburbs with the city center, more than 100 trolley lines were still in use by the 1970s. However, buses and cars—the by-products of modern prosperity—almost eliminated this important part of the city's heritage. Today, a few lines survive as vintage trips appealing mainly to tourists. From here, trolley #18 rattles to the Tramway Museum, while trolley #22 does a very handy loop through the town center—including an easy connection up to the Rua de Santa Catarina shopping street, Praça da Batalha (with another fine blue-tiled church), and the funicular down to the Ribeira (all described later, under "Sights in Porto").

• *Back out on the big square, face the university building and walk to its left end. An elevated park sits just beyond. On the left side of the downhill street that runs along the park, you'll see...*

## Lello & Irmão Bookstore

Built in 1906, the shop boasts a lacy exterior and a fancy Art Nouveau interior. It looks like wood, but it's mostly made of painted plaster with gold leaf. J. K. Rowling, who worked in Porto for a year, was reportedly inspired by this Harry Potter-esque shop. And sure enough, the interior feels like something you'd see on Diagon Alley. You'll pay to go inside (see below), then follow the quaint tracks to the book trolley. Climb the sagging staircase to find the old cash register, ogle the stained-glass ceiling, and admire the slinky hanging lights.

The Harry Potter connection—which was attracting 2,000 people to ogle the interior, but not buying anything—became too much for this little, fragile bookshop to handle. So now they attempt to control crowds by requiring that visitors buy a €3 voucher to get inside (line up to buy it at the kiosk across the street, then enter through the main door). You can apply the €3 toward any purchase—they have some souvenirs, as well as a good selection of books in English by leading Portuguese authors. The funds raised have already allowed them to restore the newly gleaming facade. Come on—support your local bookshop (daily 10:00-19:30, Rua das Carmelitas 144).

• *The cross street just past the bookstore is Galeria de Paris, lined with characteristic shops and bars. On this corner is a branch of **A Vida Portuguesa**, the Lisbon-based shop for quality, authentic local souvenirs (daily, Rua Galeria de Paris 20).*

*Across the street from the bookstore is the unusual...*

## Praça de Lisboa Park

This innovative solution shows what smart urban planners can do to camouflage an ugly concrete parking garage in the historic heart of a city: build a park on top of it. The most direct way to our next stop—the church tower—is through the modern concrete chute, which tunnels past shops and cafés underground, through the middle of the park. But I'd rather head up the stairs (just to the right of the chute) to walk across the park itself—a green respite in the heart of a con-

gested city. Up top, a hip bar called Base serves drinks, which you can enjoy at picnic tables or under one of the 50 gnarled olive trees.

• *Make your way across the park—either down below or up top—to reach the can't-miss-it...*

## ▲Clérigos Church and Tower
## (Igreja e Torre dos Clérigos)

This church, which consumed three decades of Nicolau Nasoni's life (1731-1763), shows the ambitious architect's flair for theatrics. He fit the structure into its hilltop location, putting the tower at the back on the highest ground, dramatically reinforcing its height. Nasoni worked in stages: first the church, then the hospital and the

## Nicolau Nasoni (1691-1773)

In the 1720s—a boom time in Porto—the Italian Nasoni found work as a painter here. His swirling, colorful paintings wowed Porto, and Nasoni got plenty of work. He married a Portuguese woman, had five kids, and made Porto his home. Soon, he was employed as an architect, hiring skilled local artisans to turn granite, wood, and poured plaster into his trademark cherubs, garlands, and cumulus clouds. Even stark medieval churches had their facades topped with Baroque towers and their interiors paneled and spackled in billowy gilded designs. Prolific to the max, Nasoni redid Porto in the Baroque style (much as Bernini did in Rome), creating palaces and churches throughout the area. His tour de force was the hill-topping Clérigos Church, where he was later buried.

Chapter House (residence for priests and monks). He topped it all off with the outsized tower. You can go inside the church for free, or pay to climb the tower (see page 340).

• *Take the atmospheric, traffic-free, trolley-track-lined lane to the right of the tower—an urban canyon of* azulejos *and funky shops. Heading downhill, you'll find yourself back where you started—at the Avenida dos Aliados. This time, keep going straight, one more block. You'll run right into São Bento train station.*

*Part 2 of our walk begins just inside the station (see below). But if you'd like to explore one more part of Porto's city center—the traditional market hall, bustling shopping street (Rua Santa Caterina), and* azulejo-*slathered church on Praça da Batalha—you can hike up the hill just to the left of the station (toward the pretty church you see perched on the hill). All of these are described later, on page 338.*

## PART 2: LOWER PORTO—GRAND INTERIORS AND RIBEIRA WATERFRONT

• *Begin inside the main entry hall of Porto's stately...*

### ▲São Bento Train Station (Estação São Bento)

The station's main entry hall features some of Portugal's finest *azulejos*—vivid, decorative hand-painted tiles that show historical and folk scenes from the Douro region.

Read some important Porto history in the tiles. As you face the tracks, the large, blue, upper tiles on the left show medieval battles back when Spain and Portugal were at war. Tiles on the opposite wall (far right when looking at the tracks) show a pivotal event from Porto's past: the 1387 wedding of Portugal's King João I and the English princess Philippa, which established the Portuguese-English alliance. (Notice the fine portrait of Philippa and the depiction of the cathedral as it looked in the 14th century.) Below is the result of the marriage—their son, Prince Henry the Navigator, shown conquering Ceuta for Portugal in 1415. While humble Ceuta was just a small chip of Morocco (across from Gibraltar), it marked an important first step in the creation of a soon-to-be vast Portu-

guese empire. The trackside tiles celebrate the traditional economy, such as the transport of port wine. The multicolored tiles near the top show different modes of transportation, as they evolved from Roman chariots (just to the right of the big clock), progressing counterclockwise 360 degrees to the arrival of the first train (left corner above Philippa).

Notice the words *Douro* and *Minho* overhead. These are the major rivers in this part of Portugal, and the key regions linked by these trains (basically the north of the country). All this art seems old, but it's really Portuguese revival art from the period just after World War I, celebrating the country's heritage.

• *Before continuing downhill to the Ribeira, stand in front of the station's entrance to get oriented. Consider a detour to Porto's **cathedral** and its viewpoint square (described on page 340). You can see its serrated roofline on the ridge just to the left (with the station to your back)— about a 10-minute walk away. Just beyond the cathedral is the upper level of the Luís I Bridge, which crosses scenically over the Douro to **Villa Nova de Gaia** and its port wine lodges (described on page 345). Buses to Vila Nova de Gaia leave across the street from the station's entrance (the stop closest to the Metro entrance, buses #900, #901, or #906).*

*To continue our walk downhill to the Ribeira waterfront, cross the street, turn left, then take the right street at the fork. This puts you on the delightful artery connecting the town center with the riverbank.*

## Rua das Flores

This traffic-free street is lined with iron railings, vivid *azulejos*, outdoor café tables, and enticing shops selling jewelry, antiques, chocolates, and other temptations. A decade ago, this was a deserted no-man's-land; today, it's a touristy main drag—and a great example of how Porto is blossoming all over again. And yet, some funky graffiti (a Porto specialty) and ragtag house fronts still survive, as a reminder that Porto is the result of a complex and authentic history. Enjoy this strip for a few blocks downhill.

Near the end of the street, on the right, you can't miss the elaborate, skinny facade of the **Misericórdia Church,** another confection by Nicolau Nasoni (of Clérigos Tower fame). Today you can pay to enter its Mannerist-style, *azulejo*-tiled interior, and the adjacent museum about the church's history, strong charitable tradition, and ecclesiastical art.

• *At the end of Rua das Flores, continue straight across the cobbled, busy-with-cars cross street, and head down Rua do Dr. Sousa Viterbo. Soon, on your right, you'll pass the big, red Borges Market—now a popular nightclub.*

*Just past the market, you'll emerge at the top of...*

## Henry the Navigator Square (Praça do Infante Dom Henrique)

Arguably the most important Portuguese person of all time—who put his country on the (figurative) map by putting many mysterious, faraway lands on the (literal) map—was born right here in Porto. (We'll see his house soon.) In this statue, Henry the Navigator is pointing toward the sea. For more on Henry, see the sidebar on page 183.

The building that dominates this square is the ▲▲ **Stock Exchange Palace** (Palácio da Bolsa). Commerce came to define Porto, as royalty or religion would define other cities (like Lisbon and Braga, respectively). The Commercial Association of Porto (Associação Comercial do Porto) even had its own system of courts and a representative to the king. In 1832, the monastery of the São Francisco Church (next door) burned down, and the queen offered the property to the Commercial Association. They seized the opportunity to show off, crafting a building that would demonstrate the considerable skill of Porto's tradesmen. The interior—which you can visit only with a 30-minute guided tour (see page 343)—is a proud showcase of decorative prowess, from inlaid-wood floors to plaster painted to resemble carved wood, and from the glorious glass-roofed atrium to the exactingly detailed Arabian Hall. Drop in now to see when the next tour ticket is available; the rest of this walk won't take you far from the palace.

Just to the left of the Stock Exchange Palace, you can see the apse of ▲ **São Francisco Church.** This has the finest church interior in town, and its adjacent crypt is stacked with anonymously numbered tombs holding the remains of past parishioners (see page 344; enter around the left side).

A few **culinary temptations** are around the square. Inside the Stock Exchange Palace is the **Wines of Portugal Tasting Room;** on the street just uphill from there is another wine-tasting opportunity, the **Port and Douro Wines Institute** (both of these are described on page 360). Across the street from the institute is the fine **Oliva & Co. shop,** which would love to introduce you to various olive oils and other products from Portugal, and give you a little tasting (daily 10:00-20:00, Rua Ferreira Borges 60, www.olivaeco.com).

Head down the little street directly downhill from Henry the Navigator (Rua Alfândega—the aptly named "Customs Street"). On the left, you'll see the **House of Henry the Navigator,** where the great explorer is believed to have been born. There are no Henry artifacts inside, but there is a high-tech, concise exhibit outlining some of Portugal's seafaring achievements (see page 344).

• *From Henry's pad, it's just a few more steps downhill to...*

## The Ribeira, Porto's Romantic Riverfront

The riverfront Ribeira (ree-BAY-rah, meaning "riverbank") district is the city's most scenic and touristy quarter, with its highest concentration of restaurants and postcard racks. Narrow, higgledy-piggledy homes face the busy Douro River. Head down to the riverbank and follow their example, scanning the horizon from left to right.

Begin by looking to the far left, where the **Ponte Dom Luís I bridge** rises 150 feet above the river. In the 1880s, Teofilo Seyrig, a protégé of Gustave Eiffel, stretched this Eiffel Tower-sized wrought-iron contraption across the 500-foot-wide Douro. (Eiffel himself designed a bridge in Porto, the **Ponte Dona Maria Pia,** a bit upstream—barely visible from here.)

If you followed the Douro 60 miles upriver—beyond those bridges—you'd reach a wonderland of hand-built stone terraces where grapes eke out a hardy existence (for more on the Douro Valley, see the next chapter). Port wine is harvested and stomped there, then floated downriver to age here—directly across the river from where you're standing, in **Vila Nova de Gaia** (or just "Gaia"). Until recently, the wine could be legally called "port" only if it aged in Gaia—though recent deregulation now permits vintners to age their port where it's grown. Like so many miniature Hollywood signs climbing the riverbank, you'll see the 18 different company names proudly marking their lodges here—each one inviting you in for a sample. (For more on the port-tasting scene in Gaia, see page 346.)

Looking right, the river bends as it heads out toward the open Atlantic (a long walk or short trolley ride, but not quite visible from here). To get out of the congested urban center, consider side-tripping out to the pleasant beach community of Foz, where the Douro meets the sea (see page 350).

Now turn around and face the **skinny houses** along the embankment (signed *Cais da Estiva*). Before tourism, the Ribeira was a working port. The city wall fortified Porto from the river, and (until the 20th-century embankment was built) the water came right up to the arches—many of which were loading zones for merchants. Imagine the busy harbor scene before the promenade was reclaimed from the river: cargo-laden riverboats lashed to the embankment, off-loading their wine and produce into 14th-century cellars (still visible). Today the old arcades lining the Ribeira promenade are jammed with hole-in-the-wall restaurants and souvenir shops. Behind the arcades are skinny, colorful houses draped with drying laundry fluttering like flags, while the locals who fly them stand gossiping on their little balconies. The contrast of bright tourism and vivid untouched neighborhoods within 30 yards of each other is amazing.

• *From Cais da Estiva and with the river on your right, go for a stroll along the embankment known as the...*

## ▲▲Cais da Ribeira

As you walk, notice that various interchangeable companies along this embankment sell easy, scenic, 50-minute **"Six Bridges" cruises** (rated ▲) on the Douro for €12.50. You'll see landmarks not visible from here (including Eiffel's majestic steel Ponte Dona Maria Pia). If you're interested, comparison-shop as you stroll. Cruises are generally offered daily 10:00-18:30 in the summer (until 17:00 off-season).

Soon you'll reach some distinctive boats—called *rabelos*—moored along the embankment. These were once the only way to transport wine from the Douro Valley vineyards downriver to Porto. These boats, which look Asian, have flat bottoms, a big square sail, and a very large rudder to help them navigate the rough, twisty course of the river (for more info, see page 375).

• *After about a block, you'll pop out at the bottom of the neighborhood's main square...*

## Praça da Ribeira

This vibrant, ragtag space was long the city's front door. In the mid-18th century, city leaders attempted to clear it out and make a vast wasteland like Lisbon's Praça do Comércio. But the proud people of Porto (who, remember, have granite in their DNA) asserted themselves—as they like to do—and that construction project was stopped. Today, this square is a thriving place of the people.

Stand on the riverfront and look inland: On the left is the unfinished facade of that urban renewal vision; on the right is a classic line of Porto houses that survive. (Do a "Where's Waldo?" for old ladies looking out at the crowd from their windows.) Check out the artwork in the square: the cube fountain and the statue of St. John the Baptist with his rough cloak, who overlooks the happy scene from above. For yet another wine-tasting opportunity, just a few steps above the square on Rua de São João (on the right, at #28) is **Portologia wine bar,** described in "Eating in Porto," later.

• *Our Porto orientation walk is over. There's a lot more of the Ribeira to see—just walk with the river on your right, following the rabelos. Or venture into the maze of distinctive, tiny lanes that climb up the hill from the water. At the end of the embankment is the towering bridge with a lower level that takes you efficiently to **Vila Nova de Gaia** for some port tasting. Or, to head back up to the **cathedral** area or **Porto's shopping neighborhood** (both described later, under "Sights in Porto"), ride the funicular—it departs from just past the bridge (still on this side of the river).*

# Sights in Porto

Many of Porto's top sights are connected by my self-guided walk, earlier.

## PORTO'S SHOPPING NEIGHBORHOOD

Porto's bustling, local-feeling shopping district is a wonderful place to people-watch. Most of the action occurs along Rua de Santa Catarina, which runs roughly parallel to Avenida dos Aliados a few blocks east. Begin at Praça da Batalha (just up Rua 31 de Janeiro from São Bento station), and follow this route to the Old World market hall.

### Praça da Batalha (Battle Square)

This square has a fine tiled church (Santo Ildefonso), the 19th-century National Theater (originally the Opera House), and the impressive Art Deco Cinema Batalha (now closed). The church's *azulejo* tiles, reminiscent of Ming dynasty blue-and-white ceramics, were all the rage in Baroque Portugal. But these tiles, depicting scenes from the life of the church's patron saint, aren't Baroque. They were fitted into the walls of the church during the early 1930s, an era that celebrated Portuguese heritage.

This square, while a bit seedy, has benches where old-timers hang out. If you'd like a classic little hot dog with the local gang, drop by **Cervejaria Gazela** (just to the right of the National Theater, described in "Eating in Porto").

• *At the north end of the square, branching off to the left of the blue-tiled church, is...*

## ▲Rua de Santa Catarina

Porto's main shopping street is busy and (mostly) traffic-free by day, quiet by night. A stroll along here gives you a sense of to-

day's Porto—as well as yesterday's, including the venerable Art Nouveau Café Majestic, the circa-1900 hangout for the local intelligentsia (a block down on your right). Step in. Porto's pet name for a little coffee is *cimbalino*—named for the traditional Italian espresso-making machines. Kitty-corner from Café Majestic is the FNAC department store—handy for whatever you might need.

The Rua de Santa Catarina sidewalk is a good example of *calçada portuguesa*, Portugal's unique limestone and basalt mosaic work. It's handmade and high-maintenance...but apparently worth the effort and expense to locals. Notice all the shoe stores. Along with wine, textile and shoe factories power northern Portugal's industry.

• *After two blocks, turn left on **Rua Formosa**, which is lined with little specialty shops—wine, meat, sweets, canned fish, and so on—tempting you to assemble a Portuguese picnic. At #279, you can't miss the glorious 1917 Art Deco facade of **A Pérola do Bolhão** ("The Pearl of the Market"), filled with traditional and edible souvenirs. Soon you'll run into the...*

## ▲Market (Bolhão)

Porto's traditional market still manages to stay in business, despite competition from newer shopping malls. This is a great place to wander—especially in the morning—and take in the sights, sounds, and smells of real-world Porto (Mon-Fri 7:00-17:00, Sat 7:00-13:00, closed Sun).

As you enter, the butchers and fishermen are on the left and right; produce and flowers (along with cheap eateries serving €3 sardine lunches) are dead ahead. Check out the butcher section, with half-pigs hanging from the ceiling, and display cases full of unusual specialties...such as *sangue cozido* (coagulated pig blood). Then wander through the seafood section. If it's springtime, you may see a favorite local delicacy pulled from the river: *lampreia* (eel). They say eels are so tasty because they dine on the flavorful garbage in the Douro. Climb the stairs for farmers' stalls. The market's old-fashioned sanitary conditions aren't quite up to European Union snuff, but the EU seems to be looking the other way...for now.

Inside and around the market are lively shops. At one corner is Casa Horticula, with a wide variety of seeds. In bakery windows, the big, round, dark *broa* breads, made with corn and rye, are moist inside and hard outside. The breads with bits of sausage baked in are called *folar*. The cheeses on display are either *ovelha* (sheep) or *cabra* (goat). *Bom-apetite!*

## IN THE CITY CENTER
### ▲Clérigos Church and Tower (Igreja e Torre dos Clérigos)

This oval-shaped church with a disproportionately tall tower is the masterwork of Nicolau Nasoni, a prolific Baroque architect who left his mark all over the city (see sidebar on page 333).

**Cost and Hours:** Church—free, tower and exhibits—€3, daily 9:00-19:00, free city maps at ticket window, Rua São Filipe de Nery, tel. 222-001-729. You can also climb the tower after dark (€5, daily 19:00-23:00).

**Visiting the Church and Tower:** The **church facade** displays Nasoni's characteristic frills, garlands, and exuberant cornices. Notice how Nasoni built the tower in six sections, each one more elaborate than the last, topped with a round dome and spiked with pinnacles.

The **interior** is an oval-shaped Baroque nave built out of granite and marble, but covered with ornate carvings. Look for the high altar—a wedding-cake structure with Mary on top—and the tomb of Nasoni, who asked to be buried here.

The main attraction is climbing 225 steps to the top of the 250-foot **tower**—one of Porto's icons. (On busy days, you may have to kill time waiting for your turn on the upper stairs—ask before you buy your ticket.) On the way up, you'll peek into the assembly rooms, walk along upper galleries offering views into the church interior from above, and check out the "Christus Collection," with depictions of Jesus from all over Portugal and around the world (many brought home by Portuguese explorers). Reaching the top, you get a close-up look at the carillon and commanding views of the city with its jumble of tightly packed red roofs.

### ▲Porto Cathedral (Sé do Porto)

This hulking, fortress-like, 12th-century Romanesque cathedral, while graced with fine granite stonework typical of northern Portugal and lavish 18th-century Baroque altars, feels gloomy and stark inside. But its history is palpable. Henry the Navigator was baptized here, and it was the scene of many royal weddings (including that of Henry's parents, João I and Philippa).

**Cost and Hours:** Cathedral—free, open daily in summer 9:00-12:30 & 14:30-19:00, until 18:00 in winter; cloister and sacristy—€3, daily in summer 9:00-12:30 & 14:30-19:00, until 17:30 in winter, closed Sun morning; Terreiro da Sé, tel. 222-059-028.

**Visiting the Cathedral:** The **main altarpiece** sums up the exuberance of Porto in the 1720s, when the city was booming,

the local bishop was temporarily away in Lisbon, and Italian Baroque was sweeping through town. On the side walls flanking the altar are faded faux-architecture paintings by Nicolau Nasoni, the Italian who came to Porto to paint the cathedral's sacristy and soon became the city's most influential architect (see sidebar on page 333).

Look at the chapel just left of the high altar. Inside is a dreamy, carved-and-painted limestone statue of the **Lady of Vendôme,** brought to Porto in the 14th century by monks from France. It originally stood at one of the fortified gates of the city and remains close to the hearts of the townsfolk.

Just left of the Lady of Vendôme is the **Silver Altar of the Holy Sacrament** (c. 1700)—made with 1,500 pounds of silver. When French troops under Napoleon pillaged Porto, the church guards plastered over the altar to hide it.

The **cloister** and its adjacent rooms are worth the time and entrance fee. The cloister's walls are decorated with elaborate *azulejo*

tiles illustrating the amorous poetry of the Bible's "Song of Songs." (The €0.30 pamphlet is skimpy, but the €5 English guidebook explains it all, including the text that inspired the *azulejos*.) Entering, turn right and go for a counterclockwise stroll. The adjacent **Chapel of St. Vincent,** with

17th-century painted carvings of Bible scenes, has a trapdoor into a crypt, where centuries of bishops' bones were ultimately tossed. Up the Nasoni staircase, the richly ornamented **chapter room** is where the bishop and his gang met in the 17th century to wield their religious and secular power. Note the holy figures depicted on the ceiling and the fine city views from the windows. There's also a typical **treasury**, with vestments and monstrances.

## Cathedral Square

From the cathedral's small square—until the 1920s a congested medieval quarter—you'll get a great view of the old town. The Baroque spiral pillory (20th-century copy) is a reminder of the harsh justice once doled out here. Dominating the square (and the skyline of Porto) is the massive **Bishop's Palace,** still the home of the bishop and his offices; the immensity of this 18th-century building reflects the bishop's past power. The crenellated tower just down the stairs from the cathedral square houses the TI.

Facing the cathedral, walk around to the left to the statue of **Vímara Peres,** a Christian warrior who reconquered this region from the Moors in 868. (It was lost again within two generations, and remained under Muslim control until the final reconquest in about 1100.) Step into the portico on the side of the cathedral to admire the original 18th-century blue tiles.

From the **viewpoint banister** to the left of Vímara Peres, survey the city and find the church with the blue facade in the middle ground. São Bento station is just to its right, and the green copper dome and steeple of the City Hall breaks the skyline above it. Below you spreads the seedy district called Sé (meaning "cathedral," it refers to the *Se*at of the Catholic Church). This neighborhood, the oldest in town, was famously run-down and depopulating. Things may be changing, as the government is encouraging people to move in by offering economic incentives. The streets beyond the medieval gate—once a ratatouille of drug users and prostitutes, but now touristy—twist their way down into the Ribeira district.

## City Wall View

A segment of the city wall is open and leads to a tower high above the river; from here you can enjoy a grand city and river view. To get there, walk 300 yards up the street behind the cathedral on Rua de Saraiva de Carvalho to a leafy square (Largo Primeiro de Dezembro) and through the arched doorway to the **Santa Clara Church** (with an impressive Baroque interior, decorated with carved wood and lots of gold leaf; Mon-Fri 10:00-12:30 & 14:30-17:00, Sat 10:00-12:30, closed Sun; may be partly or entirely closed for renovation). Exiting the church, go right, through another gate (Instituto Nacional de Saúde), and ahead on your left you'll see the impressive crenellated remains of the 14th-century **town wall** (free, Mon-Fri 8:00-17:00, closed Sat-Sun). From the tower you can survey the Ribeira district, see three bridges upstream crossing the Douro River (including the one designed by Gustave Eiffel), and look down at the funicular tracks (watch the cute car accordion in and out as it crests).

To ride that gadget down to the river, go back through the square to the bottom of Rua da Augusto Rosa. Here's where the

**funicular** (Elevador dos Guindais) departs for the Ribeira riverfront. Or you can hike two blocks up Rua da Augusto Rosa to Praça da Batalha (described on page 338) and the start of the shopping district. Or just hop on trolley #22, which begins its handy loop through town from right next to the funicular entrance.

## JUST ABOVE THE RIBEIRA, ON HENRY THE NAVIGATOR SQUARE

These sights are on or near Praça Infante Dom Henrique, a steep block uphill from the Ribeira district.

### ▲▲Stock Exchange Palace (Palácio da Bolsa)

This unassuming building is neither a stock exchange nor a palace, but a breathtaking monument to civic and commercial pride, with

some of the most lavishly decorated rooms in Portugal. Built over 70 years by the Commercial Association of Porto, the building celebrates Porto's renowned work ethic and dedication to international trade. For more on the history of the building, see "Porto Walk," earlier.

**Cost and Tours:** The interior can only be visited on a 30-minute guided tour (€8). Tours leave every 30 minutes in whatever language is necessary (often English plus another language). To avoid the wait, you can call to ask when the next English tour departs—or, if you're nearby, just drop in and check the screens in the lobby.

**Hours:** Daily April-Oct 9:00-18:30, Nov-March 9:00-12:30 & 14:00-17:30, these are last tour times; no flash photos inside, in big building marked *Associação Comercial do Porto* on Rua Ferreira Borges, tel. 223-399-013, www.palaciodabolsa.com. Note that the building still houses the offices of the Chamber of Commerce, and often closes when rented out for events.

**Visiting the Stock Exchange:** You'll tour several rooms, big and small. You'll begin in the dramatic main hall—decorated with the coats of arms of 20 international trading partners—then climb the grand staircase to tour a variety of fine rooms. The place is rife with symbolism and intricate, time-consuming craftsmanship intended only to impress: the complex patterned floors, carefully pieced together with Brazilian and African

wood (from Portugal's colonies); an incredibly detailed inlaid table, created over three years using wood scraps from those same floors; and a room that looks like it's made of finely carved woodwork and bronze—until you realize it's all painted plaster and gold leaf.

The knock-your-socks-off finale is the sumptuous Arabian Hall. This grand space—inspired by Granada's Alhambra and 18 years in the making—was painstakingly decorated in the Moorish style with wood, plaster, and gold leaf.

**Nearby:** Before exiting, consider a break in the **Wines of Portugal Tasting Room,** in this same building (watch for signs as you exit) and described on page 360.

### ▲São Francisco Church

This is Porto's only church in the Gothic style—complete with a rose window, stair-step buttresses, and a statue of St. Francis of Assisi on the front. Today, a visit comes in two parts: the extravagantly decorated church and its jam-packed catacombs.

**Cost and Hours:** €4, €1 guidebook describes the tiles, daily March-Sept 9:00-19:00, Oct-Feb 9:00-17:30, no photos in church, Rua Infante Dom Henrique.

**Visiting the Church:** Buy your ticket at the office across from the church entrance. Then cross over and head inside. Although the church was ravaged by Napoleon and by the Portuguese during their 19th-century civil war, the interior remains stunning, with lavish chestnut carvings slathered in gold leaf. Wander down the main aisle like a bewildered 18th-century peasant. The first big, ornate altar on the right shows how Franciscans weren't always warmly received—at the top they are being cruelly tortured and crucified by Japanese (portrayed with Muslim features), and at the bottom they are being beheaded by Moors. Still, in the center, St. Francis encourages his followers on. Across the nave, find the extremely fertile Tree of Jesse (1718), which is a very literal interpretation of the family tree of Jesus, resting upon a sleeping Jesse. Below that, Mary lies in a boat as Our Lady of Good Voyage, a patron saint of navigators. Note the wooden boards on the floor— once graves of parishioners. These graves are now empty, but you can see the bones in the crypt.

To get there, cross back over to the ticket desk. You'll walk through a modest museum, then head down the steps to the church's **crypt**—its walls and floors neatly lined with tombs. The remains of former parishioners eventually end up in an inglorious bone heap or ossuary. Peer down through the trapdoor near #32 (look for signs to the *ossário*) to see their final refuge.

### House of Henry the Navigator (Casa do Infante)

Six hundred years ago, Porto's favorite son was supposedly born in this mansion (once the largest house in town, and later the main customs house). This museum has modern exhibits that offer an insightful look at Henry and the explorations he promoted, but few actual artifacts. Still, if you're in a seafaring mood, it's a good reminder of all the new ground (well, water) that Portuguese explorers have covered over the centuries. In the entry hall (before the ticket checkpoint) you can see some Roman mosaics found on-site.

**Cost and Hours:** €2.20, free on weekends, Tue-Sun 9:30-13:00 & 14:00-17:30, closed Mon, Rua da Alfândega 10, tel. 222-060-423. For more on Hank, see page 183.

## PORT WINE LODGES IN VILA NOVA DE GAIA

Just across the river from Porto, the town of Vila Nova de Gaia—or just Gaia (GUY-yuh)—is where much of the world's port wine comes to mature. Port wine grapes are grown, and a young port is produced, about 60 miles upstream in the Douro Valley. Then, after sitting for the winter in silos, the wine is shipped downstream to Vila Nova de Gaia, to age for years in lodges on

this cool, north-facing riverbank. Eighteen companies run these lodges, holding down the port fort and offering tours and tastings. For wine connoisseurs, touring a port wine lodge *(cave do vinho do porto)* and sampling the product is a ▲▲▲ attraction; for those with a casual interest, dropping into one or two is fun, educational, and worth ▲.

Gaia is technically a separate town from Porto, even though it's just across the river and feels like part of the city. Venturing here is well worth the trip. But if you're very tight on time, consider just dropping into one of the wine tastings on the Porto side of the river (see page 360).

**Getting There:** From the Ribeira district, walk (or catch a cab or Uber) across the Ponte Dom Luís I bridge. From the city center, take bus #900, #901, or #906 (every 30 minutes, stop across from São Bento station, near the Metro stop). After crossing the bridge, the bus stops first at the Cálem lodge, then near Sandeman, then climbs the hill.

**Services:** Vila Nova de Gaia operates its own handy **TI** with information about the lodges (daily 10:00-18:00, closed Sun off-season, on the riverbank at Avenida Diogo Leite 135, tel. 223-758-288, www.cm-gaia.pt). Drinks-with-a-view options are available all along the waterfront. A pricey **cable car** links the riverfront with the hilltop Jardim do Morro, near the Ponte Dom Luís I bridge (see page 323).

## ▲▲▲Tours and Tastings

Port tasting is a subjective business, and no single lodge is necessarily the best. If you're a port enthusiast, you probably already have a favorite (or can quickly decide on one, with a little enjoyable research). Although more serious European visitors choose one lodge to visit, American tourists are known to hop between three or four in a single day...before stumbling back to their hotels.

**Visiting a Port Wine Lodge:** At any lodge, the procedure is similar. Individual travelers simply show up and ask for a tour; if it's

busy, they may assign you a time. Pass any wait time by browsing the small on-site museum or watching a video, or simply get started on the tasting. A standard tour/tasting costs €6 and takes about 30 minutes. Tours generally come with a walk through the warehouse (with wooden barrels and vats); a 5- to 10-minute video  produced by that label giving you a quick peek at their process and the scenic Douro Valley; sometimes a small museum; and, finally, two or three tastings. Tours at fancier lodges (like Taylor) take longer and cost more. At any lodge, serious students may opt for more involved tours, offering tastings of finer wines (generally €12-20, with smaller groups, 5 tastings, book in advance if possible). Before you go (or while you're waiting for your tour), read the "Port Wine Crash Course" (page 348), "Brits on the Douro" (page 371), and "Growing—and Stomping—Grapes in the Douro Valley" (page 370).

**Sandeman,** the most high-profile company, is the Budweiser of port. They were the first port producer to create a logo, which you'll see everywhere: a mysterious man wearing a black cloak (representing a Portuguese student's cape) and a rakish *Shadow* hat (worn by Spanish horse-riders, symbolizing the sherry that Sandeman makes in Jerez). Sandeman provides the most corporate, mainstream, accessible experience for first-timers—with a short walk led by a caped guide, a 10-minute video, and two tastings. It's also the most crowded, often giving times for you to return or sending you to their sister manufacturers. It's exciting to think that the entire Portuguese production of Sandeman Port ages right in this building (€6 for basic visit, €16 for 1-hour tour with 5 tastes, daily March-Oct 10:00-12:30 & 14:00-18:00, Nov-Feb 9:30-12:30 & 14:00-17:30, last tour 15 minutes before closing, faces its own little square along the riverfront at Largo Miguel Bombarda 3, tel. 223-740-533, www.sandeman.com).

**Cálem,** the first place you see after crossing the bridge, offers a fine tour wandering among its huge oak casks (€6 includes

# Vila Nova de Gaia

RIBEIRA DISTRICT

To Porto Center

100 Meters
100 Yards

PONTE LUÍS I

UPPER LEVEL

LOWER LEVEL

SERRA DO PILAR MONASTERY

Douro River

Largo Miguel Bombarda

BOAT TRIPS

Cable Car

Largo Cruz

AVENIDA RAMOS PINTO
RUA 7 PASS.

R. FERN.

R. COSTA SANTOS

R. DO CHOUPELO

R. BARÃO

R. SERRA PINTO

R. AZENHAS

R. RAMADA ALTA

RUA DE A GRANJO

R. LEO. DE FREITAS

AV. D. LEITE

RUA PILAR

RUA GENERAL TORRES

R. CÂNDIDO DOS REIS

AVENIDA DA REPÚBLICA

RUA LUÍS I

RUA JAU

CAMÕES

Jardim do Morro

Jardim do Morro

General Torres

1. Sandeman
2. Cálem
3. Taylor & Restaurante Barão Fladgate
4. Croft
5. Ferreira
6. Kopke Wine Shop
7. Adega E Presuntaria Transmontana Restaurante
8. Ar de Rio Restaurante
9. Porto Cruz Rooftop Bar

PORTO

2 samples, 25-minute tours depart 4/hour, May-Oct daily 10:00-19:00, off-season fewer tours and closes at 18:00, tel. 223-746-672, www.calem.pt). They also offer 45-minute fado shows that include a port tasting (€17.50, Tue-Sun at 18:30, none on Mon)—a handy and entertaining alternative if you show up just after most of the lodges have closed.

**Taylor**—near the top of the hill—is a good choice for more discriminating tastes. It's classy and more time-consuming than the options down on the riverbank, and comes with stunning views back on Porto. You'll follow a one-hour audioguide through the sprawling complex, including modern museum exhibits, and end with two tastings—which you can enjoy with grand views (€12, daily 10:00-19:30, last entry at 18:00, high up but worth the hike at Rua do Choupelo 250, tel. 223-772-956, www.taylor.pt). Taylor also owns Croft (described next). Their splurge restaurant, **$$$$ Barão Fladgate,** offers stunning lunchtime views along with an opportunity to recharge for more tastings. Many consider it among the best dining spots in Porto (daily 12:30-15:00 & 19:30-22:00, tel. 223-772-951).

## Port Wine Crash Course

Port is a medium-sweet wine (around 20 percent alcohol), usually taken as a *digestif* after dinner. The wine is fortified at a ratio of about 4:1 with *aguardente,* a grappa-like brandy distilled from the same grapes. The brandy is introduced before fermentation is complete—and kills the remaining yeast—which leaves more sugar in the port (standard wines ferment for 10-12 days; port for only 2-3 days). After the brandy is added, the wine ages for at least two years.

For most people, "port" means a tawny port aged 10-20 years—the most common type. But there's a whole spectrum of port, using more than 40 varieties of grapes. The two broad categories are wood ports (aged in wooden barrels or vats) and vintage ports (aged in bottles). Here's a rundown:

**Tawny,** the wood port with a leathery color, is the most typical version. It's older, lighter, mellower, and more complex than L.B.V. (described later). It's aged in smaller barrels, maximizing exposure to wood and giving it a nuttier flavor. Tawny port stays in the wood for 10, 20, 30, or 40 years. But to enhance the complexity of the flavor, any tawny is actually a blend of several vintages (for example, a "30-year-old tawny" is predominantly 30 years old, but also has components that are 10 or 20 years old). Once blended, the various ports "marry" in the bottle for about eight months.

Inexpensive **ruby port** ages in oak vats for only three years, and then it's bottled. It's deep red, fruity, and has a strong, fiery taste of grape and pepper.

**Croft,** uphill from Sandeman (and less scenic than the others), feels cozy and old-fashioned. Their traditional tour includes a look at vintage port being aged in bottles, as well as a fun "library" of dusty old ports—including one from 1834. They're proud of having invented the first rosé port in 2008 (€10 includes 3 tastings, daily 10:00-18:00, last tour at 17:00, Rua Barão de Forrester 412, tel. 223-756-433, www.croftport.com).

**Ferreira's** lodge comes with classical music "to help age the wine." It's an interesting tour and shows off some fine museum artifacts (€6 includes 2 tastings, daily 10:00-12:30 & 14:00-18:00, look for big sign at the end of the riverfront promenade at Avenida Ramos Pinto 70, tel. 223-746-107).

**Vintage port**—the most expensive—is a ruby that comes from a single harvest. Only wine from the very best vintages is selected (typically two or three per decade; 2011 was a great year, and 2000 was one of the best ever). After two years of aging in wooden casks, potential vintage port must be tested by the authorities. If they reject it, the wine stays in the casks longer to become L.B.V. (see next). If they give it the go-ahead, it's bottled and aged another 10-30 years (or more). Sediment is common, so bottles must be decanted. And if a bottle is really old, the cork may deteriorate—so the top of the bottle is heated up with a pair of red-hot tongs, then cold water is poured over it to break it off cleanly.

**Late Bottle Vintage (L.B.V.)** was invented after World War II, when British wine lovers couldn't afford true vintage port. L.B.V. is a blend of wines from a single year, which age together in huge wooden vats for four to six years. The size of the vats means less exposure to wood, which makes it age more quickly, but without losing its fruitiness and color. It's bottled after five years (later than a vintage port, which ages for only two years—hence the name). This more-affordable alternative saved the port wine industry.

You'll also see **white** ports, which are young and robust. Most are dry (similar to Spain's *fino* sherries); for a sweet version, look for *lágrima* on the label. More recently, some vintners have experimented with **rosé** ports. And **Douro table wines** are becoming a popular and respected secondary business for many producers.

Port's stodgy image makes it unpopular among young Portuguese. Lodges have not escaped the multinational conglomerate game, but new owners often retain the brand name to keep loyal customers even as they market aggressively to attract new ones. For some, port is an acquired taste—but it's one worth cultivating. As I always say, "Any port in a storm…"

**Wine Shop: Kopke** is recognized as one of the best in the business because they were the first. Unfortunately, their lodge doesn't receive visitors, but their shop along the waterfront allows people to experience—one delightful sip at a time—what they've been doing well since 1638. The staff offers concise explanations and some fine ports by the glass in an elegant, upstairs tasting room far from the crowds outside (€2-5/glass, daily May-Oct 10:00-19:00, Nov-April 10:00-18:00, next to Cálem at Avenida Diogo Leite 312, mobile 915-848-484).

## SIGHTS AWAY FROM THE CENTER
### Tramway Museum (Museu do Carro Eléctrico)

This clever museum-in-a-warehouse displays beautifully restored examples of trolleys from different eras, including 1950s buses and a brand-new hydrogen-powered city bus. You can climb aboard many for a fun, Rice-A-Roni-style experience...just ding the bell.

**Cost and Hours:** €8, Mon 14:00-18:00, Tue-Sun 10:00-18:00, Alameda Basílio Teles 51, tel. 226-158-185, www.museudocarroelectrico.pt.

**Getting There:** The most atmospheric way to arrive at the museum is via trolley #1 or #18. Sit on restored wicker seats and see a little of workaday Porto, plus some river views from up above.

### Foz

Foz do Douro (or simply "Foz") is one of Porto's trendiest, greenest, wealthiest, and most relaxing quarters, situated where the river meets the Atlantic. There's no real destination in Foz; simply wander through the park (Jardim do Passeio Alegre, with miniature golf, a fancy old WC pavilion, and a nondescript café), hike up to the lighthouse, ponder the sea, watch fishermen mending their nets, and smell the seaweed. If you have the time and good weather, take a boardwalk stroll to the beach, Praia dos Ingleses. It's a relaxing break from the busy downtown area.

**Getting There:** An antique trolley car (line #1) scenically rattles its way from the Ribeira district, along the Douro River, to the Jardim do Passeio Alegre, a 10-minute walk to the center of the Foz district. From the trolley stop, you can walk or catch bus #500 for an Atlantic coast ride. Or bypass the trolley by taking bus #500 from the Ribeira all the way to Foz (catch trolley or bus in front of São Francisco Church, departures roughly every 20 minutes, fewer after 19:00, 20-minute trip).

**Nearby:** You can combine a trip to Foz with a visit to the Serralves Museum. From Foz, either catch bus #203—it runs near the beach on Rua de Dui—or take a taxi or Uber.

### ▲Serralves Foundation Contemporary Art Museum and Park (Fundação de Serralves)

Porto's contemporary art museum, surrounding park, and unique Art Deco mansion are an enjoyable half-day excursion for art lovers—and worthwhile for anyone looking to relax in a lush green space.

**Cost and Hours:** €5 for park and villa, €10 to add the museum; April-Sept Tue-Fri 10:00-19:00, Sat-Sun until 20:00, closed Mon (except park is open July-Sept Mon 10:00-19:00); Oct-March Tue-Fri 10:00-18:00, Sat-Sun until 19:00, closed Mon; tel. 226-156-500, www.serralves.pt.

**Eating:** The museum's **$$** restaurant serves a lunch buffet from 12:00-15:00; coffee and snacks are available until park closing time.

**Getting There:** The complex is about 1.5 miles west of the city center in a wealthy residential neighborhood at Rua Dom João de Castro 210, just south of the busy Avenida da Boavista. From the center, you can reach it most easily via taxi, Uber, or on a hop-on, hop-off bus tour. Public bus service isn't great, but you can take bus #203 to the Serralves stop (less convenient from downtown—the most central place to catch it is at the big Boavista Rotunda near Casa da Música).

**Background:** The Serralves Foundation was formed in 1989 with two goals: the advancement of contemporary art and the appreciation of landscape and environment as an artistic concept. These goals, symbolized by the giant, red, hand shovel near the front gate, drive the layout of the complex: a gigantic contemporary art facility on the edge of a carefully planned park. The whole thing is based around the Art Deco villa of a count who lived here in the 1930s.

**Visiting the Museum and Park:** The **museum** presents temporary exhibits by Portuguese and global artists. The enormous, blocky U-shaped building was designed by prominent Portuguese architect Álvaro Siza, who was greatly inspired by the existing mansion.

The **park** around the museum has been designed very carefully to compartmentalize each section; when you're in one part of the grounds, you can't see the rest. This is a very peaceful, romantic place to wander. Hiding in here somewhere are a pleasant rose garden, a tea house overlooking a former tennis court, a lake, a small farm with animals, a gardening school, and Casa de Serralves itself.

The **villa** (Casa de Serralves) is, for many, the most interesting part of the whole experience: a huge pink Art Deco mansion that looks like the home of an Old Hollywood star. On two sides, long manicured hedges and fountains stretch to the horizon. Look for the private chapel in back—also pink Art Deco. You can usually go inside the villa to check out the cavernous interior. Ponder how the design of this place is reflected in the museum. The best part is upstairs: the mirrored, pink-marbled bathroom, dramatically overlooking the grounds.

**House of Music (Casa da Música)**

This landmark 1,200-seat concert hall opened in 2005. The angular, white concrete building with rippling glass windows was designed by the firm of Dutch architect Rem Koolhaas (OMA), which also built Seattle's Central Library. Contemporary-architecture fans will find it at the big Boavista Rotunda northwest of the city center (Metro: Casa da Música). Guided tours take you through the interior, or you can attend an affordable concert of anything from world music to classical to jazz to fado.

**Cost and Hours:** €7.50 tours, daily in English at 11:00 and 16:00, 1 hour, focus is on concert hall's unique architecture; info/reservation tel. 220-120-220, www.casadamusica.com.

# Nightlife in Porto

While fado is not a big deal in Porto, you can enjoy a live performance of this blues-like Portuguese music with dinner or a drink two blocks off the riverfront at **Restaurante Mal Cozinhado** (figure €35 per person for touristy dinner and show). Or drop by later to enjoy the music over just a drink (€10 cover). Music starts nightly except Sunday at 21:00 (Rua do Outeirinho 11, tel. 222-081-319, www.malcozinhado.pt).

Other music venues include **Restaurante Guarany,** which has fado on Thursdays and Saturdays and piano on other nights, starting at 21:30 (Avenida dos Aliados 85, tel. 223-321-272; see page 361). The **House of Music (Casa da Música)** offers classical, jazz, fado, and more (described above).

# Sleeping in Porto

You'll pay more to be in the scenic, atmospheric, and very touristy Ribeira district; or you can save a bit (and be closer to more interesting restaurants and local life) by sleeping higher on the hill, in the city center. The Stock Exchange Palace area offers a nice mix. You'll almost always have to climb a few stairs to get to the elevator, if they have one.

In addition to my recommendations (which are well-established), consider searching online for new boutique hotels, which are popping up all over Porto.

## SPLURGES IN THE RIBEIRA

**$$$$ Guest House Douro** is nestled right in the heart of the Ribeira bustle, overseen by charming owners Carmen and João, who are generous with local advice. It has eight small but cozy and tastefully decorated rooms with all the modern comforts (including much-needed soundproofing), and the generous breakfast is a great

# Sleep Code

Hotels are classified based on the average price of a standard double room with breakfast in high season.

| | |
|---|---|
| **$$$$** | **Splurge:** Most rooms over €150 |
| **$$$** | **Pricier:** €100-150 |
| **$$** | **Moderate:** €70-100 |
| **$** | **Budget:** €40-70 |
| **¢** | **Backpacker:** Under €40 |
| **RS%** | **Rick Steves discount** |

Unless otherwise noted, credit cards are accepted, hotel staff speak basic English, and free Wi-Fi is available. Comparison-shop by checking prices at several hotels (on each hotel's own website, on a booking site, or by email). For the best deal, *book directly with the hotel*. Ask for a discount if paying in cash; if the listing includes **RS%,** request a Rick Steves discount.

way to start your day (air-con, elevator, curfew-1:00 in the morning, closed Jan-Feb, near House of Henry the Navigator at Rua Fonte Taurina 99, tel. 222-015-135, www.guesthousedouro.com, guesthousedouro@sapo.pt).

**$$$$ 1872 River House** is a classy B&B at the far end of the Ribeira embankment. It fills old river houses with industrial-mod finishes, eight compact, stone-walled rooms (half facing the river), and gorgeous shared public spaces, including a cozy river-view lounge (Rua do Infante Dom Henrique 133, tel. 222-039-033, www.1872riverhouse.com).

**$$$$ Pestana Porto Hotel** is a stylish, overpriced, and slightly snobby top-end place, filling several colorful old townhouse buildings right along the embankment and main square with 109 plush rooms (air-con, elevator, Praça de Ribeira 1, tel. 223-402-300, www.pestana.com, pestana.porto@pestana.com).

## NEAR THE STOCK EXCHANGE PALACE

**$$$$ A.S. 1829 Hotel** is a splurge that owns a wonderfully central location, overlooking the base of thriving Rua das Flores, a long and steep block above the Stock Exchange Palace. The public spaces and 41 rooms are decorated with both a sense of style and respect for tradition—such as the vintage stationery store at the reception (air-con, Largo de São Domingos 45, tel. 223-402-740, www.as1829hotel.pt).

**$$$ InPátio Guest House,** tucked down a tiny alley just above the Ribeira scene, provides a quiet, secluded oasis of comfort away from the crowds. Five beautiful, sleek, well-priced rooms with modern interiors and unique bathrooms hide inside a renovated 19th-century building. Fernando and Olga make you feel

PORTO

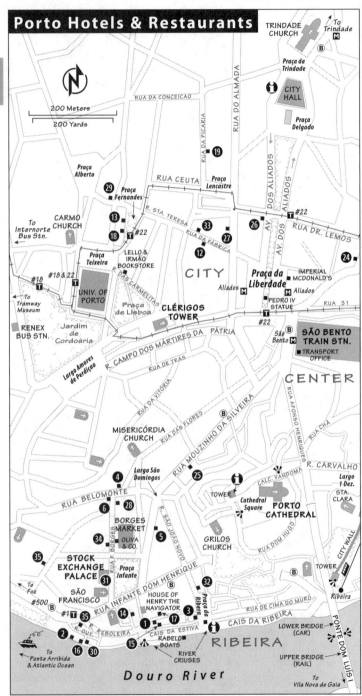

# Porto Hotels & Restaurants

PORTO

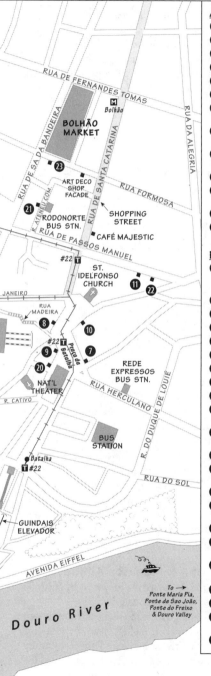

### Accommodations

1. Guest House Douro
2. 1872 River House
3. Pestana Porto Hotel
4. A.S. 1829 Hotel
5. InPátio Guest House
6. Hotel da Bolsa
7. NH Collection Porto Batalha
8. Quality Inn Praça da Batalha
9. Mercure Porto Centro Hotel
10. Moov Hotel Porto Centro
11. Pensão Residencial Belo Sonho
12. Pensão Grande Oceano
13. Duas Nações Guest House

### Eateries & Other

14. Restaurante A Grade & Restaurante Adega São Nicolau
15. Wine Quay Bar
16. Bacalhau Bar
17. Taberna Está-se Bem
18. Padaria Ribeiro
19. Taberna Taxca
20. Cervejaria Gazela
21. Restaurante Abadia
22. Café Santiago F
23. Confeitaria-Restaurante do Bolhão
24. Central Conserveira da Invicta
25. Cantinho do Avillez
26. Restaurante Guarany (Fado)
27. Ö Tascö
28. Prova Wine Food & Pleasure
29. Solar Moinho de Vento
30. Restaurante Mal Cozinhado (Fado)
31. Wines of Portugal Tasting Room
32. Portologia
33. Touriga Wine Shop
34. Port and Douro Wines Institute
35. Laundries (2)

PORTO

very welcome (air-con, luggage elevator, Pátio de São Salvador 22, mobile 934-323-448, www.inpatio.pt, info@inpatio.pt).

**$$ Hotel da Bolsa,** a few blocks above the Ribeira scene, is a straightforward business hotel, with a great location and 36 fine but aging rooms—some with views (air-con, elevator, Rua Ferreira Borges 101, tel. 222-026-768, www.hoteldabolsa.com, reservas@ hoteldabolsa.com).

## IN THE CITY CENTER
### On and near Praça da Batalha

This appealing location—on a borderline-seedy square capped by the beautiful *azulejo*-covered Santo Ildefonso Church—is close to Porto's market and shopping zone, and just uphill from São Bento station, the cathedral, the bridge to Villa Nova de Gaia, and the funicular down to the Ribeira.

**$$$$ NH Collection Porto Batalha** has converted an elegant old post office into a sleek and inviting top-end hotel. It has an open-concept lobby, 107 well-equipped rooms, and a subtle but clever postal theme (air-con, elevator, Praça da Batalha 62, tel. 227-660-600, www.nh-hotels.com, nhcollectionportobatalha@nh-hotels.com). Two other (less elegant) business-class hotels share the same square, and are worth considering if you can score a deal: **$$ Quality Inn Praça da Batalha** (at #127, tel. 223-392-300, www. choicehotelseurope.com) and **$$$ Mercure Porto Centro Hotel** (at #116, tel. 222-043-300, www.mercure.com).

**$ Moov Hotel Porto Centro** has 125 sleek, modern rooms occupying a remodeled movie theater. Black-and-white photos of movie stars decorate the walls in tribute to its former life. It's temptingly affordable and quite nice for the price, with no frills and a handy location (family rooms, breakfast extra, air-con, elevator, parking, quiet back patio, Praça da Batalha 32, tel. 220-407-000, www.hotelmoov.com, porto@hotelmoov.com).

**¢ Pensão Residencial Belo Sonho** is a well-maintained, family-run (no English spoken) budget throwback, just around the corner from Praça da Batalha. Its 15 rooms are an excellent value if you don't mind the language barrier (noisy on Fri and Sat nights, no breakfast, Rua Passos Manuel 186, tel. 222-003-389).

### Budget Options West of Avenida dos Aliados

These budget choices are on the steep streets just west of Avenida dos Aliados, mixed among some tempting eateries.

**$ Pensão Grande Oceano,** a good value in a central location, is a steep walk-up with shiplap floors. It has 15 clean, basic rooms on four floors—all but two have private baths and air-con (family rooms, no breakfast, no elevator, Rua da Fábrica 45, tel. 222-038-

770, www.pensaograndeoceano.com, geral@pensaograndeoceano.
com).

¢ **Duas Nações Guest House** is a well-run backpacker place
with 16 simple but colorful rooms—as comfy as such a cheap place
can be. It overlooks a square straight up Rua da Fábrica, a few
blocks from Avenida dos Aliados. The "two nations" are Portugal
and Brazil, still friends after all these years (private rooms available,
cash only—or prepay on Booking.com, breakfast extra—or just eat
in one of the adjacent cafés, Praça Guilherme Gomes Fernandes
59, tel. 222-081-616, www.duasnacoes.com.pt, duasnacoes@sapo.
pt). They also rent several apartments—all recently remodeled with
small kitchens, washing machines, air-con, and double-paned windows (2-person studio and apartment for up to 8).

## Eating in Porto

Porto is famous for its tripe. Legend has it that when Porto's favorite
son, Prince Henry the Navigator, set out for his explorations, the
city slaughtered all of its
mature livestock to send
along with his crew—
keeping only the guts for
themselves. Porto's cooks
then devised many inge-
nious ways of preparing in-
nards. The tradition stuck,
and to this day, people
from Porto are known as
*tripeiros*. These days, tripe

plays a subtler role. You'll most typically see it prepared "Porto-
style" *(tripas a moda do Porto):* barely present in a thick stew, with
beans, sausage, chicken, and scant vegetables. The tripe itself doesn't
have much taste—though I couldn't stop thinking about digestive
processes while I chewed.

For something easier to stomach, try *caldo verde*—a tasty soup
made with potatoes and thinly chopped cabbage.

For a quick meal, locals like the towering heart-attack sandwich called a *francesinha* ("little French girl"). While there are
many variations, a standard *francesinha* wedges pork cutlets, sliced
sausages, and gooey Swiss cheese between two thick slices of dense
bread. The whole thing is grilled and topped with melted cheese
and (often) a fried egg, and finally drenched with a spicy tomato- or
seafood-based sauce.

**Food Tours:** To maximize your eating experience, consider
**Taste Porto Food and Wine Tours** (see page 326).

PORTO

## IN THE RIBEIRA

There's a wide range of dining options in the Ribeira—and they're all touristy, with predictable tourist-trap quality and prices accompanying the fine views and fun scene. Strolling along the waterfront and following your nose is a good option. You can also try wandering the back lanes to find a spot that feels right—you'll be trading river views for lower prices and local color. The seafood's fresh, except on Mondays (since fishermen don't go out on Sundays).

**$$ Restaurante A Grade** is a small mom-and-pop restaurant on a delightful alley just off the Ribeira. Ferreria serves while wife Elena cooks good, home-style Portuguese food. The baked octopus is a favorite among regulars (big, splittable portions of seafood and meat dishes; Mon-Sat 12:00-16:00 & 18:30-22:30, closed Sun, Rua de São Nicolau 9, tel. 223-321-130, reservations smart for dinner).

**$$ Restaurante Adega São Nicolau,** next to Restaurante A Grade, is homey, small, and sparkling, with a few outside tables and a tight interior under a shiplap vault. They serve traditional cuisine with lots of fish (Mon-Sat 12:00-23:00, closed Sun, Rua São Nicolau 1, tel. 222-008-232).

**$$$ Wine Quay Bar** is a small, low-key eatery tucked into a hole-in-the-wall facing the Ribeira embankment. Their focus is wine, paired with high-quality *petiscos* (plates of Portuguese cured meats, cheeses, olives, and other munchies). Compared with some of the bombastic and touristy alternatives nearby, this is a pleasantly mellow spot to let your pulse rate slow, and focus on the wine and the company. It has a tight interior or—better—a few outdoor tables along the seawall, but they don't take reservations (Mon-Sat 16:00-23:00, closed Sun, Muro dos Bacalhoeiros 111, tel. 222-080-119).

**$$$ Bacalhau Bar** is a trendy little hole-in-the-wall at the quieter western end of the riverside rampart. A handful of tiny (unreservable) tables outside overlook the river, with more tables tucked in the mod interior (daily 11:00-23:00, Muro dos Bacalhoeiros 153, tel. 222-010-521).

**$$$ Taberna Está-se Bem** ("It's All Good") is a popular and trendy little cellar restaurant burrowed off the main inland drag, just above the Ribeira waterfront. Sit inside, or out on the characteristic alley, and enjoy good wines and a nice variety of *petiscos*—Portuguese tapas (Tue-Sun 12:00-23:00, closed Mon, Rua Fonte Taurina 70, tel. 220-900-900).

## IN THE CITY CENTER
### Basic Eateries

Good, cheap restaurants are scattered all around the city center. Menus are often handwritten (posted on paper tablecloths outside)

## Restaurant Price Code

I've assigned each eatery a price category, based on the average cost of a typical main course. Drinks, desserts, and splurge items (steak and seafood) can raise the price considerably.

**$$$$** **Splurge:** Most main courses over €17
**$$$** **Pricier:** €12-17
**$$** **Moderate:** €7-12
**$** **Budget:** Under €7

In Portugal, takeout food is **$**; a basic sit-down eatery is **$$**; a casual but more upscale restaurant is **$$$**; and a swanky splurge is **$$$$**.

with €1 soups and €5 plates. Remember that most coffee and pastry shops do double duty as lunch spots, so wander around and see what people are having. Good locations abound on the pedestrian Rua do Sampaio Bruno and on the side streets of Rua do Almada (one block west of Avenida dos Aliados). The dining's more atmospheric in the Ribeira, but these are convenient if you're staying in the center.

The charming little square called Praça Guilherme Gomes Fernandes has several cheap-and-cheery, no-pretense eateries with pleasant outside seating. **$ Padaria Ribeiro**—a bright, happy bakery handy for a breakfast, light lunch, or snack—serves savory and sweet pastries, sandwiches, and popular cookies. You can get it to go, or order inside and have them bring it to you at a table on the square (at #21, Mon-Sat 7:00-20:00, closed Sun, ample tables on square and a small indoor seating area next door, tel. 222-005-067).

**$ Taberna Taxca** is like a concrete man cave offering up beer, soup, and sandwiches. The menu is cheap and extremely basic: two soups (great *caldo verde* or the much heavier *papas*—made with shredded pork, gravy, and cumin) and sandwiches that celebrate simplicity: smoked ham with fried egg, meat from black crockpots of cooked pork *(rojão)*, or typical-for-Porto spicy shredded pork *(bifana)*. Order water and they'll hit the cowbell of shame. Hams hang with the TV from the ceiling. I like to sit at the bar to enjoy the scene (Mon-Sat 12:00-24:00, closed Sun, Rua da Picaria 26, tel. 222-011-807).

**$ Cervejaria Gazela,** a dark little hole-in-the-wall in the shopping district just off Praça da Batalha, is beloved among locals for its "little hot dogs" or *Cachorro Especial*. Sit down at the bar, order one and a beer (the Super Bock is the local favorite on tap), and watch the staff lovingly lay the sausage and cheese on the fresh buns and then grill these little snacks just right (Mon-Fri 12:00-

# Wine Tastings in Porto

In addition to the port wine lodges across the river in Vila Nova de Gaia, various wine bars and shops in Porto specialize in introducing you to port and other Portuguese wines (for locations, see the map on page 354).

The **Wines of Portugal Tasting Room**—a sister organization of the tasting venue in Lisbon's Praça do Comércio (see page 51)—offers unique wines difficult to find in other locations. Buy a rechargeable chip card and help yourself to as many wines as you like (€3 minimum, pours start at €0.50, Mon-Sat 11:00-19:00, closed Sun, inside Stock Exchange Palace, tel. 223-323-072, www.winesofportugal.com).

**Portologia,** a few steps uphill from Praça da Ribeira, is a wine bar serving flights of port wines from more than 200 open bottles, highlighting smaller producers (rather than the big, corporate outfits across the river). The menu explains how tastings can be either "horizontal," showcasing different types of port wines or producers (see page 348), or "vertical," sampling different ages of wines by the same producer (€10-17/3 wines, €25-30/6 wines, €35/8 wines—price depends on quality, daily 11:00-24:00, Rua de São João 28, tel. 222-011-050, www.portologia.pt).

**Touriga Wine Shop,** in the city center and less touristy, is well-stocked with bottles of local wines, and offers tastings. They usually have a few bottles open (affordably priced per taste), or you can do a guided 20- to 30-minute tasting of three wines for just €2 per person (available most days at 11:00 and 15:00, better to call ahead and confirm/reserve; shop open Mon-Sat 10:00-13:00 & 14:30-20:00, closed Sun, Rua da Fábrica 32, tel. 225-108-435).

**The Port and Douro Wines Institute** is a good spot for sampling an array of ports. The price per taste starts at €1 a glass (or 4 glasses for €6). If they call it "port," you'll find it here. While it's more fun to tour the cellars across the river, this is a handy one-stop opportunity to try several ports. They also give short tours for €5 that finish with a tasting (Mon-Fri 10:00-19:00, closed Sat-Sun, Rua Ferreira Borges 27, just uphill from Stock Exchange Palace, tel. 222-071-600, www.ivdp.pt).

22:30, closed Sat-Sun, facing National Theater just to the right at #3, tel. 222-054-869).

**$$ Restaurante Abadia** is a big, bright, friendly, old-school family diner, with two floors of happy customers dining on large portions of straightforward Portuguese cuisine. Split a huge half-portion of their Porto-style tripe with your travel partner, balanced with something a little more predictable, such as a sizzling hibachi of roasted chicken and potatoes (splittable *doses*, specialty is grilled cod, Mon 18:30-23:00, Tue-Sat 12:00-15:00 & 18:30-23:00, closed

Sun, head one block east of Sá da Badeira near Bolhão market to side street Rua do Ateneu Comercial do Porto 22, tel. 222-008-757, www.abadiadoporto.com).

**$ Café Santiago F** is just a basic diner, but often wins awards in the very serious competition for Porto's best signature sandwich, the hearty *francesinha* beloved by carnivores. You won't walk away hungry (sandwiches for under €10, Mon-Sat 12:00-23:00, busiest on Sat when lines can form, closed Sun, Rua Passos Manuel 226, tel. 222-055-797).

**$ Confeitaria-Restaurante do Bolhão,** which faces the market-hall entrance, has been pleasing local shoppers since 1896. This bustling bakery/brasserie offers enticing takeout items in front and an inviting old-time dining hall in the rear (the more elegant basement is less lively and soulful). You'll find fresh-baked goods, omelets, and fish, along with cheap daily specials (Mon-Sat 7:00-20:00, closed Sun, Rua Formosa 339, tel. 223-395-220).

**Canned Fish: $ Central Conserveira da Invicta** is the place to go if you're into Portuguese canned fish *(conservas)*. This pleasant hole-in-the-wall—hiding on the steep street between São Bento station and the market, facing a faded Art Deco theater facade—has shelves of colorfully packaged sardines, mackerel, tuna, and other fish, preserved in olive oil and spices. With a large and well-curated selection and helpful service, this is a good place to shop for sardine souvenirs for the folks back home—or, for a light meal, you can buy a can to enjoy at their café tables, or to take away for a picnic (Mon-Thu 10:00-20:00, Fri-Sat 10:00-22:00, Sun 12:00-20:00, Rua de Sá da Bandeira 115, mobile 912-735-241).

## Fancier Dining

**$$$ Cantinho do Avillez,** filling a colorful, upscale-casual space, is the Porto outpost of Lisbon-based celebrity chef José Avillez (see page 133). The enticing menu focuses on modern Portuguese cooking: traditional dishes, presented with contemporary flair and upmarket ingredients (weekday lunch specials, daily 12:00-15:00 & 19:00-24:00, Rua de Mouzinho da Silveira 166, tel. 223-227-879, www.cantinhodoavillez.pt).

**$$$ Restaurante Guarany,** established in 1933, has been the musicians' coffee shop for generations and is popular with tourists today. You'll enjoy Art Deco elegance with a Brazilian flair (read the brochure for the charming story of the murals) and crisp yet friendly service. They also have seating out on Avenida dos Aliados (good meat and fish plates, daily specials, daily 9:00-24:00, Avenida dos Aliados 85, tel. 223-321-272, www.cafeguarany.com). There's no extra charge for the live music starting at 21:30 (see "Nightlife in Porto," earlier).

**$$ Ö Tascö** serves affordable, traditional Portuguese food with a youthful spirit, in a trendy but accessible space—with firewood stacked in the arches—tucked on a back street in the city center. As this place has quickly acquired a following among budget-minded foodies, book ahead (daily 12:00-23:00, Rua do Almada 151, tel. 222-010-763).

**$$$ Prova Wine Food & Pleasure** is a great little wine bar. It's the passion of sommelier Diogo who speaks English and enjoys coaching visitors through his list of Portuguese wines (including ports) and then matching it with his selection of fine meats and cheeses. Dining and drinking here, you'll enjoy a jazzy interior where quality and relaxation go hand to mouth (Wed-Mon 16:00-24:00, closed Tue, across and uphill from the Stock Exchange Palace on Rua Ferreira Borges 86, mobile 916-499-121, www.prova.com.pt).

**$$$ Solar Moinho de Vento,** on a small plaza just above Praça Guilherme Gomes Fernandes, offers proper-but-friendly service and Portuguese cuisine in a tile-covered, white-tablecloth dining room upstairs (Mon-Sat 12:00-15:30 & 19:00-22:00, Sun 12:00-15:30, Rua de Sá Noronha 81, tel. 222-051-158, www.solarmoinhodevento.com).

## IN VILA NOVA DE GAIA

Eating across the river in Vila Nova de Gaia, just a 10-minute scenic stroll over the bridge from the Ribeira, is a fine option. It's basically as touristy as the Ribeira, so don't expect quality or good value—but the views over to Porto are marvelous. The last port lodges finish their tasting tours at 19:00, so working a dinner here into your sightseeing schedule is easy.

**$$$ Adega E Presuntaria Transmontana** serves up quality Portuguese fish and meat plates as well as *petiscos*—Portuguese tapas. Their tapa sampler (listed on the menu as "Mixed of Titbits") stuffs two to four people for €34. And for an education in the sweet treats of Portugal, enjoy their all-you-can-eat dessert buffet for just €7 (daily 12:00-24:00, Avenida Diogo Leite 80, tel. 223-758-380).

**$$$ Ar de Rio Restaurante,** where modern design meets traditional Portuguese cuisine, is located in a park right on the river. Their €10 *francesinha* (a local super-grilled meaty sandwich that makes a triple cheeseburger seem like health food) is considered one of the best in town. You can eat inside or out on the deck (daily 12:00-24:00, modern steel-and-glass "box" along the embankment at Avenida Diogo Leite 5, tel. 223-701-797, www.arderio.pt). Consider a drink from their bar while enjoying a lounge chair on the riverbank here.

**Scenic Drinks: Porto Cruz** has a delightful rooftop bar with a great view over both the bustle of the Gaia embankment and Porto across the river. Order a drink, find a scenic table, and watch the cable cars float overhead (lunches and light snacks, Tue-Sat 10:00-23:30, Sun 10:00-19:00, closed Mon and in bad weather, just past Sandeman at Largo Miguel Bombarda 23).

**Picnic on the Riverfront:** The Vila Nova de Gaia mayor is determined to make his city (which is actually bigger than Porto) visitor-friendly. A sign of that is the inviting waterfront, welcoming picnickers with picnic tables, grass, rockery, piers, and the best views in town.

# Porto Connections

## BY TRAIN

Regional trains use the more central São Bento station; long-distance trains use Campanhã station on the east edge of town. The two stations are connected by frequent trains (see "Arrival in Porto," page 318). All trains leaving São Bento also stop at Campanhã (the next station). Some trains only depart from Campanhã station, so check the schedule carefully.

**From Porto's São Bento Train Station to: Peso da Régua** (3/day direct, 2 hours; many more with change in Caide, 2-2.5 hours), **Pinhão** (5/day, 2.5-3 hours, transfer in Peso da Régua).

**From Campanhã Train Station:** Fast Alfa Pendular and Intercidades trains (both require reservation, buy at station) go to **Coimbra** (almost hourly, 1 hour on Alfa Pendular line or Intercidades service but 2 hours on slower regional line—confirm before buying) and **Lisbon** (almost hourly, 3 hours). Note that Alfa Pendular and Intercidades trains are similarly speedy, but Alfa trains cost more.

To reach **Santiago de Compostela, Spain,** it's faster to go by bus (see below), but you can also take a train (2/day, 5 hours, change in Vigo).

## BY BUS

Remember, each bus company has its own station; there's no central bus terminus (for addresses and telephone numbers, see "Arrival in Porto," page 318). Various companies compete on the same route (for example, four companies go to Lisbon). Ask the transport office at the TI about the handiest bus for your itinerary (see "Tourist Information," page 317; toll-free tel. 800-220-905). Don't bother trying to get to the Douro Valley (Peso da Régua or Pinhão) by bus; it takes twice as long as the train.

**From Porto by Bus to: Coimbra** (operated by Rede Expressos, Rodonorte, and others; best is Rede Expressos—almost hourly, 1.5 hours), **Lisbon** (best via RENEX or Rede Expressos, at least hourly, 3 hours), **Santiago de Compostela, Spain** (ALSA buses leave from bus terminal on Rua do Capitão Henrique Galvão near Casa da Música Metro station, daily at 12:45, 4 hours, may be additional runs in summer, Spanish tel. 34-902-422-242, www.alsa.es).

# DOURO VALLEY

*Vale do Douro*

The scenic Douro Valley—the birthplace of port wine—is a vine-draped land of otherworldly, ever-changing terrain sculpted by centuries of hardy farmers. The Douro River's steep, craggy, twisting canyons have been laboriously terraced to make a horizontal home for grape vines and olive and almond trees. Unlike the Rhine, the Loire, and other great European rivers, the Douro (DOH-roo) was never a strategic military location. So, rather than fortresses and palaces, you'll see farms, villages...and endless tidy rows of rock terraces, which took no less work—and are no less impressive—than those castles and châteaux. Locals brag, "God made the earth, but people made the Douro."

The Douro River begins as a trickle in Spain (where it's called the Duero), runs west for 550 miles (350 miles of which are in Portugal), and spills into the Atlantic at Porto. The name likely means "river of gold"—perhaps because of the way the sun shines on the water, or the golden-brown silt it carries after a heavy rain.

In the 17th century, British traders developed a taste for the wines from the Douro region. "Op-port-unity" knocked in 1756, when the Marquês de Pombal demarcated the region—establishing it as the only place that port wine could be produced. To this day, port remains the valley's top industry and top tourist draw. The 50-mile stretch on either side of Pinhão is home to some 4,000 vintners and scores of *quintas*—vineyards that produce port (and, increasingly, also table wine and olive oil). While many *quintas* are private, others offer tours and tastings, and some have accommodations as well.

The Douro hillsides change colors throughout the year, from dusty brown in winter, to scrubby green in summer, to glowing gold in fall. The 5,000-foot-high Serra do Marão mountain range guards the region, protecting it from the ocean air and creating a microclimate perfect for growing grapes. The temperature varies from snowy in the winter to arid and 100°F in the summer. Much of the Douro's dramatic ambience changed in the 1970s, when a series of dams were built

for hydroelectric power, taming the formerly raging river into the gentle giant seen today.

Although the scenery and the wines are sublime, the towns along the Douro (Peso da Régua and Pinhão) are fairly dull. If you've got wheels, consider staying at one of the many *quintas* that offer accommodations—ranging from simple rooms on family farms to modern country estates with jaw-dropping views. To many, the Douro Valley may feel low-energy and underwhelming (especially outside of September's harvest time), but some find its unique charm relaxing.

## PLANNING YOUR TIME

This area merits two days (including travel time to and from Porto, with an overnight along the river). Port wine enthusiasts may want more time. If you want only a glimpse, you can see the Douro as a day trip from Porto, either on your own (about 2 hours by car or 2 hours by train each way) or with a package tour (see "Getting Around the Douro Valley," later). While the valley is pretty, Porto is more interesting—and, unless you're a port aficionado, more worth your limited vacation time.

Drivers should make a beeline for the heart of the valley and explore at will. Without a car, you're limited as to where you can stay and which *quintas* you can tour, but you still have enough options to make the trip worthwhile. With a little extra cash for taxis, your choices multiply. With plenty of time and a desire to really slow down, take the meandering boat cruise from Porto to Peso da Régua and tour the museum (no lockers at the train station, but you can leave your bag at the museum desk, a 10-minute walk away—pack light). In the evening, take the train to Pinhão and settle in for the night. In the morning, hike to Quinta de la Rosa for the 11:30 tour and tasting, or take a taxi to wander through the vineyards at Quinta do Panascal. When you've had enough of the wine and rugged scenery, hop the train back to Porto (2.5 hours).

# Orientation to the Douro Valley

The Douro runs for 350 miles through the northern Portuguese heartland. The most interesting and scenic segment—and the heart of the port wine-growing region—is easily the 17-mile stretch between Peso da Régua and Pinhão.

Coming from Porto, the first 55 miles of the Douro are pretty and lush. When you reach the town of **Mesão Frio,** the terrain becomes far more arid and dramatic. The prized, demarcated port wine-growing region of the Douro technically begins here and stretches all the way to the Spanish border.

About seven miles beyond Mesão Frio, **Peso da Régua** (which locals call simply Régua) is the biggest town of the region and a handy home base. Seventeen miles beyond Régua is smaller **Pinhão.** Each town has a big hotel and one or two cheap *residencials,* with *quintas* nearby. Régua has better connections and services, but feels urban and functional; Pinhão enjoys more of a small-town ambience and feels more deeply rooted in Douro culture and scenery.

I've described the most enjoyable and accessible stretch of the Douro, but there's much more—vineyards stretch all the way to Spain. The train goes as far as Pocinho. Just south of Pocinho, Vila Nova de Foz Côa sits between the Douro and a fine archaeological park with cave paintings.

## HELPFUL HINTS

**Exchange Rate:** €1 = about $1.10

**Country Calling Code:** 351 (see page 422 for dialing instructions)

**Festivals:** The valley is packed during the grape harvest, which usually takes place from mid-September through early October.

## GETTING AROUND THE DOURO VALLEY

**By Boat:** Lazy cruise boats float up and down the Douro between Porto, Régua, and Pinhão. (The feisty Douro was tamed in the 1970s by a series of five dams with locks, including the highest one in Europe, the Barragem do Carrapatelo—which inches boats up and down, like a giant elevator, over 140 feet.)

The boat trip takes about seven hours from Porto to the heart of the Douro, and it comes with lunch and passage through two locks (longer trips include a third lock between Régua and Pinhão). If you've

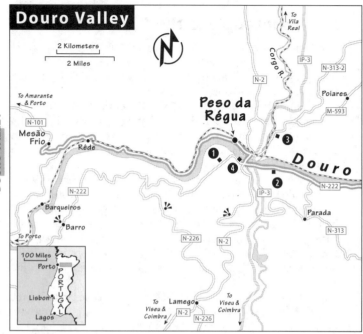

**Douro Valley**

2 Kilometers
2 Miles

To Vila Real

To Amarante & Porto

N-101

Mesão Frio

Rêde

Peso da Régua

Corgo R.

IP-3

N-313-2

N-2

Poiares

M-593

Douro

N-222

N-222

IP-3

Parada

N-313

Barqueiros

Barro

To Porto

N-226

N-2

100 Miles

Porto

PORTUGAL

Lisbon

Lagos

To Viseu & Coimbra

Lamego

N-2

N-226

To Viseu & Coimbra

got the time and don't have a car, this is a slow but scenic way to enjoy the Douro Valley.

Various companies do the trip; generally, boats run daily from March through November (no boats Dec-Feb, seniors should ask about discounts, especially on weekdays). Most travelers take a train or bus back to Porto from Régua on the same day as part of a package deal. But if you want to spend the night on the Douro, it's easy to catch a

train back on your own (or buy a two-day package, which includes lodging).

Several companies based in Porto run cruises up the Douro—from all-day side-trips to multiday cruises—including **Douro Azul** (tel. 223-402-500, www.douroazul.com) and **Rota do Douro** (tel. 223-759-042, www.rotadodouro.pt). A company called **Douro Verde** has shorter, daily cruises departing from Régua (see page 373).

**By Train:** From Porto, regional trains head to **Régua** (3/day from São Bento station, or every 2 hours direct from Campanhã station, 2 hours); all of these trains continue on to **Pinhão** (2.5

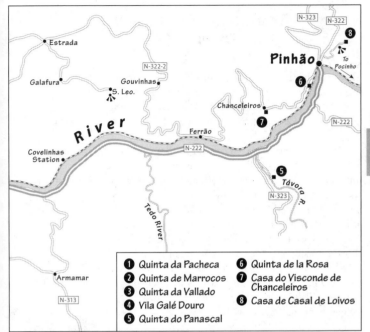

**DOURO VALLEY**

① Quinta da Pacheca
② Quinta de Marrocos
③ Quinta da Vallado
④ Vila Galé Douro
⑤ Quinta do Panascal
⑥ Quinta de la Rosa
⑦ Casa do Visconde de Chanceleiros
⑧ Casa de Casal de Loivos

hours total). On Saturdays, a **historic diesel train** choo-choos visitors between Douro towns—from Régua to Pinhão to Tua, then back again (mid-June-Oct, 3 hours round-trip, €38 round-trip—or €43 in Aug-Sept, tel. 259-338-135, www.cenarios.pt).

**By Car:** The region is easy by car. From Porto, zip on the A-4 expressway to Amarante, then N-101 through the mountains to Mesão Frio (about one hour total). Once in the heart of the Douro, the riverside road follows the north bank from Mesão Frio to Régua in about 30 minutes. From there, you'll cross to the south bank (in the middle of the three bridges) to continue on N-222 into the valley about 30 more minutes to Pinhão (where you'll cross back to reach the town). Everything I've mentioned is no more than about a 10 minute side-trip from the river and the main road. Note that bridges cross the river at Régua, just upstream at Bagaúste, and at Pinhão, but otherwise are scarce.

When passing through Amarante, it's an easy and logical pit stop to detour into the town center to check out the old Roman bridge and impressive church and convent of São Gonçalo.

If you're going between Coimbra and the Douro Valley, you'll save time and mileage by coming directly through the mountains (on the A-24 expressway, via Viseu and Lamego), rather than taking the expressway up the coast to Porto and then over.

# Tours and Tastings in the Douro Valley

## QUINTAS

The main attraction of the Douro Valley is touring the *quintas*, the farms that produce port and table wines. The best *quinta* (KEEN-tah) experiences on this stretch of the Douro are in or near Régua and Pinhão. For both towns, I've noted the best options for non-drivers.

Most *quintas* have an official program: a one-hour tour, followed by a tasting of three or four wines, for about €10. Some have tours at specific times, while others are by prior arrangement only. Ideally, call ahead and ask when you should show up. That said, it's fairly informal and easy for drivers—you could simply pull into any *quinta* listed in this chapter (or any marked *rota do vinho do Porto*) and ask for a taste. If they're not too busy, you can often get a shorter, less formal tour even outside of the official times.

Each *quinta* has its own personality. The tours of big companies' *quintas* are slick, but feel like stripped-down versions of the tours you'll do in the port wine lodges back in Porto (with the happy exception of Quinta do Panascal, where you're set loose in the vineyards). The smaller, independent *quintas* are more intimate, and offer a chance to meet the people who have devoted their lives to making the best wine they can. At *quintas* operated by big companies, it's fine not to buy. But if a family-run place gives you an in-depth tour, it's polite to buy at least a token bottle.

## GROWING—AND STOMPING—GRAPES IN THE DOURO VALLEY

Port wine can technically only be grown in the Douro Valley, which is characterized by microclimates. A few miles can make

a tremendous difference in terms of temperature, precipitation, humidity, and farming conditions. Even within the same vineyard, each parcel of land has its own characteristics. These subtle changes infuse the grapes with completely different aromas and flavors. Over the years, vintners have learned to micromanage their grapes, fine-tuning specific qualities to get the very best port for their conditions.

# Brits on the Douro: The History of Port

Port is actually a British phenomenon. Because Britain isn't suitable for growing grapes, its citizens traditionally imported

wine from France. But during wars with France (17th and 18th centuries), Britain boycotted French wine and looked elsewhere. At that time Portuguese wines often didn't survive the longer sea journey to England.

It's said that the port-making process was invented accidentally by a pair of brothers who forti-fied the wine with grape brandy to maintain its quality during the long trip. The wine picked up the flavor of the oak, which the English grew to appreciate. The British perfected port production in the succeeding centuries; hence many ports carry British-sounding names (Taylor, Croft, Graham).

In 1703, the Methuen Treaty reduced taxation on Portuguese wines, making port even more popular. In 1756, Portugal's Marquês de Pombal demarcated the Douro region—the first such designation in Europe. From that point on, true "port wine" came only from this region, following specific regulations of production, just as "Champagne" technically refers to wines from a specific region of France. Traditionally, farmers and landowners were Portuguese, while the British bought the wine from them, aged it in Porto, and handled the export business. But that arrangement changed in the late 19th century, when an infestation of an American root insect called phylloxera (which smuggled itself to the Old World in the humid climate of speedy steamboats) devastated the Portuguese—and European—wine industry.

In the Douro Valley, you'll see lasting evidence of the phylloxera infestations in the "dead" terraces, overgrown with weeds and a smattering of olive trees. During the infestations, these particular terraces were treated with harsh chemicals that contaminated the soil, rendering it no longer suitable for grapes. Other terraces were left untouched, as Portuguese vintners simply gave up. Unable to produce usable grapes for over a decade, they sold their land to British companies who were willing to wait until a solution could be found. It was, as phylloxera-resistant American rootstock began to be used throughout Europe. Port production resumed, this time on British-owned land.

Today, Porto and the Douro Valley see many British tourists. Though it's largely undiscovered by Americans, this region is a real hot spot among wine-loving Brits.

**DOURO VALLEY**

Near Porto, the Douro has moderate temperatures and a fair amount of precipitation. The vineyards north of Porto produce not port, but "green wine" (*vinho verde*—Portugal's refreshing light white wine). About 55 miles inland, around Mesão Frio, chains of mountains mark a dramatic change in climate: very hot and dry in summer, with heavy rainfall and extreme cold in winter.

The terrain around the Douro is dominated by sedimentary rocks that have been buried, heated, and deformed into a metamorphic rock called schist *(xisto)*. The easily fractured layers of schist are tilted beneath the soil at an angle, allowing winter rainfall to easily penetrate the earth and build up in underground reserves. The grapevines' roots plunge deep into the ground—up to 30 feet—to reach this water through the long, dry summer.

Building and maintaining the Douro's trademark terraces *(geios)* is expensive, and grapes plant-

ed there must be cultivated by hand. More recently, bigger companies have attempted using larger terraces (called *patamares*) that can be worked by machines, or smoothing out the hillside and planting the vines in vertical rows. Within the demarcated region, farmers are not allowed to irrigate, except with special permission.

Because the crops here are worked mostly by hand, it can be hard to find good workers (especially for pruning, a delicate and skilled task). Most young people from the Douro move to the cities on the coast. To encourage them to stay, the government offers subsidies and other incentives.

To make the finest port, many *quintas* along the Douro still stomp grapes by foot—not because of quaint tradition, but because it's the best way. Machines break the grapes' seeds, releasing too many tannins and resulting in bitter port. But soft soles against stone keep the seeds intact. During harvest time (mid-Sept-early Oct), the grapes are poured into big granite tubs called *lagares*. A team of two dozen stompers line up across from each other, put their arms on each other's shoulders, and march, military-style, to crush the grapes. The stomping can last three to four days, and generally devolves into a party atmosphere—with tourists sometimes joining in...but only later in the evening after the serious work is done.

Port traditionally stays in the Douro Valley for one winter after it's made, as the cold temperatures encourage the wine and brandy to marry. Then it's taken to Porto, where the more humid, mild climate is ideal for aging. For centuries, port could technically only be aged, marketed, and sold in Porto. But this was deregulated in 1987, and now any Douro *quinta* that offers tours can sell its port directly to visitors.

In recent years, vintners have been using their traditional port grapes to make table wines—with great success. These days, most *quintas* offer you tastes not only of port, but of their *vinhos do Douro*, which are gaining international acclaim.

The vineyards along the Douro are traditionally separated by olive trees, many of which produce fine olive oil. The farming demands of olives fit efficiently with those of grapes. There are also almond, orange, apple, and cherry trees, which locals use to make jam.

# Peso da Régua

Peso da Régua (PAY-zoo dah RAY-gwah)—or simply Régua, as it's called by locals—is the administrative capital of the Douro Valley. With 22,000 people, Régua feels urban and functional, with modern five- and six-story apartment blocks that seem out of place in these beautiful surroundings. While the town itself isn't worth the trip, the views and access into the surrounding countryside make it worth considering as a home base—or at least a transportation hub.

## Orientation to Régua

The core of Régua consists of two bustling streets that run parallel to the Douro. The businesslike upper street, Rua dos Camilos, is lined with workaday shops; the lower, main road—Avenida João Franco—runs just above the scenic river embankment, along a narrow, nicely manicured promenade. Down below is the wider, mostly pedestrianized embankment itself, where pleasure boats come and go. There are three bridges at the east (upriver) end of town.

**Tourist Information:** While Régua has a TI, it's clueless and inconveniently located (a few blocks up from the river at the west end of town, on Rua da Ferreirinha). The staff at the Douro Museum (and at bigger hotels) are more reliable sources of information.

**Arrival in Régua:** The **train** station and two recommended hotels are at the eastern edge of the center; buses also stop here. The boat dock is more or less in the middle of town (to reach the train station and hotels, disembark to the right; for the Douro Museum, disembark to the left). **Drivers** can park for free along Avenida João Franco (squeeze between the trees) or on the angled streets leading down to the embankment. There's also a large, free lot at the west end of town (as you approach from Mesão Frio). You have to pay to park along the upper street, Rua dos Camilos.

**Tours:** A company called **Douro Verde** has a near monopoly on tours here, including a cheesy **tourist train** (€7.50, two stops: mountaintop viewpoint and wine cellar for tasting, departs hourly in season); and **cruises** up and down the river. You can choose between a short 50-minute cruise (downriver to the Vale Abraão hotel complex and back, €10); a two-hour cruise all the way upriver to Pinhão with a return by train (2/week, €24); or a longer five- to six-hour round-trip lunch cruise to Pinhão and back (daily at 12:00, €60). For details, ask at one of the Douro Verde kiosks (at either end of town along the lower road—Avenida João Franco, tel. 254-322-858, www.douroverde.com). A few other companies, which specialize in longer cruises from Porto, may also run local cruises from Régua, including **Rota do Douro** (www.rotadodouro. pt) and **Tomaz do Douro** (www.tomazdodouro.pt).

# Sights and Tastings in and near Régua

Régua's sights are few, and most worthwhile for people without cars (who can't get into the countryside, where time is better spent). Along the upper street (Rua dos Camilos), you can't miss the **Casa do Douro**—the blocky, marble-clad, almost Fascist-style headquarters of the local port wine industry (ask to see the pretty stained-glass windows inside).

### ▲Douro Museum (Museu do Douro)

This museum—spanning the lower and upper roads, with a *rabelo* boat permanently moored on its rooftop garden—serves as a sort of cultural center for this little town. It has a restaurant, wine tastings (both described later), temporary exhibits, and an endearing permanent exhibit.

**Cost and Hours:** €6, daily 10:00-18:00, tel. 254-310-190, www.museudodouro.pt.

**Visiting the Museum:** The permanent exhibit, "Douro: Matter and Spirit," explains the landscape, industry, and culture of the Douro Valley. On the ground floor, you'll get a lesson in the region's unique geology, with a 3-D relief map of the Douro Valley and stuffed specimens of local wildlife. Upstairs, the exhibit delves into local winemaking and the unique folk culture that goes along with it. At the top of the stairs, the gigantic wall of wine bottles is enough to make any port lover envious. You'll see models illus-

**DOURO VALLEY**

## *Rabelo* Boats

Up until the 1970s, when the Douro was tamed by dams, boats  called *rabelos* navigated the treacherous waters, carrying port from the hillsides to the cellars of Porto. It was a three-day trip to cover the 50-100 miles. A crew of four loaded the barrels onto the 20-foot boats. For the downstream trip, the captain stood on a platform to spy rocks and shallows ahead, using the long rudder to guide the flat-bottomed boat through whitewater and hairpin turns. It was dangerous work, and the river was once lined with shrines where superstitious sailors prayed.

At Vila Nova de Gaia, they unloaded their cargo—a mere eight barrels, typically—and headed back. For the slow trip upstream, the tall, square sail helped them ride the prevailing westerly winds. Otherwise, they were pulled by ropes up the worst stretches by men or oxen on towpaths that used to line the riverbank.

Nowadays, the Douro is quiet, port is shipped via tanker trucks, and the few remaining *rabelos* are docked by *quintas* for ambience and advertising.

trating the construction of *rabelo* boats; traditional costumes and musical instruments; items relating to port production (tools, casks, barrels, decanters, and huge wicker grape-picking baskets that are supported on the forehead); and port wine labels and advertising posters. On one wall, squeeze the bulb attached to each bottle to help train your nose to the various bouquets of port: apple, honey, berry, nut caramel, cinnamon, and so on. The 33-minute film *Giants of Douro* shows the hard work in this land, past and present—showing lots of locals with grape-stained hands.

**Tastings:** Each afternoon, the museum offers four different options for sampling five or six port wines, but a reservation is required at least one day in advance (minimum four people). The price varies based on quality of the wines (€5-15, daily 15:00-17:00, tel. 254-310-190, geral@museudodouro.pt). They also have a café and wine bar on the museum terrace where you can sip port outside while admiring the vineyards...but with no explanation.

### ▲Quinta da Pacheca

Perhaps the most elegant tasting experience I list is perched near the top of the hill across the river from Régua (just under the big

Sandeman billboard). You'll drive up the elegant, plane-tree-lined driveway to a grand 18th-century manor house nestled in vine-draped hills. You can either drop by for an impromptu taste in the delightful outdoor wine bar (under a leafy canopy), or call ahead to schedule a one-hour tour of the entire process, including their atmospheric cave. While not one of the more famous labels, Pacheca is upscale and well-respected—making this a nice high-end-feeling option without the impersonal corporate glitz. They also have a fancy hotel (see page 378).

**Cost and Hours:** Tasting of 4 wines—€5, tour and tasting—€9, daily 10:00-18:00, tel. 254-331-229, www.quintadapacheca.com.

**Getting There:** It's across the river from Régua and up the hill in Carneiro—cross the bridge, turn right on N-222, and watch for the signs on the right. You'll feel like you're in Sandeman-land until you reach the driveway.

### ▲Quinta de Marrocos

This is the loosest, most informal *quinta* that I list—casual, traditional, and family-run. It's a great place to sample simple ports while chatting with the folks who made them. You'll wander through the vineyards, check out the stomping and aging rooms, and taste four different ports. They also rent rooms (see page 378).

**Cost and Hours:** €10, daily 9:00-12:00 & 14:00-18:00, mobile 918-828-785, www.quintademarrocos.com.

**Getting There:** It's easiest and safest to take a taxi (€10 each way). Hardy walkers can cross the river and follow the busy road (N-222) about 1.5 miles upstream, though there isn't much of a shoulder.

### ▲Quinta da Vallado

Although this *quinta* dates from 1716, they've recently gotten away from their rustic roots and gone in a boldly modern direction—with a new facility stylishly decorated with slate-gray schist and bold lines. They'll take you on a one-hour tour, and then offer a tasting of five types of wines and ports. They also run a fine hotel (see page 378).

**Cost and Hours:** €15, more for higher-end ports, Mon-Sat at 11:30 and 15:00, closed Sun, Vilarinho dos Freires, tel. 254-323-147, www.quintadovallado.com.

**Getting There:** Leave Régua at the eastern end of town, under the tall bridge, and follow N-313 up the narrow Corgo River Valley. Immediately after the road crosses the river, watch for signs on the right.

## Sleep Code

Hotels are classified based on the average price of a standard double room with breakfast in high season.

| | |
|---|---|
| **$$$$** | **Splurge:** Most rooms over €150 |
| **$$$** | **Pricier:** €100-150 |
| **$$** | **Moderate:** €70-100 |
| **$** | **Budget:** €40-70 |
| **¢** | **Backpacker:** Under €40 |
| **RS%** | **Rick Steves discount** |

Unless otherwise noted, credit cards are accepted, hotel staff speaks basic English, and free Wi-Fi is available. Comparison-shop by checking prices at several hotels (on each hotel's own website, on a booking site, or by email). For the best deal, *book directly with the hotel.* Ask for a discount if paying in cash; if the listing includes **RS%,** request a Rick Steves discount.

# Sleeping in Régua

You have two basic options for sleeping here: Stay in a hotel or *residencial* in town, or sleep at a picturesque *quinta* in the countryside. The in-town hotels are very handy for those using public transportation, but if you've got a car, the *quintas* offer a better value and a more memorable Douro experience. The fancier places serve meals and usually have half-board options (book ahead). If you have a car, get out of town!

The Douro is extremely crowded during the grape harvest from mid-September through early October, and good rooms are in short supply to begin with; if visiting during this time, book as far ahead as possible. Simpler places charge the same rates year-round; more expensive hotels charge more for weekends and during the busy season (roughly April-Oct).

**$$$$ Vila Galé Douro,** across the river from the town center (about a 20-minute walk), is the most luxurious hotel option within walking distance of Régua. It has 38 stylish rooms (all with river views), an indoor pool, an outdoor terrace with a hot tub, sharp service, and an elegant vibe (air-con, elevator, Lugar dos Varais, Cambres, in village of Lamego, tel. 254-780-700, www.vilagale. com, douro.reservas@vilagale.com).

**$$ Hotel Régua Douro** is big and relatively professional, with a top-floor panoramic breakfast room and 77 business-class, if somewhat, faded rooms—many of them with sweeping river views (air-con, elevator, pool, Avenida Galizia—at the roundabout at the eastern end of town, tel. 254-320-700, www.hotelreguadouro.pt, geral@hotelreguadouro.pt).

**$ Império Hotel** has a convenient, central location in a stark tower a block from the station and across the street from Hotel Régua Douro. Its 33 spartan rooms are a little musty and overlook busy streets, but the price is right (air-con, Rua Vasques Osório 8, tel. 254-320-120, www.imperiohotel.com, info@imperiohotel.com).

## NEAR RÉGUA

**$$$$ The Wine House Hotel,** at the recommended Quinta da Pacheca (described earlier), is a classy splurge filling a meticulously renovated manor house. The 15 rooms and luxurious public spaces—not to mention the stunning vineyard setting—make this a tempting top-end option (air-con, tel. 254-331-229, www.quintadapacheca.com). For directions, see the winery listing earlier.

**$$$ Quinta da Vallado** is two accommodations in one: a sleek, modern, schist-clad design hotel (with eight rooms), and a thoughtfully restored old manor house (with five rooms). The complex, perched on a hill up a little side-valley just northeast of Régua, also has a swimming pool. It's just the place for young urbanites looking for a bit more contemporary sophistication in their rustic Douro Valley experience (air-con, Vilarinho dos Freires, tel. 254-318-081, www.quintadovallado.com). For directions, see the winery listing earlier.

**$$ Quinta de Marrocos** is a wonderful option if you want to stay on a real-life family farm. The Sequeira family farmhouse operates a simple shop and a family vineyard making good ports and table wines. The four rooms include a rustic living room, where the port's always out. Staying here, with the dogs and farmhands, is a fun, authentic experience—a rare opportunity to spend time with locals who really love what they do (RS%, €25 meals with advance notice, air-con, on N-222 across the river and about 1.5 miles upstream from Régua—about a €10 taxi ride, mobile 918-828-785, www.quintademarrocos.com, info@quintademarrocos.com, sisters Rita and Catarina). They also rent a private two-bedroom family-friendly house on their property.

## Eating in Régua

**$$$$ Castas e Pratos,** next to the train station, turned an enormous railway storage facility into the hippest restaurant in this otherwise sleepy town. The interior comes with lounge tunes and low lighting. If the weather is nice, dine in an open-air freight car permanently attached to the restaurant (facing the train tracks). Their mod wine bar has a nice selection of wines by the glass; if you want a bottle, the wine list is as thick as a phone book (restaurant—daily 12:30-15:00 & 19:30-22:30, wine bar—daily 10:30-24:00; Rua

---

## Restaurant Price Code

I've assigned each eatery a price category, based on the average cost of a typical main course. Drinks, desserts, and splurge items (steak and seafood) can raise the price considerably.

| | |
|---|---|
| **$$$$** | **Splurge:** Most main courses over €17 |
| **$$$** | **Pricier:** €12-17 |
| **$$** | **Moderate:** €7-12 |
| **$** | **Budget:** Under €7 |

In Portugal, takeout food is **$**; a basic sit-down eatery is **$$**; a casual but more upscale restaurant is **$$$**; and a swanky splurge is **$$$$**.

---

José Vasques Osório at train station, mobile 927-200-010, www.castasepratos.com).

**$$$ A Companhia,** a classy dining room on the second floor of the Douro Museum, has a handy €13.50 lunch buffet (daily 12:30-15:00, Rua Marquês de Pombal, tel. 254-323-030).

**$$ Gato Preto** ("Black Cat"), next door to the Douro Museum on the lower street, is classy and affordable (daily 12:00-15:00 & 18:30-22:30, Avenida João Franco, tel. 254-313-367).

**$ Pastelaria Nacional** serves great pastries but also doubles as a restaurant popular with locals. Bubbly Paula and her family pride themselves on customer service and on their regional dishes...and her English is fun (lunch specials, Mon-Sat 12:00-20:30, closed Sun, on the upper street between the museum and the train station at Rua dos Camilos 86, tel. 254-336-231).

---

# Pinhão

Pinhão (PEEN-yow)—known locally as the "heart of the Douro"—feels like a real small town, where locals go on with their "im-*port*-ant" business, oblivious to the tourists streaming through their streets. The town—with a cobbled main street and a gorgeous deep-in-the-Douro setting—has a certain dirty-fingernails charm. Inside the big, concrete silos *(balões),* wine spends  its first winter awaiting shipment downstream to Porto.

# Orientation to Pinhão

Pinhão has virtually no sights, but it makes for a handy home base. The town has a train station along the main road (Rua António Manuel Saraiva), and a boat landing down below on the river. The two *residencials* are across the street from the station, and Vintage House Hotel is just upriver, next to the bridge. The main road rumbles through the middle of town, past the train station and a mix of practical shops and tourist-oriented wine bars. The handiest **ATM** is a block from the train sta-

tion, on the main street, just past the two *residencials* (exit station to the left, look for CA Bank).

**Getting Around:** Taxi driver **Manuel Anselmo** speaks some English and is very knowledgeable about local tourism. He can often be found at the train station. A round-trip visit to the recommended Quinta do Panascal costs around €25 (mobile 966-192-904, www.taxipinhao.com).

**Sights in Pinhão:** Even if you don't arrive by train, be sure to check out the **train station**—adorned with modern tiles illustrating the people and traditions of the countryside.

If you're not arriving on a boat, it's easy to miss the broad and manicured **river embankment** (watch for the steep, downhill road, just west of the train station, near the post office). Here you'll find boat docks, a few upscale eateries, parks, fishermen, and some public WCs. It's a pleasant place to simply stroll, with grand views to the vineyards on the opposite banks. At the west end, a modern metal bridge arcs over to another fine embankment for views back on town; if you keep going on this road, you'll reach the Quinta de la Rosa (wine tasting described later).

A popular activity in this town are **river cruises.** The top option is a round-trip cruise that goes up the river—where no roads go (accessible only by boat or train). You'll pay €10 for a one-hour cruise to a farm and back, or €20 for two hours all the way to the village of Tua (for a port wine tasting) and back. Two fiercely competitive companies both have sales kiosks along the riverfront: Companhia Turística do Douro (www.companhiaturisticadodouro.com, mobile 963-934-951) and Magnífico Douro (www.magnificodouro.pt, mobile 913-129-857).

# Tastings in and near Pinhão

### ▲▲Quinta do Panascal

This wonderful *quinta* produces Fonseca—a name familiar to port lovers for its high quality. The affordable, tasty Bin No. 27 is their best-known ruby. It's the only *quinta* that allows you to roam on your own through the terraced vineyards. From the riverside road you'll side-trip up the valley of the Távora River. Venturing up the rough gravel road, you'll feel like you're discovering a special, hidden gem. Yet upon arrival, you'll enjoy the slick efficiency of a corporate producer (Fonseca also owns Taylor, the port wine giant). Because of its delightfully remote location, and because it gets you out among the grapes, it's among the best *quinta* tours on the Douro.

The tour is self-guided, so there's no wait once you arrive. You'll be given a 30-minute audioguide and set free to wander through the winery, the cellars, and the vineyards—where you can take in the sweeping views (while listening to dry, humorless commentary about the history of port and of the company). Then you'll return to the lodge to watch a 10-minute video—which brings the otherwise still fields to life—while tasting three ports: a white, Bin No. 27, and 10-year-old tawny.

**Cost and Hours:** €7, April-Oct daily 10:00-18:00; Nov-March Mon-Fri 10:00-18:00, Sat-Sun by reservation only; tel. 254-732-321, www.fonseca.pt.

**Getting There:** This place is only accessible by car; it's well-marked off the Régua-Pinhão road (N-222), up a thrilling little side road that follows the Távora River as it branches off from the Douro (closer to Pinhão). Blind curves make this road dangerous for walking, but a taxi ride is a good value for those without cars (figure around €25 round-trip, including some wait time; see recommended driver earlier).

### ▲Quinta de la Rosa

This British-owned, family-run *quinta* is proud of its wine and eager to show it off on an in-depth, engaging one-hour tour of the facility with a finale of four tastings. I find this a nice middle ground between big and corporate, and tiny and rustic—it's unpretentious yet rich with tradition. This is perhaps the only family *quinta* that is close enough to do without a car (20-minute hike from Pinhão). Three-course dinners paired with

DOURO VALLEY

their wines cost €25 per person; reserve in advance. They also have a hotel (see page 383).

**Cost and Hours:** €10, daily at 11:30 and 16:00, one mile downstream from Pinhão, tel. 254-732-254, www.quintadelarosa.com.

**Getting There:** Drivers leave Pinhão to the west (downriver), cross the concrete bridge, turn left and look for the *quinta* on the left side, up the hill. If walking: From the boat landing, cross the blue pedestrian bridge and continue 20 minutes (or take a €6-8 taxi from Pinhão station).

### In Town

Pinhão's main street is lined with wine shops, eager to sell you a bottle, a glass, or a taste. Do some window-shopping and take your pick. For something more formal, Vintage House Hotel's lobby wine bar offers expensive, high-end, regularly scheduled **Academia do Vinho** ("Wine Academy") tastings, usually in the afternoon—call to check the schedule and reserve a spot (€30 tastings, wine shop open daily 10:00-19:00, tel. 254-730-230; see hotel listing below).

## Sleeping in and near Pinhão

Your in-town options are a plush splurge hotel or two humble *residencial*s. The *residencial*s are next door to each other, across from the train station. Both operate fine restaurants, and both have riverview rooms that don't cost extra but come with some street noise; neither has owners who speak English, but each sometimes has an English-speaking son available.

**$$$$ Vintage House Hotel** is *the* place if you want to splurge on a fancy, formal hotel on the Douro (as opposed to a hillside manor house). It's all class, with a wonderfully atmospheric bar (under tree-trunk rafters), a good restaurant with an over-the-top formal interior and riverside terrace outdoor seating, and a wine shop featuring expensive tastings for aficionados (see "Tastings in and near Pinhão," earlier). Each of its 50 rooms has a river view and a terrace or balcony, and elegant tile in the bathroom. The halls are lined with 19th-century photos of the Douro (air-con, elevator, pool, between train station and bridge at Lugar da Ponte, tel. 254-730-230, www.vintagehousehotel.com, reservations@vintagehousehotel.com).

**$ Hotel Douro** offers 14 basic, clean, and bright rooms, many with cute riverview balconies. The halls are nicely tiled, and the communal terrace provides a great, lazy-afternoon view of the river (cash only, air-con, Largo da Estação 39, tel. 254-732-404, www.hotel-douro.pt, geral@hotel-douro.pt, Oliveira family).

**$ Residencial Ponto Grande** is your basic budget choice, with 17 small, simple rooms (cash only, some with air-con, Rua António Manuel Saraiva 41A at Largo da Estação, tel. 254-732-456, residencialpontogrande@hotmail.com, Vieira family).

## OUTSIDE PINHÃO

**$$ Quinta de la Rosa,** a mile downstream of Pinhão, is a riverside winery offering 14 comfortable rooms with light, country-cabana furnishings; all but one overlook the river. Stylish but mellow and a bit ragtag, it's a fine retreat for getting lost in dreamy Douro scenery (ask in advance for the €25 three-course dinner including wine and port; tel. 254-732-254, www.quintadelarosa.com, holidays@quintadelarosa.com). For directions—and information about their tours and tastings—see tastings listing, earlier.

**$$$ Casa do Visconde de Chanceleiros** fills a manor house in the village of Chanceleiros, a glorious 15-minute drive through vineyard-covered hills from Pinhão. Stern Ursula and her right-hand woman Adelaide rent 12 rustic, homey rooms scattered over the glorious grounds, with a pristine swimming pool and extravagant views over vineyards, gardens, and the Douro. With a tennis court, hot tub, and sauna, this feels like an exclusive—but not snobby—Old World retreat (air-con, dinner-€38, tel. 254-730-190, www.chanceleiros.com, chanceleiros@chanceleiros.com).

**Getting There:** Simply follow the directions to Quinta de la Rosa (see tastings listing, earlier), then keep going past it. The road twists up to Chanceleiros, where you'll find the house on what looks like the main square.

**$$$ Casa de Casal de Loivos** hovers on a lofty perch above Pinhão, with perhaps the most dramatic views in all of the Douro Valley. The warm Sampayo family converted this 17th-century manor house into a six-room hotel with quaintly rustic furnishings and commanding Douro vistas. The family brags that when the BBC filmed a show about the best views in the world, they set up their camera right here (fun family-style dinner-€28/person without wine—reserve ahead, grand-view swimming pool, closed Dec-Feb, tel. 254-732-149, www.casadecasaldeloivos.com, casadecasaldeloivos@ip.pt).

**Getting There:** The house is in the village of Casal de Loivos, atop the mountain overlooking Pinhão. Leaving Pinhão to the west (downriver), first follow signs for *Alijó,* then for *Casal de Loivos,* and wind your way up the mountain roads. Once in town, look for the poorly marked villa on your right (with big iron grates on the windows); if you reach the overlook by the cemetery, you've gone a block too far. If you don't have wheels, catch a taxi from Pinhão's train station (about €10).

## Eating in Pinhão

Your choices are limited in this little town. If you're staying at a *quinta* outside of town, dining at your accommodations is a tempting option. Along the main drag, several hardworking restaurants vie for your business; decent choices include the old-school but popular **$$ Residencial Ponto Grande** (at #41, open daily), or the nicely tiled **$$ Bufete Restaurante** (at #13, daily). Down along the riverbank, **$$$ Restaurante Veladouro**—with a tempting menu of pricey grill specialties—is a popular choice (daily, Rua da Praian 3).

# PORTUGAL: PAST & PRESENT

Sitting on the fringe of Europe, facing the open Atlantic, Portugal has an epic history that's shaped by the sea. Here's a brief overview.

### PREHISTORY TO ROME (2000 B.C.-A.D. 500)

Portugal's indigenous race, the Lusiads, was a mix of peoples from many migrations and invasions—Neolithic stone builders (2000 B.C.), Phoenician traders (1200 B.C.), northern Celts (700 B.C.), Greek colonists (700 B.C.), and Carthaginian conquerors (500 B.C.).

By the time of Julius Caesar (50 B.C.), Rome had conquered rebellious Lusitania (Portugal), establishing major cities at Olissipo (Lisbon), Portus Cale (Porto), Conímbriga (near Coimbra), and Ebora (Évora). The Romans brought laws, wine, the Latin language, and Christianity. When Rome's empire fell (A.D. 476), Portugal was saved from barbarian attacks by Christian Germanic Visigoths ruling distantly from their capital in Toledo.

### MUSLIMS VS. CHRISTIANS, AND NATIONHOOD (711-1400)

North African Muslims invaded the Iberian Peninsula, settling in southern Portugal. The Christians retreated to the cold, mountainous north, leaving central Portugal as a buffer zone. The remnants of these Christian armies became the core of the Reconquista—the retaking of the Iberian Peninsula from the Moors—which lasted for eight centuries. During their long rule, the Moors made Iberia a beacon of enlightenment in Dark Age Europe.

But the Christians—who considered them invaders and infidels—drove them out, one territory at a time. Faro was the last Portuguese town to fall, in 1249. Afonso Henriques, a popular Christian noble who conquered much Muslim land, was proclaimed king of Portugal (1139), creating one of Europe's first modern

# Ten Dates That Shaped Portugal

**1128** "Portucale" separates from Castile.

**1139** Afonso Henriques (Afonso I) is declared the first king of Portugal.

**1498** Vasco da Gama sails Portugal into a century of wealth.

**1581** King Philip II of Spain inherits the crown of Portugal after King Sebastian dies without an heir.

**1640** The Spanish are ousted; the Portuguese gain their independence.

**1755** A massive earthquake rocks Lisbon into poverty.

**1822** Portugal loses Brazil as a colony.

**1910** The monarchy is deposed, democracy fails, and repressive military regimes rule.

**1974** A left-wing military coup brings democracy.

**1986** Portugal joins the European Community (the forerunner of the European Union), boosting the economy.

nation-states. João I (r. 1385-1433) solidified Portugal's nationhood by repelling a Spanish invasion in 1385, and established his family—the House of Avis—as kings. (For more on the House of Avis dynasty, see page 257.) Romantics prefer the star-crossed tale of João's father, Pedro the Just, and his mistress Inês (see page 269).

## THE AGE OF DISCOVERY...AND OF SLAVERY (1400-1600)

With royal backing, Portugal built a navy and began exploring the seas using technology the Arabs had left behind. These trips were motivated by spice-trade profit and a desire to Christianize Muslim lands in North Africa. From his base at Cape Sagres—at Portugal's (and Europe's) southwestern corner—Prince Henry the Navigator urged his sailors to go beyond what was then regarded as "the end of the world." Thanks to new maritime inventions—such as the mariner's astrolabe and the caravel—they finally did, slowly making their way down the coast of West Africa. In 1488, Bartolomeu Dias became the first European to sail around the tip of Africa—the Cape of Good Hope. Vasco da Gama followed the same route but continued farther, landing in India in 1498. Suddenly the wealth of all Asia opened up via a fast and cheap sea route. Much to the dismay of Venice, Portugal's new discoveries caused spice prices to drop to one-fifth of their former market value. For more

# Typical Church Architecture

History comes to life when you visit a centuries-old church. Even if you wouldn't know your apse from a hole in the ground, learning a few simple terms will enrich your experience. Note that not every church has every feature, and a "cathedral" isn't a type of church architecture, but rather a designation for a church that's a governing center for a local bishop.

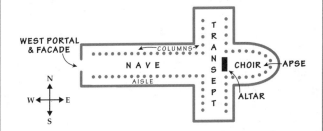

**Aisles:** The long, generally low-ceilinged arcades that flank the nave.

**Altar:** The raised area with a ceremonial table (often adorned with candles or a crucifix), where the priest prepares and serves the bread and wine for Communion.

**Apse:** The space beyond the altar, generally bordered with small chapels.

**Barrel Vault:** A continuous round-arched ceiling that resembles an extended upside-down U.

**Choir:** A cozy area, often screened off, located within the church nave and near the high altar, where services are sung in a more intimate setting.

**Cloister:** Covered hallways bordering a square or rectangular open-air courtyard, traditionally where monks and nuns got fresh air.

**Facade:** The exterior of the church's main (west) entrance, usually highly decorated.

**Groin Vault:** An arched ceiling formed where two equal barrel vaults meet at right angles. Less common usage: term for a medieval jock strap.

**Narthex:** The area (portico or foyer) between the main entry and the nave.

**Nave:** The long, central section of the church (running west to east, from the entrance to the altar) where the congregation sits or stands through the service.

**Transept:** In a traditional cross-shaped floor plan, the transept is one of the two parts forming the "arms" of the cross. The transept runs north-south, perpendicularly crossing the east-west nave.

**West Portal:** The main entry to the church (on the west end, opposite the main altar).

on Prince Henry the Navigator, see page 183. For more on Portuguese explorations, see page 91.

Another major event at this time was the European discovery of Brazil by Pedro Cabral (1500). Cabral was on his way to India, following Da Gama's route, but he headed more southwest to bypass rough waters near the Gulf of Guinea. Historians have long debated whether his "discovery" was intentional or accidental, since some Portuguese sailors had previously reported spotting land on the other side of the Atlantic. In any case, Cabral's voyage resulted in the colonization of Brazil—and more riches for Portugal.

Besides trading in spice and silk, the Portuguese also traded in human beings. The Portuguese were the first Europeans to sail to Africa, capture native people, and bring them back for sale. In 1482, they built Elmina Castle on the coast of what is now Ghana—the first of many "slave factories" (slave trading posts) that Europeans established in western Africa. The slave trade soon shifted to the New World, where new sugar plantations created a huge demand for cheap labor. Portuguese settlements sprung up in both Guinea and Angola for slavery purposes. Ships would leave Lisbon for West Africa, pick up slaves, and then sail to Brazil, selling their captives to work on plantations and in mines. The ships would return to Portugal loaded with sugar—creating tremendous wealth for the sea captains, slave traders, and merchants.

The Portuguese had a slave-trade monopoly through the 16th century, but England and the Netherlands then began their own slave trade. Historians estimate that, before slavery ended, about four million captives were brought from Africa to Brazil—roughly 40 percent of all the slaves brought to the Americas.

Through trade, conquest, and, yes, slavery, tiny Portugal became one of Europe's wealthiest and most powerful nations, with colonies stretching from Brazil to Africa to India to China. The easy money destroyed the traditional economy.

## SLOW FADE (1600-1900)

The "Spanish Captivity" (1580-1640) drained Portugal. Late in the 16th century, after the young Portuguese king, Sebastian (Dom Sebastião), died in battle without a direct heir, Portugal's throne was up for grabs. After a short reign by Sebastian's great-uncle (who died two years after assuming power), the Portuguese throne passed to another distant relative—the Spanish king, Philip II. Philip wanted the two countries to remain separate, and they did under his rule. But his son and grandson—who ruled after him—cared little about Portuguese autonomy, so they imposed new taxes on the Portuguese and forced Portugal's armies to support the Spanish military agenda. After 60 years, the Portuguese nobility had had enough, and when Spanish troops were tied up

# Typical Castle Architecture

Castles were fortified residences for medieval nobles. Castles come in all shapes and sizes, but knowing a few general terms will help you understand them.

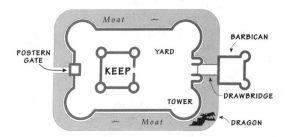

**Barbican:** A fortified gatehouse, sometimes a stand-alone building located outside the main walls.

**Crenellation:** A gap-toothed pattern of stones atop the parapet.

**Drawbridge:** A bridge that could be raised or lowered, using counterweights or a chain-and-winch.

**Great Hall:** The largest room in the castle, serving as throne room, conference center, and dining hall.

**Hoardings (or Gallery or Brattice):** Wooden huts built onto the upper parts of the stone walls. They served as watch towers, living quarters, and fighting platforms.

**Keep (or Donjon):** A high, strong stone tower in the center of the complex; the lord's home and refuge of last resort.

**Loopholes (or Embrasures):** Narrow wall slits through which soldiers could shoot arrows.

**Machicolation:** A stone ledge jutting out from the wall, with holes through which soldiers could drop rocks or boiling oil onto wall-scaling enemies below.

**Moat:** A ditch encircling the wall, sometimes filled with water.

**Parapet:** Outer railing of the wall walk.

**Portcullis:** An iron grille that could be lowered across the entrance.

**Postern Gate:** A small, unfortified side or rear entrance. In wartime, it became a "sally-port" used to launch surprise attacks, or as an escape route.

**Towers:** Square or round structures with crenellated tops or conical roofs serving as lookouts, chapels, living quarters, or the dungeon.

**Turret:** A small lookout tower rising from the top of the wall.

**Wall Walk (or Allure):** A pathway atop the wall where guards could patrol and where soldiers stood to fire at the enemy.

**Yard (or Bailey):** An open courtyard inside the castle walls.

in the Thirty Years' War, the nobles launched an uprising. One of the leading nobles, the duke of Bragança, was proclaimed king, becoming King João IV. Although it's been nearly 400 years, Spain and Portugal continue to have a sibling rivalry—with Spain often acting as the arrogant older brother—though the conflicts now happen on the soccer field rather than the battlefield.

With a false economy, a rigid class system, and the gradual loss of their profitable colonies, Portugal was no match for the rising powers of Spain, England, Holland, and France. The earthquake of 1755 (see page 54) and Napoleon's invasions during the Peninsular War (1808-1814) were devastating. Portugal was a traditional ally of England, and when Napoleon demanded that Portuguese merchants stop trading with England, they refused. Napoleon sent his army through Spain to invade Portugal, where his troops ravaged the countryside. A French coup then placed Napoleon's brother on the Spanish throne, causing a revolt across the Iberian Peninsula. British troops retook Lisbon, and a six-year, back-and-forth struggle eventually ended in Napoleon's defeat.

While the rest of Europe industrialized and democratized, Portugal lingered as an isolated, rural monarchy living off meager wealth from Brazilian gold and sugar. Eventually, the country lost its largest colony in 1822, when Brazil revolted (with the support of the son of the Portuguese king). But Portugal still had a string of colonies across Africa and Asia, including Portuguese Guinea, Angola, Mozambique, Goa, Macau, and Portuguese Timor.

## DICTATORSHIP AND DEMOCRACY (1900-2000)

Republican rebels overthrew the king in 1910, founding a republic and abolishing the monarchy, but democracy was slow to establish itself in Portugal's near-medieval class system. During World War I, Portugal joined the Allies, partly to protect its African colonies from the Germans.

The postwar years resulted in political turmoil. A series of military-backed democracies culminated in four decades of António de Oliveira Salazar's "New State," a right-wing regime benefiting the traditional upper classes. For 36 years, the former professor ruled Portugal under an authoritarian regime that banned political parties and independent labor unions. A fascist system of censorship, propaganda, and oppression kept society in order. When opposition arose, the secret police (a.k.a. PIDE—Polícia Internacional e de Defesa do Estado) imprisoned and tortured dissidents. (For more on Salazar, see page 70.)

According to Portuguese historians, Salazar didn't trust Hitler and didn't think the Germans could win World War II. He kept Portugal neutral, even allowing the British to use naval bases in the Azores under an old Anglo-Portuguese treaty. After the war,

# Portuguese Notables

**Viriato** (d. 139): Legendary warrior who (unsuccessfully) resisted the Roman invasion.

**Afonso Henriques, the Conqueror** (1095-1185): Renowned Muslim-slayer and first king of a united, Christian nation.

**Pedro I, the Just** (1320-1367): King and father of João I, famous for his devotion to his murdered mistress/wife, Inês.

**João I, the Good** (1358-1433): King who preserved independence from Spain, launched an overseas expansion, fathered Prince Henry the Navigator, and established the House of Avis as the ruling family.

**Henry the Navigator** (1394-1460): Devout, intellectual sponsor of naval expeditions during the Age of Discovery.

**Bartolomeu Dias** (1450-1500): Navigator who rounded the tip of Africa in 1488, paving the way for Vasco da Gama.

**Vasco da Gama** (1460-1524): Explorer who discovered the sea route to India, opening up Asia's wealth.

**Pedro Cabral** (1467-1520): Explorer who found the sea route to Brazil (1500).

**Ferdinand Magellan** (1480-1521): Voyager who, sailing for Spain, led the first circumnavigation of the globe (1520).

**Manuel I, the Fortunate** (r. 1495-1521): Promoter of Vasco da Gama's explorations that made Portugal wealthy. Manueline, the decorative art style of that time, is named for him.

**Luís de Camões** (1524-1580): Swashbuckling adventurer and poet who captured the heroism of Vasco da Gama in his epic poem, "The Lusiads."

**Marquês de Pombal** (1699-1782): Controversial chief minister who tried to modernize backward Portugal, regulated the port wine industry, and rebuilt Lisbon after the 1755 quake.

**José I, the Reformer** (r. 1750-1777): Disinterested king who effectively turned over control of Portugal to the Marquês de Pombal.

**Fernando Pessoa** (1888-1935): Foremost Portuguese Modernist poet, immortalized in sculpture outside his favorite Lisbon café.

**António de Oliveira Salazar** (1889-1970): "Portugal's Franco," a dictator who led for four decades, slowly modernizing while preserving rule by the traditional upper classes.

**Cristiano Ronaldo** (1985- ): Prodigiously talented soccer star, and the most famous Portuguese person alive today.

Portugal was a founding member of NATO—the only dictatorship allowed into the organization at its birth. Salazar wasn't your typical corrupt dictator. As a young man, he considered becoming a priest; as Portugal's leader he continued to be modest, pious, and celibate. Salazar—Europe's longest-serving dictator—ran Portugal until 1968, when he had a stroke and later died.

Salazar's repressive tactics and unpopular wars abroad (trying to hang onto Portugal's colonial empire) sparked the Carnation Revolution of 1974. A little after midnight on April 25, army rebels rolled into Lisbon, and by sunrise the military had taken control from Salazar's successors. They promised to restore citizen's civil liberties and conduct general elections as soon as possible. The coup was nearly bloodless. Residents disobeyed commands to stay in their homes, and instead people flooded the streets in support of the rebels, placing carnations into the barrels of the soldiers' guns as a sign of peace (hence the name "Carnation Revolution"; for more on this, see page 65).

The new regime worked quickly to free Portugal's colonies. Within a few years, Guinea-Bissau, Mozambique, Cape Verde Islands, São Tomé and Principe, and Angola all became independent. After some initial political and economic chaos, Portugal finally adopted democracy. Imagine: In just a dozen years, Portugal went from the isolation of four decades of fascism (when the Salazar dictatorship slogan was "We are proudly alone") to full membership in the European Union (in 1986).

## PORTUGAL TODAY: AUSTERITY AND CHALLENGE

The early years of the 21st century were heady days for Portugal. The former backwater was suddenly booming—building superhighways, handing out lavish bonuses to workers, and buying fancy consumer goods from the rest of Europe. Scaffolding was everywhere as the Portuguese scrambled to finish a number of projects, which were funded in part by the European Union.

The EU has worked to bring relatively poor regions (like much of Portugal) up to par with more-developed parts of Europe through matching grants and cheap construction loans. As part of the EU, Portugal was considered a low-risk bet for lenders, keeping interest rates artificially low. But with the 2008 banking crisis, things got real. Money became tight worldwide, and lenders began assessing each country on its individual merits. The risk of lending to Portugal shot up—and so did interest rates.

Today, Portugal is struggling to pay back those loans. The economy has been floundering, with unemployment around 11 percent (and as high as 26 percent for those under 25 years old). Infrastructure projects—such as plans for a high-speed bullet train

## Portugal's "Law 30"

Portugal has one of the more progressive drug policies today. In 2000, the government passed "Law 30," which decriminalized the consumption of all drugs. Although a conservative government replaced the more progressive government that established "Law 30," former opponents agreed that its benefits far outweighed its harms. Now with a center-left government, "Law 30" continues to be the law of the land.

Drug addiction was a major societal concern in Portugal in the late 1990s. A group of experts came together in 1999 to find a solution to the problem. They realized that the "war on drugs" was actually a "war on people." Similar to the US, only about one percent of Portugal's population (100,000 out of 11 million people) was actually using hard drugs.

The goal of "Law 30" was to establish a legal framework for harm reduction. Drug addicts are considered ill, not criminals. Drug use and possession are still illegal, but no longer punishable with jail time. Instead offenders are given treatment, community service, or fines.

A 2010 review of the law studied drug consumption trends from 2001 to 2009. Researchers summed up Portugal's experience this way: "Nothing bad happened." There was no change in actual usage rates, and the big negatives some had predicted, including the expected advent of "drug tourism," didn't materialize (young backpackers didn't start converging on Portugal as the new drug mecca).

Other outcomes of "Law 30" are that Portugal now has fewer people with HIV and more people in treatment. The police like the law because it frees up resources to focus on violent crime. The burden on Portugal's prisons and criminal system has been reduced. And the Portuguese government went from being the enemy of its drug-using population to being its advocate.

from Madrid to Lisbon, an additional runway for Lisbon airport, and superhighway expansion—have all been put on indefinite hold.

In 2011, the EU approved a €78 billion bailout package, but with it came the requirement for strict austerity measures. To enforce these measures, a trio of financial institutions—the European Commission, European Central Bank, and International Monetary Fund, together referred to as "the troika"—oversaw Portugal's effort to get its economy back on a sustainable track.

These austerity measures have included higher road tolls, increased health deductibles (coupled with other health care cutbacks), and new taxes, including a 23 percent tax on all restaurant income. The retirement age has been raised from 65 to 67. And a worker-friendly scheme from the Carnation Revolution, which took a year's wage and broke it into 14 "months" rather than 12 (to give workers a "bonus" each summer and Christmas), has been rescinded. Now workers making more than €650 a month get only 12 months' pay. Because this scheme was never really a "bonus" but rather a forced savings account, the change amounted to about a 15 percent pay cut.

Austerity also led to the end of rent control (a remnant of the Salazar period). While necessary, this change spurred a huge spike in rents—causing financial stress for older people, pushing out small shops, and threatening to change the character of traditional neighborhoods.

The country successfully completed the bailout program in 2014, but economic recovery remains slow. Regardless of which parties are in power, the EU retains the power to limit and guide government spending. The big discussion these days: How will the young generation pay for the old generation's consumption and debt?

Portugal's challenge of the day (along with paying off its mountainous debt) is a brain drain. Young people are thirsty for opportunity; the goal of many well-educated millennials is to get out of their parents' house, and then out of the country. In the last two years, 350,000 highly trained young people (out of a population of nearly 11 million) have left the country for more promising careers in lands offering better opportunity.

But even as Portugal struggles with its contemporary challenges, it remains open and warmly welcoming to outsiders. A visit to today's Portugal lets you personally experience the latest chapter in an epic story.

# PRACTICALITIES

This chapter covers the practical skills of European travel: how to get tourist information, pay for things, sightsee efficiently, find good-value accommodations, eat affordably but well, use technology wisely, and get between destinations smoothly. To study ahead and round out your knowledge and skills, check out "Resources from Rick Steves."

## Tourist Information

Portugal's **national tourist office** offers practical information, trip-planning ideas, and downloadable brochures on their website (www.visitportugal.com).

In Portugal, a good first stop is generally the tourist information office *(posto de turismo)*—abbreviated **TI** in this book. Be aware that TIs are in business to help you enjoy spending money in their town. (Once upon a time, they were actually information services, but today some have become ad agencies masquerading as TIs.) While this corrupts much of their advice—and you can get plenty of information online—I still make a point to swing by the local TI to confirm sightseeing plans, pick up a city map, and get information on public transit (including bus and train schedules), walking tours, special events, and nightlife.

Prepare a list of questions and a proposed plan to double-check. Some TIs have information on the entire country or at least the region, so try to pick up maps and printed information for destinations you'll be visiting later in your trip.

Steer clear of prepaid taxi vouchers sold by Portugal TIs—they're almost always more expensive than the metered price.

## Travel Tips

**Emergency and Medical Help:** In Portugal, dial 112 for English-speaking police help or a medical emergency. If you get sick, do as the locals do and go to a pharmacist for advice. Or ask at your hotel for help—they'll know the nearest medical and emergency services.

**Theft or Loss:** To replace a passport, you'll need to go in person to an embassy or consulate (see page 439). If your credit and debit cards disappear, cancel and replace them (see "Damage Control for Lost Cards" on page 400). File a police report either on the spot or within a day or two; you'll need it to submit an insurance claim for lost or stolen rail passes or travel gear, and it can help with replacing your passport or credit and debit cards. For more information, see www.ricksteves.com/help.

**Avoiding Theft and Scams:** Thieves target tourists throughout Portugal, especially in Lisbon. While hotel rooms are generally safe, thieves snatch purses, pick pockets, and break into cars. Be on guard, especially on the Metro and trolleys, and treat any disturbance around you as a smoke screen for theft. Don't believe any "police officers" looking for counterfeit bills. When traveling by train, keep your luggage in sight.

**Time Zones:** Though Portugal and Spain are neighbors, Portugal sets its clock one hour earlier than Spain and most of continental Europe. (This is true even during Daylight Saving Time.) Portugal's time zone is the same as Great Britain's: five/eight hours ahead of the East/West coasts of the US. The exceptions are the beginning and end of Daylight Saving Time: Europe "springs forward" the last Sunday in March (two weeks after most of North America) and "falls back" the last Sunday in October (one week before North America). For a handy online time converter, see www.timeanddate.com/worldclock.

**Business Hours:** In Portugal, some businesses take a lunch break (usually 12:00-13:30 or 12:30-14:00). Larger shops and museums stay open all day. Banks are generally open Monday through Friday from 8:30 to 15:00. Small shops are often open on Saturday only in the morning and are closed all day Sunday.

---

## Exchange Rate

### 1 euro (€) = about $1.10

To convert prices in euros to dollars, add about 10 percent: €20 = about $22, €50 = about $55. (Check www.oanda.com for the latest exchange rates.) Just like the dollar, one euro (€) is broken down into 100 cents. Coins range from €0.01 to €2, and bills from €5 to €250 (bills over €50 are rarely used; €500 bills are being phased out).

---

Saturdays typically have earlier closing hours. Sundays have the same pros and cons as they do for travelers in the US: Sightseeing attractions are generally open, and banks and smaller shops are closed, public transportation options are fewer (for example, no bus service to or from smaller towns), and there's no rush hour. Friday and Saturday evenings are lively; Sunday evenings are quiet.

**Watt's Up?** Europe's electrical system is 220 volts, instead of North America's 110 volts. Most newer electronics (such as laptops, battery chargers, and hair dryers) convert automatically, so you won't need a converter, but you will need an adapter plug with two round prongs, sold inexpensively at travel stores in the US. Avoid bringing older appliances that don't automatically convert voltage; instead, buy a cheap replacement in Europe.

**Discounts:** Discounts for sights are generally not listed in this book. However, seniors (age 60 and over), youths under 18, and students and teachers with proper identification cards (www.isic.org) can get discounts at many sights. Always ask. Some discounts are available only for citizens of the European Union (EU).

**Online Translation Tips:** Google's Chrome browser instantly translates websites. You can also paste text or the URL of a foreign website into the translation window at http://translate.google.com. The Google Translate app converts spoken English into most European languages (and vice versa) and can also translate text it "reads" with your mobile device's camera.

## Money

This section offers advice on how to pay for purchases on your trip (including getting cash from ATMs and paying with plastic), dealing with lost or stolen cards, VAT (sales tax) refunds, and tipping.

### WHAT TO BRING

Bring both a credit card and a debit card. You'll use the debit card at cash machines (ATMs) to withdraw local cash for most purchases, and the credit card to pay for larger items. Some travelers carry a third card, in case one gets demagnetized or eaten by a temperamental machine.

For an emergency stash, bring $100-200 in hard cash. Although banks in some countries don't exchange dollars, in a pinch you can always find exchange desks *(casa de câmbio)* at major train stations or airports—convenient but with crummy rates.

## CASH

Although credit cards are widely accepted in Europe, day-to-day spending is generally more cash-based. I find local currency is the easiest—and sometimes only—way to pay for cheap food, bus fare, taxis, and local guides. Some vendors will charge you extra for using a credit card, some won't accept foreign credit cards, and some won't take any credit cards at all. Having cash on hand can help you avoid a stressful predicament if you find yourself in a place that won't accept your card.

Throughout Europe, ATMs are the easiest and smartest way for travelers to get cash. They work just like they do at home. To withdraw money from an ATM (known as *Multibanco* in Portugal—look for the *MB* logo), you'll need a debit card (ideally with a Visa or MasterCard logo), plus a PIN code (numeric and four digits). For increased security, shield the keypad when entering your PIN code, and don't use an ATM if anything on the front of the machine looks loose or damaged (a sign that someone may have attached a "skimming" device to capture account information). Try to withdraw large sums of money to reduce the number of per-transaction bank fees you'll pay.

When possible, use ATMs located outside banks—a thief is less likely to target a cash machine near surveillance cameras, and if your card is munched by a machine during banking hours, you can go inside for help. Stay away from "independent" ATMs such as Travelex, Euronet, YourCash, Cardpoint, and Cashzone, which charge huge commissions, have terrible exchange rates, and may try to trick users with "dynamic currency conversion" (described later). Although you can use a credit card to withdraw cash at an ATM, this comes with high bank fees and only makes sense in an emergency.

While traveling, if you want to access your accounts online, be sure to use a secure connection (see page 421).

Pickpockets target tourists. To safeguard your cash, wear a money belt—a pouch with a strap that you buckle around your waist like a belt and tuck under your clothes. Keep your cash, credit cards, and passport secure in your money belt, and carry only a day's spending money in your front pocket or wallet.

## CREDIT AND DEBIT CARDS

For purchases, Visa and MasterCard are more commonly accepted than American Express. Just like at home, credit or debit cards work easily at larger hotels, restaurants, and shops. I typically use my debit card to withdraw cash to pay for daily purchases. I use my credit card sparingly: to book and pay for hotel rooms, to buy advance tickets for events or sights, to cover major expenses (such as car rentals or plane tickets), and to pay for things online or near the end of my trip (to avoid another visit to the ATM). While you could instead use a debit card for these purchases, a credit card offers a greater degree of fraud protection.

**Ask Your Credit- or Debit-Card Company:** Before your trip, contact the company that issued your debit or credit cards.

Confirm that your **card will work overseas,** and alert them that you'll be using it in Europe; otherwise, they may deny transactions if they perceive unusual spending patterns.

Ask for the specifics on transaction **fees.** When you use your credit or debit card—either for purchases or ATM withdrawals—you'll typically be charged additional "international transaction" fees of up to 3 percent (1 percent is normal). If your card's fees seem high, consider getting a different card just for your trip: Capital One (www.capitalone.com) and most credit unions have low-to-no international fees.

Verify your daily ATM **withdrawal limit,** and if necessary, ask your bank to adjust it. I prefer a high limit that allows me to take out more cash at each ATM stop and save on bank fees; some travelers prefer to set a lower limit in case their card is stolen. Note that in Portugal, the maximum you can withdraw per transaction is €200.

Get your bank's emergency **phone number** in the US (but not its 800 number, which isn't accessible from overseas) to call collect if you have a problem.

Ask for your credit card's **PIN** in case you need to make an emergency cash withdrawal or encounter payment machines using the chip-and-PIN system; the bank won't tell you your PIN over the phone, so allow time for it to be mailed to you.

**Chip-and-PIN Credit Cards:** Europeans use chip-and-PIN credit cards (embedded with an electronic security chip and requiring a four-digit PIN). Most of the chip cards now being offered by major US banks are not true chip-and-PIN cards, but instead are chip-and-signature cards, so you'll be asked to sign a receipt rather than type in the PIN code. These cards work in Europe for live transactions and at most payment machines, but won't work for offline transactions such as at unattended gas pumps.

Older American cards with just a magnetic stripe also may not work at unattended payment machines, such as those at train and subway stations, toll plazas, parking garages, bike-rental kiosks, and gas pumps. If you have problems with either type of American card, try entering your card's PIN, look for a machine that takes cash, or find a clerk who can process the transaction manually.

If you're concerned, ask if your bank offers a true chip-and-PIN card. Andrews Federal Credit Union (www.andrewsfcu.org) and the State Department Federal Credit Union (www.sdfcu.org) offer these cards and are open to all US residents.

No matter what kind of card you have, it pays to carry euros; remember, you can always use an ATM to withdraw cash with your magnetic-stripe debit card.

**Dynamic Currency Conversion:** If merchants or hoteliers offer to convert your purchase price into dollars (called dynamic currency conversion, or DCC), refuse this "service." You'll pay extra for the expensive convenience of seeing your charge in dollars.

Some ATMs and retailers try to confuse customers by presenting DCC in misleading terms. If an ATM offers to "lock in" or "guarantee" your conversion rate, choose "proceed without conversion." Other prompts might state, "You can be charged in dollars: Press YES for dollars, NO for euros." Always choose the local currency.

## Damage Control for Lost Cards

If you lose your credit or debit card, you can stop people from using your card by reporting the loss immediately to the respective global customer-assistance centers. Call these 24-hour US numbers collect: Visa (tel. 303/967-1096), MasterCard (tel. 636/722-7111), and American Express (tel. 336/393-1111). In Portugal, to make a collect call to the US, dial 800-800-128. Press zero or stay on the line for an English-speaking operator. European toll-free numbers (listed by country) can be found at the websites for Visa and MasterCard.

If you are the secondary cardholder, you'll need to provide the primary cardholder's identification-verification details (such as birth date, mother's maiden name, or Social Security number). You can generally receive a temporary card within two or three business days in Europe (see www.ricksteves.com/help for more).

If you report your loss within two days, you typically won't be responsible for any unauthorized transactions on your account, although many banks charge a liability fee of $50.

## TIPPING

Tipping in Portugal isn't as automatic and generous as it is in the US. For special service, tips are appreciated, but not expected. As in the US, the proper amount depends on your resources, tipping philosophy, and the circumstances, but some general guidelines apply.

**Restaurants:** At cafés and restaurants, a service charge is included in the price of what you order. If you had good service, it's customary to leave up to 5 percent—or 10 percent for a splurge place. For details on tipping in restaurants, see "Eating," later.

**Taxis:** For a typical ride, round up your fare a bit (for instance, if the fare is €4.70, pay €5). If the cabbie hauls your bags and zips you to the airport to help you catch your flight, you might want to toss in a little more. But if you feel like you're being driven in circles or otherwise ripped off, skip the tip.

**Services:** In general, if someone in the tourism or service industry does a super job for you, a small tip of a euro or two is appropriate...but not required. If you're not sure whether (or how much) to tip, ask a local for advice.

## GETTING A VAT REFUND

Wrapped into the purchase price of your Portuguese souvenirs is a Value-Added Tax (VAT, called IVA or *Imposto sobre o Valor Acrescentado* in Portuguese) of about 23 percent. You're entitled to get most of that tax back if you purchase more than €61 (about $67) worth of goods at a store that participates in the VAT-refund scheme. Typically, you must ring up the minimum at a single retailer—you can't add up your purchases from various shops to reach the required amount.

Getting your refund is straightforward and, if you buy a substantial amount of souvenirs, well worth the hassle. (Note that if the store ships the goods to your US home, VAT is not assessed on your purchase.) You'll need to:

**Get the paperwork.** Have the merchant completely fill out the necessary refund document. You'll have to present your passport. Get the paperwork done before you leave the store to ensure you'll have everything you need (including your original sales receipt).

**Get your stamp at the border or airport.** Process your VAT document at your last stop in the European Union (such as at the airport) with the customs agent who deals with VAT refunds. Arrive an additional hour before you need to check in for your flight to allow time to find the local customs office—and to stand in line. It's best to keep your purchases in your carry-on. If they're too large or dangerous to carry on (such as knives), pack them in your checked bags and alert the check-in agent. You'll be sent (with your tagged bag) to a customs desk outside security; someone will examine your bag, stamp your paperwork, and put your bag on the belt. You're not supposed to use your purchased goods before you leave. If you show up at customs wearing your hand-knit Portuguese sweater, officials might look the other way—or deny you a refund.

**Collect your refund.** You'll need to return your stamped document to the retailer or its representative. Many merchants work with services, such as Global Blue or Premier Tax Free, that have offices at major airports, ports, or border crossings (either before or after security, probably strategically located near a duty-free shop). These services, which extract a 4 percent fee, can refund your money immediately in cash or credit your card (within two billing cycles). Other refund services may require you to mail the documents from home, or more quickly, from your point of departure (using an envelope you've prepared in advance or one that's been provided by the merchant). You'll then have to wait—it can take months.

## CUSTOMS FOR AMERICAN SHOPPERS

You are allowed to take home $800 worth of items per person duty-free, once every 31 days. You can take home many processed and packaged foods: vacuum-packed cheeses, dried herbs, jams, baked goods, candy, chocolate, oil, vinegar, mustard, and honey. Fresh fruits and vegetables and most meats are not allowed, with exceptions for some canned items. As for alcohol, you can bring in one liter duty-free (it can be packed securely in your checked luggage, along with any other liquid-containing items).

To bring alcohol (or liquid-packed foods) in your carry-on bag on your flight home, buy it at a duty-free shop at the airport. You'll increase your odds of getting it onto a connecting flight if it's packaged in a "STEB"—a secure, tamper-evident bag. But stay away from liquids in opaque, ceramic, or metallic containers, which usually cannot be successfully screened (STEB or no STEB).

For details on allowable goods, customs rules, and duty rates, visit http://help.cbp.gov.

# Sightseeing

Sightseeing can be hard work. Use these tips to make your visits to Portugal's finest sights meaningful, fun, efficient, and painless.

## MAPS AND NAVIGATION TOOLS

A good map is essential for efficient navigation while sightseeing. The maps in this book are concise and simple, designed to help you locate recommended destinations, sights, and local TIs, where you can pick up more in-depth maps. Maps with even more detail are sold at newsstands and bookstores.

You can also use a mapping app on your mobile device. Be aware that pulling up maps or looking up turn-by-turn walking directions on the fly requires an Internet connection: To use this feature, it's smart to get an international data plan (see page 420) or to only connect with Wi-Fi. With Google Maps or Apple Maps, it's possible to download a map while online, then go offline and navigate without incurring data-roaming charges, though you can't search for an address or get real-time walking directions. A handful of other apps—including City Maps 2Go, OffMaps, and Navfree—also allow you to use maps offline.

## PLAN AHEAD

Set up an itinerary that allows you to fit in all your top sights. For a one-stop look at opening hours in the big cities—Lisbon and Porto—see the "At a Glance" sidebars. Many sights keep stable hours, but—especially in Portugal—things change. It's smart to confirm the latest by checking with the TI or visiting museum websites.

Don't put off visiting a must-see sight—you never know when a place will close unexpectedly for a holiday, strike, or restoration. Many museums are closed or have reduced hours at least a few days a year, especially on holidays such as Christmas, New Year's, and Labor Day (May 1). A list of holidays is on page 440; check online for possible museum closures during your trip. In summer, some sights may stay open late; in the off-season, hours may be shorter.

Going at the right time helps avoid crowds. This book offers tips on the best times to see specific sights. Try visiting popular sights very early or very late. Evening visits are usually peaceful, with fewer crowds.

Study up. To get the most out of the sight descriptions in this book, read them before you visit.

## AT SIGHTS

Here's what you can typically expect:

**Entering:** Be warned that you may not be allowed to enter if you arrive less than 30 to 60 minutes before closing time. And guards start ushering people out well before the actual closing time, so don't save the best for last.

Many sights have a security check, where you must open your bag or send it through a metal detector. Allow extra time for these lines in your planning. Some sights require you to check daypacks and coats. (If you'd rather not check your daypack, try carrying it tucked under your arm like a purse as you enter.)

At churches—which often offer interesting art (usually free) and a cool, welcome seat—a modest dress code (no bare shoulders or shorts) is encouraged though rarely enforced.

**Photography:** If the museum's photo policy isn't clearly posted, ask a guard. Generally, taking photos without a flash or tripod is allowed. Some sights ban photos altogether; others ban selfie sticks.

**Temporary Exhibits:** Museums may show special exhibits in addition to their permanent collection. Some exhibits are included in the entry price, while others come at an extra cost (which you may have to pay even if you don't want to see the exhibit).

**Expect Changes:** Artwork can be on tour, on loan, out sick, or shifted at the whim of the curator. Pick up a floor plan as you enter, and ask museum staff if you can't find a particular item.

**Audioguides and Apps:** Many sights rent audioguides, which generally offer sometimes useful recorded descriptions in English (about €3-6, often included with admission). If you bring your own earbuds, you can enjoy better sound and avoid holding the device to your ear. To save money, bring a Y-jack and share one audioguide with your travel partner. Museums and sights often offer free apps that you can download to your mobile device (check their websites). And, I've produced a free, downloadable Lisbon City Walk audio tour; look for the 🎧 in this book. For more on my audio tours, see page 9.

**Services:** Important sights may have a reasonably priced on-site café or cafeteria (handy places to rejuvenate during a long visit). The WCs at sights are free and generally clean.

**Before Leaving:** At the gift shop, scan the postcard rack or thumb through a guidebook to be sure that you haven't overlooked something that you'd like to see.

Every sight or museum offers more than what is covered in this book. Use the information in this book as an introduction—not the final word.

# Sleeping

I favor hotels that are handy to your sightseeing activities. Rather than list accommodations scattered throughout a city, I choose hotels in my favorite neighborhoods. My recommendations run the gamut, from dorm beds to fancy rooms with all of the comforts.

Extensive and opinionated listings of good-value rooms are a major feature of this book's Sleeping sections. I like places that are clean, central, relatively quiet at night, reasonably priced, friendly,

## Sleep Code

Hotels are classified based on the average price of a standard double room with breakfast in high season.

| | |
|---|---|
| **$$$$** | **Splurge:** Most rooms over €150 |
| **$$$** | **Pricier:** €100-150 |
| **$$** | **Moderate:** €70-100 |
| **$** | **Budget:** €40-70 |
| **¢** | **Backpacker:** Under €40 |
| **RS%** | **Rick Steves discount** |

Unless otherwise noted, credit cards are accepted, hotel staff speaks basic English, and free Wi-Fi is available. Comparison-shop by checking prices at several hotels (on each hotel's own website, on a booking site, or by email). For the best deal, *book directly with the hotel*. Ask for a discount if paying in cash; if the listing includes **RS%,** request a Rick Steves discount.

small enough to have a hands-on owner or manager and stable staff, and run with a respect for Portuguese traditions. I'm more impressed by a convenient location and a fun-loving philosophy than flat-screen TVs and a fancy gym. Most places I recommend fall short of perfection. But if I can find a place with most of these features, it's a keeper.

Book your accommodations well in advance, especially if you want to stay at one of my top listings or if you'll be traveling during busy times. See page 440 for a list of major holidays and festivals in Portugal; for tips on making reservations, see page 406.

Some people make reservations as they travel, calling hotels a few days to a week before their arrival. If you anticipate crowds (weekends are worst) on the day you want to check in, call hotels at about 9:00 or 10:00, when the receptionist knows who'll be checking out and which rooms will be available. If you encounter a language barrier, ask the fluent receptionist at your current hotel to call for you.

### RATES AND DEALS

I've categorized my recommended accommodations based on price, indicated with a dollar-sign rating (see sidebar). The price ranges suggest an estimated cost for a one-night stay in a standard double room with a private toilet and shower in high season, include breakfast, and assume you're booking directly with the hotel (not through a booking site, which extracts a commission and logically closes the door on special deals). Room prices can fluctuate significantly with demand and amenities (size, views, room class, and so on), but these relative price categories remain constant. Taxes,

PRACTICALITIES

# Making Hotel Reservations

Reserve your rooms several weeks or even months in advance—or as soon as you've pinned down your travel dates, particularly for Lisbon. Note that some national holidays and religious festivals like the Fátima pilgrimage merit your making reservations far in advance (see page 440).

**Requesting a Reservation:** It's easiest to book your room through the hotel's website. (For the best rates, use the hotel's official site and not a booking agency's site.) If there's no reservation form, or for complicated requests, send an email. Most recommended hotels take reservations in English.

The hotelier wants to know:

- the size of your party and type of rooms you need
- your arrival and departure dates, written European-style—day followed by month and year (for example, 18/06/18 or 18 June 2018); include the total number of nights
- special requests (such as en suite bathroom vs. down the hall, cheapest room, twin beds vs. double bed, quiet room)
- applicable discounts (such as a Rick Steves reader discount, cash discount, or promotional rate)

**Confirming a Reservation:** Most places will request a credit-card number to hold your room. If they don't have a secure online reservation form—look for the *https*—you can email it (I do), but it's safer to share that confidential info via a phone call or fax.

**Canceling a Reservation:** If you must cancel, it's courteous—and smart—to do so with as much notice as possible, especially for smaller family-run places. Cancellation policies can be strict;

which can vary from place to place, are generally insignificant (a dollar or two per person, per night).

Room rates are especially volatile at larger hotels that use "dynamic pricing" to predict demand. Rates can skyrocket during festivals and conventions, while business hotels can have deep discounts on weekends when demand plummets. For this reason, of the many hotels I recommend, it's difficult to say which will be the best value on a given day—until you do your homework.

Once your dates are set, check the specific price for your preferred stay at several hotels. You can do this either by comparing prices online on the hotels' own websites, or by emailing several hotels directly and asking for their best rate. Even if you start your search on a booking site such as TripAdvisor or Booking.com, you'll usually find the lowest rates through a hotel's own website.

Many hotels offer a discount to those who pay cash or stay longer than three nights. To cut costs further, try asking for a cheaper room (for example, with a shared bathroom or no window) or offer to skip breakfast.

| From: | rick@ricksteves.com |
| --- | --- |
| Sent: | Today |
| To: | info@hotelcentral.com |
| Subject: | Reservation request for 19-22 July |

Dear Hotel Central,

I would like to stay at your hotel. Please let me know if you have a room available and the price for:
• 2 people
• Double bed and en suite bathroom in a quiet room
• Arriving 19 July, departing 22 July (3 nights)

Thank you!
Rick Steves

read the fine print or ask about these before you book. Many discount deals require prepayment, with no cancellation refunds.

**Reconfirming Your Reservation:** Always call to reconfirm your room reservation a few days in advance. For B&Bs or very small hotels, I call again on my day of arrival to tell my host what time I expect to get there (especially important if arriving late—after 17:00).

**Phoning:** For tips on calling hotels overseas, see page 422.

Additionally, some accommodations offer a special discount for Rick Steves readers, indicated in this guidebook by the abbreviation "**RS%.**" Discounts vary: Ask for details when you book. Generally, to qualify you must book direct (that is, not through a booking site), mention this book when you reserve, show the book upon arrival, and sometimes pay cash or stay a certain number of nights. In some cases, you may need to enter a discount code (which I've provided in the listing) in the booking form on the hotel's website. Rick Steves discounts apply to readers with ebooks as well as printed books. Understandably, discounts do not apply to promotional rates.

## TYPES OF ACCOMMODATIONS
### Hotels
Double rooms listed in this book range from $60 (very simple, toilet and shower down the hall) to $300 suites (maximum plumbing and more), with most clustering around $120. Most hotels also offer single rooms, and some offer larger rooms for four or more

---

## Keep Cool

If you're visiting Portugal in the summer, an air-conditioned room can be essential, particularly in the south. Most hotel rooms with air-conditioners come with a control stick (like a TV remote; the hotel may require a deposit) that generally has similar symbols and features: fan icon (click to toggle through wind power, from light to gale); louver icon (choose steady airflow or waves); snowflake and sunshine icons (cold air or heat, depending on season); clock ("O" setting: run X hours before turning off; "I" setting: wait X hours to start); and the temperature control (20 degrees Celsius is comfortable; also see the thermometer diagram on page 444). When you leave your room for the day, turning off the air-conditioning is good form.

---

people (I call these "family rooms" in the listings). Some hotels can add an extra bed (for a small charge) to turn a double into a triple. In general, a triple room is cheaper than the cost of a double and a single. Traveling alone can be expensive: A single room can be close to the cost of a double. Breakfast is generally included (sometimes continental, but often buffet).

As a budget alternative in Portugal, I also list several simple, family-run hotels (listed as a *pensão* or *residencial*); they're easy to find, inexpensive, and, when chosen properly, a fun part of the Portuguese cultural experience.

Hotels can sometimes occupy one floor of a building with a finicky vintage elevator or slightly dingy entryway (addresses such as "26-3" indicate a building at #26, on the third floor). The hotelier doesn't control the common areas of the building, so try not to let the entryway atmosphere color your opinion of the hotel. Hotel elevators, while becoming more common, are often very small—pack light. You may need to send your bags up one at a time.

If you're arriving in the morning, your room probably won't be ready. Check your bag safely at the hotel and dive right into sightseeing.

Hoteliers can be a good source of advice. Most know their city well, and can assist you with everything from public transit and airport connections to finding a good restaurant, the nearest launderette, or a late-night pharmacy.

Even at the best places, mechanical breakdowns occur: Sinks leak, hot water turns cold, toilets may gurgle or smell, the Wi-Fi goes out, or the air-conditioning dies when you need it most. Report your concerns clearly and calmly at the front desk. For more complicated problems, don't expect instant results. Any regulated hotel will have a complaint book *(livro de reclamações)*, which is checked by authorities. A request for this book will generally prompt the hotelier to solve your problem to keep you from writing a complaint.

In Portugal, street noise can be high. If you find that noise is a problem (if, for instance, your room is over a nightclub), ask for a quieter room in the back or on an upper floor. You can request a room *com vista* (with a view) or *tranquilo* (quiet), but in most cases, the view comes with street noise.

To guard against theft in your room, keep valuables out of sight. Some rooms come with a safe, and other hotels have safes at the front desk. I've never bothered using one.

While it's customary to pay for your room upon departure, it can be a good idea to settle your bill the day before, when you're not in a hurry and while the manager's in. That way you'll have time to discuss and address any points of contention.

Above all, keep a positive attitude. Remember, you're on vacation. If your hotel is a disappointment, spend more time out enjoying the place you came to see.

## Historic Inns

Portugal has luxurious, government-sponsored historic inns. These *pousadas* are often renovated castles, palaces, or monasteries, many

with great views and stately atmospheres. While full of Old World character, they often are run in a very sterile, bureaucratic way, and can have faded furnishings that are a bit worn for the price range. These are pricey ($250-500 doubles), but can be a good deal for younger people (30 and under) and seniors (55 and over), who often get discounted rates; for details, bonus packages, and family deals, see www.pousadas.pt.

## Rooms in Private Homes *(Quartos)*

In touristy resorts—especially beach towns like Nazaré and Salema—you'll typically find locals who've opened up a spare room to make a little money on the side. Usually fairly private and often located in small, apartment-type buildings, a *quarto* (KWAR-too; also known as an *alojamento particular*) is less expensive than a hotel ($45-75 for a double without breakfast). In Nazaré and Salema, you can stumble into town virtu-

# The Good and Bad of Online Reviews

User-generated review sites and apps such as Yelp, Booking. com, and TripAdvisor are changing the travel industry. These sites can give you a consensus of opinions about everything from hotels and restaurants to sights and nightlife. If you scan reviews of a hotel and see several complaints about noise or a rotten location, it tells you something important that you'd never learn from the hotel's own website.

Review sites are only as good as the judgment of their reviewers. While these sites work to weed out bogus users, my hunch is that a significant percentage of user reviews are posted by friends or enemies of the business being reviewed. Ignore low and high grades. Focus on the median.

As a guidebook writer, my sense is that there is a big difference between this uncurated information and a guidebook. A user-generated review is based on the experience of one person, who likely stayed at one hotel and ate at a few restaurants, and doesn't have much of a basis for comparison. A guidebook is the work of a trained researcher who visited many alternatives to assess their relative value. I recently checked out some top-rated user-reviewed hotel and restaurant listings in various towns; when stacked up against their competitors, some were gems, while just as many were duds. Both types of information have their place, and in many ways, they're complementary. If something is well-reviewed in a guidebook, and also gets good ratings on one of these sites, it's likely a winner.

ally any day (except August weekends) and find countless women hanging out on the streets with rooms to rent. Or just ask around town, at any bar. If you have the nerve to travel without reservations, this is an excellent budget deal. Have fun looking at several places, then hem and haw until the price goes down. Your room is likely to be large and homey, with old-time-elegant furnishings (and the bathroom down the hall). *Quarto* landladies generally speak only a little English, but they're used to dealing with visitors. Given that the boss changes the sheets, people staying several nights are most desirable; one-night stays sometimes cost extra, and in the busy summer months there could be a minimum-night stay.

## Short-Term Rentals

A short-term rental—whether an apartment, house, or room in a local's home—is an increasingly popular alternative to a guesthouse or hotel, especially if you plan to settle in one location for several nights. For stays longer than a few days, you can usually find a rental that's comparable to—or even cheaper than—a hotel room with similar amenities. Plus, you'll get a behind-the-scenes peek into how locals live.

The rental route isn't for everyone. Many places require a minimum night stay, and compared to hotels, rentals usually have less-flexible cancellation policies. Also you're generally on your own: There's no hotel reception desk, breakfast, or daily cleaning service.

**Finding Accommodations:** Websites such as www.airbnb.com, www.roomorama.com, and www.vrbo.com let you browse properties and correspond directly with European property owners or managers. Or, for more guidance, consider using a rental agency such as www.interhomeusa.com or www.rentavilla.com. Agency-represented apartments may cost more, but this route often offers more help and safeguards than booking direct.

Before you commit to a rental, be clear on the details, location, and amenities. I like to virtually "explore" the neighborhood using the Street View feature on Google Maps. Also consider the proximity to public transportation, and how well-connected it is with the rest of the city. Ask about amenities that are important to you (elevator, laundry, coffee maker, Wi-Fi, parking, etc.). Reading reviews from previous guests can help identify trouble spots that are glossed over in the official description.

**Apartments:** If you're staying somewhere for four nights or longer, it's worth considering an apartment or rental house (anything less than that isn't worth the extra effort involved, such as arranging key pickup, buying groceries, etc.). Apartment or house rentals can be especially cost-effective for groups and families. European apartments, like hotel rooms, tend to be small by US standards. But they often come with laundry machines and small, equipped kitchens, making it easier and cheaper to dine in. If you make good use of the kitchen (and Europe's great produce markets), you'll save on your meal budget.

**Private and Shared Rooms:** Renting a room in someone's home is a good option for those traveling alone, as you're more likely to find true single rooms—with just one single bed, and a price to match. Beds range from air-mattress-in-living-room basic to plush-B&B-suite posh. Some places allow you to book for a single night; if staying for several nights, you can buy groceries just as you would in a rental house. While you can't expect your host to also be your tour guide—or even to provide you with much info—some may be interested in getting to know the travelers who come through their home.

**Other Options:** Swapping homes with a local works for people with an appealing place to offer, and who can live with the idea of having strangers in their home (don't assume where you live is not interesting to Europeans). A good place to start is HomeExchange (www.homeexchange.com).

PRACTICALITIES

To sleep for free, Couchsurfing.com is a vagabond's alternative to Airbnb. It lists millions of outgoing members, who host fellow "surfers" in their homes.

## Hostels

A hostel provides cheap beds where you sleep alongside strangers for about $30 per night. Travelers of any age are welcome if they don't mind dorm-style accommodations and meeting other travelers. Most hostels offer kitchen facilities, guest computers, Wi-Fi, and a self-service laundry. Hostels almost always provide bedding, but the towel's up to you (though you can usually rent one for a small fee). Family and private rooms are often available.

**Independent hostels** tend to be easygoing, colorful, and informal (no membership required; www.hostelworld.com). You may pay slightly less by booking direct with the hostel.

**Official hostels** are part of Hostelling International (HI) and share an online booking site (www.hihostels.com). HI hostels typically require that you be a member or pay extra per night.

Portugal has plenty of youth hostels, but considering the great bargains on other accommodations, I don't cover many in this book except for the stylish "design hostels" that are a Lisbon specialty. Big, convivial, and professional, these often have private rooms and appeal even to people who would normally choose a hotel (see the Lisbon chapter).

# Eating

The Portuguese meal schedule is slightly later than in the US. Breakfast *(pequeno almoço)* is often just coffee and a sweet roll. Lunch *(almoço)* is served between 12:30 and 14:00, while supper *(jantar)* is from about 19:30 to 21:30. You can eat well in mom-and-pop restaurants for about €10, especially outside Lisbon. All restaurants are smoke-free.

**Appetizers Aren't Free:** One of the most important things to remember when eating in Portugal is that appetizers (olives, bread, butter, pâtés, and a veritable minibuffet of other tasty temptations) brought to your table before you order are not free. If you don't want them, push them to the side or ask the server to take them back—you won't be charged for what you don't touch. But taking just one olive means you pay for the whole dish. Simple appetizers usually cost about €1 each, so it won't break the budget—just don't be surprised at extra charges on your bill. And it's smart to be aware of this in unscrupulous, tourist-oriented restaurants, which may use overpriced appetizers to pad the bill.

**Portions:** Many restaurants save their customers money by portioning their dishes for two people. Menus often list prices for

---

## Restaurant Price Code

I've assigned each eatery a price category, based on the average cost of a typical main course. Drinks, desserts, and splurge items (steak and seafood) can raise the price considerably.

**$$$$**    **Splurge:** Most main courses over €17

**$$$**    **Pricier:** €12-17

**$$**    **Moderate:** €7-12

**$**    **Budget:** Under €7

In Portugal, takeout food is **$**; a basic sit-down eatery is **$$**; a casual but more upscale restaurant is **$$$**; and a swanky splurge is **$$$$**.

---

entrées in two columns: *dose* and *meia dose*. A *dose* (DOH-zeh) is generally enough to feed two, while a *meia dose* is a half-portion (plenty for one person). Restaurants have absolutely no problem with diners splitting a single *dose*. *Prato do dia* is the daily special.

**Paying and Tipping:** When you want the bill, say, *"A conta, por favor."* Most mom-and-pop restaurateurs will figure the bill in front of you, so everyone agrees on the final amount to be paid.

In nearly all restaurants, service is included—your menu typically will indicate this by noting *serviço incluído*. Still, if you are pleased with the service, it's customary to leave up to 5 percent, or 10 percent for top-notch service or in a fancy place. Leave the tip on the table. It's best to tip in cash, even if you pay with your credit card (there's generally not a place to include a tip on a credit card slip). There's no need to tip if you order food at a counter.

**PRACTICALITIES**

## RESTAURANT PRICING

I've categorized my recommended eateries based on price, indicated with a dollar-sign rating (see sidebar). The price ranges suggest the average price of a typical main course—but not necessarily a complete meal. Obviously, expensive items (like steak and seafood), fine wine, appetizers, and dessert can significantly increase your final bill.

The dollar-sign categories also indicate the overall personality and "feel" of a place:

**$ Budget** eateries include street food, takeaway, order-at-the-counter shops, basic cafeterias, and bakeries selling sandwiches.

**$$ Moderate** eateries are typically nice (but not fancy) sit-down restaurants, ideal for a straightforward, fill-the-tank meal. Most of my listings fall in this category—great for getting a good taste of the local cuisine on a budget.

**$$$ Pricier** eateries are a notch up, with more attention paid to the setting, presentation, and cuisine. These are ideal for a memorable meal that's relatively casual and doesn't break the bank. This category often includes affordable "destination" or "foodie" restaurants.

**$$$$ Splurge** eateries are dress-up-for-a-special-occasion-swanky—Michelin star-type restaurants, typically with an elegant setting, polished service, pricey and intricate cuisine, and an expansive (and expensive) wine list.

I haven't categorized places where you could assemble a picnic, snack, or graze: supermarkets, delis, ice cream-stands, cafés or bars specializing in drinks, chocolate shops, and so on.

## WHERE AND WHAT TO EAT

When restaurant-hunting, choose a spot filled with locals, not the place with the big neon signs boasting, "We Speak English and Accept Credit Cards." Venturing even a block or two off the main drag leads to higher-quality food for less than half the price of the tourist-oriented places. Locals eat better at lower-rent locales.

For a quick, cheap snack, drop by a bar or café. Bars offer an enticing selection of savory treats on display, such as codfish cakes *(pastéis de bacalhau)*. Sandwiches *(sandes)* are everywhere.

Cafés also offer snacks and are usually cheaper than bars. Many cafés double as lunch joints, which locals frequent. If you see a menu written on a paper tablecloth and taped in the window, you can be assured of a quick, home-cooked meal. Just don't expect a fancy presentation (and be willing to share a table with a stranger—don't worry, it makes for great conversation).

**Seafood:** Eat fresh seafood as much as you can in Portugal (except on Monday, when the fish isn't fresh—the fishermen take Sunday off). The Portuguese are among the world's biggest fish eaters. *Bacalhau*—codfish that's dried, salted, and then rehydrated and served a reputed 365 different ways—is arguably the national dish, but definitely an acquired taste. (Strangely, the codfish aren't found in Portugal's coastal waters, but are fished in the North Atlantic.) Try *bacalhau à Brás*, a sort of cod frittata with potatoes, onions, and herbs. Fish soup *(sopa de peixe)* and shellfish soup *(sopa de mariscos)* are worth seeking out. Or, for a seafood blowout, look for *cataplana* (a feast from the sea, simmered in a copper pot). For something simpler, grilled sardines *(sardinhas grelhadas)* are popular, especially at touristy restaurants. And for a mix of seafood and land food, *carne de porco à Alentejana* is an interesting combination of pork and clams—and Portugal's unique contribution to world cuisine.

PRACTICALITIES

The Portuguese also adore *conservas*—canned ("conserved") fish and other seafood, often marinated with olive oil and spices (such as pepper, oregano, tomatoes, fennel, or red pepper). You'll see tinned sardines, mackerel, tuna, salmon, and even octopus. These tend to be less salty or pungent than canned fish back home—give it a try. The Portuguese also have a knack for decorating the tins with colorful and creative artwork, making a walk through a *conservas* shop a feast for the eyes as well. Aficionados say that the best brand for sardines is Briosa, while Santa Catarina (from the Azores) has the best tuna. Some simple eateries sell cans of fish for you to open up at a table with some fresh bread...a satisfying (and very local) light lunch.

**Other Dishes:** Popular dishes include *caldo verde* (vegetable soup), *alheira* (smoked sausage made without pork), and *frango assado* (roast chicken). The African-inspired *piri-piri* sauce—oil infused with hot chilis—is a treat if you like it hot and spicy. Don't confuse *piri-piri* with *pica pau*, a flavorful white-wine sauce with lots of garlic and bay, often served with stewed beef.

Speaking of garlic, Portuguese chefs aren't afraid of that pungent flavor. They also tend to go heavy on the salt, and many dishes come with a fresh, sweet punch of herbs—especially cilantro, parsley, and bay leaf.

Like their Spanish neighbors, the Portuguese use plenty of olive oil, love their air-cured ham (called *presunto*; *porco preto*—from black *ibérico* pigs in Alentejo—is tops), and produce some delicious cheeses (the top-quality *Serra da Estrela* is worth seeking out).

Potatoes and greens are popular side dishes. Portugal also has a variety of hearty and delicious rice-based dishes, including *arroz de tomate* (like a tomato risotto), *arroz de pato* (savory rice with roasted duck and chorizo), and the paella-like *arroz de mariscos*. Carbs never went out of style in Portugal—it's common to get both potatoes and rice with a meal.

**Desserts:** For dessert, a standard, wonderful local pastry is the custard tart, *pastel de nata* (called *pastel de Belém* in Lisbon's fancy

suburb of the same name). You'll also find various concoctions made from egg yolk and sugar, such as *barriga de freiras* ("nuns' belly") and *papo de anjo* ("angel's double chin").

**Colonial Influences:** The Portuguese have a special affinity for tropical fruits—thanks both to their own warm-weather outposts (Madeira and the Azores) and their former tropical colonies. You'll see more kiwi, passionfruit, papaya, mango, and guava here than in most of Europe. Fresh-squeezed orange juice (from Algarve-grown fruit) is also very popular...and delicious. Other culinary holdovers from Portugal's colonial days include spicy *piri-piri* sauce (described above), palm oil, and the powerful rum-like sugarcane firewater from Cape Verde, called simply *grogue*.

## Meat and Seafood

*Alheira:* Pork-free smoked sausage

*Bacalhau:* Dried, salted cod that's rehydrated and prepared in many different ways

*Bacalhau à Brás:* Salt cod and matchstick potatoes scrambled with egg

*Carne de porco à Alentejana:* Stewed pork covered with clams

*Conservas:* Canned fish, marinated with olive oil and spices

*Frango assado:* Roast chicken, commonly served with *piri-piri* hot sauce

*Percebes:* Barnacles

*Porco preto:* Air-cured ham from *ibérico* pigs

*Presunto:* Air-cured ham

*Sardinhas grelhadas:* Fresh sardines, grilled or barbecued

*Tripas a modo do Porto:* Tripe served Porto-style

## Rice, Soups, and Stews

*Arroz de mariscos:* Rice and mixed seafood stew ("Portuguese paella")

*Arroz de pato:* Duck and chorizo paella

*Caldeirada de peixe:* Like *cataplana* (see below), but cooked in a casserole

*Caldo verde:* "Green" soup of kale and potato puree

*Cataplana:* Seafood and potatoes cooked in a copper pot

*Feijoada:* Pork and bean stew

*Sopa Alentejana:* Garlic soup with a poached egg, cilantro, and bread crumbs

*Sopa de mariscos:* Shellfish soup

*Sopa de peixe:* Fish soup

## Sandwiches and Snacks

*Apertivos:* Appetizers

*Batatas fritas:* Potato chips

*Bifana:* Pork sandwich

*Francesinha:* Literally "little French girl," a sandwich of pork, sausage, and cheese, grilled and topped with more melted cheese and a spicy sauce

*Pastéis de bacalhau:* Codfish fritters

*Petiscos:* Portuguese-style tapas—cured meats, cheeses, olives

*Prego:* Steak sandwich

*Sandes de leitão:* Suckling-pig sandwich
*Tosta mista:* Grilled ham and cheese sandwich

## Desserts
*Arroz doce:* Rice pudding with cinnamon
*Barriga de freiras* ("nuns' belly"): Convent sweet made with egg yolks and sugar
*Charcada:* Eggy-almond pudding-like dessert
*Papo de anjo* ("angel's double chin")*:* Convent sweet made from beaten egg yolks that are baked, then boiled in a sugar syrup
*Pastel de nata:* Custard tart
*Pastel de Santa Clara:* Almond and marmalade pastry
*Pastel de Tentúgal:* Puff pastry dusted with powdered sugar
*Pudim:* Flan
*Queque:* Muffin
*Salame de chocolate:* Dark chocolate and broken cookies rolled into a salami-shaped log that's sliced for serving

## PORTUGUESE BEVERAGES
### Wine, Beer, and Spirits
Despite its small size, Portugal is among the world's top wine producers—bottling more than 150 million gallons in a good year. And Portuguese wines are cheap, decent, and distinctively fruity.

*Vinho verde* (VEEN-yoo VAIR-day) is light, refreshing, almost always white, and can be slightly fizzy. This "green wine" is actually golden in color, but "green" (young) in age—picked, made, and drunk within a year. *Alvarinho* grapes, from the northern Minho region, are low-sugar and high-acid. After the initial fermentation, winemakers introduce a second fermentation, whose byproduct is carbon dioxide—the light fizz. The wines are somewhat bitter alone, but great with meals, especially seafood. The best are from Monaco Amarante and Aveleda, but the one you'll see on every menu is the perfectly acceptable Casal Garcia. If you like white *vinho verde,* you might enjoy the harder-to-find red version. It's dark in color, like a cabernet, but still fizzy and light in flavor, like a rosé—a unique combination.

The Dão region also produces fine red wines, mostly from the Mondego Valley between Coimbra, Guarda, and Viseu. They should sit for a year or two in the bottle before drinking.

The Alentejo region (look for bottles labeled "Borba," a major producer) is known for high-quality reds that tend to be full-bodied and fruit-forward; the Alentejo is increasingly producing good whites as well. And the Douro Valley—best known as the place where grapes for port are grown—has recently earned an equally strong reputation for its table wines (look for *vinho do Douro*). If you find yourself drowning in choices, simply try a glass of the house wine *(vinho da casa)*.

If you like port wine, what better place to sample it than its birthplace, Port-ugal? (For a crash course on port wine, see page 348.) *Reserva* on the label means it's the best-quality port (and the most expensive). All bottles of port should have a *selo de garantia* (a seal of guarantee) issued by the Port Wine Institute.

Madeira, made from grapes grown in volcanic soil in the Madeira Islands, is fortified and blended (as is port), and usually served as a sweet dessert wine. The English and George Washington both liked it ("Have some Madeira, m'dear"), though today's version is drier and less syrupy. A Madeira called *Sercial* is served chilled (like sherry) with almonds.

The favorite Portuguese spirit is *ginjinha*, a liqueur made with the sour cherry-like *ginja* berry. You'll see shops selling shots on the street (particularly in Óbidos, where it's traditionally sold in tiny, delicate, edible chocolate cups). To take a bottle home, look for the widely available brands Espinheira or Sem Rival; for something a notch better, look for Ginja MSR.

Beer *(cerveja)* is also popular—for a small draft beer, ask for *uma imperial*. You'll see Super Bock in the north, and Sagres in the south—the Bud and Miller of Portugal. Each also produces versions that are dark *(preta)*, nonalcoholic *(sem álcool)*, or both.

Here are some common drinking terms:

*Aguardente:* Firewater distilled from grape seeds, stems, and skins, with a kick like a mule

*Cerveja:* Beer

*Ginjinha:* Sour-cherry liqueur, served at special bars in Lisbon and Óbidos

*Grogue:* Strong spirits from Cape Verde, derived from sugarcane

*Imperial:* Small draft beer

*Vinho da casa:* House wine

*Vinho branco:* White wine

*Vinho tinto:* Red wine

*Vinho verde:* "green" wine (young, white wine)

## Water, Coffee, and Other Nonalcoholic Drinks

Freshly squeezed orange juice *(sumo de laranja)*, mineral water *(água mineral)*, and soft drinks are widely available. When ordering water, fizzy or not, you will be asked, *"Fresco o natural?"* Fresco is chilled, and *natural* is room temperature.

Coffee lovers enjoy a *café*, the very aromatic shot of espresso so popular in Portugal. In Lisbon this is called a *bica*. For an espresso with a little milk (like a *caffé macchiato*), ask for a *café pingado*.

Here are some useful beverage phrases:

*Abatanado:* Black coffee

*Água da torneira:* Tap water

*Água com/sem gás:* Water with/without bubbles

*Água mineral:* Mineral water

*Bica:* Espresso (Lisbon)

*Café:* Espresso

*Café pingado:* Espresso with a little milk, similar to a *caffé macchiato*

*Chá:* Tea

*Fresco:* Chilled

*Galão:* Coffee drink similar to a latte, served in a tall glass and often sweetened

*Leite:* Milk

*Meia de leite:* Coffee with warm milk

*Natural:* Room temperature

*Sumo:* Juice

*Sumo de laranja:* Orange juice

# Staying Connected

One of the most common questions I hear from travelers is, "How can I stay connected in Europe?" The short answer is: more easily and cheaply than you might think.

The simplest solution is to bring your own device—mobile phone, tablet, or laptop—and use it just as you would at home (following the tips below, such as connecting to free Wi-Fi whenever possible). Another option is to buy a European SIM card for your mobile phone—either your US phone or one you buy in Europe. Or you can travel without a mobile device and use European landlines and computers to connect. Each of these options is described below; more details are at www.ricksteves.com/phoning. For a very practical one-hour lecture covering tech issues for travelers, see www.ricksteves.com/travel-talks.

## USING YOUR OWN MOBILE DEVICE IN EUROPE

Without an international plan, typical rates from major service providers (AT&T, Verizon, etc.) for using your device abroad are about $1.70/minute for voice calls, 50 cents to send text messages, 5 cents to receive them, and $10 to download one megabyte of data. At these rates, costs can add up quickly. Here are some budget tips and options:

**Use free Wi-Fi whenever possible.** Unless you have an unlimited-data plan, it's best to save most of your online tasks for

# Hurdling the Language Barrier

Many Portuguese people—especially those in the tourist trade and in big cities—speak English. And, in general, the Portuguese speak more English than their Spanish neighbors, since English is required in school. (Their American movies are also subtitled, while the Spanish get their Hollywood flicks dubbed.) But locals will visibly brighten when you know and use some key Portuguese phrases (see "Portuguese Survival Phrases" on page 447). You'll find that doors open more quickly and with more smiles when you can speak a few words of the language.

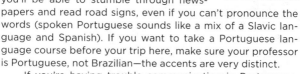

If you speak intermediate Spanish, you'll be able to stumble through newspapers and read road signs, even if you can't pronounce the words (spoken Portuguese sounds like a mix of a Slavic language and Spanish). If you want to take a Portuguese language course before your trip here, make sure your professor is Portuguese, not Brazilian—the accents are very distinct.

If you're having trouble communicating in Portuguese, try English, French, and Spanish, in that order (because some locals give Spanish speakers the cold shoulder).

Wi-Fi. You can access the Internet, send texts, and make voice calls over Wi-Fi.

Many cafés (including Starbucks and McDonald's) have free hotspots for customers; look for signs offering it and ask for the Wi-Fi password when you buy something. You'll also often find Wi-Fi at TIs, city squares, major museums, public-transit hubs, airports, and aboard trains and buses.

**Sign up for an international plan.** Most providers offer a global calling plan that cuts the per-minute cost of phone calls and texts, and a flat-fee data plan. Your normal plan may already include international coverage (T-Mobile's does).

Before your trip, call your provider or check online to confirm that your phone will work in Europe, and research your provider's international rates. Activate the plan a day or two before you leave, then remember to cancel it when your trip's over.

**Minimize the use of your cellular network.** When you can't find Wi-Fi, you can use your cellular network to connect to the Internet, text, or make voice calls. When you're done, avoid further charges by manually switching off "data roaming" or "cellular data" (in your device's Settings menu; for help, ask your service provider or Google it). Another way to make sure you're not accidentally using data roaming is to put your device in "airplane" or "flight"

## Tips on Internet Security

Using the Internet while traveling brings added security risks, whether you're getting online with your own device or at a public terminal using a shared network. Here are some tips for securing your data:

First, make sure that your device is running the latest version of its operating system and security software, and that your apps are up-to-date. Next, ensure that your device is password- or passcode-protected so thieves can't access it if your device is stolen. For extra security, set passwords on apps that access key info (such as email or Facebook).

On the road, use only legitimate Wi-Fi hotspots. Ask the hotel or café staff for the specific name of their Wi-Fi network, and make sure you log on to that exact one. Hackers sometimes create a bogus hotspot with a similar or vague name (such as "Hotel Europa Free Wi-Fi"). The best Wi-Fi networks require a password. If you're not actively using a hotspot, turn off your device's Wi-Fi connection so it's not visible to others.

Be especially cautious when accessing financial information online. Experts say it's best to use a banking app rather than sign in to your bank's website via a browser (the app is less likely to get hacked). Refrain from logging in to any personal finance sites on a public computer. Even if you're using your own mobile device at a password-protected hotspot, there's a remote chance that a hacker who's logged on to the same network could see what you're doing.

Never share your credit-card number (or any other sensitive information) online unless you know that the site is secure. A secure site displays a little padlock icon, and the URL begins with *https* (instead of the usual *http*).

mode (which also disables phone calls and texts), and then turn on Wi-Fi as needed.

Don't use your cellular network for bandwidth-gobbling tasks, such as Skyping, downloading apps, and streaming video: Save these for when you're on Wi-Fi. Using a navigation app such as Google Maps over a cellular network can take lots of data, so do this sparingly or use it offline.

Limit automatic updates. By default, your device constantly checks for a data connection and updates apps. It's smart to disable these features so your apps will only update when you're on Wi-Fi, and to change your device's email settings from "auto-retrieve" to "manual" (or from "push" to "fetch").

It's also a good idea to keep track of your data usage. On your device's menu, look for "cellular data usage" or "mobile data" and reset the counter at the start of your trip.

**Use Skype or other calling/messaging apps for cheaper calls and texts.** Certain apps let you make voice or video calls or send

# How to Dial

## International Calls

Whether phoning from a US landline or mobile phone, or from a number in another European country, here's how to make an international call. I've used one of my recommended Lisbon hotels as an example (tel. 213-219-030).

**Initial Zero:** Drop the initial zero from international phone numbers—except when calling Italy.

**Mobile Tip:** If using a mobile phone, the "+" sign can replace the international access code (for a "+" sign, press and hold "0").

### US/Canada to Europe

Dial 011 (US/Canada international access code), country code (351 for Portugal), and phone number.*

▶ To call the Lisbon hotel from home, dial 011-351-213-219-030.

### Country to Country Within Europe

Dial 00 (Europe international access code), country code, and phone number.*

▶ To call the Lisbon hotel from Germany, dial 00-351-213-219-030.

### Europe to the US/Canada

Dial 00, country code (1 for US/Canada), and phone number.

▶ To call from Europe to my office in Edmonds, Washington, dial 00-1-425-771-8303.

## Domestic Calls

To call within Portugal (from one Portuguese landline or mobile phone to another), simply dial the phone number, including the initial 0 if there is one.

▶ To call the Lisbon hotel from the Algarve, dial 213-219-030.

texts over the Internet for free or cheap. If you're bringing a tablet or laptop, you can also use them for voice calls and texts. All you have to do is log on to a Wi-Fi network, then contact any of your friends or family members who are also online and signed into the same service.

You can make voice and video calls using Skype, Viber, Face-Time, and Google+ Hangouts. If the connection is bad, try making an audio-only call. WhatsApp only offers voice calls. You can also make voice calls from your device to telephones worldwide for just a few cents per minute using Skype, Viber, or Hangouts if you buy credit first.

To text for free over Wi-Fi, try apps like Google+ Hangouts,

## More Dialing Tips

**Toll-Free Calls:** International rates apply to US toll-free numbers dialed from Portugal—they're not free.

**More Phoning Help:** See www.howtocallabroad.com.

| European Country Codes | | Ireland & N. Ireland | 353 / 44 |
|---|---|---|---|
| Austria | 43 | Italy | 39 |
| Belgium | 32 | Latvia | 371 |
| Bosnia-Herzegovina | 387 | Montenegro | 382 |
| Croatia | 385 | Morocco | 212 |
| Czech Republic | 420 | Netherlands | 31 |
| Denmark | 45 | Norway | 47 |
| Estonia | 372 | Poland | 48 |
| Finland | 358 | Portugal | 351 |
| France | 33 | Russia | 7 |
| Germany | 49 | Slovakia | 421 |
| Gibraltar | 350 | Slovenia | 386 |
| Great Britain | 44 | Spain | 34 |
| Greece | 30 | Sweden | 46 |
| Hungary | 36 | Switzerland | 41 |
| Iceland | 354 | Turkey | 90 |

**PRACTICALITIES**

WhatsApp, Viber, Facebook Messenger, and iMessage. Make sure you're on Wi-Fi to avoid data charges.

## USING A EUROPEAN SIM CARD IN A MOBILE PHONE

This option works well for those who want to make a lot of voice calls at cheap local rates, and those who need faster connection speeds than their US carrier provides. With a European SIM card, you get a European phone number—and European rates.

You can buy a basic cell phone in Europe (as little as $40 from mobile-phone shops anywhere, including a SIM card). Or you can bring an "unlocked" US phone (check with your carrier about unlocking it) and swap out the original SIM card for one you buy in

Europe. SIM cards are sold at mobile-phone shops, department-store electronics counters, newsstands, and vending machines. Costing about $5-10, they usually include about that much pre-paid calling credit, with no contract and no commitment. A SIM card that also includes data (including roaming) will cost $20-40 more for one month of data within the country in which it was purchased. This can be faster than data roaming through your home provider. To get the best rates, buy a new SIM card whenever you arrive in a new country.

I like to buy SIM cards at a mobile-phone shop where there's a clerk to help explain the options and brands. Major providers in Portugal include Vodafone, MEO, and NOS; you'll find their shops in every major shopping district and mall. Certain brands—including Lebara and Lycamobile, both of which are available in multiple European countries—are reliable and especially economical. Ask the clerk to help you insert your SIM card, set it up, and show you how to use it. In some countries, you'll be required to register the SIM card with your passport as an antiterrorism measure (which may mean you can't use the phone for the first hour or two).

Find out how to check your credit balance. When you run out of credit, you can top it up at newsstands, tobacco shops, mobile-phone stores, or many other businesses (look for your SIM card's logo in the window), or online.

## UNTETHERED TRAVEL: PUBLIC PHONES AND COMPUTERS

It's possible to travel in Europe without a mobile device. You can check email or browse websites using public computers and Internet cafés, and make calls from your hotel room and/or public phones.

Phones in your **hotel room** generally have a fee for placing local and "toll-free" calls, as well as long-distance or international calls—ask for the rates before you dial. Since you're never charged for receiving calls, it's better to have someone from the US call you in your room.

If these fees are low, hotel phones can be used inexpensively for calls made with cheap international phone cards (cartão telefónico com código pessoal, sold at many newsstands, street kiosks, tobacco shops, and train stations). You'll either get a prepaid card with a toll-free number and a scratch-to-reveal PIN code, or a code printed on a receipt.

You'll see **public pay phones** in a few post offices and train stations. The phones generally come with multilingual instructions, and some work with insertable phone cards (cartão telefónico, sold at post offices, newsstands, etc.). With the exception of Great Britain, each European country has its own insertable phone card—so your Portuguese card won't work in a Spanish phone.

**Public computers** are easy to find. Many hotels have one in their lobby for guests to use; otherwise you can find them at Internet cafés and public libraries (ask your hotelier or the TI for the nearest location). If typing on a European keyboard, use the "Alt Gr" key to the right of the space bar to insert the extra symbol that appears on some keys. Portuguese keyboards are a little different from ours; to type an @ symbol, press the "Alt Gr" key and 2 at the same time. If you can't locate a special character (such as @), simply copy it from a Web page and paste it into your email message.

## MAIL

You can mail one package per day to yourself worth up to $200 duty-free from Europe to the US (mark it "personal purchases"). If you're sending a gift to someone, mark it "unsolicited gift." For details, visit www.cbp.gov, select "Travel," and then "Know Before You Visit." The Portuguese postal service works fine, but for quick transatlantic delivery (in either direction), consider services such as DHL (www.dhl.com).

# Transportation

When deciding how to get between destinations in Europe, consider these factors: Cars are best for three or more traveling together (especially families with small kids), those packing heavy, and those delving into the countryside. Trains and buses are best for solo travelers, blitz tourists, city-to-city travelers, and those who don't want to drive in Europe. Intra-European flights are an increasingly inexpensive option. While a car gives you more freedom, trains and buses zip you effortlessly and scenically from city to city, usually dropping you in the center, often near a TI. Cars are an expensive headache in places like Lisbon. For more detailed information on transportation throughout Europe, including trains, flying, buses, renting a car, and driving, see www.ricksteves.com/transportation.

## TRAIN VERSUS BUS

Portugal straggles behind the rest of Europe in train service, but offers excellent bus transportation. Off the main Lisbon-Porto-Coimbra train lines, buses are usually a better bet. In cases where buses and trains serve the same destination, the bus is often more efficient, offering more frequent connections and sometimes a more central station. If schedules are similar, use the maps in this book to determine which station is closest to your hotel.

The best public transportation option is to mix bus and train travel. Always verify bus and train schedules before your departure. To ask for a schedule at an information window, say, *"Horário para* (fill in names of cities), *faz favor.*" (The TI will sometimes have schedules available.) To study train schedules in advance, see www. cp.pt for all domestic and Spain/France routes. Another good resource for train schedules throughout Europe is German Rail's timetable (www.bahn.com).

Departures and arrivals are *partidas* and *chegadas,* respectively. These key Portuguese "fine print" words may also come in handy in your travels: Both *as* and *aos* mean "on"; *de* means "from," as in "from this date to that date"; *só* means "only," as in "only effective on..."; *não* means "not"; and *feriado* means "holiday." On schedules, exceptions are noted, as in this typical qualifier: *"Não se efectua aos sábados, domingos, e feriados oficiais"* ("Not effective on Saturdays, Sundays, and official holidays").

## TRAINS *(COMBOIOS)*

The fastest Alfa Pendular and Intercidades trains serve the main Lisbon-Porto line with an occasional extension to Faro or Braga; these trains require seat reservations. Regional and Interregional "milk-run" trains serve most other routes, making lots of stops. On Portuguese train schedules, *diario* means "daily" and *mudança de comboio* means "change trains."

**Rail Passes:** Because you'll likely use a mix of trains and buses on your trip, a Portugal Pass doesn't make much sense, especially if you're traveling only in Portugal. Even if your trip extends into Spain, consider that Lisbon-Madrid trains leave just once a day as an overnight trip (see below)—many travelers find that flights or the bus are a better option for this stretch. Connecting Portugal and Sevilla is faster and easier by bus, which isn't covered by any rail  pass. For information on rail passes, visit www.ricksteves.com/rail.

**Overnight Trains:** If you'll be going from Lisbon to Madrid, book ahead for the overnight train (called the "Lusitânia") to ensure you get a berth and/or seat (covered by rail pass but you must pay for a sleeper reservation). No other rail option exists between these two capital cities.

## BUSES *(AUTOCARROS)*

Portugal has a number of different bus companies, sometimes running buses to the same destinations and using the same transfer points. If you have to transfer, make sure to look for a bus with the same name/logo as the company you bought the ticket from. The largest national company is Rede Expressos (covers buses both north and south of Lisbon, www.rede-expressos.pt). EVA Trans-

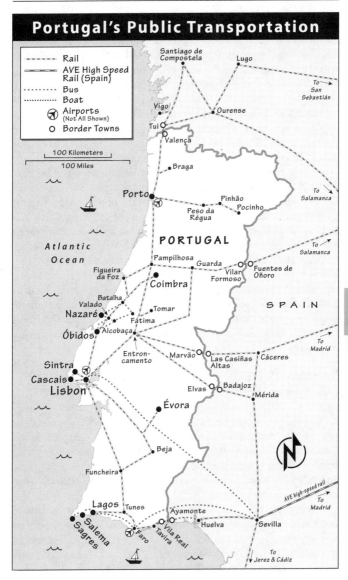

# Portugal's Public Transportation

Rail
AVE High Speed Rail (Spain)
Bus
Boat
Airports (Not All Shown)
Border Towns

100 Kilometers
100 Miles

Santiago de Compostela
Lugo
To San Sebastián
Vigo
Ourense
Tui
Valença
Braga
Porto
Pinhão
Pocinho
Peso da Régua
To Salamanca

**PORTUGAL**

Atlantic Ocean

Pampilhosa
Guarda
Vilar Formoso
Fuentes de Oñoro
To Salamanca
Figueira da Foz
Coimbra
Batalha
Valado
Nazaré
Tomar
Fátima
Óbidos
Alcobaça
Entron-camento
Marvão
Las Casiñas Altas
Cáceres
To Madrid

**S P A I N**

Sintra
Cascais
Lisbon
Elvas
Badajoz
Mérida
Évora

Beja

Funcheira

Lagos
Tunes
Ayamonte
Salema
Sagres
Faro
Vila Real
Tavira
Huelva
Sevilla
AVE high-speed rail
To Madrid

To Jerez & Cádiz

PRACTICALITIES

portes (www.eva-bus.com) covers some areas south of Lisbon, including the Algarve, as does RENEX (www.renex.pt). Central Portugal is covered by all major bus companies as well as Rodoviária do Tejo (www.rodotejo.pt) and Citi Express (www.citiexpress.eu). You can plan bus trips between cities online, but you should always confirm the schedule in person.

Bus schedules in Portugal are clearly posted at each major

station. *Directo* is "direct." Slower *ruta* buses make many stops en route. Posted schedules list most, but not all, destinations. If your intended destination isn't listed, check at the ticket/information window for the most complete schedule information. For long trips, your ticket might include an assigned seat.

If the bus station is not central, ask at the TI about travel agencies near your hotel that sell bus tickets. Don't leave a bus station to explore a city without checking your departure options and buying a ticket in advance if necessary (and possible). Bus service on holidays, Saturdays, and especially Sundays can be dismal.

You can (and most likely will be required to) stow your luggage under the bus. For longer rides, give some thought to which side of the bus will get the most sun, and sit on the opposite side. Even if a bus is air-conditioned and has curtains, direct sunlight can still heat up your seat. Long-distance (and most short-distance) buses are nonsmoking. Your ride will likely come with a soundtrack: recorded music (usually American pop), a radio, or sometimes videos. If you prefer silence, bring earplugs.

Drivers and station personnel rarely speak English. Buses usually lack WCs but stop every two hours or so for a 15- to 20-minute break. Ask the driver, "How many minutes here?" *("Quántos minutos aquí?")*. Bus stations have WCs (carry tissue), and cafés offering quick and cheap food.

## TAXIS AND UBER

Most taxis are reliable and cheap. Drivers generally respond kindly to the request, "How much is it to (destination), more or less?" *("Quanto é para* [fill in destination], *mais ou menos?")* Rounding the fare up to the nearest large coin (maximum of 10 percent) is adequate for a tip. Keep a map in your hand so the cabbie knows (or thinks) you know where you're going. Big cities have plenty of taxis. In many cases, couples can travel by cab for little more than two bus or subway tickets.

**Uber** has become popular in Portugal, especially in Lisbon and Porto. It works the same way here as stateside: Request a car via the Uber app on your phone, and the fare is automatically charged to your credit card. In my experience, I prefer Uber to taxis. You can request one without calling a dispatcher (though you do need an Internet connection), and you know exactly when they'll arrive; the drivers tend to be more courteous, with nicer and cleaner cars; and it's also usually cheaper—though "surge pricing" at very busy times can (legitimately) drive Uber prices above taxi fares.

## RENTING A CAR

Rental companies require you to be at least 21 years old and to have held your license for one year. Drivers under the age of 25

PRACTICALITIES

may incur a young-driver surcharge, and some rental companies do not rent to anyone 75 or older. If you're considered too young or old, look into leasing (covered later), which has less-stringent age restrictions.

Research car rentals before you go. It's cheaper to arrange most car rentals from the US. Consider several companies to compare rates.

Most of the major US rental agencies (including Avis, Budget, Enterprise, Hertz, and Thrifty) have offices throughout Europe. Also consider the two major Europe-based agencies, Europcar and Sixt. It can be cheaper to use a consolidator, such as Auto Europe/Kemwel (www.autoeurope.com—or the often cheaper www.autoeurope.eu) or Europe by Car (www.europebycar.com), which compares rates at several companies to get you the best deal—but because you're working with a middleman, it's especially important to ask in advance about add-on fees and restrictions.

Always read the fine print carefully for add-on charges—such as one-way drop-off fees, airport surcharges, or mandatory insurance policies—that aren't included in the "total price." You may need to query rental agents pointedly to find out your actual cost.

For the best deal, rent by the week with unlimited mileage. To save money on fuel, you can request a diesel car. I normally rent the smallest, least-expensive model with a stick shift (generally cheaper than an automatic). Almost all rentals are manual by default, so if you need an automatic, request one in advance; be aware that these cars are usually larger models (not as maneuverable on narrow, winding roads).

Figure on paying roughly $230 for a one-week rental. Allow extra for supplemental insurance, fuel, tolls, and parking. For trips of three weeks or more, leasing can save you money on insurance and taxes. Be warned that international trips—say, picking up in Porto and dropping off in Madrid—while efficient, can be expensive if the rental company assesses a drop-off fee for crossing a border.

**Via Verde Toll Sensor:** To save some hassle paying tolls, rent a "Via Verde" automated toll sensor along with your car (figure about €2/day); at the end of your rental, the car agency will charge your credit card for the actual tolls you incur. Be sure the sensor is activated before you leave the rental lot. For more on tolls, see page 433.

**Picking Up Your Car:** Big companies have offices in most cities, but small local rental companies can be cheaper.

Compare pickup costs (downtown can be less expensive than the airport), and explore drop-off options. Always check the hours of the location you choose: Many rental offices close from midday

Saturday until Monday morning and, in smaller towns, at lunchtime.

When selecting a location, don't trust the agency's description of "downtown" or "city center." In some cases, a "downtown" branch can be on the outskirts of the city—a long, costly taxi ride from the center. Before choosing, plug the addresses into a mapping website. You may find that the "train station" location is handier. But returning a car at a big-city train station or downtown agency can be tricky; get precise details on the car drop-off location and hours, and allow ample time to find it.

When you pick up the rental car, check it thoroughly and make sure any damage is noted on your rental agreement. Rental agencies in Europe are very strict when it comes to charging for even minor damage, so be sure to mark everything. Before driving off, find out how your car's gearshift, lights, turn signals, wipers, radio, and fuel cap function, and know what kind of fuel the car takes (diesel vs. unleaded). When you return the car, make sure the agent verifies its condition with you. Some drivers take pictures of the returned vehicle as proof of its condition.

## Car Insurance Options

When you rent a car, you are liable for a very high deductible, sometimes equal to the entire value of the car. Limit your financial risk with one of these options: Buy Collision Damage Waiver (CDW) coverage with a low or zero deductible from the car-rental company, get coverage through your credit card (free, if your card automatically includes zero-deductible coverage), or get collision insurance as part of a larger travel-insurance policy.

Basic **CDW** includes a very high deductible (typically $1,000-1,500), costs $10-30 a day (figure roughly 30 percent extra) and reduces your liability, but does not eliminate it. When you reserve or pick up the car, you'll be offered the chance to "buy down" the basic deductible to zero (for an additional $10-30/day; this is sometimes called "super CDW" or "zero-deductible coverage").

If you opt for **credit-card coverage,** you'll technically have to decline all coverage offered by the car-rental company, which means they can place a hold on your card (which can be up to the full value of the car). In case of damage, it can be time-consuming to resolve the charges with your credit-card company. Before you decide on this option, quiz your credit-card company about how it works.

If you're already purchasing a **travel-insurance policy** for your trip, adding collision coverage can be an economical option. For example, Travel Guard (www.travelguard.com) sells affordable renter's collision insurance as an add-on to its other policies; it's valid everywhere in Europe except the Republic of Ireland, and

## Driving in Portugal

100 Kilometers

50 Miles

To Santiago de Compostela

145m • 3.5h

60m • 1.5h

Porto

Peso da Régua

Pinhão

*Atlantic Ocean*

75m • 1.5h

100m • 2h

15m 0.5h

190m • 4h

Salamanca

165m • 3h

Coimbra

135m • 2.75h

60m • 1h

Ciudad Rodrigo

55m • 1h

**PORTUGAL**

40m • 1h

Nazaré

Fátima

240m • 4h

*SPAIN*

25m • 0.5h

Óbidos

60m • 1.h

60m • 1.25h

80m • 1.5h

125m • 2.5h

Sintra

315m • 5.5h (via Badajoz)

To Madrid

20m • 0.5h

90m • 2h

Lisbon

Évora

185m • 3h

155m • 3h

265m • 5h

m = miles
h = hours

185m • 3h

155m • 3h

(via Beja)

**Note:** Your times may vary based on traffic, construction & road conditions.

13m • 0.5h

Lagos

100m • 1.5h

Sagres

70m • 1.5h

Salema

13m • 0.5h

Tavira

Sevilla

*PRACTICALITIES*

some Italian car-rental companies refuse to honor it, as it doesn't cover you in case of theft.

For more on car-rental insurance, see www.ricksteves.com/cdw.

## Leasing

For trips of three weeks or more, consider leasing (which automatically includes zero-deductible collision and theft insurance). By technically buying and then selling back the car, you save lots of money on tax and insurance. Leasing provides you a brand-new car with unlimited mileage and a 24-hour emergency assistance program. You can lease for as little as 21 days to as long as five and a half months. Car leases must be arranged from the US. One of many companies offering affordable lease packages is Europe by Car.

## Navigation Options

If you'll be navigating using your phone or a GPS unit from home, remember to bring a car charger and device mount.

**Your Mobile Device:** The mapping app on your mobile phone works fine for navigation in Europe, but for real-time turn-by-turn directions and traffic updates, you'll generally need access to a cellular network. A helpful exception is Google Maps, which provides turn-by-turn driving directions and recalibrates even when it's offline.

To use Google Maps offline, you must have a Google account and download your map while you have a data connection. Later—even when offline—you can call up that map, enter your destination, and get directions. View maps in standard view (not satellite view) to limit data demands.

**GPS Devices:** If you prefer the convenience of a dedicated GPS unit, consider renting one with your car ($10-30/day). These units offer real-time turn-by-turn directions and traffic without the data requirements of an app. Note that the unit may only come loaded with maps for its home country; if you need additional maps, ask. Also make sure your device's language is set to English before you drive off.

A less-expensive option is to bring a GPS device from home. Be aware that you'll need to buy and download European maps before your trip.

**Maps and Atlases:** Even when navigating primarily with a mobile app or GPS, I always make it a point to have a paper map. The free maps you get from your car-rental company usually don't have enough detail. It's smart to buy a better map before you go, or pick one up at a European gas station, bookshop, newsstand, or tourist shop.

## DRIVING

Drivers in Portugal encounter sparse traffic and very good roads connecting larger cities.

**Road Rules:** Be aware of typical European road rules; for example, many countries require headlights to be turned on at all times, and nearly all forbid talking on a mobile phone without a hands-free headset. In Europe, you're not allowed to turn right on a red light, unless there is a sign or signal specifically authorizing it, and on expressways it's illegal to pass drivers on the right. Seat belts are required by law in Portugal. Ask your car-rental company about these rules, or check the US State Department website (www.travel.state.gov, search for your country in the "Learn about your destination" box, then click on "Travel and Transportation"). You may be stopped for a routine check by the police (be sure you have your rental paperwork close at hand).

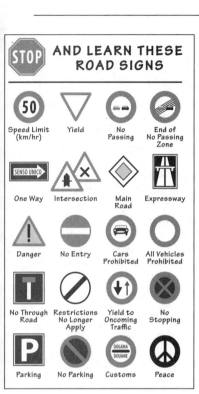

**STOP AND LEARN THESE ROAD SIGNS**

Speed Limit (km/hr) — Yield — No Passing — End of No Passing Zone

One Way — Intersection — Main Road — Expressway

Danger — No Entry — Cars Prohibited — All Vehicles Prohibited

No Through Road — Restrictions No Longer Apply — Yield to Oncoming Traffic — No Stopping

Parking — No Parking — Customs — Peace

**Fuel:** Gas and diesel prices are government-controlled and the same everywhere. Gas is around $6 a gallon, and diesel is about $5. Be careful when filling up: the words are similar for unleaded gas (*gasolina*, with green pumps) and for diesel (*gasóleo*, with black pumps). Note that your US credit and debit cards may not work at self-service gas pumps, as well as toll bridges and automated parking garages, even if they have a chip. Be sure to know your credit card's PIN, but just in case, also carry sufficient cash.

**Navigation:** On freeways, navigate by direction (*norte* = north, *oeste* = west, *sul* = south, *este* = east). Also, since road numbers can be confusing and inconsistent, navigate by city names. You can pick up a Michelin map in the US or buy one of the good, inexpensive maps available throughout Portugal.

**Parking:** Parking areas in cities generally have a large white "P" on a blue background. Don't assume it's free—check around for meters or ticketing machines.

**Theft:** Choose parking places carefully. Keep your valuables in your hotel room or, if you're between destinations, covered in your trunk. Leave nothing worth stealing in the car, especially overnight. If your car's a hatchback, take the trunk cover off at night so thieves can look in without breaking in. Try to make your car look locally owned by hiding the "tourist-owned" rental-company decals and putting a Portuguese newspaper in your front or back window. Ask your hotelier for advice on parking. In cities, you can park safely but expensively in guarded lots.

**Tolls:** Almost all Portuguese superhighways are subject to tolls (about €1 per 13 kilometers). There are a variety of ways to pay; for a rundown, see www.portugaltolls.com. But here are the basics:

First off, if renting your car in Portugal, the simplest (and recommended) solution is to get a **Via Verde automated tolling device** from your rental-car company (typically around €2/day). This lets you zip through any tolling situation—manual or electronic—

PRACTICALITIES

on any class of road and be billed later (your rental company will simply charge your credit card). With the Via Verde device, you can pass through tolling plazas using the lanes marked with a green-and-white *V* and the words *Reservada a Aderentes*.

If you'd rather **pay tolls as you go,** be prepared for two different types of tolls: ticket-based or electronic.

The majority of expressways are **manually tolled:** Simply take a ticket as you enter, and pay the toll as you leave (lanes are marked for credit cards or cash).

Other roads—such as the A-22 along the Algarve—are **electronically tolled** using cameras, which identify cars by their license plate as they zip past. Each time you drive under a toll camera, a sign tells you the fee (expect to pay about €10 to cross the entire Algarve coast, which covers the width of southern Portugal).

This electronic toll system offers three payment options, outlined below. To figure out the right option or to estimate your total tolls, start at www.portugaltolls.com (or if picking up your car in Portugal, ask for advice from the rental agency). The entire process is slick and easy.

A **TOLLCard** comes in prepaid amounts (€5, €10, €20, or €40) and is valid for one year. To use it, buy the card online (www.portugaltolls.com) or from the postal service (*Correios* or CTT), then activate it by sending a text message from your mobile phone. You can check your balance online, plus you'll receive a text message when it runs out (balance is refundable).

**TOLL Service** is a three-day, €20 prepaid card that includes unlimited travel for those driving a car registered outside Portugal. It's available online, at post offices or at the Porto and Faro airports.

With an **EASYToll** card, your credit card will be charged each time you pass a toll point. You can buy this card online and at certain payment points along the border with Spain. Simply pop your credit card into the machine (which associates your card with your license number) and take your EASYToll card. This covers your car for all toll road use for a month (or until you cancel the account). When leaving the country, be sure to close your account: Go to www.portugaltolls.com, and enter the "identifier number" (located on your EASYToll card) and license plate number. If you don't cancel the account, the next driver can zip around the country on your penny.

## FLIGHTS

The best comparison search engine for both international and intra-European flights is www.kayak.com. For inexpensive flights within Europe, try www.skyscanner.com.

**Flying to Europe:** Start looking for international flights at least four to six months before your trip, especially for peak-season travel. Off-season tickets can usually be purchased a month or so in advance. Depending on your itinerary, it can be efficient to fly into one city and out of another. If your flight requires a connection in Europe, see my hints on navigating Europe's top hub airports at www.ricksteves.com/hub-airports.

**Flying Within Europe:** If you're considering a train ride that's more than five hours long, a flight may save you both time and money. When comparing your options, factor in the time it takes to get to the airport and how early you'll need to arrive to check in.

For flights within Portugal, the country's national carrier is **TAP Portugal** (www.flytap.com). For flights between Lisbon and other cities in Europe, also try **Iberia** (www.iberia.com), **Vueling Airlines** (www.vueling.com), **Ryanair** (www.ryanair.com), and **EasyJet** (www.easyjet.com).

But be aware of the potential drawbacks of flying with a discount airline: nonrefundable and nonchangeable tickets, minimal or nonexistent customer service, pricey and time-consuming treks to secondary airports, and stingy baggage allowances with steep overage fees. If you're traveling with lots of luggage, a cheap flight can quickly become a bad deal. To avoid unpleasant surprises, read the small print before you book. These days you can also fly within Europe on major airlines affordably—and without all the aggressive restrictions—for around $100 a flight.

**Flying to the US and Canada:** Because security is extra tight for flights to the US, be sure to give yourself plenty of time at the airport. It's also important to charge your electronic devices before you board because security checks may require you to turn them on (see www.tsa.gov for the latest rules).

# Resources from Rick Steves

**Begin your trip at www.ricksteves.com:** My mobile-friendly website is *the* place to explore Europe. You'll find thousands of fun articles, videos, photos, and radio interviews organized by country; a wealth of money-saving tips for planning your dream trip; monthly travel news dispatches; a collection of over 30 hours of practical travel talks; my travel blog; my latest guidebook updates (www.ricksteves.com/update); and my free Rick Steves Audio Europe app. You can also follow me on Facebook and Twitter.

Our **Travel Forum** is an immense, yet well-groomed collection of message boards, where our travel-savvy community answers questions and shares their personal travel experiences—and our well-traveled staff chimes in when they can be helpful (www.ricksteves.com/forums).

Our online **Travel Store** offers travel bags and accessories that I've designed specifically to help you travel smarter and lighter.

PRACTICALITIES

These include my popular carry-on bags (which I live out of four months a year), money belts, totes, toiletries kits, adapters, other accessories, and a wide selection of guidebooks and planning maps (www.ricksteves.com/shop).

Choosing the right **rail pass** for your trip—amid hundreds of options—can drive you nutty. Our website will help you find the perfect fit for your itinerary and your budget: We offer easy, one-stop shopping for rail passes, seat reservations, and point-to-point tickets.

**Tours:** Want to travel with greater efficiency and less stress? We organize **tours** with more than three dozen itineraries and more than 900 departures reaching the best destinations in this book...and beyond. We offer a 12-day Heart of Portugal tour that hits the highlights of this history-rich country. You'll enjoy great guides, a fun bunch of travel partners (with small groups of 24 to 28 travelers), and plenty of room to spread out in a big, comfy bus when touring between towns. You'll find European adventures to fit every vacation length. For all the details, and to get our Tour Catalog, visit www.ricksteves.com or call us at 425/608-4217.

**Books:** *Rick Steves Portugal* is one of many books in my series on European travel, which includes country guidebooks, city guidebooks (Rome, Florence, Paris, London, etc.), Snapshot guidebooks (excerpted chapters from my country guides), Pocket guidebooks (full-color little books on big cities), "Best Of" guidebooks (condensed country guides in a full-color, easy-to-scan format), and my budget-travel skills handbook, *Rick Steves Europe Through the Back Door*. Most of my titles are available as ebooks.

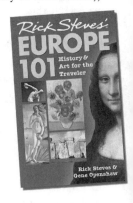

My phrase books—for Portuguese, Spanish, German, French, and Italian—are practical and budget-oriented. My other books include *Europe 101* (a crash course on art and history designed for travelers), *Mediterranean Cruise Ports* and *Northern European Cruise Ports* (how to make the most of your time in port), and *Travel as a Political Act* (a travelogue sprinkled with tips for bringing home a global perspective). A more complete list of my titles appears near the end of this book.

**TV Shows:** My public television series, *Rick Steves' Europe,* covers Europe from top to bottom with over 100 half-hour episodes. To watch full episodes online for free, see www.ricksteves.com/tv.

**Travel Talks on Video:** You can raise your travel I.Q. with video versions of our popular classes, including talks on travel skills, packing smart, cruising, tech for travelers, European art for travelers, travel as a political act, and individual talks covering most European countries). See www.ricksteves.com/travel-talks.

**Audio:** My weekly public radio show, *Travel with Rick Steves,* features interviews with travel experts from around the world. A complete archive of 10 years of programs (over 400 in all) is available at www.ricksteves.com/ radio. I've also produced a free, self-guided audio tour of the top neighborhoods in Lisbon. Most of this audio content is available for free through my **Rick Steves Audio Europe app,** an extensive online library organized by destination. For more on my app, see page 9.

# APPENDIX

## Useful Contacts

### Emergency Needs
**Police, Fire, and Ambulance:** Tel. 112

### Embassies
**US Embassy:** Tel. 217-273-300, passport services available Mon-Fri 8:00-17:00 (Avenida das Forças Armadas, Lisbon, http://portugal.usembassy.gov)

**Canadian Embassy:** Tel. 213-164-600, passport services available Mon-Thu 8:30-12:30 & 13:00-17:15, Fri 8:30-13:00 (Avenida da Liberdade 198-200, third floor, Lisbon, www.canadainternational.gc.ca/portugal)

### Directory Assistance
**Local Directory Assistance:** Tel. 118
**International Directory Assistance:** Tel. 177

# Holidays and Festivals

This list includes selected festivals in major cities, plus national holidays observed throughout Portugal. Many sights and banks close on national holidays—keep this in mind when planning your itinerary. Before planning a trip around a festival, verify its dates by checking the festival's website or TI sites (www.visitportugal.com).

| | |
|---|---|
| Jan 1 | New Year's Day |
| Feb | Carnival (Mardi Gras, a.k.a. Entrudo, Feb 28 in 2017, Feb 13 in 2018). Particularly vibrant in Lisbon and Algarve towns, some closures on Shrove Tuesday) |
| Early April | Lisbon Fish & Flavors (*Peixe em Lisboa,* gourmet seafood festival) |
| Week before Easter | Holy Week (Semana Santa). Religious processions, especially in Óbidos and Porto |
| Easter weekend (Good Friday-Easter Sunday) | April 14-16 in 2017; March 29-April 1 in 2018 |
| April 25 | Liberty Day (parades, fireworks) |
| May 1 | Labor Day |
| Early May | Queima das Fitas, Coimbra ("burning of ribbons," graduation festivities) |
| May 13 | Pilgrimage to Fátima (Peregrinação de Fátima) |
| Late spring-early summer | Festival de Sintra (www.festivaldesintra.pt) |
| June 10 | Portuguese National Day (Dia de Camões) |
| June 13 | St. Anthony's Day (Dia de Santo António), Lisbon (dancing, processions) |
| June 24 | St. John's Day (Dia de São João), Porto (fireworks, dancing) |
| June 29 | St. Peter's Day (Dia de São Pedro), Évora (dancing, processions) |
| Aug 15 | Assumption (religious festival) |
| Sept 8 | Our Lady of Nazaré Festival (procession, folk dancing, fairs) |
| Oct 13 | Pilgrimage to Fátima (Peregrinação de Fátima) |

| | |
|---|---|
| **Dec 8** | Feast of the Immaculate Conception |
| **Dec 25** | Christmas |
| **Dec 31** | New Year's Eve |

# Recommended Books and Films

To learn more about Portugal past and present, check out a few of these books and films.

## Nonfiction

*The Book of Disquiet* (Fernando Pessoa, 1982). This collection of unpublished poetry and thoughts from the great Portuguese writer, Fernando Pessoa, was compiled after they were found in a trunk following his death.

*The First Global Village* (Martin Page, 2002). Page explores Portugal's profound influence on the rest of the world.

*The History of Portugal* (James Anderson, 2000). Anderson provides a concise, readable overview of Portuguese history.

*The Last Day: Wrath, Ruin, and Reason in the Great Lisbon Earthquake of 1755* (Nicholas Shrady, 2008). The earthquake that leveled Lisbon not only destroyed one of the leading European cities of the time, but also had a lasting effect on the world at large.

*Over the Edge of the World: Magellan's Terrifying Circumnavigation of the Globe* (Laurence Bergreen, 2003). Magellan's fascinating tale of circumnavigating the globe is told through firsthand accounts.

*Portugal: A Companion History* (José Hermano Saraiva, 1997). This easily digestible primer on Portugal is accompanied by maps and illustrations.

*The Portuguese: A Modern History* (Barry Hatton, 2011). Hatton combines information on the country's history, landscape, and culture with anecdotes from his own experience living in Portugal.

*The Portuguese Empire, 1415–1808: A World on the Move* (A.J.R. Russell-Wood, 1998). Russell-Wood explores the rise and fall of the Portuguese empire.

*Prince Henry the Navigator: A Life* (Peter Russell, 2000). This biography reveals the man who helped set in motion the Age of Discovery.

*Unknown Seas: How Vasco da Gama Opened the East* (Ronald Watkins, 2005). Reconstructing journeys from captain's logs, this book explores the expansion of Portuguese trade routes.

## Fiction

*Baltasar and Blimunda* (José Saramago, 1998). Saramago's love story offers a surrealistic reflection on life in 18th-century Portugal.

*The Crime of Father Amaro* (Jose Maria de Eça de Queirós, 1875). Set in a provincial Portuguese town, this book by the great 19th-century Portuguese novelist highlights the dangers of fanaticism.

*Distant Music* (Lee Langley, 2003). Catholic Esperança and Jewish Emmanuel have an affair that lasts through six centuries and multiple incarnations; the book also delves into Portugal's maritime empire, Sephardic Jews, and Portuguese immigrants in London.

*The Last Kabbalist of Lisbon* (Richard Zimler, 1996). The author illuminates the persecution of the Jews in Portugal in the early 1500s.

*The Lusiads* (Luís de Camões, 1572). Considered a national treasure, Camões' great epic poems of the Renaissance immortalize Portugal's voyages of discovery.

*Night Train to Lisbon* (Pascal Mercier, 2004). Mercier's international bestseller-turned-2013-film follows the travels of a Swiss professor as he explores the life of a Portuguese doctor during Salazar's dictatorship.

*Pereira Declares: A Testimony* (Antonio Tabucchi, 1997). Set in Portugal in 1938 during Salazar's fascist government, *Pereira Declares* is the story of the moral resurrection of a newspaper's cautious editor.

*A Small Death in Lisbon* (Robert Wilson, 2002). In this award-winning thriller, a contemporary police procedural is woven with an espionage story set during World War II, with Portugal's 20th-century history as a backdrop.

## Film and TV

*Amália* (2008). This film captures the life of Portugal's beloved fado singer, Amália Rodrigues, who rose from poverty to international fame. (If the film is hard to find, listen to a YouTube clip of her lovely singing.)

*The Art of Amália* (2000). Interviews with the diva are highlighted in this documentary.

*Capitães de Abril* (2000). The story of the 1974 coup that overthrew the right-wing Portuguese dictatorship is told from the perspective of two young army captains.

*Letters from Fontainhas* (2010). This trio of short films follows three troubled lives in Lisbon.

*Pereira Declares* (1996). Marcello Mastroianni plays the namesake in this film inspired by the Tabucchi novel mentioned earlier.

*The Strange Case of Angelica* (2010). Manoel de Oliveira's film about a photographer haunted by a deceased bride is set against the landscape of the Douro Valley.

# Conversions and Climate

## NUMBERS AND STUMBLERS

- Europeans write a few of their numbers differently than we do. 1 = , 4 = , 7 = .
- In Europe, dates appear as day/month/year, so Christmas 2018 is 25/12/18.
- Commas are decimal points and decimals commas. A dollar and a half is $1,50, one thousand is 1.000, and there are 5.280 feet in a mile.
- When counting with fingers, start with your thumb. If you hold up your first finger to request one item, you'll probably get two.
- What Americans call the second floor of a building is the first floor in Europe.
- On escalators and moving sidewalks, Europeans keep the left "lane" open for passing. Keep to the right.

## METRIC CONVERSIONS

A kilogram is 2.2 pounds, and l liter is about a quart, or almost four to a gallon. A kilometer is six-tenths of a mile. I figure kilometers to miles by cutting them in half and adding back 10 percent of the original (120 km: 60 + 12=72 miles, 300 km: 150 + 30=180 miles).

| | |
|---|---|
| 1 foot = 0.3 meter | 1 square yard = 0.8 square meter |
| 1 yard = 0.9 meter | 1 square mile = 2.6 square kilometers |
| 1 mile = 1.6 kilometers | 1 ounce = 28 grams |
| 1 centimeter = 0.4 inch | 1 quart = 0.95 liter |
| 1 meter = 39.4 inches | 1 kilogram = 2.2 pounds |
| 1 kilometer = 0.62 mile | 32°F = 0°C |

*APPENDIX*

## CLOTHING SIZES

When shopping for clothing, use these US-to-European comparisons as general guidelines (but note that no conversion is perfect).

**Women:** For clothing or shoe sizes, add 30 (US shirt size 10 = European size 40; US shoe size 8 = European size 38-39).

**Men:** For shirts, multiply by 2 and add about 8 (US size 15 = European size 38). For jackets and suits, add 10. For shoes, add 32-34.

**Children:** For clothing, subtract 1-2 sizes for small children and subtract 4 for juniors. For shoes up to size 13, add 16-18, and for sizes 1 and up, add 30-32.

## PORTUGAL'S CLIMATE

First line, average daily high; second line, average daily low; third line, average days without rain. For more detailed weather statistics for destinations in this book (as well as the rest of the world), check www.wunderground.com.

| | J | F | M | A | M | J | J | A | S | O | N | D |
|---|---|---|---|---|---|---|---|---|---|---|---|---|
| **Lisbon** | | | | | | | | | | | | |
| | 57° | 59° | 63° | 67° | 71° | 77° | 81° | 82° | 79° | 72° | 63° | 58° |
| | 46° | 47° | 50° | 53° | 55° | 60° | 63° | 63° | 62° | 58° | 52° | 47° |
| | 16 | 16 | 17 | 20 | 21 | 25 | 29 | 29 | 24 | 22 | 17 | 16 |
| **Faro (Algarve)** | | | | | | | | | | | | |
| | 60° | 61° | 64° | 67° | 71° | 77° | 83° | 83° | 78° | 72° | 66° | 61° |
| | 48° | 49° | 52° | 55° | 58° | 64° | 67° | 68° | 65° | 60° | 55° | 50° |
| | 22 | 21 | 21 | 24 | 27 | 29 | 31 | 31 | 29 | 25 | 22 | 22 |

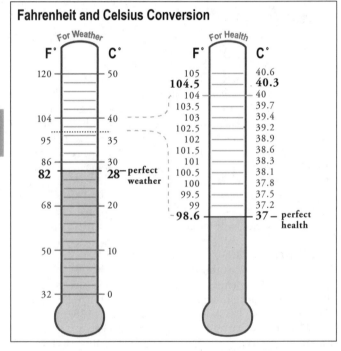

*Europe takes its temperature using the Celsius scale, while we opt for Fahrenheit. For a rough conversion from Celsius to Fahrenheit, double the number and add 30. For weather, remember that 28°C is 82°F— perfect. For health, 37°C is just right. At a launderette, 30°C is cold, 40°C is warm (usually the default setting), 60°C is hot, and 95°C is boiling. Your air-conditioner should be set at about 20°C.*

# Packing Checklist

Whether you're traveling for five days or five weeks, you won't need more than this. Pack light to enjoy the sweet freedom of true mobility.

## Clothing

- ☐ 5 shirts: long- & short-sleeve
- ☐ 2 pairs pants (or skirts/capris)
- ☐ 1 pair shorts
- ☐ 5 pairs underwear & socks
- ☐ 1 pair walking shoes
- ☐ Sweater or warm layer
- ☐ Rainproof jacket with hood
- ☐ Tie, scarf, belt, and/or hat
- ☐ Swimsuit
- ☐ Sleepwear/loungewear

## Money

- ☐ Debit card(s)
- ☐ Credit card(s)
- ☐ Hard cash ($100-200 in US dollars)
- ☐ Money belt

## Documents

- ☐ Passport
- ☐ Tickets & confirmations: flights, hotels, trains, rail pass, car rental, sight entries
- ☐ Driver's license
- ☐ Student ID, hostel card, etc.
- ☐ Photocopies of important documents
- ☐ Insurance details
- ☐ Guidebooks & maps
- ☐ Notepad & pen
- ☐ Journal

## Toiletries Kit

- ☐ Basics: soap, shampoo, toothbrush, toothpaste, floss, deodorant, sunscreen, brush/comb, etc.
- ☐ Medicines & vitamins
- ☐ First-aid kit
- ☐ Glasses/contacts/sunglasses

- ☐ Sewing kit
- ☐ Packet of tissues (for WC)
- ☐ Earplugs

## Electronics

- ☐ Mobile phone
- ☐ Camera & related gear
- ☐ Tablet/ebook reader/media player
- ☐ Laptop & flash drive
- ☐ Headphones
- ☐ Chargers & batteries
- ☐ Smartphone car charger & mount (or GPS device)
- ☐ Plug adapters

## Miscellaneous

- ☐ Daypack
- ☐ Sealable plastic baggies
- ☐ Laundry supplies: soap, laundry bag, clothesline, spot remover
- ☐ Small umbrella
- ☐ Travel alarm/watch

## Optional Extras

- ☐ Second pair of shoes (flip-flops, sandals, tennis shoes, boots)
- ☐ Travel hairdryer
- ☐ Picnic supplies
- ☐ Water bottle
- ☐ Fold-up tote bag
- ☐ Small flashlight
- ☐ Mini binoculars
- ☐ Small towel or washcloth
- ☐ Inflatable pillow/neck rest
- ☐ Tiny lock
- ☐ Address list (to mail postcards)
- ☐ Extra passport photos

## Portuguese Survival Phrases

In the phonetics, nasalized vowels are indicated by an underlined **n** or **w**. As you say the vowel, let its sound come through your nose as well as your mouth.

| English | Portuguese | Pronunciation |
|---|---|---|
| Good day. | *Bom dia.* | boh<u>n</u> **dee**-ah |
| Do you speak English? | *Fala inglês?* | **fah**-lah een-**glaysh** |
| Yes. / No. | *Sim. / Não.* | seeng / no<u>w</u> |
| I (don't) understand. | *(Não) compreendo.* | (no<u>w</u>) koh<u>n</u>-pree-**ayn**-doo |
| Please. | *Por favor.* | poor fah-**vor** |
| Thank you. (said by male) | *Obrigado.* | oo-bree-**gah**-doo |
| Thank you. (said by female) | *Obrigada.* | oo-bree-**gah**-dah |
| I'm sorry. | *Desculpe.* | dish-**kool**-peh |
| Excuse me (to pass). | *Com licença.* | koh<u>n</u> li-**sehn**-sah |
| (No) problem. | *(Não) há problema.* | (no<u>w</u>) ah proo-**blay**-mah |
| Good. | *Bom.* | boh<u>n</u> |
| Goodbye. | *Adeus. / Ciao.* | ah-**deh**-oosh / chow |
| one / two | *um / dois* | oo<u>n</u> / doysh |
| three / four | *três / quatro* | traysh / **kwah**-troo |
| five / six | *cinco / seis* | **seeng**-koo / saysh |
| seven / eight | *sete / oito* | **seh**-teh / **oy**-too |
| nine / ten | *nove / dez* | **naw**-veh / dehsh |
| How much is it? | *Quanto é?* | **kwahn**-too eh |
| Write it? | *Escreva?* | ish-**kray**-vah |
| Is it free? | *É gratis?* | eh **grah**-teesh |
| Is it included? | *Está incluido?* | ish-**tah** een-kloo-**ee**-doo |
| Where can I find / buy...? | *Onde posso encontrar / comprar...?* | **ohn**-deh **paw**-soo ayn-kohn-**trar** / kohn-**prar** |
| I'd like / We'd like... | *Gostaria / Gostaríamos...* | goosh-tah-**ree**-ah / goosh-tah-**ree**-ah-moosh |
| ...a room. | *...um quarto.* | oo<u>n</u> **kwar**-too |
| ...a ticket to ___. | *...um bilhete para ___.* | oo<u>n</u> beel-**yeh**-teh **pah**-rah ___ |
| Is it possible? | *É possível?* | eh poo-**see**-vehl |
| Where is...? | *Onde é que é...?* | **ohn**-deh eh keh eh |
| ...the train station | *...a estação de comboio* | ah ish-tah-**sow** deh kohn-**boy**-yoo |
| ...the bus station | *...a terminal de autocarros* | ah tehr-mee-**nahl** deh ow-too-**kah**-roosh |
| ...the tourist information office | *...a posto de turismo* | ah **poh**-stoo deh too-**reez**-moo |
| ...the toilet | *...a casa de banho* | ah **kah**-zah deh **bahn**-yoo |
| men | *homens* | **aw**-may<u>n</u>sh |
| women | *mulheres* | mool-**yeh**-rish |
| left / right | *esquerda / direita* | ish-**kehr**-dah / dee-**ray**-tah |
| straight | *em frente* | ay<u>n</u> **frayn**-teh |
| What time does this open / close? | *As que horas é que abre / fecha?* | ahsh keh **aw**-rahsh eh keh **ah**-breh / **feh**-shah |
| At what time? | *As que horas?* | ahsh keh **aw**-rahsh |
| Just a moment. | *Um momento.* | oo<u>n</u> moo-**mayn**-too |
| now / soon / later | *agora / em breve / mais tarde* | ah-**goh**-rah / ay<u>n</u> **bray**-veh / maish **tar**-deh |
| today / tomorrow | *hoje / amanhã* | **oh**-zheh / ah-ming-**yah** |

## In the Restaurant

| English | Portuguese | Pronunciation |
|---|---|---|
| I'd like / We'd like... | Gostaria / Gostaríamos... | goosh-tah-**ree**-ah / goosh-tah-**ree**-ah-moosh |
| ...to reserve... | ...de reservar... | deh reh-zehr-**var** |
| ...a table for one. / two. | ...uma mesa para uma. / duas. | oo-mah **may**-zah pah-rah oo-mah / **doo**-ahsh |
| Non-smoking. | Não fumar. | no<u>w</u> foo-**mar** |
| Is this table free? | Esta mesa está livre? | ehsh-tah meh-zah ish-**tah lee**-vreh |
| The menu (in English), please. | A ementa (em inglês), por favor. | ah eh-**mayn**-tah (ay<u>n</u> een-**glaysh**) poor fah-vor |
| service (not) included | serviço (não) incluído | sehr-**vee**-soo (no<u>w</u>) een-kloo-ee-doo |
| cover charge | coberto | koh-**behr**-too |
| to go | para fora | **pah**-rah foh-rah |
| with / without | com / sem | koh<u>n</u> / say<u>n</u> |
| and / or | e / ou | ee / oh |
| specialty of the house | especialidade da casa | ish-peh-see-ah-lee-**dah**-deh dah **kah**-zah |
| half portion | meia dose | **may**-ah doh-zeh |
| daily special | prato do dia | **prah**-too doo **dee**-ah |
| tourist menu | ementa turística | eh-**mayn**-tah too-**reesh**-tee-kah |
| appetizers | entradas | ay<u>n</u>-**trah**-dahsh |
| bread / cheese | pão / queijo | pow / **kay**-zhoo |
| sandwich | sandes | **sahn**-desh |
| soup / salad | sopa / salada | **soh**-pah / sah-**lah**-dah |
| meat | carne | **kar**-neh |
| poultry | aves | **ah**-vish |
| fish / seafood | peixe / marisco | **pay**-shee / mah-**reesh**-koo |
| fruit | fruta | **froo**-tah |
| vegetables | legumes | lay-**goo**-mish |
| dessert | sobremesa | soo-breh-**may**-zah |
| tap water | água da torneira | **ah**-gwah dah tor-**nay**-rah |
| mineral water | água mineral | **ah**-gwah mee-neh-**rahl** |
| milk | leite | **lay**-teh |
| (orange) juice | sumo (de laranja) | **soo**-moo (deh lah-**rah<u>n</u>**-zhah) |
| coffee / tea | café / chá | kah-**feh** / shah |
| wine | vinho | **veen**-yoo |
| red / white | tinto / branco | **teen**-too / **brang**-koo |
| glass / bottle | copo / garrafa | **koh**-poo / gah-**rah**-fah |
| beer | cerveja | sehr-**vay**-zhah |
| Cheers! | Saúde! | sah-**oo**-deh |
| More. / Another. | Mais. / Outro. | maish / **oh**-troo |
| The same. | O mesmo. | oo **mehsh**-moo |
| The bill, please. | A conta, por favor. | ah-**kohn**-tah poor fah-**vor** |
| tip | gorjeta | gor-**zheh**-tah |
| Delicious! | Delicioso! | deh-lee-see-**oh**-zoo |

For many more pages of survival phrases for your trip to Portugal, check out *Rick Steves' Portuguese Phrase Book & Dictionary*.

# INDEX

# MAP INDEX

*Our website enhances this book and turns*

### Explore Europe

At ricksteves.com you can browse through thousands of articles, videos, photos and radio interviews, plus find a wealth of money-saving travel tips for planning your dream trip. And with our mobile-friendly website, you can easily access all this great travel information anywhere you go.

### TV Shows

Preview the places you'll visit by watching entire half-hour episodes of Rick Steves' Europe (choose from all 100 shows) on-demand, for free.

# ricksteves.com

*your travel dreams into affordable reality*

### Radio Interviews

Enjoy ready access to Rick's vast library of radio interviews covering travel

tips and cultural insights that relate specifically to your Europe travel plans.

### Travel Forums

Learn, ask, share! Our online community of savvy travelers is a great resource for first-time travelers to Europe, as well as seasoned pros. You'll find forums on each country, plus travel tips and restaurant/hotel reviews. You can even ask one of our well-traveled staff to chime in with an opinion.

### Travel News

Subscribe to our free Travel News e-newsletter, and get monthly updates from Rick on what's happening in Europe.

# Audio Europe™

## Rick's Free Travel App

Get your FREE **Rick Steves Audio Europe**™ app to enjoy…

- Dozens of self-guided tours of Europe's top museums, sights and historic walks
- Hundreds of tracks filled with cultural insights and sightseeing tips from Rick's radio interviews
- All organized into handy geographic playlists
- For Apple and Android

With Rick whispering in your ear, Europe gets even better.

## Find out more at ricksteves.com

# Rick Steves has

*Experience maximum Europe*

## Save time and energy

This guidebook is your independent-travel toolkit. But for all it delivers, it's still up to you to devote the time and energy it takes to manage the preparation and logistics that are essential for a happy trip. If that's a hassle, there's a solution.

## Rick Steves Tours

A Rick Steves tour takes you to Europe's most interesting places with great

# great tours, too!

## with minimum stress

guides and small groups of 28 or less. We follow Rick's favorite itineraries, ride in comfy buses, stay in family-run hotels, and bring you intimately close to the Europe you've traveled so far to see. Most importantly, we take away the logistical headaches so you can focus on the fun.

travelers—nearly half of them repeat customers—along with us on four dozen different itineraries, from Ireland to Italy to Istanbul. Is a Rick Steves tour the right fit for your travel dreams? Find out at ricksteves.com, where you can also request Rick's latest tour catalog. Europe is best experienced with happy

### Join the fun

This year we'll take thousands of free-spirited travel partners. We hope you can join us.

# A Guide for Every Trip

## BEST OF GUIDES

*Full color easy-to-scan format, focusing on Europe's most popular destinations and sights.*

Best of France
Best of Germany
Best of England
Best of Europe
Best of Ireland
Best of Italy
Best of Spain

## COMPREHENSIVE GUIDES

*City, country, and regional guides with detailed coverage for a multi-week trip exploring the most iconic sights and venturing off the beaten track.*

Amsterdam & the Netherlands
Barcelona
Belgium: Bruges, Brussels, Antwerp & Ghent
Berlin
Budapest
Croatia & Slovenia
Eastern Europe
England
Florence & Tuscany
France
Germany
Great Britain
Greece: Athens & the Peloponnese
Iceland
Ireland
Istanbul
Italy
London
Paris
Portugal
Prague & the Czech Republic
Provence & the French Riviera
Rome
Scandinavia
Scotland
Spain
Switzerland
Venice
Vienna, Salzburg & Tirol

### THE BEST OF ROME

ome, Italy's capital, is studded with
oman remnants and floodlit-fountain
uares. From the Vatican to the Colos-
m, with crazy traffic in between, Rome
onderful, huge, and exhausting. The
ds, the heat, and the weighty history

of the Eternal City where Caesars walked
can make tourists wilt. Recharge by taking siestas, gelato breaks, and after-dark
walks, strolling from one atmospheric
square to another in the refreshing evening air.

ired **Pantheon**—which
gest dome until the
rly 2,000 years old
day over 1,500).

l of Athens in the Vat-
bodies the humanistic
ance.

, gladiators fought
another, entertaining
0.

lo Rome **ristorante.**
**St. Peter's**

a coin

Rick Steves guidebooks are published by Avalon Travel,
an imprint of Perseus Books, a Hachette Book Group company.

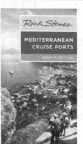

## POCKET GUIDES

*Compact, full color city guides with the essentials for shorter trips.*

Amsterdam
Athens
Barcelona
Florence
Italy's Cinque Terre
London
Munich & Salzburg

Paris
Prague
Rome
Venice
Vienna

## SNAPSHOT GUIDES

*Focused single-destination coverage.*

Basque Country: Spain & France
Copenhagen & the Best of Denmark
Dublin
Dubrovnik
Edinburgh
Hill Towns of Central Italy
Krakow, Warsaw & Gdansk
Lisbon
Loire Valley
Madrid & Toledo
Milan & the Italian Lakes District
Naples & the Amalfi Coast
Northern Ireland
Normandy
Norway
Reykjavik
Sevilla, Granada & Southern Spain
St. Petersburg, Helsinki & Tallinn
Stockholm

## CRUISE PORTS GUIDES

*Reference for cruise ports of call.*

Mediterranean Cruise Ports
Northern European Cruise Ports

## Complete your library with...

## TRAVEL SKILLS & CULTURE

*Study up on travel skills and gain insight on history and culture.*

Europe 101
European Christmas
European Easter
European Festivals
Europe Through the Back Door
Postcards from Europe
Travel as a Political Act

## PHRASE BOOKS & DICTIONARIES

French
French, Italian & German
German
Italian
Portuguese
Spanish

## PLANNING MAPS

Britain, Ireland & London
Europe
France & Paris
Germany, Austria & Switzerland
Ireland
Italy
Spain & Portugal

# Credits

### RESEARCHER
To help update this book, Rick relied on...

### Cameron Hewitt

Born in Denver and raised in central Ohio, Cameron settled in Seattle in 2000. Ever since, he has spent three months each year in Europe, contributing to guidebooks, tours, radio and television shows, and other media for Rick Steves' Europe, where he serves as content manager. Cameron married his high school sweetheart (and favorite travel partner), Shawna, and enjoys taking pictures, trying new restaurants, and planning his next trip.

### CONTRIBUTOR
### Gene Openshaw

Gene has co-authored a dozen *Rick Steves* books, specializing in writing walks and tours of Europe's cities, museums, and cultural sights. He also contributes to Rick's public television series, produces tours for Rick Steves Audio Europe, and is a regular guest on Rick's public radio show. Outside of the travel world, Gene has co-authored *The Seattle Joke Book*. As a composer, Gene has written a full-length opera called *Matter* (soundtrack available on Amazon), a violin sonata, and dozens of songs. He lives near Seattle with his daughter, enjoys giving presentations on art and history, and roots for the Mariners in good times and bad.

# Acknowledgments

Thanks to Cameron Hewitt for writing the original versions of the Porto and Douro Valley chapters, and to Robert Wright for his contributions over the years.

# More for your trip!
## Maximize the experience with Rick Steves as your guide

**Guidebooks**
Dozens of European city and country guidebooks

**Phrase Books**
Rely on Rick's Portuguese Phrase Book & Dictionary

**Rick's TV Shows**
Preview where you're going with 2 shows on Portugal

**Free! Rick's Audio Europe™ App**
Get a free audio tour for Lisbon

**Small Group Tours**
Take a lively Rick Steves tour of Portugal

**For all the details, visit ricksteves.com**

Avalon Travel
An imprint of Perseus Books
A Hachette Book Group company
1700 Fourth Street
Berkeley, CA 94710

Text © 2017 by Rick Steves.
Maps © 2017 by Rick Steves' Europe.
Printed in Canada by Friesens. Third printing March 2018.

For the latest on Rick's talks, guidebooks, Europe tours, public radio show, free
audio tours, and public television series, contact Rick Steves' Europe, 130 Fourth
Avenue North, Edmonds, WA 98020, tel. 425/771-8303, www.ricksteves.com,
rick@ricksteves.com.

ISBN 978-1-63121-615-2
9th Edition

**Rick Steves' Europe**
**Managing Editor:** Jennifer Madison Davis
**Special Publications Manager:** Risa Laib
**Editors:** Glenn Eriksen, Tom Griffin, Katherine Gustafson, Suzanne Kotz, Cathy Lu,
    Carrie Shepherd
**Editorial & Production Assistant:** Jessica Shaw
**Editorial Intern:** Meesha Sundarum
**Graphic Content Director:** Sandra Hundacker
**Maps & Graphics:** David C. Hoerlein, Lauren Mills, Mary Rostad

**Avalon Travel**
**Senior Editor and Series Manager:** Madhu Prasher
**Editor:** Jamie Andrade
**Associate Editor:** Sierra Machado
**Copy Editor:** Kelly Lydick
**Proofreader:** Patty Mon
**Indexer:** Stephen Callahan
**Production & Typesetting:** Jane Musser
**Cover Design:** Kimberly Glyder Design
**Maps & Graphics:** Kat Bennett, Mike Morgenfeld

**Photo Credits**
**Front Cover:** Tram 28, Lisbon, Portugal © Jan Wlodarczyk / Alamy
**Title Page:** Porto © Dominic Arizona Bonuccelli
**Additional Photography:** Dominic Arizona Bonuccelli, Reid Coen, Rich Earl,
Cameron Hewitt, David C. Hoerlein, Carol Ries, Jennifer Schutte, Robyn Stencil,
Rick Steves, Ashley Sytsma, Robert Wright, Wikimedia Commons—PD-Art/PD-US
(photos are used by permission and are the property of the original copyright owners)